THE LETTERS OF ALLEN GINSBERG

ALSO BY ALLEN GINSBERG

Select Bibliography

POETRY BOOKS

Collected Poems 1947–1997

Death & Fame: Last Poems 1993–1997

Selected Poems 1947–1995

Illuminated Poems

Cosmopolitan Greetings: Poems 1986–1992

White Shroud Poems 1980–1985

Howl Annotated

Plutonian Ode: And Other Poems 1977–1980

Mind Breath: Poems 1972–1977

The Fall of America, Poems of These States 1965–1971

Planet News 1961–1967

Reality Sandwiches: 1953–1960

Kaddish and Other Poems 1958–1960

Howl and Other Poems

PROSE & PHOTOGRAPH BOOKS

The Book of Martyrdom & Artifice: First Journals and Poems 1937–1952

Family Business: Selected Letters Between a Father & Son

Deliberate Prose: Selected Essays 1952–1995

Spontaneous Mind: Selected Interviews, 1958–1996

Indian Journals

Journals Mid-Fifties: 1954–1958

Allen Ginsberg Photographs

Journals: Early Fifties, Early Sixties

RECORDINGS

Howl

Kaddish

Gaté

First Blues

Hydrogen Jukebox

The Lion for Real

Holy Soul Jelly Roll

The Voice of the Poet: Allen Ginsberg

For further bibliographic information visit
www.allenginsberg.org

. . .

ALSO BY BILL MORGAN

*The Book of Martyrdom & Artifice: First Journals and Poems 1937–1952 (editor with
Juanita Lieberman-Plimpton, by Allen Ginsberg)*

I Celebrate Myself: The Somewhat Private Life of Allen Ginsberg

The Beat Generation in San Francisco

Literary Landmarks of New York

The Beat Generation in New York: A Walking Tour of Jack Kerouac's City

The Works of Allen Ginsberg 1941–1994: A Descriptive Bibliography

The Response to Allen Ginsberg, 1926–1994: A Bibliography of Secondary Sources

Lawrence Ferlinghetti: A Comprehensive Bibliography

Howl on Trial: The Struggle for Free Expression (editor)

You'll Be Okay: My Life with Jack Kerouac (editor, by Edie Kerouac-Parker)

An Accidental Autobiography: The Selected Letters of Gregory Corso (editor)

Deliberate Prose: Selected Essays, 1952–1995 (editor, by Allen Ginsberg)

*Death & Fame: Last Poems, 1993–1997
(editor with Bob Rosenthal and Peter Hale, by Allen Ginsberg)*

THE LETTERS OF
ALLEN GINSBERG

. . .

[EDITED BY BILL MORGAN]

DA CAPO PRESS

A Member of the Perseus Books Group

Library of Congress Cataloging-in-Publication Data
Ginsberg, Allen.
The letters of Allen Ginsberg / edited by Bill Morgan. — 1st Da Capo press ed.
p. cm.
Includes bibliographical references.
ISBN 978-0-306-81463-1 (alk. paper)
1. Ginsberg, Allen, 1926–1997—Correspondence.
2. Poets, American—20th century—Correspondence.
I. Morgan, Bill, 1949– II. Title.
PS3513.I74Z486 2008
811′.54—dc22
[B]
2008011054

First Da Capo Press edition 2008
Published by Da Capo Press
A Member of the Perseus Books Group
www.dacapopress.com

Da Capo Press books are available at special discounts for bulk purchases in the U.S. by corporations, institutions, and other organizations. For more information, please contact the Special Markets Department at the Perseus Books Group, 2300 Chestnut Avenue, Suite 200, Philadelphia, PA 19103, or call (800) 810-4145, extension 5000, or e-mail special.markets@perseusbooks.com.

Set in Monotype Dante
Book design and composition by Mark McGarry, Texas Type & Book Works

10 9 8 7 6 5 4 3 2 1

...more than kisses, letters mingle souls;
For, thus friends absent speak.

— JOHN DONNE
TO SIR HENRY WOTTON

CONTENTS

PROLOGUE

April 2008

Dear Reader,

Twenty-five years ago, Allen Ginsberg asked me to edit a collection of his correspondence as part of a multiple book contract. At the time, Barry Miles was working on a biography about Ginsberg, and he suggested that because he was already collecting copies of letters by Allen to various people, it might be better for him to edit the book. As a result I teamed up with Juanita Lieberman to edit Ginsberg's earliest journals, a project that was published in 2006 as *The Book of Martyrdom and Artifice*. For years the letters project languished under the overwhelming volume of material, and nothing ever came of it. Then, shortly after Allen's death in 1997, I began working on my own Ginsberg biography, also published in 2006 as *I Celebrate Myself: The Somewhat Private Life of Allen Ginsberg*. For that book I collected my own gigantic stack of Ginsberg letters, and my enthusiasm for editing the selected correspondence book was rekindled. Now, a decade later, after having unearthed more than 3,700 Ginsberg letters from every corner of the world, I've pared them down to this edition of 165 of the very best.

Gathering together the best of the best is exactly how I approached the selection process. After putting the fifteen-ream pile of letters into chronological order, I read each and made a decision based on the only criteria, was it an extraordinary letter or not? It ended up being a "greatest hits album" of correspondence. As I followed that single rule, it didn't matter whether the letter was to Jack Kerouac or Joe Blow. What mattered were the quality of the writing and the significance of the content. In the end the selection turned out to have a little of everything, including wonderful letters to Jack Kerouac, William S. Burroughs, Lawrence Ferlinghetti, and most of his Beat Generation friends. Letters to politicians from Dwight Eisenhower to Bill Clinton, dozens of letters to the editors of newspapers and magazines, and fan letters to a few of Allen's heroes also survived the weeding process. The final volume is a book that can be read from cover to cover or dipped into at random, letters to savor at one's leisure. Nearly every letter is complete in itself and therefore only needs minor editorial setup. The volume doesn't pretend to tell Allen's life story or detail his literary career, but it does attempt to show his talent as a correspondent. I would have loved to include all 3,700 letters, fully annotated, but that is a project for a future scholar with an enormous publishing budget.

Strictly speaking, a man of letters is not someone who has written a lot of letters but rather someone who is actively engaged in the literary and intellectual world. Allen Ginsberg was both. Wherever he was, whatever he was doing, he did it with paper and pen nearby. At any moment he might write a poem, make a notebook entry, or pen a letter to a friend. After seventy years, he left behind an enormous depository of documents to study. He has even been criticized by reviewers for writing too much, as if there could ever be too much material to help expand our knowledge.

The letters in this volume present a side of Ginsberg that his poetry, journals, and essays do not. Allen's letters are largely *responses* to something, quite often responses to letters from his correspondents. That sets them apart markedly from Ginsberg's other writings because in other formats Allen had an aversion to writing "on demand." At times requests to write on a particular subject became torturous ordeals for him. He experienced writer's block when it came to composing introductions, blurbs, or other writing for particular purposes. For example, in the 1960s Ginsberg promised to put together his South American journals for publisher Dave Haselwood. After years of delay, Ginsberg had to admit he just couldn't write or edit on a schedule; the mood had to be with him. A decade later the mood still hadn't struck him, and Allen gave Haselwood his *Indian Journals* as a substitute.

Ginsberg's letters were a different matter entirely. The subjects for those were nearly always determined by other people, which seems to be the very nature of many letters. Someone writes to you and you respond on the spot. If you put it off for weeks or months, quite possibly the letter will never be written, so it is almost always immediate and unrehearsed. After writing a poem, a poet can look back on it, go over it and revise it, spend as much time on it as he'd like, and then at some point declare it finished or discard it altogether. By contrast a letter is often written in haste and dropped into a mailbox without revision. Once posted it can't be recalled.

There was an enormous range in the subject matter of Ginsberg's letters. They might be a political tirade to his father, or a postcard from afar, or a reply to a young fan who hoped that Ginsberg would "discover" him. Often they were his only means of keeping in touch with friends as he or they traveled around the world. At other times he used letters to respond to media stories he disagreed with. Quite often in those cases the letter was directed to the *New York Times*, the newspaper Allen loved to hate.

It should be noted that after the 1950s, Allen was increasingly aware that his letters would be saved by and read for posterity. "Because we offhand assumed without much special thought-attention that our correspondence would make good reading for later centuries of geek poets," he said in one letter.

Ginsberg lived through a fascinating period in the history of correspondence. The great age of letters, I fear, is behind us now. The computer has been the final but not the only nail in the coffin. The history of letter-writing extends as far back as the invention of writing itself. In fact, you could make a strong case for saying that the invention of writing was for the purpose of sending letters. Some ancient merchant needed to communicate with someone in another town without going there himself, so he sent a letter. The very word "letter" can mean a piece of correspondence or a single character in our alphabet; the two meanings are intertwined.

In the chronology of Ginsberg's letters one can witness the end of the era of letter-writing. In the 1940s and 1950s, tremendous letters were written, sent, and shared by friends. They were passed around and read by many people, saved and cherished. Then with the advent of lower-cost long distance telephone rates, letters became shorter and less a means for timely communication. Allen himself wrote in a 1969 letter to Lawrence Ferlinghetti, "Alas telephone destroys letters!" Finally, as the calling charges dropped even more, his letters grew shorter still, and almost never concerned the most pressing issues. With the widespread use of the Internet, letters have practically vanished, and the golden era of letter-writing is no more. One wonders if Ginsberg lived, would he be sending cryptic email messages like "AFAIK CU 2NITE" (as far as I know see you tonight)?

Assembling this book, like each of the other eight Ginsberg books I've worked on, has taken much longer than expected. Each time the surface of Ginsberg's archive is scratched, ten times the amount of material anticipated is uncovered. The incredible volume of Ginsberg's correspondence has been both a blessing and a bother. The letters cover fifty-six years and touch on growing up, school, love and heartbreak, spiritual revelations, a nation at war, growing old and death, plus most of the intellectual and political controversies of the last half of the twentieth century. In an introduction to my bibliography of Lawrence Ferlinghetti, that astute writer likened me to a bird dog tracking the wingèd prey, the poet. I feel that I've been on the trail once again, sniffing out Ginsberg's letters in the most unlikely of places. I've written hundreds of letters myself, searching for correspondence, and have been rewarded with answers from old friends and acquaintances of Ginsberg's, all eager to help by sharing their letters with others.

Using less than five percent of those letters has caused some editorial problems. Regretfully, repetitious letters were cut, no matter how wonderful they were. Footnotes were used sparingly, leaving readers to do their own reference work if they are unfamiliar with some of the people and events cited. Editorial intrusions were kept to a minimum, but with the knowledge that excising 3,550 letters is a major underlying editorial intrusion in and of itself.

In general, spelling errors have been corrected, unless it seemed to add something to the text. I felt it wasn't important that Allen misspelled the Perseid meteor shower as "Persid." Around his office Allen was known as a notoriously bad speller, and when they were spotted, he always wanted those errors corrected before publication. He frequently didn't have a dictionary handy, so he couldn't have checked, even if he had wanted.

Ellipses [...] indicate that material has been cut from the text of a letter. Usually cuts were made for non sequiturs or asides not relevant to the text. Some postscripts have been deleted if they didn't add anything to the meat of the letter. Often they were "Did you get the clipping I sent?"–type add-ons. In the spirit of Allen Ginsberg, no censorship cuts were made. Of Kerouac's letters, Allen wrote, "I wouldn't consent to his letters being published censored. . . . . Still I want to make sure in advance that it's taken for granted by any editor of that material, that at the last minute there isn't an attempt to roughen out smooth edges or whazzit vice versa smooth out rough horny communist un-American goofy edges. . . . . In other words no fucking around with the reality." The editor has adhered to that same policy and left reality alone.

Yours truly,

Bill Morgan

P.S. I have had a great deal of help from librarians and private individuals. Those who helped most are acknowledged in the following pages.

ACKNOWLEDGMENTS

Assembling a collection of letters such as this calls for the cooperation of a legion of people. Friends, family, and scholars have all generously helped locate correspondence from Allen Ginsberg until nearly four thousand letters had been discovered, cataloged, and transcribed. From those, this final selection was compiled. The editor would like to thank everyone who helped along the way, whether their letters were selected for the final edition or not. Although it is impossible to list everyone due to space restrictions, the following should be acknowledged for their individual efforts.

First and foremost the trustees of the Allen Ginsberg Trust, Bob Rosenthal and Andrew Wylie. They must be thanked for their early interest in this project. They entrusted the project to my care, and I hope I have not disappointed them. Needless to say, without their support this book would not have been possible. Peter Hale, also of the Ginsberg Trust, single-handedly wrestled copies of hundreds of letters from bureaucratic libraries and archives. His labor was invaluable and essential to the work.

Ben Schafer and his staff at the Da Capo Press immediately sensed the importance of this book, and any success it will have is due to them. Jeff Posternak of the Andrew Wylie Agency worked tirelessly on contractual issues.

Above all, a heartfelt note of appreciation to all those who provided letters or gave information that led to the discovery of more correspondence. In particular: Simon Albury, David Amram, Alan Ansen, Antler, Karel Appel, John Ashbery, Richard Avedon, Gordon Ball, Amiri Baraka, Lois Beckwith, Jack Beeson, Bill Berkson, Paul Bertram, Steven Bornstein, Christian Bourgois, Dave Breithaupt, Anne Brooks, Andreas Brown, Eric Brown, William F. Buckley Jr., Lucien Carr, Paul Carroll, David Carter, Carolyn Cassady, Ann Charters, Andy Clausen, Steve Clay, Francesco Clemente, Jim Cohn, Kirby Congdon, Bruce Conner, David Cope, Gregory Corso, Robert Creeley, Kankabati Datta, Diane di Prima, Elsa Dorfman, George Dowden, Aidan Dun, Charlotte Durgin, Helen Elliott, Daniel Ellsberg, Istvan Eorsi, Jason Epstein, Ekbert Faas, Inge Feltrinelli, Lawrence Ferlinghetti, Leslie Fiedler, Marcia Fields, Eric Fischl, Luca Formenton, Raymond Foye, Brenda Frazer, Len Freedman, Ed Friedman, Cliff

Fyman, Chris Funkhouser, Gary Gach, Bill Gargan, Jacqueline Gens, Herb Gold, Mike Goldmark, Brad Gooch, Stan Grinstein, Arlo Guthrie, Jack W. C. Hagstrom, Nat Hentoff, Terri Hinte, John Hollander, Anselm Hollo, Michael Horowitz, Andrew Hoyem, Hettie Jones, Richard Kaplan (MacArthur Foundation), Eliot Katz, Vincent Katz, Bill Keogan, R. B. Kitai, Karen Koch, Allan Kornblum, Jane Kramer, Joanne Kyger, Robert LaVigne, Sam Leff, Winston Leyland, Hannah Litzky, Paula Litzky, Sterling Lord, Leila Hadley Luce, Lewis MacAdams, Michael McCleod, Michael McClure, Kaye McDonough, Peter McGill, Bill Mackay, Dave McReynolds, Gerard Malanga, Judith Malina, Greil Marcus, James Maris, John Martin, Judy Matz, Ralph Maud, Barry Miles, Arthur Miller, Shiv Mirabito, Abd Al-Hayy Moore, Dave Moore, Tim Moran, Ted Morgan, John Morthland, Marc Olmsted, Hank O'Neal, Peter Orlovsky, Ron Padgett, Helen Parker, Marjorie Perloff, Jim Perrizo, Tom Pickard, Fernanda Pivano, Norman Podhoretz, Janine Pommy Vega, Alice Quinn, Lee Ranaldo, Susan Rashkis, Jonah Raskin, Lou Reed, Hanon Reznikoff, Irvyne Richards, David Rome, Stephen Ronan, Ned Rorem, Jonathan Rose, Barney Rosset, Paul Roth, Malay Roychoudhury, Ed Sanders, Steve Sandy, George Schneeman, Michael Schumacher, Hersch Silverman, Louis Simpson, Vojo Sindolic, John Snow, Gary Snyder, Carl Solomon, Ettore Sottsass, Colin Still, John Suiter, Ron Sukenick, Robert Sutherland-Cohen, Miquel Tapies, Eliot Tokar, Happy Traum, Helen Tworkov, John Tytell, John Updike, Kurt Vonnegut, Anne Waldman, Barry Wallenstein, Shizuko Watari, Steven Watson, Helen Weaver, Regina Weinreich, Ed White, Les Whitten, Joan and Ted Wilentz, Bob Wilson, John Zervos, and Lionel Ziprin.

Many libraries generously made copies of the letters available from their own collections: American Academy of Arts and Letters, British Library, Brown University, Columbia University, Dartmouth University, Harvard University, Kent State University, Lilly Library, New York Public Library, New York University, Simon Fraser University, Stanford University, SUNY–Buffalo, Syracuse University, UCLA, University of California–Berkeley, University of California–Davis, University of Connecticut, University of Delaware, University of Michigan, University of North Carolina, University of Texas–Austin, University of Virginia, and Yale University.

And finally unqualified appreciation to Allen Ginsberg himself, who penned all these words in the first place, little dreaming that they'd find a home in such an attractive volume.

THE LETTERS OF ALLEN GINSBERG

[*As a young boy, Allen Ginsberg no doubt wrote letters and notes to friends and family, but none of those childhood missives appears to have survived. On summer holidays we know Ginsberg did correspond with at least one of his school chums. This is evidenced by the fact that Ginsberg's own archive contains several letters from that boy, but the Ginsberg side of the correspondence was not saved, for who would have known that this twelve-year-old would become one of the century's most famous poets? It is certain that Allen was writing letters to his aunts, uncles, and cousins during those years, but a thorough search has failed to turn up any early examples.*

The earliest letter by Allen Ginsberg that the editor of this volume has uncovered was composed in 1941, when Ginsberg was fifteen. At that young age, Allen was fascinated with politics and world affairs. Three weeks after the December 7 Japanese attack on Pearl Harbor, Ginsberg wrote a letter to the New York Times *expressing his opinion of how America had come to be involved in World War II. It was only the first of scores of letters he would send to the* Times *over the next six decades.*]

**Allen Ginsberg [Paterson, NJ] to the *New York Times* [New York, NY]
December 28, 1941**

[Dear Editor]:

I have long believed, in principle, the ideals of Woodrow Wilson and regretted that we did not choose to live with the world when the time came to 'resolve that our dead shall not have died in vain' by joining the League of Nations.

I am normally a more or less passive individual. However, I think I am growing cynical. I chuckle and feel a bit of grim humor when I read of our growing regret for the world's biggest blunder, our refusal to join the League. One can almost see a pained and astonished expression growing on the faces of America as the people now realize, under a reflowering of Wilson's vision, what they did to the world and themselves in 1920.

So now, finally we have a reflowering of Wilson's vision: witness Winston Churchill's speech before Congress; another fine speech on the 28th by Senator

Guffey; and a passionate appeal for a new league by Edwin L. James in last Sunday's *Times*. However, it seems that our futile regret is too little and too late. Our stupidity has reaped its harvest and we have a bumper crop, since we sowed the world's biggest blunder. The death toll in this war has been at least four million (including Spanish, Chinese, and Abyssinian wars). There is no preventable catastrophe in recorded history paralleling this.

That is a grim joke on ourselves, four million dead as the result of mental impotence and political infirmity on the part of a handful of U.S. Congressmen. But in the midst of all this tribulation one can gather infinite consolation by speculation as to what will happen to those Congressmen when they get to hell.

We will know better this time, but in any case, the devil has prepared a nice, hot bath ready for many more Senators.

[Allen Ginsberg]

[*Both Allen Ginsberg and his older brother, Eugene Brooks Ginsberg, were extremely interested in government and politics. On several occasions Allen took the time to write long letters to editors expressing his ideas, a habit that he continued for the rest of his life. This letter criticized the isolationist policies of many congressmen, which Allen felt had led directly to the U.S. involvement in war. It is also of interest because it is the first time that Allen made use of a literary quotation (in this case Voltaire's) to support an argument.*]

Allen Ginsberg [Paterson, NJ] to the *New York Times* [New York, NY]
June 11, 1942

To the Editors:

I should like to take issue with Mr. Emmett Oldfield[1] who protests holding their voting records against our formerly isolationist members of Congress.

Mr. Oldfield argues, first, since Pearl Harbor, many isolationists became fine supporters of the war effort. Second, Pearl Harbor did not disprove isolationism; it merely removed it as an issue. Third, the isolationists were sincere and patriotic in efforts to keep us out of war.

I shall admit that it was really nice of the isolationists to support our war effort after we had been so viciously attacked by our enemies.

---

1 Emmett Oldfield's letter to the *New York Times* appeared in the June 10, 1942, issue.

And I am also willing to admit that the isolationists were sincere and patriotic—at least, most of them. But while I do not question their motives, I do question their judgment.

Pearl Harbor and later events have disproved isolationism. It disproved and deflated such defeatist ideas as: "No matter how many fighting planes...we send to England, it is not possible to base enough squadrons on the British Isles to equal the striking power of the squadrons that Germany can base on the continent of Europe."—Charles Lindbergh, June 20, 1941. "American participation is likely to destroy democracy in this country"—"Few people honestly believe that the Axis now, or in the future, will be in the position to threaten the independence of any part of this hemisphere ..." "Freedom for America does not depend on the struggles for material power (as isolationists called it) between other nations"—An appeal to Congress by fifteen isolationists, Republican leaders, August 5, 1941. Story in the *New York Times*: "Mr. Nye described the war as...'Nothing other than a bloody mess of Communism and Nazism'." Wheeler: "I, for one, my friends, am not afraid of any of these imaginary threats." Wheeler: "German submarines are small. They were designed to operate close to their bases within a few hundred miles of England."

We are not fighting, in the long run, because of Pearl Harbor. Only a person with isolationist viewpoint would say that we were. We are not, and we should not be, fighting just because we were attacked. We are fighting because we are fighting Fascism: we are fighting Fascism, not because of what it does to us but because of what it is.

If this war is truly, as Mr. Wallace[2] has said, a people's revolution, one for democracy; and if the job of defeating world barbarism is a world problem; and if this war is not a "Struggle for material power between other nations," then the isolationists are disproved.

And before we are to have a just and lasting peace (of which Mr. Oldfield speaks) based on amicable cooperation between nations, we will have to accept and understand that isolationism, both before and after the war, is wrong. What assurance have we that pre-war isolationists if we place them in Congress, will not revert back to isolationism when the hostilities have ceased? That is why Mr. Oldfield is wrong when he suggests that we overlook the records of isolationist senators and representatives.

In this connection, I might quote a relevant, if somewhat violent, statement by Voltaire: "It is like the fire that is covered but not extinguished. Those fanatics,

2 Henry A. Wallace (1888–1965). U.S. vice president under Franklin Roosevelt.

those impostors, are mad dogs. They are muzzled, but they have not lost their teeth. It is true that they bite no more, but on the first opportunity, if the teeth are not drawn, you will see if they will not bite."

Allen Ginsberg

[*A boyhood friend, Benson Soffer, was one of Ginsberg's first correspondents. When Allen learned that he had been accepted to Columbia University, he wrote "Bense" to share his good news and to continue a debate that they had been carrying on through several letters. Ginsberg was a member of his high school debating society and loved the give and take of these exchanges.*]

Allen Ginsberg [Paterson, NJ] to Benson Soffer [NJ?] May 17, 1943

Bense:

[...] I've been accepted in Columbia University. I start work, if I live and get the money, on July 6. School in Paterson ends about June 28, or so, so I'll get about a 10 day vacation: then, back to work. No news from Columbia about a scholarship, though. I hear about that (if I hear at all) in a month. [...]

Now, I only asked you (here I digress into one of my apologizing explanations) for an ethical system *et al*, because I find it most profitable to pick other people's brains and appropriate the sum of their wisdom and experience for my own. Not that I regard you as any wiser than myself—everyman thinks that he is the superior of anyone of his acquaintance—but I compromise with my ego to acknowledge to myself that you <u>do</u> have a brain of some kind and that it is worth picking for juicy intellectual tidbits. *Comprenez?*

My own tentative philosophy is this, that man is a superior animal, that his superiority lies in self-consciousness and self-knowledge. This self knowledge includes a realization of a purpose and meaning of life (whether an affirmative, negative, or neuter meaning) and the ability to use natural force to achieve fulfillment of that meaning. What that purpose is, other than freedom from physical limitation, and freedom from intellectual limitation, I do not know. We have invented the machine in order to realize freedom from physical limitation, and we will perfect the machine. Ethics and philosophy involve the search for freedom from intellectual limitation. History—the development of civilization—is the development of the slow evolutionary search for this (excuse me if I begin to sound like Allen Ginsberg) physical and intellectual freedom. History is a river of development—slow and sluggish, pushing relentlessly onward (poetic!!!) toward the ultimate goal of human perfection: the two freedoms, there is a main current of history, and this current streams inexorably onward, there are eddies and side-streams, rapids and whirlpools, in which human progress is interrupted temporarily, but the main current pours onward in steady flux, (here I simply must be poetic) draining finally into the fathomless oceans of eternity.

I pause to inform you that I have just received the happy news (Monday afternoon, 5:45) that I've been granted a $300 scholarship by Columbia. Work starts July 6. Hallelujah.

To continue. That we are achieving the first of our freedoms, physical, is unquestionable. The one point of question is that of intellectual freedom. Have we experimented, philosophized, theorized, and conjectured our way to a place where we may say that we are on the main stream to intellectual perfection? Has our intellectual growth kept pace with our physical? It may be said that mankind was at a higher intellectual level in the time of the ancient Greeks. I do not think so, for at that time the intellect was concentrated in the minds of a few developed philosophers. The mass of humanity was very little higher intellectually than the mass mind of the primitive man. The level of intelligence is higher in our time. I do not say that by evolution we have achieved more perfect brains. Perhaps the level of intelligence in Grecian times was proportionately as high as in our times, if we base the proportion on a comparison, with the development of physical civilization and the experience of intellectual civilization as basis of their time and ours. In our time we have evolved the principles of universal democracy, and these principles are commonly accepted. The time is not far off when we shall have advanced to a stage where we will apply these principles, even as the Greeks applied their primitive principles in their times. This is one illustration of the broadening of the intellectual comprehension of the whole of humanity, aided by and allied to physical freedom.

Now this is all abstract theorizing. The practical application can be made in almost any time of civilization. The use, the application, lies in the utilization of such a philosophy of history in determining perspectives on the roles of figures of history—in other times, and in our own. We can now comprehend truer meanings for "reactionary," "conservative," "liberal," "radical." We can understand the role of a Hitler as a force of reaction. He is the embodiment of one of the side waters, the back-eddies of history—the reactionary war in a real sense wishes to turn back the clock, to pull humanity back, to dam the flood of onrushing civilization (i.e. progress) to replace the goodness of our age with the primitive perversion of principle and undevelopment of principle of ages we have long since left behind. He uses physical freedom to deny intellectual freedom, instead of helping develop intellectual freedom. He is truly the voice of barbarianism, the voice of a bestial past, calling civilization backwards, diverting it from its mission, hindering development to what is good, what is just, and what is perfect.

Somewhere along the argument I forgot to insert a general endorsement of democracy. The point of this is that the evolution toward complete self-consciousness has as a corollary democracy, for it is only by the combined efforts of all of humanity for the good of all of humanity can progress be universal, complete, and therefore perfect.

My intellectual orgasm is over. You may fire when ready, Gridley. But I retain the prerogative of changing minor definitions, words, phrases, etc. I have written this all at once in one orgiastic spasm and have not rewritten nor reread it. […]

Allen

P.S. I add that the capacity for perfection is within us, but that in a few million years we will have developed our capacities to near perfection. Also, by perfection I really don't mean god. I'm hazy on this point. Say, "more-perfect." ("To form a more perfect Union, establish justice," etc.)

[*While Ginsberg's brother, Eugene, was in the army, Allen wrote to him frequently, engaging in the same political debate and banter they had shared at home. Allen was always eager to show off his intellect to his older sibling, as this letter illustrated. It also began with an interesting historical note about Allen's plans to go to the Village and meet Lucien Carr's friends. The friends the young Columbia freshman met were William S. Burroughs and David Kammerer, two people who were to play important roles in Ginsberg's life.*]

Allen Ginsberg [New York, NY] to Eugene Brooks Ginsberg [U.S. Army] December 17, 1943

Dear Eugene::

Tonight is the 17th of December—this was my last day of school before Christmas vacation, which begins tomorrow and lasts until the 27th. I don't know what I'll be doing Christmas—nothing much I suppose, out of the ordinary. My tentative program is this—read and weep for your days of yore. Saturday I plan to go down to Greenwich Village with friend of mine [Lucien Carr] who claims he's an "intellectual" (that has a musty flavor, hasn't it?) and know queer and interesting people there. I plan to get drunk Saturday evening, if I can. I'll tell you the result. Sunday I'll be around Hastings Hall[3], probably reading *Anna Karenina*, which I've been reading on and off for a week. Sunday night I'm going to a Japanese restaurant with the Jap in the dorm here. I think I told you about him. I want to see how it compares with the Chinese delicacies. Sunday evening I'll probably go to movies. Monday I'll be either in Paterson, or at the Metropolitan Opera with Naomi.[4] Tuesday I'll be in Paterson, reading *Tom Jones*. Wednesday evening Lou[5] and I have tickets for the Met to see Lilly Pons in *Lucia Di Lammermoor*. God knows, the opera isn't too wonderful, but we want to see Cesare Sodero conduct. He's invited us to visit him backstage if we go. Thursday, Friday, and Saturday are open, except that I have to finish *Tom Jones*, and also finish the whole of Milton's *Paradise Lost*. I don't look forward to reading it.

I saw the two very interesting and very curious letters—they were epistles rather than letters—that you wrote to the family. They sounded rather bitter. Do I see you waving your arms wildly now? You sounded as if you were insulted and injured by some conscious and malevolent being. I would suggest that you favored the Draft Act[6] in 1940; that you approved the 18–45 draft ages; that you were an "interventionist." If, then, you find yourself in the unhappy predicament of being drafted and rather roughly handled by the army, you may have cause for sorrow or pained resignation, but not at all for bitterness and disgust. Meanwhile, you may as well write some good poetry while you're waiting for the war to end. If you find that you can't do that (write good poetry), why, then, go out and end the war or at least have your head shot off trying.

Well, anyway, to jump to the more abstract phases of your letters: your miraculous conversion to "realism." Sing praises to the lord, my lad! You have discovered that visions are not true! Specifically speaking, though, the idealistic vision of the war as a people's revolution, is no, no, no, not true at all. First you pull out Versailles, and discover, somewhat belatedly, that "many interpretations

3 Hastings Hall. Ginsberg's dorm at Columbia.
4 Naomi Ginsberg (1896–1956). Allen Ginsberg's mother.
5 Louis Ginsberg (1895–1976). Allen Ginsberg's father.
6 Draft Act. Law passed that made men between the ages of 18 and 45 eligible for conscription into the military.

can be placed on the same set of facts." Incidentally, the "American viewpoint," if there is one at all, is not represented by Keynes, who is an <u>English</u> historian and economist. (Did you read "Economic Consequences of Peace"? If so, you were duped by a duped liberal, an idealist, who didn't know the true facts about the economic consequences of the place.) Still I can't quarrel with you about the peace in 1918: Wilson's <u>was</u> visionary; Clemenceau was a vindictive tiger; Lloyd George was a shrewd and prostituted political philanderer. (A crappy metaphor).

However, you say "The trouble is that people disagree so widely, that a compromise or a deviation from any group's program is regarded as a victory for the other side. And obviously what happens is not as important as what people think has happened!" Your point is obscure here, because your letter immediately thereafter struck off on the point that "the emotional rationalization of the mass of the people" is the deciding force, and a variable one. I guessed that what I quoted was the expression of frustrated resignation to an inevitable evil, or realization of the sorry fact that compromise doesn't really mean anything. But you overlook, first, the fact that compromise is not always bad — either you overlook it or reject it, I couldn't figure out which — and that your Versailles illustration showed the falseness of your idea that idealists must resign themselves to compromise. Wilson compromised, Eugene, (if you read your history, you know) and compromised and compromised until he had nothing left but the most important ideal, which he retained. Then he went home and presented Versailles' Treaty for acceptance without admitting that it was a compromise, like a good politician. He represented it as ideal and defended it as such (despite your quotation) to the people when he returned to America and went on his tour. Mark Sullivan, or Frederick Lewis Allen (one of the two) declares that his mistake was in not presenting it frankly as the best the world could do under the circumstances, and asking for acceptance as a necessary compromise which might yet be justified.

I liked your point (the one I mentioned) about popular will. "The conclusion is that there is no external cause of war, because thinking is not necessarily along objective lines but deviates frequently from the actual facts." Well, who even said any differently? There was never any <u>real</u> cause for a war; no war was really ever justified. Wars come about when the opposing forces, either one side or the other, or both, were sincere but wrong, when their thinking "was not necessarily along objective lines but deviates frequently from the actual fact." War only comes about when one side or both, as I said, acts unintelligently, uninformally. Obviously, Eugene, all you have done has been to utter a well disguised platitude. Practical application? O.K. Go to it. This war: one side or the other is acting unintelligently. We are, certainly in America and Britain and Russia. Of course (no knowing smiles now) the other side is acting even more unintelligently than we, and so we are justified. Dear Eugene, if you can only persuade Hitler to act understandingly and rationally, and show the German people their error, and how they could achieve security (which they could have, if they tried) without persecution and conquest and brutality, why, then we will have removed the synthetic, the false cause of war. Because, as you know, there is no absolute, inherent cause. And when you convince the Japanese that they <u>must</u> not invade China, that they must not remedy the faults of the Western Empires by marshalling their own horrible and unintelligent apparatus for benefiting the upper feudal classes of Japan at the expense of the Malayans and Chinese and Philippines, why then, Eugene, only then have you the right to reject this war as merely a psychological knot, and a useless and unnecessary affair.

I agree with your assertion that public opinion changes, changing the purposes of the war with it, though I would add that the public opinion thinks that, of course it is perfectly consistent and whoever says so is either a radical or a crackpot. Your point about power shaping the course of history is well taken too. You conclude this with "There is no certainty in politics, no principles except as they coincide with prevalent desires, and no honesty except as it is reconciled to self interest, and thus it is no honesty at all." Oh, ho? No certainty in politics? Is it not certain that subsidies are necessary, that the greatest good for the greatest number should be the determining end of public policy, that Abramson[7] was right, that Canfield is a bad man, that Rankin and Hoffman are not good men, that Russia is making wonderful progress, that Hitler is wrong, that PM is the best newspaper in New York, that Arthur Krock[8] is a sly, slimy representative of the vested interests, that I am sincere and I have ideals and I am always, under all circumstances, at all times, utterly and infinitely right? There are no principles and no honesty? I am principled, and I resent anyone saying no. I am honest and I am angered by the aspersions you've made. You were principled and honest, too, before you were corrupted by this wicked, wicked world, and before you decided to write silly letters home. If ideals are "projections of ego," that doesn't bother me at all. They are ideals—take it or leave it, they're the best you'll get, and they are most serviceable. "Ideals," you

7 Abramson, Canfield, Rankin, and Hoffman. New Jersey politicians at the time.
8 Arthur Krock (1886–1974). Washington (DC) columnist for the New York Times.

cry "are interesting only as a curiosity, or as to which horse one shall ride to get to where one wants to go." You are excessively pessimistic here, not realistic at all in your conclusion. Does that obviate the practical use of ideals to get somewhere? Does that eliminate progress? Above all, does that eliminate the ideal political state (since we're concerned now with politics)? Why, most practically, most realistically, most truly, and most demonstrably, it does not, and you cannot pervert the conceptions of idealism to make it so. If you think that the ideals, primitive as they are, of the twentieth century, are less ideal than those of the 20th century BC, or the 5th AD, you're not looking at the world realistically. Take off your murky colored glasses, why, the world <u>has</u> made progress, God bless us, and for you to be blind to the accomplished fact is the apotheosis of your despised illusion. Eugene, your beard is on fire, you're a visionary and to say that you have proved by A plus B plus psychological X that the fatal weaknesses of man doom him to a complacently stagnant state of society and a becalmed barque of progress, a condition which has not yet occurred and need not occur in the future, is an exhibition of intemperately pessimistic presumption on your part. [. . .]

    Allen

[*In the summer of 1945 Ginsberg enlisted in the merchant marine and went through basic training at Sheepshead Bay, Brooklyn. His plan was to earn enough money to continue his education at Columbia, which had been temporarily put on hold. He kept in touch with his teachers, often writing to professors like Lionel Trilling and Mark Van Doren. Frequently he asked their advice and debated with them over the importance of writers like Arthur Rimbaud and Hart Crane, whom the academy did not consider appropriate for serious scholarship at the time.*]

Allen Ginsberg [U.S. Maritime Service Training Station, Sheepshead Bay, NY] **to Lionel Trilling** [New York, NY] **September 4, 1945**

Dear Prof. Trilling:

    I am sorry I have waited so long before replying to your letter—which was very kind—but I have been confined to the base hospital here with pneumonia in my chest for the past few weeks.

    Thank you for your criticism of the poem with the portentous title.[9] I must

---

9 Reference to Ginsberg's poem, "The Last Voyage."

admit that it pleased me to read all those nice things you wrote about it, but to tell the truth I have only a hazy idea of what you mean by 'the voice and its tone,' which you admire in poetry. As for rhyme, I usually try to make an extremely loose rhyme do if necessary where I can and find one that fits, and that I have no compunction about this because I'm increasingly pleased by the effect of the sort of 'muted' rhymes of Auden and cummings. So I would rhyme 'touched' and 'watched' and 'flesh' and 'death' or even 'birth' and 'death'—to use some more obvious situations. I wasn't aware of Shelley while writing, though I aimed at a violent semi-cerebral rhetoric. I found a copy of Shelley here (incidentally I have been reading *War and Peace* during my convalescence, with great pleasure) and on re-reading *Mont Blanc* I found the language much akin to my own desire.

That you are unable to understand why I make so much of Rimbaud, dismays me somewhat. Though I should dislike to be over bumptious about it, with your kind permission I must witness his defense. I fear that since you have read Rougemont's *Partie du Diable* you possibly approach Rimbaud viewing him as another eccentric French Satanist somewhat in a class with Maldoror, fit to be the prophet of the Mexican Hashish Surrealist Quarterly. Rimbaud had an attack of Diabolism somewhat appropriately at the age of puberty and lost it, as far as its meanings go, soon thereafter so far as I've been able to tell. I would say that, to his credit, he surpassed the more highly advertised and shallow spiritual struggles of Baudelaire-Dandyism and diabolism as puerile reactions of the puritan temper to the "vulgar complacency" of the times. I think of Rimbaud as a hero in the sense of having a violent, varied—and finally mature —response to a fairly representative social situation. Not that of a provincial 19th Century Frenchman, that of a Western man. He was flexible enough to change his ideas to correspond to his experiences, and in consequence ran the gamut of political, religious, rationalistic, and esthetic visions and verdicts that have attacked the significant figures of modern poetry. I approve of Rimbaud because unlike the heroes of the Columbia Bookstore, he survived and mastered these visions, and rose above them to a solution to the "problems" of our time which as yet our writers are first discovering. As I remember, in his earliest years he underwent the Dedalus Pontifex religious dilemma in an abridged form, and turned political after loss of faith. After divesting himself of the notions of the usual politically conscious writer (entertained in our time by the Book of the Month Club "Talentgang" perhaps) he turned, in the usual developmental groove, to the aesthetic salvation. Here the development of the poor poets of the nineteenth and part of the twentieth century seems to have stopped—unless like Auden and Eliot they have crawled back into the womb of the virgin. Pragmatic religion bores me at this point and so I continue with the fortunes of Rimbaud—who at his stage of the worship of Orpheus, with the concomitant illuminations, Satanism, *"dereglement de tous les sens,"* his physical and moral depersonalization, had the most amusing circus of them all— Yeats, Joyce, Rilke, James, Wilde, Flaubert—while it lasted. I think that he pursued this orphic wonder, experience for art's sake, the unsocializing of the animal, more effectively than any modern writer—probably because of his youth. At the same time I sense in him an ability to make contact with his culture personally, to actively live in it and be of it—and this in an artist has completed the circle of absolute artistic depersonalization, paradox or not. I think that this "realistic" contact is unknown to the other exiles at his time, except Dostoyevsky and the later Joyce. In the period of the early *Season in Hell* Rimbaud felt out his culture—his Charleville and his Paris—and analyzed it, in more primitive terms, to the same effect that Freud and Spengler later did. He went deeper than the reformism of Butler, the ivory towered amorality of Mallarme, dug deeper for a faith than Dedalus did in finding himself in art. The reason for this I think in regard to the "Aesthetic adventure" is in Rimbaud's use of art constantly as a key and not a mystical telos. He wound up with a Bohemian version of the 1920 Fitzgerald, though less provincial, less superficially idealistic, a master of exterior circumstance. He presents by implication and statement the sociological, not the abstractly ethical, "spiritual" problems of his time. His struggle concerns not merely the unpoetic machine versus faith, which is naive; nor individual power versus collective boorishness, as in Nietzschean anarchy; he presents not diffused evils to be conquered, or wicked individuals to be curbed, or heroes to emerge, and dragons to be killed—but he knows a complex anthropological unit in what appears to him to be in a state of cachexy—a whole syndrome of ills adumbrating a cultural decline. He fixes the symptoms somewhat in Freudian terms as the conflict between the anarchic impulses of the individual psyche and its needs, and the mores of a categorized, protestant civilization which is crippled because it conceives of pleasure as evil. He is interested in types representative of a neurotic culture, one ridden with anxiety and tension, the civilization of the false passport, insecure, confused, in sum chaotic. The important person is the outcast (not the literary egoist) but, as in the *Satyricon* of Petronius, the keen, levelheaded men of basic understanding. In the army, one of his practices is to gold brick. He is the type (in civilian society) that is master of his corner of reality, who cuts through the confusion of the disorderly culture to achieve his individual end—the Raymond Chandler hero, the sharp-eyed gambler, the dead-pan cardsharp, the tense tendoned gambler, the "hood"—the types which are coming into prominence now in the movies (Alan Ladd), in James M. Cain, in [John] O'Hara. There is an interest in the psychopath who moves in his pattern unaffected by moral compunction, by allegiance to the confused standards of a declining age. Rimbaud somewhere speaks of watching the skies as a criminal – *avec son idée.* And not only the criminal partakes of this attitude—even the Dos Passos intellectual, the business promoter, the political career man. These in a sense—or at least, I sense,—these have almost become our representative heroes. No longer do they rebel against society, exile themselves, romantically disdain its ways for the ways of art. Art has dropped from its pedestal; the hero moves about in society as a shadow, not menacingly or aggressively, but coolly collecting his profits and faking respectability with varying degrees of consciousness.

Yet even this stage of unrebellious anarchism is surpassed by Rimbaud. The Civilization, as he and most others seem to agree, offers no hope of personal salvation, no vital activity, no way of life within its accepted structure. His creative powers are not realized in the usual activities of the citizen—at the machine, in the office. Realizing that art was an escape—and merely an escape, a fool's paradise, a Dedalusian ivory tower—and admittedly so, considering the myths of the wound (Cocteau's) or the Wound and the Bow (Wilson's) which represent art as compensation for creative activity in life—Rimbaud amputated the wound and cast off the bow, and went to Africa. This was the exodus from society not into the futile exile of the artist, but into living salvation in the land of the primitive, unrestricted, uninhibited. And he embarked to a rigorously active public life as gun-runner and slave trader. With Rimbaud as catalyst the problems that supposedly beset the sensitive youth of the day are crystallized realistically for the first time I think. And so I look to him as "prophet" of the present literary concern with anthropology and psychoanalysis, the shift in vision of society from the simple idealism of Sinclair Lewis to the complicated, half hidden Spenglerian *Weltanschauung* of O'Hara, and, I predict, the whole crop of post World War II writers. Whether or not his pessimism prevails, his idée, his sociological approach rather than moral, has already prevailed. Secondly, he remains one of the earliest forerunners of our modern "classicism," the casting off of the aesthetic preoccupation in favor of personal activity, the relegating of art to a tool and not the salvation of battered souls. Last, he is one of the few writers whose problems are recognizably limited to his age, as Freud's psychological structure reflects the mind of the middle-European of the 19–20th Century. In this sense there is less confusion in

Rimbaud than in many other writers, who tend to universalize the conflicts in them peculiar to their time and place alone. In sum then, I admire Rimbaud not as the *poet maudit*, the decadent, but the representative hero, the sociologically concerned, and in the highest manner politically minded poet. I think there will be many more Koestlers who, reflecting their time, unconsciously participate in his ideas, look at western culture *avec son idée.*

I see I have written a great deal and I have said nothing about his poetry as poetry. *Season in Hell* seems to me the most individually expressive poetry I have run across—more than any poet, I can understand the personality—half childish, half sardonic, somewhat sentimental, furious, jealously personal and strikingly dispassionate—from the poetry. I mean, it is so compressed and flexible that it contains whole visions in a single line. To me it is pretty clearly the work of genius, and so despite your lack of enthusiasm I continue to admire Rimbaud unabashedly. [...]

I had wished to send you some poems, but I am confined to my bed out of reach of a typewriter. Everything with me is in hand manuscript form. I hope I have not tried your patience with this letter, for it is rather long; but my chiefest pleasure now, unlike Hans Castorp, is to communicate with the outside world from the Magic Mountain.

　　　Allen

[*As a seaman, Ginsberg was able to earn money, travel, and have enough spare time to continue writing poetry during the long voyages. He continued to seek Lionel Trilling's approval and advice for his work. Although he was aware that Trilling did not condone his lifestyle, he couldn't resist trying to shock his professor, as he obviously did in a letter the following year.*]

**Allen Ginsberg [SS *Groveton*, at sea] to Lionel Trilling [New York, NY]
January 7, 1946**

Dear Prof. Trilling:

I enclose a poem[10] I've been working on for about three months which has absorbed most of my literary energy in the time. I typed the manuscript under rather unfavorable conditions on shipboard, so it's the only copy I have now, though it is slightly beat-up. I hope you'll excuse its condition.

　　10　Reference to Ginsberg's poem, "Ode to Decadence."

I finally pushed myself to sail again after the first abortive Venezuelan jour-
ney. The ship I am on is a new tanker with a type of romantic young captain—
a sort of narcissistic Nietzschean, aristocrat and master of his ship, a man of
silences. The chief steward (under whom I work) is also rather interesting—a
kind of weather-beaten Prufrock with a predilection for pornographic litera-
ture (I had a long talk with him about the Marquis de Sade and another little
volume I'd not heard of before called *Lady Bumtickler's Revels*) and scatological
anecdotes. The rest of the crew is half negro—all of whom are dope addicts of
one sort or another. Then there are a few Texans, sturdy Westerners, and a
sprinkling of Cubans and multilingual Swedish seadogs.

The vocabulary of the part of the enclosed poem beginning "Right around
the block is Huncke's[11] pad" may be unfamiliar to you. It is a sort of jive talk I
found in use among the "hepcats" and dope addicts on both of the ships I've
been on—and it is also prevalent in the "Underworld" of New York, especially
around Times Square. I was first hesitant to use it, but in the last few years I've
heard it from so many various lips that I think it is very widespread and semi-
permanent in an extremely complicated culture. As such it is in a way—the
use, that is—formally justified by the Wordsworth essay.

I'm bound for Louisiana (*sans* banjo but with a lyre)—possibly New
Orleans. Right now I'm in the middle of the Gulf of Mexico, in Hart Crane
seas, amid "adagios of islands" and proverbial sunblue seas. Really, I do enjoy
sailing in these tropical waters, in watching the stars, in inventing fabulous
romances on the prow of its ship as she bounces forward. I did get seasick
about three days out of New York, at which time I experienced what must have
been at least one of the most agonizing depressions known to man—the uni-
verse dwindled to a succession of trivial absurdities, chief of which was the
pointless voyage of a group of useless men on an empty ship, not yet sure
where they were going and having no real interest in destination—all of this
involved in a seesaw nausea and a desire to return to the womb.

I expect to be homeward bound in a week or so, and I hope to get in touch
with you within the month.

I am sorry I did not get a chance to wish you a Happy New Year, at any rate
I send greetings to you rather belatedly.

Allen

11 Herbert Huncke (1915–1996). Friend and author of *The Evening Sun Turned Crimson*.

[*By 1947 Ginsberg was beginning to seriously doubt his own sanity. Events in his life led him to seek counseling, but even with his seaman's pay and father's help he couldn't afford professional psychiatric treatment. He was referred to noted psychoanalyst, Wilhelm Reich, in the hope that he could get affordable mental care.*]

Allen Ginsberg [New York, NY] to Wilhelm Reich [Forest Hills, NY]
ca. **March 11, 1947**

My Dear Dr. Reich:

I am twenty years old, have lived in N.J. and N.Y. all my life; my father is a high school teacher, as was my mother until ten years ago or so until she suffered a series of severe nervous breakdowns. She was institutionalized (Greystone, NJ) for several years, on and off, and is now living in N.Y. I live by myself in the city, and attend Columbia College, where I am a senior. When I entered school in 1943, I studied History and Economics, and then changed my course to the study of English literature. For the past few years poetry has been my major intellectual interest, and, as far as I know, writing will be my vocation, although I am now much too conscious of writing as a sort of secondary, vicarious emotion to be able to "dedicate" myself to it or any other activity. My marks have been high; though not steadily so, since I have not in the past few years been able to compose myself to any sort of consistency of action. I lead an extensive and diverse social life and have a good number of close friends, both "bourgeois" and "hip," that is, I have found myself drifting into intercourse with the periphery of criminal circles in New York. I have used narcotics pretty extensively, but not to the point of addiction to any; and by now I have stopped the use of them completely. At one time I was active in extra-curricular activities on my campus, but I found them as sterile, I suppose, as narcotics, for my own purposes, so I have dropped much of that. At present I am an editor of the *Columbia Undergraduate Literary Review* and President of the Literary Society.

My main psychic difficulty, as far as I know, is the usual oedipal entanglement. I have been homosexual for as long as I can remember, and have had a limited number of homosexual affairs, both temporary and protracted. They have been unsatisfactory to me, and I have always approached love affairs with a sort of self contradictory, conscious masochism. I have had a few experiences with women which were unsatisfactory from the start since my motivation was more curiosity than interest, and I have been pretty consistently impotent when with a woman. I have had long periods of depression, guilt feelings—disguised mostly as a sort of Kafkian sordidness of sense of self—melancholy, and the whole gamut I suppose. I have been trying valiantly to get to some psychoanalysis for years almost always unsuccessfully, mostly for financial reasons. I live on [$]15 a week provided by my father, study in school, and could not provide the necessary $40–50 a week by part time work. From September 1945 – June 1946 I underwent a sort of informal, amateur psychoanalysis, attempted by a friend [William Burroughs], who was I think trustworthy for that, as far as it went. The inevitable and unfortunate effect was that it left me washed up on the shore of my neuroses with a number of my defenses broken, but centrally unchanged, with nothing to replace the lost armor. Early this year I negotiated with Dr. Abram Kardiner (whose classes in psychodynamics I attended at Columbia) for a control analysis at his psychoanalytic clinic. They were unable to take me on mostly because, as he explained, I would have been too complicated, and my defensiveness subtle, for the unprepared control analysts. He suggested an experienced analyst with some auxiliary psychiatric training, or, as an alternate, some sort of psychoanalytic sanitarium—possibly Chestnut Lodge.

I have known half a dozen or so of the patients in treatment under your type of analysis and have been so favorably impressed by the effects of it on them that, I think, any other orthodox analysis would be unsatisfactory to me, particularly as I have had in the past sufficient interest in psychoanalysis to contemplate the possibility of practicing it myself after my own analysis and after the requisite studies. My father has provided me with a moderate amount of money for an analysis, and, though it is not really very large, it may serve in the first stages, if you see the possibility of recommending a doctor to me or (which would be more to my wish and, perhaps, more to both of our interests) having me treated under your supervision and his, at any rate, was the hope that Mr. Lowen[12] and I formulated.

Please don't think me forward for communicating to you so, I have been fearful of consuming your time and have tried to be as temperate as possible, which, you know, is not really easy. Anyway, I think you have most of the facts here. I can be reached at the above address, I hope that I may hear from you soon.

Respectfully yrs,

A. Ginsberg

12 Dr. Alexander Lowen (b. 1910). Student of the Reich method and author of *Love and Orgasm*.

[*Reichian analysis was short-lived when Ginsberg refused his doctor's request that he stop smoking marijuana. It was around that time that Allen met Neal Cassady in New York City. When Cassady went home to Denver, Allen followed him, hoping to continue their sexual relationship. By that time, Neal was occupied with several women and Ginsberg shipped out on a long voyage to West Africa. Upon his return he wrote several desperate letters to Cassady, of which this is only one example.*]

Allen Ginsberg [New York, NY] to Neal Cassady [Denver, CO] *ca.* November 1947

Dear Neal:

This is a stanza from a poem I have been writing all today, this one is after I saw your letter —

> "This was such grace, to think it is no more
> I cannot mock in dignity, but weep.
> And wherefore dignity? the heart is sore;
> True lovers have no dignity to keep,
> And till I make departure from this shore,
> My mind is sorrowful and will not sleep;
> and mockery is no good, nor mind is, nor
> Is meditation, sadness is so deep."

This letter will be different from the last and maybe different from any other, I hope for our sakes. I have protected myself, armored, since I arrived, from grief or too much self pity and as a result I saw my mind turn more than ever before, with some other circumstance, into isolation and phony goodness —to the point of retiring from the world, which I have not yet, to a furnished room to write cold hot poems. I have no place to stay yet permanently tho I have several comfortable temporary residences with others, yet I want to be by myself now. So I have been touring the city, seeing everyone I know and testing them and turned away from most—except Jack [Kerouac] and Bill [Burroughs], and [John] Kingsland. Even Jack bothers me and I think I will see not even those when I settle.

I had been writing all day a poem "The Creation of the World" on benny [Benzedrine] for the first time since I left Africa and my spirit was opened and near exhaustion when I saw your letter which slowly has broken me down. To write what I am is hard because I tend to slip into poetry or prose formalisms or even neatness of expression, or exaggeration or understatement. Even, in fact, to realistic denial of my message. Yet I was in bed a few minutes ago—it is 4:30 morning now—and I was thinking restlessly of you, allowing thought of you to penetrate deeply in me for the first time since I have arrived. Not that I neglected or even feared thought—I had just simply protected my mind before, unconsciously, because the shock was too great to allow to break in on me all at once. I think you know what is coming in this letter, it is serious; if you don't want to I won't ask you to read further or to reply for that matter.

You know or (at the moment) I am smarter than you and cleverer in ways and I don't want to be smart or clever at this point, even subtle. I must admit that I have known more or less consciously that all the "purity" of my love, its "generosity" and "honor" was, though on its own level true, not all my deeper intention toward you, which was and is simply a direct lover's. If we were equal and I were as strong as you in the relationship "I could afford to be"—I would naturally flow into common generosity. But we are not, for all my purity and abnegation is a stall and a sell out, and all my "gifts" to transmit, if they were to be any use to you which I really thought they would be, were unimportant in my mind and subsidiary to my main beggary. I would have been capable of continuing it, before, even to the point of renouncing any sexual claim on you as I did in my last letter; but that I know and knew was possessiveness taking the palatable and generous form. I had no clear ideas in mind when I told you to come back, except to follow out my agreement to the letter, though perhaps not in spirit, and wait for you to pity me again and sleep with me.

I think that you must be further removed from me than I from you but I do not care at the moment, even though that may make this letter sound out of key and insane.

I do not know how I can hope for any love for you because my own love is one compounded of hostility and submission. I don't understand and can't, your own emotions, even when explained only because my drive is so blind that I cannot comprehend even intellectually the possible realism of your statements. And I can't well plead a case of love for you truly because at my most sweet or straight or goody-goody or sacrificing or demanding, I am always conscious below of stabbing you in the back while I lead you or deceive you. This is not so much conscious as merely known, by both of us, I suppose.

But in this exposition I am losing my purpose and emotion and I must send it to you if only as an expression of my hatred. It broke my mask before to read your letter, not the content but phrases—were you mocking me? I don't think so—like "My good and lovely boy," "Answer me, sweet Allen." And for the first time I thought of you for such phrases, and for promises I made you make and which were not kept, and so I went to bed, then half forgetful and I lay half trembling, with recollected desire, breaking moment after moment, till I cried, and freed myself to think freely almost without the armor of these last weeks. I don't know what I can do, Neal, now. You know you are the only one who gave me love that I wanted and never had, as you have — this does not humiliate me any more — a number of others, and I sometimes wonder about them. What must I do for you to get you back? I will do anything. Any indecencies, any revelations, any creation, any miseries, will they please you? Or will they frighten you as this does? I mean to bend my mind that knows it can destroy you to any base sordid level of adoration and masochistic abnegation that you desire or taunt me with. This has style, and it is now so much vomit. Or do you look on it as such? I do not care what I think really, I hate and fear you so much that I will do anything to win your protection again, and your mercy.

I am lonely, Neal, alone, and always I am frightened. I need someone to love me and kiss me and sleep with me; I am only a child and have the mind of a child. I have been miserable without you because I had depended on you to take care of me for love of me, and now that you have altogether rejected me, what can I do, what can I do?

All this above is still not sincere. I cannot come down to the point where I was when I rose from bed. Neal, Neal, I am weak, now you can inflict any punishment on me you want. I can't write except with you in mind—I have two hundred beautiful lines from Dakar and I don't care about it except to show to you and have you praise me for them. I have sad lines, so sad I wept when I wrote them, and if you had any heart would weep to see all the soft torment and suffering that is in them, all the miserable torture that you made me go through. I blame you, yet I still ask for the whip.

I don't know what I am when I speak like this but it is near my true speech. Don't think that I forget myself, it is only that I have so much soul that I can rise above you not in mockery or mind but spiritual genius, for all the suffering, at the moment when I most beseech and cry. And it is my hatred for you that drives me in fear of my obscure and not known power to supplicate and kneel, to blow you and turn away unsatisfied when you are sated. What can I say but that I am not worthy of you in a real world, and that you have no cause or passion's cause to handle me and give me love, and deal with me at all. I did not mean to challenge you, I am frightened. I meant that I was impure and pure, too pure to be drowned in vomit. Yet all I am is, as well, vomit, and I am drowned.

I have never asked you for a true favor, a gratuitous gift from you but small ones once or twice when I was driven to it by your love and purposeful or unconscious frustration of me. I have always been obedient and respectful, I have adjusted my plans to yours, my desires to your own pattern, and now I do ask—I pray—please Neal, my Neal, come back to me, don't waste me, don't leave me. I don't want to suffer any more, I have had my mind broken open over and over before, I have been isolate and loveless always. I have not slept with anyone since I saw you, not because I was faithful but because I am afraid and I know no one. I will always be afraid I will always be worthless, I will always be alone till I die and I will be tormented long after you leave me. I can't give up now for this time the one chance I have of serving, not being served, the last time, my only time. Already I am aging, I feel my life is sterile, I am unbloomed, unused, I have nothing I can have that I will ever want, only some love, only dearness and tenderness, to make me weep. I am moved now and sad and unhappy beyond cold unhappiness, beyond any inconvenience that will cause you by my affection. And I will pay you back, you will see, you have never touched my intellect, I can teach you, really, what you want to know now, I will give you money. You know, or will someday learn, that you have no existence outside of me and will never be free until I free you. You have not loved yet and you have not served, and if you can you must come to love and serve me by that love: not by service, by emotions, by care and kindness that I need. I have genius, and I have had to pay for it with torment and horror; my every act is a trial of the soul, my guilt makes me mad; I have descended depths beyond depths into my own personality, even to the point of exhibition, of self-pity that is not self-pity but knowledge of tragedy. Neal, how can I change, what can I do? Don't you see that I cannot be composed, I cannot reconcile myself, because there is no other reality but loneliness for me and before I am dragged back into isolation I will clasp and grasp and claw in fright even at you without consciousness—even I—and I am afraid that I cannot survive if I have to go on into myself. You do not care, you have all genius and fortune and worldly and spiritual power and you can be happy and take what you want. I have nothing and can give little of value and don't know how and am unsuccessful and awk-ward with people. Now I call you to save me I see and I have lost my reasons. Can you do it for a love of me, even not physical? Can you do it out of pity? It is pure pity that I beg now, not comradeship or love or sympathy, sheer driven blind powerful pity. Is not my state so wretched that you who once loved me cannot think of me without guilt. Or if it is guilt that will call you, then guilt, I am not so strong that I can afford to choose my weapons. Didn't you first come to me, seduce me—don't you remember how you made me stop trembling in shame and drew me to you? Do you know what I felt then, as if you were a saint, inhuman, to have touched me so, and comforted me, even deceived me a moment in my naiveté to think I was loved. I remember that night, and it is so sad now in my mind, to think that it did happen, if once, that I think of death and only death afterwards. Do you think I am lying again? I don't mean death as suicide, I mean the unknown, the unforeseen, the horrible.

I would go on and on but in my eye I am afraid that all my emotions will only bore you and that you will turn from me with every pleading phrase, I am afraid that you could and this leaves me now as I end, speaking to you, sitting here, waiting in silence, speaking to you no more o god Neal please Come back don't be harsh on me I can't help this I can only apologize and beg and beg and beg.

Allen Ginsberg

[*In spite of his unsuccessful attempts to maintain a love affair, to enter psychotherapy, and to finish college, Ginsberg continued to write poetry. He kept in touch with his professor, Lionel Trilling, who became a surrogate father to him. As a writer Ginsberg struggled with his poetic style and had not yet discovered his own voice.*]

Allen Ginsberg [New York, NY] to Lionel Trilling [New York, NY]
June 1, 1948

Dear Prof. Trilling:

Have you had time to read the poems? I feel guilty about not having developed my art any faster and finer than I have. As you see it still has the subjective elegiac voice, but essentially thickheaded, and I'm beginning to repent, to the point of thinking that I'm altogether on the wrong track. The last poems, "Denver Doldrums and Later Dolours," is more of an improvement, because in the second part there is an intelligence communicating from within the images. But that, if you follow me, is in vain, because all I have to say in it is that I realize the fantastic nature of all that I said before. I have thought, ambitiously, of having a book, and I guess I will go through with it if it is possible, everything is finished, almost. I don't know how good the poetry is, whether it will pass. I feel for what I have done, but I know it is nowhere. What I have in mind for the future will be much less ambivalent, and easily recognizable, I am sure. I would like, at last, to work by myself, intently and with care. Conditions seem least favorable, since I will have to jump into the social abyss this fall, and I am not ready yet. I have decided that I really don't want to teach, and furthermore I'm sick and tired of Columbia University. I don't think I want to study anywhere either. The only thing good for me about the university is the leisure to study by myself, and a few directed contacts with people. I am beginning to feel sufficiently sure of myself to think that it is enough merely to write. Other work, (I'm not talking about a study) is not good for anything, particularly not discipline, psychological or aesthetic. Art is enough. It comes to me as a surprise.

Ransom[13] rejected the first poem (Denver Doldrums) and sent a letter asking for something more "compacted." The poems you have would probably fill his bill. He said that he liked the poem. I'll send him more, as soon as I get them back from you.

Also, I must tell you about St. Shapiro.[14] I finally took a course with him as you suggested a few years ago. I don't know anything about fine art and sat terrified in the front row, smiling to hear the sweetness of his discourse. I was also afraid to write his papers, but I couldn't evade the examination, for which I studied at the last moment, and I wrote him a wild sleepless book. I saw him the same afternoon to try to explain what I had meant there, though he hadn't read it yet, and held forth frantically on some mad idea about Cosmic Vibrations in Cézanne, and we parted, I suspect, mutually baffled. This morning I got a marvelous letter from him complimenting me on the exam and chiding me for not writing the term paper, and he wants to see me. Really he is a fine character, I can't get over it; I am overjoyed to find a man of such sensibility.

Now, to get off this kick, I have something serious on my mind. Jack Kerouac, whom you remember, as I produced him as a genius a few years ago, has all along been writing a novel I don't know if I told you about that. He has been working on it, in one form or another, since 1942. For the last five and a half years (since around the time he was ordered off the campus) he has been writing steadily, five and eight and eleven and sixteen hours, by night, sleeping by day, living at home etc., and has finally finished his book. He delivered it to me last week. It is 380,000 words—I know you will appreciate the labor that goes into that—and will stretch longer, with a few more chapters. I suppose you don't trust my judgment on it, particularly since I am extreme on the subject, but it is a great book, monumental, magnificent, profound, far far finer than anything I had imagined, a literary work of enormous importance, etc. I am sure you will like it, but not now, because you don't sympathize really. Anyway,

13 John Crowe Ransom (1888–1974). Editor of the *Kenyon Review.*
14 Meyer Shapiro (1904–1996). Art historian and Columbia professor.

I would ask you to read it, long as it is, if you have time, but I don't feel that there is much point since you wouldn't trust my judgment no matter how earnestly and gravely or gleefully I tell you there is a Great American Novel under our noses. Anyway I am afraid to ask you to read it, though I ask you, because you so often reject my enthusiasms for reasons beyond my understanding. Oh well, I'll get off this kick, too. Anyway, I have circulated a few chapters of it around, they have been excitedly received, and I have been trying to make some connections to get the book launched (it was rejected in messed up manuscript form by Scribner's.) The best fish I can catch at the moment, besides agents, is Alfred Kazin,[15] through some friends. But I remember reading something of his a long time ago and thought he was a deadhead, and don't want to have to trust him if I have to. Do you have any suggestions, any particular persons, we could get to without too much formal bs? I realize you may not want to take the responsibility, but I am only asking, and I am willing to take responsibility for that even if it means my "final exclusion from the world of letters." Also it must be someone sympathetic, and with lots of influence. Kerouac is a type of simpleton and the easier things are made the nicer it will be. This is really very important; the book is very great and he is tired of being pushed around, and also tired of being discouraged, I imagine. You know what the situation must be if the book is (hypothetically) any good at all.

I saw your [Henry] James essay, and thought it was the best and most beautiful criticism you have written. But I'll speak of this another time, if I may.

Regards,

Allen G.

[*Over many years Allen Ginsberg and Jack Kerouac maintained a long, philosophical dialogue through their correspondence. In this letter Allen pondered on Kerouac's oft-repeated remark, "God is love."*]

Allen Ginsberg [New York, NY] to Jack Kerouac [NY?]
ca. **November–December 1948**

Dear Jack:

Letters or speech as we speak is vague, but only because we are vague. There is no such thing as life's bitter mystery, and yet you say also that it is a

---

15 Alfred Kazin (1915–1998). Writer and literary critic.

beautiful mystery. It is a mystery to us, that's all. "None of us understand what we're doing" but we do beautiful things anyway. The something else that we are doing is always recognized by us one way or other. I want to know what I am doing / I want to recognize this. This can be recognized. That is what psychoanalysis, religion, poetry, all teaches us, that it can by its nature be recognized, sin is not recognizing. Cézanne is a beginning of recognition for me but it is not the real thing, just still an intellectual-sense substitute. All the fascination and beauty of people meeting and echoing comes from our innate instinct which is not yet emerged to consciousness, that we are here, that something specific is there that we are arguing our love about. It is one thing to accept it as such and wander around like in a dreamland struck with uncomprehending wonder of the mystery of the beauty. But if anyone throws back a direct shock of communication—not mysterious, but direct, some people are capable of that—it would be frightening to me and you because it would disrupt the whole dream of ambiguously intended beauty. What if I said stop trying to kid me, stop play acting as if I didn't know what you were talking about? You don't say what you mean, particularly in your explanation of what if anything Lu [Carr] meant by saying that he was sorry that you weren't a socially acceptable writer.

"We don't know what we are saying." "It appears that only god must know." What if we really did and were just hiding it? That is what we are doing. What did you really mean when you told me to stop peering into your soul? I was just understanding too much. Understanding sensations and feelings of gibbering idiocy that you had that you didn't want spoken of, much less enacted. Everything that you say in your letter is true, but still partial because it really tries to deceive with a gentleman's agreement. I am more afraid of a gentleman's agreement not to hit below the belt than any other. Everyone knows about the gentleman's agreement not to get to the real point, and that doubt in the back of the head is the very area of knowledge. Any attempt even to agree on the existence of this doubt and then act as if it didn't matter when it is the whole point will not bring happiness or art. "If we were god we would always feel love, only with complications." Yes that is so, and we are already in this state. The thing to do is get rid of such complications, not ignore them or explain them away as part of a meaningless business that had better be left vague, or you know what will happen. "It is just a kind of fear of being understood." True, absolutely. With love as the basic and only, exhaustive, all meaning and absolute thing that is being understood. That is why I reach out to touch people, physically. I enact the form perhaps? without content. That is because I believe in action. If you were understood, you say, completely, there would be no more meaning to the understanding, therefore the necessity of sin. "Realize Allen, that if all the world were green, there would be no such thing as the color green. Similarly, men cannot know what it is to be together without otherwise knowing what it is to be apart. If all the world were love, then how could love exist!" This is the root of your dishonesty and in a similar way mine. You try to keep it back. The point is that all thought is inexistence and unreality, the only reality is green, love. Don't you see that it is just the whole point of life not to be self conscious? That it must be all green? All love? Would the world then seem incomprehensible? That is an error. The world would seem incomprehensible to the rational faculty which keeps trying to keep us from the living in green, which fragments and makes every thing seem ambiguous and mysterious and many colors. The world and we are green. We are inexistent until we make an absolute decision to close the circle of individ-ual thought entirely and begin to exist in god with absolute unqualified and unconscious understanding of green, love and nothing but love, until a car, money, people, work, things are love, motion is love, thought is love, sex is love. Everything is love. That is what the phrase "God is Love" means. There is one law and most men try to live as if their law were different, as if they had an understanding of their own. You don't realize that your only personality not merely your true personality, which other people see, and even you see, as you, as your only personality, is not that which you set up for yourself and others to see, your individual self enclosed rebellious, egoistic mental system, your child-ishness. Your personality has nothing to do with you, what you want it to be like in your deception. It is what you are which you don't admit that I actually see you as. It would be an awful shock for you to realize that. It is also some thing you kept saying to me once. The unbelievable in the back of the head, that is the one thing that people see clearly in each other, not their reasons for not believing it which they have the gentleman's agreement not to "misunder-stand" each other. What the fuck do you actually care whether or not you know you are love in the false way that you seem to think you "know" things now? Why are you afraid to submit to the annihilation of such stupid meaning-less unreal knowledge. This is the abyss. Everything is green, love, without the logical fantastic equivocations that we invent so that we won't actually have to face each other. That is the death truly that Jesus advises, which everyman faces and dies in in different forms but never completely to the point of complete submission. They pass through the phase of possibility of such a death, face it, fear it, put it off, construe it to a meaningless verbal complex, avoid it, are changed and entrenched by the experience. Do you really believe that Lucien [Carr] totally died, or that he and Bill [Burroughs] reentrenched themselves, but stayed the same? Nobody that we know is dead.

Can this be me? Every time I see myself as I am I am staring into a cosmic mirror in which I see myself with my thoughts broken into nothing, and my unequivocal physical self weaving and gyrating in the universe in an incomprehensible monkeylike babbling idiocy, a sordid frightening picture. Actually I would at that stage be a saint, or an ordinary natural man, but so different are my mental conceptions from reality, that I think I am a monster when I see what could be. I have only faced this mirror for a few moments at a time, actually a few frightened split seconds, at maybe three different times in my life. That is what my equilibrium with L. [Lucien] is. I attempt, or flirt, with that image, a sexual one also as it is one and the same, and because I trust and acknowledge his just mind, and his love, I have only myself to blame if I do not turn before him into the monster. So instead I tell him what I saw in the mirror, and he believes me, at the same time we both realize that we are deceiving each other when we don't change into what we are. I was frightened as a kid by the transfiguration scene in Jekyll and Hyde. That is because it recalled my true self to me. So miraculous and unbelievable is this true self, is life, that it seems like an image of horror, once we accept that horror we see that it was all a fit, that horror was the birth pains, the pangs of recognition of self deception, and we are in love (in green). Blake and Emily Dickinson and lots describe this specifically.

> "To find the western path,
> Right through the gates of wrath
> I urge my way:
> Sweet morning leads me on.
> With soft repentant moan,
> I see the break of day."

This is the moment of death. This is the nectar whereof each one tells. This is why Lucien sadly hits himself on the head with a frying pan at dawn, he has never done it. I have not yet. Yes, for fuck all this, I am crazy. All this is raving babbling. I am I talk and read and write and the circle of destiny narrows and closes around me: die, go mad, what you think now is mad is really love and sane. Die, go "mad." This is schizoid. I am now monomaniacal in my preoccupation with this moment of will.

I think what I say is true in one way or another, though you can't understand it, I think, because I have not made myself clear. Perhaps I could have said all this by saying, of your letter, I understand what you are saying, more or less. I understand because not that I am smart, but that you have actually understood what you were writing. I heard what you were saying. I did not understand fully because you were not clear enough, because you were beginning to understand, but it was not complete you yet. When it becomes more complete, I will understand more. Don't say that it never becomes complete because what I am saying is that that is just the whole point, even of you, that it can be complete. All green. Abandon everything else.

Allen

[*Ginsberg was also fond of another English professor at Columbia, Mark Van Doren. In this letter Allen engaged in a literary conversation and tried to impress his old teacher with lines from his new poem, later published as "A Western Ballad."*]

Allen Ginsberg [New York, NY] to Mark Van Doren [New York, NY]
December 1948–January 1949

Dear Prof. Van Doren:

Got your letter plus enclosure. I guess you may take this as a formal acknowledgement.

My verse is weak; there isn't anything I have written which will be anything like what I will write someday, I trust. You know how I feel—as a novitiate, of the lowest order yet. I used to wash dishes on Times Square, when I would have liked to be a great criminal in some far way; and sailing the seas I also washed pots and pans. I rose from iron. I should have been captain on a slow boat to China—peg leg and all. I grew a Hebrew Rabbi's beard when I was at sea a year and a half ago. Now I am a copyboy on the A.P. [Associated Press]. If I move higher I may get to be a copyboy on the *Times*. So I am a copyboy of a poet—at the moment. I don't mean to be apologetic, but affirmative since you have heard little explicitly so from me. I'm not very explicit, but I hope to be someday. Perhaps I may be able to put some of the sun's light into my poetry, if so I have no longer any doubts as to what exactly I will be doing. It might be anything so why worry about it now? I suppose such carelessness may not be the last step to resurrection but I also trust that is on the road. I am mostly thinking of [illegible]—my own and the world's, nay, that of the very cosmos itself. Are they all the same? Or have I got my levels mixed? It's hard to keep them straight. So to get back to the point I hope someday to gladden your heart with some great-dimensioned thing of delight in celestial numbers. Thank you for your generosity and the glimmer of eternity which you have added to my horizon, even when I was not worthy of your confidence. And when alas, shall I be worthy of it?

I was "astounded" by J. [Jethro] Robinson when I saw his poems and heard of him thru [Richard] Weitzner's few words lately. Isn't there true warmth in "burly Ebenezer, home at noon?" There's no way for him to lie in such a matter, no? Imagination —

> "When I consider how the barrel hath
> contained in staves of want and misery
> sucks up in death what it spit forth in birth . . ."

a feeling for angels, tells us what it's all about. Too bad, I feel somehow, that he hasn't invented a verse, a style of his own, as well as a feeling of his own — something that talks in a modern way, and not in an old and poetically recidivist manner. But he is supposed to be a novelist and that may be inventive. "We" have got to keep the channels clear for our own time, or we will not be heard in our own time — and as for me I mean to speak to be heard now. It's got to be absolutely universal. But perhaps that is a statement of ignorance and not prophecy. Meanwhile I've started a new ballad — half western, half metaphysical. Almost true in a way, but not resolved into a clear simple image.

> "When I died, love, when I died
> There was a war in the upper air;
> all that happens, happens there.
> There was an angel at my side,
> When I died, love, when I died."

and

> "When I died, love, when I died
> I wearied in an endless maze
> That men have walked for centuries;
> as endless as the gate was wide,
> When I died, love, when I died."

I did these slowly at work. It goes by itself in fits and starts, like the warming up of a motor.

Well, so much for all this B.S.

My life is quicksanding a lot because of work and because old friends from Denver and Frisco [Cassady] came to town. I am invited to go on an expedition to New Orleans to the house of a wonderful family—the people who lived in Texas [Burroughs]—and stay awhile work, see the Mardi Gras, and perhaps move on to Nevada—work on a railroad. I gave it up—too many personal complications, though the personal complications now have really lifted me up. I wonder if a plunge back into sexual anarchy is what I need. Sometimes I think so. I get locked up in a green serious world of—for—to myself when I'm alone. Anyway I think I will sit still in N.Y. And Paris! and independence! and blind action! Scenes, tableaux, intensity, a whole wilderness to explore. But I am afraid it is only a wilderness. Right here I am at least next to the wall. But the wall travels. You see I am taking back everything I say now so I will stop. Don't answer as I also don't want you to get hung up.

Allen Ginsberg.

P.S. I think something has started to happen—love.

[During the spring of 1949, Herbert Huncke came to Ginsberg's door battered and worn out. Allen famously described him in Howl as someone "who walked all night with their shoes full of blood on the snowbank docks waiting for a door in the East River to open to a room full of steamheat and opium." He welcomed him into his apartment and took care of him until he was stronger. Then Huncke, along with his friends Little Jack Melody and Vicki Russell, began to fill Allen's place with stolen property. Allen could not, or would not, ask them to leave. He described the scene in this letter to Neal Cassady.]

Allen Ginsberg [New York, NY] to Neal Cassady [San Francisco, CA]
ca. **April 21, 1949**

Dear Neal:

Are you too occupied to write, or don't you want to for some reason concerning your relationship with us in N.Y.? No reason occurs to me that seems important, despite the usual fantasies of hassle.

The golden day has arrived for Jack [Kerouac] and he has sold his book [*The*

Town and the City]. He has a % promise, on sales, 85% on movie rights (which I believe will materialize as a matter of course after considering the nature of his work; but this has been my opinion for a long time; it now seems to be more generally accepted, and so may be true) and most important for the actual money, $1,000.00 (a thousand) cash advance, which has been in his possession for several weeks. He is not mad at you; as matter of fact 5 out of the 15 sandwiches he denied you in Frisco went bad before he could eat them.

Bill Burroughs has been arrested and faces a jail term in Louisiana for possession of narcotics and guns, etc. There is now no telling what will happen but he may get out of it without jail. Joan [Burroughs] wrote, and he wrote the next day having got out on bail quickly. If he is to be jailed I expect to invite Joan [to] NY to stay with me with children at my apartment. If he gets out, he will have to leave Texas and Louisiana as it is hot there for him; perhaps to Chicago, or Yucatan; doubtful of N.Y. as his family objects to this city, and much will depend on them financially, I think.

Claude [Lucien Carr] is writing stories and being psychoanalyzed. These are radical developments which I, at least, have hoped for and I believe it is the beginning of his regeneration and the assumption of an ideal power and humanity for him. He broke with Barbara this month. As long as I have thought of us as artists, it has been Claude who I thought of as central to any active inter-inspiring school or community of creation, and him to whom I have looked for the strength to assume responsibility for the truest aesthetic knowledge and generosity; it appears, somehow, that the unseen magnet has begun to draw him at last. And so a kind of potential millennium, that I dreamed of years ago with juvenile and romantic prophetic power, is being actualized in its truest forms, and in the only necessary and inevitable way. I talked with him all last night, heard him outline the method, plot, and technique (to give his ideas categories) and it sounded, what he had to say, essential, accurate, and so unexpected as to be inspired to my mind; and yet proceeding logically from his whole past position; but surpassing it. Anyway, another myth come true. His concern is with action and facts and things happening; but he seems (I say but because though that is the concern of all writers, ostentatiously, except crackbrained alchemists like myself) he seems successfully concerned with facts and their harmony and relationships, and all suggestion of what I would look for as the metaphysical or divine seem to rise from his stories as they do from life, and more so, because of the objectivity and sympathy and seemingly self enclosed structure of his tales; so that there is nothing extraneous or purposeless in his work; he says everything he says because he intends to. This self evident principle I discovered for my own poetry (everything must have a point and not be rhetoric) last summer consciously; but I have not been able to perfect many poems to clear realiza- tion because of my own abstract and vaporous tendencies; but I see it successfully applied in Claude potentially more than Jack. When Claude's imagination becomes freed of fear he will be a great man. I dwell so much on this because now Claude is again in the fold, the great RAM of the fold much improved from before; once again we are involved in the same work of truth and art all together. Maybe I am making too much of a good thing, however so let it pass.

I am again in a doldrums, a weak link in a chain, only surpassed in weakness by yourself perhaps. Herbert has been with me draining my money and vitality for months; now Vicki and a man named Little Jack have joined us, and are operating out various schemes successfully. Money is beginning to come in; I am to sublet my apartment to join Joan and Bill [Burroughs]: they will pay my way (Little Jack, etc.) in return for apartment for summer and now. But Bill's arrest casts a shade on that and I do not know what I will do. I would like to leave the city for the summer (June, July, August) if possible to stay with Joan and Bill. I am not writing much or well, but I have always been dissatisfied with what and how I have written; now however my artistic impotence now seems more real and radical and I will have to act someday, not only writing more, but on large scale, commercially usable (poetic dramas for television as I dream) etc. However my theoretical and visionary preoccupations—fixation, based on experience which was gifted, as it seemed, from a higher intelligence of conscious Being of the universe, or hallucination, as the doctor dismissed it when I went to arrange for therapy beginning September, has left me confused and impotent in action and thought and a prey to all suggestions, winds of abstract thought, and lassitudes and sense of unworthiness and inferiority that rise continually before my now dulling eyes, and a prey to all suspicions, my own and others, that come forth. The household set up which I both hate and desire, that I have, is an example of my uncertainty of path and dividedness. It seems that the road to heaven or back to sanity require me to deal in realities of time and circumstance which I have never done, and to learn new things, which I'm unused to. But I seem to have, like Joan, passed some point in my brain which I cannot go back from, and for the moment forward either except by some violent effort I have been incapable of since I can remember.

But perhaps therapy will help me. Anyway, I am making preparations to teach in Cooper Union College this fall, and so have some financial security more than now at A.P. Then I will be by myself and try to think unless something unexpected happens from the outside to change me or my relations with others. Next year this all amounts to saying, I will try again; now I am caught up in weariness and defeat and sterility and circumstances which have no end or meaning. Perhaps by leaving town I will activate and escape this inertia. Perhaps if you thought well of it I will come to California. At the moment however, I am not in any active suffering, and my mind is active and comparatively clear. It is long inaction and too much introspection and lack of practical ambition that weighs me down. However my pad is hot, and I expect a visit from the narcotics people since they seized several of my letters to Bill in the course of his fall. If I were able to keep clean that would be OK, but with Vicki and others pursuing their busy rounds there is always something for the law to object to. I can't seem to put my foot down, or make up my mind to, mostly because that is why they are using my pad in the first place, to operate out of, and my end is to get enough to travel off their work. Perhaps I shall find that I have been self destructively greedy on this score. But when I see the treasures rolling in I find it a powerful argument against any cautionary impulses, of mine. And maybe nothing will happen. That about summarizes what goes on on York Ave. General intimidation. Herbert was beat, and now just begins to prosper, so I can't well put a stop to it all. Or not easily anyway. I guess this sounds cowardly; or maybe it's only a balloon I blow. Claude and Jack don't seem to approve, and that is why I am concerned at all. Or what brings the concern to my mind, anyway.

What are you doing? When will your heart weary of its own indignity and despotism and lack of creation? Why are you not in N.Y.? Can you do anything away from us? Can you feel anybody as you can feel us, even though in N.Y. you did your worst to surround yourself with a sensate fog of blind activity? Or are you learning something new wherever you are now? If you wonder the motive for these questions don't undercut it with suspicion of sexual motives of mine; I have none now and was not dominated by them when you were last in N.Y. [...]

Love,

Allen

[*On April 21, the police discovered the burglary ring operating out of Ginsberg's apartment, and Allen was arrested. He was eventually sent to a mental hospital instead of prison. There seemed no other reason except insanity that would have made Allen allow the criminals to take over his home as they had. In this letter he revealed how frightened he actually was of putting his friends in jeopardy on his account.*]

Allen Ginsberg [Paterson, NJ] to Jack Kerouac [New York, NY]
early May 1949

Dear Jack:

I am back, as you put it, in the bosom of my family. It's quiet around here but I can get work done if I want to. I filled a 150 page notebook in the last 4 days with a detailed recreation of the events of the last month. This was for my lawyer who wants to get to understand me and find out why I associated with such people and did the things I did. He asked me to write him a journal. I didn't work it out carefully, but in the writing (and before) I think I came to a clear understanding at last of Huncke and his total relationship with people; something I have been seeking for a long time, and the lack of which left me powerless to act towards him before in a positive way. I (perhaps we) had dehumanized him before. The nearest and clearest of him he himself obscured to us all; he needs a mate first like anybody else. The same with me, and Neal, too. I spoke of this to Vicki and I found that she, too, had never realized just what Huncke secretly wanted from us, or we from him. I guess Bill knows Huncke.

My family problems have become more complicated and strange since my mother first was released from the hospital. She is living for the moment in the Bronx with my aunt. I saw her Monday. She is a little flighty, but natural, and my aunt doesn't understand that; but she is a sister and there are other sisterly understandings. I don't know what she will do, or be done, next. Gene and I will not live with her; I'm afraid to, and besides the doctors (at the hospital) forbid it; so that problem isn't mine. But Naomi will have to be financed by my brother and father and aunt, and so that puts an added financial strain on them. Everything seems to have happened all at once.

I don't know what is happening on my case; it is mostly out of my hands in the lawyers'. My family and lawyers are taking the attitude that I am in bad company, so that will make a lot of long range social problems for the future, since I'm so far in as far as having to (gratefully) accept their financial and legal aid. Also they would want me to betray and squeal on everybody to get myself out. It is past the point where I, like Huncke, can try to explain my position with any certitude on my part or assurance of understating, and so I am uneasy. Fortunately I know so little that I have little to squeal about. But presumably Vicki, Herbert, and Jack [Melody] will try to arrange the guilt among themselves according to their own lights, and I fear to be maneuvered into some statement which will disrupt their own stories. The situation is delicate. Of course it won't exist as anything meaningful in another (or 10) years. But at the moment I am prayerfully walking a tightrope. I would hate to have to pick up the toilsome balloon and try to maneuver my own lawyer to advance my case according to my own wishes; but that seems to be my present responsibility. At any rate, he thinks I will have to plead guilty, have charges dropped, be placed in the hands of a psychiatrist; or take a suspended sentence with psychiatrist. I saw Trilling, who thinks I am crazy; and Van Doren, who thinks I am sane but doesn't sympathize beyond a limit (he kept winking at me as we talked). He wrote Morris Ernst, a big criminal lawyer. But it is too late for Ernst for my family already have arranged for lawyers. I also saw Meyer Shapiro (Trilling sent me to him.) He told me to come over, and sat talking with me about the universe for 2 $1/2$ hours; also told me about how he was in jail in Europe for being a stateless bum. He asked about you, apologized again for not being able to get you into his class. My problem, *vis-a-vis* the above with my lawyer, would be less complicated were it not for Bill's letters, which make it imperative for me to settle on other terms than my own nearest and clearest and easiest, and get them out of harm's way before lightning strikes Bill again. It's possible; I am afraid to take chances. I have no idea how deep the Divine Wrath has been planned and will continue.

I am at present thinking a lot about Thomas Hardy's poem "A Wasted Illness," p. 139 of his *Collected Poems*, if you run across a copy. I wonder what Lucien thinks of it, or if he takes it (that particular poem) seriously? The poem is all clear, and as far as I am concerned especially the last stanza. It comes a page after the poem you drew my attention to at Lenrow's[16] house, "The Darkling Thrush." I have also been reading Shakespeare—*Macbeth*. The irony of neglected and forgotten misunderstandings and complacencies returning like ghosts to wreak vengeance.

I would like you to come to Paterson.

Write me about Lucien. Has he told you his stories? Has he begun writing them? Also, please write Bill again, telling him, if you haven't, the total situation.

---

16 Elbert Lenrow (1903–1993). New School instructor and friend.

Tell him to clear his household of crime entirely, wherever he is. I said so. He doesn't need it. Has Neal written?

Mustapha[17]

[*To protect his friends from possible legal difficulties, Allen began to use pseudonyms in his letters much more frequently. While waiting to enter the New York State Psychiatric Institute of Columbia Presbyterian Hospital, he continued to keep in touch with his friends and correspond about literary matters.*]

Allen Ginsberg [Paterson, NJ] to Jack Kerouac [Denver, CO]
June 15, 1949

Dear Jack:

I got your letter today, so add this as a postscript to one which I wrote yesterday, and which you received a week ago. Great news: Pomeroy's address [Neal Cassady] in Frisco is 29 Russell St. I got a letter from Goodyear Service requesting information, so I sent them a recommendation of his vigor and imaginativeness, congratulating them on their association with him, assuring them he'll give them satisfaction. Reminds me of the time he told [Hal] Chase's woman to leave a note in her box. Poor Pomeroy, imagine him depending on beat out refugees like me to be his solid stable reference. Oh, what we dancing masters don't have to endure. Well, write him; I will not (as with Denison [Burroughs] or anyone else) for a time; maybe just a couple of months. Give regards, explain events. Also, my lawyer tells me that I have been cleared by grand jury; no indictment, though Melody, Vicki, and Herb were indicted. I was not at hearing, did not even know it had taken place till later; fine lawyer is keeping me away from all the melee; all the war goes on in upper airs. Apparently an analyst, Van Doren, Mr. and Mrs. Trilling, and Dean Carman[18] had to be present and speak; I don't know any details. But I must say that's mighty cricket of them all. I was really worried last month; and I had reason to be, except for work of others who assumed all the burden. I feel grateful. Shouldn't I? That's what Van Doren means by society I suppose; people getting together to keep each other out of trouble (or away from tragedy) till they got an inkling of what they're getting into. Do you know, incidentally, that 22 years ago Van Doren wrote a little book on Light and E. A. Robinson, "It is not good,

17 Mustapha Nightsoil. A bit of sophomoric humor.
18 Harry Carman (1884–1964). History professor and dean of Columbia College.

one can imagine Mr. Robinson saying, to know too much of anything; but it is necessary for great people thus to err—even while it is death for them to do so. Tragedy is necessary." He ends beginning half of book so. In and out are comments like, "Bartholow, in other words, has seen too much; he is blinded by his light." And "I have spoken more than once of the image of light as being the image in which he saw life reflected. The six poems are all concerned with men who have seen a light and who are both punished and rewarded for doing so." I believe that Van Doren is talking about that specific miracle of vision which I have attempted to point to and specify the last year; his poems are about it; and in conversation with him it seems so; but since 22 years ago he has gone on beyond that light and seen its relationship to the world of time or "sober but hateful sanity"; I say gone on beyond not to mean that he has abandoned it or it him, but that it has assumed a new significance beyond its original occasional appearance as the actual existence of some transcendent fact; perhaps he has learned to see eternity in human laws, to put it bluntly, and god's ways in organized society; perhaps he even believes now without a further thought any, even to us weak willed, complaint against lawbreakers and holds the lawbreakers responsible for some outrage against other men which they really were aware of; and if they (like me) were not aware of it it's just as well that folks give them "a good slap in the face, so that they can hear the ring of iron." The quote is from his lecture to me. Maybe he sees me and the hipsters hassling against society while cream and honey pour down unnoticed. Maybe he thinks it's all a big secret joke, and that the trouble with me is that I am taking it (and myself) too seriously. In fact, these are his opinions. However he had an exaggerated idea of my self hood based on what recently he had been told by Hollander[19] and others about my fancying myself as Rimbaud. Oh those pinheads. Yes, he thinks I am taking myself too seriously. Is there anything more hateful to hear from a wise man? Jack, your book is a big balloon, you take yourself too seriously. And it's true. O Lord what temptations thous placest in the way. Deliver me from my own thoughts and the thoughts of others, too. I think Van Doren probably thinks almost the same as you, that it's all a matter for the giggling lings, so what's all this intense investigation of evil?

Remember the discussion about prayer we had? I had this week a trembling on the edges of revelation again, and came up with a fish, half flesh, half abstract; no real revelation so no true fish (incidentally I do not believe that I will have any more guideposts of Light given free for a while now). I have been

19 John Hollander (b. 1929). Columbia classmate of Ginsberg, later literary critic and poet.

praying previously for God's love; and to be made to suffer; and to be taken (I wish he'd pull my daisy); it says here in my (new) notebook, for June 14 "Say not, Love me, Lord," but "I love you, Lord!" Only lately has this aspect of the way been clear to me in its meaning. You have said this in one form or another to me a number of times; and Claude [Lucien] has told me the same. I was wrong.

Of your poetry. Yeats warns to beware of Hodos Chameliontos. You know what that is? (I was reading his autobiography, borrowed from Lenrow). That is a big dragon, all Chinese, except that it is a chameleon; and one minute you have one Chinese image, the next minute you are bumping along on a Mayan spider; and before you know it it turns into a North African porpentine, and an Indian Geek, and a Western Cat.

"Worry therefore not for green, / And dark, which deceptive signs are, / Of golden milk. / Beelzebub is just a lamb." Or "'Twas a husk of doves."

Hodos Chameliontos is also worrisomely mechanical, and very abstract. Do you know that my lecherous wink is by now become so repetitious and stale and mechanical that I am caught with my pants down? This is because I am not dealing with real things; but abstract relations between values; on the basis of a true inspiration; but the inspiration is departed, the lesson remains and is repeated by rote with many changes of symbol but not of formula. But that is the way my mind works, in its illusory Beulah. Beulaah. Beulaaah. That is the trouble I suspicion in the Myth of the Rainy Night, as far as symbols are concerned; that also was what was wrong with my Denver birds and nightingales and dawns; I got so hung up on a series of words that I went around abstractly composing odes, one after another, until even now I can't tell them apart and what they mean, and had, for instance, to throw all of the birthday ode of Willi Denison [Burroughs Jr.] out the winder, when I was making up my book. That is what is the trouble with the "Divide where the rains and river are decided." Well, you have worked out a myth for the symbol (rain being Time, events, things; the river and sea all the holy raindrops connected) (No?) and these are good and stable currency to work with; will you have trouble amplifying and extending? Eliot complains that Blake was, alas, a great minor poet, not a major one, since he made up a lot of crazy symbols of his own which nobody understands. Even I can't read the weird beautiful prophetic books because they are full of Hodos. (I'm reading a commentary on them now by Mona Wilson) whereas I get not only understanding but the actual illumination of wisdom from the short "Ah, sunflower." That is why you are so lucky and wise to be a novelist with an epic of storied events to work on; and why you are inclined (is this not so?) to leave the Myth of the Rainy Night a great big detailed fable-story, and not (as I was trying to suggest,) an allegory with a big worked out symbolism. The Giggling Ling itself is not an aspect of Hodos, for instance, because in addition to its Chinoiserie, it also winks out a stale real sound effect which gives it away; it is an actual emotion of reality recon-structed. So the thousands of details of Myth of Rain, will reveal themselves; not through an artificial system of thought. I hearken back to your letter to say, that the dirty ditty in my work comes from the feeling that I have that all I and other people secretly want is…also it's happened to me several times that while walking up a rainbow, when I get to the other side I find not a pot of gold but a bedpan, full. But I am not disappointed, because shit is gold. What else would gold be, but that, and rain? or water? So that the key, has been to remind them (people) that the shroudy stranger has a hard on; and that the key to eter-nal life is through the keyhole; and so I make great big sensual hints; and not dirty jokes, mind you, but serious hidden invocations. And when someone will read it, and see, under the surface of my poem, as under the surface of his mind, a golden pole, and a holey goals, and a silver shower; I hope to accom-plish someday an outright sensual communion; and as my love grows purer and less lecherous, when someone peeks under the surface of what I say, they will really be made love to. And not only that, I'll have this long serious conver-sation with them, just as if the two of us were in the same head. And further-more, it will only be under the surface for those who are themselves under the surface; but anybody truly akin will recognize it outright, because that's what I'll be talking about all the time right on top down front. And I will be writing about boys and girls in love in dreamland, like Blake, about the pale youths and white virgins rising from their graves in aspiration for "where my sunflower wishes to go;" and, "if her parents weep, / How can Lyca sleep?" and "absti-nence sows sand all over / the ruddy limbs and flaming hair." And if I find out any more about death, as other poets actually have, so they say, then I will have a way of communicating that too. Unfortunately, my present hang up is sexual and so I have recourse to that for key symbolism; but that in time will evapo-rate into a healthier and less frustrated truthfulness. Also, I learned from a mutual acquaintance, learned "In bodily lowliness, and in the heart's pride / A woman can be proud and stiff (i.e. love is physical) / When on love intent, / but love has pitched his mansion / In the place of excrement." That's my favorite poem of all, because it is so literal, it has really only one meaning, and that's what Yeats means. I am not just dirty to be cute; it's partly that (when in a poem I say blows, not smokes the flower superfine); but because I am calling the attention of the poem and reader to a state of fact, which is hidden, either from consciousness, or real attention, if conscious. Yes, I too see Herrick in his cups writing soft lyrics about his lady's petticoats. Remember walking down the street, reading the Bible, shouting from Jeremiah, "The filth is in her Petticoats?"

Ah, yes, I remember well the road leading to Central City, and the small hills there. I was hoping you lived there. Pommy [Neal] and I once rode around there all over the side roads leaving firecrackers under people's porches in the middle of the night. When you write, tell me how your mother is feeling about Denver, and what she says. Also, is there any difficulty about writing? I mean, about your receiving letters from me? If there is, we should do something practical to straighten out that. I could write care of general delivery.

When I next write—incidentally I will for sure be in the crazy house when I next write, so don't worry—I will probably have finished a poem about the lines I wrote a while ago

> "I met a boy on the city street,
> Fair was his hair, and fair his eyes,
> Walking in his winding sheet,
> As fair as was my own disguise."

I have some of it written: it will tell Pommy; I am writing a prophetic poem for Pommy; it will see all, hear all, know all; I am the witness for Pommy, though he doesn't know; it endeth:

> "And so I pass, and leave these lines
> Which few will read, or understand;
> If some poor wandering child of Time
> Sees them, let him take my hand.
>   . . .
> And I will take him to the Stone,
> And I will lead him through the grave,
> But let him fear no light of bone,
> And fear no more the dark of Wave..."

Followed by several more as yet unwritten stanzas describing the mansions of the Lord. Maybe I will also throw in, for good measure, that my name is angel and my eyes are fire, and that All Who Follow Shall Be Rewarded With My Favor.

May I have the title for "Tip My Cup," to use bookishly? Also, think up more, and send them to me; better we will write our own mutual poem, and I will publish it in my book under your name, and you in yours in mine, and he and she in It's. We'll call it the Natural Top. Who shall it be dedicated to? Poe? Walter Adams? Ignu VII of Egypt? Oscar Bop? The survivors of Thermopylae? Bobby Pimples? Hysterical Larry?

Speaking of epileptics (and I promise you that this is the last time I mention Pommy's name) do you know that Fyodor [Dostoyevsky] was, as you say, just like Pommy? I read a book written by Mrs. D. describing the days when he was gambling in Baden, and how she used to weep and cry alone at home, expecting a baby, while Fyodor was gambling his last ruble, his last kopeck, even, and finally coming home, throwing himself weeping at her feet, offering to commit suicide to demonstrate his love for her, and making her give him her shawl off her shoulders so that he could pawn it to play some more. She poor wretch, didn't know what to do, prided herself on being understanding, and then felt justified when one day he came home with a fortune he'd won; they celebrate, and then he goes out and loses it all the next day; and all starts up again, and happens every week and goes on for weeks and weeks and months, and a whole half year, with hysterical scenes and pacifications and entreaties every other night, like a hotel room in Denver, until at last he's so beat that he can't go on—he hasn't any more money, blames himself, cries that he is a failure. Finally he falls at her feet sobbing like a[n] injured child, helpless and in an epileptic; so she bundles him up in her coats and takes him down the R.R. station and they go to Russia. What a great, mad book, by Mrs. D. Probably in Denver Library. Years later he writes about it (in a few letters) and what he says about her, sounds like a wise and aged Pommy recollecting his own lifetime. But a wise and aged Pommy, naturally still vigorous, much more insight, on account of years. If you are curious what Pommy might be really truthfully (to self) thinking in years.

See, I have without planning, spent hours writing you. I hereby present them to you as a gift, free. No strings.

Allen

[*John Clellon Holmes, a new friend of Kerouac and Ginsberg, wrote to Allen asking him about the visions he had been having of William Blake. Holmes was interested in his friend, but he was also a writer and wanted to know about Allen's visions as source material for future books.*]

**Allen Ginsberg [Paterson, NJ] to John Clellon Holmes [Provincetown, MA]
June 16, 1949**

Dear John:

Thank you for investigating *Partisan*. The copy of the poem I sent you ["Stanzas: Written at Night in Radio City"] is dog eared, so I enclose another copy. I hope I can get some poems published soon; I have spent the last two weeks working steadily on the manuscripts you saw, and have revised them where they needed it (except for some things that are so tangled I haven't the character to untangle them) threw out a lot. There are about 50 poems left, on clean new paper (the same as this) and I am ready to go into business. I will give the book first to as many people who will read it and suggest improvements. I feel (this a most urgent specter in my poetic process) that the book is value-less, without positive content, and cannot escape that final conclusion despite the fact that I continue to work on it.

I am in Paterson; and have been since I saw you. I had intended to settle here and get a job and learn to love my family anew, and this resolution, coupled with concomitant perception of the fact that I have been harboring an enormous weight of irrational wrath, gave me a few peaceful hopeful days, but when my wrath was tried in circumstances which demanded absolute humility to my father I could not swallow my pride, without raging up again, and had to close up the wound by withdrawing from "engagement" among the family — failure of wholeheartedness without which there is no understanding—as exemplified in all the best novels. Anyway, independent of this, my lawyer, and the official analyst I saw, who dealt with the D.A. made a deal, that if I were to be given psychiatric care, charges would be dropped. I am in a few days going as an in-patient to the Columbia Psychiatric Clinic, on 168 Street N.Y. This is an experimental mental hospital, where as my analyst says (his name is Dr. Fagan), I will be given "the works," psychoanalytically. I do not know if I will be allowed out; I am to have a room, stay in the hospital, etc. Meanwhile I understand that the others have been indicted—the other day. I know nothing of what goes on since my lawyer has assumed all the burdens of activity—I had a sheltered life here. He is also following a program (in which I am grateful) of keeping from me what's going on, except the few essentials like going to the hospital I will find out about the rest later; for the moment I am at ease. At any rate, the legal weight is off.

I have been reading, too—Blake (Mona Wilson's commentaries, Dostoyevsky Diaries—his wife's comments, *The Possessed*, Yeats' autobiographies, essays, a book on E. A. Robinson by Van Doren, Racine's *Phedre*, Greek plays, Thos. Hardy's poems, Yeats' plays (Wheels and Butterflies); Pound's *Cantos*, Keats and a new book of Dr. Doolittle's adventures by Hugh Lofting. I have nothing else to do, except see movies, 3 or 4 a week, and see old friends from high school. I think a great deal—about the nature of tragedy, and the meaning or significance of light. But all such conclusions are only intellectual constructions of things which to a disciplined mind should be not obvious but palpable.

Jack and I have corresponded fitfully—I do most of the writing. In his first letter he says that he has rented a house @75$ month near Denver: "My house is near the mountains. This is the wrath of sources—The Divide where Rain and Rivers are decided...I am Rubens...this place is full of God and yellow butterflies." His second encloses a poem about a God with a Golden Nose, named Ling, one of the Giggling Lings.

> "...And the Chinamen of the Night
> from Old Green Jails did creep,
> bearing the Rose that's Really White
> to the Lamb that's really Gold..."

He is running around with Justin Brierley, an old Denver Gidean. A schoolteacher and lawyer of whom you may have heard. He is also (Jack, that is) partly running around miserably wondering, etc. His family is there. He rode in a rodeo bareback. He doesn't believe in society. "It's all wrong and I denounce it and it can all go to Hell." "So roll your own bones, I say." He reads Racine and Malherbe and Blake.

Do you remember the jingle: "I love the lord on high / I wish He'd pull my daisy?" Jack contributed another fragment to it: "Pull my daisy, / Tip my cup, / All my doors are open." This has grown into a great monster paean. His stanza begins (my hand at that) "This token mug I tup / Runneth over broken, / Pull my daisy," etc. Other stanzas added since: one he based on a recent poem of mine that has a refrain, "Take them, said the skeleton, / But leave my bones alone." And on the navy captain of another myth: "The time I went to China /

To lead the boyscout troops, / They sand my ocean line, / And all I said was oops."

So: "Tip my cup, / Roll my bones, / All my oops are doopsing."

Also there are fragments that go: "In the east they live in huts, / But they love where I am lolling; / Cut my thoughts / For coconuts, / All my figs are falling." And another begins: "I'm a pot and God's a potter / And my head's a piece of putty..." When it is all complete, we will have a great archetypical jingle, "Pull my daisy / Tip my cup, / cut my thoughts / For coconuts; / Tip my cup, / Roll my bones, / All I said was oops." And will sell it to Charlie Chaplin for his next picture or Groucho Marx. I can see it making a million dollars. Also associated, "I ask the Lady's what's a Rose, / She kicked me outa bed; / I ask a man, and so it goes, / He hit me on the head. / Nobody knows, / Nobody knows, / At least, nobody's said." Well, enough of this. Is [Ed] Stringham there? What does he do, and see? Are there artists there? I hope sometime this summer to be able to get out to visit Provincetown for I have never been there, and it would be wonderful to see you all there in that atmosphere. Marion [Holmes]? Boo! When you next write [Alan] Ansen, give him my regards and tell him what I am doing.

Now as to your request, I am glad to be able to give you any information that I have. You may not take seriously the values that I ascribe to certain experiences but since essentially I am actually involved with what I am talking of I will not bother to enervate the substance of what I say by pacifying irony.

I have attempted to put into language what I mean, events and interpretations, in letters to several people, in notebooks and miscellaneous writings, in conversation, and poems. I have not made a unified coherent or cohering statement because I am not yet ready; I do not object to a system or systematization, because that can be helpful, if properly understood; but approach through a strict rational process is not the most communicative way of transferring thoughts, or attaining rapport. Furthermore, my own use for systematization is limited because it is not system I seek (I have that, almost complete, in skeleton) but depth, value. Approach through reason, however, is one of the many ways; for some people, since it is their tool (as images are mine) it is the necessary way. We each have our own road to perfection. Also, as to your doubts in asking me, it is difficult to supply them satisfactorily (a whole history) because that is a whole mass of detailed explanations of hundreds of significant events, reasonings concerned with them, etc. There are perhaps certain "magic" formulae — recipes, religious apothegms, etc. — but what you are asking for is not so much the say abstract summary of relations between things, but elaborations of the ones I have already affirmed, explanations and details which would perhaps bridge the seemingly ungraspable theoretical abyss between theory and reality; quantity and quality, etc., all the logical polarities. Remember that I write under the paradoxical burdens, now, of not being on the other side of the trick wall, and that what I say is the result of theory made in time about the experience—which has for me been momentary—of eternity. I have been out of time, but I am now back into its illusory world; so that anything I write has no absolute value, but is just abstract imagery based on recollection of what an absolute value is like; and the modifications of what I say can go on infinitely without true timeless value, unless at some point the Paradox of Infinity is understood by an altogether different mode of consciousness. The problem of communication, here, is related and similar to the problem of accurately stating exactly the difference of thought and sensation, between the world of dreams, and the world of day. Fortunately, we have all dreamed, we all have idealistic leanings, a sensation of the supernatural, aesthetic or religious, if vague, emotions, a sense of value—deficiency, fear that is overpowering, etc. These are the experiences of the world of day, the so called real world, which I would use to suggest the underlying motif of all our lives; that these feelings are all disguised forms of another unconscious world of reality. This as you see is actually the same as the new psychological formulation, and I think that in proper hands (perhaps only Freud himself was deep enuf) it is a sufficient key; that is why I trust analysis for myself, where as most do not, really. (Jack, Ansen, etc.)

Now, to your questions. I will overlook, temporarily, the clinical details which my above paragraph might suggest, and return to a more literary, or aesthetic, or visionary vocabulary. I may say, in confession, that I do so because my experience of analysis before visions was not what I now take the possibilities of analysis to be; and I believe that most psychoanalysis is an intellectual game empty of emotional value, and is interminable, not absolute, has not understood the practice, Infinite Paradox, and is conducted on a single leveled self-enclosed world. But here, I almost end my letter, and any theoretical difference that has existed between us, by saying that my experience of analysis will change with the new analysis in the hospital and render invalid or unnecessary all the confusing mystical vocabulary that I have used. So be it, I hope so; in that case I can only say that 1. other people almost without exception never have had an inkling of what a world there is possible, or 2. I have never had an inkling of what a world other people have always been living in. In moments of actual vision, I see clearly that other people <u>don't</u> know; in moments at the edge of vision, where I am faced with problems of understanding people (as I described on page one) I feel that the deficiency in value is my own; that I am the madman in an illusory world, trying to make my abstract mechanical notions and systems stick. And I say it would be quite a miraculous and wonderful surprise if one day as the result of analysis I should have my eyes open and see that I am what is troubling me in the world at large, and in other people's conduct, ideas, etc. That, like Oedipus, I am the criminal that has been bringing on all the plague; and this is actually the experience I have had in analysis, I wake up and see that it is all my own spiteful doing. But that would not account for the psychological and sociological problems of others, which, I understand are at this point in the outside world so deep as to involve practically everyone, in extremities of wrath and physical destruction. It would, however, account for my own wrath and discomfiture of being. So there it is all wrapped up and sufficient in a system, and an accepted one at that. In fact as I write, I think it is undoubtedly true. The reason it has taken me so long to see this is because I had been so much out of contact with the world of flesh, and wrapped in my wrath and pride of intellect, that I could not comprehend, after those outbursts of the reality principle, that all along my usual unquestioned neurotic illusion world, was really a bad dream of my own, even though most others shared it in their own way, and all that I was seeing was the natural world of the organized and free senses. It was so removed from what I had known that it amounted to a miraculous change, altogether different sensations, values, even process of thought. So, seeing a light, I thought it was God. The point is, too, that that is, what everybody who had known about it before the 19th century, called god-era, had to give it a name. And those who never broke through but were still superstitious because their bound minds couldn't explain the source of being, and its irrational nature, paid homage to an idol which they invested all their reality principles in. Magic is just a subconscious expression of the sense of the real world which is in its true appearance, compared to the untrue sense of it that we have, full of vaster emotions even than the puny shadow that is summoned up by the myths of magic.

It is this very enormity, this incomprehensible difference, between the neurotic world of time and the free world of eternity, that makes me use visionary language; and it may be that I am one of a few people that has had contact with a real world, and so my language is not superfluous; if it should be the other way around I should be much chagrined, to the point of feeling it, in my pride, to be the very gate of wrath that I was always speaking about. And I feel that that is one of the keys to a final understanding of the Visionary. He only wants to be like everybody else, in the flesh, but he is afraid of love, so he makes a system which makes him prophet, confuses everybody (they all have their own systems) and forces his misdirected will into making them think the same abstractions as he.

Now I had had this construction, this system of analysis, with anthropological and sociological areas, all worked out before the visions, and I used Yeats' Unity of Being to express the psychological perfection of personality that I reasoned was possible; and I figured out rationally, schemed, even, to imitate the theoretical attitudes and activities of the happy warrior. This is, I suppose (I almost hope) what everybody does; the basis of all masks that people wear after figuring out their ideas; look to take a homely example, at Jack, with his imitation of the happy god with the golden nose; or you, with your search for a system of responsibilities, or a value in life (I am not making a joke; essentially we are looking for a value, all.) Or the New Yorker, with its concern for what it thinks is an attitude that has value; how it imitates its theoretical ideal, even to the point of absurdly forcing certain emotions and responses (mostly defensive and negative) on itself. What in all our phases we are searching for in ideas, is actually what cannot be found in a world of ideas; and that is the health of a unity of being. I and analysis (basically) and religionists and mystics, say that that health is a possible thing, and will solve all problems (or that once healthy, we will be free to solve problems that are insoluble now because we are afraid to see, act, be, clearly). I had never, before the "Vision," realized what I was saying; when I had a few momentary experiences of it (so take them to be; my doctor thinks they were hallucinations) I was so overwhelmed by the absolute wonder of the possibilities of what life was like, I suddenly realized that my thoughts, as it were, had meant much more than I thought they meant. I was quite surprised; and I felt at first that I had been wrong all along, because this attained, "ideal" was so different from what, in my frenzied dream of life, I had bargained on; I had unleashed a dragon of a reality. So in the sense that I have outlined, all I had done before, had been to make up out of my unconscious systems and images which, when they finally became substantial, at once proved them "theoretically," for all along this was what I had dreamed of—but disproved them for what they were, a reshuffled pack of cards, mere thoughts with no reality. So I abandoned making up systems and set about attempting to seek into myself for the springs of that energy, or life force, or reality, or supernaturality, that had been momentarily released—and this was no more a matter of making beautifully appealing verses, or rearranging thoughts like the furniture in a room.

Now to speak directly of the visions themselves. I told you all I could: that I saw nothing new in form, no angels, no smoke. I was in the bookstore and the bookstore was the same as ever, but with the addition of a new sense of reality, or supernatural existence, indwelling in all the forms. The sense of prescience, fullness, absolutions, and total significance of detail were all that they are in the most other-worldly of night dreams, and all that I previously might ascribe to the mystical or religious sense of the presence of the Holy Ghost. Wherever I moved I seemed to see so deeply into things that they appeared under the aspect of eternity which had been talked about for centuries, and see so deeply that I saw all there is to see, and was satisfied and peaceful. It is you might say, and I affirm, a subjective matter. "Cleanse the doors of perception," etc. Blake's phrase about eternity in a grain of sand is a literal truth. We are living in eternity. And one of the most astounding things that I saw was the souls of the men and women in the room, on their faces, in their attitudes and gestures; and what their souls were doing was hiding themselves from admitting their awareness of the all inclusive peaceful prescience, and restraining themselves from acting in accordance with the glad total community of mind and being which existed. They were all perfectly aware, as I was; their souls were opened; but they were locked in some mechanical, [coil?], withdrawal, they did not step into eternity, they refused. Inanimate objects, very substance, all partook of the prescience. The religious phrase is "God is Love." This means that substance, all, is love. And love is the stuff of substance. That I also saw, but am unable to explain, except to say that a consciousness, or awareness, or intelligence, seemed to be drifting through all things, the same in lack thing, almost animal in nature, or, as well, living. The world seemed to be alive, as a tree might be alive in a dream.

The sensation of other experiences at other times was quite similar essentially, at one time I also sensed, further, that the great beast of the universe was sick or sickening, slowly being self consumed. (See Blake's sick rose) and that human evil was part of that sickness. As if God were mad. The horror! The unspeakable horror! As if Being itself were, like the sick human mind, being destroyed. I look at your letter, the "Flesh will be the language etc." Perhaps is clear—substance is spirit. The body and mind are separated in men (theory, as in me, from meaning and reality.)

My Reichian analyst? Theoretically he ought to know the answers. In Reichian analysis, my "breakthroughs" were similar in sensation. But he says my visions are hallucination. I trust them.

My father? I have been wounding him. Perhaps he has been wounding me.

Both are unconscious, but purposeful. I do not accept him as a real entity. I must then perhaps vice-versa.

The police? The same as everybody else, including my father. To enter a world of reality, its existence must be accepted. The acceptance of the existence of another thing involves love (substance is love). Not "Love me, Lord," but "I love you, Lord." To the universe. It requires a freeing of a bloc of feeling and perception and releasing energy which is itself love. The worry about releasing evil energies is a bogey man of the nightmares of a society founded on the repression of energy and love, which might possibly be changed or abandoned in its ways when love rules. Antisocial emotions are feared because "Society" is, I believe, hostile to emotion in the first place. I feared the police because I felt guilty about the reality of my negative activity which I should have known concerned others as well of myself. I was wrong and "tried" to accept that guilt, despite my inclination of contempt, horror, ego, etc. as far as the cruel police were concerned.

Now most important is that point where I believe we have a channel of understanding. "Did the symbolisms in my poetry become, after the visions, less symbological and more actual to you? In other words, did the symbol cease to be a denotive arrow referring to something below the surface, and become, in terms of your poetry, and your thinking, an object?" This is what I mean by the word value, and my previous attempt to explain the difference between theoretical and actual reality, which share forms, but not emotion. I am greatly interested in this question because it is the key to all problems of art. I must admit I am surprised that you should be able to formulate the key question so clearly. But perhaps, as I say, I am the one who has no sense of reality, and the outside world is there all the time. Of course there is no knowing what you mean by the question. But not only in the poems, but in sensation is this process of transformation to absolute value operant. It is the same process in art as in experience, a shifting, from one level of flat valuelessness, mere symbolism, to absolute, "eternal" concreteness and substantial fullness. This has been the burden of all my poems, an attempt to use language which is pure fact, not airy poetry, to suggest to the mind of the reader that substantial actuality of Being or reality or fact, etc. that he dreams of, and to affirm it, though it may seem like madness to him (for truly our world considers it madness; and people are afraid of reality.) The difference between what I was writing a year ago and what I now attempt to write (as yet not successfully) was that before I was mouthing dreams, and now I am more aware of the meaning of the words; or better, aware that the words have meaning, and therefore, a possible effect on the reader. If I can find the true meaning, the value, the effect on the reader will be absolute. So it is in certain of Blake's poems, and they are capable of summoning up in me, the sensation of eternity. There is only one person that I know really that understands. I spoke of him, Richard Weitzner, and he is far more advanced than me. He says my poetry has little content—however he has pointed to certain specific phrases in it which are total—these are few and far between —

> O pass this passage in delight.
> Blind spectacle
> All through our land of wrath
> Dead eyes see, and dead eyes weep
> Shadow changes into bone
> The mind's forgotten meadow
> Sometime I lay down my wrath

Etc. To him it is a matter of <u>voice</u>, deep voice, prophetic voice; that's his sensual approach. The phrase "Shadow changes into bone" sums up the whole business. My poetry is not yet literal because I am not yet literal in thought, and the more literal the mind, language become, the more prophetic or true it will be. I was surprised when I realized that Blake, Wordsworth, Coleridge, Dante, etc. were in greater or lesser senses literal. Who takes them literally? Who takes the core of the Bible literally? Who even takes Freud literally? Who takes the world literally?

Now as to people. I love Neal, Huncke, etc. etc. etc., in varying degrees. They returned love, even physically. I was posed by them originally with the problem of expressing love, and what was love, etc. So they are basically instrumental in freeing me, and leading me in life. It's not presumptive to ask but I have a fear of detailed letters since my accident and so I leave that to conversation; particularly as there is too much detail, events, etc. and etc. Essentially our relations change as we grow, "L'affaire Auto," as you call it, will change things, too, welcomely. Neal, I haven't been in touch with, nor Huncke; nor Lucien, except in a few conversations by phone; Bill Burroughs I haven't written, either.

Knock and the door opens.

As ever,

Allen

[One June 29, 1949, after a delay of over a month, Allen entered the New York State Psychiatric Institute. More than anything else in the world he wanted to solve his personal and emotional problems through rigorous analysis, and at first he was eager to do exactly what the doctors told him to do.]

Allen Ginsberg [New York State Psychiatric Institute, New York, NY] to Jack Kerouac [Denver, CO] July 14, 1949

Dear Jack:

Ignore everything I said except by reading between the exaggerations to what I can't express easily. I take my madhouses seriously; it seems I have been threatening and winking for years on the same kick.

> "What they undertook to do
> They brought to pass:
> All things hang like a drop of dew
> Upon a blade of grass"
> In Gratitude to the Unknown Instructors — Yeats.

There is a pale Bartleby here, a Jewish boy named Fromm, (there are so many crazy Jews here) who sits in his chair. The first time I came in, I sat on a chair in the hall, waiting to be called to the preliminary routines of being shown my bed. He sat opposite me slumped over; he notices everything but won't say nothing. A big fat German refugee who helps run occupational therapy, a woman, came up to him and said "Don't you want to go up to O.T. today? Everybody else is there now. You don't want to sit here alone?" He raised his pale, weak head and looked at her inquiringly, but didn't say anything. Very gently she asked him again, hoping that he'd suddenly get up, perhaps, and follow her, repenting his loneliness. He looked at her a long time, pursed his lips, and slowly shook his head. Didn't even say "I prefer not to," just shook his head meditatively, after a long time in which he seemed to have been considering the question seriously; but shook his head, no, rationally. I immediately assumed that I could penetrate his mysterious secret refinement—but no—he was a poor lost wandering child of time. But the doctors (a whole hospital full of liberal minded social experimenters) have been treating him here since time immemorial trying to make him say yes. He has gone through insulin and/or electric shock therapy, psychotherapy, narcosynthesis, hypnoanalysis, everything but a lobotomy, and he still won't say yes! He rarely talks—only once have I heard him raise his voice in the wilderness. I was told that it was a great disappointment to hear him at last, because he has a nasty whining complaining voice, that's why he won't talk. When I heard him, just two days ago, he was complaining about some bureaucratic mix up. It seems he had started to shave, finished half his face, and then was called to breakfast. He came back and found the razors locked up. He stood in the hall arguing with the nurse. She was saying "Mr. Fromm, but you must realize that there are certain set hours for shaving." And he "But—But—But—I still have the soap dry on my face, I still have half my face shaved only," etc. Once in awhile they take it in their heads to drag him by force up to occupational therapy, or to the roof. He doesn't say a word, just resists; they have to bend his arm back, painfully, and take him to the elevator. But he stands near the elevator door and mournfully taps on it indicating that he wants to leave, go back to his chair. He [never] makes any trouble otherwise.

Well, last night, I heard an awful hysterical shriek down the hall and rushed to investigate. I met Fromm rushing away from the scene. He looked up at me (his eyes, walking fast, on the ground) with a half-embarrassed, half-pleased smile. I hardly smiled back, thinking he was rushing away in fear from some awful scene of psychic carnage (patients often blow their tops, alone, or attack others) and I refused to acknowledge that I was afraid, so I didn't half smile back, but half I did, because the scenes here are awesome. (The shriek, incidentally, was laughter.) What had happened? Fromm was sitting in the same chair, drooping, listless, quiet—and two other patients (one I will describe) were talking together, exchanging perhaps sarcastic jokes about the fact that they were in the bughouse—when suddenly, Fromm's face lit up, he raised himself in his chair, and without a word, he began imitating everybody in the madhouse, making bleak mimicries of even patients that just entered, doctors, nurses, me, the people he was talking to, savage, hopeless gestures that caught and caricatured everybody. I would like to show him what I have just written, but I really don't know what's under his skin. He would probably hand it back to me with no sign at all—(after reading it carefully.)

(The danger of such stories as this is that they are wishful exaggerations of possibility. *O, Les maupions de l'eternite!* But this is true nonetheless.)

There is a boy here named Karl [*sic:* Carl] Solomon who is the most interesting of all. I spend many hours conversing with him. The first day (in the chairs) I gave way to the temptation of telling him about my mystical experiences. It is very embarrassing, in a mad house, to do this. He accepted me as if I were another nutty ignu, saying at the same time with a tone of conspiratorial guile, "O well, you're new here." He is also responsible for the line: "There are no intellectuals in madhouses." He is a big queer from Greenwich Village, formerly from Brooklyn—a "swish" (he used to be he says) who is the real Levinsky—but big and fat, and interested in surrealistic literature. He went to CCNY and NYU, but never graduated, knew all the Village hipsters, and a whole gang of Trotskyite intellectuals (this generation's Meyer Shapiros), and he is familiar with a great range of avant-garde styles—also a true Rimbaud type, from his teens. Not creative, he doesn't write, and doesn't know much about literature really, except what he reads in little magazines (he had *Tyger's Eye*, *Partisan* and *Kenyon*) but he knows everything about that. Jumped ship and spent months wandering through Paris—finally at the age of consent he decided to commit suicide (on his 21st birthday) and committed himself to this place (entering a madhouse is the same thing as suicide he says—madhouse humor)—presented himself practically at the front door demanding a lobotomy. He apparently was full of great mad gestures when he first came in (with a copy of *Nightwood*) threatening to smear the walls with excrement if he didn't get a seclusion (private) room so that he could finish his book in peace. Also threatened the nurses, "If I ever hear anyone saying to me 'Mr. Solomon you're raving,' I'll turn over the ping pong table," that happened almost immediately. There is a perfect opportunity here for existentialist absurdity—he is quiet now—speaks in a sinister tone to me of how the doctors are driving him sane by shock therapy "Making me say 'momma!'" I tell him I want to be made to say momma and he says "of course (we do)." You can see what a weird sinister atmosphere here it is, Kafkian, because the doctors are in control and have the means to persuade over the most recalcitrant. Ha! I'd like to see Denison [Burroughs] exposed to these awful abysses and dangers. Here the abysses are real; people explode daily and the doctors! the doctors! my god, the doctors! They are fiends, I tell you, absolute Ghouls of Mediocrity. Horrible! They have the truth! They are right! They are all thin, pale lipped, four eyed, gawky, ungainly psychology majors from the colleges! All the seersucker liberals, dressed in the same suits, always with a vapid, half embarrassed, polite smile on their faces. "What? Mr. Solomon doesn't eat today? Send him down to shock!" All the stoops from the past years, the bloodless apoetic bourgeoisie, the social scientists and rat experimenters, the blue eyes who went to the proms, who debated about socialism—went west on bus through the rolling wheatfields to study social psychology and medicine, the squares and ignoramuses, the Jews from Bronx. They all look the same, I tell you, I can't tell one from another, except for some obviously crazy East Indian midget who also is a psychiatrist. What is he doing here in America psychologizing drug store cowboys with nervous breakdowns? These are the men who are going to fudge my immortal soul! Heavens! Where is Denison? Where is Pomeroy? Where is Huncke? Why don't they come to my rescue? It is just like Russia! The machine men from the N.K.U.D. are making me recant my rootless cosmopolitanism.

Speaking of this, because of Solomon, I am reading in all the little magazines about the latest Frenchmen. One is named Jean Genet, he is about the greatest—greater than Céline, perhaps, but similar. Huge apocalyptic novels by homosexual hipster who grew up like Pomeroy in jail—an article in April 1949 *Partisan Review* talks about him—a book called *Miracle de La Rose*, as massive autobiography, a long prose poem on prison life! The hero is the Assassin Hercamone—"Whose shadowy presence in the death cell radiates throughout the prison a mystical intensity that is taken as the standard of Beauty and Achievement and to whom the author attaches the symbol of the rose. His life lasted from his death sentence to his death..." I speak the very language used by the mystics of all religions to speak of their gods and their mysteries. I read a 3 page excerpt on the mysteries of shoplifting ending (as I remember) "and so it is that at the judgment of the apocalypse God will call me to the dolmen realms with my own tender voice, crying, 'Jean, Hean'." (Dolmen realms is my own phrase).

Also a man named Henri Michaux—interesting prose poems about the weird Aivinsikis (Heaven-seekers?) in *Kenyon* and *Hudson Reviews*.

Most of all, a madman lately died named Antonin Artaud—spent 9 years in Rodez, a French madhouse (*"M. Artaud ne mange pas au jourd'hue. apportez lui au choc."*) Solomon was wandering around Paris and suddenly he heard barbaric, electrifying cries on the street. Terrified, penetrated, totally come down, frozen —he saw this madman dancing down the street repeating be-bop phrases—in such a voice—the body rigid, like a bolt of lightening "radiating" energy—a madman who had opened all doors and went yelling down Paris. He wrote a big poem—article about Van Gogh (translated in a *Tiger's Eye*)—saying the same things about U.S. that I said about Cézanne. Solomon said it was the most profound single instant he ever had (till he came here where the doctors have insulin—and "the drugs fight it out.")

Several days ago a tongue tied boy of 20 named Bloom came in (he had been here several years before, too) talking about "concentrations of time" and eternity—he escaped, also, ran away, with attendants chasing him down the block, escaped into the subway. You see I am not unique in my formulations. I think Richard Weitzner would do well here. Before I came in I told him "If I'm mad, you're madder—and I'm mad." He looked at me, interested, and said "Really?"

What does old J.B.C. the dancing master, say about my presence here? Did he predict it before? He took me for the sane and bureaucratic type (between the 2 of us) when we were in Denver. Do you know? He said he wasn't sure about you (you were kind of Bohemian, while I was the well-groomed Hungarian.) but took you for O.K. since Ed White vouched for you (as I remember the conversation).

Van Doren asked to see my book, (after I offered to show it to him).

I haven't done any writing here at all—no pen, no place to write, no calm yet. Wrote a poem ending:

> Never ask me what I mean
> all I say is what I seen
> though it seems to be a shame,
> anyone can say the same
> anyway it happened.

It begins:

> It happened when the rain was grey,
> a gloomy, doomy, cloudy day.
> I don't remember what it was
> But then it seemed as clear as glass,
> And anyway, it happened.

This illustrates my desire to write a poem or a ballad with a real story line— but I wound up writing a poem about an unmentioned mystical "It"—a joke.

I am beginning to hate my mother. [...]

Adieu ancien ami;

Allen

[Eight months later Ginsberg was able to leave the hospital, but the cure he had hoped for had not been effected.]

Allen Ginsberg [Paterson, NJ] to Jack Kerouac [New York, NY]
February 24, 1950

Mon Cher ami Jean:

Because I left the hospital today and carried my belongings directly to Paterson, I will not see you this week, and so am writing.

I received a letter from Giroux sent February 17. He tried unsuccessfully to peddle my poems, and said that he went out of his way to do it because he liked them. He does not think the book is publishable yet, and in addition thinks that my private idiom needs a channel to the public through magazines first; and suggests prose, which he will look at, to make a name first. Half page letter, concluding with presentation of Saroyan's Assyrian, signed Bob. I went to the office and picked up my material, and also stole a copy of *Cocktail Party* [by T.S. Eliot] (the world owes me at least that $3 worth of heart balm). He also suggested I try *Poetry* magazine (now edited by one Karl Shapiro). I saw Van Doren briefly, told him the results, said I would try *Poetry* (once again, as they rejected poems this year already), and asked him to intercede with *Partisan*. It seems so far that I have not been able to make any magazine, which is not right. I will be surprised if I can't place anything at all that way in the next year at least. I do not know if, this situation has anything to do with the lack of drive I have to work. But no more complaints, I don't find that publishing has the same glory that it once had when I wanted to be supreme.

I am in Paterson and I move into the house tomorrow. As soon as I am settled and the weather looks to be warm, come out. I will be in N.Y. Monday, Tuesday, and Thursday morning for the next months to see my doctor. I can see you around 1:30 Thursday anywhere. Send postcard to my new address which is 416 East 34 Street, Paterson.

A turning point has been reached in that I am not going to have anymore homosexual affairs anymore: my will is free enough now to put this in writing as a final statement.

Verne [Neal] seems a little pathetic and dizzy from time to time as I visit him at Diana's [Hansen].[20] I had to get back home one night this week, and he refused to say goodbye or understand that I wanted to go but kept on reading me passages and pages of Hindus-Céline past my pumpkin hour; and then

---

20 Diana Hansen. Cassady's third wife.

when I forced the issue by interrupting him to apologize and say goodbye he accused me (jokingly) of wasting time. (Time, he meant by that, I should be out the door instead of explaining that I was sorry that I had to interrupt). Ah. But the monomaniacal, almost purposeful (on purpose) way in which, though he knew I had to go by the minute, he just kept reading to me, irritated me. Sheer perversion. He was trying to formulate some tender communion other than this attritive imposition; that is his trouble. He doesn't know what he is doing. I am annoyed by his insistence that he does: he thinks so because he has built a wall of mental plans. You can hardly get a word or a look in edgewise, the way he juggles Time to keep it from settling. I know this because I know from feeling-sight, as well as from the fact that when he is cool or not on edge, on some good days, he is altogether different. But there is so much invisible burden of the past on his mind that he seldom can escape. Verne is very young in spirit.

I will not speak of my creative plans (which are beginning to bud again). I am going to write non-metrical poetry for a while, I think. I have learned enough about surface. Is *The Gates of Wrath* a good short novel title? Or is it like Steinbeck?

Do you find me distant or frigid of sentiment lately? I'm not, I assure you, Jean. Not toward Verne, either.

The American myth of Wolfe and power and pathos is changing in this decade. What is happening I realized this week, reading Wolfe's credo, is that we are nearer to the edge of inevitable social transformation that is going to affect us in thought and sense: for one thing, do you realize how much nearer the alignment of east against west has become, especially since English sway in elections? If we could carry this off, it were different; but I feel in my bones that we are not really the world-spirit-power, but that Russia is actually stronger, militarily already, potentially more overwhelming, perhaps even in her myths now, and I think that Wolfe's "lost" America may be reduced to the pathetic status of self-deception. We are used to thinking of ourselves in sophisticated life and fortune power thoughts, but it may actually be that we are swollen with pitiful pride and history will bypass us (even me and you) in the next half century. We will become a sort of greater Spain, or Portugal. Dig? And not merely *Life* magazine myth, that is just the false formal consciousness of America — but pioneer America will not have the significance that it once had. [. . .]

Ton ami.

Allen of Paterson

*[Allen met a woman slightly older than himself by the name of Helen Parker. On the advice
of his doctors he tried to become heterosexual and enter into a relationship with her. For a
brief moment he felt that his sexual problems were all behind him.]*

Allen Ginsberg [Paterson, NJ, or Cape Cod, MA] to Jack Kerouac [Mexico City, Mexico] July 8, 1950

Dearest Jack:

If you are in any ennui or doldrums, lift up your heart, there IS something
new under the sun. I have started into a new season, choosing women as my
theme. I love Helen Parker, and she loves me, as far as the feeble efforts to
understanding of three days spent with her in Provincetown can discover.
Many of my fears and imaginations and dun rags fell from me after the first
night I slept with her, when we understood that we wanted each other and
began a love affair, with all the trimmings of Eros and memory and nearly
impossible transportation problems.

She is very great, every way—at last, a beautiful, intelligent woman who
has been around and bears the scars of every type of knowledge and yet strug-
gles with the serpent knowing full well the loneliness of being left with the
apple of knowledge and the snake only. We talk and talk, I entertain her in
grand manner with my best groomed Hungarian manner, and I play Levinsky-
on-the-trollycar, or mad hipster with cosmic vibrations, and then, O wonder, I
am like myself, and we talk on seriously and intimately without irony about all
sorts of subjects, from the most obscure metaphysical through a gamut to the
natural self; then we screw, and I am all man and full of love, and then we
smoke and talk some more, and sleep, and get up and eat, etc.

The first days after I lost my cherry—does everybody feel like that? I wan-
dered around in the most benign and courteous stupor of delight at the perfec-
tion of nature; I felt the ease and relief of knowledge that all the maddening
walls of Heaven were finally down, that all my olden awking corridors were
traveled out of, that all my queerness was a camp, unnecessary, morbid, so lack-
ing in completion and sharing of love as to be almost as bad as impotence and
celibacy, which it practically was, anyway. And the fantasies I began having
about all sorts of girls, for the first time freely and with the knowledge that
they were satisfiable.

Ah, Jack, I always said that I would be a great lover some day. I am, I am at
last. My lady is so fine that none compare. And how can she resist me? I'm old,
I'm full of love, when I'm aroused I'm like a veritable bull of tenderness; I have

no pride of heart, I know all about all worlds, I'm poetic, I'm antipoetic, I'm a labor leader, I'm a madman, I'm a man, I'm a man, I've got a cock. And I have no illusions, and like a virgin I have all of them, I'm wise, I'm simple. And she, she's a great old woman with a beautiful face and a perfect fair body that everybody in the neighborhood calls a whore. She's so sharp, and she never makes me shudder. She don't want war, she wants love.

Apparently I have quite respectable precedents—she was engaged to Dos Passos for over a year, he took her and kids to Cuba then, she lunched with Hemingway, knows all kinds of literary people. She was also engaged awhile and helped midwife Thomas Heggin with Mr. Roberts; he later suicided. (he-he!) But none, she says, compare to me. That's what a woman is for, to make you feel good, and vice-versa.

Then, her children, they are the most knocked out pair of flaming red haired, angelic, wise young boys (age 5 and 10) I ever saw. They need a father, which alas (this is the crux of practical problems) I am sure I cannot be, for financial and other unhappy reasons, such as not wanting to get stuck permanently with the situation. So we talk about this too.

I am in Paterson—I still work, so can't see her much, though I pine. She offered to set me up with her in Cape Cod she working, I staying home writing and caring for kids, but I can't see it as I still see doctor and want to get in a position of being financially stable somehow (though at the moment I am so beat for money I am a dog). Then to Key West for winter, if I want. Ug, so much joy!

Hal Chase sure picked himself a screwy cold chick.

Tell Joan [Burroughs] that my fair damsel originally reminded me of her, and much of their personal inborn style is alike. You must also tell me what weary, skeptical comments Bill comes on with.

I only wish you were here to talk to. Lucien is so much himself—he patted me on the back mockingly, kept buying me drinks at 4 AM the night I got back in town, asking me sardonic lascivious and practical questions, declaring that he didn't believe a word I said.

By god, I've been canorked with a feather!

Neal rearrived here 2 weeks ago, his car broke down in Texas so he planed back. He and Diana are having trouble between them, partly over practical plans—at this point he's acting slightly gruff and mean, and she weeps; he's also kind of shuddery and nervous. I would be if I were him. He never should have let her have a baby—they were doing ok till she began to try capturing him with authority and ritual, and the baby was or became a kind of trick, which he let pass ambiguously; now its marriage, they were in Newark the other day (with Holmes and Harrington) to get a license. Now he is restive, lost his job, had a call from the Frisco railroad, and is going back west in a few days. He promises to write, he will save money, he will be back when he's laid off; but she, that foolish girl, is beginning to see that she is stuck with the fruit of her too-greedy lust for him; and in the long run I believe she's fucked herself up, and him too, somewhat, by disturbing the balance they had before. She knew what she was getting into, but it was not only serious love, it was a kind of soupy insistence born of jealousy and vanity, that made her assume she would succeed in "fixing" him up.

I never saw him so detailed and rich as in his high description of Mexico, the quartz crystals, and the mambo in that side town.

Helen, I meant to tell you, knows everyone of all sorts—Cannastras, Landesmans, even the Trotskyite and hip types like bearded viper Stanley Gould at San Remo. (Know him?) I saw him the other day in Minetta, he was shrunk and thin with junk; and such a messed up youngster too, who doesn't know what he is missing, and is full of hip despair and terrible pride. I was so heart-shaken —not having seen him for half a year, and having met him on the first steps of the road downward, if I may call it such, since he's degenerating with dissipation into a mere substitute for the right, intelligent active cat that he is, that I said to him, haltingly, "You ought to eat more. Guard your health, it's the only thing you have." And he smiled on me, half hinkty, and said, "Sure man, are you carrying anything?" in the most intimately viperish tone I heard since Huncke went away to become a cowboy.

How is your novel coming along? I am going to give Helen my copy of T&C [*The Town and the City*] to read. I am poor, I write nothing. I keep fearing for the permanence of this sad nothingness of creation.

I got your letter and read it as an opera on Wotabulshit most terrible of all. Write me, make a plan for me.

Love,

Allen

[*By summer's end the relationship with Helen Parker foundered, but they stayed in touch and remained friends. One of their mutual acquaintances, Bill Cannastra, was killed in a terrible accident that prompted Allen to write to Helen who was still living in Provincetown.*]

Allen Ginsberg [Paterson, NJ] to Helen Parker [Provincetown, MA]
October 12, 1950

Dear Helen:

I do not know if by now you have heard that Bill Cannastra was killed this afternoon at about 1:30, trying to climb out of a subway window just as the train was leaving the station, somewhere on the Bowery-eastside. It was not apparently a fully conscious suicide; he was with some people, talking about a bar near there, and he tried to get out of the train, on his usual gamble that he could make it, to go back to the bar.

I don't know any details beyond that. Lucien called me up from UP [United Press] to find out how to get in touch with parents, and read me a story from the afternoon's *Post* describing the scene—Headlined something like "Loses Last Gamble For A Drink!"

There is tonight I suppose much activity in the city—I have spoken to a few people by phone, not intimates of his, and some are headed for his apartment, some to the morgue where he is now, I am told.

I will try to send you further details if I get any, though not being in the city I will miss out on some of the consternation which will be caused.

I had a long, solitary talk with him in the San Remo the night before last, and saw him home. He spoke then about "coming to an end" and I think he might have had a sense of gathering finality and possibly it was not entirely accident that he died in this way. I wonder what his face is like now in death. Apparently he was crushed by the train against the beginning of the tunnel at the end of the platform.

He reminded me, when I last saw him, of the shining pathos in inchoate awareness of the end of Crane's *Bridge*, so much so that I quoted to him a line from a stanza of the Voyages. [...]

He was a little drunk, then, but had sobered somewhat by the end of the evening, and, as we walked down Minetta Lane, spoke of how "grim" he felt. He was voluble, to a little greater sense than I'd seen him before, about his own feelings. He also said that he was in love, for the first time, with Jane Wattress, and seemed depressed and incommunicable about it, since he knew no way of love but "touching people" though he loathed the touch of flesh; and furthermore seemed involved in a characteristic inwardness and despair about loving her, since she, he said "is a lesbian." When he spoke of what dread of life he had, it was in terms of admitting and feeling like a homosexual: which surprised me, since it seems that he had not entirely absorbed that ambivalence into his awareness, after all. I had a feeling when I left him that I had seen a great deal into him, and felt his character more than ever before, almost with a kind of finality, since we came to a rapport for the first time in New York, and spoke for a long time about basic things. It disturbed me for the next day; but I thought perhaps he was coming out of his cave; perhaps he was.

He came in the San Remo, by the way, with Tennessee Williams, who left early, and I didn't get to meet him. Williams had offered him his legal executive work if he would "come off the party"; i.e. reform, and Cannastra spoke of that several times, as well as repeated several times that he had told Williams: "I liked you tonight for the first time I ever did because you got me back (readmitted) to the Remo." He was pretty triumphant over being back in "the only bar I ever liked."

I would like to meet Williams, some time, and if you are in the mood and know him well enough to recommend a meeting, drop him a line.

Lucien called me just now and said that Bill stuck his head out of the window as a joke and a dare, got struck by a pillar as the train moved, and fell to the tracks.

I think henceforth, this event being a crystallization of all that people are beginning to understand, at least of my generation, that we will be glad of the lesser joys of life and deal with the void less attracted by it, be more serious perhaps, not so tolerant and loving of the chaotic element which is ultimately death-dealing. We should at last know enough about it by now, if we didn't before. [...]

With love,

Allen

Allen Ginsberg [Paterson, NJ] to Neal Cassady [San Francisco, CA?]
November 18, 1950

Dear Neal:

I got home today from Jack's wedding to a girl named Joan Haverty, which took place last night at 6 followed by a big party at Cannastra's pad which she leased and Jack is now master of—a big quiet party which began around 7, with the arrival of the wedding party from the Judge's apartment, several blocks away, where the ceremonies took place. Claude [Lucien] and I stood as best men, fumbled around in our waistcoats for the ring, kissed the bride, who's a tall dumb dark-haired girl just made for Jack. Not dumb, really, since she's "sensitive," and troubled (trying to be on own from family in big city at age 20), and has had men (Cannastra, once for a short season), but full of a kind of self-effacing naiveté, makes dresses as vocation; but I don't know her well, but in my opinion (strictly between you and me as I am on hands off policy as regards interference with process of other's free cherce [choice]) she can't compare with Jack in largeness of spirit and so I don't know what she can give him except stability of sex life, housekeeping and silent, probably sympathetic company while he's sitting around, and children.

He has been strangely out of town the last several months, in retirement and brooding on T alone, and when he rejoined N.Y. society he seemed to me to be more settled in reality, more sober. He talked in a more disillusioned way —not making a fetish of it as I do,—but like a post 20's survivor, F. Scott Fitzgerald after the party of ego was over. Wondering what to do in the real world of men and women who were also alive and facing same problems and just as deserving of grace from above as he, tho there is no grace accorded anyone special. So, he seemed come down more than ever.

Meanwhile he's seeing this Rayanna chick (who I had my hands on till I stepped out for Jack as she is too old for me) (but who I intend to see again unless I get attached before which I doubt), and she's sharp, a real N.Y. "on the town" pro type, but all of a sudden appears on the horn this Joan, in C.'s pad, making a vulturish shrine of it (on the pretext that they had been great lovers though he thought she was an insufferable prig), next door to Claude's on 21st St.

So, with Claude's encouragement, and prodding, I start moving in on her leaving notes at her door, making meets, etc., in the hope of sleeping with her and ultimately taking over pad with her, also under impression she has money, which she hasn't. But when time comes, fuck up by being out of self control, overbearing, and impatient with her sentimentalized version of self, not wanting anything but "friendship" with men folk, wanting to be alone and keep shrine and have big parties. Anyway, I never figure her or myself out in relation to her, and return from field depressed. Next thing I know Jack ran into her, two weeks ago, slept, and stayed on, decided to marry, and did yesterday. This is a very sketchy account, not even an outline, but I am just jotting down distorted recollections.

The main things I see is this increased wariness and caution in life of Jack, and this mad marriage, they hardly know each other. But maybe it will all work out for the rest of his life. I think he hopes for permanence. Or maybe they know each other on levels which, tho I am aware of them, neglect and don't take seriously for real, so my opinion is out of the picture. Anyway I say fuck it, but we all should have beautiful intelligent wise women for wives who will know us and vice versa as well as we know ourselves (one another). I say let the home be the center of emotional and spiritual life.

And let several families gather together, menfolk and womenfolk, childfolk following, for society. Thus my ideal is everybody with telephones in each house. But maybe I want to hold together the old vain grouping of us exclusively. O dull Time. Perhaps I shall seek refuge myself someday in sull wife and exclusion of all other important society, though I do not want it now. How sullen can you get?

Be that as it may we had a big party, Seymour (and I sat on roof and blasted and talked about women); Bill Frankel (know him? fat, eyeglasses, very straight, smart, literary); the Bowmens, Hollander and little Jewish girlfriend, Claude and Lizzie, Holmes, Lindens, Harrington, Lenrow, lots of other unknown women, Solomon, and Ansen, Winnie, others from village and elsewhere, I wandered around distracted, getting into conversations and breaking them off impatiently till at three A.M. Claude, Jack and I put our heads together and kissed and sang Eli Eli and held loving symbolical conversation. But anyway, I did not feel passionate or exultant that night but dead, as did Claude and I think Jack, as we were all too old and weary to exult over anything but was new and outwidening into unknown joys beyond control, and this was not exactly like that, but anyway it did seem a big event, so that all that day Claude and I sang "Them wedding bells is breaking apart that old gang of mine," but without real sadness, since we knew that anyway we could break into each others apartment still in the middle of the night.

When I get married I want everybody I know to be there and watch including all regiments of family, in synagogue, where will be great groaning choirs of weepers, sacraments, everybody in flowers and dress clothes, slightly awed by the presence of eternal vows, chastened by tradition and individuality of marriage. Then I can go home to mad pad and have real crazy party with people jumping out of window, after. And womenfolk and menfolk separated for last goodbyes and vows of eternal fidelity too.

I got your letter today when I came home. I know you love me because you wrote such a long letter. Boo hoo I guess I'll always love you too.

Distrust my dove and vulture but trust me.

I read a letter you wrote to Jack describing (at one point) meeting early girlfriend at drugstore counter etc., and remembrance of other times meetings. I noticed then what was partly unsaid, the machinery of consciousness of place

and time, memory, at work in astonishing solidity of grasp, and so was pre-
pared for and interested in — recognizing what I found implied wearily, — your
explanation to me of gloat of knowledge of moment. Rock in the belly of the
mind is great phrase.

I wish we could talk for several days and come to understanding of memory
and phenomenology. I find my phases and interests are somewhat confused,
and I am out of touch, impatient, or inattentive to yours, because my preoccu-
pations are sometimes so different and in different directions. I feel now how-
ever that it is time for me to look around again at moment kicks of mind.
Before, they lead to centralization of thought and madness now they might be
real objective practices for me. You see, much of your train incident is "Para-
noia," desire to control world through your central perceptions. I (ahem) used
to try that myself, though I didn't always succeed, which led me to believe that
by this method, I could myself be the victim of control (thru you, for instance)
so I have been trying to achieve a less competitive not ego tack, thru Freud dis-
cipline. My doctor is an inferior intelligence who because I have seen him so
long and I allowed him to, can follow my deepest hints more strictly and objec-
tively and ruthlessly than I can myself. And so he tries to hold me to account for
them. This is in preliminary stage of process, though at this point the main
things he has done is broken me of schizoid paranoid beliefs (metaphysical
ecstasy in place of real world of dragging necessity) and queerness.

Now I am faced with dealing with world of dragging necessity. But about
you. Assuming the kid was talking out of hat, dumb, it may also be that you,
too were crazy in pushing him to wall — what if, for instance, in process of
pushing him to come down of horror, you actually choked him, woke up,
found yourself in court, and had to give a reasonable explanation of why you'd
killed? And Jack, who never knew you, was the judge you had to explain to?
And you had not built up with him already the history of thought? So we are
in relation to world of men, all different, on different kicks. But now I'm wan-
dering.

Be that as it may the account you gave was remarkably integrated. The only
possible objection to it as a short story is that the (I wander again) author's
whole view of life is, in this story, centered around the contention, in this
ambiguous world, that he is more gone and experienced than his victim. Well,
nobody would deny that from the beginning.

The right plan of action in art is to remove the self from the plot and point
of the story and write an account of what happens to other or imaginary peo-
ple based on knowledge of their attempt to make themselves the center of

universe. As it is you only beat this boy at his own braggarts' game, not at the game of impersonal Indian wisdom. But this is my own theory of myself, really, as I say. I am explaining perhaps on what terms, with what weapons I chose to battle you.

But as you say in the last page of your letter, which I understood most, "I think we all know intuitively what you generalize about tragedy and chance and death." Yes, you do know.

Enclosed find Holmes notes, but don't show him. Also, please don't show letters to anyone (my letters) but yourself, as I find I have not written as hotly as I'd like for fear that less forgiving eyes than yours would see. That goes for all your wives. O.K.? Jack is an exception, he can see them, if you see him. Secrets. Let's begin to keep secrets from the world. The beginning of impersonal wisdom.

Too much to say this moment, but to summarize, 1. my romance with Mrs. P. [Parker] is over with disgust as she is a veritable Huncke of selfishness and deadbeat hassles. I don't want a whore, I want a finished product of self education who has turned to stillness. She was in N.Y. last week but things were so tense in the end I was glad to see her go. No immediate female prospects.

2. I will not after all I said in last letter, get factory job. I'm sick of trying to be a hero of misfortune. So next I must figure out first steps in publishing career, or something.

3. I write very little and may start taking lessons from Ansen in Greek or meter of poesy, technique. Study again. Novel dead again.

4. I have 4¢ to my name and am a dead beat on my family. Doctor fortunately has come up fine and is treating me free finally. So you see he's not so bad, at least sympathetic to the cause.

5. I hope to get a job and move to N.Y. in next few months, perhaps by time you get to N.Y., so society will flourish—but please, cool kicks. We will talk over life without smirking. Hot kicks only for the war.

What courage you have.

Love,

Allen

[One of the most important documents of the Beat Generation was the "Joan Anderson Letter" written by Neal Cassady. For a brief time Neal believed he could become a writer like his friends Kerouac and Ginsberg. As an exercise, he composed a lengthy letter relating one *of his romantic affairs. It was written in a spontaneous free-flowing manner, very much like his own speech pattern and it made an enormous impression on both Jack and Allen. It became the nucleus of the style that Kerouac would call "Spontaneous Bop Prosody." Before long he adapted that style to his newest revision of* On the Road.]

Allen Ginsberg [Paterson, NJ] to Neal Cassady [San Francisco, CA]
March 15, 1951

Dear Neal:

Now: Next (I am purposely putting off what I have to say about your Tale of Joan which I read this week [The Joan Anderson Letter])

I finally got your long letter of December 17, the story by stealing it from Jack's desk when he was out. He was afraid I'd lose it.

He said to me, when he read it, "Neal is a colossus risen to Destroy Denver!"

I read it with great wonder, stopping and laughing out loud every few paragraphs, so much clarity and grace and vigor seemed to shine in the writing. I had thought, several weeks ago, in a mood of passion walking by the 5th Avenue streets that we passed when you were here, that I should write you a long letter saying that your all-salvation and joy lay in recreating the universe in a novel that you were writing, but never did, because for some reason I find it hard to write you at length now, except on flat fact matters and even now, it's hard to say (or feel, at the typewriter) how much I am impressed and astonished at the magnitude of the work you have done in the Joan Story, which seems to me an almost pure masterpiece. It's easier to speak of the flaws, which I will do.

Mainly, since it was a rambling letter, the subplots and flashbacks were a little in the way but could be easily edited to fit right in, but since you stopped short of the ending, made more chaos. Finish the story then, either to me (I'd be flattered) or Jack (also I was hung up with personal interest while reading, not tutorial as now, I was humbler then) and I'm sure you can sell it for money with practically hardly any changes as it stands now. Only changes, it doesn't need the parenthesized apologies for misspellings or word uses, certain ununiversal personal asides.

It read with speed and rush, without halt, all unified, one molten flow; no boring moments, everything significant and interesting, sometimes breathtaking in speed and brilliance — particularly serious philosophic asides like "To have seen a specter is nothing, etc." at hospital.

Echoes of Céline apparent, but graceful; wish you'd echo your own gravity-despair lunges instead.

Jack I believe has some idea of doing something with manuscript and it would be pleasure to take it to Trilling or Van Doren for magazine, *Short Story* contest set up, maybe even novelette. But it ought to be finished first, in no different way than written.

I remember you telling me story in john at Psych and Anthro building Columbia 1946. Were we looking for Chase? We looked out of window at Amsterdam and you told me about ammonia.

Take up when you got out of jail January 2 at 9AM. Dove had fled to Ft. Collins. You went to Uhl's ranch, Bull, J. Holmes, found Joan whoring in Denver, etc. Also maybe develop or add theory of sex.

Be man, not in style of writing, but in pride and presumption and assurance in idea of writing, we are all peers if you are not the master at least; not child. No be fraid of winning world, by quality mere thinking as you do, being self.

One thing: whenever you blow "alliteratively," by repetition of letters, hardy herman, hamstrung herman tit tom tight tom: beauty of music lies not in insistent repetition of letters h or t (whatever being use) nor in repetition of rhymed syllables (tantalized tipplers trooping to triumphant trash), but in rhapsodic (not nervous) fluid combination of vowel as well as first letter sounds, in contrast as well as repletion. Too much insistent beat is only nervous, not musical.

> I don't write a poem
> Take ten triumphant temples
> Teetering on Toad town,
> snickering snakily so slow,
> aping abbots along alleys.

There is such alliterative poetry (Piers Ploughman):

and with his mouth so meekly
and pity on the people
Here may you find example
how he was meek though
might
to those his heart who pierced
And tis a natural knowledge

mercy on them besought
who pain on him had brought.
by God himself may'st see
and mercy granted free
and hanged him high on tree.
thy heart may teach it thee.

See how much less straight-laced and relaxed that is compared to your insistence (hallucinatory while screwing letters) that everything seem the same, so nervous. Be care for inside of word, vowel (aeiou) combinations

if money mellowed in the	un ell owe owl
bowel	ung yon ung ane
the hunger beyond hunger's	un ade ind ane
pain	un oak ort owl
or money made the mind more	ade oan inn ain
sane	
or money choked the mortal	
growl	
or made the groaner grin	
again	

Also you force sentence phrase out of natural order and rhythm, and also out of even unnaturally pretty rhythm, dem de, for sake of repetition of tit tat toe tit tit tit etc.

The above comment applies to nothing that is in the story itself, but only to your nervous and exhausted blowing at beginnings of personal letters trying to get going; look for rhapsody rather than repetition, if you are dealing with just physical sound qualities by themselves. Or if not rhapsody (like Hawk, Coleman); then gaiety and lightness of variation (partly Parker), or even flowing clarity of sound (Lester); or brilliance of invention like Dizzy, etc. But not Jacquet, the hang up. You don't need to, you're too fabulous a story.

Be interesting to see how you would write poetry. Invent a kind of poem your own (mine is suffering from being an old steal).

Plain facts is not the alternative to unsuccessful hung up music, but musical facts is the alternative: "there are deathmasks piled, one atop the other, clear to Heaven." How that line rises from hell to paradise. ere are eath ile, op, eer eaven

Jack, incidentally, just discovered *Our Lady of the Flowers*.

But finish me the end of the tale today.

We ought to start a magazine: Bill's junk book, your sex book, Jack's nigger book, my God book; maybe Claude and Holmes.

Write me a letter.

Yours,

Allen

we are apart and I would not be

[*One of the literary figures Ginsberg most wanted to meet was Ezra Pound. Pound was being confined in St. Elizabeth's Hospital mental ward, where Allen hoped to have an audience with the great poet. He wrote several letters and tried in vain to introduce himself to Pound.*]

Allen Ginsberg [Paterson, NJ] to Ezra Pound [Washington, DC]
ca. May 1951

Dear Pound:

Don't know if it's any good writing you, but am seizing chance I thought about before. Am now almost 25, wrote a lot in college (won prizes too, Columbia) and since, but never was a scholar, guess not genius enough, atrophied mostly since, lethargy and 8 months in N.Y. bughouse.

Am occupied adjusting, trying to find place in society, work; not much ambition yet, etc. more woe.

Poetry I have written I don't know value of or not, say it is little. Started wild and full of Manhattan horns and worked down to small lyrics as good and inwardly woven as I could make them: but all concerned (pre bughouse) with externally vague schizoid mystical light. Best example is last, written as farewell to that, last of a series of similar poems, using old stock bones, blood, skeletons, etc. But believe there is some physical command of iambic 4 beat line, and some intensity.:

Ode to the Setting Sun

(Written on way back home, on Susquehanna RR,
over Jersey Marshes, in Archer season,
November December, on rainy day.)

. . .

The wrathful cast of smoke and iron
Crowded in a broken crown;
The Archer of the Jersey mire
Naked in a rusty gown;
Railroad creeping toward the fire
Where the carnal sun goes down.

. . .

Apollo's shining chariot's shadow
Shudders in the mortal bourn;
Amber shores upon the meadow
Where Phaeton falls forlorn
Fade in somber chiaroscuro,
Phantoms of the burning morn.

. . .

Westward to the world's blind gaze
In funeral of raining cloud
The motionless cold heavens blaze,
Born out of a dying crowd:
Daybreak in the end of days,
Bloody light beneath the shroud.

. . .

In vault dominion of the night
The hosts prophetical convene,
Till, empire of the lark alight,
Their bodies waken as we dream,
And put on all our raiment bright
And crown still haloed though unseen.

. . .

Under the earth there is an eye
Open in a sightless cave,
And the skull in eternity
Bares indifference to the grave:
Earth turns, and the day must die,
And the sea accepts the wave.

. . .

My bones are carried on the train
Westward where the sun has gone;
Night, has darkened in the rain,
And the rainbow day is done;
Cities age upon the plain
And smoke rolls upward out of stone.

Admittedly the whole vague reference of imagery to my own subjective experience; plus inversions and dependence on classic cadences of thought (the sea accepts the wave and raiment bright) and whole stock of post 1910 development (or whenever the magic date is) shows this up as useless as it is, except maybe the Yeatsian yoking of bare contradictory abstractions as in bloody light beneath the shroud; etc.

One other poem I give you, a song from a long projected unwritten epic in my imagination about the boogie man, a peculiar American type here, the Bowery bum, or idiot crowned with straw from Melville (Pleasure Party): called here the Shrouded Stranger of the Night. The name doesn't matter, you know the archetype. There is more machinery and habitat here: his song:

Bare skin is my wrinkled sack
When summer sun climbs up my back;
When winter racks me in these rags
I heap my lap with burlap bags.
My flesh is cinder, my face is snow,
I walk the railroad to and fro;
When city streets are black and dead
The Railroad embankment is my bed.
. . .

I suck my soup from old tin cans,
And take my sweets from little hands;
Where tigers in the alley wail
I steal away from the garbage pail.
In darkest night where none can see
In the rusting bowels of the factory
I sneak barefoot upon stone:
Come and hear the old man groan.
. . .

I hide and wait like a naked child,
Under the bridge my heart goes wild,
Shadow and bone are shriek and shiver,
I dream that I have burning hair,
Arms raised up bloody in the air,
The torso of an iron king
And on my back's broken wing.
. . .

Who'll go out whoring into the night?
I'll bare my soul for thy delight.
Youth and maid and athlete proud

> May wanton with me in the shroud.
> Who'll come lay down in the dark with me
> Belly to belly and knee to knee?
> Who'll look into my hooded eye?
> Who'll lay down under my darkened thigh?

Now this is the sum of my achievement (plus 30 other similar poems, no better, some worse).

I been reading [William Carlos] Williams and talked to him—interest there is inspiration of old W. C. Fields talking about substances and things; also some in rhythm. But he doesn't seem to me to have no system of measure (he talks about) and his poetry just isn't gone, wild, weird, whatever romantic enough— best seems to me parts of *Paterson* and last 20 lines of the pure products of America. He did everything he could to sacrifice longing for irrelevant metaphysics and imaginative splendor in language to get at truth, but that's one phase, step, for <u>him</u>, and the local scene is covered. And he has no bounce, no beat (I'm not talking about iambic). Maybe I'm asking too much (not of him but next year's poetry). Further, him and you seem to have developed up to the point of <u>narrative</u>. True Story plot which can also stand as myth grand and final for America. But not to it—that seems next year's work—making of long (ish) narrative poem in new meter which can be final summing up of metrical or measurical progress, applied to clear narrative line full of deep intense American imagery—not Buffalo Bill maybe, but (what is my own image, the shrouded stranger, post Wolfean Tom) apocalyptic, but dying of cancer in Times Square, tragic story of illusion, maybe you yourself, personally, not poetically, but certainly my own spiritual autobiog.; or Hart Crane at last moments of knowledge before he hit water. This generation (mine) has seen enough really wild personalities immolated in the subways to understand. But that's enough on that line. (I meant I knew a great shining cat who jumped out of a subway window last year).

I'm chaotic here: to get to the point. What, in measure, has been done since 1910? What've you got now, as a system, if any? Just want to know, so that I won't have painfully to search aimlessly long while. Not saying if you got anything I'm capable of using it etc. as I'm half beat already mentally, and hard to learn for me.

What I want to know, what system of sane poetic conversation have you to replace washed out beat of quantity? Ear alone? That's OK too, I just want to get an angle on where to look and work in next year(s). I understand you have some kind of worked out system (from a guy name of J. Grady, but he's full of vain bs.) Nor I'm asking you to present your system, but indicate where you've written about it, and where specifically it's best applied. I know *Cantos,* not all way down, (references, etc.) but can use them for study, but it's such a huge mass, and can find no guiding principle of measure but shifts according to sense. That's all maybe, and enough.

Also difficult to write out questions specific enough to give you something to talk to, but would be glad to make trip to Washington to see you for an hour if you have time and want to take trouble on what seems possibly aimless brain beating. Perhaps I'll write again more directly if you don't think this is clear enough. Laboring at moment under shyness of writing at all, awareness of respective learnings, demands, etc., so rushing through.

Sincerely,

Allen Ginsberg

P.S. been talking infrequently to Williams and was beginning to find the point but now he's sick and out of circulation; also he has no system but ear.

[*A few days after Ginsberg and Lucien Carr visited Joan Burroughs in Mexico City, Allen opened the newspaper to a distressing story. On September 6, 1951, William Burroughs had shot Joan in the forehead, killing her.*]

Allen Ginsberg [Galveston, TX] to Neal Cassady [San Francisco, CA] September 7, 1951

Dear Neal:

Claude [Lucien] and I went to Mexico and returned to the U.S. a few days ago. Bill was in South America on some expedition. We took Joan and kids riding all over to Guadalajara and Mazatlan—Mex Pacific Coast.

Car broke down near Houston. I spending week in Galveston on beach, Claude flew to New York. He returns in 4 days by plane to pick up me and car and dog.

Note in newspaper I saw tonight says that Bill killed Joan in accident with gun last night. "An American tourist trying to imitate Wm. Tell killed his wife while attempting to shoot a glass of champagne from her head with a pistol, police said today."

"Police arrested Wm. Seward Burroughs, 37, of St. Louis, Mo., last nite after his wife Joan, 27 died in a hospital of a bullet wound in her forehead received an hour earlier."

That's all I know.

I am sitting in a broken down shack across the street from the Gulf of Mexico. I have spoken to no one since I've been here, slept much, bathed a lot, walked around town, have an icebox.

Kells Elvins is in Mexico City. He is a great man, and on the scene so there is someone around to help Bill and take care of kids.

Claude and J. played games of chance with drunken driving, egging each other on suicidally at times while we were there. I left with him from N.Y. at last moment after Jack dropped out to go to hospital for leg and finish book.

Hope everything's ok by you. Write me 149 W. 21 Street N.Y.C. care of Claude. I'm nowhere as usual, not doing anything though this summer I worked for a month as a book reviewer for *Newsweek* magazine.

My imagination of the scene and psyches in Mexico is too limited to comprehend the vast misery and absurdity and sense of dream that must exist in Bill's mind now — or whatever he feels.

All my love,

Allen

P.S. Spent several days in Houston this trip — remembering 1947 — but didn't visit Hotel Brazos — went to look at Shamrock Hotel, drunk.

[*That winter William Carlos Williams offered to help Ginsberg publish a book of poems. Allen was thrilled, as this letter reveals. It also shows how much Kerouac and Ginsberg had interchanged thoughts and ideas, as Ginsberg clearly could not remember who was responsible for which lines and words.*]

Allen Ginsberg [New York, NY] to Jack Kerouac and Neal Cassady [San Francisco, CA] *ca.* **February 1952**

Mon Cher Jack, Mon Cher Neal:

Things is going great. Since I last wrote you I have been working steadily at typewriter piecing together mad poems — I have already 100 of them, I'm jumping. Listen to this: I'm putting together fragments of "Shroudy Stranger," with a small descriptive poem — too busy on fragments to get to the EPIC which will be next. [...]

Now, what I want to know from you: my fantasies and phrases have gotten so lovingly mixed up in yours, Jack, I hardly know whose is which and who's used what: like rainfall's hood and moon is half yours. I am enclosing copies of poems that seem to stem from you, like rhetoric at end of "Long Poem" — is "very summa and dove" yours? I'm not haggling I just want to know if it's OK to use anything I want that creeps in?

Spoke to Williams on phone, go down to River Street tomorrow. He said he already (he hasn't seen the whole hundred, just about five poems) spoken with Random House (I thought it was going to be New Directions) and book may be there. Isn't this crazy? I've been off my nut with work and giggling. Speaking of which one poem enclosed beginning "Now Mind is Clear" sounds like synopsis of Giggling Ling. Is that OK? Also I enclose, "After Gogol." Do or did you use the idea? If I use it will it screw up you? Fuck, let's both use it. [John] Hollander thinks I have burst forth like Rilke and cries whenever he looks at me, for amazement. But I tell you really, though I'll be depressed and incompetent and in a bughouse in 3 weeks, I swear I really have got the whole metrical problem at last by the balls, and that been holding me up — meter, breaking out of it, and talking like we really talk, about madtown. I was all wrong.

Listen to these "poems": (a book if any will be called *Scratches in the Ledger*; and will be dedicated to Jack Kerouac, Lucien Carr and Neal Cassady: "VAST GENIUSES OF AMERICA WHO HAVE GIVEN ME METHOD AND FACT"). [...]

[Ginsberg often acted as a literary agent for his friends. He spent years trying to get books published for many of them, but succeeded only in placing William Burroughs' first book, Junkie, *with Ace Books. In part, that was due to the fact that Carl Solomon worked for Ace, and Carl was the nephew of Ace's owner, A. A. Wyn. In the following letter about publication matters, Allen's comments about* On the Road *were references to Kerouac's book,* Visions of Cody *which was published posthumously twenty years later. Jack recycled the title,* On the Road, *for the shorter novel now associated with that title.]*

Allen Ginsberg [New York, NY] to Jack Kerouac and William S. Burroughs [Mexico City, Mexico] June 12, 1952

Dear Jack and Bill:

Will discuss theoretical questchuns at end.
<u>Junk:</u>

1. Wyn don't dig *Queer*. Can't understand it but it's just as well for moment. Does dig "Slave Trader" fantasy.

Finish *Queer* whenever you want, we peddle it as second book, and finish it whichever way you want.

2. *Junk* to come out by itself this fall. I have in next few days to write an ending on it, 6000 words. They want something covering Mexico in detail, queerness underplayed, and a theory of Yage, and a departure, or preparation for departure, for S.A. [South America].

I will use *Junk* parts of *Queer* plus letters to fabricate that, over this weekend, leaving out Joan.

Doing this despite professional disapproval of situation, want to end up all this crapping around. They say contract and advance signed etc. soon as this is done. Will work strictly within yr. own dears. Plan to publish it fall as paper covered book.

Assume this is O.K. Would have you do this yourself but they want it in 5 days to go ahead by deadlines. If you can fast write that ending as you want, and get it to me by next week, be better, but maybe too hard? Meanwhile will tack on an ending, maybe switch to yours if received immediately.

Everything a little all fucked up, they keep changing their minds.

Queer I think is a better novel and will be saleable later when you finish it, should be done out as length, as great a length as you need to cover whole history of Marker, white whale, etc., including S.A. End of *Junk* will just hint at extension into *Queer*, so will be no conflicts.

Will write soon as this is done and business transacted. This whole process has been over my head, am a little confused just what has happened. *Junk* in any case still definitely to be published.

Write *Queer*, start as soon as you get *Junk* money, which <u>should</u> be forthcoming within month. At rate things been going, anyway.

3. Situation complicated by Carl Solomon has gone almost absolutely crazy. Broke up with wife, attacking books with knives, stopping traffic on 8th and 50th St. by throwing briefcases and shoes at passing cars, been in and out of Bellevue, breaking glasses, taking planes to Cape Cod, flooding up apartments, smearing walls with paint, screaming in public. This been going on for 2 weeks and I can't get anything done at Wyn till he calms down. Gad. Seems better now.

This is shorthand description, no time for detailed explanations of all happenstance.

This agenting is getting out of hand, with your going off after your own kind of Moby Dick, Carl crazy, Jack nutty as a fruitcake. Everybody seems off their heads, blowing tops around me. Even Dusty[21] — her cat died and she had a six day drunken nervous breakdown, she's living in my New York attic with me now, I don't have a moment's peace from these people with their cats and yagis and wives and voids and anger at the universe, why can't everybody calm down, I always say, like the nice people in the booby hatch? And that bastard Davalos,[22] I trusted him, but he's a friggin narcissist, no hope there.

Agh. Send up insertions for *Junk*, that you have. Hang on to *Queer*, to work on. If possible, send up immediately a 20 page (about 6000 words) summary of Mexico and plans for S.A. trip written in first person. I hate like hell to write, myself, I don't know how I'll ever do it.

That's the situation. When you leavin? Keep me posted addresswise.

I am too hung-up on this at moment to talk about magic, I feel sick. Bah, I have my own madness.

Jeez take some of that there life insurance out in my name too, boy. Way I have luck it's a sure bet you'll live if you do.

Try that peyote again dicing it and eating it with, mixed in with, canned fruit salad. Can't taste it that way. Or is it an internal rejection from stomach?

If you leave for Panama, keep me posted addresswise like I said, I'm positive there's money forthcoming.

See Jack's letter.

Hastily, Allen.

Dear Jack:

All right, the manuscript arrived a few days ago, *On the Road* [later published as *Visions of Cody*]. Carl read it, I read it once, and Holmes has it.

I don't see how it will ever be published, it's so personal, it's so full of sex language, so full of our local mythological references, I don't know if it would make sense to any publisher — by make sense I mean, if you could follow what happened to what characters where.

The language is great, the blowing is mostly great, the inventions have full-blown ecstatic style. Also the tone of speech is at times nearer to un-innocent heart speech ("why did I write this?" and "I'm a criminal"). Where you are writing steadily and well, the sketches, the exposition, it's the best that is written in America, I do believe. I'm not stopping now to write you praise-letter, tho

---

21 Dusty Moreland. Ginsberg's girlfriend at the time.
22 Dick Davalos (b. 1935). Actor with whom Ginsberg had a brief relationship.

maybe I should etc. etc. but on my mind I am worried by the whole book. It's crazy (not merely inspired crazy) but unrelated crazy.

Well you know your book. Wyn I'm positive won't take it now, I don't know who will. I think could be published by *New Story* people in Europe, but will you be revising it at all? What you trying to put down, man? You know what you done.

This is no big letter, can't see Bill's for reason. I will, all by myself, read book second time, next week, and write you 20 page letter taking book section by section figuring my reactions.

For an on the spot minute guess:

1. You still didn't cover Neal's history.

2. You covered your own reactions.

3. You mixed them up chronologically, so that it's hard to tell what happened when.

4. The totally surrealistic sections (blowing on sounds and refusing to make sense) (in section following tape-records) is just a hang-up, hang-up.

5. Tape records are partly hang-up, should be shortened and put in place after final trip to Frisco.

6. Sounds like you were just blowing and tacking things together, personally unrelating them, just for madness sake, or despair.

I think book is great but crazy in a bad way, and <u>got</u> (aesthetically and publishing-wise) to be pulled back together, re constructed. I can't see anyone, New Directions, Europe, putting it out as it is. They won't, they won't.

HODOS CHAMELIONTOS in Yeats is series of unrelated images, chameleon of the imagination diddling about in the void or hang-up, meaning nothing to each other.

Should keep *Sax* into framework of a myth, a FRAMEWORK, and not violate framework by interrupting Sax to talk about Lucien's formerly golden hair or Neal's big cock or my evil mind, or your lost bone. The book is the lost bone, itself.

On the Road just drags itself exhausted over the goal line of meaning to someone else (or to me who knows the story); it's salvageable. I mean it needs to be salvaged. Your handing up the whole goddam junkyard including the I agh up erp esc baglooie ain't you read what I'm shayinoo im tryinting tink try I mea mama thatsshokay but you gotta make sense you gotta muk sense, jub, jack, fik, anyone can bup it, you bubblerel, Zag, Nealg, Loog, Boolb, Joon, Hawk, Nella Grebsnig. And if you doan wanna make sense, shit, then put the nonsense on one page boiled down to one intense nervous collapse out of intelligibility (like Williams did in a section of *Paterson*, scrambling up the type, and followed it real cool by a list of the geological formations of shale etc. under the fuckin falls, and then went on to say "This is a poem, a POEM.") and then go on talkin like nothing ever happened cause nothin did. Nothing jess <u>interrupted</u> something. But nothing juss keeps breaking in out all over the joint, you'll be talking along, and say "he come out of the room like a criminal —then you'll add—sike a shrouder (whoever heard of ?) then you'll add—like black winged rubens—then you'll go poetic and say—like pink winged Stoobens, the hopscotch Whiz of grammar school, hopscotch, the game of Archangels, it's hevvin, it's clouds, meanwhile he was alla time juss commin out of that room, but you got us not only up inna clouds, via Steubenville and urk ep blook, but via also I am JK interrupting myself.

Well maybe it's all three dimensional and awright aesthetically or humanly, so I will re re re read your whole buke, puke anall, (and jeez, Joyce did it, but you're juss crappin around thoughtlessly with that trickstyle <u>often</u>, and it's not so good) reread your whole book I will,

and give you a blow by blow account of <u>how it comes off</u>.

And incidentally don't be too flabbergasted flip at my foregoing because I Allen Ginsberg one and only, have just finished cutting down my book from 89 poems to a mere perfect 42, just to cut out the comedy and crap and personalia jackoffs, for leanness, and humanness, it is ACTION WHICH IS DEMANDED AT THIS TIME. That's what he sez, though god know what kind of action he talkin about.

[*Cassady lived in San Francisco and Ginsberg kept in touch by letter, confiding in Neal about his life in general, his plans to make it with women, and his plans to re-enter therapy. He also tried to find a publisher for Cassady, but Neal could never find the time to sit down and write.*]

**Allen Ginsberg [New York, NY] to Neal Cassady [San Francisco, CA?]
July 3, 1952**

Dear Neal:

Whyn't you answer my last letter? Too flip?

I have your manuscript beginning of novel from Carl. I would send it to you but I think there's a chance of publishing the section beginning with your own remembrances (excluding the historical preface) in the New Directions annual anthology. I'll give it to them, they may not take it, or they may—we'll see.

I reread it incidentally. I thought the parent's intro was too tight and in a way dull, except for moments like the porch—or Harper's dump house. Maybe it's the strain of point of view or strain of writing; and maybe as it is it would still be appropriate for a beginning when the whole thing is done.

The main body, where you begin with yourself is very good and swings and is actually interesting to read (to a total objective outsider's eyes). I think it's ripe enough to try to publish as is.

I don't know where your long autobiographical letter is [the Joan Anderson letter]—has Jack got it? or you? I don't, maybe you know who does.

New Directions took a few (2 or 4) of my poems—ones which were prose-poems, in paragraphs—for this same annual.

I haven't heard anything from Bufford at New Story, he must have thought I was crazy maybe. That's O.K. as I have new U.S. connections slowly opening up.

I am writing Kenneth Rexroth today. He lives in Frisco, believes in Williams, has a lot to do with New Directions poetry selections, and with a big new international magazine named Perspective. Lamantia (Philip) gave me his address. I ask him to publish my own poetry and Jaime De Angulo's (great poems) in his connections. If he says he'll try, I'll send you my book (with W.C.W.'s introduction) for you to read and then deliver to him by car if you'll do it. He's an old guy, not really great as writer, too hung up on booklearning, but he does dig all the young subterranean cats like Lamantia.

I saw Lamantia for an evening—he's a nice boy like I thought and intellectually experienced but he's not big enough and is all hung up on being a cabalistic type mystic. He's no ignu,[23] but nice. He couldn't give me much account of your visit, which I tried to get from him—sure sign of lack of soul on his part.

Carl and I may also start our own magazine, and call it Crazy; but only hi-class stuff in it, no Lamantia bullshit about the green guts perched on the churchpole and "real reality redness of the real" on peyote. That don't say nothing much. Lots of young kids like us got the right idea but don't have no reality in what they put down on paper.

Jack's book arrived [Visions of Cody] and it is a holy mess—it's great all right but he did everything he could to fuck it up with a lot of meaningless bullshit I think, page after page of surrealist free association that don't make sense to

23 Ignu. The group's name for a kindred spirit.

anybody except someone who has blown Jack. I don't think it can be published anywhere, in its present state. I know this is an awful hang-up for everyone concerned—he must be tired too—but that's how it stands I think. Your tape conversations were good reading, so I could hear what was happening out there—but he put it in entire and seemingly un-unified so it just skips back and forth and touches on things momentarily and refers to events nowhere else in the book; and finally it appears to objective eye so diffuse and disorganized—which it is, on purpose—that it just *don't make*. Jack knows that too, I'll bet—why is he tempting rejection and fate? Fucking spoiled child, like all of us maybe, but goddam it, it ain't *right* to take on so paranoiac just to challenge and see how far you can go—when there's so much to say and live and do now, how hard it is albeit. Jack is an ignu and I will bow down to him, but he done fuck up his writing money-wise, and also writing wise. He was not experimenting and exploring in new deep form, he was purposely just screwing around as if anything he did, no matter what he did, was O.K. no bones attached. Not purposely, I guess, just drug out and driven to it and in a hole in his own head—but he was in a hole. I don't know what he'll say when I say this to him—he comes back to N.Y. this week or next I think—and how he'll make out, with all this shit to shovel around, I dunno. I will try to help but I feel so evil when I not *agree* in blindness. Well shit on this you git the point.

Bill's contract is signed and sent down to him, so that's all over. I haven't heard about my own book.

My unemployment compensation is running out; Dusty and I are separating residences (on friendly basis); I will be poor again in 2 weeks and don't know where to turn. I started trying to get back to work kicks yesterday, but nothing's turned up and I'm feeling weak. I guess I will find something by next week however, I have to, and I feel it closing in on me.

I will stay on in N.Y. longer. When I begin wandering in space, and among the subterraneans, and into the hung-up literary corridors, I get hung up on everything but the real pressures—money, love. Anyway I want to set myself up independent again, with a small apartment, a steady secure job, start laying again. With Dusty I seldom lay and it is no good really, though I like her alright.

I still have love longings and yet have not in my lifetime founded a relationship with anyone which is satisfactory and never will unless I change and grow somehow out of this egoistic grayness and squalor. Drifting like I am or could would leave me with no hope but stolen fruits. I had begun to get hung up on the metaphysical image and the subterranean peyotelites here. Must stop *play-*

ing with my life in a disappointed grey world. Maybe go back to analysis. I am miserable now—not feeling unhappiness, just lack of *life* coming to me and coming out of me—resignation to getting nothing and seeking nothing, staying behind shell. The glare of unknown love, human, unhad by me,—the tenderness I never had. I don't want to be just a nothing, a sick blank, withdrawal into myself forever. I can't turn to you for that any more, can't come to Frisco for you, because how much you love me, it is still something wrong, not complete, not still enough, not—god knows what not—you know how I was before and what I am, my hang-ups. Do you think that is all I shall get ever, so that is why I should come out? Maybe that is not bad idea but I still want to seek more. I suppose maybe I'm looking too hung-up at a simple sociable proposition.

I guess that's true, too—I haven't reread this—but I started off trying to say what I'm feeling. I just *want* something, beside the emptiness I've carried around in me all my life. Bliss of tenderness I think of, but that's too monomaniacal and soft-hearted—maybe I should go out of myself somehow here and keep trying to get back to life.

So anyway I will I guess stay here and live it out like a man. What this doesn't sound like.

I am real tired, but it is sleep-fatigue, not work fatigue. I live in an inactive lethargy of thinking and running around and doing everything but what I need to do to keep myself comfortable and happy.

Well write me, I would like to hear from you, dear Neal.

Yours,

Allen

Whatever this letter means I have just given you the picture as it runs thru my mind.

Maybe a change of scene would be good. I may come out there yet. I suppose someday I'll regret not just jumping out there on a rainbow.

Allen Ginsberg [New York, NY] to Jack Kerouac [San Francisco, CA]
February 19, 1953

Dear Jack:

On the reverse is rough draft of news gossip item for the *Times* that Carl and I and Wyn publicity figured up. I read it to Holmes and it's OK by him. Will be given to *Times* gossip litterateur, David Dempsey.

Please give your permission for your name to be used, and also please send me, for now or later use, with this item, a two sentence plug for Bill as intense and hi-class as you can make it. 25 words or so. Holmes will contribute also—emphasizing literary value, whatever it is, personality, or perhaps balloonish foolishness of whole project of JUNK.

I am expecting to go out of town this weekend to Paterson on Saturday tho I may be here Fri nite.

John never made it last week to Birdland in time anyway, he came in from Queens, or wherever, $^1/_2$ hour late and thought perhaps it was his own fault.

I will call Lu tonight and move into his apartment in a few days perhaps Monday or Tuesday. He'll go away for a month so perhaps we could see him again once before.

Adios. Write that please and send me this week. For dear Will's sake.

Yours

Allen

"JOHN KEROUAC AND Clellon Holmes, both experts on the Beat Generation, Holmes through his recent *Times Magazine* section controversy, say that they "dig" the pseudonymous William Lee as one of the key figures of the Beat Generation.

"Lee first appeared lurking in the shadows of both of their books, respectively *The Town and the City* and *Go*, portrayed as an underground character. Lee's professional debut in the open on his own as an author is announced by Ace Double Books with the publication of *Junkey: The Confessions of an Unredeemed Junk Addict*, which comes up from underground April 15.

"Author-Junky Lee has not stayed around to gather whatever plaudits are due and was last heard from on an expedition into the Amazon basin in search of a rare narcotic."

[*Always eager to promote his friends, Ginsberg was surprised when Kerouac refused to allow his name to be connected with Burroughs' new book,* Junkie. *Although he liked Burroughs, Jack did not want to be linked to John Clellon Holmes, who had already written words of praise for the novel. Holmes' book* Go *had been published with a large advance, while Kerouac's books languished on the shelf without a publisher, so he was jealous of Holmes' success. Jack was also afraid to be associated with a memoir by a drug addict, albeit fictional. He felt it would hurt his own future chances for publication. All that put a strain on his relationship with Ginsberg. Rejected by Kerouac, Allen replied with a formal, sarcastic letter.*]

Allen Ginsberg [New York, NY] to Jack Kerouac [Richmond Hill, NY]
February 24, 1953

Mr. Jack Kerouac
94-21 134 Street
Richmond Hill, New York

Dear Sir:

Thank you for your two prompt replies of the 21st to my letter of the 20th. I am sincerely aggrieved that my original appeal appeared to violate certain proprieties of your situation which you explained in your letters, and I hasten to set this matter right on all counts.

Before I proceed let me congratulate you on the charm and incisiveness of the quotation which you authorize; which quotation I will naturally submit to your agent for his (her) approval before making use (there)of.

There are two delicate matters which I wish to mention: While I approve your wish to dissociate your own literary position with that of the author of *"Go"* (who incidentally gave his general permission, etc. without consulting MCA) and while I will do everything in my power to aid you in doing so, especially in this instance, it behooves me to remind you as a friend that, adopting your suggestion of separate statements, no further reference will be made by me to anyone that it was at your request. In other words, let us do this as quietly as possible, so as not to risk offending Mr. Holmes. If you wish to make a public matter of this, of course, that is your privilege, and I will follow suit.

Secondly, you know of course that great secrecy is desirable *vis-a-vis* your new relationship with MCA, particularly as there is still a delicate situation to be dealt with at A. A. Wyn. Solomon knows nothing of your recent activities. I have, by your express instructions, said nothing to him of any import on anything remotely concerning your present publishing position. So, if you do see him, and speak of this matter, or any other, I beg you for your own sake to breathe not a word about MCA. And certainly, if you wish to see him, avoid MCA as intermediary, until they say so.

I applaud your discrimination in choosing the method of praise which you have consented to accord to Mr. Lee's writings. I am sure that he, as well as myself as his agent, would be gratified by this instance of your esteem, were he apprised of the facts. He is, as you know, traveling in South America now and cannot be reached for consultation on matters of publicity. I have been proceeding carefully as possible on my own in his behalf, though mistakes are to be made and unmade I am sure.

A further question, perhaps to be decided by your agent: do you really feel the possibility of threat of persecution for drug reasons as a result of your contribution to the publicity? The pseudonym conceals the author's name as he confesses, as you know, to a number of statutory crimes. This does not involve a threat, except perhaps of social disapproval, to anyone who choose to praise his writing.

A further word as to my own position: though your name is being cried on the streets for book trade reasons, I would not dream of participating in this particular request to you except for reasons of high literary seriousness. I have faith in the quality of the book I am dealing with. I would not, as well, make use of your name for any other purpose publicly. The motives of the publisher, A. A. Wyn, are, as far as I am concerned, for the most part beneath my interest; and I do not find it necessary for my purposes to concern myself with their motives except infrequently for tactical reasons. As evidence of the latter I adduce my paragraph consulting you to keep silent about your arrangements with MCA until MCA makes it public.

I cannot close this letter without thanking you once again for your paragraph which seems to combine all the proper elements and catch the spirit of admiration which I hope one day will be universally accorded to the work we are dealing with.

Yours most respectfully and in the spirit of strictest commerce,

Allen Ginsberg

P.S. Once again let me apologize for bothering you on this matter. I will of course follow your suggestion and clear such matters with MCA first, on this situation and on any others to come.

[*Ginsberg kept in touch with Burroughs who was in the South American jungle experimenting with the drug yage. In his letters William enclosed various "routines," his term for short prose vignettes. Carefully, Allen saved them, and those became the foundation for* Naked Lunch.]

Allen Ginsberg [New York, NY] to William S. Burroughs
[Colombia, South America] May 13, 1953

Dear Bill:

I have all your letters. Forgive me for not writing sooner but I have been busy getting a new job, trying to work it and getting fired again. So I am out of work again, and have time to tend to affairs.

The job was with a literary agency, Scott Meredith by name: they handle Mickey Spillane and B. Traven. My job was what was called on the Fee desk as opposed to the Pro desk. Fee means all the Miss Lonelihearts who want to be writers send in their stories and novels, etc. plus $5.00 (or more) to cover the attention paid to their creations, and I had to read it—shitty, sorry, stupid, inane feebleminded stories—and write a 2 page letter of criticism according to prescribed pulp-slick-quality fiction market formulas; but not discouraging them enough to stop, encouraging them to send us more business. Sort of a Célinish literary con. I was very good at it, as I have all the proper qualities of a high class brilliant robot to be able to grasp the essentials of the formula and apply it instinctively (I had to compete with about a hundred Ivy League would be litterateurs in giving a sample analysis and did the best) (and so got the job). But after about two weeks it was discovered that my spelling was lousy (didn't for didnt') and so I got sacked. Most of my time was spent typing out these complicated letters, and so secretarial efficiency was a requisite. Also I was working on a piecework basis and I am a slow typist; so it wasn't working out from my end anyway. Well I don't know what I'll do next, maybe try to get a better job now. No real bad financial worries as I can always pick up $30 per week for typing for my brother a few hours a day, and I have old market research jobs to go back to. But I think I'll take it easy and look around for something high class. I learned a lot out of this last job though, in a Balzacian way, about the immense self-absorbed world of pulp-fiction; and also I read a lot of puerile fantasies of all kinds, Western, Romance, etc. that those poor fools from the hinterlands (surprising all the people in Peoria who'll write inferior sad stories year after year hoping for criticism and final acceptance which they'll never get but are encouraged to believe is at the "end of the road" for them) dream up in their more introspective moments. One story was about a man 50 years old fired from job, decided to become a writer, the climax of the story being he gets his first acceptance check. This was titled *The Chance Of A Lifetime,* was autobiographical, and was this person's first story. Horribly written trailed all over the map and full of confused clichés. Like reading letters to lonely hearts column in Nathaniel West's book (do you know it?)

Skip further on for information on ss and *Junkie*, meanwhile I am writing you a letter.

The preoccupation of my last two years has been with restoring to my eyes the sight of the material universe in all its surface grandeur and familiarity. This is the world without ideas, so to speak, of which I made so much when you were in New Orleans. Resulting from this my thought was depressed (the consciousness of an oyster, as you said) and my vision totally obscured, so also for the most part feeling and Eros and poetic inspiration. The title of the book I wrote then was justly *Empty Mirror*. That is mirror uncolored so far as I was aware by rainbow of one's own imagination and desire.

The last few months I have become more aware of the proper role of my own feelings and imaginations. That is to say, the next step as I see it is to deal with reality as plastic, recreate the world after my own mind's image of what I want it to be like. By world I mean the flat surface data sans interpretation which is given to.

Well anyway so much for that.

I am getting a confused idea of the Colombian political situation. There isn't much in the papers, but *The Times* has been carrying some stories lately about it. I enclose their editorial today, if it's of any interest. They seem to disregard the liberals altogether in their moderate "hopes." Why don't you write a letter to the *Times*? I'll see that it gets published if it's possible, as Lucien is the son-in-law etc., and perhaps he'd be interested. If you want to enlist yourself in aiding the cause this is a real way to do it. Those *Times* letters influence a lot of people here, on subjects like this.

Junk is out and I am sending you a few copies. Reaction has been very good from Junkies. I sent your check to Florida ($270.00) at a time when I thought you were headed there and could cash it. I expect that, since you mention the letter it has been forwarded to you in Lima. [. . .]

Anyway, this partially solves the financial problem of the expedition, temporarily. We are all incidentally terribly impressed by your dealings with the higher ups. It's so much more romantic than being beat. How much more money do you need to do Yage work? I'll try to get some more out of Wyn. Send me a 1-page summary of plan of the book, types of things it covers, time it covers, places (perhaps if it is in chapters a list and description of chapters). Then I will try to raise the money. I may be able to mortgage your future royalties to my brother Gene, or maybe get gelt from Wyn.

Stretch out book with much detailed adventure and politics as you like, it's interesting reading and somewhat in the news. I wouldn't come on too campy though, that'll lessen its chances of publication. Keep that to one or 2 specific chapters, as in *Junk*, or make it manly or something. Any detailed camp should be kept for the book *Queer*.

So Jurado[24] is out? I thought his goose was cooked? Your letter of May 5 speaks of preparing a manuscript in part. Send it up, and enclose please if not too much trouble the 1 page prospectus of the whole book. They always ask for those and I never know what to say. It makes them feel securer to believe the writer knows what he is doing.

What were you sentenced to, by the way? Can't Jurado erase that somehow?

If you have a chance get a map and show the route of your travels chronologically in red or blue for different trips. I can't keep straight where you are at or going. Where the hell are the Ancas located for instance?

Jack is in Frisco, after another break with all publishers, and a trip through Canada. He says Neal nearly killed himself falling off a train and broke an ankle (bent back double) and slashed his chest. On crutches around the house. But surviving. Jack wants your address which I'll send him today. He also wants to know Kells address so he can go yachting with him. Jack is at 103 Santa Barbara Street, Hotel Colonial, San Luis Obispo, Calif. Malcolm Cowley wanted to publish Jack's first Harcourt-rejected version of *On The Road* and Jack refused since they wouldn't publish *Dr. Sax* and another subsequent novel about a high school love affair. (Cowley worked for Viking Press). So I am back as Jack's agent again. The *Sax* and other are worth publishing I think, and so will try.

Lucien having a baby in 4 months or so, maybe less, and is moving to a big apartment in a nice building on Sheridan Square. His wife is big with child and has stopped working at UP.

Has the *Life* man returned to U.S. What is his name? I'll look him up and find out what I can, and see what's what.

Write me, I'm freer to answer letters now.

As ever,

Allen

If you have any spare gelt like 12¢ or whatever it costs send me some fucking artifacts from the jungle, or Chile, or anywhere. What kinds of artifacts have they? Anything but Moa Moa swords and machetes.

24 Bernabé Jurado. William S. Burroughs' lawyer in the case involving the death of Joan.

I forgot to say above I am reading Zen Buddhism and looking at Chink and Jap paintings, scrolls and poetry in museums and liberries. Very interesting.

[*Ginsberg remained political, although much of his time was devoted to literary matters as well as the necessity of earning a living. In this telegram he speaks against the government's decision to execute the Rosenbergs. In the years to follow, Allen wrote letters to every president from Eisenhower to Clinton.*]

Allen Ginsberg [New York, NY] to Dwight Eisenhower [Washington, DC] *ca.* June 16, 1953

Rosenbergs are pathetic, government will sordid, execution obscene, America caught in crucifixion machine, only barbarians want them burned I say stop it before we fill our souls with death-house horror.

Allen Ginsberg

[*After a visit from Burroughs to New York, Ginsberg decided it was time to get out and travel the world himself. Neal and Carolyn Cassady had invited Allen to visit them, and he decided to make a grand tour of the south and Mexico on his way to California.*]

Allen Ginsberg [Mérida, Mexico] to Jack Kerouac, Neal Cassady and Carolyn Cassady [San Jose, CA] before January 12, 1954

Dear Jack and Neal and Carolyn:

I am sitting here on the balcony of my Mérida "Casa de Huespedes" looking down the block to the Square at Twilite—have a big $5 peso room for the nite, just returned from 8 days inland. Came by plane from horrid Havana and more horrid Miami Beach. All these tropical stars—just filled my gut with big meal and codeinettas and am sitting down to enjoy the nite—first rest I've had in longtime.

Saw Bill's Marker[25] in Jacksonville—a sweet fellow who donated $12 to my trip on his own hook, very simpatico—but, and, I *must* say Bill's taste in boys is macabre—(to say the least etc.). He is so starved looking and rickety and pitifully purseymouthed and "laid"—French for ugly and with a disgusting birth-

25 Lewis Marker (1930–1998). Friend of William S. Burroughs.

mark below left ear—and skin the texture of a badly shaved hemophiliac. The first sight of him was a shock—poor poor Bill! To be in love with that sickly myopic pebblemouthed scarecrow! Had great long talk about mystical ignu's personality and drank rum and stayed in big moldy apartment in slums house that he owns.

In Palm Beach I called up the Burroughs family and was given big welcome—Xmas dinner and put me up at fancy hotel and drove me around town sightseeing and asked me about Bill, who I told them was "a very good and perhaps become a very great writer" which I think they liked to hear said, and was glad to say it in most conservative Bob Merims considering manner. Old Burroughs very nice, some of Bill's innate wisdom-tooth. Miami Beach I stopped overnite for $1.50 and saw all the mad hotels—miles of them—too much for the eye, the lushest unreal spectacle I ever saw. Also ran into Alan Eager at a Birdland they have there. Key West pretty like Provincetown, nothing happened there, rode on Keys on truck at nite. Havana I won't talk of—kind of dreary rotting antiquity, rotting stone, *heaviness* all about and don't dig Cubans much even in Cuba. Got lost penniless 20 miles out of town in small village and had to be sent home on train with man who bought me drinks. So sad, so hospitable, but I wanted to get away, can't dig his fate. Marvelous first airplane air vistas of the earth, Carib Isles, great green maplike Yucatan Coast maplike below with sinkholes in earth of limestone crust and narrow road and trails like antpath down below and little cities like mushrooms in pockets and hollows of afternoon hills, and windmills.

Stayed in Mérida 3 days at this place, ran into 2 Quintana Roo Indians and drove in horse carriage round city, met mayor's brother so got invited to big City Hall ceremonies New Years day—free beer and sandwiches overlooking plaza on balcony City Hall; that nite, New Years, formal dress—New York-Paris-London society type "Country Cloob" (Club) champagne free and French and English and German speaking industrialists and young Yucatan Spanish girls fresh from New Orleans finishing school—all dressed in tux and party evening dress at tables under stars—nothing happened I just wandered around and talked to people, then after went downtown and heard poor mambo in dancehalls and drank little and slept at 5 AM. Next day to Chichén Itzá where I got free house next to pyramid and spent days eating in native hut for $7 pesos a day, wandering around great ruins—at nite take hammock up on top of big pyramid temple (whole dead city to myself as living in archeologists' camp) and look at stars and void and deathheads engraved up on stone pillars and write and doze on codeinetta. Free guide from where I eat, and drink every nite before supper at Richman's Mayaland Hotel talk to rich Americans, meet 35 yr old Ginger B. all hung up on Yucatan songs and costumes, dumb, drag, talking bitch sad. Stars over pyramids—tropic nite, forest of chirruping insects, birds and maybe owls—once I heard one hooting—great stone portals, bas relief of unknown perceptions, half a thousand years old—and earlier in day saw stone cocks a thousand years old grown over with moss and batshit in dripping vaulted room of stone stuck in the wall. A high air silent above niteforest —tho a clap of hands brings great echoes from various pillars and arenas. So then left for Valladolid—money already running out—in central Yucatan and nite there with amigo speaking English who showed me the tower and I ate at his middleclass family house where his wife bowed respectful and a movie about ghosts—and next day awful miserable 10 hour train to town name of Tizinia [sic: Tizimin] for the oldest fiesta of Mexico; most venerable Indians from Campeche and Tabasco on train with great sacks full of food and babies and hammocks; started on train at 4 AM morning rode till afternoon cramped no place to stand, train ran off rails, hold-ups, arrive at really crowded small town middle of nowhere—with silly bullring and 400 yr old cathedral, mobbed by old Indians, candles, 3 wooden kings old as the conquest they came to see (3 Mages [Magis])—the air of cathedral so smoky and so full of candles the wax on the floor was inches deep and slippery—thought I was the only American in town but later found a Buffalo optometrist on train back who said famous documentary film maker named Rotha was there with movie cameras —(I saw Rotha pix in Museum of Modern Art once)—trip back horrible—the *boxcars* with benches on sides and down center, wood, Mex-made and all crude, 110 people to car, people hanging on platform and even *steps* for hours—me too—so uncomfortable to sit it was insane, for 10 hours—and had left my codeine behind! (*No* have habit by the way only used 2 times) old women and babies falling asleep on my shoulder and lap, everybody suffering meaningless hour-long stops in the nite to change tracks or engines.

Had met priest at Tizimin Cathedral who took me backstairs and smoked and cursed native pagan rite of the feast, and so went with him to his village "Colonia Yucatan" a lumber town *à la* Levittown or Vet housing project—and he drove me by jeep next day to forests of Quintana Roo and back—then to train and horrid ride. Then another day at great silent Chichén Itzá—recalling a dream I once had about a future world of great plateaus covered with grass and levels and plains of plateau leading to horizon with grassy roofs on many levels of dripping stone chambers and wild sculptured ornament all round the sides—stood up and looked from top at jungle spread all around circle to horizon, dream actualized. Who came up but the optometrist, with his nice camera?

Came back to Mérida today. Met bunch of Mexico City painters on junket to study provinces and talked French and will go to a big *gran baille* (dance) tonite (Sat. nite)—and tomorrow look up Professor Stromswich for info on Mayapan ruins—also must pick up letter from Bill from Rome at Consulate and telegram perhaps with money from home—down to $25 dollars, enuf to get to Mexico City but not much more and want to see more Mexico south so sent for some more $ from Gene. My Spanish is got to point where I can find out what I want easily but I keep making mistakes that have cost me money from time to time—enough to wish I knew—like I bought the wrong kind of hammock and so lost out 9 pesos the other day.

Also in Mérida a "homeopathic druggist" i.e. I don't know, different from pharmaceutical druggists—name of George Ubo been everywhere in U.S. and Yucatan and told me how to get everywhere on big 10 foot map he has. So far everywhere I have run across someone or other who showed me the town in English or French or English-Spanish mixture but have not met anyone great— except one nite in the rich hotel in Mérida last week, wandered into bar for 1 peso rich-man's tequila and ran into a drunk brilliant elderly Spaniard who talked to me in French in great world weary monologue full of filth and Paris and N.Y. and Mexico City and who was later led off by his bodyguard to be sick in the urinal—later found out he was the richest man in the area Yucatan Peninsula—famous character who married a whore 20 years ago and owns everything everywhere and gets drunk every nite with venerable looking Jaime de Angulo white bearded spic internationalists at the hotel—who were there that night winking and calming him down—sort of an old evil Claude he was, full of misery and rich and drunken disregard of life.

Mosquitoes down here awful—all beds come with M-nets and I have bought one for my hammock.

Jack, incidentally—they won't let you past customs in Mérida without health card and all the Indians have vaccination marks they wear "proudly"— it's really a 50-50 necessity. Have had dysentery and took pills and it went away, so no suffer. No such thing as a natural man untouched by medicine around here—it's not for *touristas*, tho it's a *tourista* routine—it is for everyone.

If I had more money, I found a way to get thru Quintana Roo involving busses and narrow gauge mule driven R.R. and an afternoon walk 13 kilometers on rocky mule path thru jungle—or else a 40 peso boat around peninsula —but cannot go cause too costly for my purse. But will be fine trip for someone someday. Many people all over ready to help the traveler—it's like a frontier—with engineers building a road thru that never gets done.

The man here, head of archeology, name given me by Museum Natural History in N.Y.—turned out valuable—gave me pass to stay on archeologist's camps, free, everywhere there's a ruin I go. Great way to travel and see ruins. Write me note to Mexico City Embassy.

Love,

Allen

[*Ginsberg spent several months in Chiapas, Mexico, where he had adventures and wrote long letters during the lazy afternoons. In the summer of 1954, he arrived on the Cassadys' doorstep. With the same enthusiasm he had shown Mexico, he recorded his first impressions of San Francisco and the nascent literary scene he discovered there.*]

Allen Ginsberg [San Jose, CA] to Louis Ginsberg, Edith Ginsberg and Eugene Brooks [Paterson, NJ] July 10, 1954

Dear Louis, Edith and Gene and *Kinder* [Edith's two children: Harold and Sheila]:

I applied at the railroad for brakeman's job. A good job if it works out and I can do it, which would be difficult but valuable experience and good pay (3–5 hundred month) but no hiring going on at present. Will reapply in a few weeks the situation I am told fluctuates rapidly and I have friends on RR who recommend me (who got Jack similar job). Meanwhile no worry and I can wait beyond summer if necessary without strain.

I looked up Rexroth's connections here, he's away on vacation but sent me name of a Prof. [Ruth] Witt-Diamant at San Fran State College who runs a poetry institute or club. Moderators are Kenneth Patchen (of all the creeps) (I have been spared meeting him so far but will see him for the sake of my universal conscience), Norman Macleod who is white-haired and has a speech defect and is sucking around the course to see if he can get a job in the school there, apparently he's taught a lot but in S.F. is presently unemployed, and Robert Duncan, a young Pound student, about 30 and smart but sort of a pathetic type, tries to browbeat these poor nowhere would-be student poets at round table workshop type meetings, admission 50¢ and not worth a nickel. Macleod most simpatico of the trio. I gave him my book unintroduced and he wrote me a letter next day saying he liked it and would pass it on and suggesting a nasty little local magazine named *Inferno* to send some to. But he's a nice guy. Rexroth apparently the only real brain around here except for [Yvor] Winters at Stanford, I haven't met him but will soon. I have a meet[ing] to discuss metrics with Duncan some afternoon when I get to town.

I've also seen a lot of Chinatown: the food is more excellent varied tasty and original than NYC Chinatown, it's easier to get, and it's about half as cheap as NYC. They have basic dishes I never heard of, a brand of Won Ton soup new to me and better than original NY style, 40 cent fried rice and tea, etc. I also hit all the North Beach bars — their Village — and found more life even than in NYC, more bars even anyway, and the same people as NY or their spiritual cousins; a very depressing sight in some respects and I'm glad I'm in San Jose where I can be protected from the temptation to run around to wild surrealist movies, art shows, jazz bands, hipster's parties, cellar lounges filled with hi fidelity Bach, etc. All in all a very active cultured city the rival of NY for general relaxation and progressive artlife. Probably a very fine place to live if you like cities. When I get money I'll move there for a while, at least a few months to absorb it all. Spectacular views of the bay, bridges, Alcatraz, whiteroofed city on hills, clean, expansive horizon, ships in the toy harbor (really so huge). Communist murals in the tower (Coit) where sightseers go to observe, but they've decided after much public bitching, to let them stay, and they're funny and charming as they are. Also keeping the cable cars, a big issue here.

I have unnecessary piles of correspondence, with Kerouac at the moment a monumental exchange of descriptions of SF-Mexico trip and him sending news of NY. Plus long dissertations on Buddhism which he's been reading in for a year and is all hopped on. In between I work daily on poems but still not really shoveling at the mountain of notes yet.

Eugene sounds positively angelic. Louis sounds happy too. I had a haunting sense that most of my Mexico letters were gibberish since there's no map around, as Edith tipped me off. The parakeet is really a new and shocking development. I never dreamed . . . . . But why not go whole hog with a monkey and really get some animal inspiration. Incidentally I traveled with a monkey for several days on the way out and if you think parakeet crap comes anywhere near the nuisance value of a monkey's bowel movements . . . I should say, you could have done worse. I hope Louis is behaving himself with the animal. I've always suspected him of having a strange unnatural savage fascination with the little dears. It was one of his poetic eccentricities, one of the few he allows himself. Let me warn you about him. If you find the bird dead like some mystical swallow under a rose bush one summer morn. I will write Harold. Regards to all, Sheila. Tell her (again) to dig Gerry Mulligan's music. He must be playing around the Apple (as NYC is referred to from afar).

Nothing new special to report. I visited the Rosicrucian meeting here and met some old lady spinster Rosicrucians. They keep seeing imaginary auras and talking about their lousy karmas. (You pay in one life for what you do in the last few, you keep getting reborn) and they keep having dreams about when they were in Egypt and Atlantis. This is the occidental Rosicrucian center. I sure would have liked to pick up on them in the Middle Ages but now they're a bunch of mystical bobby soxers.

Everybody appears to be either off their rockers or getting religion. Cassady has some mediumistic cult [Edgar Cayce] that has changed him so that he kneels and prays with his children; the doctrine is screwy and absurd, almost on a *Readers' Digest* level, but the seriousness of the search for uplift is real enough and respectable; Kerouac seems all hung up on a Buddha doctrine of life as a dream; even Burroughs in far off Tangier appears to have undergone a humanistic conversion and Jack sent me a letter from him declaring, "I say we are here in <u>human form</u> to learn by the <u>human</u> hieroglyphs of love and suffering. It is a duty to take the risk of love. I <u>know</u> that ultimately the forces of death will destroy themselves." Such generalizations belong in a Nobel Prize speech. As for me sanctity is a worn out suit. I've been reading everything from theosophy to W. C. Fields' biography and Eliot criticism. I hear WCW [William Carlos Williams] has a new book out. Jack's recommending me some Buddha books so I'll eventually read those too. Nothing like a wide range of information.

Well enough of this prattle. Forgive me if I don't write too often but I'll keep well in touch, it's just that when I get started like this I wind up spending hours instead of writing book.

Love,

Allen

Allen Ginsberg [San Jose, CA] to Eugene Brooks [New York, NY]
August 14, 1954

Dear Gene:

Received yours of the 12th rapidly today, fast service. Thank you for the check, really thoughtful. My expenses are not very much and are taken care of. I'll hold on to the check in case I need it but I don't think I'll cash it, at least in the immediate future. If I do I'll let you know. I am still negotiating with the railroad for the job, it's not settled yet one way or the other. I was turned down by the doctor in a physical for what I thought were phony reasons. Since writing to you (or Louis) last on the subject I appealed his decision to the Southern Pacific hospital in S.F. to his superior and found that I was right; they passed me. The score as far as the doctor remains a bureaucratic mystery too involved and tendentious to go into here (he's just an old fart slightly anti-Semitic is the nearest I can get to it). At any rate having been ok'd by the hospital has set off some small bureaucratic war in one of the smaller offices of the RR Co. and I am waiting the results. I expect to know this week. Maybe favorably, but you never can tell. At any rate since I want the job I've been pushing it with more vigor than my usual wont. (As to the 4F deal, first doctor said no ex 4F's employed on orders from his superiors. His superiors told me Merchant Marine made up for that and passed me.)

Hope you enjoy Cape Cod. Helen Parker introduced me to the place; the late Wm. Cannastra and a whole pile of Remo types hung around there and still do, those that survive. There should be lots of chicks around. San Francisco has a huge highly organized bohemia, in fact it's a big institution sympathetically treated in the *SF Chronicle*, a good paper. I spend a day or so a week there looking up people. I met Kenneth Rexroth who is the big cheese poet here except for Jeffers and spent an evening talking with him. He used to know or knew of Louis. A real learned man, translates Chink, Jap, Greek, Latin, French and is an editor at New Directions. Also an anarchist self-professed with a whole line of dreary self pitying ARTIST hangups. I'm no one to talk but he makes a profession out of it which is really embarrassing to listen to. However he knows a lot about literature when his taste is not corrupted by this kind of hangup.

That's a good idea about investing small sums in plays. I never heard of Yvelvington (YVELVINGTON?) and somehow the name smells of bankruptcy. However if by the investment of a small sum you could get to dig the scene (is it Sheridan Square Circle?) [Circle in the Square was a theater on Sheridan Square] (and maybe some of the dolls) even if as seems likely you lose the money you might be buying yourself some useful experience in the field. Anyway that's a good way to circulate some of the banked money and probably good for some kicks, be worthwhile. I don't know personally of any small group or author in whom I think investment would be remunerative, except by some such chance as might come thru with Quintero, though I should think with the success they had they had enough backing by now, unless he's passing off on you a long shot he don't want to back. But these are thoughts on no basis of personal knowledge.

Speaking of investment, have you thought of putting some money in an investment trust (like Investment Trust of Boston?). They take your money, you buy stock in them, that is, and they take their total assets and invest it in stocks, spreading out the investment all over the map to give it a safe base. You get monthly interest (about 45 dollars on 5 thousand) and a yearly dividend. Interest and dividend you can spend or reinvest. You can sell it anytime, and you can borrow in it cheap anytime. On the basis of the last 20 years a 10,000 investment becomes worth 80 thousand. Presuming the economy is going to be stable and not take a stock nose-dive, it's one of the safest and most remunerative forms of investment. Bankers and insurance companies say they're a good thing, safe that is. They also provide you with perpetual economic advice on major moves, like buying houses, cars, etc. with personal service, that is they assign you an advisor. Neal has about 6000 invested in above mentioned fund and seems to be getting his money's worth. I myself have 'grave' doubts that the U.S. will stay stable and economically upswinging. But I think barring a bomb you could probably tell when things were going to get really bad and withdraw. At any rate you should do something with your money to make it work for you instead of letting it sit. For instance in Santa Clara Valley here the population and building is going fast and people are building on all the old peach etc. grove land. Well you buy yourself a few acres of that and resell in a year or so and make money. The areas of development and the certainties of it are much clearer to the eye here than in more confused and developed East. While looking around for a house to buy here we ran into such possibilities. However undoubtedly the international situation is such that you're wise enough to keep your money in your pocket or bank.

As for international situation it seems to me that since Indo China the whole deal ought to be much clearer. Eisenhower's recent statement modifying and limiting U.S. policy to cooperation seems to have put the final nail in the coffin. Just think a few years ago *Life* was talking about the American Century. It's obviously the Asiatic century, if it's anybody's. Spengler etc. The U.S. with all its phony stupid realpolitik has just about put itself and me behind the 8-ball and at this point I don't see any way out. We're too stupid, people here seem to think they can get away with the usual shit to the end of time. Seven years ago we still had time for a total reversal of egotistical direction in favor of an all out Point 4 UNRA etc. super policy of cooperation and relief and rehabilitation involving us with as much energy in a positive program of world development as we have spent in a negative series of armed retreats from an untenable imperialistic selfish position. The policy has at this point definitely failed, as anybody then could see, we never had a Chinaman's chance to limit or ignore India, China, Russia, socialism, etc. All we've done is fucked everything up by forcing them to fight us and become as monstrous as we are. Confucius said: "Rule an empire as you would cook a small fish." The only hope for peaceful survival we ever had was obvious years ago and simple as cooking a fish. However the U.S. is lost in a mad dream of plastic lampshades. There's an obvious relation between the evils of competitive usury capitalism and the whole senseless self righteous psychology that goes with it and the present fact of our being humbled and beat down by the rest of the world who are plain sick of us. Everybody from Europe to India has been saying that for years and we still haven't caught on. And as far as I can see it when we go down any possibility of a really constructive cooperative future goes, everybody everywhere will wind up in bureaucratic armed misery. I'm writing a poem on the subject. I never saw the possibility of political poetry before but the international political situation seems to me to have at last palpably revealed its final necessary relation to moral or spiritual justice. Finally for the fiftieth time, I declare, the so called higher ups, the military authorities and industrial experts and government experts, etc. etc. who have been shrouding their plain stupidity all along in the Time-type myth of realpolitik—trying to tell everybody that they know more than anybody else and that their decisions are mathematically predicated on the given data of power and policy—trying to browbeat everybody else who has any plain common sense at all into handing over to them the mystic power to make mistakes—well I don't know where this sentence goes but my point is that the men who are running the government are playing it strictly by ear whatever they think and they have the worst ears. This government would be better run by a bunch of irresponsible tea heads from the San Remo. Ezra Pound says a politician who is not an accomplished musician and doesn't understand Greek prosody is unfit for office. At least Mao Tse-tung spent 10 years in a cave studying Confucius, and writing odes.

I haven't seen *Caesar*, *Waterfront* or the hot-rod motorcycle picture with Brando, yet. They're all supposed to be good.

Give my regards to Levy if you see him, and Klein if you write him. How is the minister's daughter's [Connie, Eugene's future wife] mother and brother? From what I see of wives and husbands you might be making a good bargain if you do marry her. At least she'll appreciate it and take good care of you. If you can't find a great love to marry, I think, your wife should be humble. She's all right. You thinking of marrying her? I would hate to say one thing or another but since she does seem to like you sincerely for yourself and have a great many potential wifely virtues, that is to say, she knows what she's doing and getting into and seems to like it—why then if you feel like getting hitched you might as well.

I am reading a lot: *Troilus and Cressida* (disillusioned bitter Céline-ish Shakespeare), Pound Eliot Winters Leavis criticism, Chinese and Latin poetry, books and articles on prosody. You would like Catullus. I read a collection of translations edited by an Aiken, and am reading him in Latin now with aid of a pony. Selections in anthologies won't give you the idea. Get a book of translations from all times, from library. The Aiken book is good, includes translations by Ben Jonson, Byron, Landor, Campion, etc. I am doing some real study on metrics and maybe will come up with something. It's already improved the music of my free verse. Trouble is a real study involves knowledge of music, Provencal, Greek, etc. It all relates directly to history or basic theory of metrical practice and notation. I don't know how far I can go with the crude education I have. I mainly miss music. There is a difference between the kind of fine classical education you can get in private school and the vague generalities of public high schools. Write sometime. I'll let you know when anything happens.

Love,

Allen

P.S. I bought the new Céline—it's opening is great but I haven't finished it yet. It seems so disordered in the writing it's hard to read like the more hallucinated parts of *Death on the Installment Plan*—but still worth the trouble and very funny. The translation is not by the same person and is more awkward— that's part of the trouble I think. Look at it and tell me what you think.

[*While staying with the Cassady family in San Jose, Carolyn discovered Ginsberg in bed with Neal. The next day she drove Allen to San Francisco, gave him twenty dollars, and left him out in North Beach at the corner of Broadway and Columbus.*]

Allen Ginsberg [San Francisco, CA] to Jack Kerouac [n.p.]
September 5, 1954

Cher Jean-Louis Le Brie:

Thank you for your letters, all so kind, all so sweet to get, such a pleasure that tho it's a waste of time etc. I get more kicks from reading them than almost anything else,—but don't write if not so set up, natch. Hard to write with burn-blister on thumb (of pen hand) and no typewriter. Well: what has happened out here, afterward will express my joy at the [Malcolm] Cowley news, so right for the occasion. Sooner or later as I opined (in a prophetic tone) in first or other letter it was bound to break sooner or later. Yours is assured, I wish mine were equally so. Show Cowley my poetry if you can without embarrassment when there is a ripe time, but not if it involves a hassle. But more of this later.

I have a lot to relate but hard to write with bad hand—Carolyn caught me and Neal—screamed,—she is I think a charnel—yelled,—reversed her original hypocrisy—was it?—or I shouldn't maybe judge—but it was not comic, the intensity of insult and horror and even I think spite, indignation, etc. (She burst into my room one 4 AM at the house) (though you see I was hiding nothing—told her in fact—it was O.K.'d—but all the details are not for here can't write fast enough) but anyway a horrible scene—ordered me gone—Neal went blank, ran out to work—I sat and faced her. She talked and I thought her face waxed green with evil. "You've always been in my way ever since Denver—your letters have always been an insult—you're trying to come between us" and more, horrible—such force, Célinish, I went cold with horror—felt steeped in evil. They hate each other, charnels to each other she and Neal. But I can't picture it to you as I really see it, no Levinsky sacerdotalism involved. I was glad to get away. So took 20 dollars and went up to Frisco to the above address—(I had said nothing back to her—went blank with a kind of hopeless feeling she was mad—though tried to hold with some kind of in-sad sight to it all—I didn't come to screw her up) and here moved into Sublette's hotel (he moved to the Marconi up a few blocks Broadway can see Vesuvius from his window) and pounded pavements madly. Got a job in market research, $55 a week, 9-5 next month—on Montgomery financial street—found a girl the first night—a great new girl who digs me, I dig—22, young, hip (ex-singer big buddy of Brubeck, knows all the colored cats, ex-hipster girl) pretty in a real chic classy way, straight—she works in high teacup emporium store writing advertising—digs me—she has a wild mind, finer than any girl I met—really—a real treasure—and such a lovely face—so fine a pretty face—young life in her—and real sharp agenbite of inwit thoughts like Lucien—Thos. Hardy. So have been seeing her for a week we talk and neck and will make it sure—but she has a kid (married at 18, kid 4 years old) used to sing in San Jose roadhouses and knows Mrs. Green [marijuana], etc. What a doll. And she's not a flip thank god. Not a stupid square in any way but not a flip. Sheila Williams. She tried to get me a crazy job at store the first nite I knew her—instant digging each other—how wild and great. O well, to see how this proceeds—nothing ugly can happen anyway thank god, she's too fine—she dug Sublette, etc. But we wander around alone and sit and drink coffee at her apartment and talk—and she digs the <u>really</u> good lines of my poetry, not just generally digs, but digs the <u>specific</u> tricks—well enough.

So to continue otherwise: I live in the Marconi hotel—run by dykes—first night they say to me —"here's yr. key. You want to have anybody in your room go ahead and have a ball we're drunk all night ourselves"—and they are. Middle size room $6.00 carpet soft on floor privacy, Sublette upstairs and—horrors! Last Friday night Sheila takes me to big party of nowhere engineers on Telegraph Hill. I come home 4:30 AM meet Sublette, and Cosmo (a weird egotistic small poet smart aleck) go and get coffee, the cops look at us, search us, find white powder on Cosmo. To jail, all night, my first week here, as a vagrant (tho I have $18.00 and a job for Monday to come and a room and party suit on) in tank, me and Sublette horrified (I had a pipe in my room but they didn't look) but actually great kicks—set free the next day, Cosmo doesn't get out for 4 days—the powder was foot powder not junk all along—he kept telling them but didn't believe and had it analyzed and finally let him go. So Bill better be careful.

I went saw Pippin, Gene Pippin, at Berkeley—he real smart you know on archaic styles and respects invention too (tho he's limited like Ansen, etc.) but served me big meal, glad to see me, we talk all eve till 1 AM about Cannastra and N.Y. and he reads me Fulke-Greville etc. and is not tied up and private snit like he used to be—has graying hairs even (31 yrs.)—so a happy "occasion."

Yes, of course I am a <u>Taoist</u>, I know about that and I dig it in relation to yoga —guilt—discipline—absolutes like you do for the same reason, the big fact is there in Taoism and it's much more relaxed—as I dig the <u>first</u> poem in *The Way of Life*—"Whichever way you slice it etc." Zen Buddhism is also a very <u>late</u> sharp humorous version—though it has sinister disciplinary undertones I understand. I will though definitely do what I have never done, following your example, and read the books you named, I have a library card here now (and am reading Latin poets too. I like Catullus) (Big passionate sharp feelingful love poems to Dusty [Dostoyevsky] and also to his <u>boy</u>, Juventius).

I am writing among other things a series of Roman—saintly—"realistic" —platonic etc. some pornographic poems from Neal pages too. I have a <u>lot</u> of fine things in my journal—50 good poems maybe—still trying to get them typed up and add more and measure them out in lines and it will be O.K. But my writing isn't gone enuf yet.

I at last enclose *Siesta in Xbalba*. It won't be finished (I won't quit trying to add) for a while but this is the best I can do with it after 4 months—5 months. The handwritten part still doesn't get a vision of Europe like I hope for but just mentions it and signs off. Show this to Lucien maybe and Cowley maybe? if you dig it—maybe it's too revised and formal now.

Yes, Rexroth was only an idea just in case nothing else was happening, Cowley much better. By the way the Ansen type poet round here name of Robert Duncan, friend of Pound, runs a crappy tho sincere Pound type poetry circle here part of S.F. College came to my room and saw a typed copy of your "Essentials" of Prose (remember, you wrote it down on E. 7th St.) and dug it (strangely particularly the part of no revision and the general conception of spontaneity) and asked to borrow it to make a copy and wanted yr. address and wanted to know who you were etc. Well he's a funny guy, queer, his poetry is all crazy and surrealist and he's a friend of Lamantia and his poetry also is no good because too aesthetically hung up all about his sensibility faced with the precise tone of his piddle—Light, etc.—that's the subject matter—but it's all right he's nice a curious person, talks too much in front of his young Corso students.

Neal—he played chess with Dick Woods and was blind, etc. except in a weird way very nice to me, but he is mad—the thing is Jack he really is suffering some incipient insanity—the charnel Carolyn, the frantic sex—now it is terrible pathetic mad rushing around and can't even make it—getting caught masturbating by his conductor—fucking 70 yr. old spiritualist woman in S.J.— the crackpot Cayce which he holds on to like some doctrine in an asylum— half serious obsession—I see him driving now frantic with empty hatreds of other drivers on Bloody Bayshore—he hates Carolyn I think—but nowhere else to go—no way out of the 3 children R.R. After I left they both went and took (o comedy horror) the Rorschach Ink Blot Test (which is maybe more or less accurate in determining degree of clinical insanity if you believe in the word, which I don't for me and you, but sort of do now for Neal) and he told me, jumbled, four conclusions: 1.) sexually sadistic 2). pre-psychotic 3). "delusive thought system" 4). intense anxiety prone. Well as to number 3 that means if anything he has some kind of mad "Cayce—sex—driving—T"—system which is operating independently sort of convulsively compulsively running him around a kind of rat race. He don't write no more "I was writing about sex and you dig it's sinful, I know etc." he says. And Carolyn agrees "What good is that sort of thing, you call that art? It's just dirt." I tell you that household is— and so much gold in trash now, the chess, maniacal. He won't talk to me, except in a sort of dissociated way. Comes to my room in Frisco gets in bed and

plays with self. You know how I [like] sex my way any kind but there's some-
thing wrong in the total sense of masturbatory insistence and franticness of
that. He says generally "I have no feelings—never had." I mean we ball as ever
still but read on. His stomach is bad—nausea at meals, maybe ulcers. His suf-
fering is—well not suffering, his pain or dissociation from contact or good
sweet kicks is more and more autonomous, more overloaded, heavy. He sees it,
no way out for him he says once in a while, drives faster. I do all I can to make it
with him—as friend I mean,—I don't really care about the cock—it seems too
dislocated for that. (I mean this judgment does not come from morbid lusting
turning sour exactly.) Would be willing to take vows of leave him alone etc. if
he only would be sweet and care-ful again and open to gentle kicks and images
and poetry and digging things of all natures—and no time for kicks on jazz—
he's too busy—Chess. Or if we did go it would be a ragged fury of being too
high driving too fast, all too hot and horrible. Well he and I love each other, it's
all there no doubt, but everything seems impossible as far as any real contact
and natural enjoyment. He really gets no kicks from me as Allen or Levinsky or
poet or old memory friend. I mean he does and I too from him but it's so fast
it's unreal and most of the time driven into the background grim reality noth-
ingnesses that happen. As for Carolyn, I know or imagine she has suffered as
wife perhaps to justify any way she is now but I have strong impression she's a
kind of death—she doesn't dig new things (statues or paintings when pointed
out)—I mean she has no active curiosity or aesthetic or kicks interests and lives
by this ruinous single track idea of running the family according to her ideas
strictly, ideas which are mad copies of *House Beautiful* and are really nowhere in
addition to being unreal on account of the horror of the house and the need for
some real force of compassion or insight or love or Tao, or whatever. Maybe it's
impossible. She's a hysteric type—that is, shifting layers of dishonesty which I
first didn't dig but do so now. Will take it or leave it, it is only my reaction to the
general scene. I felt relieved to get out to poverty—work worries free of the
mad hassle of anxiety at the house, alone in Frisco. And if I feel relieved to get
out of a situation with Neal there must be something screwy somewhere. I
know what I was doing there with Neal sounds on the surface like a monstrous
thing, as Carolyn with some justice suddenly exploded out with, but that isn't
the cause of their woes, she forbade me by the way to ever see him again. I have
horror of such insensitivity to the total situation insisted on as the right, self
righteous final eternal etc. Oh well enuf of this it is too nasty and I can't give
the picture as I saw it. But I mean I felt evil around me—her vehemence and
the feeling of horror I had reminded me of moments in the N.J. hospital when

my mother was seized by a fit of frenzied insistent accusation and yelled at me that I was a spy. If you remember the story I told you about the sense of finality and absolute tired despair and hopeless futility I felt when at age 14 I took my mother on a mad horrible trip to Lakewood where I left her to fall apart in paranoiac fear with shoe in hand surrounded by cops in a drugstore. I felt the same tired inevitability and impossibility of fact and mad horror listening to Carolyn, and afterward—tired exhausted feeling in the back, want to go off somewhere else from the impossible end of communication and sleep it off. That's disappeared since I've been here running around, but it hasn't disappeared in San Jose, for Neal who lives in hell and for her who lives in hell, and I guess the children. The thing that is bad about it all is that unless he or she can do something anything almost I don't see how he will not be injured—wracked wrecked, destroyed—life fucked, I thought when I read *Visions of Neal*, "You haven't told me anything new" because I didn't understand how he could "just go blank"—he's too great—too much natural force, sweetnesses, divinity in fact, soul,—power, perception, mental beauty, gravity, greatness—simply to blank it up—it would have to drive up and out of him. I mean beauty would have to spring out of him somehow—he could not live without life, tender sweet springing gaiety, mental gaiety life, imagination all that he has like the colossus of old which he really has—it can't just go blank, it would have to go blank into a divine Tao silence—but not an unholy mean blank. If so he would have to suffer a madness for the lost feeling, lost love, lost whatever that is holy and is there. The force will drive itself out to expression even if it be madness, suicide, nastiness, T., chess, driving, harsh sex—arguing with Carolyn. (I wrote in Harlem:

> A very dove will have her love
> 　Ere the dove has died
> The spirit craven in a cove
> 　will even love in pride
> And cannot love, and yet can hate
> 　Spirit to fulfill
> The spirit cannot watch and wait
> 　The hawk must have his kill.

The hawk must have his kill.)

I may be nightingale, you may be gull, Neal may be hawk—though we are all does at soul.

But if this were all—Perhaps nothing is really lost in life, I mean, it all evens out, he will be alright—but I have seen my mother gone beyond conceivable human horror in living death and it is not all right there—horrible things happen. I see I am making it maybe worse than it is with Neal. He will survive and maybe something will happen to deliver him from torment, or perhaps it is not unrelieved torment. Essentially all he has to do really is realize everything is all right if he can only start living as far as seeking feeling and worth again according to his heart or imagination. But it is so tangled and unrelieved the monotony of the drear to him. Do you dig what I mean? Like a kind of madness, a living dream he is dreaming that has taken over his body. I am not sure how you will think of this—too hung up and not disinterested enough in a Tao-acceptance way watching ants devour a worm—but though there is nothing we can do I say fuck the Tao, I am the Tao and my life doesn't live for this kind of drear or trash or lack or whatever bitch it is—ain't no reason to be indifferent to Neal's woe, the fucking worms. He ain't no dream he's real. Only worry is, here—am I exaggerating—have I the wrong slant? Have I misinterpreted what I see? Am I Levinsky yapping in a cafeteria about madness? I'd almost rather take that cross, I'm used to it, than understand that what I am saying about the life of Neal is true, god knows if it is, it seems so now. Yes there is an edge of Levinsky in all this. My standards of what he <u>should</u> be like and what he is like are so personal, but beyond that there is something really fucking up like Blake's worm or a Hardy tragedy in San Jose with King Neal. Lucien who never dug Neal's kindness or pathos or communication empathy or aspiration would take this above I suppose for immature shit and there's a lot of it there but there is also, I think, something more basic than that.

Well, Bill writes he leaves September 7 from Gibraltar and he'll get here sooner or later. God knows what will happen. Jack boy now get on the ball. I will be trying to make it perhaps with Sheila, trying anyway. I will do everything I can for and to Bill, anything he wants, but the impossibilities of his demands are ultimately inescapable unless I let him carry me off forever to Asia or something to satisfy his conception of his despair and need. You must try and now straighten him out, you know. I'm not that [much] a bitch or unwilling to go to any lengths to help out. I do like him and would love to share a place with him here if it could be done which it will be, but he is going to be frantic and possessive you know. He was (against his own will) having tantrums of jealousy in N.Y.C., even over Dusty he was annoyed. The situation with Sheila will be a madhouse. I don't know how to manage it. Bill will enforce his idea so much he will <u>make</u> me reject it and take it as a hopeless horror. He has of course calmed down a lot since midsummer, but he still puts all his life in my hands. Even <u>I</u> never went that far. So you must make him understand to go easy. It's not a crisis of final communication, etc. Whatever it is—it is whatever he sees it as of course, except for the basic mutual bond which is so final and permanent which seems now unreal to him unless he possesses my very thoughts equal to his—it's a real bitch man. So you <u>must</u> try to give him some kind of strength or Tao and O.K. hipness to the situation so that he doesn't make a horror of it. I can't be his one sole and only contact forever, I can only be his nearest and best. Well you know, whatever so long as everybody's happy with the resources that are at hand. Christ what a situation. Surrounded by mad saints all clawing at each other and I the most weird? And tell Lucien to talk to Bill. He certainly knows about symbiosis and ought to have a helpful constructive word. As for me I am resolved to be patient and as un-evil as I can manage.

No time to describe—too tired—North Beach—characters—one mad Peter DuPeru (who has gestures and same tone as Peter Van Meter and <u>both</u> are from Chicago). But DuPeru (what a mad Subterranean name!) is also like Solomon a Zen ex amnesia-shock patient who wears no socks and is always beat and <u>sensitive</u> and curious and interested and has the best mystic mind I've met here. Digs me too. We talk—have walked together him telling me about various Baroque and Regency and City Hall weirdness of architecture all over S.F.

And our friend Bob Young, why my dear I <u>believe</u> it is the very same little black angel I once <u>did already</u> make it with on E. 7th Street no less perhaps a year ago—ask him. Wears fine clothes? very sad sweet, yes it must be he, even the name I <u>seem</u> to remember. We met drunk at the White Horse. Actually a sad occasion, it made me shudder.

As for the American Revolution it <u>was</u> a revolution wasn't it? The "traditional dissenters"—well the Tories weren't dissenting it was our forefathers, the Paines. But Hinkle[26] (nor I) don't favor revolution or conquest of U.S. by Red-East. Maybe Hinkle does, come to think of it. All I am saying is that the U.S. is in the hands of people like the publishers you hate and they are fucking us up in the rest of the world's Spenglerian schemes. We should be feeding Asia not fighting her at this point. And if we actually do (for some mad reason) fight,

26 Al and Helen Hinkle. Friends and neighbors of the Cassady family.

it'll be the <u>end</u>. The Reds are what Burroughs thinks they are—evil—probably
—but enough bullshit on this. Yes, Al is kind, and so Helen too at time of crisis
in Cassady household—they put me straight on the horror. I thought I might
be going mad. They knew.

No more long letters, but short notes occasionally when there's news. Keep
me informed on pleasant news of publishing. No space to talk about Shake-
speare. I like your Tao, it's more humane. I also have read some Chinese cloud
mountain—for as said in the *Green Auto*, "Like Chinese magicians, confound
the immortals with an intellectuality hidden in the mist." And my poem also by
the way on Sakyamuni (who brought Buddhism to China) coming out of the
mountain. I got most of my titles about it all from digging the <u>pictures</u> of
the cloudy mountains and the sages that the arhats[27] painted—<u>dig dig dig</u> at
the N.Y. Public Library Fine Arts room the great collections of Chinese paint-
ings—visions of the physical Tao, if one can get a spiritual insight from the
painter's material vision of the mountains receding into vast dream infinities
series of mountains separated by infinities of mist. The paintings of the infinite
worlds of mountains were my favorite, and next the great belly rubbing or beat
or horrible looking W. C. Fields arhats in rags with long ears or giggling
together over manuscripts of poems about clouds.

<u>Also</u> there is a book, *The White Pony*, ed. Robert Payne, which is translation
of all kinds from thousands years Chinese Buddhist—Taoist poetry—easy to
read, such a pleasure, so many—and Bill Keck has my marked copy of this
book, unless he's given it to someone. Tell him "I ask him for Balloon's sake to
recover it and give to you if it's not an impossible hassle"—if you see him.

When you send me essay on Buddha? I read it with pleasure.

Quite right about No Direction in Void—Bill too eager for that and there's
no place to go but where he is and I am already and that's what's causing the
hassle. [...]

[*In October 1954, while Ginsberg was living in Sheila's apartment on Pine Street, he had a
vision in the lights of the Sir Francis Drake Hotel's upper-story windows. He felt the mighty
presence of Moloch, the Old Testament god of the Ammonites and Phoenicians to whom
children were sacrificed, and it inspired him to write his most famous poem, Howl.*]

---

27 Arhat. A Buddhist monk who has attained Nirvana.

Allen Ginsberg [San Francisco, CA] to Jack Kerouac [n.p.]
November 9, 1954

Dear Jack:

My rage was annoyance but I generally understood and took it as a minor
thing. Certainly not enuf to make me think of not writing. Yes Bill has become
too strange for me to live in such close quarters with—not absolutely frighten-
ing but I knew it would end in some kind of absolute sad idiocy, particularly
with me off all the time with Sheila. But even without chick [woman], too
much. Still I invited him finally to come here, I didn't want to put him down at
soul. We are corresponding again. He's more distant. It's easier to read his let-
ters. How hard it all is—I have to confess that as far as I'm concerned I dig Bill
as ever and have no objection to anything and feel like an ego fool for the whole
season but what could I do or should or whatever. I don't care really about
straightness with chick or anything like that—I first knew he'd come here and
I'd get him all involved and vice versa and there'd be a bust with the cops ulti-
mately and I'd be coming late to work and have to sit and listen to him and rou-
tines mercilessly applauding and so on. I wasn't interested enough, I might be
sometime when I want to return to saintly solitude and brotherliness to Bill. I
lack solitude here and Bill is a power of solitude—got to give him <u>all</u> attention,
I had my attentions turned in other (lesser) directions.

Oh, as to what he wrote, he kept saying in letter after letter you agreed with
him, I was being coy, I really wanted/needed him then—a burlesque. I was
mad because it isn't is it?—really a queer matter, but Bill was like making it
one. My objection wasn't to queerness but to the wild strange frightening
(antipathetic symbiotic) uncanny Bill chill thrill. Too much. Also the horrors
with Caroline [Carolyn Cassady] and thru the affair with Sheila—too much.
My formal reject letter was distracted, I don't regret it, Bill was driving me to
distraction (purposely?) by letter—how much worse in person? But as for <u>why</u>
I got so mad, man you should read his letter specter zipping around me. Enuf
of this draggy matters. I made it against my will in N.Y.C. by the way. I'm not
sorry but no more.

Sure I'm crazy. I begin at the local analytic clinic tomorrow—$1.00 an hour.
Don't bust a gut.

I'm not a devil neither are you, stop saying things like that. I just thought
you were on an angelic type jig so to speak, gleefully siccing Bill on—but really
he's so far gone or was, you might just as well have humored him. In the long

run the same thing that made you tell him white lies—the same madness—made me yell at him. I did everything I could not do for half a year.

A cat by the way, sits on my shoulder as I write this. Me and Lucien were secretive because we were sinning and joyful and ashamed and abashed in front of you, afraid you'd look sour on us—if you'd any likelihood of joining the ball we'd not have been secretive—perhaps you would have anyway—but we were only secretive 5 minutes at a time when you were knocking on that door remember? That doesn't count as secretive, we were just goofing the flesh away in secret. He'd laugh at me for admitting we were secretive probably.

Sheila has a Canuck brother-in-law Paul Tremblay of Boston environs. We talk Kanuk [Canuck] together on occasion. Big sad sweet salesman whose wife hasn't laid him in 3 months, about our age (30-33) and generation. I told him to read T&C [The Town and the City].

Because of living in splendor with girl I do no reading no writing. Probably coming to the end of this, I'll move in a month or so and get secret nice pad on side street run-down height of Nob Hill I've elected, under a great concrete basement of the next top-of-hill block for $35 a month save money and read and write and pray to solitude. Have you yet seen Liang Kai's (Southern Sung) Chinese picture of Sakyamuni Coming Out of the Mt. of Enlightenment? It's on the cover of Edward Conze's book on Zen—in any metaphysical book-store—and in some of the collections of classic Chink art in the Fine Arts room at Public 42nd St. Library. Do look at the pictures. Remember how you dug the Bacchuses and bosoms of Titian and Hals, those of the West? Dig Chinese art—(paintings). But dig particularly that portrait of an arhat at the very moment of enlightenment. It will fit in your picture I mean also. So when I move, anyway, I promise to begin reading Buddha for you according to instruction.

Rexroth has Bill's book reading it. He advises at New Directions. He invited me to reading poetry at a series he's a manager of connected with a college here. Auden, Williams, local poets including me. Sometime next month perhaps.

Damned Belson[28] read Yage and put Bill down, refused to read Queer, the movie is all off. What madness inspires these semi-ignus? He gave me some peyote, I got hi with Sublette and Sheila and we dug S.F. midtown cable cars clanging skyline—looked out my living room vast window down into the bldgs.—especially the Sir Francis Drake hotel—which has a Golgotha-robot —eternal—smoking machine crowned visage made up of the two great glass-

28 Jordan Belson (b. 1926). Friend and avant-garde filmmaker.

brick eyes on either side (the toilets men and women of the Starlight Room)—upstarting out of the paved mist ground—I wrote on it.

Skeletons have no cocks—no cunts in the cemeteries, great line, and Sublette made it with Sheila behind my back weeks ago. Well, that's the way the ball bounces (as Al. S. says all the time.) He read yr. last letter. I'll write Burford.

What Cowley article? I wrote asking, hearing some rumor of it, but never saw—when and where? Neal wants also to know. We ran to San Jose Library while I was there and I thumbed thru back issues of *Saturday Review of Literature*. So send copy or name and date of mag. for my interest please? I will send or bring you *Naked Lunch* in 1 month after Rexroth is done with it. I am going to type up my poems and reproduce them on a machine I have in the office (Ozalid machine) and make up and bind 25 copies of a book and send you 1 in a month. My brother Eugene is getting married and will send me plane fare. So I will be in N.Y.C. for a week (possibly) around the 18th of December. He's marrying "The minister's daughter" if you remember her, a sort of meek blonde he's been making it with for 2 years. Both families somewhat miffed but accepting it. Anyway I will be there, you must come too (Riverside Church 125th St. I think)—So I mean, I hope to be in N.Y.C. in a month for a week, see you, confess, talk Buddha. I've told Bill. He may be on his way thru NYC to Tangier by then. So there may be a convention. [...]

As to Neal: Since I been settled down here he comes by every week to borrow Miss Green [marijuana] or bring Miss Green. Last few times rushed in and out with Lucien, a high grotesque black man from Howard St., his pimp for Miss Green, unrolled her on the floor and proceeded to manicure and blow in midafternoon while I wandered around turning on and off lights and carried garbage downstairs and picked up child's toys. One thing I must say, I can see what a strain it has been for him to try and maintain a family household and at the same time run a mad pad. Sheila digs him, of course, but he's been very good about not coming on with her. He came up one nite, settled comfortably on the white rug, got hi, and in the shadow of the Dank Monster looming in the window (which he dug immediately) read aloud from Proust for an hour, a quiet sweet nite. Standing by the imitation fireplace: Peter DuPeru (whom I've described?) DuPeru has been here 2 weeks and we've finally gotten his finances straight and he's in a hotel now. Very great cat, worthy of the best of N.Y. Rexroth calls him the White Plague. I think he's very droll—a sweeter thinner Solomon, more forgetful, full of curious innocuous obsessions—spends hours in bathroom (Huncke-like). Sleeps with pillows on foot, walks around with bottles of Vicks or J&J Baby Oil or garlic filling pockets, has an income (18 a week), learned in Zen, most front teeth out, growing a French 19th century thin Balzac beard (sideburns running along edge of chin, not under or over) wears dirty blue suede shoes, lumberjack shirt, frayed Levis, no socks, walks all over town, knows Yeats by heart, completely bumbling and innocent toothless smile on young face—as the time he turned on the radio too loud and (unobserved) fumbled with it inefficiently and began saying shush, making a shushing gesture impatiently humbly with his palm. Then smiled toothless (unobserved) smile at self secretly.

Well Neal says I shd. write you for him. He is always rushing around. So he keeps telling me—"you know what to tell him, we're buddies, etc." He will be cut off the R.R. sometime early January. He wants to go to Mex City for kicks for a week or a few days, then go booming in Florida, and then go rush up to N.Y.C. for a day or 2 and then return to Frisco to job. Carolyn threatens to quit if he goes booming, wants him to get a filling station job in Los Gatos. He as yet seems undecided whether or not he can get away with it, but he's been talking about it since I first arrived. So he wants you to know his general plan. I don't think I'll go with him to D.F.—Scared of his driving, and I'll be working still, then, I suppose. Saving $ for Europe or the East. Anyway he wanted me to write you for him. Consider him. He's up for 3 investigations, everybody on the R.R. whispers about him blasting, "everybody knows I'm a cunt hound," Carolyn hasn't laid him in 3 months. I'll tell him I wrote. He seems lately a little cooler however than in the Hotel Marconi days—a few months ago. I even played him a game of chess. He's taught chess to Sublette and half of North Beach. Sublette beat him. He's still on Cayce, will bring it up out of nowhere on every visit. If I say something other than Cayce he says with a forbearing smile, "Well that's because you don't really understand Cayce." No news from Carolyn. Do you have his Los Gatos address? 18231 Bancroft Los Gatos.

Gerd Stern and MacClaine came up the other day and spent a spooky midnite. I didn't recognize MacClaine for an hr., kept ignoring him. He said there were only a few great poets lately "Lamantia, John Hoffman and himself (& Stern) and Ginsberg." How polite. Then I talked on phone to him called him up a week later and he ran on and on breathlessly making surrealist jokes. Wha!? Well I'll go make it over to his house in N. Beach later. And to Stern's in Mill Valley. And Pippin in Berkeley. And all thru, slowly. I haven't had time to myself to run around on account of domesticity which as I say is coming to an end soon, so will soon now that I know the city be taking long fog shrouded walks into the valleys between hills here. By the way I dug by sight the site of your Transcontinental Tootsie Rolls! Yes! Is it not below San F. in South S.F. or nearby visible "marching" up the weird brown hills on the left side of the road coming by auto visible up Bloody Bayshore "the ribbon of death" from San Jose to S.F.? Your poems I still will not write on yet, closing this long letter, but they are good I agree and truly believe not to be shrugged off for unevenness of them by me (or you as in last letter)—seeds of nakedness are there which is the pure inspiration of poetry and without which not valuable at all, with which anything goes. You (and perhaps I) will begin a literature with them.

What is happening with yr. art? Send me, yet, the Buddha book to read.

Love to Lucien, Dusty,—how is J. Kingsland? etc? I saw N.Y. subterranean painter loft owner Paul Beatty (friend of Anton [Rosenberg], Keck etc. at whose loft the Alan Eager—Bru Moore sessions were once held) here at the wino opening of a new stable art gallery great evening.

Love,

Allen

[*One of the most important occurrences in Ginsberg's life was the day he met Peter Orlovsky. Peter became Allen's companion for the next forty years. The following letter, written just after they met, described the event in detail.*]

Allen Ginsberg [San Francisco, CA] to Jack Kerouac [NY?]
December 29, 1954

Dear Kind King Mind:

> I'm sick, kind Kerouac, your hallowed Allen
> Is sick in eternity! laboring lonesome
> and worse and worse by the day by the hour...
> but I need a little sweet conversation
> sad as the tears of that great prince Sebastian.[29]
>   (after Catullus)

Fraid you were mad then because of me unkind, the paper, was unkind. Never yet have seen Alistair Sim, I'm sick, home a day from work, deep cold, penicillin, I'm deaf almost, sick with love again also, moved to Gough Street artist bohemian pad, Sheila comes surprise dressed up on her lunch hour to

---

29 Sebastian Sampas. Jack Kerouac's childhood friend who was killed in action during WWII.

find me in clothes sweating in cell on pallet on floor, Neal is giggling and play-
ing games with redhead [Natalie Jackson] in other room down the hall, I'm in
love with 22 year old saint boy who loves me, lives there too, but terrible scene
is here. I ran into painter Robert LaVigne, ignu-deep souled 26 year Polk-Sutter
beard a month ago, we went up to see his paintings, walking up Sutter from
Polk-Sutter Fosters Cafeteria where I went one night drunk to dig subterranean
scene and look for Peter Carl—Sol DuPeru (who I met first nite in Sublette's
room here in SF), so I went up to beard lonely to ask after DuPeru who he did-
n't know, we talked, he invited me to see paintings, went to house on Gough St.
I walked in room—this was a month ago—and saw huge modern true paint-
ing of naked youth, and others of same, clothed and unclothed. Then in
walked the boy his model, who painter, made it with too, gentle souled tall
Russian red Kafka, respectful, silent, and so I came back that week, expected,
and began season—great house, I told you, I brought Neal to dig the redhead
girl, he made it with her last week and thereafter—long hall, big messy rooms,
tea in kitchen, just like youth, we gather, talk, Neal rushes in 9AM WC Fields—
Oliver Hardy pulling on or off his pants, makes it with girl, laughs again, puts
on her clothes, she his vest, they blast,—and he and I agree on nostalgia of the
front door, we've both gained so much tender youth kicks in last 2 weeks enter-
ing the apartment first floor of huge Victorian wood house, big smell of paint-
ings and studio for LaVigne up front, Peter Orlovsky studying in a room in the
middle (he's the boy) and Natalie the ex-Stanley Gould girlfriend here for 4
months in the back—so sweet and promising 115th St. tender joys entering the
house again, for me, Neal feels same like I say, so one night before I leave for
NYC—LaVigne telling me he's leaving, mysterious, leaving town to go paint
(after his show running now, wild colored nudes and pix of Fosters) near San
Diego, end of his season with Peter as perhaps mine ended when I left Houston
for Dakar Doldrums, so he says he's leaving, will I see please Peter much when
he's gone, needs a friend, needs sweet companion, I shudder, I see the love, I'm
doomed, my heart melts again—how I hate women, can't stand not to be in
love, can't stand not to be melting with real tenderness, childlike need sweet-
nesses, that's what's wrong with me and Sheila, I don't love like sad love can be,
my heart's chill there. So I tell LaVigne, OH, god not again, what lord are you
asking me for? I can't kneel and cocksuck forever like of old—but he says Peter
knows and digs me, mind, man, I'm changed in Calif., like a dream—I've
waited for. So I went to NYC with that in mind, except also a night I spend there
and talk to Peter who tells me he dreamt that he had walked up to me, put arms
round my waist, I was surprised in dream. Then in hall in life, embraced, real

sweetness in my breast, too much, I'd almost cry, but it's such poor pitiful fleet-
ing human life, what do I want anyway? Nature boy — to be loved in return. So
followed a night of embraces, not sex. Then NYC, then I return, move out of
Sheila's to here —meanwhile, she suddenly digs Al Hinkle in my absence (in
fact had before I left one evening when I was out all night, Al came visiting, got
some wine, they talked on the floor rapport) — so in absence she made it with
Hinkle, sweet, I am pleased — so she waits for him one night, I'm in NYC, then
she goes out, he cuts by, doesn't know where she is, nor know I'm in NY, he
goes up to Polk and Sutter Fosters looking for me or her, she has just left there,
he goes up to the Gough street house, looking for Ginsberg, redhead says I'm
away, he asks to flop for few hours, sleeps, wakes up, goes to take a piss, turns
hall corner, there's naked Neal bumping into him (he didn't know Neal ever
was there — all in my absence) they laugh, the circles of Dostoyevsky in this
house. I return, everybody making it full blast, Peter having got hi first time
with Neal and redhead Natalie and suddenly DUG also, in strange drooling
Peter Lorre way — he's a Myshkin too — BUT alas, now the sad horrors begin,
LaVigne also digs me, I make it with him in bed, for life's sake tho not really
want to, then when I move here we set up bed, all three of us making it in same
bed, but I only dig Peter really, Peter begins guilty only digging me, tho all love
Robert LaVigne for sad genius ignu self and beard he wears — and one thing, I
can't understand why he's bowing out, what genius of sad knowledge of loss
he had (as I had with Neal in Texas) — meanwhile Peter and I have mad conver-
sations about Thought, I read *Visions of Neal* aloud to Natalie and all, Neal
expected hourly again, night of wild balling with Peter with Bob there too —
and then Bob (LaVigne) goes mad, sees self losing, Peter changing, I seem
smug and over bestial, he's angry, won't speak, locks self in room with Peter to
plead, threaten? I never heard, we try to talk, Bob and I being more or less equal
souls, fruits, can't say, hate and love each other, Peter scared and guilty and
faithful to Robert, I suffer now, anger in the house, all wrought up for days,
who will kill who? But I not want to deceive or offend Robert so drag pallet into
my lone room, tension yet mounts, Bob feels I've betrayed him, I'm falling
more in love, he's falling more in despair — love though he is leaving any week
now, still can't give up hope for golden love boy, he thinks I'm evil mocking
(Hal Chase thought) grabbing kid fast for kicks, Peter meanwhile promised to
me, promise fades, we finally all three meet in kitchen and evil hate scenes,
Peter loving both, old fidelities, new sensual mental kicks, Bob and I digging
each other perhaps the most yet thru clouds of fear, the maya mists, irony
between us, he accusing, I can't stand it as he thinks I'm being dirty toward

Peter, but I love, meanwhile Peter more and more offended by scene we can't stop as it's in cards—Robert saying "You're both waiting for me to kick off so you can make it together." I saying, "We can't have a rose without your blessing —rose requires perfection which you added don't take it away now." Robert saying, "I won't again" irony, Peter saying finally ah comedies, "You're both a pain in the ass"—only Burroughs would appreciate. But finally we all melting in sadness, I can't hide that I want, Robert can't hide that he too wanted, Peter that he didn't need—his innocence going to see us old farts go woeful, he also wants girls, after all, as well as teacher kind king mind yet sweet prince would love us too, and me after all these hopeless years—that is to say, this be some self deception but actual promise of Peter nature more harmonious for kind of sweet comradeship than any other I had yet met, I having given up hoping long ago, so now hardly begun to thaw to the rue and sadness of love, just beginning tonight in my sick bed. Well we all made up in a kind, Peter to go alone, Bob to go alone, I alone, Sheila appearing at noon digging my kick sadly, she loves me, I dig her but can't make it, with final conversation neither of us really wanting to betray Robert between self and Peter, that we would wait and see—but already in sad old love hear I know it never came that way, that easy, unless this was prelude of torments to some bliss, will never manifest with such innocence again, I'm sad, lay in bed sweating with cold, too olden to really remember self pities of 18-20 again, but unhappy till I began thinking of the unlikely possible accidental sweetnesses of life, maybe that's all they are, transient. And in his journal (where I peeked tho he would have killed me) Robert writing suffering lines about god shaping him with torment to bareness and true beauty, he really digs, though we can't talk.

So the situation stands now, Natalie making me tea to drink, meanwhile rent is due, Robert due to leave, house to break up, I have to find new pad or hotel—will move in or near area near Peter and Polk Gulch in some hotel for two weeks till paycheck comes enough to get small pad, meanwhile reading *Visions of Neal* and *San Francisco Blues*.

Yes, I know maybe you will wind up throwing up arms at life's mess and accept it Dickens' way but I still say Jack that though I did not attain sanctity because I was too egotistically hung upon the idea of pure vision continuous in order to be saint, and had no stern bare guru who KNEW, just Van Dorens who made me doubt—there is the goal of the Nameless that is the most worthy for us if we've the faith or insight to persist (I wait for life like this to break me down to no attachments maybe because none so sublime as I can emotionally imagine exist

not even the human
imagination satisfies
the endless emptiness
of the soul

(This silly simpleminded after all our conversation and your last letter) maybe to a point where as before I'll sit in silence cooking vegetables again as I did in 49 in Harlem hopeless till my door was silent and silently swung open and let in heaven's light) to persist in seeking it whatever way is offered, directer the better. But what a madness gamble it is. I'll try to live it up first, then die again, when I'm sure there's nothing left in life for me to dig of beauty, but that's almost endless, at least sadness is, recurrent. So practice the Dhyana[30] and bring me holy news. [...]

Allen

[*In this short letter Ginsberg mentioned his new poem,* Howl, *and the Six Gallery reading, famous as the place where the Beat Generation first appeared onstage together. Allen also mentioned that Peter Orlovsky has just returned from New York with his mentally handicapped brother, Lafcadio.*]

Allen Ginsberg [San Francisco, CA] to Jack Kerouac [Mexico City, Mexico] mid-August 1955

Dear Jack:

Received your letter several days ago, then Peter Orlovsky blew into SF with kid brother, 15 years old hungup on toilet rituals, and getting everybody settled.

Robert LaVigne the painter is somewhere near Mazatlan, if I get his address I'll send it to you, on your way up you can sleep on his floor and eat.

If you still have dysentery, you know the Enteroviaforma brownpill cure, if it persists I understand a heavy shot of antibiotics is good—Terramyacin, I believe.

I enclose first draft scribble notes of a poem I was writing, nearer in your style than anything. My book has 50 pages complete and another 50 to go still

30 Dhyana. Meditation.

I think. It won't be finished by summer end. I will unless you persuade me that my sight saver lies elsewhere go to Berkeley, I found a cheap house ($35 per month) one room, a Shakespearean Arden cottage with brown shingles and flowers all about, big sweet garden, private, apricot tree, silence, a kitchen and bathroom too, windows on sunlight, near Shattuck (Key System trolley) Avenue, 6 blocks from school, perfect place to retreat be quiet, which is my desire since I am more absorbed in writing than before. I will have to go to work in compassionate hospital possibly to support self, and start MA work, course on Anglo Saxon they require and whatnot, not, and so will be alone there and so you will be welcome to settle there for 1 year 2 years, a month, however long, there'll be all foods around, I eat well, little money, but enough to get into SF, we'll make out alright. I will be here at 1010 Montgomery Street for 3 more weeks or perhaps more, and move across bay around September 5. Neal has apartment in town for you to stay in if you want to flop over in city anytime. My original invitation to come stay here etc. still same except now the cottage with garden makes it more Shakespearean Bhikku retired, better.

An art gallery here asked me to arrange poetry reading program this fall, maybe you and I and Neal one night give a program; also we can record and broadcast whatever we want on Berkeley radio station KPFA.

I have been seeing big Berkeley professors but I am anonymous nobody and can impress no one with nothing so I will have to work for a year, after I can have money from schools and make it thru PhD's Fulbrights to Asia Harvards wherever I hope. I guess I have to do this route for the moment, otherwise just work anywhere when money runs out and not be preparing for anything as far as money future. What you think?

Letter from Bill, he wants me to go to South America bisexual tribes, but how can I? no gold.

Come up here keep me company, there's no one to talk to. I am continuing Surangama Sutra. Also I am reading surrealist poetry and Lorca, translating Catullus from Latin.

I will see [Karena] Shields the Mexico woman and tell her you'll leave your address at the U.S. embassy for her, she'll probably pass thru Mexico City in a week or two.

I was thinking, would you be able to order Mescaline Sulfate from the Delta Drug Co. thru Mexican pharmacy and bring it up here? I'll send check for that, find out? Delta Chemical Works, 23 West 60th Street, NY 23, NY, it costs $7.00 a small bottle.

I'll write soon. Write, come for sure.

Love

Allen

[...] I also want to get piano and study basic music, write blues poems.

Since Peter been away I've been writing a lot, solitude after all this year is good for me though I go blue depression mad in it too. I can't stand life.

Don't get mad at me, come when thou wilst, don't come only on account of Eugene's $25, but come anyway, soonest, make it in peaceful milk in Shakespearean house.

I am trying to shepherd 15 year old Orlovsky around thru life right now, like being married and having overgrown problem child, crazy kicks, pathos of real life. They'll take an apartment in town here, I'll move to Berkeley and get away from it all.

Guy Wernham the translator of Lautreament is in furnished room across street, comes over and translates Genet for me, Genet poetry, drinks tea and shudders dignified and lost like Bill, looks like a sort of Bill without Bill's genius charm.

I'm alright, actually sort of happy.

Also we'll have a car to loll in.

Love

Ginsberg

[*The following is the first letter in which Ginsberg quoted lines from his new poem,* Howl.]

Allen Ginsberg [San Francisco, CA] to Eugene Brooks [New York, NY]
August 16, 1955

Dear Gene:

Heard about your accident from Lou last week & meant to write; received your letter. I wonder what Woodstock looks like now—is the old cottage by the stream by the bridge we lived in still standing, and is that monstrous superhighway traffic circle in town center still as vast as it once seemed? And is that copy of *Eyeless in Gaza* still on the table downstairs in the cottage? Were the rocks in the swimming hole still as fantastically worn by water? And that meadow infinity behind the house? & does the poison ivy bloom behind the moon still? [...]

I'm expecting as of now barring troubles to settle at Berkeley for a year or so, have put in bid for $35 per mo. Ivy-covered one room (plus kitchen & bath) cottage on side street, garden and apricot tree around, private and Shakespearean. Will have to get job, in hospital or restaurant nearby, work part-time. Still haven't been accepted but sent in registration $5 fee and got Columbia records etc, etc.

Senora Shields of Mexico in and out of town, have seen her a few times. Kerouac out on road on way here, he received your money, thank you for sending it.

Thanks for the manuscript I had a duplicate. Am over the hump on a collection of last 4 years' work and writing in a new style now, long prose poem strophes, sort of surrealist, & reading a lot of Spanish and French modern poetry, Lorca, Apollinaire, & some Latin, still on Catullus. Catullus really worth looking at in edition an anthology of all translations edited by someone named Aiken, probably in Columbia library, if you liked Tacitus. The new style: example: referring to Carl Solomon

"... who presented himself on the granite steps of the madhouse with shaven
    head and harlequin speech of suicide demanding instantaneous lobotomy,
and who was given instead the concrete void of insulin metrasol electricity
    hydrotherapy psychotherapy occupational therapy pingpong & amnesia,
and who in humorless protest overturned only one symbolic ping pong
    table..."

    and other Who's Who's & images (this from a long catalogue)

"who screamed on all fours in the subway, and were dragged off the roof
    waving genitals and manuscripts,
who loned it thru the streets of Idaho seeking visionary Indian angels who
    were visionary Indian angels,
who copulated ecstatic and insatiate with a package of cigarettes a bottle of
    beer a chick or a candle and fell off the bed and continued on the floor and
    down the hall and ended fainting on the wall with an ultimate vision of
    cunt eluding the last come of consciousness,
who bit detectives in the neck and howled with delight in police cars for
    committing no crime but their own wild cooking pederasty and
    intoxication,

who digested rotten animals lung heart tail feet borscht and tortillas dreaming
     of the pure vegetable kingdom,
who plunged under meat trucks looking for an egg,
who tramped all night on the snowbank docks with bloody feet looking for a
     door in the East River to open to a room full of steam heat and opium,
who picked themselves up out of alleyways hung up with heartless Tokay and
     horrors of iron and stumbled off to unemployment offices,
who ate the lamb stew of the imagination or digested crabs at the muddy
     bottom of the rivers of Bowery,
who chained themselves to subways for the endless ride from Battery to holy
     Bronx until the noise of wheels and children brought them down wide eyed
     and battered bleak of brain mouth wracked all drained of brilliance in the
     drear light of Zoo,"
etc. etc.

   goes on for 5 pages. This is more or less Kerouac's rhythmic style of prose,
ends "the actual heart of the poem of life butchered out of their own bodies
good to eat a thousand years." Elegy for the generation, etc.
   also, "who mopped all night in desolate Bickfords listening to the crack of
doom on the hydrogen jukebox."
   I have been looking at early blues forms and think will apply this form of
elliptical semisurrealist imagery to rhymed blues type lyrics. Nobody but
Auden's written any literary blues forms, his are more like English ballads, not
purified Americana. Blues forms also provide a real varied syncopated meter,
with many internal variants and changes of form in midstream like conversa-
tional thought. Most of my time is actually occupied with this type thought
and activity, writing a lot and therefore beginning to change style, get hot,
invent and go on interesting kicks thanks to courtesy of U.S. government
leisure. I never spent it better. Still have quite a few weeks left but will cut short
probably for Berkeley.
   Still having trouble collecting $$ from Wyn Co. royalties on Burroughs
book, they're holding out present royalties against possible future returns and
in addition by estimating next 3 yrs. returns wind up with figures with him ulti-
mately in red. This is strictly shyster publisher practice. I would sue them for
the 88s they presently owe but it seems technically hopeless — tho I'm not sure
— Rexroth says to forget it since they're infamous shysters (he's had trouble
with them in past too). Do you have Burroughs' contract on file anywhere?

He's in Tangier, writing, doing alright, unhappy, like an old rubber tire inde-
structible, his letters piling up, pathetic, brilliant, Kafka-Céline comedy, great
Rabelaisian appetite for seedy humor, writing a sort of surrealist satire fable
about life in decadent Tangier. Cowley is writing an introduction for a Kerouac
novel and asked to see Burroughs' work so I sent him 3 vols. of opus called
Naked Lunch. After that he looks at my book. Have you seen Céline's *Guignol's
Band* published last year yet? It's as good as best Céline.

Sheila [Williams] my old lovedoll here got married last month. My old boss
is writing a cookbook. The fog's in on SF hills. I went to the planetarium today.
Had steak for supper.

Love.

Allen

[*The end of the summer of 1955 was a seminal period in Ginsberg's life. He met many of the
people associated with the Beat Generation and it was the Six Gallery reading that brought
many of those poets together for the first time.*]

Allen Ginsberg [San Francisco, CA] to John Allen Ryan[31]
[Mexico City, Mexico] mid-September 1955

Dear Johnny:

Your letter September something received, and also your previous one, and
the poems, and I think one of mine crossed in the mails; and I also wrote Uni-
vac (no relation to Kerouac) (latter a Breton name) you would be in D.F.; I hope
you did meet; and that you were not too much of a cool Zen and that he was
not too much of a Mahayana sourpuss; and that Garver put you on one way or
another. [...]

Hendrix asked me if I wanted to organize a poetry reading at the Six, and I
didn't several months ago, not knowing of any poetry around worth hearing,
but changed my fucking mind, and so you will be glad to know the tradition
continues with a gala evening sometime in a month or so or shorter, the pro-
gram being Rexroth as introducer McClure reading new poems (he thinks, it's

31 John Allen Ryan. Bartender from The Place in San Francisco.

partly true, he's found his own natural voice—it sounds a little tightassed to me but he is writing well and that's maybe the way god built him), Lamantia putting in an appearance to read John Hoffman's work (which I haven't really seen for years, if it isn't poetry it'll be a great social occasion), myself to read a long poem the first scraps of which I sent to Kerouac, you might look at it if you see him again. I don't have a copy or I'd send you a piece (it's more or less up the alley of your SF recollections in tranquility), and a bearded interesting Berkeley cat name of Snyder, I met him yesterday (via Rexroth suggestion) who is studying oriental and leaving in a few months on some privately put up funds to go be a Zen monk (a real one). He's a head, peyotlist, laconist, but warmhearted, nice looking with a little beard, thin, blond, rides a bicycle in Berkeley in red corduroy and levis and hungup on Indians (ex anthropology student from some Indian hometown) and writes well, his sideline besides Zen which is apparently calm scholarly and serious with him. Interesting person. IF anybody else turns up along the way to read we may add somebody else. When Kerouac gets to SF probably I'll try set up another program, Myself, Jack and Neal Cassady (whom you didn't know in SF?). You might send this bit of 6 gossip to [Jack] Spicer, he'll probably be pleased that something is being done to continue there. And you might send me any advice on organizing these readings that you can remember from previous experience.

Yes, I'm studying literature at Berkeley, I may be able to make a self-supporting proposition via some kind of sinecure in 6 months, according to what vague promises I've wheedled out of Miles Shorer and a nice one named [Thomas] Parkinson, ex SF Anarchist now English Professor here. I'll be working scholarly like on prosody problems.

I have a house here for $35 a month, backyard cottage and private backyard, quite big, filled with vegetables and flowers, ideal Camden Whitman cottage, I write a lot, depression, solitude, last night a rare half hour of a kind of animistic ecstasy and weeping in the garden, the vines with leaves turned top up in the night as they were left during the hours of day when the gracious sun rayed on them, the father is merciful; I had a vision of that as I haven't had in maybe 7 years; a relief, a drop of sweetness. I did some writing and it looks like Christopher Smart. Tell Jack if you see him; but well I'll write. [...]

Love, as ever

Allen

Allen Ginsberg [Berkeley, CA] to Eugene Brooks [Plainview, NY]
December 26, 1955

Dear Gene:

Received your letter and news and $15; (also same day $10 from Louis) very munificent, just like old-fashioned Xmas—I spent the day and had turkey at Cassady's down the peninsula—and am working (for last 2 weeks Xmas) at Greyhound Bus baggage room, and so now have sizeable small bankroll for short trip northwest. Taft-Hartley act has (lord works in subtle ways his wonders etc.) opened up the shipping unions, so I think I'll be able to catch ship in 60 days and make some real money for real travel. Also possibility of 4 month round-the-world type cruise job thru unions, tho that's slight. Anyway I've been wondering how to make it to Europe and a 3 or 4 month stretch at sea would set me up for 7 or 8 months on the continent, so I'm applying now, and will wait around here after return from northwest for a ship. When I leave here I'll probably forward a load of books and phonograph records to you—can you take them? After return from trip (if trip comes off) I'll head for short stay in NYC (or Plainview) and then take off for Europe. Prospects there are fine, I have friends scattered around, places to stay and people to see and show me around, especially Paris.

Kerouac left here several weeks ago and probably was in Rocky Mount when you were there. He stayed with me for several months, dug the scene, had a good time for awhile, but then got broody and touchy, I got mad at him one night, and Rexroth showed him the door the following week, he left down the road to hitchhike home with sleeping bag and knapsack for Xmas. He got a grant of $300 from National Academy of Arts and Sciences thru Cowley, I signed libel release and Neal did on his 5 yrs. old novel [*On the Road*] which Viking seems ready to publish, at least they sent out big legal forms. By the way I have a problem. Legal—my own book is due, the manuscript is due, before I leave here, to be printed in England for economy's sake, costs only $150 there for 500 copies of 40 page booklet (comprising single poem, Howl for Carl Solomon, Lou saw it)—however City Lights, the people here publishing for me, are afraid it will be held up in customs for obscenity, since I use cunts, cocks, balls, assholes, snatches and fucks and comes liberally scattered around in the prosody—the question being, do you know anything about the customs law, appeals, etc. in case there is trouble, or (as I am told) are they likely if they notice it to forthwith burn the books without notice for appeal? The problem is whether I should cut out (which I don't want to do), chance it, or request book printed here, which City Lights is also willing to do. The problem is not with publisher but with possible customs laws, I expect there will be further use later, as I have been making arrangements for possible cheap publishing to be done for Self, Jack and Bill in Japan, where a friend is going next month—costs only $50 to print a book there. Amazing. Burroughs is getting fantastically dirty in his manuscript but it is high art, but he doesn't shilly-shally, in fact he's been writing pornography with a vengeance lately, and my own work is full of orgies.

I'll probably not need any of my furniture or books for a long while, so get them from Paterson and use them as you will, there are some nice pieces that were in my bedroom, a file chest and low bureau that were finished in very good taste and are built modern and low, they were custom-built for someone who liked low furniture in fact. There's also probably an extra bed leftover in Paterson now?

Statuary: why not wait till I get to NYC? Art objects are an investment, if you go to a regular commercial store you pay very dearly for monotonous *Sat. Eve. Post* moderns style, you should get some individual work by a young genius, there are probably dozens of such in NYC starving. As I said in letter some time ago, there were people in NYC in 1952 and 1951 whose paintings were selling for 20-40 dollars who are getting 500-1000 now, the situation is still the same. Meyer Shapiro knows who they all are, when I get to NYC I can ask him, or you can look him up in the phone book give him a line about wanting to buy something interesting from good young unknown types, you haven't much to spend, I think he'll be happy to connect you—it does everybody a favor. If you want paintings, there is this really great painter Robert LaVigne here, and he sells his from 40-60-80-100, and never gets to sell any even at that price. He also has great interesting drawings. I have a small collection (about 20) of them which I'll send on with my records, you can use any you like. I mean, as an investment, I myself gave him 60 dollars when I was working in exchange for drawings, and wish I had had more money to get the more elabo-rate ones I liked even more. The people I knew in NYC are now too expensive to recommend—Wolf Kahn and Larry Rivers. Rivers by the way does some sculpture, it's probably excellent, maybe expensive now (he's better known as a painter)—and he has a gallery, Tibor De Nagy on 53rd and 3rd Ave. S.E. corner, but that means $$. I don't know how much you want to spend, but if you're asked over a hundred for a piece from a retail commercial store for a hack job, you can obviously do much better elsewhere. Anyway don't buy anything you don't really like yourself, that's the only test. But you won't be ready till say summer so why not wait. There's nothing I'd like better than to go shopping for sculpture in the dens of Lower East Side. Also it would be better to pay a great deal of money for an interesting minor piece of sculpture from a master like Lipchitz or Giacometti (whose works can be seen at Museum of Modern Art) than waste a cent on meaningless uninspired commercial pieces. Also if you want cheap sculpture reproductions of classics, you can find out about them from the museums, there are companies putting out Greek, Medieval, Mayan, and Chinese copies in heavy Tootsie roll type plastic, cheap. Also, Tibetan scrolls and mandalas, good ones, are cheap (under a hundred) (if you shop well) and are one of the best investments of any kind of art. They are classic, rare, undervalued, the commies are in there prohibiting further exports, little has reached the U.S. since the war and little likely will and the tradition there if kaput probably will raise their value even more. Also they are extremely interesting to look at, the U.S. taste hasn't found them—tho they'll be or have been in *LIFE* this decade—and are generally unknown except by connoisseurs of Asiatic art, hipsters, etc. More popular here on the west coast of course, and prices in NYC better. There's a shop around 55th and Park-3rd Ave., I don't remember, small shop, has good ones, not too good condition, but finely painted. I mean there are good and bad Tibetan brushworkers, the condition not too important, like medieval art. I dig their sculpture the most, it's hair-raising, maybe you have to develop a taste for it tho,—however you can buy incredible 12 armed seated Kali gods with their Shakti smaller paramours seated on their laps screwing, ancient Indian–Tibetan statuary tradition, not at all shocking to have around when you look at them, could have on desk, etc. only a noticing or trained eye could see and even then it's so unbelievably demonic-classical it's socially quite unobjectionable, all museums have them. By the way, for an idea of all this Tibetan, the Newark Museum top floor has a great small collection—supposed to be the best in the east. If any of the above sounds at all interesting, look at what they have in Newark and inquire where in NY you can get similar type works. However Tibetan sculpture begins to run into the hundreds. The point about buying Asiatic art, is that as yet it's not in demand really at U.S. prices, it's future is $$ very good, Asia being so important to the cultural future, being the thing in fact: and that pieces comparable to the great Greek-Roman-Medieval Praxiteles-Rembrandt classics are not nearly so high priced, so on down the line to more modestly priced minor pieces.

　　Were you asking me how I acquire library here or how to do so in NYC? If the former, I borrow books and keep them. If the latter, figure out what you want yr children to read and what will amuse you in old age and go down to

4th Avenue 2nd hand bookstores and buy big sets of Shakespeare, Dickens, Tolstoy and Balzac etc. You can buy 10 vols. of Flaubert for $5.00, and complete Balzacs (25 vols?) for under $25, etc. Also you can use the hundred or so books I left with you and I'll send a few more. You can also buy complete Miltons, Popes, Drydens, Johnson's, Jonsons etc. cheap on 4th Avenue, 10¢ apiece if you put in a little time—take the day off and visit every store on 4th (between 8th St. and 14th).

I'm reading Whitman, who seems to me now a great personal Colossus of American poetry—am on page 450 of 550 page complete *Leaves of Grass*. Also reading all I can of translations of XX Century French poetry, Apollinaire, Cendrars (Blaise), Cocteau; also a little Gertrude Stein. The kick (includes Lorca) is: 1) spontaneous method of composition, 2) a long imaginative line, 3) subject: the immediate consciousness of the transcriber (or writer). A great release of imagination takes place among these writers, like jazz musicians suddenly ON and making it wildly. Little of this has been absorbed (after Whitman) into American poetry, everything now is mealy-mouthed, meaningless, abstract, tight, controlled, tight-assed, scared, academic, uninventive, attitudinized, afraid to show feeling, too "Cool." Mainly this stems from lack of constant writing, fear of revealing self (which is all a writer can do) (so that others may be themselves too, recognizing it in the writer) (which is Whitman's great bardic kick in Song of Myself), and lack of technical experience in composition as free invention. Tight formal poetry seems to me result of basic lack of technical understanding and not subtlety, mastery, control etc., which academic poets like to think of themselves as "exhibiting." Like trained dogs. Who else is writing active? Burroughs and Kerouac. Then there are 3 minor poets around here, all influenced by us. Williams, who's better in old age than ever. There is a group made up of Robert Creeley, Charles Olson (the best), Robert Duncan and Paul Blackburn who publish their books from Majorca and run 2 little magazines, *Origin* and *Black Mountain Review*, whose work and attitude (hip, bop, free, imaginative, Zen, anarchist, sensual modern and sane) I like tho they are too tight-assed as a group from what I read and have not enough human magnanimity in their work. I'm answering your question somewhat pedantically I realize of a sudden. [...]

Merry Xmas, happy anniversary belated, write when you can, see you probably sometime in spring or early summer.

Love,

Allen

Allen Ginsberg [Berkeley, CA] to Louis Ginsberg [Paterson, NJ]
ca. April 1956

Dear Louis:

Not written for long since I've been running around and busy. I'm working full time at Greyhound in the city, but haven't made decent living arrangements, so I only get back to Berkeley a few times a week where all papers and letters are on desk in big mess. I stay over in city on various couches on workdays, since I've been back I haven't had time to really sit down in leisure and figure out what to do about living arrangements, I almost moved back into SF tho I hate to give up this cottage, and was in fact supposed to this weekend but too many things came up and I can't find time. I am really all up in the air.

Mainly I'm waiting for a ship or some equivalent moneymaking project since I do want to leave here and take off for Europe sometime this year. Meanwhile the Greyhound job brings in 50 a week, Seattle debts are being cleared off this month. I'm also surprisingly enough teaching one class a week at S.F. State College — State is the school that's been promoting poetry workshops, readings, etc. and I am now the local poet-hero so was invited to occupy the chair of guest gorilla at their writing class. I work with another regular teacher who handles all the details, registration, mimeographing of poems to be handed out and discussed etc, and I act as pro in conducting discussions. The class is about 20, half old ladies and half hip young kids who have been attracted by all the recent activity. My teaching technique could shock you undoubtedly and certainly get me kicked out of anywhere else or not be countenanced, I bring in bums from North Beach and talk about marijuana and Whitman, precipitate great emotional outbreaks and howls of protest over irrational spontaneous behavior — but it does actually succeed in communicating some of the electricity & fire of poetry and cuts through the miasmic quibbling about form vs. content etc. and does this phrase "work" and is that line "successful" and are all those "p & f" sounds too intense, etc. The woman who runs this program is a Prof. Ruth Witt-Diamant who has dug my work — there appears to be, according to Rexroth, a semi major renaissance around the west coast due to Jack and my presence — and Rexroth's wife said he'd been waiting all his life hoping for a situation like this to develop. The thing I do in class is get them personally involved in what they're writing and lambaste anything which sounds at all like they're writing "literature" and try to get them to actually express secret life in whatever form it comes out. I practically take off my clothes in class myself to do it. The students all dig it and understand and the class is now grown weekly to where it's too big to handle, starting with 8 and ending with 25.

W. C. Williams read *Howl* and liked it and wrote an introduction for the book; and meanwhile there is the possibility of expanding and making a whole book of poems. We put on another reading in a theatre here in Berkeley, I read some other poems, Whitman, The Sunflower, and a new poem called America —a sort of surrealist anarchist tract—all of which came off very well, so the publisher is now interested in a book full of representative work not just the one poem. The reading was pretty great, we had traveling photographers, who appeared on the scene from Vancouver to photograph it, a couple of amateur electronics experts who appeared with tape machines to record, request from State college for a complete recording for the night, requests for copies of the recordings, even finally organizations of bop musicians who want to write music and give big west coast traveling tours of *Howl* as a sort of Jazz Mass, recorded for a west coast company called Fantasy records that issues a lot of national bop, etc. No kidding. You have no idea what a storm of lunatic-fringe activity I have stirred up. On top of that the local poets, good and bad, have caught up and there are now three groups of people putting on readings every other week, there's one every weekend, all sorts of people—this week Eberhart (Richard) arrived in town for readings at State, there is a party for him tonite, I was invited to give a private reading, refused (sheer temperament), and so the recordings will be played. Tomorrow night Rexroth invited me over to meet a group of jazz musicians and discuss the possibility of making some form of jazz-poetry combo. There is also another group of musicians, the leader of which used to arrange for Stan Kenton who wants to record with me. Finally I was asked to write an article which I haven't gotten around to do for *Black Mountain Review*, & also contribute to 2 literary magazines starting here. Bob LaVigne, a painter whose work I've been buying and digging, has been putting up wild line drawings to plaster the walls of the readings and painting fantastic 7 foot posters *à la* Lautrec. Really a charming scene. My big problem now is not having enough time to do all I could, working at Greyhound and not having moved out of Berkeley, so I get little time for actual writing anymore— it will be a relief to get out from under and away on a ship or up to Alaska possibly on a fishing industry job.

Rexroth's house—Friday evenings, open house, 2 weeks ago Malcolm Cowley, I got drunk and made a big inflammatory speech denouncing him for publishing Donald Hall as a commercial snot and neglecting & delaying Kerouac, a funny scene, no blood spilled; last weekend [Richard] Eberhart there, a long non drunken recollection of a party we'd met at in NY 5 years ago, he remembered the conversation in detail, I'd just got out of hospital and was hung-up on the religious experience in the Groundhog poem.

English publishers won't handle *Howl*, that is English Printers (Villiers) and so there is now difficulty in getting it through unexpurgated. I revised it and it is now worse than it ever was, too. We're now investigating Mexico, if necessary will spend extra cost and have it done here tho. Civil Liberties Union here was consulted and said they'd defend it if it gets into trouble, which I almost hope it does. I am almost ready to tackle the U.S. government out of sheer self delight. There is really a great stupid conspiracy of unconscious negative inertia to keep people from "expressing" themselves. I was reading Henry Miller's banned book *Tropic of Cancer*, which actually is a great classic—I never heard of it at Columbia with anything but deprecatory dismissal comments—he and Genet are such frank hip writers that the open expression of their perceptions and real beliefs are a threat to society. The wonder is that literature does have such power. [. . .]

Allen

[*The following is Ginsberg's most famous letter, written to poet and critic Richard Eberhart, in which Allen took a good deal of time to explain the construction of* Howl.]

Allen Ginsberg [San Francisco, CA] to Richard Eberhart [New York, NY] May 18, 1956

Dear Mr. Eberhart:

Kenneth Rexroth tells me you are writing an article on S.F. poetry and asked for a copy of my manuscript. I'll send it.

It occurred to me with alarm how really horrible generalizations might be if they are off-the-point as in newspapers.

I sat listening sans objection in the car while you told me what you'd said in Berkeley. I was flattered and egotistically hypnotized by the idea of recognition but really didn't agree with your evaluation of my own poetry. Before you say anything in the *Times* let me have my say.

1) The general "problem" is positive and negative "values." "You don't tell me how to live," "you deal with the negative or horrible well but have no positive program" etc.

This is as absurd as it sounds.

It would be impossible to write a powerful emotional poem without a firm grasp on "value" not as an intellectual ideal but as an emotional reality.

You heard or saw *Howl* as a negative howl of protest.

The title notwithstanding, the poem itself is an act of sympathy, not rejection. In it I am leaping *out* of a preconceived notion of social "values," following my own heart's instincts—*allowing* myself to follow my own heart's instincts, overturning any notion of propriety, moral "value," superficial "maturity," Trilling-esque sense of "civilization," and exposing my true feelings —of sympathy and identification with the rejected, mystical, individual even "mad."

I am saying that what seems "mad" in America is our expression of natural ecstasy (as in Crane, Whitman) which suppressed, finds no social form organization background frame of reference or rapport or validation from the outside and so the "patient" gets confused thinks he is mad and really goes off rocker. I am paying homage to mystical mysteries in the forms in which they actually occur here in the U.S. in our environment.

I have taken a leap of detachment from the artificial preoccupations and preconceptions of what is acceptable and normal and given my yea to the specific type of madness listed in the Who section.

The leap in the imagination—it is safe to do in a poem.

A leap to actual living sanctity is not impossible, but requires more time for me.

I used to think I was mad to want to be a saint, but now what have I got to fear? People's opinions? Loss of a teaching job? I am living outside this context. I make my own sanctity. How else? Suffering and humility are forced on my otherwise wild ego by lugging baggage in Greyhound.

I started as a fair-haired boy in academic Columbia.

I have discovered a great deal of my own true nature and that individuality which is a value, the only social value that there can be in the Blake-worlds. I see it as a "social value."

I have told you how to live if I have wakened any emotion of compassion and realization of the beauty of souls in America, thru the poem.

What other value could a poem have—now, historically maybe?

I have released and confessed and communicated clearly my true feelings tho it might involve at first a painful leap of exhibition and fear that I would be rejected.

This is a value, an actual fact, not a mental formulation of some second-rate sociological-moral ideal which is meaningless and academic in the poetry of H–, etc.

Howl is the first discovery as far as *communication* of feeling and truth, that I made. It begins with a catalogue sympathetically and *humanely* describing excesses of feeling and idealization.

Moloch is the vision of the mechanical feelingless inhuman world we live in and accept—and the key line finally is "Moloch whom I abandon."

It ends with a litany of active acceptance of the suffering of soul of C. Solomon, saying in effect I am *still* your amigo tho you are in trouble and think yourself in a void, and the final strophe states the terms of the communication

"oh starry spangled shock of <u>Mercy</u>"

and mercy is a real thing and if that is not a value I don't know what is.

How mercy gets to exist where it comes from perhaps can be seen from the inner evidence and images of the poem—an act of self-realization, self-acceptance and the consequent and inevitable relaxation of protective anxiety and self hood and the ability to see and love others in themselves as angels without stupid mental self deceiving moral categories selecting *who* it is safe to sympathize with and who is not safe.

See Dostoyevsky and Whitman.

This process is carried to a crystal form in the *Sunflower Sutra* which is a "dramatic" context for these thoughts.

"Unholy battered old thing O sunflower O my soul
I LOVED you then."

The effect is to release self and audience from a false and self-denying self-deprecating image of ourselves which makes us feel like smelly shits and not the angels which we most deeply are.

The vision we have of people and things outside us is obviously (see Freud) a reflection of our relation to our self.

It is perhaps possible to forgive another and love another only after you forgive and love yourself.

This is why Whitman is crucial in development of American psyche. He accepted himself and from that flowed acceptance of all things.

The *Sunflower Sutra* is an emotional release and exposition of this process.

Thus I fail to see why you characterize my work as destructive or negative. Only if you are thinking an outmoded dualistic puritanical academic theory ridden world of values can you fail to see I am talking about *realization* of love. LOVE.

The poems are religious and I meant them to be and the effect on audience is (surprising to me at first) a validation of this. It is like "I give the primeval sign" of acceptance, as in Whitman.

The second point is technical. This point would be called in question only if you have not Faith. I mean it is beside the true point and irrelevant because the communication, the *sign* of communication if successfully made should begin and end by achieving the perfection of a mystical experience which you know all about.

I am also saying have faith that I am finally referring to the Real Thing and that I am trying to communicate it.

Why must you deny your senses?

But as to technique—[Ruth] Witt-Diamant said you were surprised I exhibited any interest in the "Line" etc.

What seems formless tho effective is really effective thru discovery or realization of rules and meanings of forms and experiments in them.

The "form" of the poem is an experiment. Experiment with uses of the catalogue, the ellipse, the long line, the litany, repetition, etc.

The latter parts of the first section set forth a "formal" esthetic derived in part incidentally from my master who is Cézanne.

The poem is really built like a brick shithouse.

This is the general ground plan—all an accident, organic, but quite symmetrical surprisingly. It grew (part III) out of a desire to build up rhythm using a fixed base to respond to and elongating the response still however containing it within the elastic of one breath or one big streak of thought.

As in all things a reliance on nature and spontaneity (as well as much experience writing and practicing to arrive at spontaneity which IS A CRAFT not a jerk-off mode, a craft in which near-perfection is basic too) has produced organic proportion in this case somewhat symmetrical (i.e. rationally apprehensible) proportion.

This is, however, vague generalization.

The Long Line I use came after 7 yrs. work with fixed iambic rhyme, and 4 yrs. work with Williams' short line free form—which as you must know has its own mad rules—indefinable tho they be at present—

The long line, the prose poem, the spontaneous sketch are XX century French forms which Academic versifiers despite their continental interests (in XIX century French "formal" forms, Baudelaire) have completely ignored. Why?

This form of writing is very popular in S.A. and is after all the most interesting thing happening in France.

Whitman

Apollinaire

Lorca

Are these people credited with no technical sense by fools who by repeating the iambic mouthings of their betters or the quasi-iambic of Eliot or the completely irrational (tho beautiful) myth of "clear lucid form" in Pound—who works basically by ear anyway and there isn't any clear mentally formulizable form in him anyway, no regular countable measure* [an error here, as Pound attempted to approximate classical quantitative measure. Allen Ginsberg, 1975] —I'm straying—people who by repeating etc., are exhibiting no technical sensitivity at all but merely adeptness at using already formulated ideas—and *this* is historically no time for that—or even if it were who cares, I don't. I am interested in discovering what I do *not* know, in myself and in the ways of writing— an old point.

The long line—you need a good ear and an emotional ground-swell and technical and syntactical ease facility and a freedom "esprit" to deal with it and make of it anything significant. And you need something to say, i.e. clear realized feelings. Same as any free verse.

The lines are the result of long thought and experiment as to what unit constitutes *one speech-breath-thought.*

I have observed my mind

I have observed my speech   1) Drunk

                                        2) Drugged

                                        3) Sober

                                        4) Sexy etc.

And have exercised it so I can speak *freely,* i.e. without self-conscious inhibited stoppings and censorships which latter factors are what destroy speech and thought rhythm.

We think and speak rhythmically all the time, each phrasing, piece of speech, metrically equivalent to what we have to say emotionally.

Given a mental release which is not mentally blocked, the breath of verbal intercourse will come with excellent rhythm, a rhythm which is perhaps unimprovable.

[Unimprovable as experiment in any case.

Each poem is an experiment

Revised as little as possible.

So (experiments) are many modern canvasses as you know. The sketch is a fine "Form."]

W. C. Williams has been observing speech rhythms for years trying to find a regular "measure" —

he's mistaken I think.

There is no measure which will make one speech the exact length of another, one line the exact length of another.

He has therefore seized on the phrase "relative measure" in his old age.

He is right but has not realized the implications of this in the long line.

Since each wave of speech-thought needs to be measured (we speak and perhaps think in waves)—or what I speak and think I have at any rate in *Howl* reduced to waves of relatively equally heavy weight—and set next to one another they are in a balance O.K.

The technique of writing both prose and poetry, the technical problem of the present day, is the problem of transcription of the natural flow of the mind, the transcription of the melody of actual thought or speech.

I have leaned more toward capturing the inside-mind-thought rather than the verbalized speech. This distinction I make because most poets see the problem via Wordsworth as getting nearer to actual *speech*, verbal speech.

I have noticed that the unspoken visual-verbal flow inside the mind has great rhythm and have approached the problem of strophe, line and stanza and measure by listening and transcribing (to a great extent) the coherent mental flow. Taking *that* for the model for form as Cézanne took Nature.

This is not surrealism—they made up an artificial literary imitation.

I transcribe from my ordinary thoughts—waiting for extra exciting or mystical moments or near mystical moments to transcribe.

This brings up problems of image, and transcription of mental flow gives helpful knowledge because we think in sort of surrealist (juxtaposed images) or haiku-like form.

A haiku as the 1910–20's imagists did *not* know, consists of 2 visual (or otherwise) images stripped down and juxtaposed—the charge of electricity created by these 2 poles being greater when there is a greater distance between them — as in Yeats' phrase "murderous innocence of the sea" — 2 opposite poles reconciled in a flash of recognition.

The mind in its flow creates such fantastic ellipses thus the key phrase of method in *Howl* is "Hydrogen Jukebox" which tho quite senseless makes in context clear sense.

Throughout the poem you will see traces of transcription, at its best see the

last line of *Sunflower Sutra,* "mad locomotive riverbank sunset Frisco hilly tin-
can evening sitdown vision."

This is a curious but really quite logical development of Pound-Fenelossa-
Chinese Written Character-imagist W. C. Williams' practice.

I don't see the metrics or metaphors as revolution, rather as logical develop-
ment, given my own interests, experiences, etc. and time.

This (explanation) is all too literary as essentially my purpose has been to
say what I actually feel, (not what I want to feel or think I should feel or fit my
feelings into a fake "Tradition" which is a *process* really not a fixed set of values
and practices anyway—so anybody who wants to hang on to traditional met-
rics and values will wind up stultified and self-deceived anyway despite all the
sincerity in the world). Everybody thinks they should learn academically from
"experience" and have their souls put down and destroyed and this has been
raised to the status of "value" but to me it seems just the usual old fake death,
much under Professor T–, whom I love, but who is a poor mental fanatic after
all and not a free soul—I'm straying.

2) *The poetry situation in S.F.*

The last wave was led by Robert Duncan, highly over-literary but basic
recognition of the spontaneous free-form experiment. He left for Mallorca and
contacted Robert Creeley, editor of *Black Mountain Review,* they became friends
and Duncan who dug Williams, Stein, etc. especially the Black Mountain influ-
ence of Charles Olson who is the head peer of the East Coast bohemian hip-
ster-authors post Pound. Olson's *Death of Europe* in *Origin* last year (about a
suicide German boy)—"oh that the Earth / had to be given / to you / this
way." is the first of his poems I've been able to read but it is a great break-
through of feeling and a great modern poem I think.

Creeley his boy came here [San Francisco] last month and made contact
with us—and next issue of *Black Mountain Review* will carry me, Whalen and:

1) William S. Burroughs, a novelist friend of mine in Tangier. Great Man.

2) Gary Snyder, a Zen Buddhist poet and Chinese scholar 25 years old who
leaves next week for further poetry study in a Zen monastery in Kyoto.

3) Jack Kerouac, who is out here and is the Colossus unknown of U.S. Prose
who taught me to write and has written more and better than anybody of my
generation that I've ever heard of. Kerouac you may have heard of but any
review of the situation here would be ultimately historically meaningless with-
out him since he is *the* unmistakable fertile prolific Shakespearean *genius*—lives
in a shack in Mill Valley with Gary Snyder. Cowley (Malcolm) is trying to ped-
dle him in N.Y.C. now* [Cowley as editor at Viking was having difficulty per-

suading the management to publish *On the Road*. Allen Ginsberg, 1975] and can give you info. Kerouac invented and initiated my practice of speech-flow prosody.

I recount the above since anything you write will be irrelevant if you don't dig especially Kerouac—no shit, get info from Kenneth [Rexroth] or Louise Bogan who met him if you don't take my word.

The W. S. Burroughs above mentioned was Kerouac's and my mentor 1943–1950.

I have written this in the Greyhound between loading busses and will send it on uncensored.

I've said nothing about the extraordinary influence of Bop music on rhythm and drugs on the observation of rhythm and mental processes—not enough time and out of paper.

Yours,

Allen Ginsberg

Summary
I. Values
1) *Howl* is an "affirmation" of individual experience of God, sex, drugs, absurdity, etc. part I deals sympathetically with individual cases. Part II describes and rejects the Moloch of society which confounds and suppresses individual experience and forces the individual to consider himself mad if he does not reject his own deepest senses. Part III is an expression of sympathy and identification with C. S. [Carl Solomon] who is in the madhouse—saying that his madness basically is rebellion against Moloch and I am with him, and extending my hand in union. This is an affirmative act of mercy and compassion, which are the basic emotions of the poem. The criticism of society is that "Society" is merciless. The alternative is private, individual acts of mercy. The poem is one such. It is therefore clearly and consciously built on a *liberation* of basic human virtues.

To call it work of nihilistic rebellion would be to mistake it completely. Its force comes from positive "religious" belief and experience. It offers no "constructive" program in sociological terms—no poem could. It does offer a constructive human value—basically the *experience*—of the enlightenment of mystical experience—without which no society can long exist.

2) *Supermarket in California* deals with Walt Whitman, Why?

He was the first great American poet to take action in recognizing his individuality, forgiving and accepting *Him Self*, and automatically extending that recognition and acceptance to all—and defining his Democracy as that. He was unique and lonely in his glory—the truth of his feelings—without which no society can long exist. Without this truth there is only the impersonal Moloch and self-hatred of others.

Without self-acceptance there can be no acceptance of other souls.

3) *Sunflower Sutra* is crystallized "dramatic" moment of self-acceptance in modern terms.

"Unholy battered old thing, O sunflower O my soul, I *loved* you then!"

The realization of holy self-love is a rare "affirmative" value and cannot fail to have constructive influence in "Telling *you* (R.E.) [Richard Eberhart] how to live."

4) *America* is an unsystematic and rather gay exposition of my own private feelings contrary to the official dogmas, but really rather universal as far as private opinions about what I mention. It says—"I am thus and so I have a right to do so, and I'm saying it out loud for all to hear."

II. Technique

A. These long lines or Strophes as I call them came spontaneously as a result of the kind of feelings I was trying to put down, and came as a surprise solution to a metrical problem that preoccupied me for a decade.

I have considerable experience writing both rhymed iambics and short line post-WCW [William Carlos Williams] free verse.

Howl's 3 parts consist of 3 different approaches to the use of the long line (longer than Whitman's, more French).

1. Repetition of the fixed base "Who" for a catalogue.

A. building up consecutive rhythm from strophe to strophe.

B. abandoning of fixed base "who" in certain lines but carrying weight and rhythm of strophic form continuously forward.

2. Break up of strophe into pieces within the strophe, thus having the strophe become a new usable form of stanza—Repetition of fixed base "Moloch" to provide cement for continuity. *Supermarket* uses strophe stanza and abandons need for fixed base. I was experimenting with the form.

3. Use of a fixed base, "I'm with you in Rockland," with a reply in which the strophe becomes a longer and longer streak of speech, in order to build up a *relatively* equal nonetheless free and variable structure. Each reply strophe is longer than the previous I have measured by ear and speech-breath, there being no other measure for such a thing. Each strophe consists of a set of phrases that can be spoken in one breath and each carries relatively equal rhetorical weight. Penultimate strophe is an exception and was meant to be—a series of

THE LETTERS OF ALLEN GINSBERG

cries—"O skinny legions run outside O starry spangled shock of mercy O victory etc." You will not fail to observe that the cries are all in definite rhythm.

The technical problem raised and partially solved is the break-through begun by Whitman but never carried forward, from both iambic stultification and literary automatism, and unrhythmical shortline verse, which does not yet offer any kind of *base* cyclical flow for the build up of a powerful rhythm. The long line seems for the moment to free speech for emotional expression and give it a measure to work with. I hope to experiment with short-line free verse with what I have learned from exercise in long.

B. Imagery—is a result of the *kind* of line and the kind of emotions and the kind of speech-and-interior flow-of-the-mind transcription I am doing—the imagery often consists of 1920s W.C.W. [Williams] imagistically observed detail collapsed together by interior associative logic—i.e., "hydrogen jukebox," Apollinaire, Whitman, Lorca. But *not* automatic surrealism. Knowledge of Haiku and ellipse is crucial.

**Allen Ginsberg [USNS *Sgt. Jack J. Pendleton,* Wainwright, Alaska]
to Robert LaVigne [San Francisco, CA] August 3, 1956**

Dear Bob:

Settled down in trip more, now up at a place in Arctic Circle called Wainwright, Alaska—so far no ice, snow, icebergs, aurora, whales, dolphins, seals, fish—nothing but grey sea and occasional bright day, and day which truly does last all night. The light if you're interested of these northern nights has a kind of deadbluish-grey immanence, as if not out of sun (usually hidden behind solid cover of clouds also dead grey color past midnight) but lunar reflected out of the water. But it is enough to think it's day by.

Reading mostly pious works, the lives of the Saints and the Bible, tho small comfort all that since I feel my own egotism and irresolution more painfully for the striking though doctrinally confusing examples set up in my imagination by St. Francis (have 2 different biographies aboard). Death of my mother[32] has brought me more close to understanding inevitability of death feeling that already I see a part of me my childhood in the grave, a piece of my own life gone and the rest surely to go, and rereading my own writings the skimpiness and hollowness of most of that. Enclosed a pamphlet of Mexican poem I mimeographed last weekend. Really I feel miserable the isolation not so much

32 Naomi Ginsberg died in Pilgrim State Hospital on June 9, 1956.

as the continual sexual attrition and voluptuousness of my night dreams and the broad daylight out of jointedness of it when I dress and come to breakfast with the men I dream of, making me feel as if life is wasted in Kafkian sexual dreams, or else the broad daylight is wasted in fear of homosexual martyrdom, which it would be if I began acting like I feel: added to that the continual ignoring of this whole problem in the Bible and Saints except for admonition to disregard and suppress entirely all objects of the sense and put yr. love to the fear of the lord, whoever or whatever that is, tho It certainly exists in some form I am no longer able to guess about. Anyway the dumps.

Send me a pretty picture envelope size you can send without folding for me to tack up on my bunk and contemplate.

Not allowed off ship, tho we've been anchored here for several days half a mile off shore where thru field glasses I can see a village on a cliff of 70 houses ramshackle, Eskimos live there without measles or colds and that's why we can't visit. Northern latitudes look flat and the land of Alaska a pencil line on the edge of horizon from where we are, and the further Northward stretches up another thousand miles to the pole in the daylite streaked with clouds.

What's happening in SF? I wrote Ferlinghetti to see if a drawing could be arranged with you for my book but I guess it's too late, I don't know. Maybe check with him if he hasn't contacted you. Send me a gossipy letter.

Love,

Allen

Allen Ginsberg [USNS *Sgt. Jack J. Pendleton,* Alaska] to Rebecca Ginsberg [Newark, NJ] August 11, 1956

Dear Buba [Allen's grandmother]:

I am sorry not to have written you earlier. I have been traveling and in strange places but I have thought of you often, as I know you have thought of me: and I love you for that, and have not forgotten.

Naomi's death made me remember my own generation, and how it must pass. She wrote me to marry, before she died, as you have spoken. I take that to heart, but my path is too far from home yet and will be a while more, while it is still dark. This to your heart. But there is time left me for many summers of grass on earth, I am not impatient.

I am on the sea north of Alaska 1000 miles from the Pole. The sun is up all night, and ice flows by on the edge of the ocean day after day. I spend my evenings reading through the books of the Old Testament—and from Genesis I have read to Samuel and the story of David who danced naked before the Ark. I am sorry I am not able to talk with you about your memory of the family, time, and the Jews.

I hear that Clara [Allen's aunt] is getting married—give her my love and say I will see her this year; and will see you too for I will return East before the end of the year.

I will go to Europe after awhile and hope to go to visit Russia. If you know of any of our family there please try to find out where they are, I would like to visit them, and see their faces. Travel is now permitted there by both countries —it may not be so forever, and train fare costs little, and I can live like a hermit, so I see no reason not to try a pilgrimage to Pinsk and Vitebsk. The captain of this boat, by the way, is an old White Russian.

San Francisco and the West Coast has been a good place for me—I have found money easy to make, and so have become less concerned with having it, and my needs are small, so I have had freedom to study and look at the sun and laugh at the summer grass.

Give my love to the whole family, send me your blessings, and I will see you soon.

As ever, love

Allen

[*Once back in San Francisco, Ginsberg learned that Carolyn Kizer had been asked to write an article on the new literary scene just beginning to unfold in San Francisco.*]

Allen Ginsberg [San Francisco, CA] to Carolyn Kizer [?]
September 10, 1956

Dear Carolyn Kiser: [*sic*: Kizer]

Greetings once again. Rumors you are doing an article for *Nation* on San Francisco Poetry. This is absolutely absurd, how can you know all the essential details? Most of the poetry here is illustrious unknown. Therefore this letter. IF you are doing an article allow me to intrude. Get the facts straight. Eberhart wrote good article, since it was inclusive, in last Sunday *Times NY*. But not being on or of scene nor being acquainted with material how could he do anything but vague journalism, and you must realize that newspapers get all the facts screwed up anyway even say murder stories, so how can anything straightforward informed and understanding be wrote about so cockily and silly a thing as poetry; like love affairs—imagine a review of the season's love affairs. Well it must not be in condescending tone, that's first paramount. Must be simple without attitudes, and if possible without aesthetic bullshit about manners and form. Above all no yelling about revolt or immature kicking against form by ignorances. We is not ignoramuses. But I am writing this not essentially to argue (we've already argued and I'm sick of it) (too much basic understanding of the basic words we argued about like the word "form" by which you mean one thing and I, or we, if there is a we, which there really isn't, mean another). Now to some pertinent facts and read these please as they are really so.

The greatest writer in San Francisco who has unquestionably lifted the whole scene to joy is unknown but will not be so long, his name is Jack Kerouac and he is a novelist and poet. He just returned to town an hour ago from spending the summer in Desolation Peak, Baker National Forest, as a fire-watcher. Author of a number of books mentioned in my dedication to *Howl*. Cowley is diddling with a long manuscript of his and Grove Press will now probably if all goes well carry out an offer to print everything of his in chronological order. A great genius of method of spontaneous writing—a style like mixture of Melville and Céline—a story of his "The Mexican Girl" in *Paris Review* earlier this year and under pseudonym of Jean Luis a story "Jazz of the Beat Generation" in *New World Writing* 8 I think. He is a Buddhist. Generally the method is as in Buddhist Zen Archery or Koan Response, long continued practice at spontaneous exactness of expression requiring years of 10-16 hours a day practicing uninterrupted transcription of the droppings of the mind upon a page—until form, deep form, begins to appear, emerge out of the sea. Requires native genius to do however and emerge as anything but conscious chatter. Now Jack is actually the great seminal spirit here, who transformed my earlier work, and gave me what power I have. This same influence at work in last hectic productive year on Gary Snyder, and also on Philip Whalen. Snyder's work you know, at least heard some of tho I don't think you paid attention. There is also, from Reed, Philip Whalen, mentioned by Eberhart as one of the "bookless" poets. [Stanley] Kunitz saw him and his work here. Also under Jack's debt.

A poet whom Jack and I dug, a young Wop ex-jail kid with angelic mind,

Gregory Corso, who learned perhaps a little from us of self acceptance and how to blow natural, was in Harvard, bumming around Cambridge, they put a play of his at poets theatre and collected money to put out an early book poems of his there. I enclose that book. Note the free-swinging strange verbal style. It of course looks goofy and uneducated to you but you must also dig what he has, as well as what you think that he doesn't have. Well he just hit town a few weeks ago to see me and Jack with a pile of new manuscript and City Lights man dug him immediately, so did Ruth Witt-Diamant and everybody around, so he will give reading here next month, and City Lights is getting a book out for him, perhaps six months will take for that. He is of the same ground and style, you'll have to see for yourself how it follows a method and differs from say a random [Kenneth] Patchen type blathering. You must not misunderstand this all as pure ignorant mental bohemianism else you miss the gist and don't grasp the existence of a method, which I keep saying requires considerable mental discipline and above all as with any skill extensive free practical practice. For clearest simplest poems in Corso's book, these two: In the Morgue and on p. 13 In the Early Morning. The elegy for or Requiem for Bird Parker (Charlie Parker the great musician I'm sure you know of him) is the most important poem in the book—read it aloud, forget the few obvious absurd or crude elements and dig the hip tone, the humor and the fine imagination. Yeh, yeh. This is his own emergent swinging style. Imaginatively swinging as the hipsters say.

I enclose Mike McClure's book. He has his own formal delicacy, unlike Corso or me but he also possibly has undergone some affect from my Sunflower Sutra style—see particularly the poem the Greech. W. C. Williams thinks the Death of the Whales, last poem is a great statement, I rather agree. He's cooler and perhaps less magnanimous as a spirit than others but an intense married young man and what can you do with such having babies and all except hope for the best, that they don't get dry and nasty and critical and attempt to keep an open perhaps even religious exuberance of nature. Not against criticism much, except as it reflects an unbalanced character—out of fear of own nature, criticizing self and others. Read Whitman. Any way I send you McClure. The only thing that counts is examples of energy or perfection in work, that's what corrects, but not theoretical criticism that's useless for improvement mostly you realize. Think of Rembrandt, and don't be afraid to think of Beethoven and Rembrandt. No quarrels, just examples of Art. This also is classical Zen not primitive ignorance of tradition. The tradition remember is not what you are taught in school. There is a tradition however. What that is is another matter but please like I say don't write about tradition if you are just going to write about what is taught in school, any school. No matter how charming a school.

I also enclose samples of other City Lights publications. Ferlinghetti as you know who he is, runs City Lights. The others you know already, they are not new and I have no axes to grind in that direction.

And Robert Duncan. Ever hear of him??? He has been running SF poetry, holding fort, immense intelligence and learnedness, just been to Europe, returned last week, will be asst. director of Witt-D. Poetry Center this year now, as had been before less officially. He also, with greater learning than any- one else of us, tho not so great spirit perhaps, greater classical preparation tho, been tackling for years the problem of the transcription of the droppings of the mind on the page. Some of his work in print somewhere. Contact older issues of *Black Mountain Review* or *Origin* magazine. Well he has always been the spir- itual leader here, before, but Jack and I came from east, 3 years ago, and Corso, and Gary and Phil emerged from the Northwest Seattle, see, and the local woodwork while he was in Europe, without much connection with him, tho I've always been interested in Duncan, but all respect his great learning and his long practice of a sort of smaller can purity of approach to the blank page, his clearing of his mind of chatter, meditation, and then transcription of the end- less sentences of his consciousness. So he's back now to help complete the pic- ture his own way.

Then Robert Creeley—ever know of him? Editor of *Black Mountain Review*, connected with Duncan in Mallorca, and so this summer came out here to see me, Kerouac, Rexroth, Snyder, Whalen, all became buddies, lots of drinking marijuana jazz and discussion of eastern (Black Mountain Creeley-Olson hip cool Mallarmé style) and recent western (me, Jack, blowing hot and frantic) (and romantic)—meeting of minds, he left town with huge pile of manu- scripts for next edition of *Black Mountain Review*—an earlier intro to my work by W. C. Williams, an expanded version of "America," a poem of mine, the poems of Whalen that Eberhart mentions, a mess of Snyder's work, some prose of Kerouac, and a short piece of explicit instructions by Kerouac, titled "Essentials of Modern Prose" showing exactly how to meditate and transcribe in dudden or Chan or Zen fashion the perpetual prose or poetry of the mind, the ordinary or elated mind, a statement of method you see, this too to be pub- lished, plus Creeley took along poems of McClure, etc. and an unknown railroad brakeman from Southern Pacific named Neal Cassady who taught me and Jack that the mind has its own flow and rhythm—this is too much for you to absorb maybe for an article if you have any intention of absorbing I hope you do anyway—but I do want to indicate the real sense of things here not some phony formal la do da about literature and groups and crap which has nothing to do with nothing.

Actually to do an article you should read Whalen's work, and Jack's and get a hold of Duncan and Creeley's publications. However at least do indicate that there is a rumor or a conscious ascription of true originality by me and Whalen and Snyder and Corso and others to king Jack Kerouac.

Is it true that you are going to write an article by the way?

IF not this is all silly. But won't do no harm and took me 10 minutes. When you are thru with the enclosed material send the Corso and McClure books to Louise Bogan c/o *New Yorker Magazine,* who may possibly do a review of my book, but I want her to see these, too, for her own edification. She by the way knows and digs Kerouac, I mean this to say he isn't my myth, or an irrelevant myth, he's central. Dig him, write of him and you have a magnanimous lovely poetical SCOOP. But I guess it don't make much difference because from what I see of articles articles articles they're just articles irrelevant to the creation of poetry which has nothing to do even with publications, or nothing, just God and Buddha who don't read the newspapers, or whatever.

There I have written a letter of some length requiring attention and tried on my part. Remember I have nothing to lose or gain one way or the other by your paying attention to what I have explained here, but you do have something to gain if you trust me and will understand that I have been trying to be helpful and tried not to bug you but set forth and communicate out of the blue which wasn't necessary for me to do, except it was ordered by angels from above, so your duty lies you believe in angels is to try accept this intervention if it seems unseemly.

Yours

Allen Ginsberg

Note also the rather clear tho light images in Ferlinghetti's book.

[Carolyn Kizer's article did appear and Ginsberg was quite happy with the results. He felt she made fair and balanced statements. On November 1, 1956, Lawrence Ferlinghetti published 1,000 copies of Howl and Other Poems *as the fourth in the City Lights Pocket Poets series.]*

Allen Ginsberg [Paterson, NJ] to Lawrence Ferlinghetti [San Francisco, CA] December 7, 1956

Dear Larry:

Well, finally here in NYC. We left Gregory waiting for money order to arrive in Mexico City; it was sent the worst and slowest way possible, mail money order, several weeks ago, he was still waiting December 3. Money order from his girl so he could fly home fast, to [Randall] Jarrell.

Reading we gave in LA was the most wild ever, I disrobed, finally, been wanting to onstage for years.

Peter, Lafcadio and Jack Kerouac and I came up here together. Gregory by the way filled a whole huge Mexican notebook full of beautiful strange poems and silly pictures, writing more and better than ever. His book for you ought to be really great, individual and solid—he surprised me even by his great voluminousness and copiousness and freedom of imagination all the way down on the trip, writing poems all over everywhere in bus stops and restaurants. His style developing looser and more far out toward an imaginative wop surrealism. He's as completely tough and original now as anyone I can think of. I was really kind of aghast and amazed how fertile and curious everything he wrote seemed at the moment.

Well anyway, this letter from Laughlin.[33] Open all letters you think necessary, personal or not, I don't care. I hope to give him something new, rather than reprint, *Howl.* So the reprint of 1500 *Howls* is safe. Grove Press has an *Evergreen Review* upcoming and they asked for reprint of *Howl* too, but I'll give them other material. Maybe later on if there's still demand, in a year or so, I don't know. Why 1500 copies?? Can you sell them? There are a number in the 8th St. Bookshop, buried under Rexroth's title, but nobody I know in the Village has seen or bought it. So I don't imagine you'll dispose of many in the Village. Need some kind of advertising or distribution but that's out of the question.

---

33 James Laughlin (1914–1997). Owner and publisher of New Directions Books.

Send me please the remaining 25 copies (as per 1000 reprint) due me, I can use them here now. I keep giving them away. If any more are due me since the reprint is 1500 send them too, to bring to Europe. Or do you have any now, and are you waiting for reprint to arrive? If have few send me 5 at least if you have them.

Spent a long time talking with Williams yesterday, he heard little about the SF scene and was interested. I read him some Gregory which he liked.

Denise Levertov we stopped and saw, she was nice to us, we liked her a lot. I was surprised how much a good Joe she was. What ads in *Nation*? That is, what dates for *Nation* and intro?

Just spoke to Laughlin, told him to reprint Sunflower [Sutra], if he wanted, and will send him some new poems. I guess that would not harm book, might do it some good in fact.

Levertov is a good poetess, certainly, I read a lot of her work there. Regards, I'll write a clearer letter later.

Allen

Allen Ginsberg [Paterson, NJ] to Robert Creeley [Albuquerque, NM] December 11, 1956

Dear Robert:

Sorry we didn't get to New Mexico—I left S.F. a month ¹/₂ ago with Peter, Lafcadio his brother and Gregory, who had no money, and we were worried about time and money. Passed thru LA with Gregory, alone, preceding Orlovsky brothers, to give reading for Anaïs Nin, [Stuart] Perkoff, silly Lawrence Lipton and 70 other assorted strangers from *Coastlines* magazine and friends of Lip and Nin. Someone heckled Gregory so I drunkenly screamed take off your clothes and be naked, which then realizing what I was saying I went and did myself, to my great surprise. They made me put them back on before reading *Howl*, which I read with great wildness and lovely abandon so the night turned out fine. We went straight to Mexicali then, to take desert all night buses with wetbacks and Corso complaining and fighting with Lafcadio over who sits near the window. This saved us 20$$ U.S. cost bus fares to El Paso or other further bordertown, Albuquerque was out of reach—Neal was originally supposed to drive us, but he skinned the sole off his foot in a RR accident a few days before departure and I loaned him some money for family, so we were strapped and since traveling with so many it made immediate dive for border necessary. Nonetheless I flew over Albuquerque by ghostplane and saw you struggling drunkenly in the moonlight out of car which ran out of gas in desert and watched you alas rip your leg on barbed wire crawling with friend to the highway. He (I no remember his name) told me about it. We spent a drunk night arguing with him about Peter's soul, argument *à la* Black Mount. In the morning we watched dawn come up over Chinatown and Peter picked up a huge board and killed a cat which was writhing and gasping in painful death throes, a kitten, on the pale dawn sidewalk.

We went to Guadalajara and visited Denise Levertov for several days, and liked her. Her husband read halting prose to us—so embarrassed to read he kept stopping to tell involved complete story of the novel. He's very simpatico. Gregory read his poetry to her, she kept laughing happily at it, we walked thru markets together and held hands and watched mad longhaired Mexicans selling cure-all liquids for blindness amid church rubble.

Found Jack in Mexico City and woke him up and spent two weeks drunk, high often (all except me I can't stand it anymore) (tho the one great time we all got high on top of Pyramid of the Sun and stared at the sky and the whole shining valley of Mexico and ring of mountains and intelligent little Indian boys climbing all the way up to us to sell Aztec images—Gregory surpassing the scene by trading his Harvard belt for all they had). Then all rode by car north 5 days thru great mountains and valleys and deserts and half of U.S. to New York and arrived last week. Viking printing Jack, as well as Grove in *Evergreen Review*, a novelette called *Subterraneans*. I saw W. C. Williams for long 3 hour talk last week and will return to read him Jack, Philip and Corso and Snyder and Lorca's ode to Walt Whitman—he says he don't remember it. He asked about you, said it was alright to use those sketches I sent you in *BMR* asked also how you read, wanted a description, I tried imitating the terminal breathgulp, and articulation of separate words. Is Snyder's manuscript back with Whalen yet? I want to read him some, and also have opportunity of placing chunks of it with Grove *Evergreen Review* and also Laughlin. If you need any agenting (poetry) done send me manuscript and I'll pass them along too. Send me some poems to read anyway. I've written a little but nothing revised and typed so later. [...]

Love as ever

Allen

[Ginsberg was always eager to meet other poets whether famous or obscure. This is a good example of his attempt to visit one of America's most famous poets.]

Allen Ginsberg [Paterson, NJ] to e. e. cummings [New York, NY]
December 20, 1956

Dear Mr. Cummings:

Came to your door, you were out, am writing, will be in NY for a month, then leave for Europe with 2 other poets, Jack Kerouac and Gregory Corso. Came from San Francisco where we held big crazy drunken poetry readings. I sent you my book, *Howl*, from there, to 8 Patchin Place, did you get it, did you read it? Have manuscript of Corso, Kerouac, Snyder (25 year old Zen hip young cocksman who lives, with a sweet mind, in Kyoto monastery translating the Zen Lunatic poets) and other SF recent poets, to read to you, a few poems, write me a postcard, I'd like to come by.

Sincerely,

Allen Ginsberg

[P.S.] Rexroth gave me your address, said you never read your mail anyway so that's why I knocked on door before.

[As they had feared, U.S. customs officials seized the second printing of Howl *as it was coming into the country from the British printer. Ginsberg was visiting Burroughs in North Africa at the time and wrote to his publisher and friend, Lawrence Ferlinghetti.]*

Allen Ginsberg [Tangier, Morocco] to Lawrence Ferlinghetti
[San Francisco, CA] April 3, 1957

Dear Larry:

Received your letter of March 27 and was surprised by news of Customs seizure. [. . .] Offhand I don't know what to say about MacPhee.[34] I don't know what the laws are and what rights I got. Is it possible to get them in at New York P.O. and have them shipped on to you under other label or address? Transshipped from NY that is? Is it also possible to have any copies sent to me here from England? I suppose the publicity will be good I suppose — I have been

---

34 Chester MacPhee. San Francisco Collector of Customs.

here with Jack, Peter and Bill Burroughs all hung-up on private life and Bill's mad personality and writings and on digging the Arab quarter and taking majoun (hashish candy) and opium and drinking hot sweet delicious mint tea in Rembrandt dark cafés and long walks in lucid Mediterranean coast green grassy brilliant light North Africa that I haven't written any letters (this is the second in 2 weeks) or thought much about anything. I'll write to Grove to Don Allen and let him know, and he'll tell the lady from Time-Life. If you can mimeograph a letter and get some kind of statement from W. C. Williams, [Louise] Bogan, [Richard] Eberhart and send it around to magazines might get some publicity that way. Also let Harvey Breit at *NY Times* know for sure definitely—he'd probably run a story maybe. My brother is a lawyer and has recently done some research on the subject, I'll write him to get in touch with you and provide any legal aid—if any is useful from him in New York. I guess this puts you up shits creek financially. I didn't think it would really happen. I didn't know it was costing you 200$ for reprint, I thought it was $80.00 each extra thousand. Sorry I am not there, we might talk and figure up some way for a U.S. edition, I guess that would be expensive tho. Be sure let the *Life* people in SF know about situation, they might include it in story. The woman in NY is Rosalind Constable c/o Time-Life, Rockefeller Center. She is very simpatico and would immediately call it to attention of Peter Bunzell who is (I heard) writing up the story for *Life* in NY. Send story too to *Village Voice*, they've been digging the scene. By the way I heard there was a lukewarm review in *Partisan Review*, could you send it to me? Might let them know, too, as they took a poem of mine for later. I guess the best way publicity wise is prepare some sort of outraged and idiotic but dignified statement, quoting the Customs man, and Eberhart's article and Williams, and *Nation* review, mimeograph it up and send it out as a sort of manifesto publishable by magazines and/or news release. Send one to Lu Carr at United Press, too. If this is worthwhile. Also write, maybe, [Randall] Jarrell, at Library of Congress and see if you can get his official intercession. I imagine these Customs people have to obey orders of their superiors; and that superiors in Washington, D.C., might be informed and requested to intercede by some official in Library of Congress. Maybe I'll write my congressmen—is there a friendly congressman in SF? This might be more rapid than a lawsuit. Copyright it under City Lights name—only thing is, if you ever make your money back and make some profit from all your trouble, and we go into a 4th or 17th edition, we divvy the loot. I don't think Grove book will knock out sales. They'll probably carry note about the full book. Send me clippings of reviews—I haven't got anything besides the *Nation*, if anything comes through; also any further news of the Cellar[35] etc. sounds charming. Everybody must be having a ball. How's Duncan. Regards to DuPeru, etc. *Ark III* out yet? Send one? I must say am more depressed than pleased, disgusted than pleased, about Customs shot, amusing as it is—the world is such a bottomless hole of boredom and poverty and paranoiac politics and diseased rags here *Howl* seems like a drop in the bucket-void and literary furor illusory—seems like it's happening in otherland—outside me, nothing to do with me or anything. Jack has a room I move into next week, full of light on a hill a few blocks above the beach from whence I'm writing now, can look over the veranda redstone tile, huge patio, over the harbor, over the bay, across the very sunlit straights and see the blue coast of Spain and ancient parapets of Europe I haven't been to yet, Gibraltar small and faraway but there in brilliant blue water, and a huge clear solid cloudless blue sky—I never saw such serene light as this, big classical Mediterranean beauty-light over a small world. I'll write Senor MacPhee myself, ask him to let my copies go, big serious poignant sad letter.

Write me and I'll answer, let me know how things go, if there's anything you want me to do let me know and send along any clippings if you can. These aerogrammes are only 10¢ postage if there are no enclosures.

Thank Kenneth [Rexroth] for efforts and say I hope he enjoys the scene—it is pretty funny, almost a set-up, I imagine they can't bug us forever, and will have to give in. Let me know what the law is.

Rock and Roll on all the jukeboxes here, just had a rock and roll riot at the moviehouse here a few weeks ago, and in fact before I left NY me and Peter picked up on the historic stageshow at the Paramount. I brought a few Little Richard and Fats Domino records here in fact.

Only interesting person here besides Burroughs is Jane Bowles whom I have only met with once.

As ever,

Allen Grebsnig

Allen Ginsberg [Tangier, Morocco] to Robert LaVigne [Spokane, WA] June 8, 1957

Dear Bob:

Received letters, and drawings. The brushwork with the flower I thought beautiful and in some ways better than the others, though the head with moon

---

35 The Cellar. Ferlinghetti and Rexroth did a series of poetry readings to jazz at this North Beach nightclub.

and star in eye looks like the product of much previous doodling and thought. I like the poetic tricks in the faces (do you know Cocteau's double faces of Marais?) but I don't like the faces themselves—though that has nothing to do with the line—I guess you mean the faces to be somewhat imaginary sylphlike stylizations but I showed one to Burroughs and his immediate comment reflected my own earlier unspoken noticing—"Gawd," he said "who the fuck is that effeminate asshole (the imaginary poet you drew)—it looks like some Greenwich Village fairy xmas postcard!" The actual postcard Orpheus was supposed to [be] funny, but was the chap with the moon in mouth supposed to be so faint (washed out looking?). All these unobtainable agricultural beauties must be driving your sex-mythologized imagination off its rocker. Are there no tough angels in Spokane? Well soon I will be seeing El Greco's stylized fairy Christs in Toledo so I've no right to complain.

There is a painter here Francis Bacon, I must have mentioned, just met him the last few weeks, he's very good, I'd seen a few (only 3) pictures by him in NY and SF—in Museum of Modern Art, what looks like gorilla in black tuxedo with his head chopped off over the mouth sitting under a deathly black umbrella, with a bunch of Rembrandt butcher cadaver cows hanging around him. He's friend of Bowles and we see him every other day on street and stop for coffee or tour bars. Very strange nature, looks like 35 or so, rather fat boy but tough, but he's actually 47 with his English sneakers and levis and curly red hair —rather spoiled tragic face like Thomas, D. [Dylan]—and quite a sport. A good cook and has worked around, didn't start painting till thirty and now the best painter in England I think, and says his reputation is a lot of chic shit and will decline and he don't give a shit, he's a gambler, won 4000$ at Monte Carlo, spent it all in a summer ten years ago, villa, autos, champagne, likes to be whipped and had six year affair with Peter Lacey an ex-RAF cocktail pianist in a large western empty chic bar here—anyway, a very serious painter, has a funny approach. Doesn't dig abstraction, thinks DeKooning the great man in U.S. for his attempt to plant an image on the canvas busting thru abstract smash of paint—his approach to painting is gamblers, says he is waiting for some way to paint a picture of someone, but not representation, psychic representation, the eye and a nose and the mouth, all formed somehow on the canvas, by accident, then the trap shuts on him, and by an accident of sudden brushstroke inspiration and slip of arm the eye takes on inconceivable painterly and poetic magic—not poetry he's after, but some dangerous game with the canvas where by patience and long work and wild splashing of canvas painting a face all of a sudden some spontaneous brushstroke gesture will make it, a great image...and is so hung up on the expressionists, Soutine, and Van Gogh,—in fact finished a series of seven pictures modeled on a Van Gogh, showing him walking down the road, the landscape looking upside down, Van Gogh in different ghostly slumping positions on the road with a big shadow hat. Got drunk here and hurt his arm, and so not painted here yet but will stay a year or so. Spends money like child and enjoys "gilded gutter" and is really interesting form of man—said he enjoyed, gambling, knowledge zenlike that he was making it, so in a half hour piled up winnings, and watched the spirit leave him and exhilarated equally by reverse of fortune and watching the whole pile fade and flow back where it came from—"life is a lie."...Burroughs prose much the same, pure free association of visual images, a sort of dangerous bullfight with the mind, whereby he places himself in acute psychic danger of uncovering some secret which will destroy him—of course this not really exaggerated—dredging up unpublishable mad routines about talking assholes, a whole section of the book dedicated to recurrent image of the hardon and spurt come when the hanged man has his neck snapped (a physiological fact) even finally vast paranoiac theories of Agents and psychic Senders taking over the world in bureaucratic conspiracies located in Interzone, with Lee (Burroughs) the Agent and Author, the great Factualist, witnessing and killing assassins and being followed.

I got your letters and read them but haven't time much to sit down think and answer because I am so swamped with work other than my own, cleaning up remnants of correspondence via publishing etc. and working with Bill on his manuscript and mediating between him and Peter who are somewhat antipathetic and trying to read the Koran and Melville and dig the scene here and at the same time have time to sit and think—so far very little. Every time I have free time I have the specter of letters to answer and so it takes me a long time to get around—I'm sorry if I try you by being so silent, I'm not being spooky I just am screwed up—I thought Europe would mean leisure and I've been hung up on backlog details since been here. Not written one good word except something like this letter and don't know where I'm going writing.

We leave here, Peter and I, in a day, tomorrow morning, to train thru Spain, Seville, cathedrals and first Europe town, then Cordoba the great Mosque, and then the Alhambra at Grenada, then Toledo, El Grecos, then Madrid and the Prado, Bosches, and then up north to Riviera France, Marseilles and Aix en Provence Cézanne country, then to Venice—should arrive in Venice to stay with friend Ansen there in a month or less, be on the road continually till then. I've been sick, some kind of liver or stomach trouble on and off but that seems gone so I'm ready to travel and work on Burroughs manuscript is temporarily ended.

Short letter, rare, from Corso, complaining he's starving in Paris, he took trip to Nice, saw Miro show, saw Picasso and yelled at him in French "I'm starving I'm starving" and got in garbled conversation, was dragged away, went back thru Barcelona to Paris and waved a pistol in an existentialist cave cafe and got took to jail for drunk and let out next morn. Sounds like he's having wild trip what? Says he finally sent his book to Ferlinghetti. IF you have drawings, one or a series, you think publishable why not send letter to Don Allen, *Evergreen Review*, and describe them and find out if he can use any, I told him about you but he hasn't seen more than a few drawings, say I told you to try him, he might pay a little.

New poetry magazine from one John Wieners, Boston, should be the great one, he's trying to draw all threads together and is good poet himself, sort of an east coast Creeley-Olson axis but more humane digs Williams and Kerouac, and Gregory. Write him subscribe if you have loot or tell him you have none and ask for free copy—*MEASURE* magazine.

Glad you wrote Peter he pleased with your letter—the one you wrote him seemed more intelligible and real than mine in fact. Tho you may prefer your less simple expressions.

This my last day here, it's raining, company coming over in an hour signing off. I'll write you from new address when I get to Venice where there are many a great Bellini too, I hear.

Love, as ever,

Allen

[*When Ferlinghetti decided to have* Howl and Other Poems *printed in the United States, the Department of Customs dropped their case against the book. However, it wasn't the end of the problem. On June 3, 1957, two plainclothes policemen purchased copies of* Howl *and a little magazine called* The Miscellaneous Man. *Then they arrested Ferlinghetti and the bookstore manager, Shig Murao. Both men were charged with publishing and selling obscene material.*]

Allen Ginsberg [Tangier, Morocco] to Lawrence Ferlinghetti [San Francisco, CA] June 10, 1957

Dear Larry:

Received your June 4 letter today, with clipping. I guess this is more serious than the customs seizure since you can lose real money on this deal if they find you guilty. What does it look like? I guess with ACLU should be possible to beat

—except this is local law—does that give police complete discretion to decide what's obscene? If so that may make it difficult.

Presumably a matter of local politics—therefore can anything be done to call off police through politicians at City Hall thru State College thru Poetry Center thru Witt-Diamant? If it is a matter of purely interpretive local law and juvenile bureau, perhaps somebody at Berkeley and State College know some-body at City Hall that can call a halt. But arrest and formal charges have been filed already, so I guess open showdown is inevitable.

I remember your speaking of troubles with local police on Henry Miller—and not being able to beat the cops on that—is it possible also in this case? It was all funny before but could be very difficult, for you, you actually stand to risk so much, money. In any case if you get fined I'll try to help raise loot to pay it—you've put yourself out financially very far already.

Had awful fantasy of being in SF and putting on big reading sponsored by State College at museum and inviting cops and ending in big riot scene. I wish I were there; there could really, we could really have a ball, and win out in the end inevitably.

There seems to be good ground for expecting to win out—but I haven't seen the *Miscellaneous Man*—if you can convince them my book is "Art" will you get hooked on M.M.? I wonder if that will prove a stumbling block—you didn't seem to think much of the M.M. story when you mentioned it sometime back. Does it make things harder or more confused with two separate issues to deal with?

Who or what is behind all this attention? It appears like Customs were burned up when they had to let go and someone must have called juvenile police from customs, and asked them to take up and carry the ball from there.

Well these are just vague ramblings, I don't know the situation, you must have chewed it all over already.

One thing occurs to me—re *Evergreen Review*. They're carrying *Howl* complete and are due out soon if not now. Will they get carried in SF bookstores? Will you be able to carry them (Are you still selling *Howl* from the store)? And if Grove can't distribute *Evergreen* in SF for their special SF issue, Grove will be in a hell of a spot and the police are likely to have the whole poetry population of SF personally with all their mothers and aunts up in outraged arms. Well I guess the more the merrier. Really it's a ridiculous mess. Have you got in touch with Grove? Or maybe they can just slip thru unnoticed and not ask for trouble. Too bad Gregory Corso is not there to make an anonymous phone call to the juvenile authorities tipping them off that Paul Elder is carrying same obscenity in *Evergreen*—infiltrating thru every channel—by the way is Elder selling *Howl* or any other store in town—and what are they doing about it—pulling their necks back in or continuing to sell? I'm really sorry I'm not there to take part in this latest development. I never thought I'd want to read Howl again but it would be a pleasure under these circumstances. It might give it a reality as "social protest" I always feared was lacking without armed bands of outraged Gestapo. Real solid prophetic lines about being dragged off the stage waving genitals and manuscript, biting detectives in the neck etc....I wonder by the way if the communist propaganda in America will further confuse the issue, the police, the judges and even ACLU. I really had some such situation as this in mind when I put them in, sort of deliberately saying I am a communist to see what would happen...burning bridges (not Harry) you might say. Well if they do send you to jail I'll make haste to return to SF and wage war in person, join you in next cell. Poor Shig, after his motorcycle bust up to get busted on this kind of bum rap...give him my thanks and apologies...I hope it was not grim. Strange to see his name in the paper.

I don't know what to suggest, I guess you already got testimonials from WCW and *Poetry*, etc., judging from the article you sent me. Are local newspapers being sympathetic? I have a friend on the *Oakland Tribune,* named Jim Fitzpatrick, who is quite literate...might try calling him for some kind of local pressure publicity—give him a statement or something. Did Harvey Breit carry anything on the original customs seizure? He ought to be informed about this, I guess he'd write something and you might get in further angles there about what is Grove *Evergreen* going to do—and the fact that you've put out the Levertov and Ponsot and are expecting Gregory next. As far as testimonials and official types, I imagine Jarrell might be rung in and make himself useful. He don't approve of the dirty words in my book so I understand, but he is Poetry Consultant at Library of Congress and gets paid for it and he has visited your store and he did dig it as cultural center and he is interested in Gregory publication, so he should be conscience bound to make some kind of official Federal statement for you to use in court. With testimony from someone with his <u>official</u> title and ACLU backing you would have strong case, even if the judge had never heard of WCW Patchen Jarrell or Rexroth or anyone since Ambrose Bierce. I'll write him; it might be good for you to get in touch with him and tell him what you need. Has *Village Voice*, who knew me and Greg in NY, followed the case?

Who else—man I got the greatest—get Josephine Miles—no one can suspect her of any but most respectable judgment—to court in person—star witness. Well I'm rambling. [...]

Would like to see the Hollander review in *Partisan*. Any other reviews I don't know of, of interest? [. . .]

Have written very little but will sooner or later. When I have a manuscript I will send it to you to look at and publish if you can and want to; I won't go whoring around NY publishers I promise. The trouble is, what long writing I've done is more or less unpublishable lately—some autobiographical sexual history—send us all to jail. Burroughs' influence has been to open up even more extreme areas and much more questionable taste, as far as subject... God knows where I'll end up, elegies in the asshole of some Istanbul hermaphrodite, odes to cocaine (the connection is finally coming tonite—had hash and tea and opium here but no coke till now)—anyway, I don't know what next—talking with Francis Bacon, a painter, a good one, interesting man, sort of an adventurer in regards to his painting (and won and lost 4000 at Monte Carlo and didn't paint till he was 30) (and can always work as a cook)—and get idea of art as a funny sort of psychic gamble, an experiment with subjective areas and psychic material that can be dangerous personally—to say nothing of its publishability (its worth or its legal worth). This is some-what romanticized, but I guess it could be also literally true—if you stumbled on some de Sade like or saintly absolutism in your own nature—or sexual compulsion or whatever—in the act of writing. Something like that happens on small scale with Howl which gives it power. Would like to develop that, tho it perhaps means sacrificing any foreseeable audience—which I see Burroughs has done—and to some extent Kerouac in his solitary vigils over notebook.

Expected to leave here today, so would have missed your letter, but Peter came down with the grippe, so remaining till tomorrow or perhaps another day—then off thru Spain several weeks to Venice and settle there awhile. I'll be out of touch more or less till I get to Venice. [. . .]

I'd go to Paris but I have only 150 dollars and have to hole up with friend in Venice cheap. Paris costs even more in summer. Don't know where the next loot comes from, but I guess things will work out alright, whatever happens. All mail previously sent to me here or Paterson will ultimately be forwarded to Venice—Burroughs remaining behind here a month more and will take care of that. I guess I'll receive the books (25 copies) in Venice. Gave [Paul] Bowles my last copy. He's been very nice, dug the poetry, still follows little magazines where he can get them. Add him perhaps to your list—next time you send out a list of works. He isn't sinister; his life is safe and rather comfortable; but I suspect he would like to make it on wilder greater level. He reads WCW and would maybe order *Kora in Hell*.

Will you ever be in position to print some pocket prose? The Burroughs manuscript is pretty great. It's more than the law will allow—as he commented, he'll probably wind up with the distinction of being banned not only U.S. but also France. Sooner or later we'll start circulating the publishable parts in U.S. IF you're interested I'll send you a block of it to look at when we have copies. I sure would like to see a reading of this at 6 Gallery, Kerouac might do it if the police were barred. I don't think any court anywhere would uphold Burroughs. I can see ACLU reeling back aghast and audience staring in horror —and Burroughs leaning back laughing with a lushed up hashhead mad intelligent gleam in his Shakespearean eye. [...]

As ever,

Allen

[*Jack Kerouac was the person who most influenced Ginsberg's writing style. For a while even Allen's letters to Jack took on the more spontaneous travel narrative of* On the Road. *This letter is typical of that form before telephones became their favored method of communication and put an end to the great era of letter-writing.*]

Allen Ginsberg [Venice, Italy] to Jack Kerouac [n.p.] August 13, 1957

Dear Jack:

Got your letter today, of Garver's death, and the other letters before, and answering with big long letter now, I've been putting off, it's such a big terrible letter, telling all about Europe, I'm sorry I waited so long, but thought every day and couldn't sit at typewriter for fear of not writing something beautiful. But Bill is only in Copenhagen, after London, after Spain, waiting what to do, we (me and Peter) in Venice with Alan Ansen, Gregory (we hear from oftener) in Paris still (with big apartment someone loaned him and broke and hungry we sent him 5 dollars but he ate with Genet and met Brandos), and now we are all ready to take off. It costs only 20 and go to Greece and further Istanbul, before even seeing Paris—but all our plans are not fixed, so when you are ready in October after NY where else is there to go, come join us in Istanbul or Paris or live free at Ansen's (pay for your own food rent free and lots free liquor) in Venice—we been here month and half now.

Peter and I left Alan [Ansen] and Bill [Burroughs] in Tangier and took off on our own with knapsacks into Spain, crossed straits, dolphins and rainbows at prow of ferry, wandered around in heart at Algeciras—June 5 [*sic*: June 11] it was—digging first European Spanish sidewalk cafés and gay mall life with no negroes and Tangerians and how cheap, 10 peso meals, cheaper than Tangier; we bought a 15 dollar railway ticket that gave us 4000 miles all over Spain reduced rate, and stood on long lines in shacks by ferries and got 2nd class train to Grenada, because I'd read about it in grammar school, gardens of Spain, and rode through Lorca sunset thru mountains and red sunset between castle hills without dragons, carrying T with us, enough for a few highs here and there, got to Grenada the same night, south of Spain, Andalusia they call it, especially because Peter wanted to dig gypsy caves there—big Paterson town with main streets and bars filled with cheap food, 5 peso fish soups, Peter got sick, something stomach. First thing a big cathedral so we went inside and stood under a vast dream machinery marble pillared arch that looked six blocks long, huge marble floor, and wandered around looking for St. Francis painted by El Greco, supposed to be there, he's looking up to Heaven with long glistening eyes and long fingers hands crossed over grey breast, when we found it. Afternoon Peter slept and I took long walk up hills to castle on top of town, Alhambra, at nighttime, in the trees I couldn't see where I was going, huge battlements and endless castles and walls I couldn't get into, finally came to great Arabic looking gate and got on 20 foot wide parapet and looked over city and down on big gypsy hill, Lorca learned singing there, came down and walked into Sacramonte gypsy hill, big carloads of tourists rolling up road and many caves hung with copper frying pans and whitewashed roofs and neat doors entrances, pretty chairs with 20 German tourists sitting in circle and fifty mad gypsies singing and clapping hands and dancing Flamenco style (sound like Mar Chica but faster and weirder and more Jewish)—costs 50 pesetas to get in so I hang around door—beautiful thin gypsy came up to me in black silk pants and said he danced in Radio City Music Hall. I told him I had no loot so he put his 2 fingers and pulled down sides of his nose said "Sec," meaning dry, meaning broke, so that's the sign, the Zen sign in Spain, if you want to stop shoeshine boys from berating you. Great hill we both went there next day and drank wine silent in cheap cave bar where off duty entertainers go and young boys dressed like gypsies come in and make play dances like doodling while elders guggle wine, straw from bottle right down into throat, steady stream. Then finally made the Alhambra, they charge, but it's free Sunday, huge six layer castles and gardens and finally the best part near where old wry cranky Washington Irving lived, an imaginary Arabian dream palace full of rooms of Arabesques, crawling up the walls and all over the ceiling, huge rooms every square inch filled with late Spenglerian magian three dimensional gold filled painted delicacies, every square foot changing as eye sweeps up to the starry domed ceiling blue, sat down and got high on purest eyeball kicks abstract—and while I'm writing sad Ansen still in his living room beslippered and afternooned in pajamas is putting on old 78 records of melancholy Wagner—Peter sick then, so I wander around the gardens and climb ramparts and overlook the gypsy hill and can see clay paths honeycomb it for centuries and gypsies and bicycles and mules winding up and down and still cock crows from hidden bottom of valley between and autos horns in the city below too, so I'm sitting in this vast quiet ancient garden where they used to have harems and smoke tea until exactly the year 1492 in fact when the Arabs was finally driven out of Spain. Then we took train again because Ansen wanted us to, see Seville, I always read about the big cathedral there—meanwhile getting more hipped on seeing every city everywhere—hit Seville it's hot they got high narrow streets with white awnings spread from roof to roof over alleys so you can walk in cool, and a big black cathedral inside, and a huge tower we climbed and looked over Munich spires and church tops and Europe awnings and weathervanes and Dr. Mabuse. By this time we're getting tired and money going too fast, we walk by rivers I've forgot, and arrive in taxis at museums which're closed and sit exhausted in parks and walk cross-town by towers and Peter digging pretty girls but we don't know what to do, so we go to Cordova, next stop and walk there late at night disgusted with heavy knapsacks and get another cheap nice room on narrow windey street, and next day go dig the Great Mosque, huge labyrinth inside of colored arches and more roomfuls of arabesques and a big church choir for Christ set up in the middle—and this was the biggest place in the world once too—great university center for remembrances of Aristotle and Jewish and Persian mystics holding hands and reviving classical learning and millions of people living in town—so down street to long quiet Guadalquivir River, and we sit down on embankment exhausted and look at washerwomen across stream and Roman bridge 2000 years old still sitting there motionless— only the trees have risen and fallen and millions of crops of grass waved and disappeared since Arabs sat by Guadalquivir, and later said a plaque, Cervantes rode by and stayed over and mentioned next door house where Don Quixote killed a monster—and so we crossed the bridge to a big nameless tower—ugh it's too much to go through in detail—big clean tower peopled by state curators who took us around and said it was a million years old and Góngora the poet lived here like Williams on Passaic so had written big sad poem about how he always remembered the Guadalquivir washing dirty Spain, they got a stanza of it on a plaque by the river by the older Roman mud stone bridge, I sat down and cried and copied it down on postcard and sent it to Williams who loves Góngora, who had a big high domed brow and probably lived with candles and stepped in mud and horseshit every time he walked across centuries old bridge at night to the broken down mosque (where Ansen says he's buried). But I sat by the river tired for two whole hours watching the water float by and old Spanish washer ladies drubbing in it. The Moon! the police! Klaxons across the Atlantic! Phaeton's chariot falling in the sky! Time shifting with a million insects! Thousands of winters! Trees rising and falling on the riverbank! Old trees and new trees invisible and visible! The big muddy river in the sun! O Lorca's góngora'd guadalquivir! Big vision on the riverbank by the million arched mosque, ancient Europe. Ran on, ran on, took train to Madrid all night, arrived morning Peter sick, I walk around with him hours looking for cheap room up and down old streets and leaky arches and tilted slums through the big Puerta Del Sol Times Square mobstreet full of buses and subways and artistical bookstores full of Spanish translations of Eliot and Picasso books, finally Peter sits in cafe while I explore RR station furnished room areas and we get one for 50 pesetas for 2 nothing cheaper, we're disappointed, money going, we collapse in bed and I wake up and walk at nite, and next day run out in morning and run into Prado vast museum, halls of big glorious nowhere Rubens and Goobins, I run thru all the hundred halls digging everything as I pass out of corner of eye till all of a sudden I see the great magic picture of the West, I never dreamed of it before, none other than Brother Beatifical Angelical (Fra Angelico) his Annunciation—a huge picture made out of clearest pearly ivory white and shining green and delicious red full of delicate hand touches of long gowns and lines and kneeling angels and rosy virgin cool, and god's gold small hands ushering out radiances of long golden streams of light from the upper left corner, thru which rides a dove with a halo down to the virgin kneeling and bowing down with her robes settling round her like in a dream underwater; all brilliant pearl surface colors outlined with fine exquisite sweepy lines and loose folds in angels robe showing turquoise angel-petticoat beneath; and great heavy gold wings; all against a bright new background of gold leaf on which Angelico's made thousands of little etched lines with a stylus or pin, arabesques and designs inside the haloes, the design formulas of magical graces in the wings and halos, you got to stick your nose an inch away to even notice the detail all over, never see it in picture books at all—and on the left side off the porch which has high thin imaginary columns and starry blueblue ceiling, a shot of paradise and Adam and Eve simultaneously being ushered weeping out of the garden of Eden, floating along on a carpet of violet buds and greeney grass and angel over them with gold leaf sword—and on the bottom of that, along the border of the bottom, a series of magic box solid gay red and blue and green paintings in miniature of other scenes from life of Virgin: —the only Angelico in Spain. Guard saw me digging it and nodded and said it was the best picture in the whole Prado. I never saw such a beautiful painting, and immediately got all lit up about Angelico and hunted thru bookstores to see more reproductions, and learned thereby there were whole collections of them in Italy, Florence (where we went later, now, but later). Meanwhile (because at that instant I got Europe hungry and museum hungry and realized all the treasuries of Europe all over, in Italy and Spain and Moscow and Paris, all the vast collections of infinite pictures) Peter meanwhile broke out through bad sandwiches or something with hideous blotches of hives red and purple and ankles and knees swoll, swoll, and I'm running around, how're we going to dig Madrid while he's sick, we get doctor who says it's something he et, so we live near market and Dr. prescribes cheap yoghurt and fresh fruit and zweiback —so I buy great baskets of strawberries (so cheap) and melons and pears and peaches and apples and bananas and tomatoes and grapes and ah cherries and juices and zweiback and yoghurt—which we eat for a week (except I sneak in some Spanish salami which gives Peter a relapse,) meanwhile we got this room in Madrid and privacy and we occasionally ball and dig each other and are depressed and coo out window on street naked, a big hailstorm comes up too, I try Prado high next day with Peter and don't dig Angelico this time but stumble on the endless novels in the canvasses of Breughel—Triumph of Death—a million skeletons emerging from drum beats and bells tolled by skeleton and mountain opening and skeletons legions marching out and attacking everybody, the king fainting and ascetic in one corner, being upheld by skeleton with hourglass, poet in right-hand corner lutanisting his girlfriend, and behind her a skeleton playing violin, and behind him a table full of picnic hams and apples and a fine lady screaming while a skeleton in waiters cap brings up a silver plate with a picnic skull on it, and a cowardly looking jester crawling under the table, and Hal Chase lothario with sword and buckler turns around on the horde of advancing skeletons and draws his sword with his eyeballs popping and hair on end and in the middle an old lady fainted and her baby on her bosom yelling and a lean and hungry black long skeletal dog beginning to sniff at baby, and these maybe 10 details of a huge picture full of a thousand details, like a great poem, an epic, the Triumph of Death, Breughel, way off on a mountain a couple of skeletons tolling huge bells, and great crowds of people being herded into a black mine hole by an army of skeletons, and a big cart drawn by skeleton horse and driven by skeleton on riders seat drags a huge wagonload of skulls; and millions of skeleton armies more waiting behind a hole in the mountain to emerge and join the battle, numberless skeletons, and a lone skeleton up on a hill with a big sword whacking off the head of a man kneeling blindfold praying, and a skeleton over the mine hole banging away ecstatic at huge tom toms even a guy lying half asleep or sick in a nightmare right on the ground and a big mean skeleton bending over him looking in the eye and cutting his throat (like the other day hitchhiking out of Perugia we came thru a small town and passed by butcher and we stopped and saw a cow lying down on concrete garagelike floor and man bending over it with a knife, hacking away at its live throat, and he gave one cut, and the cow groaned and lifted up its ass and bled and fell, but only a cut an inch deep, and the whole neck's a foot thick, so he bends down, like a small razor, and sliced another inch—he didn't have the right knife, or the right business, or the right world, the cow lifted up, he gave another scratch, getting into the tendon by now, but nowhere near the death center, the cow snuffled and vomited blood and bled from nose like bull in bullring)—and I confess I shame saw another fucking bullfight in Madrid, with Peter—not again—(and kept hacking away at the huge tender neck, the cow still conscious and whacking up with ass and hind legs, tho bound down, every time, an old black Italian lady passed by stopped and cried out, *"Niente de compassione"* and shook her head and looked us in our eye to see if we were evil too, we all shook our heads—and it kept on for 10 minutes the man attacking the cow and the cow protesting and neck slowly being cut thru till finally it snapped, the cow stopped struggling, wriggled and bleed and fell astill suddenly, lump.)—and a dank brick well like behind factories at Paterson with 3 skeletons on the edge shoving a screaming knock-kneed warrior in, and a whole shipload of white robed skeletons blowing trumpets and supervising the battle, like the communists suddenly rose up in the factories and took over the means of production and killed everybody and turned into skeletons, and way back miles in the distance a big sea, with human ships burning and sinking, and castles in the water and skeletons overwhelming them on the towers and a thatch house surrounded by skeletons on the shore like cannibals in Africa, getting the men inside, and even the very trees in the landscape being burned and hacked down by lonely skeletons who got nothing else assigned to do and some vultures wheeling around in the sky faraway. And Bill was in Madrid last month he said, and didn't even set foot in Prado alas. The thing is in Breughel you have to see the actual canvasses (or a life-size perfect photo which doesn't yet exist) to see all the details, with your eye sometimes an inch away to see way in the distance a minute skeleton of a horse dragging a distinct but microscopic perfect brushwork wagon of skulls, that's just as great and important in the picture as a big detail you can see from 20 feet away, a mountain or tree. Same goes for the other master Bosch whose great Garden of Delights we saw, in fact we were high, and we got up close and spent hours in Madrid digging just those two pictures — and the whole rest of Prado — El Greco rooms, and Poussin whom I dug for 3 dimension as he was loved by Cezanne — and the Great Deaf Man's Room of Goya — walls of his old age rich lonely house he painted deaf for himself — big black fantastic Saturns eating own beautiful boy, battles of ugly giants, campfuls of negro witches — his big secret madman's pictures, transported, huge 20 foot walls. So we spent several days digging all that at Prado and endless more, Botticelli and Roger Vander Weyden and Velasquez and other Dutch and Spanish dullards and French refinements we got a good education now. But there was only one Breughel in Prado. But we read there's seven huge great Breughels nearby in Vienna, we go there in 2 weeks. But so we also took train out to Greco's Toledo for a day and walked up and down in and out and around city looking for magic spot of his View of Toledo, only we didn't have postcard picture of the picture, and couldn't find the spot, tho the scenery was great, and we walked miles on the other side of river around cliffs and walls of piled high Toledo, and asked people, but nobody knew where it was or even knew the picture — it's in NY — so came back to town — and saw in book he made up the scene — changed the composition of the town around to fit his sky I guess — we kept getting mixed up where the church was in relation to river and bridge, but he mixed them up on purpose — but I took a picture of us overlooking moody sky Toledo and we also saw all his great paintings there. Including big orgasmic explosion of a last judgment The Burial of Count Orgaz. I took long walks and double deck buses by big filmy fountains and wide Mexico City downtown Madrid streets and back to Porta del Sol old-time center and new hep center of town and looked up hip movie producer who introduced me to job hunting Lafferties and Crus working for construction companies but it was too many slow papers to fill out so we left next for train to Barcelona and rode up the Mediterranean coast by rocks and arrived and walked into Barcelona's Barrio Gothico, high dark stone tenements look like fortresses with alleys in between and up the Great Rambla, huge street for walking and benches cost a peseta to sit all day and look at flower sellers, and into Genet's Barrio Chino, swinging cheap slum, half gothic, half bombed out (Spanish Civil War, and my father'd written a poem then "When Bombs on

Barcelona Burst (1937) / I was 10 thousand miles away / but all the walls around me cracked / and fell apart in disarray"), whorehouses, little art restaurants a place like Valeska Gerts and expensive for old Babylonians and Giroux, and dark downstairs Rembrandtesque workingman's restaurants where we ate whole meals, great soups, for 8 pesetas only—got a hotel room like garret at Paris, high up, huge room with little window sunset came thru all orange and red on the sheets, went out but couldn't find any wild Genet life—so went to ancient old stained glass cathedrals, vast pillars and caves, and a museum Meyer Shapiro'd have dug, or did once, best collection Romanesque painting in world, now prepared to dig all primitive old colors and cartoons and christs and saints as depicted by mysterious ancient figures with paintbrushes in castles and monasteries, don't remember any great sexy piece there tho lots of half naked thin angular leering christs hanging on crosses and later sophisticated smooth virgins and mages. Wildest monument in Barcelona is a fantastic unfinished church by mad architect Antonio Gaudi, elder and inspirer of Dali and Picasso, started 1885 thereabout—only got four weird inter-connected towers full of holes like gingerbread castle, but huge skyscrapers, you can climb around on, filled with strange beastly stone carvings and already after 50 years so weirdly balanced it scares you way up inside especially as it's already cracking and huge windows held together only by lately acquired rusty pieces of wire and whole balconies crumbling with jagged cracks in soft stone—need 25 million dollars to finish it they said, and still had workmen banging away downstairs at another part of the church (Sagrada Familia) constructing another door— what we were on only a door, planned to be biggest church in world, down- stairs a mad plaster model looks like secret communist Kremlin RR station mosque instead of a church, but apparently all real at least they're building it— elsewhere in Barcelona a big children's park with strange name (Guell Park) he built, acres of gingerbread castles and strange balconies rising out of hills and flowerpots 10 feet high made out of rough stones cemented together with flowers (real) growing out top and big octopus-like soccer fields surrounded by thousand foot mosaic snake bench for mommas with baby carriages. Also we went up a cablecar up a mountain overlooking city to strange heavenly amuse- ment park with roller airplanes and sideshows and jukeboxes full of rock and visions of Harlem in penny arcade theatre miniature showboxes, and Arizona in the penny movies, movies of "Far West," and we walked past and looked in a big fascist silent radio station in the bushes guarded by police, but what we were doing there I dunno so we got bored and went away after staring at them in plate-glass window at huge apparatuses and dial machines and IBM switchboards—3 men needed a shave drinking coffee and playing ticktacktoe and an amusement park outside and twilight deepening over the city below in the fog and lights of yellow going on in the great boulevards and everybody getting the funicular train go home so it fell silent on the mountain and got dark. Mt. Tibidabo. And saw a strange silent boy with a beard, full black strong beard talking to an Austrian on streets of Barrio Cjine, just a glimpse. Spent another day goofing around, at huge paella meal, saw more painting museums, and at nite took off finally for the great border of France, bought ticket to Perpignan, and thought to hit there at midnight—train rolling along at nite approaching Pyrenees disappointing foothills.

Arrived at border town finally big excitement we still had pocketful of T but nobody at any borders searches Americans, didn't even look in knapsacks, and changed money at lousy rate of 350 having goofed totally and neglected to get Francs in Tangier—and rushed on new modern electric streamlined roomy French train to Perpignan, an hour ride ahead, for we knew (from poet Blackburn in Mallorca whom I'd contacted for info) that Perpignan center for fruit growing industry sends trucks all nite to Marseilles and Paris to hitch on. But when we'd arrived in Perpignan and walked a mile down dark quiet streets thru center of town to wholesale district it was dead night three and nobody around and big huge trucks asleep with no drivers, and cafe truck stop all folded up for nite, chairs piled up, no yelling mobs of electric lights all nite like we thought, so walked two blocks to park, unfolded sleep bags first time in Europe and lay down under high old trees to sleep on bench, and mosquitoes buzzed later, and dawn light began came, we pissed and walked 3 miles out in country, still no trucks, till about 5AM they started rolling thru, but nobody picked us up, we stood in front of old outskirts of town Raimu cafe, watched him open at morn and read paper and have coffee on outdoor table and stare at us, but not bugged, all the trucks roll past and no private cars but little Europe midget cars not big enuf for 3 people and 2 huge lousy knapsacks, so hiking lousy, in fact, inexistent, stood there till noon and maybe got a 10 km. ride and stood in another small town by a river and waited another 5 hours watching farmer's horse cart drag up huge wagon size casks to fill with water under a shady elm by well and roll out to water field, us drinking cheap fine milk and cakes and eating salami and bread and pastry and cheeses and fruit and water. Finally picked up and got to Beziere, a town mentioned by Pound as haunt of Provencal poets and Jongleours so stopped there and walked uphill to the town to look at church and arrived in middle of Dr. Mabuse funeral with tall pillars and tall black parishioners and a wild loud organ screeching against the stone and longhaired organist and the whole town full of old black ladies lined up around a coffin like in T.C. [*The Town and the City*] and a rose window shining down on the scene from faraway upstairs. A big plaza outside, a stone balcony and beyond panorama of intimate green valley all French and cultivated with shining rivers and microscopic mules and roads winding thru trees and ancient charms of country Provencal. Down again to Rue George Sand where we left knapsacks and another hot walk past RR station to outskirts and waited in dust on bad hitch spot, cars whiz by too fast, it's been all day and we only got 40 km, so we give up, money getting low, can't dawdle like that thru So. France, take train to Montpellier (realized we couldn't make it hitching) and arrive at nite midnite and go walking looking for food now beat with heat and sleepless tired and stumble on a big bookstore filled with French communists having an intellectual party, like old bupkis [*sic*: bumpkins], except also selling Mayakovski and Cocteau and Picasso—a cell leader looked like Frankel come up and began asking us who we were and we said artistes and got into argument about whether world existed to be communized or whether world didn't exist anyway, I said no. But they hold meetings and are evil mentalists but at least there they're free to have open meetings, it was amazing to see like shift back in time to U.S. 1934 near River St. Paterson when reds were only innocent bumpkins I thought. So we're just wandering around waiting for a train to Marseilles and run down streets and stairways to lower older part of town to university crowded district and the cathedral there, which somewhere I'd heard of, I turn alley and see a vast pillar 20 feet thick like a gothic tower going up high as eye can see at nite, and roof on top and another sister pillar, dream pillars, supporting porch of great cathedral—that's all I saw except walls and crooked streets all around, a glimpse and rushed back to RR and there was the same youth with black beard from Barcelona adjusting his great knapsack—heavy as iron, with fur on outside, I went over where he was and talked in Spanish and he looked up with big sweet eyes and talked back, about knapsack heavy, and led him to Peter (who also had big red beard) and he recognized him from Barcelona streets, so we all went across street to park (where earlier on bench Peter got in big incomprehensible conversation with drunk old crone in black) bench to hold hands and wait for train, and he (John by name) short built like iron angel, said he from Zurich and had walked six months across the Alps and down France all the way to Barcelona, working everywhere in farms and cities and reading Nietzsche and maybe was a painter—but we couldn't talk much, except for strange sudden love reasons dug each other, I didn't understand how he carried 120 pound knapsack, and totally alone, all over, had walked thru Italy and Austria and was then heading finally back home to parents in high mountain town in Alps, actually, Zermatt maybe not Zurich; after hour our train come and we exchange addresses, he should live in McCorkle shack I think, (Peter sleeping drowsing on bench). Time for train and he carries Peter's sack into station to wait there bid goodbye, in fact when we shake hands suddenly, as Peter puts arms round him, bashful, he suddenly kisses him on neck and to me the same farewell, a great sad bearded European youthtime stranger truelove comrade kiss, I felt great thrill of meeting face to face reality of heart again —and as train was pulling out he reappeared in our compartment, with strange trifle gift, a bag of grapes for thirst, tender and looked at us and said goodbye and disappeared with his huge knapsack. That's how we should all love each other.

Big hallucinated night full of train—(on the Riviera Cezanne Coast)

September 5. Never finished this—Leaving for Paris day after tomorrow and cleaning up desk—will pick up from there and tell you everything else we've done so you don't miss nothing of Europe.

Love

Allen

[*Once in Paris, Ginsberg settled down for a long residence and was finally able to get back to writing poetry. He played with some lines about his mother, which eventually became* Kaddish, *perhaps his greatest poem.*]

Allen Ginsberg [Paris, France] to Jack Kerouac [?] November 13, 1957

Dear Jack:

Gregory brought his letter over, I'll add a page and save stamps and reassure you, we are all still here, not bounded over Atlantic—reason I'm so still is I'm confronted with great backlog of unanswered letters, have just been sick in bed with Asia flu for 2 weeks, ago to now and been reading book on Apollinaire and learning more French. Suddenly I can read French a little better—not enough to read books, but enough to read poems I see quoted in books—I am all hung up on French poetry, I went into a big bookstore, saw French translations of whole plays by Mayakovsky, pamphlets of fine funny poems by Esenin, then the big bookshelves of XX century French bohemians, Max Jacob, Robert Desnos (a French girl said I looked like Desnos profile) Reverdy, Henri Pichette

—all their huge books, Fargue, Cendrars, etc., names, I never read them, but read a few by each, all personal and alive, Prevert, and all the funny surrealists, so I want to improve French and dig them, none translated, and all fine fellows, I can see from the pages of loose sprawled longlined scribblings they've published for 50 years here now—what sad treasuries for Grove or City Lights if anybody ever were able to have time and intelligence enough to organize and edit and transliterate them all, would be marvelous to read in U.S.—most of it almost unknown really. Anyway my French I happy to say, getting better so one day I'll be like R. [Richard] Howard with French books in my house in Paterson and be able maybe to enjoy them.

Gregory as you can see, he improved in Frisco, and he improved since, and now is even riper, and is like an Apollinaire, prolific and golden glories period for him, in his poverty too marvelously, how he gets along here hand to mouth, daily, begging and conning and wooing, but he writes daily marvelous poems like the enclosed—enough already for another huge book since last month's City Lights manuscript Gregory is in his golden inspired period, like in Mexico, but even more, and soberer solemner, calm genius every morning he wakes and types last nite's 2 or 3 pages of poems, bordering on strangeness, now he's even going further, will enter a classical phase soon and possibly construct structural poems and explore big forms, his genius showered with strangeness.

We are getting lots of great junk too, better than anything I ever had with Bill or Garver, so pure horse we sniff it, simply sniff, no ugly vaginal needles, and get as good almost a bang as a main line, but longer lasting and stronger in long run. Very cheap here too, and this around for Louvre visits.

Not yet explored Paris, just inches, still to make solemn visits to cemeteries Père Lachaise and visit Apollinaire's menhir (MENHIR) and Montparnasse to Baudelaire.

Granite surrounded by ivy.

I sat weeping in Cafe Select, once haunted by Gide and Picasso and well dresst Jacob, last week writing first lines of great formal elegy for my mother—

> "Farewell
> with long black shoe
> Farewell
> smoking corsets and ribs of steel
> farewell
> communist party and broken stocking
> O mother

Farewell
with six vaginas and eyes full of teeth and a long black
    beard around the vagina
O mother
farewell
grand piano ineptitude echoing three songs you know
with ancient lovers Clement Wood Max Bodenheim my
    father
farewell
with six black hairs on the won of your breast
with you sagging belly
with your fear of grandma crawling on the horizon
with your eyes of excuses
with your fingers of rotten mandolins
with your arms of fat Paterson porches
with your thighs of ineluctable politics
with your belly of strikes and smokestacks
with your chin of Trotsky
with your voice singing for the decayed overbroken   `
    workers
with your nose full of bad lay with your nose full of the
    smell of pickles of Newark
with your eyes
with your eyes of tears of Russia and America
with your eyes of tanks flamethrowers atom bombs and
    warplanes
with your eyes of false china
with your eyes of Czechoslovakia attacked by robots
with your eyes of America taking a Fall
O mother O mother
with your eyes of Ma Rainey dying in an ambulance
with your eyes of Aunt Elanor
with your eyes of Uncle Max
with your eyes of your mother in the movies
with your eyes of your failure at the piano
with your eyes being led away by policemen to ambulance
    in the Bronx

with your eyes of madness going to painting class in night
    school
with your eyes pissing in the park
with your eyes screaming in the bathroom
with your eyes being strapped down on the operating
    table
with your eyes with the pancreas removed
with your eyes of abortion
with your eyes of appendix operation
with your eyes of ovaries removed
with your eyes of womens operations
with your eyes of shock
with your eyes of lobotomy
with your eyes of stroke
with your eyes of divorce
with your eyes alone
with your eyes
with your eyes
with your death full of flowers
with your death of the golden window of sunlight…"

I write best when I weep, I wrote a lot of that weeping anyway, and get idea
for huge expandable form of such a poem, will finish later and make big elegy,
perhaps less repetition in parts, but I gotta get a rhythm up to cry.

Re Lafcadio: Good news, suddenly the long-lost father Orlovsky appeared
on scene, visited, promised $10 a week support family, talked gravely and digni-
fied with Laf, the crises in household still go on, but now not critical, no mad
deeds will be done, so it can wait Peter's return—we wrote you unrealizing
you were already out of NYC—meanwhile Joyce Glassman wrote us and pro-
posed she investigate with Donald Cook, so the situation's there in hand and
we got sensible fine letter from Laf, he has beard he says and will be great artist
of space and time and draws constantly and sent us a burning red face in crayon
of Laf-spaceman-mystic with eyeshields of red glasses.

Let me know when plays are ready. I think play down the Beat Generation
talk and let others do that, it's just an idea, don't let them maneuver you into
getting too hung up on slogans however good, let Holmes write up all that,
just as "S.F. Renaissance" is true, but nothing to make an issue of (for us). I

mean I've avoided generally talking in terms of SF as if it were an entity. You only get hung on publicity-NY-politics if you let them or be encouraged to beat BEAT drum—you have too much else to offer to be tied down to that and have to talk about that every time someone asks your opinion of weather —it'll only embarrass you (probably already has). Let Holmes handle that department. Next time someone asks you say it was just a phrase you tossed off one fine day and it means something but not everything. Tell them you got 6 vaginas.

Ron Loewinsohn wrote, and sent me one great poem, he's really finally got something wild he wrote, a short poem "The White Rhinoceros," good a Whalen good poem—this for later reference—he's the youngest active person of generation (and a half) younger than us—already he write me putting down *Howl* as a museum piece like Baudelaire but of now no use—his reactions be interesting—but in long run he's not sad and mad enough.

Peter on junk dreamed of a funeral all the taxicabs went to in Paris, one taxi had died.

Ansen on a surprise visit to Paris for a week arrives in 3 days.

Bill's manuscript [*Naked Lunch*] was read by Mason Hoffenberg who pronounced it the greatest greatest book he read of all time, Mason brought it to Olympia and assures me it'll be taken (Mason wrote a porno book for them [*Candy*] and knows them and is also an advisor) he is astounded by WSB and his reaction I gave great sigh of relief, I think everything'll be alright with the book, it'll be published here in toto intact. Meanwhile Bill sent me another 30 pages and says he has another hundred coming up with new final character like Grand Inquisitor who will wrap the whole book up in one unified theme and stream and interspace—time plot and fill in all lacunae and unify everything into perfect structure and delight, so.

I guess it will be published here then in the Spring. I wait to hear word this week and then will notify Bill. If. I think it'll work out they'll buy it tho terms are lousy, they only pay $600 per printing (i.e. if reprinted he gets another 600) but I'll try get a formal contract reserving all mag. rights for *Evergreen* to Bill etc. I have to contact [Sterling] Lord and get name of his Paris office and have them arrange legal details as I personally don't want to be responsible for another fuckup like Wyn. However with fugitive shady Olympia, the terms of publication seem bound to be disadvantageous and nothing much can be done, except the great main thing get book into print once for all. Perhaps I'm proceeding too nervously and in too much haste merely to get book in print irregardless of business hallucination dignities Bill deserves and might demand—what you think? I don't know, I be relieved to see it actually accepted. But I'll try to have Lord's Paris office protect Bill. [...]

I get lots of letters, also from many unknown young businessmen who tearfully congratulate me on being free and say they've lost their souls. I have to answer them all and have several dozen letters to write—which is why I seldom go near the typewriter, which is why I haven't written you. And then I owe Levine [LaVigne] 6 letters, and Whalen, and McClure started writing me again (he was seized with madness when he saw your Blues book, evidently Ferl is showing it around) and called it the great poem since Milton—also said he wept reading Road, in urinal scene with Neal, where you quarrel. And I always owe letters to Bill—and my unfinished project to finish another 50 pages letter to you recording continuing our Europe tour—still have all Italy and Vienna and Munich and Amsterdam to tell you about—which will do soon—and typing up poetry which I rarely do—there isn't enough time for all the great flowery tasks. You must be snowed under, more than me, I wish I knew all details. (Oh, I found Lord's address, never mind).

Still no sign Genet. What novel you writing? ("Zizi's Lament" is incidentally about a new disease we sent Bill a clipping about) KURU, a relative to Asian Amok and Latah, a laughing disease, "whole villages laughing themselves to exhaustion and death."

I thought record was rotten (I played it in front of painter hipsters here and cringed) but Ferl says I should make a new full length LP he'll put out with Fantasy records (it's all signed up and arranged) so as soon as I get voice back after flu will record whole book and new poems too. My record with Grove is censored and I'm mad and I got embarrassed, by my own tone because where I really rescued tearful seriousness in that particular reading was in parts 2 and 3 (which continued upward in beauty and non-goofing intensity tears)—and I asked Grove to print those parts on record—which advice ignored—so far as I think it's all a goof that record—they missed the big meat, those vultures. However it don't really matter. Besides I put out good record in time, or not, but will. So disgusted I sold my copy of record here for 800 francs to eat with (less than $2 to someone who was going to England). Bookstore friend of Ferl here has big window display of 50 copies of my book and sells a few a week so I get small income from that.

What number best seller are you nowadays? How dreamy that all is. Thank god. Neal wants $5000 or has he not written? We were talking about your money, our own fantasies and demands, but nothing we grub for will match Neal's final Great Demand for 50 or ten thous for the hosses. Whatcha gonna

do? I should write him a letter. I wonder what he's thinking. When *Howl* trial
was over there was a front page banner headline all across page of *SF Chronicle*
announcing results—wonder what he thought—and did he see you on TV?
[…]

My father and brother write you seemed confused and nowhere on TV,
were you high? I supposed they missed the mad drama, dream.

I got mad long Rimbaud letter from boy in Bordentown Reformatory [Ray
Bremser]. I wrote mad Rimbaud letter to [Rosalind] Constable at time saying
[Henry] Luce should send me (and you) (and Peter and Greg) on secret trip
Russia. She said she passed letter along, who knows? And wished us well, was
sad, in our greatness. I wrote Gary. Whalen in N.W. [North West.]

Love, Tears and Kisses

Allen

[*Orlovsky had to return to New York to take care of his family's mental health problems.*
Ginsberg stayed in Europe for another seven months and kept in touch with Peter via air-
mail letters.]

Allen Ginsberg [Paris, France] to Peter Orlovsky [New York, NY]
January 20, 1958

Dear Petey:

O Heart O Love everything is suddenly turned to gold! Don't be afraid
don't worry the most astounding beautiful thing has happened here! I don't
know where to begin but the most important. When Bill came I, we, thought it
was the same old Bill mad, but something had happened to Bill in the mean-
time since we last saw him. I did not realize it that first evening and day, nor for
another day after you'd left, but last night we stayed up till 3 AM talking, like
you and I talk, clearing up everything—first we started arguing and misunder-
standing as usual, I afraid he had come to claim me now you'd left, he still
sherlock-holmes poker-faced impassive, I thought he was tormenting cats still,
was worried, felt depressed, I sat on bed cried realizing you were gone and I
was alone in this miserable situation, I even got hi on T which made it worse,
Francine came in too and leered at me and tried to climb all over me, I was at
my wits end, I fell silent terrified on the bed—then a knock on the door—this
is 2 nights ago, Saturday nite—and Gregory walked in with great publishing

news from Germany (about that, later)—I was so glad to see him, he seemed so familiar and reassuring, only one left from when we were together here, when you were still here, I thought he would save me from sordid sorrows with Satanic Bill—but last night finally Bill and I sat down facing each other across the kitchen table and looked eye to eye and talked, I confessed all my doubt and misery—and in front of my eyes he turned into an Angel!

What happened to him in Tangier this last few months? It seems he stopped writing and sat on his bed all afternoons thinking and meditating alone and stopped drinking—and finally dawned on his consciousness, slowly and repeatedly, every day, for several months—awareness of "a benevolent sentient (feeling) center to the whole Creation"—he had apparently, in his own way, what I have been so hung up on in myself and you, a vision of big peaceful Lovebrain—said it gave him (came sort of like a revelation slowly) courage to look at his whole life, me, him more dispassionately—he had been doing a lot of self-analysis. Said his whole trip to Paris not to claim me but visit me now and also see an analyst to clear up psychoanalytic blocks left, etc. We talked a long time got into tremendous rapport, very delicate, I almost trembled, a rapport much like yours and mine, but not sexual, he even began to dig my feelings about that, my willingness but really I don't want to, has stopped entirely putting pressure on me for bed—the whole nightmare's cleared up overnight, I woke this morning with great bliss of freedom and joy in my heart, Bill's saved, I'm saved, you're saved, we're all saved, everything has been all rapturous ever since—I only feel sad that perhaps you left as worried when we waved goodbye and kissed so awkwardly—I wish I could have that over to say goodbye to you happier and without the worries and doubts I had that dusty dusk when you left—that you could have heard the conversation, taken part—I'm sure now henceforth when you meet again there'll be no more anxiety between you and Bill, all this is gone from him—the first day there, between us here, when we 3 were together—Bill was still very hesitant and unsure of himself, still hadn't come out—still doubting perhaps but knew inside, as we did not yet, that everything was OK, but still too withdrawn to know to clear it all up—but I know for sure now he's OK and consequently I feel like a million doves—Bill is changed nature, I even feel much changed, great clouds rolled away, as I feel when you and I were in rapport, well our rapport has remained in me, with me, rather than losing it, I'm feeling to everyone, something of the same as between us. And you? What's happening inside Dear Pete? I read Bill your poems, I'll type them and send them soon, everything is happening so fast. I feel like I can write even. Are you OK? Write me happy letter, don't be sad, I love you, nothing can change love, beautiful love, once we have it. I cried the other night realizing you'd gone, thinking that love would go away with you and I'd be alone without connection—but now I see Bill is really on same connection as we are—and I begin to feel connected with everything and everyone, the universe seems so happy. I made it with him the other night, to be good, on junk, before he and I talked, treated him sweetly, as you once treated me, but after our talk and new understanding, there's not even any more need for that, we get along on nonsexual level—maybe occasionally later an overflow we make it—but he no longer needs me like he used to, doesn't think of me as permanent future intimate sex schlupp lover, thinks even he'll wind up maybe after difficulties, with women, we slept apart in different rooms last night, both happy, first time I was alone in bed, I was happy, I missed you (jacked off even), Bill woke me up in the morning, had happy breakfast, talked more, the rapport real, Bill's change real, I changed too, no longer suspicious and worried of him, he doesn't even bother the cat—I'm continuing to keep your calendar—Bill will accept you—have no more fear, remember Nature is really kind, loves you, he's getting to be as kindly feeling as you and I do at our best when we're not worried—he said he was still sunk and irritable when we were all together in Tangier—the doubt and uncommunication still hung-over unresolved your last day here maybe,—but absolutely it's really now gone, have big peacy happy slumber dreams—Life is so great, and best of all Bill completely aware of this. So we took long walk, it was a blue fine unfoggy day, downtown. Jack wrote nice letter from Florida, sent me all the money, arrived this morning ($225), so we walked downtown to the Opera to Amer Express, cashed it into Travelers checks, now I got plenty money and Bill has, I repaid him what he loaned us. Don't send me money, I have all I need—maybe later in a few months I be poorer, but right now I have plenty plenty and small expenses, shared with Bill, he no longer lives high anyway so we live cheap henceforth—don't send me the $10, keep it now you'll need it, in fact, if you really get in hole tell me I'll send you some. So Jack says he's in Fla. and movies look like they'll buy his book now and he asks where you are, so write him a card (Enclosed find Lafcadio's letter to you arrived 2 days ago).

Also Gregory: he came back, happy, he and Bill got along great, Bill likes him, and Alan Ansen wrote Gregory great warmhearted letter saying don't worry about money, come to Venice and stay happy there and safe awhile, let me know if you need money for RR fare there. How strange, Alan suddenly woke up too? I don't know, but it was a great letter from him to Greg. Meanwhile in Germany, Gregory made arrangement for Gregory (not me, it's better this way leaves me free in fact. good deal) to put together one small anthology of me Bill Jack Greg, expensive, and to help in a larger volume of Amer and SF poetry to be published in a few months. So he's going to work on that now in Venice. Furthermore the Germans offered him an apartment in old university town of Heidelberg, for 6 months after Venice, thru the summer, so now he knows where he can go next. He also sending another long Coit-Tower type madpoem to fill out his book for City Lites, so that's going to be good too.

Meanwhile also, a letter arrived from America saying Bill's *Junky* had been finally sold and published in England and Bill is due some more money (under a hundred) from that.

Got on big discussion with Bill of means of extending Love-Bliss to others and spreading the connection between us (told him we had intended that in Tangier with him, even if it didn't work) without sacrificing intimacy. We'll solve that problem too before we're done. I feel so good today it don't seem hard. It's just that there aren't many people who've experienced the freedom that we have. Jack's letter today was nice, and more friendly—but I think he still is doubtful and secret—or doesn't know that we know, or something. But that'll turn to gold later and we'll all get straight with Jack next time we see him too.

So money's rolling in, honey, and love's rolling in. I'll see you in 6 months like I said. Are you alright? Write me as fast as you can. I'm worried you're unhappy and got too much trouble in front of you in NY. Julius will be hard to help. We'll see what we can do. But don't let your own sweet tender knowing Pete be eat by worry. I'll always be with you, and so will the trees and all the rainbows and angels in Heaven be singing last happy cowboy songs with shiny eyes at us.

Tell Lafcadio to stop being Christ of Mars and I'll stop being unhappy Christ of poetry. No more Crucifixions! Regards to your momma and Marie.

XXXXXXX. How's the ship? Don't take too much horse. I've quit T entirely it's a bringdown and I doan want no more bum kicks. Bill smokes less too. But it varies with everyone. *Black Mountain Review* came out, Creeley editor.—get it at 8th St. Bookstore—send me a copy maybe.

Love,

Allen (with your green pen)

Allen Ginsberg [Paris, France] to Herschel Silverman [Bayonne, NJ]
February 22, 1958

Silverman, Silverman, why are you writing me mad letters full of extravagant
neon imagery in long versicles like hiccups

Silverman, Silverman, what you expect, I should get involved in politics
about bricks and cultures when I can fly off on the nearest golden cloud of
meditation and find myself giggling by the Seine?

Silverman, Silverman, it was never sex and jazz and trains and booze I
loved,

It was boys full of light and trains full of black music and the voice of
William Blake roaring in my ear in Harlem

reminding me of Silverman, Silverman, woeful in Bayonne dreaming of
frank symbols exploding horrible truths over New Jersey

while the silver wooly lamb came in his lunch cart sat down and shyly
ordered vegetable hamburger from Silverman, Silverman weeping at the ice-
box of systematic Meat.

Allen
Merry Xmas
Happy New Year

Allen Ginsberg [Paris, France] to Gary Snyder [Corte Madera, CA]
April 2, 1958

Dear Gary:

Glad to hear from you, got your card, I wrote you a few letters, long some,
to strange address Don Allen sent me but I guess they never got to you Gary.
Anyway I been here in Europe all this time, to sum up, 2 1/2 months in Tangier
being Burroughs' slave typing up his manuscript and cooking for everybody,
awful routine, good time there, met Bowles and Francis Bacon painter, took off
with Peter thru Spain and toured all great monuments mosques of Cordoba
and Alhambra and Toledo Madrid Barcelona then to Venice, stayed at Ansen
(friend from NY—Jack describes weekend in his house in *Subterraneans*) for 2
months, more museums and more cooking, then trip with Peter to Florence
and Rome and Assisi, slept on grass and bugged the monks hand in hand beg-
ging food and conversation, then back to Venice and trip alone back to Rome
and Naples and Capri and Ischia (saw Auden a few nites and only argued

lunacy), then with Peter again thru Vienna so to see Breughel paintings, then a few days in Munich, then here in Paris got a room with cookstove gas and went sightseeing and settled down but didn't write much, then Amsterdam visited Gregory there for a month, nice quiet Dutch canals and calm whore streets girls in windows like legal mannequins, then back to Paris, goofed for a few months doing nothing, then Peter left for U.S. to take care of brothers (and now has job in my old Langley Porter type bughouse as attendant in NYC), Burroughs arrived here (all full of new fine enlightenment, for him, all his old evil Baudelairian ennui begone — he meditated for half a year alone in Tangier and said he experienced first time the "indifferent benevolent sentience at center of things" — sort of a late life crisis for him, came to Paris to get last frazzles psychoanalyzed and has room downstairs, and Gregory went to Frankfurt where he contacted German poets who commissioned him to make anthology of young U.S. poets, then he went stayed with Ansen in Venice; now he's back and also has room in this hotel — which is right near Place St. Michel, on left bank near St. Germain Center, my hotel itself only a few steps away from the Seine near Notre Dame Isle de Cité, — great — tho I don't go out too much, lately, I sit and loom and gloom and brood, don't know what's the matter guess I'll come off it sooner or later — too much poetry or self or publicity or ideas about myself, hard to get out of, particularly as I was so involved, self involved, well anyway hope I'm getting out of that, so then took a trip to England, 3 weeks, slept on Parkinson's couch, visited Turnbull, Gael, doctor near Stratford, and drove to Stonehenge with Parkinson and wife, and made weepy BBC record, then back to Paris been here a month or 2 getting restless and hope, tho broke right now, to take off for Berlin-Warsaw, maybe Moscow, if I can get any money. Bill has income so no starvation now. Never did really starve, just ran out of money, so got fragments of loot from family or royalties or records or selling books or BBC — actually have been getting quite a lot of money in this last half year — almost maybe 70 a month or more — so no real problems. I get royalties from City Lights, they sold about 10,000 I hear, so owe me another 200 this month, will use that and take off for more travel — still not seen eastern part Europe nor Greece. After that sometime in summer, July, will go back to NYC, rejoin Peter, and figure off from there what next. Not written anything very great, that's bugged me, overanxious to please I guess and follow *Howl* up, obsessional, so just a lot of self conscious long lines about politics, horrid, some funny tho — I don't know I have a lot of manuscript. But maybe there's something left I'm afraid to begin typing it all lest it stink. Meanwhile I am about the same a little more withdrawn and frightened in a way can't smoke tea I get paranoiac and read the newspapers thru every day worrying about politics—they got cops with machine guns on every block here now, like Berlin 1934, after the Arabs, the Algerian war nobody talks much about but it's a big drag it's happening and the soul of Paris seems dead—frightening tho to walk out at midnight near Notre Dame and run into a black street full of thousands of nightmare cops with machine guns sitting smoking waiting inside huge black Maria vans expecting some kind of military coup or Arab riot or student demonstration god knows what—shout in the streets here I keep feeling, run wild in the streets and you never know what would happen. America from here after year and half seems like your "This Tokyo" poem only worse, sort of unconsciously perpetuating a war, Dulles spouting about saving world for white Christians etc., gave France half a billion dollars so that keeps the Algeria war going which is insoluble now anyway everybody so filled with hate there, newspapers suppressed here in Paris, Sartre magazine seized etc.—well a lot of bullshit but very oppressive so close up, I guess you got some kind of an idea traveling around the east—in fact what kind of an idea did you get I wonder about present history, seems to me America's taking a fall, i.e. all Whitmanic freedom energy all fucked up in selfishness and exclusion like a big neurotic paranoid that's about to crack up. Talked to some of the 41 U.S. students who made it thru Moscow youth festival to Red China, they shot all the junkies and prostitutes there and I read some Mao and Khrushchev announcements about literature, all brainwash party control—seems to be a different world. I sure would like to go traveling thru that red world and see what it's like. Burroughs very interested in Japan so, me too, I guess next world wander I head east— you any plans for going back there—or for that matter coming here? Jack writes you maybe off for hike tour with him thru West that sounds fine. But what happened, to you? Anything great from monastery? I saw some of your poems, that Phil sent Gregory for the German anthology, liked them they're fine, some I'd seen before in NY, most in fact. Read thru Phil's again last night and they really picked me up, I was depressed I wound up feeling real great after finishing them including some new series called Takeouts he has...By the way, if can dig Ron Loewinsohn, he sent Gregory a whole mess of really good poems, amazing, I didn't think he'd so forcefully come up with out of his 20s or 23s year, seems he has a girl and some kind of terrific great love match with her, and writes a lot, more or less isolated in SF says it's empty except for fairy poet clique he can't make, maybe true—sometimes he sounds a little like Whalen, but he seems at least in poetry very much an enterprising spirit and very alive. Also heard from McClure who's changed somewhat for better, shipped out, read thru Jack's *Mex City Blues* and flipped over them and got a room in 〔 Wentley, Polk and Sutter, LaVigne there and Neal around there too says La-Vigne, and McClure been writing weirdly and more free. How is Locke, and Sheila? Give them my best. What's happening around SF now I wonder? NY is strange, Jack and Peter write, everybody in the Village is giving poetry readings, lots of excitement, even Lamantia there reading, all sorts of small clubs and bars, strange—I saw some of the poetry by young people tho it looks lousy, but with spirit. If you have manuscript you want to send out there are a few places Gregory, Phil, Jack and me have been sending to the last few months; *Chicago Review, Climax, Yugen, Partisan Review, Black Mountain Review, Measure* —John Wieners, interesting Olson type, in SF somewhere, Loewinsohn or Whalen or McClure know, I haven't his address. *Chicago Review* picked up on Burroughs with great enthuse, only place so far, *Partisan* and *Evergreen* both so far put him down. I left his whole manuscript with Spender in London for *Encounter*, who I think just lost it. Also gave a reading for 25 poetry types at Oxford—read pieces from everybody and they picked up, like at Reed [College].

So anyway that's the sum of me right now, not much, wish there were some Buddhists here to get drunk with. What your plans, you have any yet? Regards to anybody I know if you see them, Rexroth, Neal, etc. Tonight I go to movies see Rosselini's St. Francis picture, never saw it in States. Saw Chaplin's King in NY—did you in Japan? I hear you've been everywhere from Ras Tamara (wherever that mighty name belongs to) to Okinawa, including Bombay—run into anything or anybody fiery or flippy? Or floop? Even. Flow! Write, I did write you—about 2 big letters they're lost in the Pacific somewhere—all about Fra Angelico and the cocks of Florence—oh yes, got high in the Forum at Rome, and climbed afoot Vesuvio and walked down 12 mi. to Pompeii, I saw a lot of classical Europe got all hung up on painting for the first time—and also saw huge exhibits of the greatest all time painter I decided, Van Gogh—in Amsterdam—like a museum with 150 Van Goghs all at once. Plenty weed here, also lots of cheap excellent high quality heroin, sniffed an enormous amount and stopped when Burroughs came to town—he's kicked completely for the last 2 or 3 years after being on for a decade—so you see his whole scheme of things has changed a lot, "I've told no one to wait for me" he saith, quoting Perse. Had here, myself, a nice enlightened doll of an Indonesian girl was making it with, ach, but she found someone else last month—but anyway realized the future world's going to be colored yellow or brownish after everybody winds up all intermarried and happy—never really realized that before.

Wrote one nice line over English Channel "the giant sun ray down from a vast cloud sun light's endless ladders streaming in eternity to ants in the myriad fields of England bearing minute gold thru smoke climbing unto heaven over London."

As ever,

Allen

Allen Ginsberg [Paris, France] to Eugene Brooks [New York, NY]
ca. **April 20, 1958**

Dear Gene:

Received the check—that was very rapid, I wrote and asked Nick Orlovsky for the money only about a week ago. Thanks for the extra $25. The money was repayment of money I'd loaned them for lawyer's fee to get Nick out of bug-house. Looks like it all worked smoothly, and well, and nothing lost but a little time for that particular good deed. Kind of renews your faith etc. etc. and Kerouac's all paid up. So out of loans outlays etc. I've only lost 10 or 20 dollars out of my original pile. Also this week received $180 dollars from City Lights, royalties on last thousands sold. They printed up another 5000 copies (now 15,000) in all practically a best seller, so there's more due, enough to get fare home this summer I guess, plus a small bankroll for NY. I can also make some (not much) money reading in NYC so won't be immediately hit by depression, bad scene in market research, shipping, etc.

Interested to hear your reaction to *Subterraneans*. Yes it is *sui generis*, tho it has roots in a tradition of Miller-Céline-Wolfe-Anderson etc. Its value seems to me to lie in that, he [Kerouac] trying to find new personal intimate direct mode of expression. It's obvious he has a lot of foolishness and idiot in him and psychological hang-ups like anyone, but he doesn't try to revise them out, hide them or make an objective phony facade—you really are in contact with a man himself—that's an interesting development—and it affects the prose. The sentences sound like someone talking long and excited all night telling an immense personal anecdote—with interruptions, additions, halts, stops, confusions, confessions, strangeness. It's not his best writing (a relatively weak book compared to *Dr. Sax* and others unpublished) but it is unmistakably real and his own and in time. Lou's reaction, he read and put it down, lost interest, "mutilated in its English, wretched abominable English sentence structure that makes a hodgepodge and mishmash"..."wreck of English language." "I'd flunk any pupil of mine who mangled the language like that." He has a new book due this fall, *Dharma Bums*—about hitchhike thru Northwest 2 years ago with Zen Buddhist friend Gary Snyder. I haven't read it, it's last year's writing, Viking bringing it out. Those publishers will screw him up since they ignore the deeper solitary paeans of prose he wrote earlier like *Dr. Sax*—want to rush out books all out of chronological order to fit Beat Generation propaganda bullshit they've created themselves—it's all mis-taken. (Taken wrong). However maybe *Dharma Bums* is solid. *Sax* is great like Melville's *Pierre*.

I wrote Russia writers group and Warsaw. Doubt if Russia will bite hook, they're puritanical and edgy about anything that doesn't follow their idiot line —lately attacks on Rock & Roll. I wrote them a letter all about Rock & Roll poetry screw that up for them in advance. Warsaw is another matter, I wrote them too, and sent some books (as I did Moscow). I spoke to people who were in Warsaw, also to French littérateurs who attend international conferences etc. also to German avant-garde editors—there is a wild literary life raging in Warsaw now, things are comparatively free—only place behind the iron curtain where there is a large vocal hip minority—they get all English and U.S. papers and books there—a lot of literary life, above and underground—(It's not visible anywhere in Moscow or Yugoslavia, etc. but it is out in open in Warsaw). Because of this weird situation it's supposed to be the most jumping city in Europe now. Chances of my being invited to live there free by official group is good, if I wait around long enough. See, Gregory wrote long article in a Dutch mag the equivalent of *Sat. Review*, it was reprinted in Germany, Beat Gen material has hit France, and there is a lot of cultural intercommunication. I have distinguished credentials already—read on BBC and that caused attention, etc. If I can swing Warsaw before summer will go there, waiting to hear. Meanwhile taking another England trip, invited to read (paid $20) some society—have to make a respectable appearance before Spender and Herbert Read to beat down opposition to uncensored tape of *Howl* to be broadcast over BBC. A part was already broadcast and well received in papers, they are even rebroadcasting it this week, or soon, but the Talks Dept. there is now engaged I'm told in a conspiracy to broadcast the whole thing uncut as I read it (weeping, wailing)— they stick their necks out. Gregory come to England with me this time probably, he also record. This is all sort of a ball. Well I'll write later—be in England early May for a week or so then back here.

As ever, love

Allen

Allen Ginsberg [??] to Louis Ginsberg [Paterson, NJ] *ca.* **April 20, 1958**

Dear Lou:

Can't write much, have been preparing manuscript for an anthology Grove is bringing out of young poets 1948–1956, looking at old poems of mine & figuring what's best. Will go to England around May 1, give reading there for some small poetry group, $20 pay, Corso go along too for kicks maybe read or record for BBC. "Transmutation" is very good, that's one of the best of your poems recently, I guess a lot of the material you've used before but here all adapted well together & has considerable power. 4th line cater I like 6th line also, 8th line, last 3 best & sharpest for me. Great you could do that on phone.

Happy that you found Corso's book interesting. I was always really impressed by that lost watches too (and similar phrasing in other poems). It's his particular weird gift—an almost surrealist phrasing that makes strange sense. The line means, as I understand it, in context, since he's revisiting unhappy scene of garbage dirty ears loss poverty, and sees the same poverty still there, tho he's escaped it, when it's image raises up to attack him (dirty ears aims a knife at me), he realizes he's now free, escaped on the road of his own beauty desire thru time, time has passed, he's no longer a kid involved with same ugly conditioning, he's escaped free of the tragedy of lower east side, he's aware of death & time, he no longer attacks back with a vicious gun or knife, but pumps him full of lost watches—lost watches being time gone by, realization of mortality, old forgotten contemplations (as the hours of watches on ships)—while Dirty Ears, still caught in the environment, doesn't realize the immense change—the lost watches, then, basically, as human consciousness—achieved by Gregory, denied alas to Dirty Ears who's still hung up. What I like about that is the language and images—the most unpoetic, garbage cans, lower east side realities, Dirty Ears, stairways, hand on gat (fantasy of returning a big Italian successful heroic hoodlum—which he is, hoodlum of poesy)—all so realistic, and yet thru strange combinations capable of expressing very lucid and eternal thoughts. That's really making poetry of everyday life, the strangeness of the commonplace, writing about real things. He has a peculiar imaginative second-sight. There's another example in the poem "Italian Extravaganza" —the weird almost frightening beauty of "small purplish wrinkled head"— followed by the last two lines, comparison of the small coffin, a cause so small & real, and the 10 immense black Cadillacs of sorrow, almost pathetic the great display from the funeral home. Yet all done without abstraction, in simple images.

In the poem "Coit Tower," the language is at its most imaginative—the situation is here he, the poet Gregory who was in jail in youth, is looking down on Alcatraz from a hill: "And I cried there in your dumb hollows O tower (Coit tower up on Telegraph Hill) clutching my Pan's foot (imagination, life, & consciousness & experience) with vivid hoard of Dannemora"—that seems a line worthy of Dylan Thomas's Fern Hill. (Dannemora Gregory's prison). I've cried reading that, his grief & understanding seem so great (underneath his facade of childish egotism).

The sun poem is an experiment at pure wild images without direct sense, just fantastic combinations—they do make a kind of mystic sense actually, since the mind has its own secret language, as in dreams, we're not always aware of the significance of certain compelling phrases—from another poem there is the line "Rose is my wise chair of bombed houses"—which I don't at all understand—but it's a line that haunts me like some of Kubla Khanish mysticdoms. That's poetry. It takes a weird gift to imagine up a wise chair in a bombed house.... Spring started here too, a few trees in flower tho it's been chilly last week—I have a cold. Re Jack's prose, well I like it of course, my reason being that it has the same syntactical structure of fast excited spoken talking—this is an interesting event in prose development, and it's no less communicative to me than heard speech, mine, yours, his,—when you speak you also talk a little like that, especially when you're moved, excited, angry, or dizzy with happiness etc. etc.—heightened speech in other words. Normal conversation does not necessarily follow formal syntax, nor need it as long as it's communicative. So written prose. Perhaps you find it uncommunicated or uncommunicating because you expect to see a different written order of syntax. But it actually gets across very well, what he's describing, faithful to his own way of talk. It's obvious from On Road or Town & City that he can write normal prose, simple & straightforward. So if he writes experimentally one has to give credit for it being you know at least sincere & even intelligent, an approach, a try—most people don't even try—and it isn't as if he hasn't personally sacrificed a lot to pursue his sense of craft—that book was written long ago without a hope of publication—as On the Road was written 8 years ago. I do find it interesting though—I know the girl he writes about—who took off her clothes & flipped—I heard her story about it—that was the way she spoke, the syntax even, her style of speaking—a very common style—he's caught her very well—and if you add his interpolations & private thoughts which he records semi-simultaneously with her monologues, & their conversation—you have a very complicated but very real structure of events to try and get down on paper. Hemingway tried simplification & reduction (and was attacked for being too inhumanly stripped down)—Jack trying (as Proust & Céline) to include all the little private thoughts you normally wouldn't mention—so he arrives at a complicated sentence structure. It's not trying to be English sentence structure. It's trying to be American actual speech—and thought—reproduction. So it shouldn't be judged by standards of a high school or college grammar course. It's not meant to be grammatical <u>that</u> way, it's meant to be right <u>another</u> way. Nor can one say that standard English syntax is the fixed and only standard way of transcribing human thought—all languages have different syntax structures—the Latin ones are one group—the German type inflected is another—and many primitive cultures have approaches to syntax that are almost almost incomprehensible to us (but make perfect sense to them—no verbs for instance in some languages, no adjectives in others). And there is Chinese syntax which I'm told is of a totally different order from ours. Syntax is only a tool to speak with, there are many syntaxes, & many variations possible to our tongue, common in use even, in talk—English grammar is only the formal way tied to fixed habits of feeling & communication—Jack, broken free of these fixed habits of thought, has to think & write his own way, find a mode. Look at the sentence I just wrote—it's crazy, but it followed the spontaneous convolutions of my thought very flexibly—would I change my thought to fit the sentence structure better, or alter my thought & pare it down neat & leave out the hesitations, changes, and halts, interruptions, to make it fit a school copybook? I'd wind up writing gibberish if I tried to halt in midstream & box it up neat to fit some imaginary standard. The ideal is for me a sensitive prose or poetry syntax or metric that is practical & follows the changes actually going on in the process of thinking or writing—where a normal metric or syntax works, fine—but where it doesn't apply, why? I no longer worry about that so much—just go my way—that's all any man can do—live—and do what he thinks practical. And real. See now that that last bit, and real, added on to the sentence. I thought it up next and added it—you can follow my actual process of composition—what I mean is there directly no less and no more—I just thought to say, and real, and added it in, just like that. What freedom—and why not? Language is to use not dictate our thoughts. But so much of our lives & feelings are tied down to the limitations of what we're taught—this is the importance of striking out into variation & experiment—this is not nihilism but courage—not really that—Joy! Well I'll end on elevated note. Love to everybody—wrote Gene tonite—will try Warsaw yet see under skirt of iron curtain perhaps. There is no Beat Generation, it's all a journalist hex.

Love

Allen

**Allen Ginsberg [Paris, France] to Hannah Litzky (Ginsberg's aunt) [NJ?]
June 20, 1958**

Dear Hannah:

Making plans to return—hope to be back next month sometime, tho how and when I haven't figured yet, but so anyway I guess I'll see you soon. Spent a kind of gloomy uneasy winter not doing much but sightseeing in the rain and writing a little but since spring the city has opened out a little and I just gave up writing schedules and wander out every day now with friends here, go to parks, drink wine and coffee in outdoor cafés, St. Germain mostly, goof around all day and evening, write letters and poetry when I feel like, meet Frenchmen. If I stayed here another year I guess my French would be good enough to get around more socially—I'm just beginning to come into contact with literary types here—also with a strange young Rothschild heir who takes us (Corso me and Burroughs) riding to expensive nightclubs (us still in spotted rags) up the Champs Elysées. So far mostly have been hanging around with Americans mostly. We all live in the same hotel, others (a tall bearded motorcyclist method actor Brando type fellow from LA) around the corner—I have a large room and do the cooking, Burroughs and Gregory or whoever supplies the gelt when I'm (as usual) broke—so there's always people around, I don't actually have too much time alone, in fact beginning to develop a taste for solitariness and long hours staring at the ceiling just emptying my mind of junk. Sort of a floating existence, I'll be glad to get home and settle down for a year.

If you see Saltman—Is he still working for NJ Parole or does he know anyone on it? Tell him, I've been getting some letters from (and answering them) a fellow name Raymond Bremser—who's been in Bordentown Reformatory for 4 years and has another 22 months to go (armed robbery when he was 18)—writes extremely hopeful energetic wild poetry, definitely a gifted individual—he shouldn't be hanging around Bordentown Reformatory. Saltman ever run into him? I'll show Eli his letters when I get back. In fact I sent him some care of you a few months ago, misaddressed, and it returned here to me. But I get vast

30 page poems from Bremser that sound like jazzy awkward Hart Crane dithyrambs—very sweet and religious nature—tho rather scared (of where he is) and hiding his light under prison shades. He just sent me a letter with poems out of the blue a year ago, bold trust.

Went watching mobs parade against end of 4th republic a month ago—reminded me of days in Journal Square with Milgram. Otherwise, except for cops, street-life is normal and in fact indifferent to the whole political scene. The honest people here have all given up, powerless, tho DeGaulle sounds like he's trying to order a basically contradictory and insoluble problem. The Algerian poets here say, "but, man, we're not French—when are these squares going to get it thru their heads?" or words to that effect, in French. But had a vision of prewar Europe, with all the putsch excitement.

Lou says some of your students write papers on Beat Generation material. Alas, the whole scene is strictly a literary scene, basically, with technical literary practical meanings (shifts in prosody of verse and experiments and progress in prose forms)—and most of the great manuscript are still unpublished and will be for 10 years or more (like in 1910 with Pound, Joyce, Williams, etc.)—most of the sociological generalizations and middleclass publicity discussions ("What does beat mean? is it positive or negative? why do they steal hubcaps?) are false issues created by journalistic minds, hung up with meaningless habitual categories that just do not fit and never have been the concern of artistic (or spiritual) creation, i.e. square.

If you're interested in the origin of the phrase (and it's actual context and actual meaning) it was a word Huncke used to use, or we used to use about Huncke, to describe the peculiar physical and spiritual depression he used to get into—typical of a junkie (heroin addict, not marijuana which is harmless) —during and after which he (Huncke) used to experience a kind of religious illumination—that is being beat down to his naked human core (similar in a sense to the experience of the Dark Night of the Soul described by St. John of the Cross—or any classical mystic—or for that matter any psychoanalyst in describing the anxiety and depression that precedes a flood of basic insight) he had his soul sort of cracked open to admit the light. I'm using Huncke as an example, tho I think he's the archetypical beat type. But actually, later, I think Kerouac walking down the street digging a ragged skeletal but illuminated junky girl we knew (a painter named Iris Brody[36]) looked at her amazed and said, very casually, off remark—"This isn't a lost generation it's a beat genera-

---

36 Iris Brody. Painter and friend from New York City who died of a drug overdose in 1961.

tion." The remark was picked up (by a writer named Holmes) and made the title of an article long ago in the *Times* and it spread there from. But so you see there isn't any beat generation, there's only a casual remark and a lot of journalists trying to make money by writing articles about sociology. That's why there's so much misunderstanding of the word, and overplaying of it, it's ridiculous. It's meaningless out of context—or has any meaning you want to give it, all equally arbitrary. And publishers use it to sell books, or TV interviewers use it to peg Kerouac (simple journalistic device) and sociologists use it to promote career by editing anthologies (good gimmick)—but that's not art —and it's not hip, and definitely not "beat." So where are you? a great mass of literature, mostly unpublished…and a greater mass of misunderstanding. Like, there is not one reviewer of Kerouac who has noticed the basis of his prose nor the basis of structure in his writings (spontaneous unrevised prose and structure automatically rising out of the natural series of associations on a subject, without attempt to follow any other order than what passes thru his mind in recollection.) But all of them are worried about, and talk endlessly about, whether he's serious or not, and whether he has moral concerns, and whether he steals hubcaps, or whatever. This may sound like a rather technical pre-occupation but actually most of our preoccupations are in this sense technical. So nobody really knows what we're doing and an endless stream of bullshit flows thru *Time* and *Commentary*, etc. authored by ignorant sellouts who have absolutely no artistic insight or interests and are writing silly college debate society arguments for money attacking us for nihilism. I don't know if you (or they for that matter) realize the real corruption of the intellectual community in U.S. and the trashy commercial level it operates on. Kerouac a victim, rather tired, of that now—his publishers avoiding all his later mellow golden immense works (*Dr. Sax, Visions of Neal*) (and his vast series of poems) (and a life of Buddha) (and a book of prayers and meditations—500 single-spaced pages) and playing him for the Beat Scene. The point is however the works are written, tho unknown, Burroughs's also, unpublishable in U.S. for censorship reasons, my own later poetry ditto,—a whole raft of poets unacceptable for commercial reasons in NY—so this if anything is what is Beat. The illumination is there (the classics are written) despite the dark night of the soul in America, the illumination is intact in the poets and lovers—which was the message of Whitman. And Melville writing Billy Budd in solitude of his failure attic. That was "beat." So you see the question of positive or negative values is not relevant. It is the questioner who's a lost idiot, not poor beat saint, who knows (trembling) GOD. No less. Ancient Hasidim Rabbi would weep and agree. High school students and teachers, BEWARE! (End with diabolic crazes laughter and fadeout to dark rainy streets of Paris, gargoyles atop Notre Dame)...can show this page to interested students but don't forget the mad beware. Love, see you in a month.

As ever,

Allen

Allen Ginsberg [Paris, France] to Jack Kerouac [n.p.] June 26, 1958

Dear Jack:

Wrote you last month, no answer, are you mad at me? Write honey, I'm full of snow right now, strange interesting rich acquaintances here, one a young Rothschild junior Burroughs, he and Bill will go to India someday together, I'll —somebody, another blonde young millionaire just brought up some old suits, Bill now smoking Green [marijuana] all drest in distinguished Averill Harriman black worsted flannel, thin, graying temples: he brought me my first suit in years, fine English grey wool, last a thousand winters—but later—Alas Alas Jack I got final word from LaVigne today, long letter, Neal is in jail, LaVigne not seen him, talked to Carolyn on phone to find out for me and wrote me—he's in San Bruno County jail, waiting trial, "Two facts are 1) that he was arrested selling to narco agents, has been tied (mistakenly) into series of other arrests as source of supply (since he comes up in trains from south), there is a long list of charges against him (tho Carolyn didn't enumerate them), 2) that he is discovered as Dean M. of *On the Road* by the fuzz." That's what LaVigne says Carolyn says, though I doubt the latter means anything, maybe just her paranoia. Tho I hear scene in SF is very bad, saw a girl from there who showed me evil Herb Caen column innuendos about marijuana smoke stronger than garlic these days on North Beach, anyone can pick up Columbus and Bway, fuzz is all over on account of all the publicity, city officials cracking down, The Place raided, and its balcony use forbidden and only 35 people at time allowed in LaVigne was having a show there and they ordered him off balcony—some guy name Paul Hansen fall off a building last Sunday, and finally skull struck again, Connie Sublette was strangled last "Tuesday AM by a spade seaman who confessed that PM." I met someone here 2 months ago that knew her said she had a codeine habit and was slightly crazy, calling cops to arrest people, I don't know what—long saga of drunken week following her around feuding with some evil tea heads or something, I don't know. Haven't heard anything of Sublette, I guess he's ok—in jail I had heard for a burglary....everything I hear from there sounds evil...except letters from Gary who's in hospital for ball operation, and Wieners who's living at Wentley with LaVigne, they're friends now, I guess I think even making it...but what to do about Neal—I wanted to write Carolyn, don't any longer have address on Bancroft, got letter back—LaVigne forgot to send it—you have it? I'll try write him in jail—Carolyn added that she thought he'd get 2-5 yrs maybe—god knows what he's thinking—I had a shuddery premonition, thought he was committing suicide, yesterday when hi, suddenly thought of him maybe in jail, then got this letter today. But little doomed Connie is sad.

I'm coming back to New York in a few weeks, hope to leave here, have to get up the fare but that'll come, or else family said they'd send it if no other way. Gregory and I interviewed by Buchwald, Art, silly interview, he tried to be sympathetic but we were drunk and kookie, but next night I sent him big serious prophetic godly letter, said maybe he'd publish that, and Gregory will send him another Luciferian sweet one—but at end of article he said we were trying to raise fare, I was, for return, maybe someone send it. Long letters from Peter, he OK, you see him? His brother Julius strangely better, will get pass to leave weekends, no more mad sneakings into grey halls with stolen keys, he talks and reads to Peter a little—P discovered in bathroom he eats his shit off fingernails after washing with hand—"what am I getting in to" says Peter—I dunno, I come back, hope for best. "Allen, now Julius' shit is in my mouth and yours," says P.

Paris Review, Nelson Aldrich, came weeks ago, asked for Burroughs manuscript, I gave him County Clerk and some others he said he'd try to publish, also gave him my Lion poem, Peter show you that? and Gregory gave him Atom Bomb poem and I typed out his selection from your scroll—Choruses #19, 112, 126, 226, 228, and 240—a nice round selection with the magnificent sonnet "Love's multitudinous boneyard" (It's got end couplet Shakespearian like sonnet). Is this OK by you—they want some prose from you—send if can to Nelson Aldrich at *Paris Review*—send parts of *Visions* or wild prose from *Sax* —that a good way to get *Sax* going into world—I think they'll take all—crazy selection, the best so far in one magazine—but if they don't take the County Clerk or something of Bill's we'll take back our poems—OK? Let me know if these poems are OK to give them—Bill and I all dressed up alone in room here, drawing of Horn and Hardart by Peter taped on mirror, we're sniffing coke, I'm high now, so trying to write on this, never did before—lovely feeling, like benny a little, and last longer than I thought—keep sniffing every so often you can stay happy for whole hour, just came down before and starting up again—haven't had any since Norman-Vicki 1949 or 48 rooms or was 47?

But is there anything we can do about Neal? Character witnesses—he'll be all alone only haggard Carolyn probably angry at him, Gary's in hospital can't find out anything, he's wise enough to know if anything to do, no one to write to there who could help—thought maybe Ruth Witt-Diamant or Rexroth, just some letters that he's a writer or something, say—he being crucified, evil laws on T, trapped by decoy cops, all nothing for him to suffer for—and probably big mistaken spider web paranoias by cops—though I guess maybe he's having some peace and have plenty time to meditate and stay way from horses and RR and T and Carolyn and house and his life, forced vacation, maybe blessing in disguise and he grim and peaceful in jail, or writing prayers to Saturn, maybe he write again, die, I'll stay in NY-Paterson-Long Island Eugene's, wherever, a year, maybe Peter get Veterans apartment in Bronx—have endless notes, poems, to type, finish Fall of America poem, maybe, Bible Jeremiah book, China have billion people by 2000, we'll see it, be industrialized as much as England in 14 years I read, must call for Holy America make it on beat angel soul promote Walt [Whitman] comrade to Budh ambassador—otherwise maybe paranoia machine sink down on us from new Asia—we may be visionary island America after all—still interested in *Democratic Vistas*, he says if we don't produce bards and spiritual America and if materialism greed takes over we be "the fabled damned among nations"—can see it happening from year and half in Europe, from Europe,—yes I see the vast virtues but family Sunday house with eternal TV like *T&C* solidity strength—even that and spume in history waves—white race too small—smooth metallic faced chinamen in space suits maybe go to Mars—Burroughs horrified by all tales of communist dullness, we hear here in Paris from travelers, shot all hop smokers in China etc. etc.—now T is banned (legally and slightly enforced) in Tangier (Arabs have to hide their pipes under table in cafes now)—so America got to be peaceful wiseman among nations, and survive—maybe take vow of poverty and give away empire state bldg possessions to India—I dunno, just a gleam—Melville and Whitman both worried about albionic Jerusalemic prophetic America—our? are you beyond that? magic dream of ladies moving in advertisements. Well, that's what's happening outside, I read it in papers, I mean about politics China, see police in streets here—we were all here thru 1936 headlines about dogauullep—I saw my mama and Aunt Elanor marching huge street crowded with Naomi and Maxes, didn't know what they were doing, a month ago, vast mob rally against DeGaulle, Gregory and John Balf who's like a student calm DuPeru—we climbed on the ledge of a bank on Place Republique and watched the thousand headed streets walk—chain of organized (communists? or anyone) joining arms to prevent crowd from advancing further—and down the block, suddenly glimpsed, waiting, a "hoard of silver helmets" Gregory said, cops waiting to break riots—but the crowd never transgressed and people said it was nothing to compare to the great aroused weeping mobs of half a million 1938. Went just now with Harry Phipps (Marshall Field daughter grandson something blonde boy 24 writes Copelandesque jazz) to his big apartment and wife with Bill and Greg on Baudelaire's nearby Notre Dame Isle St. Louis, house Voltaire and Chopin lived in—Gregory sat at Chopin's piany—next door a big party—Elsa Maxwell—we didn't go in, peeked thru keyhole to see vast candelabra red rugged hall lights, vast tables for Princes—so big a party a map of table seats at door made by LaVigne artist—we went to Phipps next door, met his wife, she went for cucumbers and he pulled delicate enamel box of snow (other day Harry I'd had from same box in bathroom of Club St. Germain—he'd took me—heard Kenny Clarke and Sonny Clarke had been in my room 2 months ago talking interminable junktalk to Bill, me and BJ and Gregory drunk arguing and hinctying in front of my room-kitchen table, where he sat with Bill, audience, we stood up fronta them and they talked serious we enthused by 12 people in room put on play me asking BJ to give me his life, he with big beard saying yes, but, Gregory drunkest rolling around us encouraging Clarke and Bill to listen—I explaining my prosody lines to Clarke asking him if it's like his drums—he told me come down free to St. Germain—I never went—till Phipps took me (Phipps a friend, went to India with Rothschildic Jacques Stern, 25 yr old, crippled, braces on poliac thin hips and feet, one crutch aluminum, I carry his 95 pounds oft upstairs 4 flights to my room so he see Bill) (all the latter is Stern whom I'll describe)—Phipps took me to hear great excitement jazz with Clarke and Bill—everybody on Harry in Paris busted, including Clarke, great raids everywhere—he playing that night suddenly shaved headed and I beard sick—he waved at me after 2 months—high later that night after can visit with enamel junk box, talked with narcissus Yale strange boy blond Phipps, he told me he made it with Jimmy Dean, had backed his first show, fell in love with Dean lounging openbreast and feet outstretched in chairs—screwed Dean and blew each other, Dean no screw him. (Door just knocked, I got it locked so I can keep private 3 AM feed of coke and write you letter.) You ever get a coke letter before? Dear Jack, you love me still, I love you, don't be mad I make long remark last time and about mother—

that why you no answer? Bill say not to, he say it's meaningless to make such generalizations, i.e. even if true you know anyway accept or reject on one level or other, such insights, psychoanalytic, naive of me to think they have emotional meaning anyway to you—but was I wrong—I old ami trying to talk to you Lucienesque *à la* Carr—as we might dig Neal apattern from afar— tho his I can't fathom—anyway door knock, just turned away Arab acquaintance Bouraba, wrote 7 novels in Arabic, from Algiers, sensitive Arabic even Bill thinks is good intentioned, one maybe translated I dunno in French— wanders around Paris no place to sleep slept here last nite—I wanted to be alone with Coke Jack—said was typing. He showed me his wet shoulders from rain and said *"mais in tout cas mieux que vous travillez sans distraction."* I said *"Pardon, c'est vrai—a bientot."* My room like a RR station, we all get up different times, Bill now unaccustomable 1 PM for tea bread breakfast, Greg wakes 10 or earlier and don't eat breakfast but writes types or walks—he has little green (8 mille) attic room upstairs last week he asked Jacques Stern for sudden $50 for rent etc. and Jacques peeled it off his daily junk-taxi-chauffeur-Tour D'argent roll—I get up noon mostly, talk to Bill 1-3 PM, walk out with Gregory, Bill goes in late afternoon to buy paregoric (he has 2 oz. small habit) or see analyst. I shop at 5 and cook we all eat early—7PM-8 or 9—we go out to St. Germain for coffee maybe all, with BJ or anyone else who comes over, sometimes 5 people, I come back at 10 maybe and type letters, rarely write with empty mind, don't write much poetry, sometimes scrawl notes in new green notebook and leave them, have a lot now. Anyway, just got back from Phipps house visit first time all three of us—first time know rich—he came as I said, earlier to bring us his old suits—one for each of us—Bill looks like great sober Palm Beach chess player private genius in his new black flannel suit, fits him exact—saw him framed tonight in huge 18th Century drawing room, his hair thin, he thin (PG) and retired, making speedy psychic gestures with his palms, stiff armed junky explanation gestures, of some scientific theory of chess—probability, and horserace betting, indifferent to vast Elsa alas Maxwell Party actually going on next door (shades Kingsland). Jacques Stern, I haven't explained, Gregory heard of him at Harvard, a rich young Frenchman—crutches, 95 lb., polio—had read *On Road, Gasoline, Howl, Junkie* (not realizing the latter was Bill)—he writes, prose, very good, not totally mad, but amazing, so desirous of explaining soul of dead Peter la Nice, fellow 20 yr old junkie with Alan Eager, who died, Stern says he was his saint (Peter)—studied, like Bill, anthropology at Harvard, like Bill, descended from noble (Rothschild) Jewish strange huge Champs Elysées apartment—like Bill, an endless experimental junkie, had same kafkian idea of junk as Bill—writes prose like Bill's anthropological images of Yage City—also lived in India with guru 14 months—going back next fall (wants to go with Bill) Like Bill, being psychoanalyzed by multilingual famous analyst in Paris—he was sick, we went to his vast apartment, his tall sexy lovely wife hates us, he lay in bed junksick (everybody busted) reading Bill's manuscript—he loves Bill and says he's the great teacher—reading me Tristan Tzara dada poesy too—lay in bed thin and pale and ashen, huge room, butlers outside door, told us go to library get licker—rolls joints—drove us in huge chauffeur 50 foot convertible, cream, top down (Gregory asked that) up Champs Elysées—immense intellectual knowledge, years in polio bed reading Pareto and Roman history and anthropology and Spengler—wants to be saint—said in India, with guru, meditated daily 10 hours—reached what he thought was nirvanic void—would stay there 2 hrs—suddenly evil voices Why! Why! began creeping in void, his guru told him he was Not Ready, and sent him away—yesterday he came to hotel—he too finally busted by cops for possession, they came and questioned him at 8 AM in his huge ruggy bedroom, 5 hours in the library with them, he big black sheep for years, may go jail, short term 2 mo., probably not, just fine and expensive doctors and lawyers testimony—he wanted to know from Gregory if jail was necessary spiritually for him—we told him no anyway poor cripple—Like Bill (this year) he gave up sex, indifferent, tho he has this solid Ava Gardner wife who digs him, loves him, and 3 year old baby, or 4, boy—never saw kid, in nursery of vast duplex apartment.—His friend buddy millionaire boy, went to India with last time, Harry Phipps, who came by tonight for us with old clothes and cocaine. Bill digs Stern, his mind, factual information, on junk and on anthro, and advanced experimental thoughts on brainwashing and evil—so suddenly Paris getting interesting, Stern knows Dali and Cocteau aristocracy types, bored, wants Corsoesque Romantic Age—but I want to come home, have no fare, wondering where it will come from—got to come in next two weeks or I hide in Rotterdam looking for ship free workaway—almost might ask Stern or narcissusist Phipps but don't want to don't know them yet besides my father offered it if no other jokefate gold appears. Will send a batch poems to *Botthege Oscura* and elsewhere and try collect $30 each, should work. Gregory might come back, but scared of cops and doesn't think anyone needs wants loves him there anyway, so would as well go to India—tho when the other day I told him I wished he'd come home—thought how beautiful he would be a great known poet in NY, with Fried Shoes and H Bomb wrapped in Ermine with mustache of Gold, I want to eat your Boom, etc.—he seemed moved he said, nobody asked him to come back before. He's homeless, Bill is another matter, he says "I have told nobody to wait," or "I have told no one to wait" and seeing him suddenly look old, I added "Not even my body." He wants to finish analysis here in a few months, then no plans—he's long gone from interest in sex me loveboy—tonight in his black suit in his room he looked so lone I kissed him all over his cheeks goodnight, he smiled impassive and shy as if in Asia, and bowed me out good-night—then after, maybe with Stern in fall, go to India. Just sniffed last of my pile of coke,—about 20 nostrils-full all today since 5 PM—no tzinging noises around ceiling and walls—just a sustained energy and want-to-talk.

Well, yesterday Art Buchwald, we were looped, I see not much gets across in interview that way, tho he was simpatico, I wrote him serious prose poem letter last nite for his column—I see what you had to go through, wish I'd been there, I feel now too tired tongue stricken to blow, afresh, when I get home, my virgin kicks and energy and sense of mission like I had with Gary in North-west, or earlier in SF, seems gone—nothing new to say, repeat poetry novelties—wonder how I'll do in NY and if I'll have to do anything wild— don't even feel like reading, *Howl,* can't even make ecstatic tape in soundproof French Vogue studio room, tho I've been paid $50 advance on it, can't make it right now, maybe in Newman's studio in NY can get drunk—make last weep record. Help me. What you do—I heard your record (records?) out—Steve Allen? Tho not heard anything about it. Enclosed find letter from Terry South-ern, friend of Mason, wrote pointless tho hip N. West book [*Flash and Filigree*] published by your Deutsch in England—perhaps you can answer him—I'll write him that queer sections, some libel characters, and whole scroll long syn-tax of *On Road* was tampered with by Viking—they take out any tea? I seem to remember they broke up prose a lot to shorter sentences often and disturbed the benny flow. He (Southern) seems well meaning and interested in prose and took trouble to write and investigate and so I feel like answering information-ally. You seen review of *Road* from England *Times* and *Observer*? One (John Wain) quoted both of us at length attacking etc.

Buchwald said he'd introduce us (and Bill especially) to John Huston who's here, making picture. Bill has idea for Tangier panorama film (episodes seen thru eyes of bill-junky looking for drugstore sick on Ramadan holiday, street boy looking for a score from fag, effeminate tourist with mother), town seen thru different Burroughs eyes, juxtaposed. Or maybe Greg and I make travel loot in bit-parts—or maybe just watch Huston Burroughs talk.

Lentil soup and Bayonne hambone on stove, blue dawn rainy cloudy sky all week, coke descending, been grinding my teeth all night, cat's on bed washing his breast, grey calm cat Bill no longer torments at all, why don't you write me love letter, you ashamed of me I don't write enough or not sufficiently entered void ready for death? Ah Jack, are you tired—you have been writing long solitudenous halo for Sax? I'll be home in NY see you within a month, lets meet like angels and be innocent, what are you brooding about in Long Island, hold my hand, I want to see Lucien again and shade of Rubenstein and London Towers and 43, 1943, our walk by 119th St. to Theological Seminary when I told you about saying farewell to Lucien's and my door on 7th floor and adieu prayer to stairway there, is not Sebastian faithful to the end? [...]

Goodnight,

Allen

[*After receiving the news that Cassady had been arrested, Ginsberg wrote to him immediately offering to help in any way he could.*]

Allen Ginsberg [Paris, France] to Neal Cassady [San Bruno, CA]
July 7, 1958

Dear Neal:

I hear you're in San Bruno County Jail, so taking a chance with this note in hope it will reach you. I'd have written before but had lost your Los Gatos address. How are you—what's happened? I got letter from LaVigne telling me news of you and North Beach. Neal, Neal hello, write me. I leave here in 10 days and return home to join Peter in New York—everything's ok here, Bill's with me in same hotel. We met young 24 year old genius millionaire, digs Bill, same kicks as Bill, anthropology and Harvard and horses you know—they'll go to India, this young Frenchman and Bill (he's married a beauty and has kid)—he's crippled and thin angel, polio—a Rothschild—writes—and he'll set up a big house for us to join them, outside Calcutta—study Yoga and meet the Sages of India at last (he been there 14 months a year ago). So next year after a year home I will head Far East with Peter I hope. But only fragmentary news of your difficulties reached here—tell Carolyn to write me if you can't, with details, and what future looks like and what family situation is, and what arrangements have been made for house, etc. Is there anything I can do, I mean get together any character references or witnesses—Witt-Diamant from State College or whoever I can arrange for, I don't know if that's any help? I will be in NY around the 25th of this month—if there's anything I can do on the spot tell me and I'll come out there and be what help I can. I have no idea of the situation. I wrote Gary Snyder, he's the only one with strong sense (he's in hospital for operation right now) to find out the score and find what need be done. [...] Bill sends his love, Gregory sends his, he left yesterday for trip to bullfight fiesta in Pamplona, Hemingway backwater—he's glowing nowadays and very funny. We made an English trip together, read in Oxford, explored Soho head area. I guess you're OK, hah? Bill you know lay alone in Tangier for half a year 1957 and finally meditating all afternoon alone in darkened room, for months, received his first perfect bliss, that is he says, he felt, after long despair, a new sense of "indifferent benevolent sentience at the center of things"—his first real faith. So came here to Paris to clear up early tangles in a last mop-up psychoanalysis. He's changed a lot, very balanced, kind and gentle. Now even tender. His whole hang up with me completely disappeared, miraculously, it was only a last ditch grab at some connection before godliness, now he's alone with the Alone. Me, I have got too hung up with my identity as poet-power and after yearlong hassles with publicity and pulling wires of Beat behind scenes to get poetries published, got to give up again, and go be nobody again and regain my god calm prophecy feelings. Life here been frantic and second rate, everybody in my room all the time, I never get alone enough. But I've seen Tangier, Spain, Italy, Vienna, Munich, Paris, Amsterdam, London. Tomorrow night Bill and I go make visit to Céline, I spoke to him on phone, he has shy reticent young voice, almost quavering, very delicate voice and hesitates, no ogre. I said, "How lovely to hear your voice." He said "anytime Tuesday after 4." But I never got to Warsaw and Moscow, tho I tried.

What have you been doing all this time? I hardly could get news of you and asked everyone I wrote in SF, write me a note at least, here or to Paterson, when will we see each other again? Come fly over ocean at night and meet me in mid Atlantic sky in a dream—or I'll arrive and hove in clouds over San Bruno shedding prayers in the moonbeams. Keep Neal—I'll keep Allen as ever, write me.

Love

Allen

[*That July, Ginsberg sailed for home. As soon as he could he wrote to his friends Paris to bring them up to date on events in New York.*]

Allen Ginsberg [Long Island, NY] to William S. Burroughs and Gregory Corso [Paris, France] late July–early August 1958

Dear Bill: Gregory:

Been home a few days, nothing much spectacular happening, I'm out at my brother's Levittown-type house in L.I. where nothing works, the chrome type-writer table rattles, dishwasher machine puffs steam and ties you down in the kitchen 45 minutes till it finished, walls are plasterboard so you can't hang pictures or put up shades, all the sliding new-type closet doors have been off their rails for years, you can't get them moving, none of the other door handles catch, sink has a special modern faucet you pull up handle instead of turn it, but the pull-up handle goes out of commission and you can only get scalding water, now my brother's gone out Sunday to canvas neighborhood, collect Democratic votes for local district committeemen because he's caught in middle of small town personality squabble between two irritable competing factions of ambitious Democratic politicians. He has to do this to get business as local lawyer and political appointment job later since it costs $10,000 a year to keep his household running, and it's not even far enough out on L.I. to be out of bomb area.

Missed Peter at boat and had supper with Lucien, he had ulcer and quit drinking, he has house in country, his wife stays up there all week with three children, he stays here works, I was quiet, he says he has special pipeline to God, ain't no rules in his religion except "You don't mess with people" (he says that covers the ten commandments etc.), and his religion don't allow no prose-lytizing either, it's just for him, and his special pipeline (like in Arabia he says)— woke up one morning on 33rd birthday felt like he'd just been taken down off the cross—also his God don't have nothing to do with human ideas about malevolence or benevolence—no special point to life except that if you get a special pipeline like him it's pretty interesting, that is, life is at least interesting, but there is no moral. This his sermon to Jack, me, Peter, and a collection of UP drunkards at his house. Last night, before last

Found Peter next day and key to apartment on 87th on loan (87th and First) for a few weeks from friend Elise [Cowen] and went there and had long sweaty ball, and midnight woke up with strange feeling in my kidney I'd had all day and realized I was in line for a kidney stone attack, called up Dr. Perrone in

Village, he phoned pharmacy, I sped down in taxicab and picked twelve Demerol tablets, so scored early after arrival. Took three and it killed the pain and knocked me out for the next day, gave some to Peter and Jack (to keep Kerouac from boozing). Saw him the next afternoon, down at Lucien's, he seems a little wider, face and body, arm wrapped dirty poison ivy bandage, he was a little drunk and insisted on lifting up my brother (I want to lift the Ginsbergs) we took long walk around the Village, fragments of endless details about movie money (*On Road* sold for $25,000 to shysters who won't pay up), interviews, says he don't know what to write now. Yes, I got that letter from his mother you forwarded, he says he know about it, she read one of my letters (the long cocaine one) he says it don't make any difference between us, but I suspect it does. He going to stay out in L.I. not see anyone all summer. I went out yesterday to Peter's in Northport—turns out Jack lives two blocks away, Peter went over to fetch him out, I hid in bushes, Jack wouldn't come out said he was afraid his mother would suspect, anyway "What good would it do?" whatever he meant by that—something Buddhist—so I went away feeling rather bad— so far can't seem to reach him, emotionally—just shout maybe when drunk. He said he was restless in L.I. and wanted to get place somewhere else, I suspect his mother not happy there either, I don't know, he stuck with her like wandering Kike.

We went to Don Allen's, he said he'd look up you, Michaux book and find out about Céline latest book, he was interested in publishing both—also there's a new *Evergreen* out with some Artaud and Jack's essay on essentials of prose. Also told him about Stern's book, have Jacques send him or me a copy, he was interested. Also said he was printing a poetry series and would publish everyone, Snyder and Whalen and Creeley, etc. Said the publishing scene is taking care of itself now, I think. Olson now digs my poetry and Whalen's and recommended them publishing the Xbalba. Grove disaffected with Duncan and so is Olson—too much campy clique???, I gather (these last gossips for Gregory, not you, Bill)—Met Peter's father, they're living on 84th near Riverside in one room. After long talks, what we'll do is get a pad in town, Peter leave his father to shift for self (says he can), and we settle down for unknown year ahead. Lafcadio in Northport will stay there and get job he says though he's invited to stay with us—but he talks about seeing Mars rocket which swooped over Northport and signaled to him when he ran out of house in woods naked —they're coming back get him, the one perfect man, to save him from the coming bomb apocalypse when the earth will go too near the sun "just like

Mars came too near earth last year." We gave him long frantic astronomy lesson all afternoon and he got it through his head about regular orbits of Mars etc. but there's nothing much to say to him about spaceships rescuing him since says he waved to them and saw them. Altogether screwy. At same time painting a great deal—I bought his first oil for $10—a lone doll like adolescent (him) painted orange sitting at small round table dreaming and gazing at an empty chair with a wall opened in a window and writhing green Matisse-like vegetation entering the room. Odor of personal dreamy loneliness in the picture almost like a Balthus dream picture—he's very good, and the colors varied and inventive, a natural talent. We bought him more oils and canvasses and what happens next don't know. Meanwhile got to find a pad. Julius no great problem since if he's well enough he can be brought home weekends tentatively; if not, not. Peter's submerged in all that and seems glad to take my advice to disentangle where his help's doing no good. Don Allen publishing one of his poems in the anthology too.

So that's all I've done, seen Jack, Lucien, Peter, my family one day in Paterson, and now out here in L.I. with brother for Sunday. I'll go into the city Monday and get X-rays for kidney stone possibilities—probably nothing permanent—meet Peter, go up to apartment on 87th and ball, sleep, and figure what next. Peter works nights. I haven't sized up or contacted much of the literary entertainment world money scene and don't know how real that is yet here actually, meanwhile trying to get part-time job dishwash or Gallup Poll research til I see what is up. I don't know what I'm doing here except for Peter, I don't understand Jack, the newspapers are too many to read and the cars roll by in the rain outside on the highway in L.I. Guess I'll just settle down if can find an apartment and see what happens. [. . .]

I'll write as I go along. Not showed Jack his mother's letter yet but he seems so ambivalent, I will next time. She's mad and he seems to be picking it up. Says he's a Republican. I don't know what's wrong. Nobody seems to be dependable but Peter, I'm going to analysis, if I can find one.

Skyline is stunning in the mist, when I came in—like all the spires and architecture and cathedrals of Europe all put together on one shelf and more massive height—you get a sense of eternity looking at Manhattan from a boat arriving—the buildings look as if they were manufacturing cosmic jazz. [. . .]

Love

Allen

[*Ginsberg was always bothered by criticism from the academic world, but when his old classmate, John Hollander, began to criticize the Beat Generation in print, Allen wrote an epic-length letter in which he tried to set the record straight.*]

Allen Ginsberg [New York, NY] to John Hollander [New London, CT] September 7, 1958

Dear John:

Got your letter, slow answering since writing a little and invasion of people in apartment and too much mail, a lady in Michigan wanting to know if I believe in God, I have to answer everything, it's difficult. No, of course, communication's always there, why not, only a shit would be bugged, besides I've seen too much, I'm tired. It's just that I've tried to do too much explaining and get overwhelmed by the vastness of the task, and sometimes what seems to be all the accumulated ill-will and evil vibrations in America (Kerouac got beaten up at the San Remo for his trouble in coming down there and making himself available.) But to begin somewhere, I should might begin with one thing, simple (I hate to go back to it over and over, like revolving around my corpse, the construction of *Howl*). This may be corny to you, my concern with that, but I've got to begin somewhere and perhaps differences of opinion between us can be resolved by looking at that. See, for years before that, thinking in Williams line, which I found very helpful and quite real for what it is doing, the balance by ear of short lines formed of relatively natural ordinary notebook or conversation speech. Xbalba is fragments of mostly prose, written in a Mexican school copybook, over half a year—then rereading, picking out the purest thoughts, stringing them together, arranging them in lines suitably balanced, mostly measured by the phrase, that is, one phrase a line—you know it's hard to explain this because it's like painting and unless you do it like practicing a piano, you don't think in those terms and get the experience of trying to work that way, so you don't notice all the specific tricks—that anyone who works in that field gets to be familiar with—that's why I'm interested in Blackburn, Levertov, Creeley, Oppenheimer, all the Black [Mountain] lit people—they work steadily consistently trying to develop this line of goods, and each has a different interesting approach—they all stem out of Williams—but I can tell their lines apart they really are different just as you can tell the difference between styles and approaches of abstract painters. When you tell me it's just a bore to you, that just cuts off communication, I mean I don't know what to say, I get embarrassed to retreat and go about my work and stop explanations. Of course you may not be interested in this field of experiment, but that doesn't mean it's uninteresting to others, that it's categorically a bore. I ALSO believe it's the main "tradition," not that there is any tradition except what we make ourselves. But basically I'm not interested in tradition because I'm more interested in what I'm a doing, what it's inevitable for me to do. This realization has given me perspective on what a vast sad camp the whole literary-critical approach of school has been—basically no one has insight into poetry techniques except people who are exercising them. But I'm straying at random. But I'm now getting bugged at people setting themselves up as scholars and authorities and <u>getting in the way</u> of continuous creative work or its understanding or circulation —there is not one article on the Beat or SF scene yet that has not been (pro or con) invalidated (including yours) by the basic fact that the author is just a big windbag not knowing what he's talking about—no technical background, no knowledge of the vast body of experimental work, published and unpublished (the unpublished is the best), no clear grasp of the various different schools of experiment all converging toward the same or similar end, all at once coming into intercommunication, no knowledge of the letters and conversations in between, not even the basic ability (like Podhoretz) to tell the difference between prosody and diction (as in his PR diatribes on spontaneous bop prosody confusing it with the use of hip talk not realizing it refers to rhythmical construction of phrases and sentences). I mean where am I going to begin a serious explanation if I have to deal with such unmitigated stupid ignorant ill willed inept vanity as that—someone like that wouldn't listen unless you hit him over the head with a totally new universe, but he's stuck in his own hideous world, I would try, but he scarcely has enough heart to hear)—etc. etc. —so all these objections about juvenile delinquency, vulgarity, lack of basic education, bad taste, etc. etc., no form, etc. I mean it's impossible to discuss things like that—finally I get to see them as so basically <u>wrong</u> (unscientific) so dependent on ridiculous provincial schoolboy ambitions and presuppositions and so lacking contact with practical fact—that it seems a sort of plot almost, a kind of organized mob stupidity—the final camp of its announcing itself as a representative of value or civilization or taste—I mean I give up, that's just too much fucking nasty brass. And you're guilty of that too John, you've just got to drop it, and take me seriously, and listen to what I have to say. It doesn't mean you have to agree, or change your career or your writing, or anything hideous, it just means you've got to have the heart and decency to take people seriously and not depend only on your own university experience for arbitrary standard of value to judge others by. It doesn't mean you have to agree, that Free Verse is the Only Path of Prosodic Experiment, or that Williams is a Saint, or I have some horrible magic secret (tho god knows I have enough, this week with that damned Buddhist laughing gas, everybody has). Just enough to dig, you to dig, what others besides yourself are trying to do, and be interested in their work or not, but not get in the way, in fact even encourage where you can see some value. And you're in a position to encourage, you teach, you shouldn't hand down limited ideas to younger minds—that was the whole horror of Columbia, there just was nobody there (maybe except Weaver) who had a serious involvement with advanced work in poetry. Just a bunch of dilettantes. And THEY have the nerve to set themselves up as guardians of culture?!? Why it's such a piece of effrontery—enough to make anyone paranoiac, it's a miracle Jack or myself or anybody independent survived—tho god knows the toll in paranoia been high enough. All these grievances I'm pouring out to you. Well why revise.

Back to *Howl*: construction. After sick and tired of short line free verse as not expressionistic enough, not swinging enough, can't develop a powerful enough rhythm, I simply turned aside, accidentally to writing part I of *Howl,* in solitude, diddling around with the form, thinking it couldn't be published anyway (queer content my parents shouldn't see etc.) also it was out of my shortline line. But what I did thought my theory, I changed my mind about "measure" while writing it. Part one uses repeated base who, as a sort of kithara BLANG, Homeric (in my imagination) to mark off each statement, each rhythmic unit. So that's experiment with longer and shorter variations on a fixed base—the principle being, that each line has to be contained within the elastic of one breath—with suitable punctuatory expressions where the rhythm has built up enough so that I have to let off steam by building a longer climactic line in which there is a jazzy ride. All the ear I've ever developed goes into the balancing of those lines. The interesting moments when the rhythm is sufficiently powerfully pushing ahead so I can ride out free and drop the who key that holds it together. The method of keeping a long line still all poetic and not prosey is the concentration and compression of basically imagistic notations into surrealist or cubist phrasing, like hydrogen jukeboxes. Ideally anyway. Good example of this is Gregory's great (I swear) Coit Tower ode. Lines have greater poetic density. But I tried to keep the language sufficiently dense in one way or another—use of primitive naive grammar (expelled for crazy), elimination of prosey articles and syntactical sawdust, juxtaposition of cubic style images, or hot rhythm. Well then Part II. Here the basic repeated word is Moloch. The long line is now broken up into component short phrases with !

rhythmical punctuation. The key repeat BLANG word is repeated internally in the line (basic rhythm sometimes emerging—/—) but the rhythm depends mostly on the internal Moloch repeat. Lines here lengthened—a sort of free verse prose poetry STANZA form invented or used here. This builds up to climax (Visions! Omens! Etc.) and then falls off in coda. Part III, perhaps an original invention (I thought so then but this type of thinking is vain and shallow anyway) to handling of long line (for the whole poem is an experiment in what you can do with the long line—the whole book is) —::: that is, a phrase base rhythm (I'm with you etc) followed as in litany by a response of the same length (Where you're madder etc), then repeat of base over and over with the response elongating itself slowly, still contained within the olsstic of one breath —till the stanza (for it is a stanza form there, I've used variations of it since) building up like a pyramid, an emotion crying siren sound, very appropriate to the expressive appeal emotion I felt (a good healthy emotion said my analyst at that time, to dispose once and for all of that idiotic objection)—anyway, building up to the climax where there's a long long long line, penultimate, too long for one breath, where I open out and give the answer (O starry spangled shock of Mercy the eternal war is here). All this rather like a jazz mass, I mean the conception of rhythm not derived from jazz directly but if you listen to jazz you get the idea (in fact specifically old trumpet solo on a JATP Can't Get Started side)—well all this is built like a brick shithouse and anybody can't hear the music is as I told you I guess I meekly informed Trilling, who is absolutely lost in poetry, is got a tin ear, and that's so obviously true, I get sick and tired I read 50 reviews of *Howl* and not one of them written by anyone with enough technical interests to notice the fucking obvious construction of the poem, all the details besides (to say nothing of the various esoteric classical allusions built in like references to Cézanne's theory of composition etc. etc.)—that I GIVE UP and anybody henceforth comes up to me with a silly look in his eye and begins bullshitting about morals and sociology and tradition and technique and JD [juvenile delinquency]. I mean I *je ne sais plus parler*—the horrible irony of all these jerks who can't read trying to lecture me (us) on FORM.

Kerouac has his own specific method of construction of prose which he has pursued for a decade now and I have yet to see one piece of criticism taking that into account, or even interested enough to realize he has one and its implications and how it related to the rhythm of his prose,—much less how his method alters and develops chronologically from book to book, and what phases it goes thru, what changes one would encounter in so prolonged and devoted an experiment as his (rather like Gertrude Stein)—but nobody's interested in literature, in technique, all they think about is their goddam lousy ideas of what they preconceive writing to be about and I'M SICK OF LISTEN-ING TO THAT AND READING ABOUT THAT AND UNLESS THERE IS MORE COOPERATION FROM THE SUPPOSEDLY RESPONSIBLE PAR-TIES IN UNIVERSITIES AND MAGAZINES I ABSOLUTELY CUT OUT AND REFUSE TO SUBMIT MY HEART WRUNG PSALMS TO THE DIRTY HANDS AND MINDS OF THESE BASTARDS AND THEY CAN TAKE THEIR FUCKING literary tradition AND SHOVE IT UP THEIR ASS—I don't need them and they don't need me and I'm sick of putting myself out and being put down and hit on the head by jerks who have no interests but their ridiculous devilish social careers and MONEY MONEY MONEY which is the root of the EVIL here in America and I'm not MAD.

Footnote to Howl is too lovely and serious a joke to try to explain. The built in rhythmic exercise should be clear, it's basically a repeat of the Moloch sec-tion. It's dedicated to my mother who died in the madhouse and it says I loved her anyway and that even in worst conditions life is holy. The exaggeratedness of the statements are appropriate, and anybody who doesn't understand the specific exaggerations will never understand Rejoice in the Lamb or Lorca's Ode to Whitman or Mayakovsky's At the Top of My Voice or Artaud's Pour En Finir Avec Le Judgment de Dieu or Apollinaire's "inspired bullshit" or Whit-man's madder passages or anything, anything, anything about the interna-tional modern spirit in poesy to say nothing about the international tradition in prosody which has grown up xarnor the tradition of open prophetic bardic poetry which 50 years has sung like an angel over the poor soul of the world while all sorts of snippy cats castrates pursue their good manners and sell out their own souls and the spirit of god who now DEMANDS sincerity and hell fire take him who denies the voice in his soul—except that it's all a kindly joke and the universe disappears after you die so nobody gets hurt no matter how little they allow themselves to live and blow on this earth.

Anyone noticing the constructions and the series of poems in Howl would then notice that the next task I set myself to was adapting that kind of open long line to tender lyric feelings and short form, so next is Supermarket in Cali-fornia, where I pay homage to Whitman in realistic terms (eyeing the grocery boys) and it's a little lyric, and since it's almost prose it's cast in form of prose paragraphs like St. Perse—and has nobody noticed that I was aware enough of that to make that shift there. Nor that I went on in the next poem Transcription of Organ Music to deliberately write a combo of prose and poetry some lines indented which are poetical and some lines not but paragraphed like prose to see what could be done with absolute transcription of spontaneous material, transcription of sensual data (organ) at a moment of near Ecstasy, not, nor has anybody noticed that I have technically developed my method of transcription (as Cézanne developed sketching) so that I could transcribe at such moments and try to bring back to the poor suffering world what rare moments exist, and that technical practice has led to a necessary spontaneous method of transcription which will pass in and out of poetry and so needs a flexible form—its own natural form unchanged—to preserve the moment alive and uncensored by the arbitrary ravenings of conceptual or preconception or post-censoring-out-of-embarrassment-so-called intelligence? Anyway there is a definite experiment in FORM FORM FORM and not a ridiculous idea of what form should be like. And it is an example that has all sorts of literary precedents in French poetry, in Hart Crane, in—but this whole camp of FORM is so ridiculous I am ashamed to have to use the word to justify what is THERE (and only use it in a limited academic context but would not dream of using this kindergarten terminology to poets from whom I learn—Kerouac, Burroughs or Corso—who start to new worlds of their own academic tribe that is so superciliously hung on COLLEGE that it has lost touch with living creation.)

The next problem attacked in the book is to build up a rhythmical drive in long lines without dependence on repetition of key words and phrases, who's, Moloch's, or Holy's, a drive forward to a climax and conclusion—and to do it spontaneously (...well I've broken my typewriter on this explanation I continue on Peter's—a 20 minute task) (Sunflower) with 15 years practice behind —to ride out on the breath rhythm without any artificial built in guides or poles or diving boards or repetition except the actual rhythm, and to do it so that both long long lines, and long lines, and shorter 10 words lines all have the same roughly weight, and balance each other out, and anybody take the trouble to read Sutra out will see it does that and the come of the rhythmic buildup is "You were never no locomotive Sunflower, you were a sunflower, and you locomotive (pun) you were a locomotive, etc." And furthermore at this point in the book I am sick of preconceived literature and only interested in writing the actual process and technique, wherever it leads, and the various possible experiments in composition that are in my path—and if anybody still is confused in what literature is let it be hereby announced once for all in the 7 Kingdoms that that's what it is—Poetry is what poets write, and not what other people think they should write.

The next poem America takes off on the free line and is an attempt to make combinations of short and long lines, very long lines and very short lines, something I've always wanted to do but previously had to depend on sustained rhythmical buildup to carry the structure of the poem forward. But in America I rely on discrete separate statements, rather than one long madbreath forward. Here as always however the measure, the meter, of each line, the think the thing that makes it a complete line, and the thing that balances each line with its neighbors is that each (with tactical exceptions) is ONE SPEECH BREATH —an absolute physical measure as absolute as the ridiculous limited little accent or piddling syllable count. And in this I've gone forward from Williams because I literally measure each line by the physical breath—each one breath statement, dictated by what has to be said, in relations and balance to the previous rhythmic statement.

The next task the book includes is the Greyhound poem which is attempt to apply the method with all tricks, long with short lines mixed, some repetition some not, some lyric, some Bardic, some surrealist or cubist phrasing, some pure imagistic-Williams notation—to apply all this to a realistic solid work proletarian common experience situation and come up with a classical type elegiac poem in modern rhythm and tricks etc. Also to make a nonhowling poem with separate parts etc.

So all this adds up to handbook of various experiments with the possibilities of an expressive long line, and perhaps carries on from where Whitman in U.S. left off with his long lines. At least I've in part III Howl attempted one visible organic stanza construction. Pound complains that Whitman was not interested enough in developing his line, I have tried to rescue long line for further use— tho at the moment (this last year I've abandoned it for a totally different mode than I've ever used, a totally wild page of free verse dictated by the immediate demands of spontaneous notation, with its appearance or form on the page determined by the structure of thought, rather than the aural quality primarily.

Latter's unclear I'll start over. Tho poetry in Williams has depended a lot on little breath groups for its typographical organization, and in Howl an extension into longer breaths (which are more natural to me than Williams short simple talks)—there is another possible approach to the measure of the line— which is, not the way you would say it, a thought, but the way you would think it—i.e. we think rapidly, in visual images as well as words, and if each successive thought were transcribed in its confusion (really its ramification) you get a slightly different prosody than if you were talking slowly.

This still not clear—if you talk fast and excitedly you get weird syntax and rhythms, just like you think, or nearer to what you think. Not that everybody's thinking process is consciously the same—everybody's got a different consciousness factory—but the attempt here is to let us see—to transcribe the thought all at once so that its ramifications appear on the page much as the ramifications of a sentence appear on the page when it's analyzed into a paradigm in grammar books—example, from last poem (Laughing Gas—an attempt to transcribe that experience of the dis-appearance of chilicosm when consciousness is anesthetized, as an instance of what maybe happens at death)

The Bloomfield police car
With its idiot red light
Revolving on its head
Balefully at eternity
  Gone in an instant
— simultaneous
appearance of bankrobbers
at the Twentieth Century Bank
The fire engines screaming
Toward an old lady's
Burned-in-her-bedroom
Today apocalypse
  Tomorrow
Mickey mouse cartoons
          . . .

I'm disgusted! It's unbelievable!
How could it all be so
Horrible and funny?
  It's a dirty joke!
The whole universe a shaggy dog story
With a weird ending that
  Begins again
    Till you get the point
"IT was a dark and gloomy night"
"in every direction in and out"
  "You take the high road
and I'll take the low"
  everybody in the same
fantastic Scotland of the mind —
consciousness
          . . .

> Gary Snyder, Jack, thou Zens
> Split open existence
> And laugh and cry —
> What's shock? What's measure?
> When the mind's irrational
> - following the blinking lights
> of contrariety —
>   . . .
>
> etc. etc.

Well I haven't done enough work yet in this direction, I want to get a wild page, as wild and as clear (really clear) as the mind—no forcing the thoughts into straightjacket—sort of a search for the rhythm of the thoughts and their natural occurrence and spacings and notational paradigms. Naturally when you read it aloud it also turns out to have intricate aural rhythm. But this is just an experiment—and naturally, this type writing gives thought an artificial form—the mere crystallizing it on page does—but to attempt to reproduce the droppings of the mind on the page—to work freely with this kind of direction—you see—you see—it's fascinating to me.

Now if I have you at all intrigued with this as a possibility—to spread out into the field—there's Olson's interesting essay on projective verse, and Kerouac's handmaiden article on approaches to prose—and all his experience in organizing whole novels with mad complicated structures (*tres* formal you see) built on the process of his mind in composition—novels say about Neal (unpublished *Visions of Neal*) which take off from the first shining memory, (irrespective of chronology) and take their form from the deep sublime symmetries that are to be found in following from naked recollection instance to another one to another I mean—I mean that in watching natural thought (like in meditation Buddhist type) you see the structure of your random seeming thought—and you can build whole prose or poetry structures on it. Not without effort at first, for it takes immense self discipline and effort to learn to not think (IBM) but to meditate and <u>watch</u> thought without interrupting it by literary self-consciousness and embarrassed preconceptions and rules.

So the most authoritative handbook of forms for me in modern poetry is Kerouac's immense sonnet sequence *Mexico City Blues*, they're not sonnets, they're a series of 280 short (10-30 line) poems written sequentially in Mexico City, each has its own form-universe, all interrelated, being pieces of the same mind,—they look roughly like the piece of verse above I typed out—very weird and zigzag on the page—tremendous rich language and imagery too—nobody except the poetic hepcats in SF and *Chicago Review* picked up on this yet, nobody will publish it, a dirty rotten shame, but fuck everybody they don't desire it it's their Karma and they'll never learn how to write. (This is for real and important).

Gary Snyder and Phil Whalen from SF we lived with, they're learned Zens, Gary speaks Chinese and Jap and translates and taught anthropology and just got back from monastery etc. and specialized in comparative mythology, etc. etc. and peyote and T etc. he has a little beard, 27 years old rides a bicycle and has vow of poverty and likes girls—well him and Whalen (who just sits like a Buddha) also have vast unpublished manuscript. Well their work is great too tho who would know because who's interested except those advanced enough in same line and similar experiences in composition? Jack myself Gary and Phil originally read together in SF and that was the renaissance and any evaluation of the poetry is incomplete without FULL authoritative account of their work and not one of these shits who presumes to write on the subject for MONEY or EGO reasons has taken the trouble to investigate, and I've tried some of their work out on *Hudson* and *Partisan* and all the so called responsible journals and been put down so I conclude the whole official publishing scene in the U.S. is a vicious camp and Rhav and etc. and Morgan at *Hudson* etc. etc. and all those people are ENEMIES of culture and civilization and a bunch of perverted fairy amateurs and will get theirs anyway when the universe collapses on them so why worry in any case.

Then we have the case of Gregory who has absolute genius at elliptical hilarity, great natural phrasing, and is as good a poet now as Dylan Thomas, his great Bomb poem and Army and Coit Tower in his book which is powerful and pure and rich like Fern Hill and why nobody gives him the respect and money he deserves I'll never understand except a peculiar kind of ungrateful ill will of mediocrity which is always the enemy of the muse and will wind up poisoning Corso except that he's too mad—yet I haven't seen one responsible review of his book, an epoch making original book, tho much richer and better has already been composed by him—we are living in a very rich period of poetry in the U.S., it may be the very cracks in consciousness appearing over the fall of America is the concomitant of such a flowering—and his book's been out years now, a year and half—without official notice people have picked up on it about 2,000 copies already—not one review. I can't stand the pharisaical attitude of the whole treasonable intellectual group who think they are the civilization—basically the problem is they are not free, they have all sold their souls for money ego security conformity prestige university maturity social integration of the most spiteful and chicken kind—to have to endure the attacks and ignorance of these people is more than I should have to bear with the load I have to carry already it's not fair and it's asking too much of me, and to do that and have done that in a kind of ridiculous self imposed safety-poverty where I don't have stamps to communicate with Corso half the time oh well I'm complaining like Hitler. But not one inch of understanding! And the vulgarity of the kind of opportunistic publicity so called friendly from the same intellectual types—in another guise or job—at *Esquire* or *Time* —stories which ball up the real prosodic and spiritual issues—halfwit interpretations of "negative values" of Howl—all the Highetss that are pain paid thousands of dollars a year to there and yatter out their opinions opinions opinions the screwy band of opinionated clunkheads that run everything from the *Daily News* to the *Hudson Review*—you should see the insulting letters I get from that Morgan lame duck poet. And Simpson reviewing Howl and an inept and prosodaically inaccurate parody and rejoicing (with Podhoretz) that Burroughs and Kerouac and other SF manuscripts are unavailable and unpublished—and you resolving your conflict by taking the angle that Howl is rather "vulgar"—I mean I sent it to you hoping you'd have the technical knowledge to deal with it as a piece of construction and that you'd fuck the whole sociological-tone-revolut whatever bullshit that everyone else comes on with—and to have Gold (Herb) mocking me for dragging myself around the magazines and publishers trying to go out of my way to introduce new materials, explain, spread some light—in the face of the worst civilized shits that ever ran so monstrous a conspiracy as America mass communication at all— to have to tackle all that single-handed practically and then be put down for all that—I DIDN'T HAVE TO TAKE THE TROUBLE—to have to listen to Rhav in Venice giggling that there's no poetry in U.S. so that's why they didn't have a poetry editor at all 2 years ago—which was just his ignorance and the ignorance of all non-poets—yet he's RUNNING this so called mental newssheet! ? and to call that responsible culture? And to have them and everybody else ignoring totally the productions of the Jonathan Williams' Jargon series which for 8 years was the only respectable publishing company for experimental poetry—and total ignorance of all the work developed out of Black Mountain—the fucking sneers if anything—total incomprehension of Creeley's funny volumes of verse, nobody reviewed or heard of Blackburn's book (Dissolving Fabric—not GREAT but real), nor Levertov's nor Zukofsky's books there reviewed, *Black Mountain Review* the only decent mag operating for poets in America circulating 300 copies and nobody supposedly responsible at Columbia or anywhere taking the trouble to HELP, and the other BM poets minors, Oppenheimer, Perkoff, maybe Duncan etc.—and the great new young ones John Wieners and Edward Marshall—whom nobody ever heard of—or will investigate—and don't think I haven't written this to anybody I could get hold of, Gold, Rhav, *Mademoiselle*, *Hudson*, *New World Writing*, endless conversations and letters and explanations and trying to spread some good news, *Life*, and have them fuck it all up with their indifference or vulgar money journalism—and the whole problem of the Burroughs manuscript legally uncirculatable here in the U.S.—to say nothing of the great unknown Boston group around John Wieners (got a magazine *Measure* out in SF now)—and the beginning of interconnection of all these with the NY people, O'Hara Ashbery and Koch—at least these latter three pick up on something, and have some sympathy and openness, and respond to original attempts at composition.

The key and interest of Creeley's verse incidentally is this. Whereas in short line Williams generally or mine, runs forward in the line like actual speaking, Creeley has an ear of his own that's peculiar and laconic. He has got lately to using the most simplified forms, two lines together, free verse type couplets, trying to listen and balance them—his line tends to run backward, so to speak, rhythmically, the words very separate from each other and halting and stoic, effort of difficult nuts of speech, little pure sayings. A very peculiar subtle ear I'd say, NOT AT ALL like Williams, more like Pound writing Williams. Also a great historic literary grasp, used well and incisively as editor of the *BMR*—he's a great figure—sort of the great connection between the BM-Olson-Williams school and the SF Williams-Beat-Zen types—and also the Bostonians, (Wieners and Marshall and others). That you say these people have poor or inadequate preparation, education, to write poetry—considering their individual respective learnings, languages, skills, etc. etc. educations (to say nothing of their radical approach)—I mean I don't see how you come on like that, or why. They're all perfectly literate. Snyder is more learned than you or anybody, except maybe Ansen. Creeley teaches Latin. Blackburn Provencal. Olson you know. Whalen's reading everything both occidental and oriental. Kerouac knows everything intuitively. But also he's read extensively in Buddhist specialties. I don't see where you think you're better educated particularly than, well I was going to say me, but that gets us into tendentiousness. I mean it isn't really education that's at issue, never was, I don't know what illiterate jerk brought that point up, probably Podhoretz. But this kind of incredible corny crap has served for literary discussion at endless length. The scene is too corrupt.

Well what's all this leading up to? I don't know yet I'm just obviously blowing off steam. Yes, back to Xbalba. If you, one, is interested in a certain awkward natural style, for reasons, then the fact that Xbalba is "carefully made" is its most minor virtue—it's technically no improvement on Williams, except it's application of free verse to Wordsworthian meditation long poem—Tintern Abbey type, or Byronic meditation on ruins. But the real technical advance is in the long line poems, they proceed inevitably and naturally from the earlier poems, it's just a sort of COMPOUND imagism—compounded cubist images, and compounded rhythmic long lines. By hindsight. If I ever worried about technique in advance I wouldn't be able to write a line— THAT kind of worry. My worries are more practical having to do with the problem of breath and notation and the freeing of myself from preconceptions as to literary style. The beauty of writing is as Williams says, the invention, the discovery of new appropriate forms, the discovery of something you DON'T know, rather the synthesis repetition of things you do already know. It's a jump up forward into life, unknown future life, not—not an old spinster hung up on her one virgin experience and endlessly crooning it to herself (while the robber unknown's waiting under the bed). Any poem I write that I have written before, in which I don't discover something new (psychically) and maybe formally, is a waste of time, it's not living. I mean to get to the point of finally being frank and including queer material in the poems was a liberation, socially and psychically etc.—of expanding the area of reality I can deal with in the poems rather than shrinking back—(one reason I dig Gregory—he'll write about anything, socks, army, food, Arnold, Loony—so he also now writes the One Great Poem about the Bomb. He's extended the area of poetic experience further out than anyone I know—my own area is still rather limited to literary aesthetic hangovers from stupid education experiences. At least he writes, (as Koch coincidentally demanded in poem Fresh Air) a poem about PANTS. Williams precise real images are such a relief after affected iambics, but PANTS is such a relief after hard real Williams—a new Romanticism in bud. But expanding the area you can deal with directly, especially to include all the irrational of subjective mystic experience and queerness and pants—in other words individuality—means again (as it did for Whitman) the possibility in a totally brainwashed age where all communication is subject to mass control (including especially including offbeat type talks in universities and places like *Partisan*)—means again at last the possibility of Prophetic poetry—it's no miracle—all you have to know is what you actually think and feel and every sentence will be a revelation—everybody else is so afraid to talk even if they have any feelings left. And this kind of Bardic frankness prophecy is what Whitman called for in American poets—them to take over from Priests—lest materialism and mass production of emotion drown America (which it has) and we become what he called the Fabled Damned among nations which we have—and it's been the cowardice and treason and abandonment of the poetic natural democratic soul by the poets themselves that's caused the downfall and doom of the rest of the world too—an awful responsibility. It's not that Podhoretz and the rest of the whores are just a passing phenomenon of vulgarity like transient editorials in the daily news, it's the very poison that'll permanently sicken the mental soul here and has sickened the nation beyond recovery already—simply nobody taking responsibility for their own real thought—nothing but a lot of Trillinguesque evasions with communist doubletalk about moral imagination, a cheap trick to suppress their own inside irrational Life and Poetry and reduce everything to the intellectual standard of a *Time* magazine report on the present happiness and proper role of the American Egghead who's getting paid now and has a nice job and fits in with the whole silly system—well it's no loss to have it already blown out from under them by the ridiculous collapse of the American Century after Sputnik—I suppose there's a new "examination of conscience" going on somewhere in their heads and they'll come up with a new worried bald set of polemics while gay prophet Corso starves ignored in Paris. And I'm not overstating Corso's magical importance. So anyway there is this Grove anthology of all these poets (about 30) coming out in a year and if you call that a BORE again I swear I'll write you a letter goofier than this and twice as exasperated—unless you really <u>believe</u> that—in which case I give up but god knows I have tried—and while I'm on the subject, I'm sick of reading articles on Beat or SF poetry accusing me or anyone of inability to express myself, incoherence or jimmydeanesque oral blocking, inability to communicate etc.—I certainly refuse to get any more involved with the stupidity of other people in petty mad literary arguments and so for that reason have refrained (tho god knows I get messianic critical article impulses) from writing insane long articles refuting this and that misunderstanding, etc. etc. better save my energy for god knows what, at least something real, a letter, or a poem, agh, I wind up fuming in solitary. Well I know

I'm raving, but I've saved it all up for you. And is Trilling behind all this mass stupidity about poetry, at least in NY?

Then there is McClure who started out as a narcissist but seems to have grown some, there was a gleam in him earlier, now it's a fire. Long poems this last year very good. He has his own way.

All these people should have long ago been having books out in NY and reviewed seriously everywhere and the lack of their material has left the atmosphere poisoned by bad poetry and bad people and bad criticism—and the criticism! Incredible after 2 decades of new criticism and the complete incompetence to evaluate and recognize anything new—nothing but lame sociological bullshit in response to Jack's prose or my poetry—or total amnesia with Gregory's or Creeley's and Olson's etc. All the universities been fucking dead horses for decades and this is <u>Culture</u>!? Yet prosody and conceptions of poetry been changing for half a century already and what a Columbia instructor can recognize in Pound he can't see in Olson's method, what he can see in Lorca or Apollinaire he can't see in Howl—it's fantastic. You call this education? I call it absolute brainwashed bullshit. Not saying that either Olson or Howl are Lorca or Pound—I'm saying there's a recognizable continuity of method—yet I have to listen to people giving me doublethink gobbledygook about why don't I write poems with form, construction, something charming and carefully made. O Lawrence thou should be living at this hour! And Diana Trilling in public correspondence with that eminent representative of the younger generation Podhoretz about Lawrence! It's a vast trap. And god save the poor young students who know nothing but that mad incestuous atmosphere.

I could go on all night. What else, what else? I don't have your review here or I'd try and work in and out of that. And some jerk named Brustein who TEACHES at Columbia writing in a new money money money magazine *Horizon* attacking the Cult of Unthink, grandscale vicious attack on Stanislavsky Method, abstract painting (bedfellow!) and beat writing drooling on about how I express every degradation except the one humane one Loneliness—I mean some completely inaccurate irrelevant piece of journalism! Ignoring bi queer lonely lyrics about Whitman and Moloch in whom I sit lonely cocksucking— just goes on and says this here vicious incoherent Ginsberg refuses to admit he's lonely. He TEACHES! Is such shit allowed on this earth? The whore of Babylon's befallen us! Run for your life! And in highclass *Partisan*, Podhoretz (I keep coming back to him it seems he has collected all the garbage in one mind, archetype) quoting me about Jack's "spontaneous bop prosody" proceeds to attack it instead of trying to figure what I mean—because I put it there as a tip, a helpful hint to criticism, a kindly extraverted gesture—and winds up all balled up confusing Jack's <u>diction</u> and use of the mind's hip talk to itself with the <u>rhythm</u> of the consequent sentences. This sort of ignorant Babel in *Partisan Review*—and they tell me he'll be editor someday? Could that be true? Well they deserve it if they put up with that Yahoo type creepy mentality. I'm sick of the creeps bugging the scene, my scene, America's scene, we only live once, why put up with that grubby type ambitious vanity? Ugh. It's too ignoble. Take it away. I'll take a sick junky any day to this horde of half educated deathly academicians. Not one yet, not ONE in all the colleges, magazines, book pages has said anything real, has got the point, either of spirit or prosody prosody (what a campy word—I'm sorry I keep using it—it really is that—but <u>another</u> way) NOT ONE. And this is the product of the schools of the richest nation of the earth, this is the intelligentsia that's supposed to run the world, including moon? It's a monster shambles.

Complaints, complaints, you hear them on a summers day. Pound is absolutely right... With usury. The whole problem is these types want money and security and not ART.

Well I don't know where to go from here, I've unloaded it all on your head... tho you asked for it... on the other hand that's what we're here for, why not have a ball.

I did all this so I wouldn't be involved in endless statements when we met, explanations, better shit it all out at once.

Tell me what's happening. Write a note. See you later in the month. I'm snowed under with work and don't go out much actually and hope to retreat and do nothing but stare at ceiling and write a little... have a manuscript to assemble inside a year... and Peter's brothers worrys... looking maybe for an analyst, but they're caught in the moneywheel too... have to get a part-time job... and letters from fairies in Oshkosh wanting salvation... and the Woe of Laughing Gas.

Yours in the kingdom of music
Nella Gregsnig

Allen

The birds have eaten the berries.

Haven't I sent this letter before in another life? And haven't you received it?

Incidentally this letter is a sample of spontaneous bop prosody for prose—what happens when you let it all out and don't censor too much—note mad rhythm of sentences—you blow.

[Ginsberg's friend, the painter Robert LaVigne, wrote to him. LaVigne was worried about artist's block, a lack of production. Allen did his best to calm his friend's worries by giving personal examples and told him of his recent completion of the poem, Kaddish.]

Allen Ginsberg [New York, NY] to Robert LaVigne [n.p.]
ca. January 15, 1959

Dear Bob:

Got your letter, started to read it and couldn't because of the thin pencil, finally finished today, squinting. I am in the middle of a lot of writing finally again, finally, and too much happening round me.

One definite thing I felt—Gregory is back, we were talking about it the other day—these periods of productivity and lassitude are inevitable. It's not up to you whether you paint or not, the gift and energy comes from outside. When you have something to do you will do it. I mean literally from <u>outside</u>. It has nothing to do with our conscious choice. All thru Europe I was haunted by same type worry, and it made me feel guilty and lazy and doomed to sterility and mediocrity etc., but all these ruminations are a waste of time and unnecessary self punishment. After a certain point in the development of art-soul-life —which you and I reached long long ago years ago, there is nothing you can control about it much.

Like, the more I shut people out and make peace in house to work, the more I worry about "work," the less I do, I wind up sleeping in midafternoon.

The more I run around get drunk fuck up waste time and lose touch with my writing, the more I wind up putting down on paper. It's amazing. It's not under our control. Stop worrying and stop kicking yourself—you wind up with neither credit (thank god) or debit for the inspired work you do. It's inspired and it's not you.

Gregory agrees. He's gone thru many periods of non-invention and decided he was finished and a week later he surpasses himself—or 3 months later as the case may be.

I spent 2 years since *Howl*—or is it 4 years by now?—worrying whether I'd be able to make higher than that—finally have (thank god) with huge poem about my mother [*Kaddish*]—but that was not the subject I planned on, or foresaw, would carry me up, nor was it written in a way I thought likely. Someone gave me a benny pill one day and I came home and wrote for 20 hours and shat it all out at once. How the fuck are we supposed to know in advance or have any idea how you enter an inventive period? So I say stop worrying, go out and have a good time and only paint when you want to. It's not up to you, whether you make it or not. You're destined to make it on some guiding angel's terms. No? [...]

Love,

Allen

[*Ginsberg continued to use his influence to have his friends' work published. In this letter he offered to pay for the publication of books by Gary Snyder and Philip Whalen himself.*]

Allen Ginsberg [New York, NY] to Lawrence Ferlinghetti [San Francisco, CA] January 23, 1959

Dear Larry:

Thanks for your encouraging telegram, it made me feel fine, for 2 days and Gregory's upset you haven't responded to his poems, help him too.

Enclosed find "Ignu."

A book of these poems in May would be a good idea, if they are all finished by then, but let us plan on a book when I'm done with them, I'd rather not work by deadline, it doesn't help composition, and I'm trying them out for defects at readings. But there's no rush, actually, from commerce angle.

Grove said they'd print Snyder and Whalen but only if in a book with some poems of mine or Jack as third part, and neither Gary or I or Phil dug that, each for his own reasons. Don Allen wanted to print separate books, but [Barney] Rosset nixed it. So Allen gave them to Laughlin who said he dug the books but was too busy, too full up, and wanted to give Denise Levertov's upcoming books special promotional attention, and not confuse his salesmen with too many poetry books at once. So they are left out again. I don't think it's good, all this, everybody getting books and books and nobody willing to print the two central Classicists. LeRoi Jones proposes to and that's a good idea but he has hands full and no apparatus as yet. Won't you please put their books out? They are good poets, they write and deserve audience after all this time, they are important in the U.S. poesy renaissance and their poems still get nowhere as far as publishing. I be willing to finance the costs for both of them if you are too overloaded with other manuscripts in preparations you can use my future royalties on the new 10,000 *Howls* for that—should cover Villiers costs for 2 books. I mean they are so historically important for SF muse and you are the historically important SF pioneer so it would work out madly great if you'd relent. Besides they'd sell enough to pay in long run and be well received prestigious items, etc. I remember originally you said you just weren't that moved by their poetry, I'm writing this now in hope that acquaintance and recent readings of last 2 years in their visits have made them any more dear to you. Otherwise it means me running around spending more time, LeRoi overburdening his shop, etc. and sadness a little for them too. I mean, the romance, of us all having the same publisher and United Front. Well put this under your pillow dear Larry.

Leaving for Chicago next week to read several times to raise money for [Irving] Rosenthal's independent magazine, he has almost enough now and the manuscripts are at the printers already. Mag to be called *Big Table* and that issue lovely, the Burroughs selection is very good. Also read this Monday night for the Living Theatre with Paul Goodman, another benefit to raise money for them, they're putting on Williams (WC) *Many Loves* play. Then February 5 with Gregory big free attack on Columbia at MacMillan Hall there, maybe Jack join us. Then with LeRoi, Raymond Bremser and Ed Marshall to read to the shades at Howard U in Washington, DC. Gregory to Chicago and Washington, too. Then April 25 be in SF for a few weeks, read for Poetry Center and UC. I tried to get both to try arrange for Corso and O'Hara and said I'd share costs out of my loot but they are too bureaucratic and/or slow or unwilling to put themselves out so I'll come alone, I guess. OK. Write about the Zenmasters' poetry.

As ever,

Allen

[*Scathing media attacks continued to plague Ginsberg and the Beats. Whenever Ginsberg became fed up with the biased reporting, he'd fire off a letter to the editor hoping, usually in vain, to reach a sympathetic ear.*]

Allen Ginsberg [New York, NY] to Editors of *Time* [New York, NY]
February 17, 1959

Sirs:

Your account of our incarnation in Chicago was cheap kicks for you who have sold your pens for money and have no fate left but idiot mockery of the muse that must work in poverty in an America already doomed by materialism.

You suppressed knowledge that the *Chicago Review*'s winter issue was censored by the University of Chicago; that the editors had resigned to publish the material under the name *Big Table*; that we offered our bodies and poetry to raise money to help publish the magazine; we left Chicago in the penury in which we had come.

You quoted what was charming in our speech out of context; you altered chronology of the evening of the party; your ignored the main event the reading at the Sherman Hotel, which was a religious intellectual exposition of poetry's truth; you perverted the beauty of Orlovsky's tears; you mocked the reports of your own employees on the scene who were moved by the reading; you spat on the appearance of the soul of poetry in America at a time when America needs that soul most; you brainwashed your millions of readers.

What you do to pervert the significance of larger public events which I do not witness I now can know: you are an instrument of the Devil and crucify America with your lies: you are the war-creating Whore of Babylon and would be damned were you not mercifully destined to be swallowed by oblivion with all created things.

Allen Ginsberg, Peter Orlovsky, Gregory Corso

[*It wasn't always in Ginsberg's own defense that he wrote to editors. Often he wrote to defend his friends from harsh criticism.*]

**Allen Ginsberg [San Francisco, CA] to Editor of the *New York Times*
Book Review [New York, NY] May 11, 1959**

To the editor of the *NY Times Book Review*:

I have read Kerouac's *Dr. Sax* for seven years as a grand luminous poem. David Dempsey's review of it in May 3rd's *Times* seemed inconsiderate and mixed-up. Mr. Dempsey's first paragraph may have confused readers: *Dr. Sax* was written after, not before, *On the Road*, which he referred to as having "established Jack Kerouac as a young man of considerable talent."

The prose experiment begun in *On the Road* is carried out further here. High-speed improvisatory composition—and when the mind bursts into flame the language is sublime. Here the method is applied to very gentle, comprehensible material: small town boyhood recollected in humane and mournful detail, side by side with development and resolution of a vast comic puberty fantasy.

Perhaps Mr. Dempsey read the book with almost no attention. He refers to Dr. Sax as "an elusive symbol of evil," whereas on the contrary Dr. Sax is the good guy. In the daytime he is football coach, at night he puts on his prophetic Shadow costume and goofs around with magic trying to stop a giant snake from invading the world.

Most of the review is too generalized to examine in much detail. Mr. Dempsey's consistent insults to this work of art ("bad taste...incoherent ...mishmash of avant-gardism...depths to which a style can sink...mildly clinical...typing...perverse") strike me as journalese stereotypes—mostly rather ill-mannered—to which the writings of many historically important literary originators have been subjected. This book is specifically a case in point.

I am writing this letter to warn readers that *Dr. Sax* is a work of Genius which will be lost to them if they accept Mr. Dempsey's shallow reading. The structure in the book is modeled on the structure (i.e. the succession, order, speed, interruption, juxtaposition, rhythm, form) of thoughts flowing thru the normal mind, as far as they can be transcribed spontaneously with practiced concentration on the object.

This is related to, but is not the same as, Joyce's attempt to synthesize a stream of consciousness thru slow revised invention. Kerouac relies for his materials on the actual "mindflow." And it's quite easy to read, delightful. He does not rely on the arbitrary, and for prose-creative purposes, ossified syntactical conventions that are taken for granted as standard writing by less imaginative and I might add less practiced stylists. The latter conventions are not (or were not in their time) standards of composition in most of the great 20th century works of prose (or poetic) invention, Proust, Céline, Faulkner, Pound, Williams, etc., have all made adjustments in this direction, according to their own interest.

The areas of origination and experiment have only begun to be explored. Primarily, among my contemporaries, it is Kerouac who has led the way. For him, with his courage and solitude, in the grand tradition of individualistic experimental composition, to be subjected to a continuous barrage of philistine hostility by petty critics, the "illustrious obscure" of Keats' day, is a literary scandal which has poisoned the intellectual life of this country for three years.

The foul word "beatnik" is used several times to describe either Kerouac or his characters—even the innocent ghosts of Lowell. Must this journalistic sneer continue to be directed at artists? It is shameful. Then well may Kerouac continue to be Beat in America, a lone creator, like Melville, among generations of stereotypes. His Art's a wonder. To be Beat this way is noble.

But the "beatnik" of mad critics is a piece of their own ignoble poetry. And if "beatniks" and not illuminated Beat poets, overrun this country, they will have been created not by Kerouac, but by industries of mass communication which continue to brainwash Man and insult nobility where it occurs.

Prophetically,

Allen Ginsberg

[*Ginsberg had sent a copy of* Kaddish *to his father, who complained to him about some of the explicit lines. In his reply to that letter, Allen also encouraged his father to try LSD, a drug Allen had recently discovered.*]

Allen Ginsberg [San Francisco, CA] to Louis Ginsberg [Paterson, NJ]
May 20, 1959

Dear Louis:

Got your letter & poems, which I return as per instructions. They are all fine. I'm OK, I will be here another few weeks, then start home slowly, overland. I went down to Stanford University the other day to be subjected to a research experiment with a new drug—LSD-25 (Lysergic Acid) which Huxley described in his books *Doors of Perception* and *Heaven and Hell*. It was astounding —I lay back, listening to music, and went into a sort of trance state (somewhat similar to the high state of laughing gas) and in a fantasy much like a Coleridge world of Kubla Khan saw a vision of that part of my consciousness which seemed to be permanent and transcendent and identical with the origin of the universe—a sort of identity common to everything—but a clear and coherent sight of it. Rather beautiful visual images also, of Hindu-type gods dancing on themselves. This drug seems to automatically produce a mystical experience. Science is getting very hip. It's a very safe drug—you ought to contact someone at Rutgers who's doing experiments with it and try it—like a comic movie.

The line about the "beard around the vagina" is probably a sort of very common experience and image that children have who see their parents naked and it is an archetypal experience and nothing to be ashamed of—it looks from the outside, objectively, probably much less shocking than it appears to you I think—it's a universal experience which almost everyone has had though not many poets have referred to it but it can do no harm to be brought to consciousness.

Caw Caw I still rather like since it's the climax of a sort of musical form, a fugue—two themes Caw Caw and Lord Lord—representing realistic bleakness-pain-materialism, versus Lord Lord which is mystical aspiration that alternate and in the last line merge into one <u>cry</u>. I've read it aloud here and it sounds alright.

I'll be here till around June 1 (I'm going back to Stanford then for another bout with the Lysergic Acid) and then see if I can find someone with a car driving east—would like to see the Southwest and Grand Canyon on the way home.

The jet plane ride here (5 hours) was like a movie of topographical geography.

This Saturday all the poets get together to give a reading to raise money to resuscitate *Measure* magazine and so that'll be on its feet again at least for another issue.

Partisan asked me to reply to Diana T's[37] article but I am busy with other worlds so I'll shut up and let things take their own course. Hope you are O.K. and having nice springtime.

Love,

Allen

[*Even though Ginsberg's letters did not always elicit positive responses, he continued to write them.*]

Allen Ginsberg [New York, NY] to Richard Eberhart [Washington, DC] October 20, 1959

Dear Dick:

Thanks for live letter. I never had a public stance of any kind, I haven't got that kind of mind, please don't get me further confused with the image of a beatnik disseminated via mass media, I am not responsible for other people's bad poetry (Philistine journalism) and have done my best to confute it, i.e. for the most part shut up and not replied except to continue reading and writing poetry. I was actually sort of offended by Diana Trilling's essay despite the evil joy I felt at being taken so seriously at such length because she misunderstood

---

37 Diana Trilling. "The Other Night At Columbia."

and perverted everything, missed the point really—but there's too much to explain. I mean I have stomach trouble now, too much evil opinion around, I get it all on my head—I'm not a social protest poet I'm a reader of Blake and an angel's poet. Guggenheim [grant] is not castles, I can have castles already if I want, I don't want castles, I want to go to India and need fare there for me and Peter Orlovsky and a few other people. I have no vow of poverty, I have a vow of penury—i.e. live cheap and buy clothes at salvation army and not get things complicated with too many possessions, this is strictly a personal convenience and not a public stance. Have been broke mostly the last 4 years and will continue to be broke in India despite Guggenheim in any case. One thing I have now, is a semi permanent small income from City Lights, about $800 a year, which is convenient and I have got by on, without other work—so I do nothing now but read and write and goof around and think, which is fine by me.

What gave me the stomach trouble I think was a series of readings at various colleges trying to get over the heads of academy to the student and read works of various new poets—Olson, Creeley, myself, Corso, Kerouac, Snyder, Whalen, Wieners, etc. I think Diana Trilling didn't realize what had really been going on and had accepted a *Time* magazine version, which I suppose is no fault of hers except her imagination and trust faults her.

I'm outnumbered by journalism—that is I've continued to talk to people as individuals rather than taking crafty public stances and so that's led to my being open to all sorts of ridicule. Rather continue to do that and play by ear than be shut up, silent and moody, or suspicious continually, like Greta Garbo. Whatever is genuine will come thru in the long run and surprisingly I think has despite all the vulgarization and academic malice.

I've mainly not been at war with the society, the society if anything has been at war with me. All I've done which seems on outside like war or social protest is maintain my sympathies where my sympathies were, i.e. with the god-seekers, and experimental poets.

I'll send *Big Table* and *Yugen* under another cover. *Yugen* is I think the best avant-garde poetry magazine in the country—surprised the Library [of Congress] doesn't have it. Is there any possibility of the poetry room now beginning to amass and distribute info on the variety of really important new work coming out of little presses in the last 2 years? There is too much for me to explain in a letter, right now. I'll send you *Yugen* and *Big Table*.

By the way the Library has a tape I made with Corso and Orlovsky, I wish you would listen to it—we made it last year. All new poems, and we were pretty high and gay when we read.

I have a new book about ready for City Lights—should be about 3 times as thick as *Howl*.

I'll write again soon

Allen

Your letter was really so nice to get—I thought you might also be annoyed with me thru mis-understandings etc. Rexroth having been away 2 years thinks I'm living with millionairesses and hanging around in Hollywood. Main change is that I've gotten a little sadder, and perhaps paranoiac.

I had some Lysergic Acid (LSD-25) in Stanford this year and had a very beautiful experience of total transcending precipitated by it, have you heard of or tried this? I had had some earlier <u>without</u> drugs and have something to check on, as experience—this drug is amazing.

[*In 1960 Ginsberg and Ferlinghetti were invited to a writer's conference in Chile. Allen took advantage of his open-ended roundtrip ticket and stayed in South America for another six months.*]

Allen Ginsberg [Santiago, Chile] to Peter Orlovsky [New York, NY] January 24, 1960

Dear Peter:

Came down here to Concepción, sat part way in front pilot's seat in control cabin and saw the Andes far away on left. The Conference lasted a week and ended yesterday. I seem to be the only bearded man in Chile, so my photo was in all the newspapers—and children on the streets thought I was Fidel Castro's representative. Most everybody at Conference was un-poetic but one thing was most interesting, all the communists seemed to take over enough to make the whole week a big argument between pro and anti political writers. Everybody from every country got up and made fiery speeches about the workers. Everybody wanted revolutions. I delivered an address also on Wednesday—in broken Spanish, English, and French—and had translated and read them Wiener's queer poems, Lamantia's "Narcotica" and Gregory's "Bomb"—plus a long lecture on prosody, jazz, drugs, soul, etc. It was a big mad interesting speech and they dug it—I think it was probably the best of the speeches. Then 2 nites ago Ferlinghetti and I read—he did very well but my reading was without real feeling but had some force. So I was depressed afterward tho the audience seemed to enjoy it. But was unhappy not to deliver the lamb to the communists. But anyway withal we were big hit and now Beat Generation is considered great new American poetry and all the professors will bring it back to Uruguay and Argentina and perhaps Colombia.

At same time there are some interesting people here like in Tangier—the best friend I've had here is a strange roly-poly philosophy professor at the university who talks English and is called Luis Oyarzún. "Luce" (lu-cha") (little light) is a big telepathic botanist, naturalist, fairy, astronomer and poet (tho not a great poet—too shy)—he's like a small Ansen but funny. He has various queer friends including an old man named Hyde who has a house here and is very brilliant and lost like an old lady with books. Also a young couple of lovers, boys, whom they all know—so there's a whole semi-hip queer secret society here. Oyarzún is also a big head of the Fine Arts School and is leaving for China in a week. He says he will get us invited (expenses paid by Chinese) to visit China—everybody here visits China. He sends you regards.

I've slept with nobody and masturbated twice. The land is like California. Tomorrow I'm taking a 3rd class train south towards an island called Chiloé near the broken islandy bottom of the continent. I'll stay there a week and eat fish and maybe finish *Kaddish*. Then return here, fly to Santiago, take a round trip bus ride across Andes, return and fly to La Paz Bolivia—see Machu Picchu—then to Lima Peru for a week. Then to Panama City for a week. So I will be here about another month or month and a half and then be back.

How are you and Lafcadio? From here it seems you must be in a labyrinth of his worries. Tho I have been in a labyrinth of communists which is just as bad. [...]

My writing here is simplified down because I am so used to talking simple Spanish I feel as if I were translating everything to basic explanations. I have been a little lonely but feel good anyway. The unfinished book bothers me so I may try it here more. I hope you are not feeling trapped in N.Y.C. Perhaps we can all go to Mexico later in the Spring or further on. Is Lafcadio showing any signs of independence and feeling?

My plane ticket is good for side trips to Bolivia so it's very cheap for traveling.

Another person I like is Nicanor Parra, a poet about 45 years old who is always falling in love with Swedish girls, writes intelligent and sincere poetry and is also a big mathematics professor who studied in England and U.S.A. He too went to China last year and believes and accepts Mao Tse-tung's Yenan literature theory. City Lites just put out a book of his translations—not bad, at least readable. I'm sorry you did not, could not, come—you'd have been the most amazing person here.

Well OK for now—I haven't written anyone but you and I should send postcards to everybody so I will today. I am generally confused, by the communists and by being alone, but it feels good to be wandering solitary in South America. No cocaine yet but still have to get the Chilean yage-like drugs and try them.

Love,

Allen.

[*Ginsberg extended his trip to South America month by month. He was determined to find a source for ayahuasca, the drug Burroughs had discovered in 1953 on his own South American travels.*]

**Allen Ginsberg [Huanuco, Peru] to Eugene Brooks [New York, NY]
June 2, 1960**

Dear Eugene:

Happy birthday, so today I am rapidly approaching your age and you're moving on too. I'm stuck for the day in a little town on the eastern slope of the Andes called Huanuco, waiting for a bus or truck to take me further down to the jungle and a town called Pucallpa on the Ucayali river, where I'll settle for a week or so. The roads are so crude that traffic moves only in one direction on alternate days, and I came here yesterday so have to wait a day for the next connection. I left Lima, where I stayed 3 weeks, a few days ago, crossing Andes by railroad and bus. This town is I guess typical of all I've seen in Peru and Bolivia —I have a hotel room that cost me 40¢, there are Chinese restaurants here (many Chinese in Peru) where I can eat huge meals (a plate of steamed trout with soy sauce, fried wonton, and diced chicken w/vegetables plus pot of tea) for 70¢. The town has one square with City Halls and bureaucracy buildings, a lot of streets of adobe houses for 10,000 people, and a big open air market where they sell everything from magic talisman bone deaths heads to weird tropical fruits. Also local Indian blankets. I tried to buy one for $2.00—huge white wool blanket with colored designs in it—but on inquiring found that the Peruvian postal system is so rudimentary I can't mail it outside the country. So can't carry it into tropics in knapsack, or, too much trouble to do so. I've been getting money all along from City Lights and various other small checks from magazines so still have $140 which is quite a lot here, in travelers checks. So far have been in Southern Chile—all the area now destroyed by earthquake from Concepción down to Isle of Chiloé—and Bolivia and all over Peru—mainly Cuzco and Machu Picchu where the Inca ruins are. All along the coast of Peru it's desert, filled with pre-Incan ruins and graveyards. One of the big illegal local industries is robbing graves for the funeral pottery buried with the dead —some 2,000 years old, others newer. I have a few pots I've bought for a buck each and will try to get government permission to bring them back. Good pottery is worth up to $2,000 in the states and cost $100 here or less if you buy directly from the grave robber. I have some painted bowls worth maybe $50.00 each, and some clay figurines—paid $2.00 for the lot. One could make good money smuggling them out. I get to take a few out legally since I'm an official literary guest of a government cultural institution—gave a reading here, and am having a small book of translations published in Lima soon. But I've been all hung up on archaeology and pre-Incaic pots.

Anyway, 2 or 3 days more travel overland brings me to Pucallpa,—there I go visit a local <u>curandero</u> or witch doctor who is a specialist in preparing a native brew called ayahuasca—which is similar to peyote, mescaline and LSD-25. Only stronger, I have heard. It's part of an ancient jungle tradition, and the curanderos use it to invoke visions or cure physical ailments. I'm going to study witch-doctoring for a few weeks at the source. Then I don't know—I can take a 5 day raft or launch trip down the Ucayali river to Iquitos which is the big Peruvian port on the western end of the Amazon River. From there I can get a boat 2,500 miles all the way down to the Atlantic on the Amazon for $50.00. However I think I'll save that trip for the next time I get down here if ever. Takes several weeks and my money's a little low—I'd have to fly back to Peru to get my free plane home. Anyway I'll see a little jungle and few days of riverboat travel. —I've been writing a lot, especially lately, which is why I write so few letters. Every time I sit down there's a new town to describe in diary. [...]

Economic conditions here are real dirty, in Lima there's a mile square mountain of garbage (the only of its kind in the world I think) where Indians live and work,—whole communities and streets in the garbage, scavenging wood and broken glass and pig food for a living. The average Peruvian income is $120 a year, caused mostly by stupid laws like the above preventing me from mailing a Peruvian-made blanket abroad. That's $ American $2 I don't leave in this town. I've been well except for some piles, very slight. Got a long black beard still. Love to you as always, and love to the children and Connie. As ever. Yr. weird brother.

Allen

Allen Ginsberg [Pucallpa, Peru] to William S. Burroughs [Tangier, Morocco] June 10, 1960

Dear Bill,

I'm still in Pucallpa, ran into a little plump fellow, Ramon P—who'd been friend to Robert Frank (photographer of our movie) in '46 or so here. Ramon took me to his curandero, in whom he has a lot of faith and about whose super-natural curing powers he talks a lot, too much, about. The Maestro, as he's called, being a very mild and simple seeming cat of 38 or so, who prepared a drink for 3 of us the other night; and then last night I attended a regular Curan-dero all night drinking session with about 30 other men and women in a hut in jungly outskirts of Pucallpa behind the gaswork field.

The first time, much stronger than the drink I had in Lima, ayahuasca can be bottled and transported and stay strong, as long as it does not ferment, needs well-closed bottle. Drank a cup, slightly old stuff, several days old and slightly fermented also, lay back and after an hour (in bamboo hut outside his shack, where he cooks), began seeing or feeling what I thought was the Great Being, or some sense of it, approaching my mind like a big wet vagina, lay back in that for a while. Only image I can come up with is of a big black hole of God-Nose thru which I peered into a mystery, and the black hole surrounded by all creation, particularly colored snakes, all real.

I felt somewhat like what this image represents, the sense of it so real.

The eye is imaginary image, to give life to the picture. Also a great feeling of pleasantness in my body, no nausea. Lasted in different phases about 2 hours, the effects wore off after 3, the fantasy itself lasted from $3/4$ of hour after I drank to $2\,1/2$ hours later more or less.

Went back and talked to The Maestro, gave him 35 soles ($1.50) for services and talked with him about peyote and LSD, he'd heard of peyote. He's a mes-tizo who studied in San Martin (upper Huallaga territory). He gave me samples of his mix, uses young cultivated ayahuasca plant in his back yard, and mixes that about half and half with a catalyst known as the 'Mescla' which is another leaf known in Chama Indian language as Cahua (pronounced Coura) and locally by him in Pucallpa is called Chacruna. Said he'd get me more samples to bring back to Lima Natural History Museum to identify. Cooks the mixes together all day and strains the broth, gives the drained leaves a second cook too. Anyway the preparation is not excessively secret. I think Schultes [Peruvian botanist] saw and knows the preparation. Can add other leaves of other plants, too, I don't know these combinations to try out. He seems generally interested in drugs, serious, and not mercenary at all, good type, has quite a following here, does physical cures, his specialty.

Anyway to make long story short, went back to formal group session in huts last night, this time the brew was prepared fresh and presented with full ceremony, he crooning (and blowing cigarette or pipe smoke) tenderly over the cup-mouth for several minutes before (enamel cup, I remember your plastic cup) then I light cigarette, blow a puff of smoke over cup, and drain. Saw a shooting star, Aerolith, before going in, and full moon, and he served me up first, then lay down expecting God knows what other pleasant vision and then I began to get high, and then the whole fucking Cosmos broke loose around me, I think the strongest and worst I've ever had it nearly. (I still reserve the Harlem experiences, being natural, in abeyance. The LSD was perfection but didn't get me so deep in nor so horribly in). First I began to realize my worry about the mosquitoes or vomiting was silly as there was the great stake of life and death. I felt faced by death, my skull in my beard on pallet on porch rolling back and forth and settling finally as if in reproduction of the last physical move I make before settling into real death, got nauseous, rushed out and began vomiting, all covered with snakes, like a snake seraph, colored serpents in aureole all around my body. I felt like a snake vomiting out the universe, or a Jivaro in head-dress with fangs vomiting up in realization of the murder of the universe, my death to come, everyone's death to come, all unready, I unready, all around me in the trees the noise of these spectral animals the other drinkers vomiting (normal part of the cure sessions) in the night in their awful solitude in the universe, vomiting up their will to live, be preserved in this body, almost. Went back and lay down. Ramon came over quite tender and nurse-like (he hadn't drunk, he's sort of an aide to help the sufferers) asked me if I was OK and 'Bien Mareado' (Good and drunk?). I said 'Bastante' and went back to listen to the specter that was approaching my mind. The whole hut seemed rayed with spectral presences all suffering transfiguration with contact with a single mysterious thing that was our fate and was sooner or later going to kill us, the Curandero crooning, keeping up a very tender, repeated and then changing simple tune, comfort sort of, God knows what signified, seemed to signify some point of reference I was unable to contact yet. I was frightened and simply lay there with wave after wave of death-fear, fright, rolling over me till I could hardly stand it, didn't want to take refuge in rejecting it as illusion, for it was too real and too familiar, especially as if in rehearsal of last minute death my head rolling back and forth on the blanket and finally settling in last position of stillness and hopeless resignation to God knows what fate, for my being, felt completely lost strayed soul, outside of contact with some thing that seemed present. Finally had a sense that I might face the question there and then, and choose to die and understand, and leave my body to be found in the morning. I guess grieving everybody, couldn't bear to leave Peter and my father so alone. Afraid to die yet then and so never took the chance, (if there was a chance, perhaps somehow there was), also as if everybody in session in central radiotelepathic contact with the same problem, the great being within ourselves. Coming back from vomit saw a man knees to chest I thought I saw an X ray his skull I realized he was crouched there as in shroud (with towel mosquito protection wrapped round his face) suffering the same trial and separation. Thought of people, saw their images clearly, you, mysterious apparently know more than I do now and why don't you communicate, or can't you, or have I ignored it? Simon seemingly an angel in his annihilation of vanity and giving forth new life in children. If any interplanetary news comes through he said 'I'll be the first to be relaying it over the wires in a way that won't get it fucked up'. Francine his wife, sort of a seraph of woman, all women (as all men) the same, spectral creatures put here mysteriously to live, be the living gods, and suffer crucifixion of death like Christ, but either get lost and die in soul or get in contact and give new birth to continue the process of being (tho' they themselves die, or do they?) and I lost and poor Peter who depends on me for some heaven I haven't got, lost, and I keep rejecting women, who come to minister to me, decided to have children somehow, a revolution in the hallucination, but the suffering was about as much as I could bear and the thought of more suffering even deeper to come made me despair, felt, still feel, like lost soul, surrounded by ministering angels (Ramon, the Maestro, yourself, the whole common world of diers), and my poor mother died in God knows what state of suffering. I can't stand it, vomited again (Ramon had come over and told me to vomit off the porch where I was lying, if I had to later, very careful kind situation). I mean, is this a good group. I remember your saying watch out whose vision you get, but God knows I don't know who to turn to finally when the chips are down spiritually and I have to depend on my own serpent-self's memory of merry visions of Blake, or depend on nothing and enter anew, but enter what? Death? and at that moment, vomiting still feeling like a great lost serpent seraph vomiting in consciousness of the transfiguration to come, with the radio telepathy sense of a being whose presence I had not yet fully sensed, too horrible for me, still, to accept the fact of total communication with say everyone an eternal seraph male and female at once, and me a lost soul seeking help. Well slowly the intensity began to fade, I being incapable of moving in that direction spiritually, not knowing who to look to or what to look for. Not quite trusting to ask the Maestro, tho' in the vision of the scene it was he who was the local logical ministering spirit to trust, if anyone. Went over and sat by him (as Ramon gently suggested) to be 'blown', that is he croons a song to you to cure your soul and blows smoke at you, rather a comforting presence, tho' by now the steep fear had passed. That being over got up and took my piece of cloth I brought against mosquitoes and went home in moonlight with plump Ramon, who said the more you saturated yourself with ayahuasca the deeper you go, visit the moon, see the dead, see God, see tree spirits, etc.

I hardly have the nerve to go back, afraid of some real madness, a changed universe permanently changed, tho' I guess change it must for me someday, much less as planned before, go up the river six hours to drink with an Indian tribe. I suppose I will. Meanwhile will wait here another week in Pucallpa and drink a few more times with same group. I wish I knew who, if anyone, there is to work with that knows, if anyone knows, who I am or what I am. I wish I could hear from you. I think I'll be here long enough for a letter to reach me, write.

Allen Ginsberg

Allen Ginsberg [Iquitos, Peru] to Louis Ginsberg [Paterson, NJ]
June 21, 1960

Dear Louis:

Wrote two weeks ago or so—by now I've crossed over Andes and spent 10 days in Pucallpa, a small town on a huge river big as the Hudson—The Ucayali —which winds 1000 miles up to the Amazon—so took a small steamboat 6 days ago and, sleeping in hammock with mosquito net on passageway on deck, spent the week traveling up to the Amazon thru huge flat area of jungle—on riverside small grey thatchroof huts and every 20 or 50 miles a small cluster of houses and every 100 miles a little town, frontier towns, of several thousand gents. Cost of boat trip including 3 meals a day is $6.00 which is cheap—am now on last day of trip and just a few hours ago entered the Amazon proper— big wide flat brown shining water wide as a big lake with sticks and greenery floating on surface, balsa rafts and canoes paddling near shore—we dock at Iquitos this evening and I go find hotel, stay a week, and then fly back to Lima, to catch plane home a week later. Iquitos is the river port at western-Peruvian end of the Amazon. From Iquitos one can take another steamer down thru Brazil and the Atlantic, 2500 miles, for $50—but I haven't the money or the time, and have to get back to Lima.

While in Pucallpa my main purpose was to look up a local Curandero or witch doctor and try a native herbal brew named ayahuasca which reportedly gives visions—similar to peyote, Mescaline and Lysergic Acid. Well I tried it 4 times and with remarkable results as far as I was concerned subjectively. I certain saw "visions."

What the drug seems to do is activate the unconscious without putting the regular consciousness asleep—so that you can both be awake <u>and</u> dream real solid dreams at the same time—a neat trick, but quite possible. The local Indians use it for curing illnesses, finding lost objects, communicating with the dead, religious visions, etc. and I'm sure they can do all that, from what I've seen. It was like stepping into a voodoo movie and finding it was all <u>real</u>.

Anyway the main dream or vision I had, was of the condition of my own death, i.e., how it feels like to die—and I don't think I've ever (except once before having "visions" in Harlem) been so terrified before in my life while awake. It seemed that death was a <u>thing</u>, not mere emptiness, a living being— and my whole life was being judged and found a vanity, as in Ecclesiastes, and I saw as in x-ray my skeleton-head settling in final position on pillow to give up the Ghost. A <u>familiar</u> feeling, strangely, with the realization that I had known all along, but avoided consciousness, of the fact that I am flesh and that flesh is crass. The main after effect, aside from a desire to widen further the area of my consciousness, and realization that my life so far has been relatively empty, was resolution to bear children sooner or later before it is too late. The question is to be or not to be—and also, what <u>Thing</u> is beyond Being. I saw something—a sort of great consciousness which was familiar, but unhuman—as if in one being were united an Elephant and Snake and Mosquito and Man—and all the trees—nothing like the terrible hidden Lord of Moses or Revelations, it felt like. Whether this is vision or hallucination makes very little difference. I passed thru several hours of intense suffering awareness of the worm at my ear. I thought of you and the whole family—everyone I knew passed thru mind at one time or another—with tears and love—realization that sooner or later, I, or everyone, enters a great solitude and give up everything—which was painful to realize, which is why I said my life seemed a vanity, for I as yet had thought of it as semi-permanent and had not considered the inevitable. It also seemed that until I were <u>able</u> to freely give myself up, entrance into some great joy (in life or beyond life) would not be seen—but that there is some kind of inhuman harmony yet to come. But this is speculation. In any case the universe did seem like one Being.

Well that's enough of that for awhile. I wrote a great deal this month, huge ranting wild poems, psalms, notes, sketches, drawings, a whole book actually. I'll have to reread it in a year and see if it's still hot. But poetry doesn't seem enough — "in the vast strange and middle of the night."

Also bought a lot of native pottery — hand-painted ceramic ashtray types — for souvenirs, which I'll bring home — and a hammock and mosquito net.

I thought of poor Williams, living so long on the edge of death — "for this is the first — and last — day of the world" — he wrote. Had a dream of him entering Non-Being with huge snowy-feathered angel wings. And saw you Louis as a sort of elephant-nosed seraph or deity with old human eyes. Well the Indians in the jungle certainly don't lack a huge metaphysical inner civilization, half the town of Pucallpa drinks ayahuasca every week and has its own secret life aside from radios and movies of the A-Bomb. So that's I suppose the proper poetic climax of my trip down here — it's been almost half a year and I am nostalgic to get back to N.Y.C. and see everybody and see you.

Love,

Allen

[*Ginsberg had met Timothy Leary, a young psychology professor who taught at Harvard. In 1960 Leary invited Allen and Peter to visit him in Cambridge to take some of the hallucinogens he had been experimenting with. In this letter to Corso, Ginsberg described the effects.*]

Allen Ginsberg [New York, NY] to Gregory Corso [Paris, France]
December 8, 1960

Dear Gregory:

I am in doldrums and don't know what I want to do — how to go to Sweden with Peter — and what to do with Lafcadio? And Peter has girlfriend who really likes him who would be sad if we left right now with fates unsettled — and this week Konstantin Simonov and Russian writers visited us, we took them walk on Brooklyn Bridge and showed them your educational alliance street — and they said come to Moscow and live with us free. We could go there from Sweden — I haven't heard from the Swedish Museum — but I guess I would go as soon as I read proofs of my book — or before. Last week Peter, Laf and I went up to Harvard — two weeks ago. We gave great reading for psychoanalysts, 100 of them. They invited us to try cylocybin (mushroom drug) so we did, second time I got on (it's like mescaline) in bed with Peter naked, I was afraid to come, lest I spurt out imaginary beings into the void, I realized I was a God, I am the God I always longed for, I could make same babes in this dimension, or imaginary ones in others, wouldn't let Peter blow me (till I came down)—was naked, saw star of Bethlehem like Giotto miniature outside New England window, realized all consciousness was waiting for me the Messiah to make a break, all were waiting for one to say I am One, and announced to all the new Birth of Millennial Union One Mass Of Endless Consciousness, to paragraphed spaceship to leave the earth for the sun and explore this dimension this universe, instead of vomiting and seeking in invisible mental universes for fear of being one and only Gods in one and only this, I rose in all my Hebraic nakedness followed by Peter in Russian nakedness and strode downstairs King without robes into the midst of a party of psychologists, commandeered the telephone and began to carry out my mad scheme for announcing the new birth by telling the operator—yes, who is this?—G-O-D and get me Kerouac in Long Island—and after him I was going to interlink by electrical telephone communication with Bill and you and Khrushchev and Mao and Lucien and Mailer in Bellevue behind thick bars—all on phone system, is really set up for the interlinking of consciousness when the time comes—finally got Jack on the line from Boston—shouted to him, "Come up to Boston—I saw Milton's Lucifer in vast dark space! Take a plane and come up here immediately—the revolution is beginning—gather all the dark angels of light at once—it is time to seize power over in the universe and become the next consciousness —" And he laughed and says, "Whazammater, are you high?" "I am high and naked and I am the king of the universe. Get on a plane it is time!"—"But I got my mother..." "Bring your mother" I command—serious—I really have the answer—"Ah I'm tired"—But he was interested and strange—"What do you want to do?" I ask and he says, lay down and die, so I shout, "What's the matter with you, are you AFRAID?" And that's it, he really is afraid of God, he don't know that he already is God, everybody like me looking for power outside them, afraid to be the authority of the universe—who else but us if IT the life force—is God?—and was he surprised hearing that in my voice—first time in ten years—yes, you are, were, right, it is man (published in *Nomad* I think?) ME is IT—I was rapturous on the phone I made him promise not to die—I thought I would save everybody. Take over the universe and freeze it in permanent eternity present, Williams not die, I almost called him too—convoke all the consciousness at once over radio, telephonetelevision electronic thinking

machine hooked into myriad eyes and ears and TURN ON THE UNIVERSE—
Great horns of *Die Valkerie* were on the phonograph inspiring me—da dam, da
dam da da dee! Revolt in paradise, the messiah has broken loose—Finally the
psychologists prevailed on me to lie down naked on couch with Peter and stop
piling up their private phone bill and we listened to Joyce's voice Finneganing
through time. I realized sooner or later that drugged consciousness would
wear off. I didn't have strength right then to break through the massed negative
consciousness of the whole world, the time would come, all is well, I got the
great inspiration, I'm through magic psalming outside myself to find the great
power of being. I am the great magician henceforth. I'm reading Milton and
will go back to Blake's Milton too.

That was Lafcadio's first plane ride too by the way. Peter when high saw all
the dinosaur battles of yore and foretime. Then we rushed out to Gloucester
and dragged Olson back to Boston and turned him on a mighty dose of mush-
room. He lit up and turned into Santa Claus, kept calling the psychologist
coach—psychologist a nice coach-type guy who digs getting high, wants to
start a pyramid club and turn America on, free the drug on the market, we're
starting a conspiracy, next week we turn on Rosset, [Robert] Lowell, Muriel
Rukeyser, David Reisman, etc. etc. (we'll think up) believing his eyes and ears
and repeating—"DID YOU SAY THAT?" Incredulously happy. First time he
ever got high and he immediately understood me for the first time ever.

Love

Allen

[*Ginsberg had always been interested in the effect drugs had on the human mind, but
from this period on he took a leading role in efforts to have mind-expanding drugs de-
criminalized.*]

Allen Ginsberg [New York, NY] to Kennett Love[38] [New York, NY]
February 2, 1961

Dear Kenny:

Thanks for your letter, I haven't had time to answer, which I wanted to,
till tonight. There is one important thing in your letter which I wanted to

---

38 Kennett Love (b. 1924). *New York Times* columnist.

communicate information about: "she [Emily Harrison] says Anslinger[39] is a nasty type but she says Anslinger only administers the law and that the law and the narcotics bureau is the root of the problem." See, this point is basically Anslinger's con—it is Anslinger and his Bureau, not the law, which is the big block. I don't know where to begin to illustrate this and make immediate sense but will try to outline the facts sketchily.

First the original law is just a tax stamp to control narcotics use, that's why it is under Treasury Department (Anslinger and all). Anslinger got in as head administrator and by administrative practice added more and more drugs to the ones originally named in the Harrison Act—by his decrees and practices the control of addicts was taken from medical hands and put in police hands.

The actual law now on federal books allows doctors to take on addicts as patients and give them steady narcotics if they deem medically wise.

But Anslinger has conducted a continuous 20 year campaign to extend police control by harassing and tripping and tricking doctors, he takes every doctor that openly opposes him and treats addicts and by every means legal and illegal gets them out of business. The AMA has as usual shut up and not defended the doctors, so that hardly any doctor anywhere will treat an addict as a private patient, tho legally he can. But if he does he does so at expense of a huge legal battle with the treasury dept attorneys, he may win or lose (the narco agents do not hesitate to fix such doctors with bum raps) and has legal expense, professional shame, crusade etc. no support from the profession, and possibility of losing his license. So all the doctors have collapsed and thrown in their cards.

The AMA-ABA-Ploscows report is outline of above legal situation, and comments, tho mildly, on the attempt of narco department to extend their power by lawsuits and harassment, and rebukes narco department for trying historically to force the Harrison Act to mean that doctors can't treat patients with junk. The narco department has been put down on some crucial test cases —tho generally if a crucial case which will CLEARLY determine their limits is going against them, they do not prosecute further but drop action so no clear decision gets on record.

For outline of above situation see series of articles by Prof. Lindesmith[40] in the Nation, and in various learned journals. He develops in detail the calculated

39 Harry J. Anslinger (1892–1975). From 1930 until 1962, the Commissioner of the Treasury Department's Federal Bureau of Narcotics.
40 Alfred R. Lindesmith (1905–1991). Professor of sociology and drug reform advocate.

steps the narco department took to put the whole medical scene under their control. If can write Lindesmith and digest his information IT'S A SCANDAL. Further corroboration of same in the new book by Indiana University Press pps. 70–82.

In addition there are a few doctors here in NYC who have taken the bull by the horns and tried ambulatory treatment—and I spent a month with one in situation I mentioned in last letter. Well this Dr. Gilbert Grossman has 15 years battling Anslinger and has an AWFUL tale to tell—constant agent harassment of him and his patients, the agents go to wholesale drug houses and warn them against this Grossman. They burn down all the pharmacies (i.e. warn pharmacies on him)—send Treasury Tax agents to trip him up on fees—try to set up legal pitfalls where they can get him in jail. He's under half a dozen counts of indictment now. I presume he's actually quite honest—as honest as any doctor anyway. The other Dr. Freyman who treated addicts for a while was finally forced out of business by pressure from hysterical junkies and agents. Also a Dr. Nyswander an analyst who treats junkies has her harassment tale to tell. Also Lindesmith in Indiana has been pressured indirectly to shut up—thru complaints to his State Univ. trustees etc.—there's been a shakeup there, so he's free again. At least that's the pure rumor I hear. Also Dr. Bowman who authored the LaGuardia Report on marijuana speaks of all sorts of pressure to suppress his report, etc. etc. all the way down the line anybody who's had anything to do with narco problem from a non-Anslinger bureaucracy angle.

The second thing to understand is that the whole narco hysteria and confusion is as result of Anslinger's control of INFORMATION that gets channeled thru mass media, congressional committees, etc. Only in last few years has there been a non-official breakthrough of people getting up on their hind legs and yelling, like now. The narco department feeds narco stories and statements to the papers and they are published as patriotic duty. The information fed thus has been way out of line, absolute lies sometimes. Like there is an Anslinger statement in the thirties that marijuana was a more vicious and destructive habit than heroin even. This when he was expanding narco bureau activities to take in marijuana in the face of the LaGuardia Report which for all practical publicity and informational purposes was suppressed. Beyond that there is active effort to distort and suppress information, such as this Indiana U. book.

The reason for all this surrealist activity is that the larger Anslinger's position and bureau, the more power he got. Simple case of a cancerous type bureaucracy. If junk were legalized à la England, i.e. junkies went to doctors to get cured or supplied, the whole junk black market would collapse and all the crime attendant on it would disappear, there'd be no more illegal junk or junkies, and the narco bureau of how many thousand people would have no function at all. They'd all be out of a job. The point is they know it, and the narco bureau's activities are consciously (with rationalizations etc.) intended to perpetuate the problem so they don't go out of business. This isn't hot air I've seen documents to prove it. Or at least make it obvious. For instance Dr. Grossman has a friend, a retired federal agent, who kept a diary, the Treasury men broke into his house stole a copy, he made it into a fictional novel with Grossman, I read it and am handing it on Tuesday to Rev. [Norman] Eddy of the East Harlem Protestant Parish—a friendly liberal who works with junkies but doesn't know what he's up against because he thinks the whole narco mess is not intentional and so like Miss Harrison thinks it's just a confusion of laws, with Anslinger a fall guy and not the real monster operative he is.

The point is how did this immense mass of misinformation brainwash the whole public on two facts (1) that marijuana is both vicious and habit-forming and 2) that junkies are criminals and not medical cases? Aside from lunatic prudes, the whole smog of misinformation comes directly from the propaganda activities of the federal narco bureau.

Well, in the last few years enough people have smoked pot to know the score on that, and the heroin problem has got so bad it's becoming a J.D. problem and the whole structure begins to collapse and so there's the beginning of independent activity, the few liberal groups, judges, etc. in NY begin to speak up and now exchange info in NYC and now on a larger national basis.

I think that there is sufficient info now at hand so that if someone intelligent could investigate and integrate it all and get everybody's story, it might be possible to blow up the whole federal narco system.

However the simplest way to solve the problem would be to get AMA to take a stand that henceforth they will back and defend doctors who treat junkies—the government would then have to back down because the Law is on the doctors' side. But getting the AMA to do anything like that is perhaps more difficult than making a public scandal of Anslinger's activities.

Below is a partial list of people who have assembled information of all kinds, historical, legal, personal—who have never gotten all together to pool their information—tho some such movement seems on the way now. [...]

I went to all this detail above to give ground and reason and sources of information to indicate that the narco problem is not the laws but the narco bureau and Anslinger as head of it, because having been in and out of junk-pot etc. scene for 15 years, I was actually surprised that my understanding of the problem was not similar to Emily Harrison's as regards Anslinger—and hope that she, or someone, could take time to check on the actual situation— because until that's understood, if what I say above is true, nothing will solve the narco problem but complete overhaul, backtracking and/or demolishment of the federal narco bureau by means of a Pulitzer Prize type <u>political</u> examination of the activities of the bureau in the *N.Y. Times*.

I've gone rushing around the last month trying to interconnect as many sources of information as I could as fast and sloppily as possible because I think I'll be leaving the country in a few weeks for long trip and the more I've talked to people the more opens up the possibility that something could be done. There are plenty of doctors and psychoanalysts and judges and experts and junkies who are willing to help. [...]

Center for Personality Research, Dr. Tim Leary, part of Harvard Grad school—also be helpful for statements etc. I have been up working with them on psilocybin—magic (hallucinogenic) mushroom synthetic—[Aldous] Huxley, Alan Watts, [Arthur] Koestler, Robert Lowell, etc. also. One further problem is, research and spread of use of the really great useful non-habit forming chemicals like peyote and lysergic acid and mushrooms will be balked as long as government bureaucracy controls national psyche on subject of drugs, doctors and analysts are bad enough without getting politicians on top of that. Government control of benevolent drugs like marijuana means government control of perception. Means government control of STATES OF AWARENESS. (I think this is the significance of the whole problem.)

I better quit,

Allen

[...] Furthest and worst horror is attempt by Anslinger to apply his methods and thinking to world drug problem thru the UN. You should see what's been going on there. He's taken over the UN drug committee, apparently. It's really incredible that Harrison should think he's just trying to do his best as victim of a bad law. He's MAKING IT INTERNATIONAL.

While all this mad hypocrisy is in control there are at this minute 25,000 junkies here in NY sick, stealing, scoring furtively, getting busted, suffering the tortures of the damned.

The way to avoid further spread of junk addiction particularly among young—as it is now becoming a big thing in NY—is to cut off the black market supply of heroin. The way to do that is to take the profit out of it. The way to do that is to have doctors supply the junk to junkies who need it, and will get it legally or if necessary illegally. That eliminates likelihood of new users spreading.

If junk addiction is permanently curable—nobody even is really sure of it —then let doctors, hospitals, psychos try any way they want. That prevents confirmed junkies who should be allowed to maintain from being victims of bureaucratic system.

It also encourages medical and social experimentation toward cure for those who can be cured. Cops and jail totally irrelevant murder here.

Marijuana is totally other problem and has no relation to junk use any more than alcohol does except under present system where they are both purposely confused as interchangeable dope by Anslinger. General public doesn't even know the difference due to narco bureau and newspaper fictions.

[*Ginsberg had the ability to cram a lot of information into a brief letter.*]

Allen Ginsberg [Paris, France] to James Laughlin [New York, NY]
late April 1961

Dear James L:

How am I supposed to address you? Dear Jim?—am in Paris, so's Gregory, he got your letters and has replied?? already. Yes fine to use the 2 prose poems in antho—sooner check comes the happier I'll be, every little bit helps we're down to $10 as it is—tho I expect money soon from *Kaddish*.

Been correcting proofs on new Burroughs book the *Soft Machine*—also remarkable—and yakking with Gregory. Orlovsky here too getting laid and going to gym classes and French classes and writing down dreams.

Saw your remarks re [Thomas] Merton in letter to Gregory and was fascinated by possibility that he had not ever actually experienced some breakthrough visionary state. I would be curious his reaction to the Magic Psalm poem in *Kaddish* since it's practically a catholic type prayer. If you see him again and if he ever sees my book.

Everything absolutely lovely here—we'll go off somewhere and write new epics—see Burroughs in a few weeks, he's back in Tangier—maybe Kerouac come soon if all well—hope to go to Moscow too have invite to stay with Konstantin Siminov a Steinbeck type Moscow government bureaucrat.

Cuba thing [Bay of Pigs Invasion, April 17, 1961] really is the bankruptcy of U.S. "liberalism," at long last, now maybe some kind of real Left get started. Seemed all incredible here and the unanimity of assent to Kennedy also nuts.

Can always reach me thru City Lights or American Express Paris will forward—am in haste or would relax and write goofier.

Love

Allen

[Ginsberg's letters to his father were always filled with political conversation, and the Bay of Pigs fiasco gave him plenty to write about. In this letter Allen began by remarking on his Uncle Max's death, but quickly moved on to the political situation.]

Allen Ginsberg [Tangier, Morocco] to Louis Ginsberg [Paterson, NJ] June 12, 1961

Dear Lou:

Sad to hear Max had died—and whom to write condolences to now? I saw less of him the last few years but when I did we were pretty close and I always felt for him, in thought, and that apartment in the Bronx was landmark always —was there last year again looking at it knowing I'd not see it much ever more, it was a mellow place for Max-Elanor then, Eugene must be sad too.

Say hello to everyone at picnic—I wrote long letter to [Aunt] Honey yesterday, details on Paris, for Ruth and her.

Glad you had poem in *Second Coming* and *Liberation*—I also had prose piece in *Second Coming* — I hear it is out. I haven't their address. Can you send them a card or note telling them to send me a copy of the issue with my and your writings and also remind them they owe me money which I have not received and which I need—so tell them to send it here to above address. They said they'd pay me I think it was $50 and that payment is overdue by now if the piece is out. Have you time to drop them a note? I would but I don't have the address.

Glad you are getting *Liberation* as it is a sincere magazine compared to most. [interruption, Corso typed a page to Allen's letter and Allen continued] Gregory just came upstairs, read your letter and sat down at typewriter so that was the result—he's very funny—I live on top of a roof, a little tile room in hot Mediterranean clime, and that leads to a glass enclosed sun-shack, and that leads to a little terrace overlooking rooftops and Tangier Bay and parapets of Spain (as last time, I'm around the block from hotel I was last time)—all this costs $20 a month. Gregory has a slightly larger room downstairs for $14 a month. Peter walks around the Arab streets and keeps diaries. Burroughs around the corner in his old room just finished novel (*The Soft Machine*) now

cuts up newspapers and photographs to make collages in spare time (weird jux-
tapositions of news stories, Kennedy stepping off airplanes onto Queen Eliza-
beth's forehead)—everybody busy. I'm typing up journals and answering
letters. The weather is great. Lots of young beatniks suddenly in town swing-
ing with the poor Arabs buying old clothes and smoking pot (it's legal). Paul
Bowles takes us to his favorite cafe on mountain-cliff overlooking vast blue
crawling hide of the sea and we sit silent watching the universe, everybody
tranquil. Gregory and Peter and I at nite on roof discuss galaxies. We eat 50¢
shish kebab meals in dark Arab fry restaurants—sometimes go to European
quarter and get high-class French meals for a buck—cheaper than Mexico here
—in fact this place is more interesting and weirder to live in and happier than
Paris at the moment for me—so everything's fine. Since independence Tangier
no longer is international free port trading post and so's more tranquil less
paranoiac less Europe-Arab conflict, calmer fewer people less business less
tourists less surface confusion, more calm to live in and cheaper. You can get
$180 Yugoslav boat here from NY—ought to come for a few weeks sometime.

Anyway as I say glad you reading *Liberation*, seems more active radical than
the old-time-radical-new-liberal-weeklies. I agree generally with Finch the guy
who resigned more than the other editors in disapproving of Castro dictator-
ship; and Finch's ideas on that are based on more specific and accurate informa-
tion than generally circulated in U.S.—excellent detailed accurate info in
previous issues of *Liberation* attacking Castro by Cuban anarchist-pacifist
groups who are persecuted there. Do you ever see *I.F. Stone's Newsletter*? That's
the most balanced political comment and reporting I see from the U.S.A. I get it
regularly, someone put me on sub list. Enclosed if I have sample around.

Now this above (disapproving of Castro police state) not to be taken as
change of opinion on my part as to complete vileness of U.S. government and
U.S. people in last year regarding Cuba. Nor if I were Castro am I sure I'd be
able to do any better with Cuba than he's doing, given the U.S. for neighbor.

All last year I was complaining about the CIA and I think by now what
sounded in me to be eccentric has been put into perspective by events and
come to general public consciousness, realized—the whole complaint I had
then is now the general U.S. complaint. What sounded in Castro as Mussolini-
hysteria—his screaming about U.S. attack—has also been justified by event.

I wondered how you reacted to the Cuban invasion and if that made sense
of what you had taken to be mere communist propaganda before, i.e. accusa-
tions made by Russia and Castro that U.S. was preparing military blow at Cuba?
This was dismissed as paranoia for a year before it happened.

According to Gallup poll at invasion time 80% of U.S. people, on basis of U.S. mass communication data—including *NY Times,* etc.—thought that Cuban masses were against Castro. I remember [Uncle] Leo thought so, too. I disputed that point wildly and was put down for it, as a "dupe." I was merely reporting fact and amazed to realize that all the liberals even were completely misinformed to the point to mind-control or brainwash on the facts of the case. Now the fact is no longer ambiguous and it is generally reported in U.S. press (*NY Herald Trib, Times,* etc.) that majority of Cubans are behind Castro. I been warning, this total reversal of public information is the result of a deliberate manipulation of information reaching the U.S. public and until people stop believing the newspapers in the U.S. they will have as inaccurate information and opinions on the cold wars as they have on the beat generation, to give an example close to home.

What was really shocking was that the old-line liberals and socialists like yourself after 20 years of McCarthyism are completely out of contact with any kind of perspective on what's happened to America.

Put it this way—to my generation, the Cuban scene is similar to the old Spanish Civil War scene—with many of the same stresses and interior conflicts.

I don't see any way out except full public investigation of CIA activities in Guatemala, Iran, Cuba, Formosa, Korea, Laos, Congo etc. for the last 10 years —total reversal of policy of secret manipulation of foreign policy and hiding or withholding news and info from public—the extent of which nobody knows fully but what I already know has made me gasp with horror and has justified the worst Russian tirades in the U.N.

I also see last week's banning of Communist Party as formal police state action by the U.S.

In fact at this point I think the U.S. is too far gone and now useless to com-plain since I don't see the people of the U.S. wake enough to take their own life up again and begin to swing politically in some imaginative free expression.

The reason I kept yelling at you is in a sense you represent the intelligent lib-eral symbol in my mind—the people who are supposed to be depended on to be able to defend themselves from right wing police state—the stable progres-sive old school—and I see you inundated by History, by a U.S.A. that would have been inconceivable in Roosevelt's day, by a U.S. that is suicidal and unable to straighten out in time to prevent itself from being blown up by the commu-nist world, and that will steadily lose ground and degenerate and get more right wing every year, no matter what party is in power.

The only way out for America now as far as I can see is socialism, return of government power from oligarchic holding companies and military power groups that run things—industry <u>and</u> information-propaganda. (We do NOT have a free press. Period.) (Actually about 8 people in the U.S.A. determine policy for majority of newspapers and TV and radio) (that's why it's possible to have such massive factual misinformation as on Cuba) (i.e. one year of constant information totally at variance in factual data as attitude from British, French and Moroccan papers, to say nothing of Russian or Chilean)—and shift of U.S. economy from present monopoly capitalism to some relaxed socialistic form wherein a shift can be planned from conspicuous consumer and military production to world-integrated useful production for undeveloped countries. (This be [Arnold] Toynbee's suggestion too). Which means a lower standard of living for U.S. and a more meaningful life maybe, at least be of some use to the rest of the world instead of a mockery and horror of fake democracy gone nuts. More and more from outside U.S. everybody digs U.S. as approaching some vast crisis which people inside U.S.A. are almost completely unconscious of, as if everything was well in the refrigerator and history be escaped.

I.e. to French socialists, the "world struggle" is not the cold war at all but struggle against "power" monger groups in U.S. and in Russia both, and it makes very little difference if the U.S. power group loses, in fact it might be preferable for the red power group to win since at least it's a power that's still ALIVE in the sense that the U.S. is dead from the neck up and more retrogressive and less promising of flexible development than the red power groups. I could imagine the world developing and relaxing (maybe) after a total red victory; but after a total U.S. victory I would see nothing but medieval scenes of Cuban-Guatemalan horror sort of, a McCarthy-Kennedy–Max Lerner police state, I'm not making sense.

Anyway, what I'm saying is, some new sense of a serious fix is coming into consciousness on the American scene, is it not? Something's got to give, I hope it's the right wing not the left—at least there's the beginning of some open fight—Republicans calling for war on Cuba and Democrats beginning to draw back from that and be neutral.

It simply is a shame that there is no real progressive party because now there is a progressive scene possible, i.e. historical demand for reversal of U.S. policy on Latin America so that we encourage peaceful socialism—which neither party is willing to admit—outside the U.S.A. and even inside if necessary.

OK, Love,

Allen

[*Ginsberg was able to fill even the smallest postcard with a lot of detail.*]

Allen Ginsberg [Marrakech, Morocco] **to LeRoi Jones** [New York, NY]
ca. July 18, 1961

Dear LeRoi:

Spending a week here in Marrakech with Paul Bowles, this is the maddest teahead city I've ever seen, a vast plaza where at dusk when it's cool all sorts of acrobats, fortune tellers, snake charmers and shade drum and dance groups gather circles of crowds and collect coins—also a huge labyrinth market with alleys covered by bamboo against sunlight, selling Aladdin lamps and clothes. Can wander for hours lost—and outside the walled city is the desert and Atlas mountains. The people are all heads spiritually and modernization here is killing the best and most humane aspects of the life—nationalistic "progressives" want to close down on pot, close the markets and square and rebuild with U.S. style supermarket architecture. Also everybody sleeps with everybody.

Allen

[*While in Tangier, Ginsberg and Orlovsky decided to go their separate ways, due in part to William Burroughs' treating Peter like Allen's prat boy. Allen was unable or unwilling to defend Peter from Burroughs' abuse, so Peter left Morocco with the intention of touring the Mideast alone. Immediately, Allen hoped they would reconcile and connect at some point in the future. Within a few days Allen forwarded Peter's mail to him and included the first of many letters written during their separation.*]

Allen Ginsberg [Tangier, Morocco] **to Peter Orlovsky** [Athens, Greece]
August 2, 1961

Dear Peter:

Just got up—have to run to PO to send this so be short—been up 2 days on O [opium] with [Timothy] Leary and Gregory [Corso]. Enclosed note from Buenos Aires. How are you and how's Athens? No other mail come but this so far, will send anything on as it comes. Beautiful to see you ride off and I felt good that you were off into world alone, just tearful that we had been quarreling with each other and separating in soul but that will be OK I hope next time we meet. I felt lost when you said "years" [from now] but if years alas, then years alas I'll still cry to see yr old eyes. Leary came in, said he saw you at airport—living downstairs in hotel, lots happened, he dug Gregory, gets along with Bill [Burroughs] politely and vice versa. He invited Bill to Harvard in September and Bill accepted so that will take place in September, he pay Bill's way over and small salary but not the $2000 planned because no money. We all went to Ahmed's[41] new apartment (great balcony view) last night, and had been going to fair to listen to music. I took a few mushrooms and felt sick and began kissing Pamela Stevenson on Blvd Pasteur, I think I will start chasing girls again. Leary off to Copenhagen [LSD Conference] later today; Ansen also leaving this morn for Venice, that leaves me and Gregory here and Bill and the boys there—still a sort of cold war. They gave Mark (the friend of Mike Portman lives downstairs) majoun and he got panicked at Bowles because everyone was ignoring him, so Jane [Bowles] and I and Paul and Leary held his hand and got him back and the next day on O I sat up with him and had long talk and now he is much more sociable and open and independent and I also gave him my flute since he is a musician. Gregory and I started article on Cannes [Film Festival 1961]—an interview, was OK but boring all about Sal Mineo. Then we cut it up and it sounds wild—sample:

"Emptiness haunted by Jack Kennedy. Talking about windowsills of cold Sal Mineo Liberace secrecy, how would world war 2 clodhop strange? Assuredly American film presents films of attention. Musically they're really enough. Hollywood is reporters and roses? And a producer in a slimy flower festival, he got into string bean conversations." This was done by taking cut pieces and reweaving poetic sentences from words—that is, half cut up half mental reweaving.

Bill still cold, so that's that, I feel depressed in that I've lost touch with you, and also out of direct contact with Bill, and Mike Portman mainly in the way, tho maybe it's just my own schemings. Greg and Leary went to Casino last nite with [Francis] Bacon and lost a few bucks—I'm down to a hundred dollars. Leary says he'll send us railfare from Paris next week, so Gregory and I will go to Copenhagen I think. Leary says lots of girls there so I'll try girlies. Ansen made date with me for to try his boys but not done that yet. From Copenhagen can get to Berlin etc. or Scandinavia. But I don't know what I do

41 Ahmed Yacoubi (1931–1985). Moroccan artist and storyteller, friend of Paul Bowles.

next. Bill can't take mushrooms he says he gets horrors. Ian [Somerville] built a flicker machine it's easy—Gysin made it sound hard. You just get a cylinder of black paper and divide it in twenty squares and cut out 10 of them around the roll and that's that. Gregory afraid I'll fall for cut-ups I think and I will experiment more than I did, since it was useful to hop up and intensify the Cannes interview. Bill leaving for Paris in a week and we'll leave probably around then too—I'll keep writing you gossip. How is Parthenon? I mailed your letter to [your sister] Marie Monday. I haven't writ Jack yet. I feel lost but I guess that's good for me I'll have to grow up like Lafcadio and learn to be independent. The maid sick, so I sent her to the doctor again and bought her $2 worth of medicine, some kind of sulfa drug for her pussy and vanilone pills for liver like you had. Please write me soon so we keep thread unbroken, at least a little diamond thread.

XXXXX Love,

Allen

[As Ginsberg traveled he kept up correspondence with dozens of friends. One of these was Philip Lamantia, who had experienced visions of his own. At the time Philip was in the process of becoming a much more devout Catholic.]

Allen Ginsberg [Athens, Greece] to Philip Lamantia [San Francisco, CA] September 7, 1961

Dear Philip:

What is this abstract calling on Christ all the time? How can there even be one (I'm talking to myself as usual), much less called a name like god christ all that? Been with Burroughs for several months, & he says cut up language in order to get out of mere word consciousness, leave behind the hypnotic logos which is a lie located in the cortex—cut up a practical means of annihilating poetry too. A koan type mind-breaker. I've separated from Peter. Cut up Love! Nothing sacred, Zen-man! I vomited from fear, as usual, like an aging soprano. I'm going on to see the Sphinx—how are you?

Love

Allen

[*After several months traveling alone, Ginsberg and Orlovsky decided to team up again. Allen's plans were to meet Gary Snyder in India and travel with him and Joanne Kyger for awhile. He wanted to live in India for awhile, and Allen hoped that Peter would stay with him.*]

Allen Ginsberg [Athens, Greece] to Peter Orlovsky [Haifa, Israel] October 21, 1961

Dear Peter:

I had been sending you mail Amer Express Istanbul from Tangier, including magazines and a package (letter and book gift Fra Angelico) from Janine [Pommy Vega]; when I got to Greece there were two earlier letters from me I also had forwarded to Istanbul (but here they told me the real address was Turk Express Istanbul not American Express)—so there is a lot of stuff following you that way. Then finally after trip to Crete earlier this month and after I wrote your mother with a letter for her to send you, I received all your letters from Beirut and around the 10th or 12th of Oct I sent you letters and postcards there including a 20 dollar bill in one letter since it sounded like you were broke selling your blood and your check not arrived according to your mother; then I received yesterday your last note from Beirut saying you were heading off to Damascus, Jerusalem, and I should write you in Haifa. I don't understand how you going to pick up mail in Haifa which on map is way up north in Israel; but I guess you will be there around the 2nd or 3rd of November to receive V.A. check from your mother.

I not sure what plans are for me but will make sure I am in Haifa then and be around, and will leave note in Amer Express address you sent me there, saying where I am living. You do the same yes, so we not lose contact again. I can get boat from here to Haifa for 20 dollars with bunk-bed. So I will go there and wait. I hope you get this or I will be waiting there forever? I also wrote you extra postcard to Embassy Beirut saying I would try to reach you at the Haifa address you sent me October 15. Your note sounded like none of my letters had reached you by the time you were leaving in "Taxey" to go to Damascus.

Gary Snyder says he and Joanne his wife will be in Bombay on Jan 1, 1962 and I should meet them there, go on tour meet monks with him. He says he'll need money and will give poetry readings in universities there and wants me to do it too, I wrote him okay. Tho I don't feel like singing any more. I guess you read if you want. He, Gary, sounds great, I wrote him what happened with Bill etc. in Tangier. Enclosed letter from Irving [Rosenthal] I got this month with

NY gossip. Ferlinghetti's *Journal* came out [*Journal for the Protection of All Beings*], so did issue of *Kulchur* and I have them; I mailed you a copy of New Orleans *Outsider* with your [Snail] poem in it. Ferlinghetti writes me where are you he wants to publish yr poetry, I sent him yr Beirut address; Gregory keeps asking why you don't write him, Amer Embassy London, he sad thinking you disappeared. He was broke and lived with Colin Wilson on south coast of England. Then sent article to magazine and got some money and now lives near zoo and finishing manuscript of poems *Apples,* and hit Norman Mailer for insulting beatniks at a London party one night. Bill was in Harvard and Leary wrote that all was quiet and OK but you see what Irving says. Leary sounds a little sad, send him a postcard encourage? I got to write Jack still.

I have 250 dollars when I get to Israel. Prefer to go overland but want to get there by New Year in Bombay, meet Gary, because he'll know all the monks and I said I'd read with him.

I stopped smoking for 2 weeks solid, then started again, but can stop anytime now, it's just that it makes me nervous. To stop. I get irritable touchy. I got some O [opium] from friend coming from India and used it twice, once I wrote huge letter about Politics and Consciousness to Howie Schulman (Hotel Presidente, Vedado, Havana Cuba) for his magazine there (*Arriba*). He wants yr poems too.

I packed up books and papers and mailed them back to States; also packed up rock-and-roll and mailed them all to Romanova in Moscow. So now my knapsack lighter. I got some shirts. Meanwhile I been here in Greece all along, read *Odyssey* and *Iliad*, and been in country most of the time to ruined cities and shepherd goatbell music valleys—Mycenae, Crete, Delphi, Olympia—I was going up north to Mt. Athos monasteries but time getting short for India and want to meet you in Haifa and it save money if I take this cheap boat. Had a lot of strange dreams in which I had amnesia or was whirled around by winds. Made it with a few boys here but cost money a little and they weren't so interested but I dig the cock. I live across street from bar where whore boys gather, I know them all. Also hang around Zonars and Flocas cafes and see intelligent old literary men here and they all like me. They're all bugged at Gregory who apparently teased everyone, threw fits etc....

Lessee what else to add. I get endless mail and still answer. Not wrote much poetry but lots of dreams, and some notebooks. *Empty Mirror* book is out and looks okay. Money I got is advance on Italian translation plus 20 dollars Gregory sent me back plus 10 dollars from New Directions. I sold article to *Show Business Illustrated* on Cannes, had 750 dollars, Gregory lost 200 gambling and owes me that, spent the rest traveling plus 100 extra was his for helping; now they want to censor the word shit so I wrote them no even if I have to pay them back 450. Still waiting to hear. [It was never published.]

Sorry I did not see Istanbul and Cairo and Damascus but maybe see strange places inland overland to India if do that. Be sure and send for your mail in Beirut and Istanbul and send Amer Express 1 dollar they charge nowadays for forwarding. I read Melville [*Holy Land Travels*] notes years ago and don't remember them except that was my idea, to see the Bible landscape he mentions, also he has long poem "Clarel" I read parts of about his trip to Jerusalem area. Okay Petey I sign off and see you in 12 days I guess if you finally get this, and you not delay forever in Petra. I have 2 huge maps of Middle East to Persia. Also possible boat from Israel to India. Maybe I, we, miss further Arab countries and rush to India fast. They say Bombay and India is expensive because dysentery dangerous to eat native food and there are no hotels like in west, just big hotels cost 3 dollars a day but with good food included. That Bowles says and all others I met.

Thank you for all letters sorry you not receive mine, some were crazy. I was lonesome for you.

Love to you from your old Lover,

Allen

Allen Ginsberg [Tel Aviv, Israel] **to Eugene Brooks** [New York, NY]
November 25, 1961

Dear Gene:

Think I wrote you sometime back but not heard nuttin except thru Louis. Been in Israel a month now—traveled a little, spoke to lots of people, lived with businessmen and artists as guest, so not spent much money, got interviewed a lot, earned a little loot with poem in *Jerusalem Post* newspaper and getting my poems translated into Hebrew. Basically it's kind of a strange scene here—for the very reason that you, for instance, wouldn't necessarily think of moving to Israel. Well imagine the psychology of a bunch of Jewish folk who think that all Jews <u>should</u> come here and get together. So it's a little uncomfortable this excessive hang up on invisible Jewishness. Main justification for Israel is as place for refugees and for that it's good. But then once all those Jews get together they stare each other in the face and wonder what's it all about? So the main opinion you hear here is that this is the place to forget about being Jewish once and for all, this from the intelligent sensitive types (all but the wild orthodox religious). For the rest there is plenty dissatisfaction that the old idealist socialist Russian kibbutz spirit which first settled the land is fading at advent of prosperity, new middle class, American and German money flooding the holy land with Western-Hollywood styles of living, slow loosening of PURPOSE, which once everyone felt. Arab pressure holds things together spiritually. But there are some contradictions here that aren't settled and will have to be — huge Arab minority, with lots of guilt feeling for the refugees who were (I now learn) pushed out with considerable unofficial Jewish terror. Some Jews say, good riddance to bad rubbish. Others, my god, we're raping democracy. Every- one agrees the Government is hypocritical however in its official goody-goody attitude as far as propaganda. Meanwhile the Arabs are repressed here (partly for military reasons, mostly for old fashioned middle class Yiddish intolerance) —and anyway it's a Jewish state, so even if an Arab is patriotic and wants to integrate he can't really in the long run without become a Jew, which is absurd. So the "good" Arabs are all neurotic, that is, goofily displaced socially—they're not really part of the country since it's a Jewish state. That's 10 percent of the population. Another 50 percent is arabized oriental Jews who are more like Arabs than Europeans. (From Yemen Morocco etc.)—and since the Europe whites run the country (tho they're a minority) they're big cultural chaos—i.e. it takes more than clothes and radios and cars to "educate" the Orientals— who don't want to be educated like that anyway, but who slowly slip into the pattern. I haven't been to Kibbutz yet. Will go this week and in 2 weeks hope to catch ship to India from Israel port of Elat. Still vague exactly how, investigat- ing now. Meanwhile saw the spot where Christ changed bread [*sic:* water] to wine and multiplied loaves and gave sermon on mount, stood on the mount in fact, and wandered in Galilee and even tried (unsuccessfully) to walk on Lake Galilee.

Listen, here is cause of this letter. I received a note from Marie Orlovsky saying that her mother Kate AND Lafcadio both had been taken to Central Islip hospital and shut up. Peter Orlovsky arrived here a week ago and is writing her to find out what happened and what if anything needs to be done. Marie sounds a little bewildered. It's a weird stroke, two at once. I thought they'd finally have to put Lafcadio in. But I didn't expect they'd take the mother— she's not nuts at all and doesn't belong there. I think he must have got violent, she hysterical and by the time cops arrived they both looked crazy. Presumably after short observation period they will send her out. I wrote Marie to call you up and see you if she needs any law advice. Also told her to borrow a few dol- lars (5 or 10) from you if she needs and is broke—if she does I'll send it to you. I don't know what her situation is, she probably needs someone to talk over the whole problem with, and figure what she should do. Main practical problem I think is Mrs. Orlovsky's apartment. I think Marie is there now—she wrote she might have to give it up. Could you drive over there if she doesn't call you, and see if she is handling the situation alright, and give her any advice she seems to need? I told her, if she moved, to leave Peter O's manuscripts with you, they're valuable, shouldn't be lost.

The welfare people were taking care of her mother and probably would make sure that the apartment was kept for her till she gets out. I am assuming there's nothing serious wrong with Mrs. Orlovsky—I doubt there is. But she's deaf and may have trouble explaining herself at Central Islip Hospital. But the welfare people should be able to get her out since they know her quite well over long period of time. I just don't know if Marie has enough savoir faire to know who to contact and what to do in the situation, so I wrote her to talk it over with you (or Connie maybe)—maybe she needs advice. So if you can drive over and see if she's at the apartment in Northport—it's 155 Main Street, Top Floor, I think. I'll get right address before I close letter. Send me a note if you can. OK—Later.

Love,

Allen

[*For political reasons Ginsberg and Orlovsky were not able to leave Israel through any of the neighboring Islamic countries, so they had to go to India via Africa. In the meantime Allen's brother, Eugene, was able to help straighten out the difficulties with Peter's family back in New York.*]

Allen Ginsberg [Mombasa, Kenya, Africa] to Eugene Brooks [Plainview, NY] January 27, 1962

Dear Gene:

Been in Kenya and Tanganyika the last few weeks—Dar Es Salaam and Mombasa the port towns in East Africa—Arab, Persian, Bantu, Swahili, Portuguese, German and English talk and architecture left over from 12 centuries of shipping and colonization. Mombasa a charming town—live in an Indian hotel with mosquito nets and eat curried prawns for 45¢ a dish. We took bus inland to Mt. Kilimanjaro and around thru national game reserves and thru Masai warrior territory—saw giraffes, zebras, ostriches, lions, hippos in big savannah grassland plains—thru to Nairobi and living around in cheap African hotels eating and mixing with negro Africans—all week there. Also attended huge political rally at Nairobi African stadium and saw Jomo Kenyatta himself make big speech. Also was in town for Tom Mboya (local politician) wedding and went to his wedding dance and met all sorts of politicians and hangers on to new negro nationalism here. Also hitch-hiked with member of Kenya special police who told me how he used to torture Africans in the old Mau Mau emergency. (Stand them all nite in cold mountain air in a barrel of cold water or shoot them up till confessions of information.) Now back in Mombasa, and in about 10 days, cheap $50 deck-class passage to India. Should land in Bombay around the 15th of next month, leaving here February 6 also saw the Masai as I said above—big tall funny negroes like Lucien's friend Miles Forst—wear dry-blood colored robes and carry spears and hang huge rings from their ears and eat naught but milk, blood and meat. But very friendly and funny types—awkward, intelligent, always poking each other in the ribs and making funny remarks, with those wild ears. A far cry from the duty-ridden sadist from the Kenya Special Police.

Reading a huge load of Indian books now—old Hindu classics and modern novels and Gandhi *Autobiography*—that last would interest you—when he got out of English law school he was lost about how to start a career, reminded me of you (or myself for that matter when I first looked for a job after college.) Anyway finally, about ready for last leg of India trip and be there soon.

I bought a pair of khaki shorts so am all equipped for 3° below equator where I am. Also take anti dysentery and anti malaria tablets and got all kinds of smallpox yellow fever and cholera shots.

I hear via Marie that Mrs. Orlovsky is still in the bughouse. Sounds like the bureaucracy wheels are still grinding slow and small. Does it look like she'll be hung up there very long? When you think that this kind of hopeless victimage is compounded a billion times all over Asia and Africa to say nothing of Russia and Balkans and Baltics, etc.! Does it still look like police want her too? Marie and Peter to write you some family history, which he says he'll do this nite. He received letter yesterday from his sister.

OK—That's all for now. Gregory Corso is living at Hotel Albert on 10th Street in Village, if you have time to call him up and maybe see him. He's charming. OK.

Love,

Allen

[*Finally Ginsberg and Orlovsky arrived in India and found Snyder and Kyger in Delhi. Having left the manuscript for a new book,* Reality Sandwiches, *with City Lights before he left, Allen kept in close touch with Ferlinghetti via the mail.*]

Allen Ginsberg [Delhi, India] to Lawrence Ferlinghetti [San Francisco] February 25, 1962

Dear Larry:

India is MORE, yes, we met Gary a few days ago here in New Delhi and we leave day after tomorrow for Himalayas, go stay in Yoga forest school, talk to the Dalai Lama maybe, climb in snows, everything is fine. India has everything Mexico has, poverty and dead dogs, I saw a body scattered on RR tracks like toe cover of *Kulchur* only it was in 6 pieces, also it's got hoods like Morocco and Moslems and shrouds and Indians like worse Bolivias and garbages like Peru and bazaars like Hong Kong's and billion of people like nowhere I seen. So that's all fine. I also have this backlog of 2 months mail, I'm woozy what with 16 cent morphine you can get here easy here, and sitting in a Jain temple dormitory to answer. Gary's down street in the Hindu YMCA.

I got the check, fine. Actually cash is the best thing here since you get best black market rate for that exchange, but it's too risky I suppose to send hundred dollar bills in mail so send on the other money in same type check. American Express cashes them, no trouble, and gives me travelers checks ok. I'll be back in Bombay the end of March with Gary and Peter and Gary's wife, so will pick up next mail there, I guess send the money on there by then.

Gary looks older and a little more domestic-acting now that he's married; his face is more seamed and wrinkled and the baby look is gone, and he comes on very straight and simple—I haven't seen him for 6 years and change is noticeable. He's staying here till end of March, we'll travel till then all together; and then he to Japan and Peter and I stay here till seen enough maybe a year, then go to Japan-Kyoto. Music here is great—night before last we went to hear farewell speech of a holyman who's going to stop talking for the rest of his life —he's 32 now—and a couple of the greatest musicians is a drummer (tabla finger drums) and lady sarod (guitar drone sound) serenaded him improvised for an hour straight, ending in trance-celestial speed—such classical music as I never heard.

So far spent 2 days in Bombay and sped here to meet Gary and we've hung around met a few writers, walked thru alleys and streets and saw Nehru give election speech and shopped for a little Tibet statue for Whalen and ate cheap 25 cent curry dinners, I haven't settled into any routine here yet and am disorganized and got too much unanswered mail. Anyway India got more than anywhere else, especially great cheap horse carriages to take you around cities for 15 cents a hop, lovely to lean back and clop clop thru fantastically crowded streets full of barbers and street shoe-repairmen and bicycle rickshaws and Sikhs in turbans and big happy cows everywhere stealing cabbages from pushcarts.

Your spring list Lowry and Russians is great. *Poems of Thaw* is, comparatively, drear title. If the poems are really lively why not something lively like *Thaw Heads* or *Moscow Gold* or *Beat Moscow* or *Hip Moscow* or or *Red Cats* — yes *RED Cats!*~ (subtitle *Poems of the Thaw*) *Red Cats* sell better.[42] But are the poems good? I hope.

Send my proofs, or have Villiers send them, to Bombay. I think the book's OK. If you think anything should be left out, do it, and let me know. Have you got from LeRoi [Jones] the tape of Artaud's voice I mailed him? That may help, for translation.

Make next check even 250 and send me a few copies *Howl* and *Kaddish*, 9 dollars' worth. First thing I found in Bombay when stept off ship was messages from *Time*, apparently they're finally reviewing *Kaddish* — so maybe it sell better hence? Apparently it's selling less than *Howl*.

That's astounding about your being a poppa after all.[43] The rich get richer, good thing you adopted that babe, he [*sic*: she] brought you blessings. Doubled congratulations to Kirby from the Indic depths of bacheloral morphia. Send interesting books and pamphlets slow boat to Bombay, they'll eventually reach me. [. . .]

Love,

Allen

If anyone wants to sell Tibetan cheap statuary rajput nice miniature paintings and Indian dancing statues, you can get crazy copies and originals here real cheap for export. Be a good business. I'll send you some souvenirs when I get settled long enuf to pack and ship gifties.

---

42 *Red Cats* became the title for this book in the City Lights Pocket Poets series.

43 After trying for a while to have a baby without any luck, the Ferlinghettis adopted a baby, and within a short period of time his wife became pregnant.

[*Allen's year and a half in India was a period of most intensive correspondence as he tried to stay in touch with friends and carried on his literary life from halfway around the globe.*]

Allen Ginsberg [Bombay, India] to Gregory Corso [n.p.]
April 19, 1962

Dear Gregory:

Received letters today about Phipps.[44] Yes, that's a strange note. Weirdly harmonious. I guess every death is, from afar. Last week I heard from Irving [Rosenthal] and others that Elise Cowen committed suicide and that really gave me a turn. I had felt a little responsible for her welfare and hadn't been much help to her when I was around. Always felt revulsion for the death smell in her hair and so always held myself distant from her when she lived upstairs on East Second St. I wish you'd sent me more details about Phipps. I don't get it. Was he taking liquid amphetamine regularly? And did that wind up in overdose? I never heard of that before. Though everyone else that took amphetamine regularly wound up a thin-faced paranoiac nervous wreck like Elise. Peter's girl Janine was making that scene with Bill Heine, and Huncke and Elise. What has happened to her? Ask Irving. Peter wants to know if she's alright. She last wrote she was down to 95 pounds. Horror's sure hung his hat in New York of late. I wrote Wilentz[45] I'm glad I didn't stay. I would have surely come down with a broken leg or measles.

I feel fine. Last night I even gave a little poetry reading with Peter and Gary and read well and feel a little more okay nowadays, and I'll begin writing again. I didn't much since Tangier. Luckily, I still have the negative of the photo you asked for, plus some others you may not have seen from same roll. I enclose five of them. You can get them developed and use whatever. That old pix of you on Acropolis also I sent. I also got the nude ones of us. I'll keep those negatives, did I ever send you copies? They're real funny. Listen, things are very interesting and comfortable in India for living. All the things people said about horrors and heat and disease are a lot of exaggeration. It's now mid-April, well into the hot season. I'm in Bombay and it's warm, but not at all uncomfortable. If it ever got uncomfortable, all I got to do is get a third class train (third class very comfortable — you reserve a sleeping bunk 24 hours in advance, and settle down on train unbothered by crowding like settling on comfy private space on

---

44 Harry (Henry) Phipps. Wealthy young friend from Paris who died of a drug overdose in 1962.
45 Ted Wilentz (1915–2001). Co-owner of the 8th Street Bookstore in Greenwich Village.

ship.) And costs nothing to cross all India that way, maybe $5 for a 2-day, 2,000 mile ride. Cheaper than hotel. And great huge cheap meals—Indic or European style for 45 cents in 19th-century appointed dining car. And ride up to Kashmir hill coolness or Darjeeling and Sikkim and Nepalese snows. All sorts of Himalayan summer resorts, cheap to live in with interesting Tibetans nearby camping on roadsides and selling prayer wheels. Anyway, if it gets hot, just go to Himalayas. I've been all over western foothills of same with Gary. All sorts of nice old British hill stations to retreat to. But I doubt it's so hot it's necessary. I'll in any case probably head towards Sikkim up above Calcutta on Tibet border in a few weeks, for kicks.

Food quite good, we've been eating everywhere in meanest, dirtiest holes and delicious air-conditioned deluxes rarely. The cheap food—15 cents a huge vegetarian meal—I've lived on for weeks at a time, is boring but sufficient and not poisonous as everyone told me. Hardly been diarrhetic here even as much as Paris and I've really eaten the worst. Maybe I'm immune, immunized by Peru, Mexico, Tangier. But ritzy restaurants are cheaper than Tangier even. Bombay has great food all over. I've even drunk water practically all over and not been bugged. And everybody tells me it was instant death. So, what I mean, the inconveniences and terrors of India are a lot of silly gossip by old ladies. Come here and have a ball in the greatest, weirdest nation of history. The structure at Ellora, the missing noses, Moslems knocked off all the noses in this part of the earth, is greater than anything in Greece. Mt. Kailash, Temple Allora, cyclopean bas-relief of six-armed, five-headed, wild haired sex goddesses, demons shaking mountains where the gods are playing dice, Shiva dancing the cosmic dances to create universe, huge mythological great world, elephant-headed god, Ganesha, my favorite, he rides on a rat and is household divinity, every morning pious Hindus give him cornflakes. So, we've seen the Dalai Lama, Sanchi stone girls and Ajanta caves and all that and clumb 9,000 feet up Himalayans and seen Maharaja palaces at Jaipur and vast mosques in Delhi and ruined cities and minarets in Aurangabad and met swamis and seen fakirs covered with dust in marketplaces. And talked to gentle, intelligent hermits in caves and watched a parade of naked saddhus, ash-smeared holy men, come down to bathe in Ganges where it emerges from Himalayas and talked to yogis who are all over. And we've moved around now for two and half months—two days here, three days there, comfortable traveling and now in Bombay, seeing Snyder off to Japan, sailing tomorrow.

India also great for tourist travel, as nowhere else. Left behind by British, a series of rest houses everywhere. Huge comfortable rooms with all wood furniture, costs 40 cents a night or less to stay in. Can stop over several nights almost wherever you go or else stay in 20 cent hotels attached to railroad stations everywhere for convenience of travelers. Huge rooms with enormous shower bathrooms and ceiling fans and armchairs, spotlessly clean — usually — all these places specially reserved for tourists like us and folks. Or, you can settle down in civilized downtown Bombay or Delhi in big rooms for $20 a month, and write hymns to Kali, in fall and winter and spring quite civilized up to now — it's April. If the heat and rains come on, just retire to hill stations in mountains. Also almost everybody talks English. And whole world of new literature. Mahabarata and Ramayana equal Homer but are more magical. I'm all involved in huge kiccuppy readings of Indian classics. On top of that Madame Hope Savage[46] is on the scene. Ah, yes, I forgot. All the signs point to your having a fine time in the Orient, Gregory Corso. Come and get your kicks in India. And as for drugs, my dear, eek, shit, you can score for morphine in ampules, neat and hygienic, in almost any drugstore in Delhi. Plenty black O around. I haven't tried the pot here, but it's all over for asking. And best of all, opium dens for real. I finally went to one in Delhi with Peter. Imagine the beautiful drama, back alleys up a ladder to a narrow attic, laying on our hip with our head on a brick while the dealer cooked and prepared a classic old smeary black pipe for us which we inhaled six times about each, and began to feel high in about ten minutes. But six hours later, in hotel room, it was beginning to reach its height. It grows on you, and smoking O is different from eating it or shooting H, and three times better than both combined. Peter, the H fiend agrees emphatically. A new world, a new dimension of junk, better and smoother and sweeter and dreamier and more relaxed and subtler and stronger than mainline H. Yessir, it's a new kick I never experienced and I thank the kindly gods who reserved that charming surprise for my middle age. Only had the opportunity once so far though. Maybe this week we find a den in Bombay. Fortunately, Peter been mostly well-balanced with all the opportunities around and we been sparing of use and moderate in all indulgences. So the hop is a pleasant diversion and not an omnipresent monster. It's really bad for you to get involved that way, excessively, as you know. Simply takes too much of your world up and ends crappily.

Hope [Savage], I left note for her in Delhi. She appeared, talking hypnotically, as ever breathless and nervous. We treated her nice and took her to eat Chinese. Then she showed up here in Bombay and we took her to poesy read-

46 Hope Savage. Gregory's first real love.

ing we gave. She wandered around anonymous, full of spy plots, indifferent, she says, to anyone she knows two years ago. Regularly cuts herself off from acquaintances every so often, but seemed almost wanly eager to be courteous with us the few times we've met. She admires Gary, but independent, and made a lot of lonely great scenes. Winters in Himalayan Kulu Valley, alone in cabin in village with fire, she speaks a little Hindi. No message for you except hopes you are well, she's not quite human but very hyper-bright, in good health. Probably see her in a few days. She disappears. Can reach her c/o American Express Bombay, and she also gets mail c/o same Delhi. Going to Calcutta in a few weeks to renew passport. She has bureaucratic troubles always, attracts insane consular officials to persecute her occasionally. From Aden to Kashmir she wears shawl and boots—she's same. So there's your Hope, still savage. [...]

[*Once they found an apartment in Calcutta, Ginsberg took a trip into the mountains and lost his passport. Orlovsky stayed behind in Calcutta awaiting news about his Veteran's Administration disability benefits, which had been discontinued. Even though they were drifting apart again, Allen wrote each day to Peter.*]

Allen Ginsberg [Darjeeling, India] to Peter Orlovsky [Calcutta, India]
June 6, 1962

Dear Peter:

Just got back from Kalimpong today and found your 2 letters (June 1 and June 5)—always thrilled to carry it down the street and sit down and read— makes me feel old time romantic to you. No letter from consulate or U.S.I.S. but that is OK since I did get Sikkim permit (for only 3 days) and will go the day after tomorrow (Friday) (June 8)—stay till the 10th or 11th and then be back in Calcutta several days later. Calcutta and your room and guitar wang sound great and things here also very lovely. I went and visited head of the whole (Zen type) N'ying ma pa sect (red hat tantric) and asked for wang[47] and talked to him an hour about visions and he said he had asthma and had to prepare a week or 2 in advance praying and building up powers—so said he couldn't but would definitely if I could come back in September. Well it's a long journey. I been reading many Tibet books and getting better picture and figuring out

47 Wang. Meditation initiation mantra.

what goes on: you get this wang, plus a mantra (short verbal formula) and a text to follow, and meditate like on LSD conjuring up image like on tankas and then eating it up like Ganesh ate the bad giant. So apparently it's a long process like Zen. Except the initial wang is supposed to be a real splash. Who knows? He the lama said of the vomiter and other visions: "Watch them and let them go, don't get hung on visions beautiful or ugly, even the wheels within wheels: the point is that all are conjurations of the mind, and so, unreal and to be enjoyed and not grasped at." The thing I always did with LSD, ayahuasca, was get hung up thinking the visions were <u>real</u> in the sense of realer than everyday —but neither are "real" says the Tibetans.

Also made good friends with head Lama of a yellow hat monastery and taught him some English and he told me about his gods and invited me to stay in Lamasary and said if I want he'd get me a Tibetan boy—apparently lots of boy love in the yellow hat (official sect) monastery. It's supposed to be a real little sin, don't count much. Said next time to bring you also. This is 34 yr old English speaking lama-scholar who's head of the big monastery in Kalimpsong. So I heard all the gossip about all the sects (he said, forget what Dalai Lama's interpreter said, we should have got wang from Dalai Lama's guru—teacher in Dharamshala and he'd write them a letter if we ever went back there)—(See all these sects gossiping against the other sects it's a big comedy.) Also met English monk I mentioned and the Lama told me he likes boys too, one of the big meditation exercises is to imagine fucking the red goddess you have on your tanka.

So I was frustrated and sat down on the edge of a cliff overlooking huge mountain abyss and began demanding my consciousness open and sure enough I began hearing the locusts sound like electric cosmic serpents for a few minutes like on yage. So felt good—the night before on 37th birthday I had dream of seeing the earth like Harry Smith—from afar in space—but exactly one / half earth like this and couldn't figure it out. Later realized 37 is half of 74 and if I live to be 74 I'll see the year 2000 I always wanted to.

I stupidly bought a tanka for 200 rupees. I regretted after since I rather keep the money and may run short. But anyway it's a nice tanka (except it was torn and repaired) like a 4 or 500 [rupee] tanka. Couple lamas at opposite corners watching 3 blue devils appear in flames in air, and some walls in back—and 2 devils are surrounded by yellow, green, red and blue flying witch women each. Painting is not too fine, but not too crude. I've also collected about 5 yab-yum statues, plus finally got a copy of those little printed tankas. [. . .]

Your red goddess with skull cup is a Dakini, and her skull cup means you got to die and get yr skull brains et up to be her lover. She's supposed to be Wisdom. I saw nice one of her here.

Love

Allen
Xxxx

[*After Corso insulted Ferlinghetti's poetry, Lawrence wrote to Ginsberg. Corso had told him that Ginsberg didn't like his poetry or take him seriously as a poet. Allen quickly set the record straight with this letter. Ferlinghetti was sensitive about being pigeon-holed solely as a publisher and amiable business man after Kerouac described him as such in his books.*]

Allen Ginsberg [Calcutta, India] to Lawrence Ferlinghetti [San Francisco, CA] July 5, 1962

Dear Larry:

Our letters must have crossed in the mails. I got your July 1 sad letter today, and had written you one on July 27 [*sic*: June 26] or something, so you can see even without your saying anything I did hold your hands and look in your eyes soulfully and said I liked D. H. Lawrence poem [*The Man Who Rode Away*] and told you about Jyoti Datta Bengali poet who also said how nice he liked your poetry and said you should send him your books. I don't consider you a business man honey (I'm full of chandul—opium—we just got back from the Chinese Den here). Larry I do "consider" you a poet and I do and always have I admit complained about your loose pen but I wouldn't complain to you about it if I didn't think you were fine enough to complain to and your poetry solid enough to complain about non-solid frills in it. Don't feel so bad! Remember, Gregory is a narcissistic put-down artist and he doth exaggerate his put-downs —i.e. for instance he was putting down Peter and telling him he was no poet and should stop writing poetry forever and accept position as my prat-boy and weak sister friend. And that sure bugged Peter because Gregory was drunk and absolutely serious at the time. Actually however Gregory changed his mind as usual a few weeks later. He (Gregory) just claims the right to put people down occasionally to preserve his own independence and let off some steamy insight in usually exasperating and momentarily unfair manner. He do it to Jack too, and Burroughs and (rarely) me (because I got him by the balls in some other way, like hold his head and dry his tears when he gets hysterical like when we all arrived on Tangier dock last year and his passport had expired and they wouldn't let him off the boat for 48 hours.) So that's Gregory, neither take him seriously nor don't take him seriously.

Not seen Jack's *Big Sur*—is it out??? But remember he puts almost everyone down in kind of crude subtle way, including me and Peter. I mean, the pictures he paints of me in *Town and City*, *Subterraneans*, *Dharma Bums*, etc. is actually sort of a creepy image and sometimes I got quite bugged, except I figure (by insight and hindsight too) that there's a basic sympathetic intention under-neath and some real insight ("Ginsberg, you're nothing but a hairy loss," he said to me 3 years ago looking up from my kitchen floor drunk)—so God knows what kind of good time Charlie lost Denny Dimwit he saw you as—but it isn't, like, a sophisticated coterie type exclusion hatchet—it's strictly Jack's own genius—grotesquerie, home made in his mama's attic. Probably it's actu-ally funny.

Jack seems to save his full range of understanding sympathy for the few heroic hero-worship loves he has. That is, the only people he pictures in full 3-D as human round heroes are I think Neal, Burroughs occasionally, his father and mother, (himself less directly)—Gary almost—one or two Huncke others—the subsidiary characters he generally treats with rough impressionist sketches, almost caricatures—including myself and others close to him. You too I guess. It bugged me at first but after all it's only a novel and, alright, his main energy and reality goes to his obsessive hero, he hardly has one now? I am always so amazed and gratified he has the power and energy to be recording angel of so much detail of the last 2 decades' seasons,—more work and drive and inspira-tion than I have summed up in my couple books of poems—that I don't feel right to be mad at him he hasn't seen me thru my eyes, or you thru yours, or make completer pictures of everybody. He done what he could do—with all his own needs and inner crazy—and that, when I read his books (the sum of them) seems so much, that the faults seem inevitable. I mean at times I was bugged, he didn't treat me right. Tho some characters do catch him eternally, like Huncke. Anyway I just mean, don't be bugged, there is no lasting ill here.

Starting from San Francisco either you never mentioned or I never noticed. I didn't know you have a new book poems, please send us and we'll send you big letters of criticisms—send airmail and here's one dollar for postage. I don't want you should stop writing or shut up poesy and neither does Peter. I think maybe it's the too closed-in local literary atmosphere that's putting you down so low in soul. It bugged me in S.F. last time, it's a local malady and not too seri-ous tho, it's like a cold, persistent and unobtrusive. Whether Rexroth is being sympathetic or obtuse, whether Duncan etc. or letters from afar are being understanding or shitty. So don't feel bad—well anyway, you know all that. I should have written you more seriously line by line about your poems (as I almost did D. H. Lawrence) but it seemed to me your intention was to be hazy-sloppy (as in Fidel Castro poem [*One Thousand Fearful Words for Fidel Castro*]) and so no point detailing what you know already, since you did not mean for each line to be perfect poesy, or try to be at least.

What occurs to me is that you're more perfect as poet when you're nearer the bone pessimistic, than when you are being wiggy and hopeful and social-anarchist-revolutionary-lyrical-optimistic. So maybe you should write now some strictly private and anti-social melancholy poems. Anyway that always struck me as your natural vein, that and a kind of empathy-nakedness which is rare.

The solidest element I always thought was apt precise images like the classical butterfly in and out of open boxcar door or the naked objects at the end of the Lawrence poem—rather than puns or ironic references to Dulles. And that the pattern of the lines should be arranging themselves into intuitive shapes, as end of D. H. Lawrence poem.

Well anyway, this is all opium—diarrhea. Glad you got the statues. You want more? They're only 3 or 4 dollars each and another 2 bucks to ship. For 20 or 40 dollars I could get you some big snazzy Kalis or Yab-Yums.

I'll work on <u>Aether</u> and send it in a week. Yes, *Bunch of Poems*, *Hiccup*, all too flat.[48] I don't dig *Alba* either, because one little stinky poem is *Alba* the whole book isn't. It's actually a decade of poems. I'll come up with something yet. I wish it was *Red Cats*, like that. [. . .]

I realize I'm getting sizeable extra royalties from you, but I thought we were sharing profits 50-50. Is all of your share of my books proceeds going to pay expenses? If so that is obviously not proper and you should readjust royalty rates so that we share the net not gross profits equal, which means it's ok by me if you cut my royalty scale down. Despite all previous discussions I had not got it thru my skull that you or City Lites Inc. were making no direct proceeds from my books. That should be readjusted! Take it up at the next Board Meeting and rearrange things as seems fit and fair and businesslike. There is, after all, aside from fairness, no long range future with me in your firm if the firm is not making some profit thereby, otherwise I just wind up in 5 years a draggy sea-anchor and dead weight of unremunerative responsibility. I'd rather be one

48 These were suggested titles for Ginsberg's next book, which was published as *Reality Sandwiches*.

of the (at least modest) moneymakers and have my position assured by more than sentiment. That's that. But aside from that, since I turned down Knopf and Penguin offers, you can't entertain the thought that I (and Peter) think of you as $ pimping poesy! Banish the thought, Chairman of the Board, and full speed ahead! S.F. must really be bugging you. Or is it babyshit all over your living room floor? What's baby doing? Is it any good?

Meanwhile (contradictory as it may seem)—as I said in last letter, if there may be any money practically speaking due me for last half year, send it this way. Don't send me any theoretical advance, and if you have no midyear inventory any more, just what McBride guesses is already sold, not to be futurely sold. Reason is we're about broke. I have a couple ways of getting other loot saved for emergency, so don't send me what is not, practically speaking already due.

Well this is all too much handwriting—I hope you're feeling better. I'm still on the hop, that's why I ramble on so. [. . .]

Enough, enough, goodnight, love always

Allen

[Kerouac was still Ginsberg's most important correspondent. Allen continued to write long, descriptive letters to Jack. He often said he wrote especially for Kerouac's ear and in the correspondence he treated Jack as his sounding board on almost every topic.]

Allen Ginsberg [Calcutta, India] to Jack Kerouac [n.p.]
September 9, 1962

Dear Jack Ti Jean:

Happy happy you answered. To be or not to be? I say to be, whatever we can make of it, I been laying in death arms all last year, now suddenly feel better. Ferlinghetti sent me proofs of new book (*Reality Sandwiches, 1953–60*, includes Green Auto, Xbalba, Over Kansas, Sather Gate, Aether and lots short tasty scribbles—no big pronouncements, just a wind up book of uncollected poems so I get done with them—and from now on go on)—big future epic plans, first "a poem including history," all my rantings about politics and newspapers I'm going to put it all together I got pages and pages of that, except now I don't feel doomy so it's a big peaceful no hate manifestor—I'm rambling, also big open sex autobiog poem, and also one long poem describing each major "vision" I've had in chronologic order, as best I can, including all major drug insights etc., beginning with Blake. Also in 2 weeks the monsoons be over and weather nice, I go travel seek sex temples and then settle down in Benares and type up ayahuasca Peru notebooks for Auerhahn, get that off my back I promised them 2 years ago and been too depressed and poetry-hating to do.

I got to write you another long letter, now I'm opiated tonite and too scattered to, just to answer—re mushrooms, I don't know what to think, no Leary is a nice man my heart tells me that, he may be overenthusiastic. Yes they make identity meaningless as you said in previous letter—but after all that's a good thing at times and a religious thing (no ego, etc.) so in long run the experience has something interesting to contribute, no? Needn't plunge into any abysses immediately, we got time, Man, the race got time to amplify and learn how to use and live with these new feels, after all it's an interplanetary future and everything's going to be alright. No hate to Leary and not even suspision suspicion—can't even spell the word right—don't want to see anybody go be sent to doom or hell, that's not the way things should work out. As I said I get cosmic paranoia on mushrooms so I don't take now, tho I got a stock with me for later feels, but my mistake before was to hang too much urgency and crisis on it instead of whatever relax and dream.

John Foster Dulles you're right I got mad at him and Ike, truly they will go to heaven—assuming when you die everything just disappears in Nice Quiet—which I assume—Dulles is in Heaven—with Stalin and my momma—it's all free—but you got to remember to include all sides of the parties and folks in scheme. No more hate, name callings etc. At the same time if we're going to live together—I mean U.S. and Russia—and China—if we not going to blow up the world—and we're not—that means we got to make up our mind to really live together and the communists stop hating us—and that's as you see already beginning on the Russian side with Yevtushenko poet meeting dear old [Robert] Frost—and means the Communists got to relax and gentle up, and the U.S. really got to relax and get gentle to them—and no more paranoias—and that also means everybody really got to change,—that means our foreign policy got to change from brink of war containment, etc. We got to realize that the Russians have as good or almost as good a case against "capitalist warmongers" as we got against communist slave state aggression. Both sides are right and wrong. If this too vague, I been studying the papers U.S., English, Indian, Greek, Russian mags, South American, etc.—I can give you a sloppy but serviceable outline Berlin Vietnam Korea Formosa Hungary etc. etc. Cuba is clear —how both sides have justified serious complaints—isn't that true?—and I think that Dulles and Eisenhower were too much hung up on the black and white war scene, I'm right, you're wrong, to be able to resolve the situation peacefully, just made things worse at the time. The whole world has been in a really nerve wracked state the last 15 years—I think it's only just beginning to clear up—but it is.

Bertrand Russell makes sense, more than anyone, on straightforward What To Do. Last couple days, I think he makes it. All he saying is, use your head, compromise and don't commit suicide everybody.

Trouble with LeRoi [Jones] and youngers is they see no way out and see clearly the injustices America has pulled but don't think the U.S. will make it up in time. So he's got hate and is trying to push thru emotionally that way, mad at cops etc.

But the situation is serious enough for everybody should sit down and think and not scream pro or anti any more but try solve the problem. Russell is at least trying. I think Kennedy and Khrushchev are at least trying to try also. Frost thinks so too, I see by the papers.

All that John Birch scene is really in wrong direction and just emotional and making the problem worse. Incidentally some girl 16 in Chicago wrote me she visited local Nazi Party (Rockwell) HQ over a bookstore there and they are talking about killing me. (I wrote them nice air letter inquiring what they were thinking about and do they really want to kill me? I'm only me and asking them send me their literature and application form maybe I join them.)

And all the left wing hate is also no help, and it isn't enough for your heart to break because everybody's heart is broken now.

Gregory says title of his new book is Long Live Man. How lovely of him. He says TO BE.

Assembling huge Aether Notes poem I kept trying to find out what it was all about, all that pain of so many different universes and realization each depends on the brain consciousness. What I came out with, finally, was that the ether high and dissociation of eye ear touch taste smell and final disappearance experience of the blackout was like a little death. So meanwhile we are in this form, not the other, yet, so we got to work with this form, what we got. If we can improve it thru brain changes fine, but meanwhile best to live with what we're born with and stop suiciding it prematurely. The death will come in its time. Meanwhile the Big World Problem, really is, the whole race of man doesn't know whether it wants to continue or not, to be or not to be, and that's why everybody is so Hamlet-helpless in front of cold war crisis. Well the answer is like in the koan, of the man hanging on by his teeth. They asked him what's the meaning of life and he, there was, no answer, he just hang on to branch with his teeth that's what he was doing. So I think Russell Bertrand is making the right scene, as far as practical politics concerned. And wish him well. See his point is he does want the race to continue — in whatever universe we be, as of now. Really there is a lot of death wish in everybody's heart, my heart your heart — it's been dogging me the last year especially — probably in everybody the same trouble, well I'm making a move. Not shit or get off the pot exactly, but anyway, time to lay the immediate world-hate bane, no?

I won't burden you with long explanations of how and where the U.S. is in the wrong and where Russia is in the wrong. You need them? But it do mean America is no more and Russia is no more and the whole world _is_ more, and that's OK. I think wandering around outside U.S. does enlarge perspective. Because, really, why should it be that only the U.S. be right and saved? Do we want to damn the rest of the folks to limbo? But most U.S. thinking is in that way ego-centric. And Russian and Chinese I suppose, it's all got to go.

Anyway I think what's happening, Russia is changed enough, softened enough now, to begin to make hope possible, and like that, the U.S. got to change too. The Birch and Conservative scene is just last gasp abreaction to the insight that's coming thru. So I'm saying I think you too shouldn't be so rigid about politics, not rigid exactly, just all your poetry politics so isolationist — can't anymore, the world networks are now all interconnected, the U.S. got itself involved and so we should make a good show of it and get on with the epic. It'll all be alright.

I'm rambling on too much too vaguely, that's not what I started to write you about, I said above you're rigid, well I been rigid too hating Dulles, rigid isn't the word, just what, paranoia emotionalizing, conspiracies, etc. World too scared and sick for Hitlerian Wagnerian ego pronouncements on any side. Anyway, I say, yes, To Be, let's go on living till we die. Maybe if everybody decide that, some of the pressure relax. This O makes me ramble, STOP. [. . .]

I not received your _Big Sur_ book, who published it? I'll write them myself and ask. Dying to see what you been think-writing and what pages you got holy. Time we all got together and felt good again.

I will actually write you a long letter soon as I clear off my desk — not answering mail the last month, OH — YES — I just did finally fix up a great paean of love I wrote in 1957 [_The Names_], I think I once showed you, about Huncke, Cannastra, Joan, Morphy and Joe Army (completely disguised) and ending with Neal — 7 pages — probably can't publish it — have to show it to Lucien for his opinion — but even so the sheer pleasure of concentrating all the emotion gave me a whole new lease on life, writing. I revised it cutting out all participles and crap and discovered a little method for super-imposing one image on another:

"His dream, a mouthful of white prick trembling in his head" makes

"His dream mouthful of white prick etc."

Something I hadn't noticed so clearly before, makes lines sound Kerouacky-Shakespearean. I think I don't generally write <u>well</u> enough for first statement always to make it. With this poem I did explode and write great (but repetitive and loose) first draft in 1957—then, now 5 years later, able to cut thru it with knife and superimpose all the scattered parts of one glimpse together. I try that with all the political material I got accumulated, when I get to Benares. Gregory does that a lot, that combining, par excellence.

I getting bored with the flatness of my writing and this seemed to interest me (all these you see and forgive excuses for revising I guess) at least I spent last 2 weeks happy at desk again after a year of aversion.

Re: Cut ups—Bill. Well, he does have a great technique worked out there, I think—surely—I read *Soft Machine*, a year and half ago in Paris—have you received that from Olympia yet??—and it is especially exquisite, page after page of heroic sinister prose poetry—that is to say, it worked and made an Art Gem. He's doing other things now. The pure cut up random phase is over and —I think it altered his EAR and mental eye for imagery, so that he writes naturally now like cut up, without mechanical razor recourse, once he trained himself to hear the music, by practice.

Incidentally, you hear about this great Edinburgh Writers Conference? Mad scene—Miller, Durrell, Mary McCarthys and Angus Wilsons and Trocchi and Mailer etc. and Burroughs officially invited and he made a great dignified scene, W. S. Exterminator. I read all about it in English papers in British Council reading room. They had *The Scotsman* by chance, an Edinburgh newspaper, which gave huge local coverage. So Bill gave two great speeches, one on censorship, but full of his own weird strange ideas. Then next day "The Future of the Novel" and everybody saying well we're trying but the novel is a dead form, etc. old sociological and moral bullshits and then Burroughs' turn he gets up looking like an impersonal royal physician and delivers technique-logical scientific demonstration lecture on his experiments with cut ups and new thing "fold ins" reading them prose the like of which beautiful you can imagine—all of them attending serious and slightly shook up—Kushwant Singh in turban asks "Are you serious?" thinking to get a humanistic laugh and Burroughs looks him in eye with St. Louis undersea face of genius—"Of course I am." He do know what he's doing, for him. Anyway it made a big impression and McCarthy and Mailer had been praising him in big speeches days before so when he came on with his own mind people were listening and apparently heard. Lovely to see Burroughs in the World, time he made great high scene like that. Anyway got me all excited reading the papers so far away. Not in contact with him the last few months. Stories mentioned a new—two new—novels he's writing—*Nova Express* (I think it's finished) and *The Ticket That Exploded*. Fucking great Flower.

All right, everything fine in world, you alright too, cheer up old patriot, the country don't need be defended, the WORLD needs us to defend it, that's what. We all going to be saved and die happy! I mean leave a harmonious dream behind not another old nightmare. Les Preludes (List) heroicking trumpets in my head all day. Thou'rt the Guard!

Love,

Allen

and forgive me everything else and we'll think together.

[*While in India, Ginsberg wrote to Nobel Prize laureate Bertrand Russell about the arms race. He received a reply in which Russell stated that world-wide nuclear annihilation was a near certainty. That comment unnerved Allen since he respected Russell's opinion, so he wrote back for clarification. Since both Ginsberg and Russell had studied William Blake and had even experienced visions of Blake, there were several references to Blake's work. Even as Ginsberg wrote this letter, the Cuban Missile Crisis was unfolding in the waters off the coast of Cuba.*]

Allen Ginsberg [Calcutta, India] to Bertrand Russell [England]
October 4, 1962

Dear Earl Russell:

I wept to receive your letter, while walking back to room on Calcutta street.

What does Blake do? My experience is 1948, alone on couch in NY had masturbated, then reading The Sunflower suddenly <u>heard</u> ancient tender voice speak aloud, "Ah Sunflower weary of time" (Blake sounded like the Ancient of Days)—bliss answered yearning—felt "Eternity"—out window building corners, images of sentience everywhere. Then "The Sick Rose" poem, auditory presence again and sensational consciousness / limitless behind Death—body physical lightness also. Continued with "Little Girl Lost" (How can Lyca Sleep / if her parents weep / if her Hart does ache / then let Lyca wake)—Kafkian madness doom event, my deepest sense data experiences age 22. Same flashes continued a week, catalyzed by Blake poems, I anticipating them, even precipitated epiphanies by yelling alone in room. Finally days later isolated walking on Columbia Univ. path, same sensation crept over me, but without Fatherly voice—suddenly a new feeling of cosmic cancer (universe will eat me alive)—scared me and ended recurrence of these sensations.

Later, with hallucinogens, approximation of same "events" of consciousness, sometimes absolutely ecstatic and sometimes absolutely frightening. Complete literal dissolution of Self seemed to lead to immediate physical death. Never stabilized a continuously enlarged or widened area of consciousness.

That's what I meant when I asked if you knew any "scientific step of consciousness."

What happened to you with Blake? Any further significance to the sensation that nearly made you faint? Any hint of alternative to "the world of politics entailing lifeless organization...and...diminution of individual sensibility..."?

"Act or Perish!" I've tried as poet 6 years to catalyze in others the sensation Blake woke. Meanwhile assembling long anti-bomb-politics poetry—which leads maybe action but not to awareness and depth consciousnesses.

But now you say "Imminent nuclear annihilation...this is the priority...the nuclear technology is faulty...Rockets hair trigger...problem in elementary mathematical statistics: nuclear war is a matter of statistical near certainty..."

I thought a week, hesitating to burden you with my individual sensibility and ambivalences. No time, no time. You're blowing Gabriel clarion, it wakes individual hopes. Everybody's entranced with death wish: Coffeehouse westernized Indians for instance: "What difference, does the universe really need Man?....Who'll care when it's over?" or "I'd rather die a goofy disorganized human me than be compelled to organize against organization." I feel that also natural, the bomb-doom and dissolution of my separate Ginsberg consciousness. I loathe to get involved in even friendly anti-bomb organizations. Even you gather power, by frightening or compelling (act or perish) individuals into accepting your evaluation reality and "statistical near certainty."

Vague suspicions...I don't want to become a monster ego gathering organization power by scaring people about death,....introducing another factor into the mass of statistics, namely my own hysteria and ego scream contributing to the high tension that makes the military jittery.

Laughing at death, laughing at bombs better reduce tension. Would Blake say that Tiger be scared by bomb? Yet your letter made me think that doom sounded serious.

Einstein and Buddha say that "all conceptions" of the universe are "arbitrary," i.e. conceptions of a Conceiver, it doesn't matter except to Man. To Be or Not to Be, is the question. You say, To Be? Why? This question is central, is the cause of the whole Apocalypse. Can anyone answer, except by acting, to blow it up, or stop it from being blowed up?

I mean the cancer at the heart of history right now is, disillusion with this life in space. That's why I wonder if there is any deeper answer than "Priority." What does Blake say to you?

All I know is, I've lived in the midst of apparent worldly events and apparent transcendental insights, and it all adds up to I don't know what. I hardly trust any appearance anymore, statistical or intuitive. I'd rather drift and see.

How exact is your statement of statistical probability? Has comprehensive survey of bomb networks been possible to make, sufficient for anyone to project a date of "probable" occurrence of network error?

Can you boil down your awareness of danger into a verbal formula (not a slogan) of several sentences factual data and conclusion that can be plastered on walls everywhere, memorized and passed from mouth to ear. This might penetrate public consciousness in U.S. and Russia.

That is, if there is statistical near certainty that machine will explode, can you PROVE it SUCCINCTLY enough in public for basic facts to move thru mass media?

If you can't do this, can you formulate a succinct request to governments that they provide you (or Pugwash) with enough data on bomb networks to make a specific projection of likely date and probably error that would precipitate holocaust?

The urgent request itself, even unanswered, would formulate the probability problem, and government equivocation of same, in public awareness.

I enclose some money—please have sent me any printed documents that back your assertion of probability. The assertion is powerful, coming from you, but I would like more basis to judge.

I hope you put your experience of Blake on verbal record in more detail, it may be helpful.

Koan of student off cliff.

Love or teeth and counting the steps of the sun Kali worship in Bengal next week.

Allen Ginsberg [Calcutta, India] to Robert Creeley [Vancouver, Canada] November 3, 1962

Dear Robert:

All last months I've been hanging around the burning ghats watching corpses burn—empty—meat dolls—and reading religious books (Ramakrishna's conversations especially, great book, 1000 pages mystic gossip with disciples 1880–1886, Calcutta excursions and people of those days, technical discussions of Hindu traditions and doctrines, strange scenes in which Ramakrishna suddenly goes off into Samadhi and comes out babbling to Krishna or Kali—photographs of him in that state even) and visiting saddhus (wandering holymen) and swamis (disciples of disciples of Ramakrishna) and Avatars of Kali (one lady Anandamayee) (big black haired woman whom Nehru visits supposed to be great bhakti (faith) saint)—long discussions with octogenarian healthy yogis. Best thing though, visiting burning ghats Tuesday evenings, all the saddhus and their householder visitor friends sit around in circles near the pyres and prepare little altars of flowers, incense and prasad (candy offered to Gods then distributed) and a little 3 inch fire, and they pass around big red clay pipes full of ganja and all get high with corpse smoke rolling round their heads. I sit with them and turn on and walk around the fires and look at ivory-yellow pudding of brains blackening in flame, skulls with flesh burning away leaving teeth gleam like movie horrors and eye sockets—detached feet swollen and toes spread in the heat and fat dripping down ankle pushed into center coals by bamboo pole attendants—nothing but a "pillow" I mean like burning a pillow —Ramakrishna's remark. Then last week went up to village Tarapith (goddess Tara—pith means place of pilgrimage of which there are 54 in India, spots where breast cunt teeth hair eyes or other parts of body of Shiva's first wife fell —big complicated legend the gist of which, she died and he danced wild tandava destruction dance with her corpse on his shoulders and parts of her body fell all over India—her Yoni in specially holy place in Assam Chittagong.)— Anyway Tarapith is little sleepy village miles from roads, walk there thru woods and paddy fields crossing rivers—finally a settlement on riverbank with a few dozen grassroof mud houses and tea stalls and a small old temple and altars nearby to different gods, and lots of tombs crowded in saints graveyard next to temple—half naked or saffron robed saddhus come pilgrimage here or settle down a few months or years to do yoga in peace and quiet. Last century a famous saint Bama Kape—naked lushing pot smoking madman—renewed the millennial holiness of the spot—so saints come now to meditate on his image, marble statue of fat man with fox and snake at his side, pink flesh colored marble. Anyway, the main thing everybody does all day here is smoke ganja, everybody, that's all I did 4 days straight morn till nite, sitting around in huts and tomb-cells with saddhus, singing Baul religious songs and passing the pipe—just like Mill Valley writ large and 1000 years old tradition. These saddhus, I mean the saddhu network is nothing but a classical teahead network, I shoulda known it all along. That's the whole basis of Indian mysticism. Advanced yoga or mystic possession rules out tea, sex, meat, travel, etc. but the massive preliminary conditioning, the general scene is nothing but a lot of perfected lifelong homeless hepcats wandering from holy place to holy place with their red ganja pipes and meeting other wanderers and sitting down with them to turn on, and exchange hobo information and breathing exercise techniques and sing to each other, "the sea has overflown with the milk of worms...the fish of water have given birth to the young ones upon the tree and while the dog was looking at it the cat took them away...an elephant is tied to the foot of an ant...this is the primal teaching, says wise Kabir" etc. "The completely barren one has given birth and the child wants milk of the dove...by the kick of the mosquito the mountain is broken and the ant goes on laughing...the pond cuts the workman...The skillful man who can wreathe the peak of sumeru with a thread and snare elephant in spiderweb becomes eligible for secret love, etc." Well I leave here and go visit another place Navadip (where saint named Chaitanya or universal bliss comes from—big saddhus convention there next week.)[...]

Love,

Allen
India gets better and better.

[Although he was in India, Ginsberg was not isolated from issues back home. His friends kept him informed, and he was always quick to express his opinion and lend support.]

Allen Ginsberg [Calcutta, India] to the *Harvard Crimson* [Cambridge, MA] December 5, 1962

To the readers of the *Crimson*:

I have seen a statement by Harvard officials on LSD and other drugs, and offer a few comments based on about thirty experiences (with LSD-25, psilocybin, mescaline, peyote and banisteriopsis caapi) spaced out over the last decade. Circumstances of ingestion varied from solitary trial to controlled academic setting at Stanford University and Harvard to watchful supervision by native curanderos in the Peruvian Amazon.

The statement is marred by faulty terminology: to label the above substances "mind-distorting drugs" is to make a mistake which confuses thinking. It's an inaccurate epithet; it's not precise language at all. More accurate to write "mind expanding" or "consciousness-widening" drugs in conformity with the experiences by almost all who have tried them. There's sufficient mass of data published and unpublished to bear this out.

Wiser still to adopt neutral terminology "consciousness altering drugs." The phrase "mind-distorting" pushes forward an arbitrary evaluation. It's unnecessarily prejudicial.

The Harvard statement should be amended to exclude this impropriety of phraseology. The circumstances under which these drugs are taken inevitably affect the subjective experience. Unfortunately the formal warning against "mind distorting drugs" is now part of the setting in Cambridge. The echo of this official Sound will cause all sorts of nervous crises, not the drugs.

Good intentions abound; an alteration of only the direction of official concern is in order. It would make sense for Harvard to provide the situation where those interested in the effects of the consciousness altering drugs may have the experience in a secure and friendly atmosphere.

One concludes that although many circumstances such as final examinations, Ph.D. theses, love affairs or the reading of poetry "may result in serious hazards to the mental health and stability even of apparently normal persons" it will not be found necessary to warn Harvard men off limits in these areas.

With good cheer to all,

Allen Ginsberg

[*Frequently Ginsberg's letters from his trips contained detailed travel writing, such as this one to his old friend, Lucien Carr.*]

Allen Ginsberg [Benares, India] to Lucien and Francesca Carr [New York, NY]
***ca.* January 15, 1963**

Dear Lucien and Cessa:

Moved here to Benares a month ago, found a fine old room with black wood beams in ceiling, 9 wood-slat French doors and balcony surrounding—2 flights up—overlooking market one side and steps of Dasaswamedh ("10-horse-sacrifice-by-Vishnu") Ghat, can see Ganges flowing by from balcony, little 3 story temple-peaks across street, constant noisy street all day, vegetable-basket women squatting on curb along the road, lines of leprous beggars with aluminum bowls set out before them, monkeys jumping in room to steal bananas, cows hanging around on street making sneak attacks at vegetable-greens and the old ladies beating them off every 2 minutes with a stick, like a great Breughel play, same scene every day, I recognize which cows steal the smartest by now even. Rent $9 a month—pandits (brahmin priest caste with little string looped around ear to belt) sitting watching bathers' clothes on waterfront. It's supposed to be holy ritual to bathe, so the pandits guard yr watch and put a little red third eye of incense-paste on your forehead when you come out to dry up. Too cold for me to dip much tho, have to wear wool sweater at nite, haven't had a bath in weeks in fact. Holiest burning ghat in India (Manikarnika Ghat) is ten minute walk along waterfront which looks like Venice Grand Canal, Maharaja's palaces and pilgrim rest houses with high stone walls against river towering over the bathing steps and little boats. I go there to get high with friendly Naga (naked) saddhu who got a little den for himself in basement cave under a Dharamsala (rest house for dying people who want to be burned here so they come here to die) overlooking the ghat—now been here long enough to settle back at desk. We took off for two weeks to Agra, spent Merry Xmas eve at Taj Mahal, slept inside for two nites (death anniversary of the lady buried there, the Moslem hereditary guardians of the Taj throw an Urdu singing-poetry party and throw the doors open for those two nites.) Taj Mahal an awesome surprise, the picture postcards don't tell the vibrational story, it really is a sublime joint, like being inside a perfect symmetrical 3-D DeChirico canvas, you get that particular infinity sensation around it, like a time machine. Fortunately we <u>lived</u> in it for three days and never went out so got quite an exposure, plus as usual plenty ganja to sharpen the metaphysical thrill, and friendly atmosphere, most stupendous motel in universe I'm sure. Worth a trip to India just for that, as I've read people say, it's true. Then we spent a few nites camping in abandoned Mogul city (carved red sandstone palaces and courts) some miles away (built by the grandpa of Shah Jahan who built the Taj. Shah Jahan incidentally had planned a black marble mirror image of the Taj set across the Yamuna river, both to be connected with a golden bridge, they finally put him in the boobyhatch before he went too far, actually locked him in a tower a few miles downriver where he could see the Taj Mahal). (He must have been a really great man, I can't conceive how he ever got such a project, so fantastic in idea but so perfect when you look at it up close, completed, he must have laid down some strange con to get far as he did. Actually it was a sort of WPA project in its time and great economic benefit. But the idealism of the project is what's so obviously striking, breathtaking because he got away with it) etc. — anyway first building I ever saw in the world I could call "glorious" without a doubt for the word. Then we spent a week in Lord Krishna's homeplace, Brindiban, met some saints, it's the center of Bhakti Yoga Cult in India, Bhakti meaning faith-love devotion yoga (as distinct from jnana yoga — knowledge — or karma yoga — works). They told me to practice Bhakti to Blake as he was obviously my GURU and stop looking for a human guru, best oriental wisdom I heard yet from any of the (many) holymen I've met. I was intrigued they'd come up with that as a path. Then came back here. I'm supposed to sit still and type a book of South American Journals I owe to a press in San Fran, I had promised it a year ago, but I'm too lethargic at desk now, probably get to it this month. My hair still growing, haven't cut it for a year and it feels alright, looks right for the streets here. Will be flying back to Vancouver this June and then NY in fall so see you then. I hope with all that hair except it's scary for the U.S., streets are so violent and juvenile delinquents etc., to say nothing of cops perhaps. Received friendly letter from Bill B. after year's silence, sounds like he's back on the planet — says he does nothing but write — and Gregory gossips that Bill stopt smoking pot; I'm intrigued. How's Jack? We're going to share a Penguin poetry book together. So everything here is fine, Peter says hello, he's peeling a guava on the balcony watching the cows comedy. Happy New Year to all. My brother's wife Connie *enceinte* again, they'll be Brooks running all over Long Island when my hair turns gray.

Well, the world didn't blow up, I guess [Bertrand] Russell miscalculated. But there now seems to have been a conscious decision by Kennedy Khrushchev also to compromise. I guess they got scared too finally, so Russell didn't totally miscalculate, his urgencies did some good I imagine. All meaning I suppose that secretly the cold war is actually over except nobody been told yet and they still have to tell the Chinese. Incidentally the Indian War effort would really turn yr gut to see, creaky World War I style patriotic bands playing off key and chink restaurants scared.

Love

Allen

[*Although Ginsberg's poetry had been declared not obscene by the U.S. courts in 1957, censorship issues plagued him elsewhere.*]

Allen Ginsberg [Benares, India] to Arno Hormia and Pentti Kapari [Finland] April 29, 1963

Dear Mr. Arno Hormia and Mr. Pentti Kapari:

Forgive my addressing you directly although I do not know you; but I understand that you were kind enough to plan to publish translations of my poetry in Finnish—work done by Pentti Saarikoski and Mike Rossi and Anselm Hollo.

I received a letter from Mr. Hollo saying that you wrote to him to inform him that you would have to alter the book as planned to exclude certain poems (including *Howl*), for reasons of "obscenity"—tho the details are not clear.

I am familiar with the problem since the U.S. government and the San Francisco municipal government at one time tried to prohibit the circulation of these poems—that was almost ten years ago. Some reactionary bureaucrats, mostly Catholics, intruded into the literary field. We took them to court, the judge declared the poems to be NOT obscene, and we had no further trouble since then. The poems have been printed in various languages without difficulty, most countries being less neurotically Puritanical than the U.S.A.

Therefore I was surprised to hear that there was some hesitation (at this late date) in of all places the civilized land of Finland. I had always heard that Finnish people were less tied up in an adolescent approach to sex and literature than my own country America, which has been notorious for its prudery earlier in the century.

I am eager to learn what specific pressures you have upon you that makes you hesitate to print these poems which by now seem to me very mild and tame. Is it an external legal problem you are facing, or is it a question of your own internal taste? And what sort of legal problem specifically?

In any case you will understand that I do not wish, and cannot be expected to allow you, to publish a book of my writings in Finnish if the writings are censored or if the most important poem of the set, namely Howl, is to be excluded for reasons of censorship, particularly on the grounds of what they call "obscenity." It is too old and tired and silly an issue to waste time on any more. If your country is so backward that it is impossible to see a representative selection of my poetry safely thru to the public, then I would prefer to wait another decade before seeing a book of mine in Finnish, if ever.

In other words DO NOT PUBLISH my book if you have to castrate it in the way that you propose. I am not blaming you, God knows you may have troubles of your own. It may not be your fault personally. Meanwhile you understand that I withdraw my poetry from your hands—under the circumstances that you have communicated to Mr. Hollo.

I should explain, in case you are not aware, that the basic method of my writing is to explore and communicate sections of my own consciousness, in other words to make a graph of all the movements of my mind in a particular space of time. To alter the graph, to exclude certain data therein, as "unpleasant" or "unacceptable" or "obscene" would be as dishonest as trying to alter or "doctor" industrial statistics. In addition I regard such tampering with the actual contents of my consciousness as a direct attempt to brainwash me and the reader. In addition I regard the accusation of "obscenity" as a filthy sort of personal insult. I don't like it any more than you would if someone called the contents of your brains "obscene." Actually it's too stupid to consider, but I wanted to be sure you understood clearly.

I'll send a copy of this letter to Mr. Hollo, and I leave it up to his discretion to make any further decisions, if the publishing situation in Finland becomes more reasonable in the future. He seems to know what he is doing, and was kind enough to offer to deal with the problem for me, since I am so far away and speak no Finnish. Whatever he decides I will back him up.

Thank you for your original good intentions and your present attention, and long live the human revolution!

Yours,

Whoever I may be, this time named

Allen Ginsberg

[*Ginsberg had been reading about the new generation of Russian poets and was surprised to learn that the Communist Party bureaucrats didn't believe the new poets were political enough. In recognition of his Russian kindred spirits, Allen wrote to Corso.*]

Allen Ginsberg [Benares, India] to Gregory Corso [Italy] May 5, 1963

Dear Gregory:

Well, listen, yeah, I'll be back soon, waiting now to get tix, fly Japan and Canada and month in Frisco. So figure before Christmas anyways, but isn't that a scream about Russia? I've been reading all I could get my hands on, *Encounter*, and *Soviet New Times*, Khrushchev March 8th speech. But *Evergreen* number 28, Voznesensky is a genius about hotels on the moon and 17 Voznesenskys now, that's a really worthy futuristic poem with even some soft mechanical paranoia. Gregory, those Russian poets are probably our brothers and Voznesensky I bet a great young poet, that is judged from [Anselm] Hollo's translations of Fire in Architectural Poem, moving on from one burning lot to another, and the fragments of Triangular Pear in *Evergreen*. So now we got more great souls, but this time, I think at least Voz [Voznesensky] really great word mouth, and I read somewhere in a Russian mag, *Soviet Literature* in answer to a questionnaire he says he writes spontaneously, and also his poesy a probe or exploration of his consciousness. Something is cooking. Just that one poem about New York hotels of the moon, and aluminum forests in one eye robots staring up at him from urinal. Unless it's Hollo's talent, and not Voznesensky's genius. Ain't that welcome, to have a whole nother world of poets in Russia? Some weird touches in Aksiev's prose and Céline stupidity, in that guitarist-poet's story about hopeless pants-sweating soldier in *Encounter*. I wrote to this Yolana Romanova lady of Writer's Union and big novelist Simonov last week saying as fact that Yev [Yevtushenko] and Voz have converted me to Marxism, so they were good propagandists. Not the bad propagandists like we read in the mass media *Time* and *Pravda*. If these lovely young geniuses is Marxism I buy it, real exciting conspiracies in Moscow, if you follow. They making weird statements in Polish literary journals. Interviews just like our interviews, but they more sensible as bureau pistols hanging over their heads, yet they've said great things, like poesy will save man from technology. And explore consciousness, *etc.* Do read up on all that what you can find, it's just like a big super-dooper *Big Table* Slavic scene, but they've got backs to wall.

Can you find Elizabeth Gurley Flynn, head of U.S. Communist party? She in New York City, cousin of Pete Martin, I met her once in restaurant and told her about metaphysical pot, and make her send privately or publicly, information to Moscow Writer's Union and novelist Sholokov who said Yev was callow bad propagandist, that the young poets of U.S., meaning at least me, certainly LeRoi, for all his fuckupness, will have to love to swing on this as he met Yevtushenko. Hereby declare that Yev and Voz are their best propagandists ever, and made everyone sympathetic to communist Russia and catalyzed all sorts of new hope in despairing youth. Because actually the Podhoretzes of Russia are getting them on a bum rap in fact, accusing them of anti-Russian, or misinterpreting Russia creepily, when actually, from communist point of view, from their own Marxist point of view, the young poets were great 20th century diplomatists, which is not actually a lie. We should help them, and we maybe can, with comedy methods, announce we're all Marxists, on account of their moon hotels.

Really, it's all so vile. Podhoretzes with guns. Also E. G. Flynn should protest, in behalf of American Negroes, that their common people's folk music, jazz, being attacked like that, more white shit, as Miles Davis saith, Khrushchev not making proper Marxist interpretation, hung on his own dreary hook, and LeRoi should contact his Cuban poets and make them ask Castro to intervene. Everybody now got to show their hand and be judged in the flower show. Curious how LeRoi will come up on this, because he can help them. I wrote him, care of Hettie, care of Wilentz and wrote Russia, and wrote all the Bengali and Hindi communist poets I knew. I got all excited in fact. If you got rhyme can you make up with him and we all everybody can throw some poetry at Russia? See, it needn't be anti-American or anti-communist. Here is the scene where these artists are making communism come true and be a success like it's supposed to be, historically. Like everybody waiting for. And, if in their spirit, Russia and communism grow into big modern spirituality and gentility, nobody can be unhappy over that, not even Jack, Jack's mama. I think we should try help them, I mean serious. So not be big public nasty, anti-state statements. But by writing say to personal contacts, and explain to the afraid Russians that there's nothing to be afraid of, gad, I'm glad I got that ticket to Moscow or will have it, except I figure to go there quiet like tourist, not to make big readings or publicity, but sneak around, see the poets, and the sights and explain Blake. Let's go to Moscow, if they'll let us, on New Year's Eve, or Easter, yes, Easter in Moscow. Big symphonies and ballets and onion domes and handsome Russian poets and plenty girls, and we be gentle to everybody and have no official connections. And come on surprising, privacy angels again.

From what I read there's a whole base of young souls there, very free and sad like us. We see the future, too. As they're a younger group than ourselves and roughly, I divine, they're on same cosmic vibration. Actually, wouldn't it be a gas if they were? Wouldn't you be happy? The world becoming true again. There was always something missing. The other half of our mankind hid under Cold War aluminum wallpaper.

New development here. After 5 months in holy Benares passing the leper beggars lined up in my street one day last month, noticing one particularly hideous skeleton-like Buchenwald covered with brown loose feces and flies on huge yellow sores on hips and elbows, crouched in fetal position, naked in curve of urinal wall nearby, obviously dying, like several I've seen and given milk to, and they died, I saw their great-eyed bony corpses on street, days later. This one, I couldn't stand seeing like that and cheerfully gave him some milk. Broke the ice. He too weak to take rupee I put in his hand. Dumb-mute, can't talk, and yellow eyed pus couldn't see, a brown shirt stuck to ulcerating shoulder and filthy shit and piss and mouth all old curry dribbles and one paw like a rabbit's, withered and swollen, shiny skinned feet hung on end of stick-thin legs, literally that Buchenwald look, been there weeks, finally too weak to move, even if I gave him change, and dysentery and God knows what cancer and one swollen toe, leprous, and flies all over his eyes, and ass and maggots coming out of his right ear, all this literal photo not metaphor, couldn't talk, but I heard him from my room, a high piercing wail-scream in quietness of street night, finally withered so he looked like another 10 or 20 hours left. Breathing heavy, gurgling. Next day we, Peter and I and an orphan boy, lives in that leper park where saddhus smoke ganja, nice looking healthy kid, his parents died there and he grew up there serving the beggars, we carried this man-corpse in his rags, to the Ganges and bathed him and got doctor to look, who said nothing but starvation was wrong, with its complications, so started feeding him milk and food and bought him a dollar mattress and hired boy to wash him in river every noon, Peter the nurse showed how, and put penicillin and afterward talcum on the open wounds and hydrogen peroxide in ears to sterilize and kill the maggots, bought him a sheet and pajamas and looked to him every day, under shade of big Bo tree in the park, branches over the ghat street where the beggars sit, so he slowly began stirring and writing in the dust, couldn't talk, *dude*, that is milk, I bought him a notebook and pencil, he wrote in English first thing, "Sir I want to died because hearing anybody magi saying to me, he is thief Hardwar then some scrawls in Urdu and Hindi and couple letters Sanskrit, I want to go to my house where my family is, I want to Hard-war. I want my bed and clothes." Hardwar being place, holy, upriver. One com-mits suicide there. So I hired the boy to feed and wash him, for 50 cents a day, a fortune, actually a laborer's day's wage, and got him new pajamas, white, he sat in, stupefied, shitting on the mattress, incontinent, smelly, but we undressed him every day and washed the shit off, and dried in heat on Ganges bank and finally I went away to go to Bodh Gaya two weeks ago and left money behind, Peter stayed and supervised. When I came back, he was a little stronger, and one day, in high squeaky pierced voice, spoke in English, his tongue'd been cut out during partition by Moslems, and he knifed all over crippled, but still so sick, still amazing to hear him talk. Finally, this week, sneaked him into hospital to get him off our hands, a nuisance, and he much better now and will live. One saintly Hindu postal clerk watching us one day on street, cleaning him, squat-ting down and got his family address and wrote letter. Tonight came by to say the family actually existed and answered saying the skeleton's mother was cry-ing alla time, missing him. He disappeared six months ago, they're sending the brother down to Benares from Punjab 1000 miles away to get him. Fantastic, in that I wouldn't've believed anyone in that condition could survive, much less the fortunate accident of our intervention succeeding and then the family appearing like in weird movie.

Meanwhile, I got all familiar with the beggar scene and been investigating around and visiting hospitals and corrupt beggars' homes and even the mayor and health commissioner here, trying to set up help for the few really helpless street skeletons. Most beggars and lepers okay in that they can move and beg and make out. Lazily, not bad. But a couple a week are really in clas-sic shit-rag death throes. A few nights ago, one just like junkie Iris Brody teeth and skeleton face and bones thin as my thumb, her legs and arms, but bright eyed, chattering and appealing to me in Hindi for help. Another today, I got some medicine for, been there a month, but last week lost all his flesh and down to bone, also dysentery. We get him in rickshaw tomorrow, I mean to hospital.

Anyway, regarding death, I keep seeing people dying in front of my eyes. I talk to them and give loot where I can or milk or food. See, my money is more than enough for that minimal 2 cents milk and oddly, just as I was worrying about loot, for payment, this one beggar's care arrived. $100 gift from Nanda Pivano.[49] All the beggars together only cost $25. So it's not money. If I stayed

---

49 Fernanda Pivano (b. 1917). Ginsberg's Italian translator.

here I'd organize a Schweitzer brigade. Anyway, that's my soap opera for the month. An orange robed zedanta saddhu connected with puritan Hindu group came up while we were bathing him and said, "Young beardy guy with evil nail-biting frau, you're committing sin to intervene." And so I said, "Yes, probably, I thought so, but I can't help it. Pray for me." Because obviously, that did cross my mind. The poor skeleton will get better and then you have to go all through the same horror later on anyway.

"Your sins are too big." He's still pacing around, staring at me, fascinated. I see him on the street. But it says in Bhagavad-Gita, don't look to the fruits of action. So I don't have to worry if it's meritorious or de-meritorious, helping the skeleton. It's not my business. I got no way of knowing. Only time I got emotional about it, except for a drag depression anxiety, followed me around for days as I got deeper involved. Realizing now I was hooked with the man in as much it was all up to me whether he lived or died, i.e., I wanted to get out of the situation, not be faced by thought of the skeleton lying under the tree in street, with a dwarf cow that hangs around him, which has crippled legs. It's really a scene I didn't want to face, but fortunately solved by getting him into the hospital. Tho worried what happens when I leave in a week. And now, like miracle, the family appears on horizon, like some kind of mysterious clock-work, the whole thing. Meanwhile, there's this other man to take tomorrow, to hospital. India is a big mess. There's money and beds and people enough just indifferently starved to death or rheumatic fever, t.b., waste away in front of the post office. Or milk shack, or lie there under the tree, there's a city health office on the same block, with five men filling out forms about some-thing else. Complete bureaucracy stasis. Like a parody. I still not sure how it all so fucked up, I mean why everybody's so totally inefficient. People hanging around cigarette stall, like lawyers saying, "Oh, he can't be starving, he's prob-ably got t.b." So there's nothing to do about it anyway, they think to them-selves. Also, I've been discovering not to get mad and flip. Useless though enjoyable histrionics.

Okay, I go to bed,

Allen

[*Robert Creeley arranged for Ginsberg to attend a poetry conference in Vancouver, British Columbia, in exchange for a round the world airplane ticket. On the way to the conference from India Allen took his first jet and stopped in Vietnam, Cambodia, and Japan. In Kyoto he stayed a few weeks with Gary Snyder and Joanne Kyger.*]

Allen Ginsberg [Kyoto, Japan] to Louis Ginsberg [Paterson, NJ]
June 17, 1963

Dear Lou:

Traveling by jet plane kind of a gas, you do get in and out of centuries from airport hangars & glassy modern downtowns to jungle floating markets & 900 year old stone cities in a matter of minutes & hours instead of weeks & months. Like space cut-ups or collages, one minute paranoiac spy ridden Vietnam streets the same afternoon quiet Cambodian riversides. I spent a week in Vietnam talking with opium poets & U.S. directors & State Department spokesmen & Army public relations sergeants & most of all with newsmen & also the Buddhist priests. Horrible mess as you can read in the papers. Curious [thing about] the reporters is that they are all young & relatively eager there unlike most "hotspots" so this a rare instance if you follow the politics war there one can get a relatively straight account within the limits of assumed anticommunist slant & the euphemisms of ticklish situations (i.e. Diem government not referred to outright as Diem dictatorship, but as "Diem Government which has been called dictatorial" etc.) (i.e. phraseology picked to suggest idea rather than say it outright as is done with red dictatorships). Anyway I'm glad I saw what little I saw of that. Gave me nervous stomach after a week. Then spent a week in Angkor Wat ruins in Cambodia & now here in Kyoto with Snyder & his wife in neat little Jap house sitting typing on the floor. Big week of Zen meditation in the monastery, I've been going with Snyder & sitting 2 1/2 hours immobile cross-legged the last 3 nights & learning proper belly breathing for that kind of sitting. Hard on the ankles but interesting subjective effects. I'll be here a month & thence Vancouver. Japan amazing after all the other Asian & Arab countries—not much police state, everybody neat & keen stylish & motorcycles & transistors & cameras & civilized nobody starving in his shit in the street like India & everywhere else practically. Native Japanese quickness plus the fact they aren't saddled with active participation in cold war so all their energy goes into self-improvement. Lucky they lost the war. Jap style living very lovely, houses with sliding walls & clean food & mat barefoot on floors leave shoes at door & sense of taste & cleanness in all the woodwork

& carpentry & weird little careful gardens everywhere, and all the young peo-
ple real chic like they stepped out of an Italian fashion magazine with girls
Jackie Kennedy hair mops & the men hip downswept over forehead like
Brando as Marc Anthony—just amazing to see all these Asians prosperous.
Quitting now, 6:30 PM going out to sit early eve in temple.

    Soon—Love,

    Allen

[*After leaving the Snyders in Kyoto, Ginsberg took an express train to Tokyo. En route he
had another epiphany which led to the poem, "The Change." He wrote about that to Ker-
ouac from San Francisco. By that time he had decided not to return to India.*]

Allen Ginsberg [San Francisco, CA] to Jack Kerouac [Northport, NY]
October 6, 1963

Dear Jack:

    Kept thinking I should write you back fast huge love lovely belly flowers let-
ter, received yours in Japan, I just got TOO MUCH to tell you. TOO TOO
TOO much whoops where could I begin Japan or somewhere? India, Ganges
I'm bathing all the time and praying for transcendentalist Blakes and visiting
holymen and all they got to say is "Take Blake for your guru," or "Your own
heart is your guru," or "O how wounded you and Peter are, Oh how wounded,
Oh how wounded," till finally I left when time was up and flew to Viet Nam
and everybody killing everybody else hardhearted America paranoia and
weeks in Cambodia ruins Angkor Wat and pot and Bangkok Chinese boys and
finally peaceful Kyoto, sat in monastery with Gary and did belly breathing and
that calmed my mind and then the sweetness of all those gurus sinking in to
me and then Joanne and Gary both so nice to me both took me to bed even
Gary made love to me and all of a sudden I dug Joanne since it was alright for
me to feel what anyway I felt, I want a woman wife lady, I want I want, want life
not death, wound up crying on train from Kyoto to Tokyo and wrote final
poem: "On My Train Seat I Renounce My Power: So That I Do Live I Will Die"
therefore accepting Christ see also, and no more mental universe arguments: I
am that I am and what exactly am I? Why I'm me, and me is my feelings by
gum and those feelings are located to be exact in my belly trembling when eyes
say Yes and in my breast all along that's my me NOT my head not Christ ideas

not Buddha — Christ and Buddha are in my body not no where else. And every-thing else is arbitrary conceptions. So from now on I won't take nothing but love and give same, in feelings, except — well I came back weeping to Vancou-ver and there was Olson Duncan Creeley Levertov all to teach together and I said, I can't eliminate them from my universe or anyone even Norman Pod-horetz they are all selfs too like me alas we been arguing and seeing each other like beatniks and poets and everything but crying self so I just cried and didn't teach just went around feeling everybody up till we were all there together hav-ing a happy earth picnic with no ideas in head about put up poetry or put down poets NO MORE WARS all are immortal laugh and lie down no superior poets no inferior poets furthermore no more need ayahuascas or peyotes because already flowing from belly and breast is infinity when feeling's open and that feels good not scary — all I saw in Blake 1948 finally came true, lasted weeks and weeks, lovely Jerusalem blisses, I even realized (finally) my mother died having seen and told me her last day the key is in the sunlight, but I didn't realize what she meant and felt till I felt myself back home in my own body on earth and knew she had been there and knew it. So all's well, I go get married and have lit-tle hairy losses someday — and I am not a hairy loss, I'm me, and me's name-less, but certainly not a bad feeling OOK like hairy loss,[50] you put me under a spell for years, and Burroughs about killed me off with his cut ups. His cut ups fine since it cuts up the head but he wants to cut up his body feelings too, and that don't feel good at all. Your hairy loss served to get me down off my high head too, but you coulda saved me faster by calling me tender heart, honey — everything's fine we're all going to be what? be what we is! ain't that great. I'm too mental and hungup to explain right, but anyway Jack I'm telling you like you tell me, yup, everything is alright, in fact I can't explain it anymore I just FEEL it and that's better than explaining so next time we meet I'll make you feel good. I'll kiss you and pet you and read you little poemlets about ispy did-dle and I'll also kiss your mama and ask her forgiveness and ask her to love me and I done already prayed for your poppa and I go see my poppa and thank him for borning me and make him feel it's all alright and I go back to human uni-verse just as in prophecy of *Dr. Sax* (last chapters of which I read to class in Van-couver) THE SNAKE'S ALL TOOK CARE OF. And your letter full of tenderness so I won't sermonize you anymore either, despite I do detect doubts in your mind whether it's alright for you to have been born, well you go right

---

50 Years earlier Kerouac had told Ginsberg that he was "nothing but a hairy loss." That phrase haunted Ginsberg for decades.

over to your mother and REASSURE her that she did right giving life to you. And why right? Because god is feeling and it makes her feel bad you complaining alla time you didn't want to be born. Wouldn't you feel bad if your son told you he was mad at you for borning him. And wouldn't you feel good if son came home and said, dad, we made it, I'm glad I'm alive you did right. Wouldn't you feel better? and what else have we got but feelings, have we got some big ideas, or something else to be? besides our hearts? All the gurus in India say Abhya mudra[51] and so says Buddha and so I say to little English Kerouac, except we NOW are in the tents of god so let's like lambs rejoice: and no more specters.

So now I'm here in SF going around asking everybody if I can kiss them. Pathetic isn't it, asking everybody to love me? Which seeing I'm such a fucked up longhair goof naturally they melt and do, except it gets to be hard work. Nonetheless you look in those faces everywhere and what's to be seen but same self all over been wounded and pissed on—and Lucien was here and we blessed each other anew—and Neal now. Well I'm in a big apartment with some quiet young Kansas poets I got backroom and Neal and his girl have another room (same Anne [Murphy] you saw in Northport) and he understands why it was too difficult there (in Northport)—and beginning I hope Monday we sit down and Neal actually write his blop again, anyway he quit job and Carolyn divorced him (I spent days with her) and I singing hours of calm hindoo mantras to him soften the air till he get back in his body from racetrack specters and unfeeling frenzy and we all be back together again *o la tierra est la nostra*. I come see you Xmas without hair if you so desire me or with hair if you so accept me, if you want calm weeks come here reunion NO LUSHING it destroy feeling in fact get off that lush. I no take drugs no more nothing but belly flowers. I sleep with girls I reborn I happy I sing harikrishna lords prayer ipsky diddle I weep Sebastian[52] knew all we know nothing unless we do love. Now we go out save America from lovelessness. I reverse *Howl*, I write white *Howl*, no more death. O Walt [Whitman] Hello Jack!

I make movie of *Kaddish* with Robert Frank later you help me with dialogue?

I'll write you soon again. Will you love me ever? Peter heading his footprints across Pakistan toward Persia and New York by Xmas.

We are all babies! Feels good. The word at last!!!

51 Abhya mudra. Ginsberg defined this as "a mudra of reassurance, fearlessness."
52 Sebastian Sampas. See page 113.

[Ginsberg had a large stack of unanswered mail on his desk, but he took time out to defend Philip Lamantia against Richard Howard's negative review in Poetry.]

Allen Ginsberg [San Francisco, CA] to *Poetry Magazine* [Chicago, IL]
October 14, 1963

To Readers of *Poetry*:

"...and Ginsberg already have written the poems these spasms so relentlessly parrot..."* Philip Lamantia and I share old friendship and similarity of sources—our insight into an American <u>weir</u>, its mechano hells (his words): our longing for breakthrough into the more natural universe of Self, all our true feelings: our experiments with alterations of consciousness catalyzed by drugs: our prayer, public communication, poetry. His interest in techniques of surreal composition notoriously antedates mine and surpasses my practice in a quality of untouched-ness, nervous scatting, street moment purity—his imagination zapping in all directions of vision at once in a cafeteria—prosodic hesitancies and speedballs—the impatience, petulance, unhesitant declaration, machine-gunning at mirrors nakedly—that make his line his mantric own.

Since I'm cited as stylistic authority I authoritatively declare Lamantia an American original, sooth-sayer even as Poe, genius in the language of Whitman, native companion and teacher to myself. "And for years I have been absorbed in contemplation of the golden roseate auricular gong-tongue emanating from his black and curly skull. Why Not." Says Philip Whalen, and many poets his admirers Michael McClure and Robert Creeley others have spoken—thus I've composed this letter returning to Lamantia the last word:

"There is no agrarian program it is all economic war!

I make war! I declare this tribe, cool! this nation, spared!

this stupidity unlimited, put down! this slumbering beauty, waked up!

    this heap, fuckup, dead bitch—run down, put down, finished!

        I liquidate by magic!"

Allen Ginsberg

*A.G. Note—*Destroyed Works* by Philip Lamantia (Auerhahn Press, S.F. 1963) was thus bugged by Richard Howard—an excellent friendly fellow otherwise—in his review, *Poetry* July 1963 review of it.

[Orlovsky returned home from India overland via Persia, Turkey, and Eastern Europe. When he arrived in London, this letter awaited him.]

Allen Ginsberg [San Francisco, CA] to Peter Orlovsky [London, England] November 1, 1963

Dear Peter:

Received cards from Yugoslavia and Istanbul—today November 1 maybe you in London already. I sent letter to Anselm Hollo and you at his address, enclosing poem I wrote in Japan—please look. If you have time stay a couple weeks in London look around it's worth it. Blake in Tate Museum, British Museum, Blake's grave in Bunhill Fields, Simon Watson Taylor 33 Tregunter Road—at least he used to be there. Visit Stephen Spender in London maybe too—*Encounter* office. Also look up Dame Edith Sitwell c/o Sesame Club for Women and bring her this poem I sent you and Anselm. She be interested in our India and is a nice holy old lady.

I be in NY first weeks of December for sure—we probably arrive around the same time. I rush out and mail this. Neal's OK.

Neal says "tell Peter how much I liked his last postcard well—as I sit in the kitchen on cold mornings looking at the grease in the frying pan that he once licked on a colder morning—in fact the first time we met stands out in mind— tell him we all love him."

Love

Allen

I made picket sign for Madame Nhu here. I carried it in front of her hotel on Market St. 14 hours last week singing harikrishna mantra and Buddham Saranam Gochamil:

> Man is naked without secrets Armed men lack this joy
> How many person without Names?
> What do we know of their suffering?
> "Oh how wounded, how wounded" says the Guru
> Thine own heart says the Swami
> Within you says the Christ
> Till his humanity awake says Blake
> I am here saying seek mutual surrender tears

> That there be no more Hell in Vietnam
> That I not be in Hell here in the street.

That was on one side of the sign, on the other I painted 3 fish with one head at LaVigne's using gold and silver paint on scales of fish and red white blue tails and wrote also:

> War is Black Magic
> Belly Flowers to North and South Vietnam
> Name Hypnosis and Fear are the Enemy — Satan Go home!
> I accept America and Red China to the Human Race
> Madame Nhu and Mao Tse-tung are in the same boat of Meat.

Show to Anselm, I gonna write propaganda picket sign poems slogans like Mayakovsky, this was the first.

[*By the beginning of the year, Ginsberg and Orlovsky had reunited in New York. They found an apartment together on the Lower East Side where Allen began a decade of heightened activism. Not only did he continue to write poetry, but he generously helped other people in their battles against the establishment. The government tried to shut down the avant-garde Living Theatre on trumped up charge of unpaid taxes.*]

Allen Ginsberg [New York, NY] **to Robert Morgenthau** [New York, NY]
January 30, 1964

Dear Mr. Morgenthau:

I am writing in behalf of Julian Beck and Judith Malina of the Living Theatre. I understand that the government has prepared a legal case against them. I have been away (in India) several years so have not followed the controversy. However I have been interested in the Living Theatre for a number of years, have given poetry readings there to raise money for the continuation of their work, and have contributed holograph manuscript of a poem *Kaddish* which was auctioned for their benefit for about 600 dollars. This was done at a time when I had very little money for my own use. I am saying this so that you will understand that I have a so to speak old time emotional/personal/artistic investment in their theater and their activities for many years in the center of the avant-garde artistic community in New York.

I understand that Julian has been proposed with 33 years in jail, if the government succeeds in its prosecution. The whole situation is so unthinkable that I certainly feel involved.

Difficult to know how to involve myself properly in a way that would do them any good, and at the same time not deny any ultimately legitimate grievances the government may (or may not) have.

The first thing I would like to know is, is the Government (which is to say the people and yourself, your staff etc.) aware of the cultural importance that the Living Theatre had, in its time, and of the present cultural importance of the Becks as theater dynamos and experimenters? And, do you and your staff look on their work with sympathy or antipathy?

I understand, from the violence of the language of the charges presented against them, that there is an element of cultural antipathy present, which must be dealt with, before any reasonable thinking on the problem can be done.

My request for information from you on this point is not irrelevant, since it is after all a matter of policy who to prosecute, how seriously to prosecute. And that policy would in any case be determined by the sympathies or antipathies of the government officials involved.

I understand you are an intellectual fellow and so take the liberty of asking you seriously for information and requesting reply.

Whatever actions I take in regard to this case in future will be determined by how the attitude of the government people feels when it is communicated. If I conclude that underneath the technical-tax-financial hang ups involved, that the basic problem is the city or federal government's emotional antipathy to the work the Becks have been doing, or to their personalities, then my only conclusion can be that the case has definite social and political importance, and may be the beginning of a threat against many other avant-garde organizations in the city. In which case, despite my own aversion for hung-up hassles of this kind, the government may in the end have to put me in jail also, as well as a lot of other people in the artistic world in NY who may feel their artistic existence as citizens definitely threatened.

I am aware that from your point of view my attitude may seem alarmist and extreme, but I assure you that from my observations of the NY scene since returning from India, the government handling of the Living Theatre situation has already put a chill in the soul of several other organized groups, (magazines, movie writers, etc.) and already had a bad effect on that part of the avant-garde which has to deal with Government and public in an organized way such as Living Theatre tried. In other words the damage I speak of has already been done in a small way. If Beck actually goes to jail, there is no telling what kind of Pandora's box the government will have opened in NY.

I have assignments or requests to write for various publications—*Playboy*, *Esquire* etc., as well as access to letter columns in *NY Times* or *London Times*, and I maintain correspondence with large magazines in India, Russia, France and England. It will be my duty to go all out and start screaming if I judge that the government policy decision ultimately amounts to political and/or cultural fuck up.

If you think I am misinformed or fucked up myself, please let me know. I'm not interested in fighting. Simply that the Becks are important cultural property and I want to know definitely if the people acting for the government are aware of it, sympathetic to the fact, and acting so, or if they are not aware, or feel that that awareness is a matter of indifference in the automatic cut and dried legal necessities involved. That's really the crucial point involved, particularly for foreign readers observing the process of the case.

You may have noticed that in the Russian government persecutions of Pasternak, his girlfriend, and Yevtushenko etc. the poets, there was always also a legitimate legalistic point involved in the eyes of the authorities, who said publicly that it was not a political matter but a question of the rules, etc. From distance of perspective we here in U.S. could see that the "rules" were an excuse for bureaucratic action on the basis of emotional, cultural, political antipathies against the artists involved. I suspect that such appears to be the case in regard to the Becks, and that's why I'm writing you so openly, to give you chance to consider this point, and give me the benefit of a clear statement on your part as to your own sympathies and that of your staff. I assure you that your own feelings are not irrelevant, as after all they are what makes you a man, and what after all, must finally determine your policy, your phraseology in dealing with the problem, your very tone of voice and the feelings which you communicate in person or by letter or private discussion or official conference, on this matter.

Thank you for your courtesy, I await your reply before taking any further action.

Yours,

Allen Ginsberg

[*Due to Ginsberg's national and even international celebrity, his participation was sought for a wide variety of causes. He tried to help wherever his name could be of use.*]

**Allen Ginsberg [New York, NY] to the *Wichita Beacon* [Wichita, KS]
April 16, 1964**

To the Editor:

I understand, from several clippings from your newspaper that have been sent me, that local police have banned or threatened to take steps to ban the sale of poetry by me and several other writers—fellows from Wichita as well as San Francisco and other places.

Almost a decade ago there was a similar attempt to ban a book of mine in San Francisco, and my work was found to be NOT obscene by the courts. That settled that. Subsequently my writings have been included in anthologies, translated into a dozen languages, recited on television and movies, studied in English courses in universities. Meanwhile, I have taught or lectured in University of British Columbia, Concepción University in Chile, Oxford in England, Harvard, Columbia, Berkeley, Yale and Princeton here in the U.S. This month I find myself listed in *Who's Who*. Now what the heck is going on in Wichita?

Is the mayor's office so provincial that it has no judgment and no control over local police officers and cannot better advise its captains? Are the citizens of Wichita so apathetic they have no control over their own bureaucracies in matters like this? Is the faculty of the local college so indifferent to the community that it cannot intervene and straighten this hassle out? Are the local patrons of arts and local lawyers so buried in their TV sets that they can't bring moral suasions to bear on city officialdom to be more reasonable where such a crucial constitutional matter as freedom of expression is concerned? Is nobody home in Wichita?

I am writing a letter to your mayor to ask for an explanation. It certainly shouldn't be left to me thousands of miles away to have to do that. Ladies and gentlemen, take good care of your own city.

Allen Ginsberg
New York City

[In support of comedian Lenny Bruce, Ginsberg cut off his beard and long hair. He sent them to New York's Assistant District Attorney, Richard Kuh, who was prosecuting the Bruce case and other cases against Jonas Mekas and various underground film venues. Receiving Ginsberg's shorn locks and beard did not soften the D.A.'s heart.]

Allen Ginsberg [New York, NY] to Assistant District Attorney Richard H. Kuh [New York, NY] *ca.* June 16, 1964

Dear Mr. Kuh:

Please don't be confused by all these goodwill offerings...please accept the enclosed offering of my shorn locks as a sort of spiritual bribe that you look with friendlier kindlier heart on the earnest strivings of the artists of N.Y. to communicate with all men including myself and yourself. I think you have misunderstood the message thru mistrust and/or earlier bad experiences and so take amiss the real tenderness in the new movies and bodies. There is a definite social value I think you are going to be happily surprised to find. Meanwhile accept and guard this part of my head which I have cut off in your honor, as a devotional offering to the God in you.

    Allen Ginsberg

[In a letter to Michael McClure, Ginsberg revealed how quickly he had been swept up into the hectic life of New York once again.]

Allen Ginsberg [New York, NY] to Michael McClure [San Francisco, CA] August 29, 1964

Dear Mike:

LaVigne got your hard-skin'd beast. [Lyndon] Johnson won't get in so may Mailer follow thru. He veritable patron of arts, approved and token invested in *Kaddish* film says Robert Frank but I not seen Mailer in whiles and whiles. Went down to Atlantic City [site of the Democratic National Convention] with Peter and Ed Sanders on silent Vietnam picket vigil. Hot dogs Negroes klieg lights TV cameras Texan hats boardwalks bible-protestors Mississippi protestors leaflets and vast facade of convention hall we never went inside of but bussed back to NY before midnight.

Gregory here on floor and so also another Orlovsky *nee* Julius who been in bughouse last 12 (twelve) years Bartlebying—been with us a month now talking blue streak but hard to figure what next. The house is a chaos, 4 people in 3

$^1/_2$ rooms, just the nightmare I was hoping to avoid—in addition Peter's girls and now a little 19 year old LSD nymph moviemaker girl that shares my foam rubber mat. BIG heterosexual secret I finally learned after all this time is, if I lay back passive and let myself be made love to from nipples to knees and all over, I don't have no trouble sloping getting with it and screwing later. But if I have to do all the work as I generally thought I was suppose to, or, no didn't think that but somehow always wound up being on top and active, mainly because either I or the girls I was making it with were too inept to understand I wanted to be made love to first to at least get me going—anyway this little girl found the secret and now all's pleasantly relaxed more so than before. Meanwhile plenty jizzum spurting around the house. Got some nice Indian records too, before borrowed phono collapsed. Totally broke and my type-writer in hock till Monday. I applied for a Carnegie Fund grant (that's $500 to aid distressed writers) and got turned down. LaVigne got a gallery I think lined up and a patron and now moving into nice NY studio, so I guess he'll be alright. Neal and Ken Kesey arrived in their hallucination bus and we all rode out to World's Fair, some gang. Jack in town once and moved this week to Florida again. Finally I began screaming at him about politics—he's always so sadistic to me yelling that I'm a fairy kike pinko and Goldwater's a patriot from Arizona—and told him to tell his mother to eat her own shit—and that broke the ice a little so we were able to talk better—Ugh—Saw a chapter in "Signal" of Kirby Doyle I thought was energetic, not seen him around a month now. Damn earthquake never came off, I was took in.[53] You see Gary? Lower East Side turning into community, now there are 4 bars where poets photographers musicians meet, all around Avenue B. I registered to vote. You? So did Peter. If everybody in Lower East Side did that would be a huge voting bloc and could get all sorts of action. I guess that will come, tho it be hastened by someone's energetics. All these cats who can't write poesy, what do they do? All falling on poetry's shoulders.

I been writing desultorily and wrote some poems but all this time in NY no time to type much up. Bonnie Bremser after me to save Ray from jail... agh...no peace here I get so easily sidetracked. At the moment un-ease, other-wise all's well.

Love to Joanne,

XXX

Allen

53 Someone had told Ginsberg that a major earthquake would hit California, and he repeated the prediction to his friends on the West Coast, but the date passed without incident.

[Even though Ginsberg was world-famous by the 1960s, he was also broke. He wrote to Lionel Trilling for a grant reference. The letter revealed that Allen still held his old professor in high esteem.]

Allen Ginsberg [New York, NY] to Lionel Trilling [London, England] September 30, 1964

Dear Lionel:

I am applying again this year for a Guggenheim grant—I did once 1960 before unsuccessfully (& if memory serves correctly you & W. C. Williams were among my references)—have you any objection to writing a letter for me again? (Have you any ideas who <u>would</u> be helpful?) If it is inconvenient or you can't conscientiously recommend etc. please don't worry about it. I'm not sure who to ask at this point, actually. Most of my connections are among younger people who won't be of much help. I've tried several places, the Merrill Foundation, Carnegie Fund, Author's League, P.E.N. etc. and seem to get nowhere. What burns me up is that there is actually about a million dollars a year handed out (one way or another) to poets in the U.S.—some connected to institutional duties, some not, a great deal not. I'm totally broke so going about it more systematically this year. "Project" proposed is to type & edit another book of poems 1960-64-5 continue writing &, hopefully, visit Prague, Milan, Warsaw, Berlin, Moscow. I have books (collected or selected poems) prepared or in preparation in Czech & Italian & Moscow so want to correct consult translators while I'm at it. Also have not been in Eastern Europe before & been everywhere else so it's about time. Might even do east-west relations some good. The State Dept. sent [Richard] Wilbur & Peter Viereck a while back but I doubt they'd send me and in any case it would not be a good idea to go under any official auspices Russian or U.S. (However the Guggenheim application is not necessarily centered on that trip—I just want money to subsist whatever I do.)

Happy to hear you're traveling. I visited Oxford in '58 with Corso & read for the Henry Vaughn Society and stayed a week with an Indian young poet Dom Moraes & met Edith Sitwell who was at the time very friendly, (said she adored Blake, Shelley & Whitman).

Saw final text of your letter re [Leslie] Fiedler[54] & myself in *Partisan*. I thought his book had a lot of insight into new material—i.e. new dissociations of American literary sensibility & "alterations of consciousness" & simply new

---

54 Leslie Fiedler (1917–2003). Writer and literary critic.

sense of life mid-century & acknowledgement that something curious had happened in poetry & Burroughs prose—but the book was so badly written and so filled with gossipy secondhand information and egotistical theories & used-up academic attitudes—attitudes at which he's not even a sophisticated past master in any case—and anyway he really lacks background in Stein Dada Transition Marinetti French poetry Mayakovsky Neruda Pound prosody Williams—i.e. XX century avant-garde—so the book was hopelessly sluggish. To think of college students reading up on modern writing from him, using his versions as source for their generalizations—ugh nightmare. If you think he hoked up our relationship—by gum its only one small detail in a mass of pre-suppositions & gossipy errors Augean stablic in proportions. Augean stables.

My opinion (which I know you didn't ask for) of present day English poesy is: that unless & until there is a complete renovation of British prosody comparable to what went on in U.S., France & even Russia (to say nothing of Spanish changes) they'll never get anywhere & the Beatles are more interesting. That is most English poets are still trying to write literature, as they once knew it, derived attitudes expressed in derived arbitrary accentual meter. Till they begin scoring the line on the page to follow as notations of breath, or some other basic physiological measure, standard—or some design that graphs the actual process of thought during the time of writing—they'll just keep on repeating themselves more & more weakly. I haven't read one really new great English poem for decades have you? It's a simple matter, that all the energy is enclosed in old iambic box & till that box is broken open nobody will know what's inside not even Pandora. Actually Pound & Lawrence & others made classical advances in how to compose, how to write, or approach writing little poems, which younger English poets just ignore & I suspect that's a fault of emphasis in the educational system. There's one English poet here in the Lower East Side Harry Fainlight who's going back in half a year, he has poems in Encounter sometimes, he seems interesting, tho from texts he has here & not what Encounter has published.

Give my best to your wife [Diana Trilling]. While I have more space & apropos of nothing presently at hand I wish you would confirm for her my recollection that the message "fuck the Jews" was not the only message I left scrawled on Livingston Hall window. I also wrote "Butler has no balls" (a common gaga saying among the students at the time) & punctuated it all with a pirate's skull-crossbones. I think later commentators on these esoteric graffiti have entirely misunderstood the intention—possibly thru reference to woefully incomplete text. And lack of subsidiary documentation. You see, the charwoman on that

floor in Livingston was a real grumpy old freak who read Westbrook Pegler &
took *Daily News* editorials for Bible. A slovenly little old lady in tennis shoes,
who never cleaned my windows & made sour comments about kikes. I was
hoping she'd get so upset by the message in the thick dust on the window she'd
finally clean it off. So did roommate Bill Lancaster, who also thought the gesture
was funny, tho admittedly we did have a normally irresponsible sense of college
humor. What actually happened was that the charwoman was so freaky she did-
n't clean the window but instead thought it was important enough to report to
the dean. And—the dean thought it important enough to send the director of
student-faculty relations up to investigate the shocking phenomena. Unfortu-
nately when he burst into my room without knocking at 9AM that Saturday
morning he found me snoring in bed with Kerouac at my side (not even naked,
it was all too innocent, at the time I was so inhibited I'd not had sex with men or
women). Everybody immediately suspected the worst & later that morning in
Dean McKnight's office the first thing he said to me was "Mr. Ginsberg I hope
you realize the <u>enormity</u> of what you've done." (Kerouac had been banned
from campus as an 'unwholesome influence'). Lancaster who'd been with us all
night went to the dean & explained, Lionel I think intervened sympathetically,
my father came in tears, and in the end (a year later) I was able to get back into
school with a letter from a friendly psychiatrist who avowed to the dean that I'd
been treated for my morbid diseases. Really I felt surrounded by madmen.
About that same year I first developed a taste for Céline, who's very good
describing that kind of humiliating chaos. I think this description will conform
to yr recollection, if you show to Diana. Fiedler's book reminded me.

As ever

Allen

[*1965 was a pivotal year in the life of Allen Ginsberg. In a long letter to Nicanor Parra, who
had shared the stage with Allen at a poetry conference earlier that year in Cuba, Allen gave a
detailed description of those events.*]

Allen Ginsberg [Portland, OR] to Nicanor Parra [Santiago, Chile] August 20, 1965

Dear Nicanor dear:

I got your letter from Santiago July 9 and am now up in Northwest with
Gary Snyder an old friend poet who's been living in Japan studying Zen Jap

tongue and Chinese for last 8 years. We're camping with sleeping bags in forests and beaches and preparing to climb snowy glacier mountains for a month. Then back to San Francisco and October 15-16 I take part in anti-Vietnam war demonstration and maybe end up in jail or maybe not for a month or so. Well I'll see. Happy to hear from you, I had some very mad adventures since I left Cuba, I even spent a few evenings till 4 AM with Alessandro Jodorowsky in Cupola Cafe in Paris. But anyway to begin where we left off.

8:30 AM after the party at the Havana-Riviera where I last saw you in your pajamas giggling I woke up with knock on my door and 3 *miliciano* entered and scared me. I thought they were going to steal my notebooks, they woke me up in the middle of hangover sleep I'd only been in bed 2 hours. Told me pack my bags the immigration chief wanted to talk to me, and wouldn't let me make phone call, took me down to office in old Havana to a Mr. Verona head of immigration who told me they were putting me on first plane out. I asked him if he'd notified Casa[55] or Hayden [*sic*: Haydee] and he said no, they had appointment with Hayden that afternoon and she would agree after she heard their reasons. What reasons? "Breaking the laws of Cuba." "But which laws?" "You'll have to ask yourself that," he answered. As we drove to airport I explained I was simpatico with revolution and embarrassed both for self and for them and also explained that my month was up, the rest of, most of, the delegates were leaving that weekend anyway, wouldn't it be more diplomatic and save everyone entanglement if they left me to leave normally with the rest for Prague, and why act hastily without notifying Casa? "We have to do things fast in a revolution."

When I landed in Prague, I wrote Maria-Rosa long letter and mailed it at airport explaining what happened and asked for advice and said I won't talk to reporters etc. and would keep quiet so's not to embarrass her or Casa or Cuba but thought ultimately I'd have to tell friends. It would get out and look silly of Cuban bureaucracy, so perhaps best ask Hayden to invite me back, at least formally to erase the comic [expulsion] and so have been in contact with her and Ballagas ever since. Saw [friends] in Prague and later in London and they opined the police were using me to get at the Casa. Meanwhile I hear there's been increased wipe-out of fairies in university and finally this month Manuel Ballagas wrote that Castro at university had spoken badly of *El Puente* and now *El Puente* is dissolved and he's depressed. I certainly didn't know what I was getting into consciously but I seem to have been reacting with antennae to a shit situation that everyone was being discreet about. I doubt if things would not have come to a head without my bungling, I mean it would probably have ended the same way if I weren't there, the hostility and conniving was in the works all along, that was what I was sensing and yelling about.

Well anyway in Prague I found I had royalties for a new book, and back money due me for foreign Lit. mag and 2 years back royalties for stage performances of my poesy in Viola poetry cafe, enough to live well for a month and pay for 3 days intourist and train fare return to Moscow via Warsaw. Met a lot of young kids, heard all the gossip conducted myself discreetly, sang mantras all over the streets and literary offices, gave a poetry reading and answered questions for audience of 500 students at Charles University. They let me loose, I talked freely, the walls of the State didn't fall, everybody was happy, sex relations with anyone male or female is legal over age of 18 (in Poland all [sex] over age 15 is legal) and I left for Moscow. See, when I came I explained to Writers' Union friends what had happened in Cuba to forewarn them so they wouldn't get into trouble over me, I also tried to be as little abrasive as possible and confined my criticism to ideological doubletalk instead of saying directly what I thought in my own terms. So that worked out fine and I went off in a train to Moscow. Spent the first few days with Rominova and Luria and little girl interpreter and got 2 weeks invitation, saw Akaionov and Yevtushenko night after night and briefly one day with Voznesensky and visited Akhmadulina in country and his Buba and Aliguer who remembered and asked after you. I had hotel transferred to Bucharest below Moskovskya bridge and passed thru Red Square every morning and evening and wrote poems in snow by the wall and stood there at midnight watching the guards and yelling Slavic lovers in GUM [largest department store in the world] doorway, fast 4 days train to Leningrad Hermitage, saw my old cousins in Moscow ("It wasn't Stalin's fault, it was Beria, Stalin didn't see, and Beria was in the pay of Scotland Yard" explained my uncle—and K. Simonov commented "Yr uncle is a very naive man"). Yevtushenko was godly reciting drunk one nite in composer's house after midnight profiled golden against wall his neck cords straining with power-speech, but at first meeting very funny, "Allen I have your books you *gran poeta nosotros respectamos mucho, consego hay mucho escandalo sobre su nombre, marihuaniste, pederaste, perro yo conosco no es verdad."* "Well, er—*pero is verdad pero yo voy explicar"* so I spent 15 min. trying to elucidate scientifically the difference between effects of alcohol marijuana heroin ether laughing gas lysergic acid mescaline yage etc. His gaze wandered, he had a headache, popped a codeine

pill in his mouth, and finally said, "Allen I respect you very much as poet but this conversation demeans you. It is your personal affair. Please, there are two subjects do not discuss with me: homosexuality and narcotics." Despite all this comedy I saw a lot of him while I was there and he was very open and sim-patico with me and took me out a lot evenings and his wife and I were all drunk in the Georgian restaurant and he came to train to see me off the last day with Aksenov—another weird scene, as that very last day I'd succeeded in contact-ing [Alexander] Yessenin-Volpin and spent all day with him at his house talking philosophy of law, relations of individual and state. He's working on big proj-ect to define socialist legality inasmuch as they put him in bughouse for com-plaining about police treatment. His sanity certification depended on him signing statement that police had not abused him at one point. He has fine sen-timental sense of humor and human mind—in fact because of his position as sort of writers-union-rejectee he has more recognizably real sense of social humor and reality than anyone else—at least by my heart's standards—very reassuring to see a completely natural mind working on basic emotional reac-tions rather than thru the medium of what's socially acceptable for the season. So there was Yessenin-Volpin the comic pariah at night by the train door and up rushes fur-collared heroes Yevtushenko and tipsy manly Aksenov and they stumble on each other and meet socially for the first time as I waved goodbye from iron door as the train pulled out for Warsaw. I'd not had a chance to meet much younger people or even give a reading there, toward the end they let me meet a group of Univ. Satiric Club theater youths, and there were a few formal conferences with select professors and editors at Writer's Union and Dan-gulov's staff at Foreign Literature Institute and Foreign Literary Club but no opening for big poesy reading like kindly Prague. So I sang mantras to any-one who'd listen and Romanova listened and all the girls at Writer's Union, in taxicabs.

Quiet month in Warsaw, I stayed alone mostly or drank with Irridensky a young rimbaud-ish marlon brando writer at Writer's Union and long after-noons with editor of *Jazz* magazine who'd printed my poems, a Jewish good man who'd been in Warsaw Ghetto, escaped, and covered rest of war as jour-nalist with Russian Army and stood across river from Warsaw at end and saw the city destroyed by Germans and nationalist underground killed off; appar-ently Stalin didn't want to move his army across river to help them because he didn't want competition in postwar control of Poland. Then a week in Krakow which hath a beauteous cathedral with giant polychrome altarpiece by medieval woodcarver genius Wit Stoltz, and car ride to Auschwitz with some boy scout leaders who were trying to pick up schoolboys hanging around the barbed wire gazing at tourists.

Then by train thru Poland to Prague again April 30, and called up friends to walk with on next day May Day parade. Students heard I was back, and this year on May 1 afternoon they were allowed to hold Majales (Student May Festival) for the first time in 20 years—last few years students had battled cops with dogs and fire hoses, so this year Novotny President had stepped forth and reinstated the old medieval students fiesta. They have parade to park and elect a May Queen and May King, and the Polytechnic School asked me if I'd be their candidate for May King—each school proposes one—so I asked around if it was nonpolitical and safe and writer friends said it was OK so I waited in my hotel after marching in morning May Day parade past the bandstand on Wenceslas Street with the Chairman of the Ideological Committee and the Minister of Education and economics and shoes all waving down on the crowd —and a gang of polytechnical students dressed in 1890s costumes and girls in ancient hoopskirts came up to hotel near RR station to get me with a gold cardboard crown and scepter and sat me up on creaky throne on a truck and took me off with wine to the Polytechnic school where there were hundreds of students and a jazz band crowded in the courtyard and I was requested to make speech—which was short "I want to be the first naked King"—and we set out in procession thru the backstreets of Prague to the main avenues downtown. By the time we'd gone half-a-mile we had a crowd of several thousand trailing behind us singing and shouting long live Majales; stopping every ten minutes for traffic and more wine and so I had my cymbals and sang every time they put the bullhorn loudspeaker to my mouth for a speech—mostly sang a mantra Om Sri Maitraya—Hail Mr. Future Buddha—a mixed hindu-buddhist formula for saluting the beauty that is to be. By this time there were more and more people and by the time we moved into the old square in old town Staremeskaya Nameske where Kafka used to live there were floods of people crowding the huge plaza maybe 15,000 souls and I had to make another speech "I dedicate the glory of my crown to the beautiful bureaucrat Franz Kafka who was born in the building around the corner here." (Kafka was published finally in Prague in '61) and the procession moved on past the House of the Golden Carp where he wrote *The Trial*, which I pointed out to the crowd and got drunker on beer and sang more and louder, finally we crossed the bridge over the Vltava River people lining the bridge and the huge dragon-masses of cityfolk following before and after our trucks and Dixieland jazz playing ahead and citizens sitting on the cliff ahead watching it all with their children—everybody in Prague who could walk came out spontaneously. When we got to the park of Culture and Rest there were over 100,000 people and half a dozen rock-and-roll bands and everybody happy and amazed. They'd only expected 10 or 15 thousand out that afternoon. So finally at 3 PM the medical school candidate wrapped in bandages got up and made his speech in Latin and the law school candidate in kings robes got up and made a long sexy speech about fornication as his campaign speech, I got up and sang Om Sri Maitreya for 4 minutes and sat down, and finally was elected May King by the strange masses. So realized it was a politically touchy day and behaved myself, wandered around soberer than any one else with a gang of Polytechnic students. Meanwhile in this Garden of Culture and Eden the Chairman of the Ideological Committee and Minister of Education were wandering around complaining. I had slipped off to be alone a few hours and listen to music, I later learned they were looking for me; that night we all reassembled on the podium to elect a May Queen, I was sitting in my throne looking out at the crowds and floodlights and opened my notebook and wrote a poem and dwelled in my Self for a yogic fifteen minutes. Meanwhile the bureaucrats had given an order to the Student Festival committee to depose me, I didn't know that, suddenly 10 brown shirted Student Police lined up in front of me and the master of ceremonies spoke a few sentences into loudspeaker saying I was deposed to be instead Prime Minister and a Czech student would be put in King's place, and the police lifted me up off my chair and put me on the side with the May Queen judge and a drunken Czech student who didn't know what was happening was put on the throne where he sat for an hour confused and embarrassed. But the crowd thought it was just another student prank and didn't hear or know the difference everybody so drunk anyway the gesture was too late and small to be understood and May Queen was elected by I didn't get a chance to marry and sleep with her as was tradition for the night. In fact I was supposed to have the run of Prague and do anything I wanted and fuck anybody and get drunk everywhere as King, but instead I went to the Polytechnic dormitories with 50 students and we sat up all night singing and talking—along with a couple of business-suited middle-aged fellows who brought some Scotch and a tape recorder. Said they were trading officials but I supposed they were agents, perhaps I'm paranoid. But anyway we made them welcome. Meanwhile I figured I'd better leave in a few days so at Writer's Union next day made inquiries bout whether I had money in Hungary, next stop maybe, and waited for telegram answer, and wandered around Prague making movies with filmmakers and singing Hari Krishna and making tape recorded interview on consciousness evolution and sex logic and space age feelings for student magazines and had some secret nighttime orgies here and there and went to rock and roll concerts and wrote poems—and suddenly lost my notebook, or suddenly it disappeared from my pocket. But anyway there wasn't much in it, it was sketchy and vague, names of people disguised, a number of dreams and six poems including the one I'd wrote under klieg lights and some political gossip ("All the capitalist lies about communism are true and vice versa") and descriptions of orgy scenes with a few students and an account of masturbating in my room at the Hotel Ambassador kneeling on the bathroom floor with a broomstick up my ass—things I wouldn't necessarily want anyone to read and for that reason have never published my journals so as to keep them raw and subjectively real—but nothing illegal and nothing I wouldn't be happy to have read in Heaven, or by Man—embarrassing to a police ear or a politician's—fortunately not detailed like in Cuba or Russia as I was enjoying myself too much to write anything but concentrated Poesy. That nite I went to Viola and met the two business suits who gave me vodka till I was drunk and went out at midnight singing Hari Om Namo Shiva on Narodni Street. Police car picked me up asking for identification—which I didn't have since the hotel had my passport for registration. I explained at station I was May King Tourist Poet and they let me go I really wasn't so drunk just happy. Next nite however, since I saw I was followed around all day by bald plainclothesmen, I stayed sober visiting the Viola, and left with a young couple to go to all night post office to mail postcards to you or someone and as we turned midnight corner on lonely street a man came up from around corner, hesitated, saw me and suddenly rushed forward screaming *bouzerant* (*maricon* [fairy]) and knocked me down, hit me on the mouth, my glasses fell off, I scrambled up and grabbed them and started running down the street, the couple I was with tried to hold him, he chased me and had me down on the ground again in front of the post office and a police car full of captains pulled up immediately and I found myself on the ground with 4 police rubber clubs lifted over my head, so I said OM and stayed quiet, they pulled me into police car and we spent all nite in police station telling the story, the couple I was with said what happened accurately, the Kafkian stranger said we'd been exposing ourselves on the street and when he passed we attacked him. Finally I asked to call lawyer or U.S. consulate and they let me go and said it was all over, nothing more would be heard of it, I was free. Well I reported all that in to Writer's Union and Foreign Literature mag. friends and decided I'd better leave town, tarrying foolishly for Hungarian telegrams, still, and next day I was followed again and in evening in remote cafe with student friends on outskirts of town was picked up by plainclothesmen: "We've found your notebook, if you'll come to lost and found with us and identify it we'll return it to you and you'll be back here in half an hour." So I went to Convictskaya Street Police and identified and signed paper for it and soon as I signed the detective's face froze and he spoke, "On sketchy examination we suspect that this book contains illegal writings so we are holding it for the public prosecutor." Next morning at breakfast downtown I was picked up with student friend I knew slightly who volunteered to stay with me that day make sure I didn't have troubles and taken to Convictskaya Street again, same plainclothesmen, brought upstairs to office with 5 pudgy-faced eyeglassed bureaucrats around polished table: "Mr. Ginsberg we immigration chiefs have received many complaints from parents scientists and educators about your sexual theories having a bad effect on our youth, corrupting the young, so we are terminating your visa." They said the notebook would be returned by mail, may be. I explained that I was waiting for Hungarian telegram, and if that didn't work out had plane ticket to London so could leave on my own the next day, and it would be more diplomatic and spare them the embarrassment of exiling the May King if they left it to me to go voluntarily. I certainly didn't want to get kicked out of ANOTHER socialist country. And it might be difficult to explain to the students etc. Deaf ears, incompetent bureaucracy again. So was taken out to hotel and sat in my room with detective all afternoon and not allowed phone call to Writer's Union or U.S. Embassy or friends and put secretly on plane for London that afternoon and pretty girl I knew who was receiving LSD thereby at state mental hospital met me at hotel door wanted to speak with me but cop stepped in between us. At airport the eyeglass bureaucrat said humorously "Is there any last message you want to deliver to the young lady who met you at the door of your hotel?" Also the last I saw of my student guard from breakfast, he was being pushed around a little and asked for identity papers by the police on Konvictskaya Street as I was being led upstairs in elevator. So I flew off to England on plane, and kept my mouth shut again. I didn't want to make a stink or get anybody I knew connected with me in scandal there, so was discreet from May 7 on when I flew in air to England and also wrote a nice poem *Kral Majales*, I'll send you in a month when printed—big paranoid hymn about being May King sleeping with laughing teenagers—and landed in England and found Bob Dylan (folk singer, you remember, I had his record in Havana?) was there spent days with him watching him besieged by a generation of longhaired English ban-the-bomb girls and boys in sheepskin coats with knapsacks—and in his Savoy hotel spent a drunken night talking about pot and William Blake with the Beatles, gave a few small readings in London Liverpool Newcastle Cambridge and met my NY girlfriend there, made more film and had a birthday party after reading at Institute Contemporary Arts, took off all my clothes at 39th birthday party drunk singing and dancing naked, the Beatles came at midnight and got scared and ran away laughing over their reputations, then Voznesensky came to town and we met again—we'd seen each other another night in Warsaw—and Corso and Ferlinghetti came over from Paris so we hired Albert Hall and filled it with 6,000 hairy youths and bald middle-aged men of letters, Indira Gandhi and Voznesensky sitting at my side holding hands, 17 poets English German Dutch all read, Voznesensky shy to read because *Daily Worker* wrote it up as anticapitalist antiwar demonstration and perhaps too political for his visit, Neruda said he'd come read but didn't, went to some official university scheduled for him alas instead, big funny night all the poets filled with wine, a lot of bad poetry and some good, but everybody happy and England waked poetically a little. A few nights later Ferlinghetti, Corso and I read at Architectural Assn. together and Fernandez and Voznesensky and another Georgian poet came, I read from *Kaddish* and Gregory read *Bomb* poem and last Voznesensky got up and read like a lion from his chest, poem dedicated to all artists of all countries who gave life and blood for poesy, poem imitating sound of Moscow bells in Kremlin towers, he read better than anyone and was happy and came up and kissed me after and stuck his tongue in my mouth like a Russian should in Dostoyevsky, we said goodbye, then I flew to Paris but had no money left I'd taken no money for Albert Hall or other readings so had to walk street all night with Corso first night and finally slept a week upstairs in Librarie Mistral bookstore room with customers sitting on bed reading Mao Tse-tung at 10 AM when I woke, and flew back to NY on still-valid Cuban ticket, arrived in NY and as I entered customs was stopped by U.S. guards and taken into room and searched, they collected the lint from my pockets looking for marijuana. I was scared, I'd stayed with Tom Maschler a few weeks in London and he'd given me his old clothes and I didn't know what he'd ever had in his pockets, but they found nothing tho they stripped me down to my underwear. I saw their letter of orders they negligently left on the desk face upwards "Allen Ginsberg (reactivated) and Peter Orlovsky (continued)—These persons are reported to be engaged in smuggling narcotics..." and meanwhile back in England on May 18 I heard rumors and got phone calls from journalists and found that the Czech Youth Newspaper had big article attacking me as dope fiend homosexual monster who'd abused Prague hospitality, so they didn't have enough sense to shut up about their own idiocy. They didn't report any accusations I hadn't already said myself publicly in my own way, I never made a secret of the fact that I smoke pot and fuck any youth that'll stand still for it, orgies etc., that's exactly the reason they elected me May King in the first place—aside from Mantras and Poesy—the journalese rhetoric like in an old creaky movie—and they published a drawing and a few selected pieces of dirty writing from my notebook —properly censored so as not to be too offensive—suppressed the fact that I'd been elected May King while they were at it. Anyway the police there still have my notebook and some poems I didn't copy out—fortunately they can't destroy it or they destroy their own evidence so it's safe—probably in fact copies of it are being passed around and read by amused littérateurs in the Party, it'll find its way down to the students in time even and back to me in 1972 in Outer Mongolia from the hands of a lamaist monk who practices ancient tantric sex yoga or Neruda will find it in his Ambassador hotel room drawer next time he visits Prague.

So back in NY after I got thru Kafkian customs search I came home, dopefiends had visited and robbed Peter Orlovsky's Indian harmonium and my last typewriter and then we came out to San Francisco to a Berkeley University poesy conference with Creeley and Olson and Gary Snyder and more raving barefoot apocalyptic teenagers. This country slowly revealing its total madness also, I wound up with the Berkeley student sit-in demonstrators singing mantras thru microphone to them in front of courthouse where they were going to be tried by judges. I'm supposed to take part October 16 in more teach-in protests, meanwhile with Guggenheim money award I bought Volkswagen transistorized camper miniature bus-trailer that rides 65 mph and lasts 10 years or more with bed and icebox and writing desk and radio and tiny closets inside and now riding thru redwood forests and reading maps and visiting Snyder's northwest youth country to climb maybe Mt. Olympus before he goes back to Zen monastic studies this fall. We get up in morning with his girlfriend and read a chapter of the 100,000 Songs of Mila-Repa (Tibetan 12th Century saint poet all about illusion and dream stuff of universe) (and flying thru the air)— stopped over in friend's household with children and cats and typewriter, everybody now asleep but me it's midnight past, so I shut up with *abrazos* and *saludos* and *dosvedanyas* and *laegitos, feliz* and *fatiguado, adios por uns momentito Shri Shivati Comrade Comanchero* Sir Zeus Nicanor, *Senor.*

Love

Allen

[After his trip to the Northwest with Gary Snyder, Ginsberg stayed in San Francisco for a few months and became more involved with the anti–Vietnam War movement. That involvement led to renewed correspondence with his father about the morality of the war.]

Allen Ginsberg [San Francisco, CA] to Louis Ginsberg [Paterson, NJ] November 19, 1965

Dear Louis:

Been even more involved in Berkeley march than I expected; all the poets here got together to give a reading & raise money for the Vietnam Day Committee. The last march a swastika-studded band of crazy motorcyclists, the Hells Angels, attacked the march & were threatening to turn tomorrow's into a riot; all the newspapers played up the threat, the Oakland police opposed the march & so everyone was afraid the police would let the Angels through as they did last time; all the VDC Marxists began talking counter violence and a dangerous situation was developing. I went down 70 miles to San Jose College to get on a platform with some representatives of the Hells Angels last week and did what I could to head them off; then the other night Neal Cassady & I and Ken Kesey went privately to their house, had a party with a lot of marijuana and LSD, sang and danced & talked to them till some kind of communication began getting thru. They're paranoid, the police state conditions here fall heaviest on them as they're stupid and brutal and sensitive, all products of the last Korean war, they think the communists are going to come here and liquidate them, that the march is a communist march (both last opinions they picked up from the *Oakland Tribune* & U.P.I. and A.P. and SF Hearst *Examiner*) and so the only way to defend the country and themselves is to attack the marchers (mostly apolitical teahead pacifist bohemians) with chains. At San Jose State I began singing Buddhist hymns, tried not to debate or argue but to inquire & explain. The audience mostly hostile, laughing & cheering—1000 young healthy Americans—when the Angels promised to come out & attack the march, I got up and asked if they really wanted to see wounds blood unhappiness on the march and a great youthful roar of "Yeah!" came up out of the crowded cafeteria where we were gathered with news photographers & TV cameramen. "You want to see UNhappiness?" "Yeah we want Unhappiness!" This a specially conservative provincial school with second-rate teachers, not like the larger universities, but the temper of the crowd was so sick I was surprised—the corruption of U.S. consciousness now advanced to a point enough to make even you ashamed. At the party a few nights later we did better & the

Angels promised nonviolence & anyway the Oakland mayor got a court order he had to protect the march and so called out the State troops & National Guard—to protect a political parade! This sickness is the same sickness as your constantly reverting to calling me a communist—the same screams of the crowd "Pinkos, cowards, Commies, draft dodgers, etc., etc."

I'm not an absolutist and naturally everybody has different opinions and sees things different but even THAT role-playing is over inasmuch as at this point it is necessary for everybody to compromise and come to one mental place where the diversity can exist, lest the earth be destroyed by this vast bomb which is not the atom bomb but the egotistical rage & frustration which you see daily in the editorial columns & screams of parade attackers. Free to his own opinion etc. but the U.S. has carried that too far in Vietnam at this point and now it's not Johnson or McNamara at fault it's the whole U.S.A. and how this country will ever get out of its Karma, how it will ever get out of having to pay for all that suffering and blood, I don't understand.

As you remember a year or more ago we differed on other matters but one thing we did agree on, you agreed on, that the Vietnam War was a farce and stupid policy. Since then we've totally changed policy—at the time we were only advisors to a South Vietnam effort. The rationalizations are now all different, it's our war now even if the South Vietnamese don't want it—(and if you can find any scrap of printed paper saying the South Vietnamese DO want it you'll send it to me despite that every day you can read exactly the opposite in the foreign press or even in the U.P.I. dispatches—that Vietcong would win an election because the people are so sick of the U.S.A.—that South Vietnam army no longer interested, many deserters, that there's no Government except one general who likes Hitler as an ideal, etc.), but now I don't understand how you changed your position to correspond to this last year's government change of tactics???????????? You began against the war, now that it's got serious thru U.S. escalation you're suddenly for it? In 12 months? Now you're saying it's not a civil war? It's Chinese absolutism threatening world peace? It's EVERYBODY'S stupid absolutism threatening world peace including yours, Louis Ginsberg, and now you got blood on your hands.

And if you don't like that, sit on it. You're just like the Germans under Hitler and all your talk since 19Alpha is the same hypocrisy. They were trapped in history and so are you. And if I get my head busted tomorrow in Oakland walking along singing with my finger cymbals it'll be a piece of the same television-hypnosis hysteria you carry in your heart that did it. That's what Karma is.

Okay, enough of my own hysteria on you. I was kinder to the idiot Hells

Angels than I am being to you. But you're supposed to be more responsible so the frustration I feel is—ugh, I give up. This kind of screaming at you certainly doesn't change your mind because it backs you up into a position where you have to defend yourself. And that, as usual in our letters, only brings violence back from you in answer to my own violence.

But I see why LeRoi Jones gives up on the U.S. whites.

This prophesy Merlin shall make for I live before his time: the next great war crises for the U.S. will be in South America. For the last 8 years since everybody including you got conscious of the fact that there was a severe economic problem there, and that the answer would be either Communism or U.S. sponsored total reform, the U.S. has been putting in small amounts of minimal reform, not enough even to make up for the increasing social degradation, and pouring in large amounts of military energy there, cultivating right wing juntas etc. Dominica a perfect example. In ten years there'll be a large scale war with U.S. on one side and nationalist communists on the other side. And the reason it'll be all communist (at worst) is because the U.S. refused to let the steam escape any other way. And at that time it'll be the same paranoid U.S. cry, "It's us or them folks hurry up and get in the barroom brawl." Exactly as now in Vietnam. Even though even you know (or knew a year ago) that North Vietnam was trying to ESCAPE from Chinese domination and was taking the soviet side of the sinosoviet dispute. The one consequence of the war you're approving will be to FORCE on the Vietnamese exactly the thing you think you're trying to prevent. You'll force them to side with China. And then you'll blame China for having paranoid world-conquest ambitions. Meanwhile the idiot masters of Communism and Capitalism will be rubbing their hands and gathering police state power everywhere. The Pentagon & McNamara, etc. are mirror images of the Chinese bureaucracy. But I must say it's disgusting after years hearing you complain about flip-flops in the party line to see you doing a total flip-flop in your opinions on the Vietnam war. Which should show that the old party line you were so angry about was not an EVIL thing, just a thing of subtle belief & exposure to imagery, as your flip-flop has been.

And don't say it hasn't been a flip-flop because we discussed this for the last years and you were always very dubious of the Vietnam War, and there's been nothing since (including the Stevenson last conversations) to change one's mind except a continuous barrage of overheated imagery in the papers & a lot of pictures and soft soap on television.

And if for 10 years I've been screaming like a paranoid nut about Mass Hypnosis—this is a perfect example of it in action.

I also saw it in action at the first Vietnam march, attacked physically, attacked by "patriots" as seditious—attacked by Humphrey as seditious—and now suddenly in the last week now that war-dissent has become respectable in the newsprint of Reston Lippman & The Courts—suddenly legal and healthy. But there were a few dangerous days last month when those who organized the march were preparing for sedition trials. And if the wind had blown that way, I could not have depended on you to know the difference.

And that's why I always get so bugged! MY OWN FATHER caught in the same mass hysteria and sadisms that is dragging planet to radioactive shit. My own high minded ex-socialist liberal family!

Well enough of my vomit. I'll write in a few days. I spent the last week running around from VDC to Hells Angels to newspapers to insure the march would be peaceful so I wouldn't get my skull bashed on the streets.

"Apollinaire: now is the time for prophesy without death as a consequence."

as ever

Allen

This is a disgusting letter to write you. At least it's better than the napalm you're paying for and approving and justifying to your son. Oughta be ashamed of yourself at your age. But this tone of letter leaves no room for someplace to agree in. Forgive me. I'll be more calm when the parade anxiety's over.

[With Ginsberg's encouragement, many of his old friends had become authors. At long last Herbert Huncke's book, Huncke's Journal, *was published by Diane di Prima, and Allen wrote to congratulate Herbert.]*

**Allen Ginsberg [San Francisco, CA] to Herbert Huncke [New York, NY]
December 5, 1965**

Dear Herbie:

Everything here building toward more harmony, hints and scattered glimpses of the last 2 decades now becoming more manifest and natural making a continuity of high awareness and a public community emerging each person contributing his own privately experienced unthought-of discovery of light/unity/self nature to the common outer world by action or talk or song or print, and the Them of all we envision begins to show up in bookstores and airwaves and even on the hats of kids in gas stations. I begin to feel the societal meanness and pain—like the China war—as just fear and suffering which grows acute because changes are coming on so fast one after another. Things unthinkable 10 years ago like our Word spread serious, like, I'm bald browed, or astronauts with long hair soon, or the *Eve of Destruction* broadcast to teenage home ears, or Dylan's mysterious spirit speech, or Russia turning young again, or sexual blackout for teenagers ended with high school kid flashlights on cancer lunch under the covers or on the bedstead, Hells Angels high on LSD listening to Cosmos-is-Maya songs chanted to them / as if it were all pre-arranged by Universe-Cinemascope in déjà-vu, movies of world's end apocalypse or else Buck Rogers space universal coming true scene by scene. Anyway seeing your blue first edition journal cover with "Huncke's" in gay nineties-twenties type unexpectedly in City Lights was like seeing a comet or climbing a snowy mountain and reaching clear rock peaks and sitting down to look at the blue earth-gas in panorama low land valley floors and wondering how it could be so that the big heavy mountain was finally climbed to its grogtop since when we began way down below looking up at a real earth-god big mountain such as there were only library pictures of in Junior High School.

Your own book is the most interesting new truthful word-text I've read in recent years-era. You can't imagine how awesome it is, how helpful, how magically influential on our same life as I know it, that what seemed real drops seeming and is here now for good. Once you completely manifest yourself in these detailed fragments, and the world has you out front like a big elephant-rock you can actually see and point out and look at up close.

What's truthful in the book is that it's a writing that's by itself, for god knows who, which makes it raw (not like most art objects) nature, a part of life itself like on Uncle Fireside Story told so the family could know really who felt what in Newark some recent years. It feels truthful, the truth being an accurate record of you, a close version of whatever you know you are, close enough to be identical with your self-thought and inside noticing of all the scenes, written the only way it comes out without trying to "improve" your real nature's image by calculated rearrangement of your story. So it's like nature of things.

I keep getting glimpses of that, like recognitions of the actual scene as we know it so familiar but rare in conscious reflection and rarer in permanent writ-memory.

What I mean is your original self as I've always contacted it to be, is the same as the way the book is; and the closeness between your nature and your written version of what you're minded of, is a rare thing in art (somehow not many people can come up with that simple such-ness in prose or poetry) and is absolutely precious vital social serum against the effects of mass-bulk false (like mis-comprehending mis-interpreting mis-reporting mis-taking) word products wholesale broadcast Niagaras an hour in everybody's consciousness.

I'm meaning to say, one straight record like <u>Cuba</u> or <u>In the Park</u> or <u>Youth</u> to take the most obvious, (or <u>Old Elsie</u>)—one straight account like that is so recognizably true to what lie is, and true to what everybody's natural sympathy feels like—true even to what one time or other at least, everybody has experience in his own scene—true to everybody's first native mammal reaction—true to everybody's inside knowledge—that it has the effect of waking or reaffirming that sleeping or timid self-recognition—and (offhand or incomplete, or dubiously or hastily jotted as you may have felt them to be during or after writing, unsatisfactory) because it does so clearly show some real, native, undisguised self to any reader's obscure unaware self, that it can cut thru all the illusions of prejudice identity opinion—Cut thru millions of copies of official Time Digest Righteous Viewpoint language—and touch the actual huge nature underneath even the worst heart in the long run—and bring lost people back to them selves, back home to the original feeling for life.

Now all this I guess is really obvious to you, I'm only scribbling to you at such length the same repeated thought because (maybe out of some lack of confidence in your efforts) you always do say when low down that maybe your writings have no real value or function or purpose to yourself or anyone else for that matter, and why bother to publish them? I'm trying to explain clearly what is the value function purpose to the whole central population organized nation community. Which is now as you know so lost in the head it's like to be the end of the whole show. Or the mind could be clarified in us and we transmit that clarity as you do in the book and it will certainly have an effect on others, that will return to you in the long run too.

So the point is, you have good reason to do something now about the larger manuscript—how many pages now 600?—and make an active effort to be sure all the scattered fragments are collected and arranged in some indicative order, and maybe whatever lesser material there is (less lively) cut out,—or better blue penciled in but retaining only associated phrases and sentences that are lively and pure, linked with "…" to show you painted out the background for the gems. That's the easiest most natural way, Williams recommend it—(if a poem has only 2 good lines, get rid of the poem and publish the 2 lines, there's no reason a poem should be look finished or complete if the completion is shitty or unreal or just to make it look apparently complete) (he said and that's how I prepared manuscript of *Empty Mirror*, from masses of journal jottings I boiled it down to those essential lines and fragments of writing that were interesting).

The present journals volume looks to me all high order writings. Is the rest of 600 p. manuscript the same as good? I thought of the title *Confessions* years ago but don't know now if it's appropriate. (I meant like St. Augustine's or Rousseau's *Confessions*).

Is the manuscript ready to submit to a publisher? I won't be back in N.Y. till February or March but no reason you or Ella or Clive or someone—Sanders perhaps—could not start circulating it. Perhaps try Grove first. Ferlinghetti wants to see the manuscript too. You could give him an hundred page book; and then arrange to have that and Di Prima's volume reprinted with the rest of the bulk by a hardcover NY publisher in a year or 2 or just go directly to Fred Jordan at Grove Press; or Jason Epstein at Random House etc. etc. I can send you more names and places but why not start there now? Probably 3 or 4 will reject it before one finally can see in the book what it is. If you do go to Grove or Random, tell them I advised you to and show them this letter too if they need any convincing.

Please send me a card (before the week is out because I'm leaving here December 15) let me know what the status of the manuscript is.

(If you feel that there's more editing to do, Irving Rosenthal you know is really handy at that if he's willing. If publisher wants to edit, better have it checked with Irving anyhoo.)

Everything socially here is very dramatic and charming. I see a lot of McClure, a lot of new young poetry and LSD and longhair anarchist boys, I've been active in the Berkeley Vietnam (anti?) war manifestation, mainly showing up, talking tranquilly to cool the revolutionary radical righteous hysteria freaks and singing peaceful mantras (I've learned some new Zen ones from Snyder) on the parades—to marchers and police both. Got in the middle of a Dadaist Happening, the Hells Angels (genuinely anticommunist motives but all sensitive dumb paranoid) versus the marchers. Now made friends with the Angels and cooled them out—sang mantras to them too—while Neal and friend novelist Ken Kesey turned them on to LSD—we had a big party 2 nites before the threatened riot scene and that (plus threat of state troops) cooled everything for peaceful communion march thru spade section of Oakland.

I see Neal all the time, he and Anne [Murphy] his love slave dearie stay over

here in Julius' bed several nites a week. Neal has entered new space-age dimen-
sion—all his old energy still full steam but after 13 years railroad 2 ^{1}/$_2$ years jail
and now divorced and years of intensive pot and then all the reincarnation spir-
itualist cult monomanias and several years obsession with the racetrack where
he lost about $10,000—and now several year's omnivorous absorption of
amphets by mouth ("jumpers" he says) and company with huge crowds of
young Zonk-minded admirers, lovers of his legend, like, devotees of his energy
and speed—he's become a sort of fantastic continuously talking (on 7 or 8 lev-
els of simultaneous association) teacher plus the fact that for 2 or 3 years he's
gone into the LSD mind too, also omnivorously more than even Barbara Rubin
and friends did. Super expert master of Acid and Dar T etc.—in company with
a huge clownish Utopian gang at house—commune in peninsula back roads
woods of a novelist, friend Ken Kesey, who's taken over appreciating him in his
later phases as Jack once did. I think I told you or you heard about their big bus?
all painted psychedelic ultraviolet orange green blue covered now with
swastikas and hammer sickles and U.S. eagles and every conceivable identity
emblem painted neatly along sides of the bus—and they go on trips to Idaho
or L.A. everybody on acid including Neal the super-driver (it's on the road in a
mad '60s dimension) hallucinating the gas pedal's turned to spaghetti, but able
to find his way thru side phantom cockroaches and deliver everybody safely—
him sweating and talking furiously with tape microphone hanging over his
head in driver's cab and movie cameras grinding and radio hooked to loud-
speaker atop the bus (where 6 or 7 youths and maids dressed in red white blue
striped sweatshirts and pants and purple magic shoes lie around on mattress
smoking grass)—and on this trip, said Neal the bus had no clutch, brake or
reverse—he got all the way to Idaho and back, and thru a Calif. forest fire burn-
ing on both sides of the road.

   Bob Dylan here a week and I see him every day and talk about poesy and
fame and Eden Desolation—we may do something together, he produce a
record of my mantras or a TV show or I act in a movie or who knows.

   I wrote a lot, poems, letters—and a huge First Manifesto to End the Bring-
down on the subject of pot. Maybe we'll break thru soon, I do think—on
many levels—work hard.

   Love,

   Allen

[*Throughout his life, Ginsberg continued to promote his friends and fellow poets, as in this letter to Philip Lamantia. The proposed anthology he mentioned here never materialized.*]

Allen Ginsberg [New York, NY] **to Philip Lamantia** [Malaga, Spain]
August 20, 1966

Dear Philip:

Thanks for your letter & anyway post-belated answer to universe questions, all our sad language so charming, the effort. Can you reprint text of the *Poetry* mag letter? I hate bullshitting and I sorta codified formulated articulated thoughts about you there. Anyway, also, following project: for Random House, they asked me to do an anthology, I said no too much work & I haven't finished editing my own scribbles, but did propose an easier maybe more useful book: put together 5 or 6 poets whose work is great but not much yet published or if finely published not sufficiently available & circulated among 1966 youths like on street or in colleges. They said OK and I specified 40 pages each about, of 1) Sanders Russell because tho he write recent interesting Harlem works he never had much out, & Rexroth fiendishly urges; 2) Ed Sanders because he's funny 3) Lew Welch because he's readable in 40 pages; 4) Ted Berrigan because he's exemplary of a whole new generation style growing out of O'Hara (now dead run over by a beach taxi in Fire Island *aetat.* 40 a month ago), Ashbery & Koch, and also because Berrigan's poor & never had book but mimeo 5) Orlovsky because I sleep with him and he has about 40 pages perfect collected works & noplace students can find him in bulk 6) yourself Lamantia because tho you have books they are hardly in circulation in the provinces. The volume would be a handy gas for younger & older heads, because all the poets are different, eccentric & rare one way or another—there's no consistency of purpose except a handy place to set forth under-circulated blossoms in sufficient bulk to attract bees. Then I'll have to write some general preface or short note on the poets, each.

Is this alright with you? My only requirement at Random was that there be no censorship, any shit goes, and that I do no work but their editor (Richard Billow) take care of all details & correspondence—he may have written you already.

So if it's agreeable for you to make that scene, can you put together your signal classic work from youth to now, or else any mass of 40 pages new compositions, or what you will, or do you want me to select out of *Ekstasis* & *Destroyed Works* & *Blue Grace*, etc.? I have my favorites that I think would please or teach readers but maybe you got some special idea what you want. The book in any case is free & open. Let me know what to do. Money I guess will be routine, royalties divided equally 7 ways including me. Please address all correspondence except high esthetic or urgent to Billow. He'll collect manuscript or books for me, like, secty. [...]

Can't find anything to differ with in your summation. I just don't know what's going on. We've all seen visions, & they come & go & fade; and the world fades too; so either way it's all mysterious & apparently beyond my 1:30 AM Aug 20 '66 brainbody comprehension. Jack calls drunk from Massachusetts. He wants to move to Florida and I'm stealing his prosody; Peter went out to get second crazy brother to live with us (Julius and Lafcadio) tonite; Bob Dylan is a wizard; & my father's 71 yrs old.

Fatigue tonite

Allen

[*Ginsberg also continued to lecture politicians about their various mistakes.*]

Allen Ginsberg [New York, NY] to Leo Cherne[56] [New York, NY] December 3, 1966

Dear Mr. Cherne:

According to Mr. Scheer's pamphlet you were considerably involved in creating the situation that led to the authoritarian violent rule of President Diem in South Vietnam.

As you know and as it says in both Western and Eastern wisdom books, violence leads only to more violence. Use of the word Freedom on the House over which you are Chairman is an abuse of language inasmuch as the House is not promoting freedom by continuing to promote violence. As in most cases, proposals for the use of force and violence on the general polis are projections of internal psychic conflict by the proposer.

It would seem proper that you begin purifying your own motive and sense of self hood, rather than continuing to further complicate the original mistakes made a decade ago in the external world, as a consequence of your own misjudgment.

This letter rises as consequence of a letter signed by you in *Times* December

56 Leo Cherne (1912–1999). Presidential advisor on economics.

3, 1966, in which you continue to sanction the use of violence in resolving our primarily emotional problems in Vietnam.

The war is, and all war is, and always was, a consequence of personal aberration, not some mysterious consequence of non-human forces. Your own and my own personal aberrations are involved here as well as the obvious personal aberrations and fantasies of Eisenhower, Dulles, Max Lerner, etc. as well as the rest of the body politic.

Certainly after so many false starts, I should think you would be willing to be quiet for a while and more introspective, and try to make yourself peaceful. It will do you no harm to be able to die-in-life as many virtuous men have done. Continued justification of your own past Karma (Action) serves neither you nor me nor our fellow citizens any peaceful purpose.

Thank you for your attention.

Yours,

Allen Ginsberg, Poet.

[*Ginsberg could not sit still and ignore poor scholarship and criticism when it came to the Beat Generation. He continually corrected authors wherever he perceived errors. In this letter to the publisher of one critical text, Allen documented the precursors and visionary importance of his own generation of writers.*]

Allen Ginsberg [New York, NY] to Monarch Notes [New York, NY] December 3, 1966

Dears Messrs. Roy, Cooperman, Leavitt and Violi:

I wandered thru 8th Street Bookshop in NY last night and encountered your Monarch Notes "Beat Literature" pamphlet which I purchased and read with a good deal of dismay.

I realize that the author Mr. G. Roy was sympathetic and had friendly and objective intentions, and had done some research; but the scholarship displayed in the book is so incomplete, and the judgments and perceptions therefore so inaccurate (albeit sympathetic), and the inclusions and exclusions so arbitrary; and, finally, the information so dated—circa 1960 I'd guess—that the book will prove a stumbling block to understanding for young people rather than an educational help. In brief, problem with the book, is that it reflects the limited relatively unscholarly popular arguments pro and con circa 58–60: many of the arguments have been clarified or rendered obsolete by documents, events, texts, and changes of mind by the very critics cited, since those days—so that in effect, what is presented to students 1966 is an anachronistic and misleading critique, very vague in its generalizations, and worst of all, lacking even an out for the students to do their own research since the bibliography presented is so dated and meager and journalistic and, simply, incomplete.

I would not bother to write, as I have more urgent personal business preparing texts of collected poems for Grove and collected essays etc. for Random House and a lot of other projects. Besides since you have already issued your pamphlet there's little hope of changing it or its effects on young people. But I am interested in education and for that reason do teach and write prose and give readings of poetry in colleges, and I despair when I see the incompetence of your Monarch pamphlet and realize that it will set another whole generation of unspecialized innocent students off on the wrong track again. And it will make more work for me and other artists who follow to clarify, over and over again, a few simple ideas, and inform, despite or in spite of your scholarly efforts, where texts are to be found and what texts are relevant.

So I thought I would write anyway.

In brief the flaw of the book is that the thinking, reading and analysis is all dated, as I said the book smells of popular yatter of 1959–61, discussions like "are they positive or negative?" "Do they abandon form?" "Are they posing?" etc. This is all such dreary irrelevant occupation for eager contemporaries. For instance the main insights presented by the beat writers of the 50s 1) the literal possibility of new modes of consciousness 2) the literal bankruptcy of Cold War society—these are themes by now much more clearly realized and taken seriously and experienced by the generation grown up during Vietnam War and LSD. The whole wasted discussion of "is their rebellion a pose?" etc. was possible in 1960 but less useful circa 1965–1966 when professors of English at Columbia also take LSD and marijuana and march desperately in peace marches.

Regarding serious purely literary matters: The best anthology, the most famous anthology, containing all our work, also containing expositions of literary method and composition and prosody, is the Don Allen *New American Poetry 1945–60* — which is completely ignored. It is the one invaluable reference book—instead your students are given journalistic trivia like Manville's *Saloon Society* which not even I have read.

The choice of representative "Beat" writers is localized primarily to those represented in a pre-1960s issue of *Evergreen Review:* heavy emphasis on Levertov,

Everson (Brother Antoninus) and Duncan as Beat writers. They were always friendly poets and associates, but disclaimed often the Beat label for themselves. On the other hand poets like Robert Creeley, Gary Snyder (mentioned but hardly discussed), Philip Whalen, Philip Lamantia, Charles Olson and a whole raft of others, all now very influential and respectable even, who did not disclaim the Beat label, but participated in readings with us and magazine publications, and who were, early (1957–62) damned with Corso, Kerouac, etc. as mere Beats, are completely excluded from consideration. Naturally it is hard to decide on who to label what: but if Duncan, Levertov, Antoninus are examined as specimens of Beat, it is hard to understand what happened to Creeley and Snyder, etc.

This is important because we now find Snyder after 10 years Zen study in Japan leading psychedelic ritual-tantric movements in San Francisco and marching with me in NY Peace Parades, carrying his Bollingen Award for scholarly studies under his arm. And we find Creeley reforming English studies at NMU and Buffalo U., armed with Guggenheim as myself, the unmentioned LeRoi Jones, etc. This obviated a good deal of the 1958–60 argument as to what our relation to "society" is.

The point I'm making is—the choice of representative poets, criticism of them, etc.—all dates to that issue of *Evergreen*—and that is not scholarship on Mr. Roy's part—that is, in effect, as if he read cursorily in the popular items of that day and then stopped reading except to add a few books to Burroughs' or my list of bibliographized items circa 1965.

Further, the dead horse of what is acceptable lasting literature—kicked over and over—seems to depend on texts 1956–7. Hardly anything on *Kaddish* or later works of mine; nothing about Burroughs' work after 1960 which now seems the most influential among young—the cut-up method—obviously nothing of Olson's *Maximus* or Creeley's prose or poetry, much less Hubert Selby Jr. much less that later appearing but earlier described Herbert Huncke. In short a misleading mess for a young kid trying to get into the actual literature. In fact this book will lead students away from the material rather than draw them in to explore for themselves.

No technical discussion of methods of composition and prosody is even approached: a major defect. Nothing but the vaguest generalizations. Whereas there are innumerable reference documents at hand especially in the Grove Press Anthology edited by Don Allen—which might have clarified the whole specific problem of "form" so much loosely gossiped about in your Monarch pamphlet.

In regard to prose the lacunae are amateur again. Brossard, Broyard and a few others were considered hip Beat writers around 1956–7 but have not figured in much actual literary history. Prose by Creeley, Selby, Burroughs' *Naked Lunch* and after—all the writers anthologized in LeRoi Jones' anthology *The Moderns* such as himself and Mike Rumaker and later Kerouac—are all ignored and supplanted by the dated middlebrow publicity of 1957. And page one's introduction to prose doesn't even mention the work of Burroughs, who historically and categorically was and is considered much more integral to the whole movement than Brossard. His influence is mentioned as if his texts were of no account or didn't exist.

On page 7 a slipshod account of prosody presents Charles Farber as representative, as a "sample" but it simply is not, historically, a "sample" major text of the "movement" if we are considering "beat" literature to be a movement. Why of all people Farber? What happened to the major writers like Lamantia and McClure and Whalen and Snyder, etc. Farber's work is—well, again, I heard of him in late 50s but don't even know his work. Why are you referring students to this irrelevant and almost unobtainable text as a relevant typology?

Page 10 Historical Background is completely ill-informed with the inclusions of Mallarme and Verlaine as salient influences, Yeats, Baudelaire, etc. None of the poets mentioned as primary "Beats" used much Mallarme, much less Yeats or Verlaine. Creeley, unmentioned in your sketch, did use Mallarme however.

Had you included Snyder and Whalen as Beat poets you might justifiably have used Rexroth as a forerunner: as it is he is not a forerunner of anybody you do mention except Antoninus and Levertov—the latter however disclaims Beat connections. Your list of favorite forerunners leaves out the real influences on me and Kerouac—in fact it's just a mess. No reality to the generalizations, just a composite of vague 2nd rate uninformed patchwork which doesn't indicate any real direction. Kerouac for instance has as primary source Shakespeare, so has Corso and Burroughs and myself—yet Shakespeare is discounted as a source. Gregory Corso and I did like Marlowe and Shelley—and I, Keats—and Smart particularly, and Apollinaire and Blake, and Melville's poetry, and Thomas Hardy, and Basil Bunting, and Catullus—all this is spelled out in various essays published. Why are we referred, contrariwise, to Kenneth Patchen and e. e. cummings? Patchen and cummings had NO influence on 1) Kerouac 2) Corso 3) Burroughs 4) Myself much less Snyder Whalen McClure. They did have some influence on Ferlinghetti.

St. Jean Perse, Céline and Genet did always have influence on Kerouac myself Burroughs and everybody—they're unmentioned. The traditional stable of U.S. influences mentioned are so irrelevant and vague as to be misleading to the student. Gide Kafka Hemingway etc. Just ridiculous. Of course we read all that, but we practically advertised for 10 years Melville's prose, and Céline and Genet, and Dostoyevsky.

In sum your literary background paragraphs are ill informed and will misinform the young reader—who would be better pointed to Korzybski, Spengler, Suzuki, Yeats' *Vision*, Smart, Céline, Genet, Artaud, Michaux, Shakespeare, Melville's poetry and prose in *Pierre,* Emily Dickinson, Apollinaire, Cendrars, Perse, Mayakovsky, Yessenin, Lorca's *Poet in New York,* etc. Your analysis is so vague and ill informed as to be totally useless. To the student.

Furthermore Lewis and Fitzgerald (p. 11) had no influence on those you cite as prose beat writers. Flat and simple as that. Wyndham Lewis yes, Gertrude Stein yes obviously influenced the dissociational improvisation of Kerouac, the speech of Selby, the psychological-state scientism of Burroughs. But all of this scholarly notation is on record by 1963 in various essays by everybody.

The main misconception of course, which leads to the overemphasis on Sinclair Lewis as a precursor, is that we are primarily concerned with rebellion or social protest—this was, again, the dated terminology of 1958–60 used by popular essay writers who still didn't understand the basically MENTAL TRANSCENDENTALISM we are and were working out; i.e. visionary. Blake was also a social critic and rebel etc. but the ROOT of his work as of ours has been in exploration of modes of consciousness. If this isn't by now obvious then I suggest you all update yourself to what I and Burroughs have been saying for 20 years and actually take a flyer with some LSD. If you can't get the point thru our language then try some extraliterary means. Lewis' basically political materialism is and was basically more inspirational for a political revolution—so he is popular in Russia and Genet unknown—but not for a revolution of psyche in space age.

Yet you have irrelevant page after page on Lewis and Fitzgerald. It's maddening, and reflects the education of Mr. Roy, and not the specificities of the subject he's chosen to examine, namely OUR influences, not his. This inaccuracy reduces the whole study to a nonspecific vague pointless repetition of generalities no different from any other academic school of composition.

Page 27: Mr. Corso is not mad. What a thing to inform students.

Accusations of "phony" madness against Oscar Wilde, whom I find an immensely sympathetic figure of letters, run thru the book as if it were important to the subject at hand. It isn't.

The William Lee referred to on p. 35 will not be recognized by the student as the same Mr. Eminent Burroughs.

1966 why spend so much time on Angries when you have the whole Voznesensky-Yevtushenko Russian complex more parallel; as well as Provos, Stilyagi, mod-rocker London generations, etc. everywhere? Your sociologic evaluations, again, are dated 1958/9. In any case I myself wasn't elected May King 1965 in Prague for any psychic reason or social reason elected by Mr. Roy as relevant.

Page 53 disclaims transatlantic influence while, contrariwise as I have pointed out, Artaud, Céline and Genet, as well as the whole Dada-Surreal-Gertrude Stein scene, were essential to Burroughs, Lamantia, myself, Kerouac, etc.

Paul Dreyfus mentioned p. 55 as "Genuine and effective" beat poet along with di Suvero and others is absolutely ridiculous. There were millions of—or hundreds literally—not very good poets publishing as beat. The ones Mr. Roy mentions were singularly ineffective. Dreyfus! What kind of nonsense are you laying on students 1966? Absolute uninformed claptrap.

I was kicked out of Columbia for being found sleeping in bed with Kerouac not for the reason given p. 61. The whole book is inaccurate literary generalization and gossip. Nor, even, once, did I refer to a bughouse as a laughing academy, same page. Someone else may have. Not my language. Then I'll have to face students in 3 years and answer questions based on this Monarch pamphlet? Ye Gods what horrors you're condemning us all to.

Page 63: The generalizations about my poetry really being iambic are so hopelessly ill-informed and so generalized as to be absolutely misleading to any innocent student trying to figure out what the fuss is all about. Dumb ideas like that because they sound easy will be picked up and passed from head to head like trench mouth exactly as they passed from Mrs. Trilling's head to Mr. Roy's. It's not an accurate comment, and, in addition, not a comment that Mrs. Trilling would stand by 1965–6, actually.

The discussion on poetry-jazz again is dated, and inaccurate: based mostly on Rexroth-Patchen's practice rather than Corso, Kerouac, Ginsberg, Lamantia, John Wieners, etc. AD 1966 the real significance could be found in the developments that lead to Donovan and Dylan—all of which is unmentioned, tho it would be the one aspect that students nowadays have recognized and discussed —relationship between my own practice and Dylan. And mutual influences. Yet this is completely left out in favor of minor attempts (by older others) circa late 50s. In this sense all the data, texts, gossip, and arguments of the book, from Ciardi down, are all obsolete. Because of lack of scholarship since, I would guess, 1960. For a book published 1966 about a living movement, some time-lag is natural, but not such an obvious misjudgment about matters that are not only common knowledge these last few years but popular mythology even in *Life* magazine.

Page 65: Prose "No Revolutionary Developments." This is of course debatable, what is a revolution? But Burroughs' cut-up method—a number of very influential books *Soft Machine* etc.—are not even considered, tho many do consider them revolutionary as I do. Kerouac's spontaneous prose method is obviously influential and revolutionary—affecting my own poetry as well as dozens of others who have Guggenheim grants. So this is generalized over and scanted without proper consideration. Of course since Mr. Roy takes Brossard, Broyard, as his salient beat prose writers and elides Burroughs, Selby, Creeley, Rumaker, etc. then no wonder he sees no change.

Constant reference to Lipton and contemporaries 1960 also dates the book to the first period of the most popularistic uncomprehending criticism. Newer work such as *Paris* or *Partisan Review* begins to put ideas into clearer order (as the middle class moves desperately left Vietnam).

Pages 69–70: Dr. Rigney's book is completely misinterpreted. He concluded that the beats were trying to do something about it mostly. Mr. Roy's emphasis is just the opposite, as will be read by high school or college soph.

Page 69: Venice West is not in San Francisco, it's in L.A.

Counter arguments regarding religion, use of Zen etc. disregards the fact that someone like Snyder (hero of Kerouac *Dharma Bums*) is practically the only U.S. intellectual to have actually spent 10 years in Zen monastery and is now on learned Bollingen; much less the fact that Orlovsky and I spent years in India, learned something, and are now spreading the teaching of mantra chanting with cooperation and approval of qualified swamis, over the U.S., and helping translate and apply Tibetan works, in cooperation with qualified Tibetan Buddhist functionaries here. Thus the arguments and counter-arguments about our use of oriental tradition as amateurs circa 1958 have already been rendered obsolete by public activities quite well publicized since 1963. Instead of factual material your student readers are presented with commonplace generalized debater's point arguments which can lead to no useful knowledge, no practical understanding—not even to useful texts.

Arguments and counterarguments p. 106 as to the durability of texts are arguments that were going on 6 years ago before work by myself Burroughs Kerouac Creeley Lamantia McClure etc. etc. Olson were substantially included in grad school and now often even high school studies, so the information on which this argument proceeds (Ciardi's expostulations circa 1961?) is already obsolete. Furthermore the reference to Burroughs' single work *Naked Lunch* itself. Your students are presented with anachronistic generalizations and half-baked history. How can they make any sense of the whole shot? I couldn't finish reading your book. It didn't really touch on any central spiritual center, the whole psychedelic movement is really left out tho it is a major "social concern" in the U.S. right now to the students that will read the book.

I have written longer than I anticipated when I started this letter. I don't mean to devalue Mr. Roy's intentions and goodwill, I especially appreciate his clear understanding and sympathy in such a controversial consideration as it revealed p. 89. "The beat is a spiritually constructive entity dwelling in a society apparently intent on its own destruction," and that is perhaps the most contemporary insight in the book, or hindsight, as may be.

But it is terrible to think that if students interested in the subject take their verbalizations and articulations and facts and estimates and reasonings and bibliographies from this book they will be left with a completely anachronistic dead horse, instead of a living literature which needs glossing, bibliography, scholarship and mature explanation to protect such literature from the distortions of the popular lowbrow media who would see nothing but rebellion eccentricity and poor manners. Tho lately, the media have been more kind—it's taken a decade and a lot of pot.

A useful book with inclusive survey and discussions of influences from Smart to Céline, Buddhist Tantra, Amerindian Peyotism as influences, a book which puts into perspective the real career of Burroughs, which included McClure and Whalen and Creeley and Olson's influence rather than such poor lost samples as Dreyfus or di Suvero would make sense. But as it is I am afraid your book confuses more than it clarifies and, personally, I hate to think of all the future wasted breath we'll all have to expend trying to undo the vague language the Monarch series is fostering under the guise of scholarship. Alas this book will likely lead students away from texts rather than into them.

I don't know what to suggest you do: scrap it and rewrite it, or forget it altogether. In the long run, while flattered to have my position in letters considered at such length and basically so sympathetically in your pamphlet, I would rather not see it happen at all, and would rather see the book scrapped. It is not only inadequate—it is a stumbling block to understanding. And you have to remember, many youngsters already understand a great deal more than they are given in that book.

Sincerely yours,

Allen Ginsberg

[Ginsberg wanted reporters to be accurate when it came to articles about the use of drugs. In this letter he took the New York Times *to task for referring to marijuana as a narcotic.]*

Allen Ginsberg [San Francisco, CA] to the *New York Times* [New York, NY]
January 24, 1967

Dear Sir:

In a front page report from Tangier, Morocco on December 26, 1966, *Times* reporter Ralph Blumenthal mentions a substance which he refers to as "narcotic kief" and defines as "a local powdered leaf that is mixed with tobacco for a marijuana smoke." He goes on to say that "after Mexico, Tangier is possibly the closest place to the United States where such narcotics can easily be bought."

In its coverage of the drug problem the *Times* has frequently referred to marijuana as a narcotic. In so doing it reflects and helps to maintain a popular misconception about the drug which is also reflected in existing legal penalties.

On October 9, 1966, in a story headed "Marijuana Laws Held Too Severe," the *Times* quoted Dr. Donald Louria, chairman of the New York State Council on Drug Addiction and a professor at Cornell University Medical School as remarking at a Cornell-sponsored symposium on Drugs and the Campus that marijuana, as a mild hallucinogen, must be legally distinguished from heroin, a narcotic. Dr. Louria's classification of marijuana as non-narcotic is not unique in medical circles; as a matter of fact, impartial medical authorities tend to view the drug as a relatively harmless hallucinogen or anti-depressant which differs from narcotics like heroin, morphine, etc. in that it is not physiologically addicting.

The distinction is important because there is a growing body of responsible opinion to the effect that marijuana is a potentially useful drug which has been the victim of a well-intentioned but ill-informed propaganda campaign, and that it is time the harsh penalties for its mere possession were reevaluated. In September, 1962, for example, President Kennedy's White House Conference on Narcotic and Drug Abuse found "long criminal sentences imposed on an occasional user or possessor of the drug" to be "in poor social perspective."

In this period of rapid social change and resulting public confusion, the *Times* can help to improve our understanding of this emotionally loaded subject by using scientifically accurate terminology.

Sincerely yours,

Allen Ginsberg

[Ginsberg did have a sense of humor about some things as he displayed in this letter asking the CIA for $10 million in funding for liberal projects to counterbalance money awarded to conservative groups.]

Allen Ginsberg [New York, NY] to Richard Helms[57] [Washington, DC] *ca.* May 29, 1967

Dear Mr. Helms:

I do not know the appropriate section of your organization to apply to for monies so I am addressing this letter to you.

I am the treasurer of a tax exempt non profit corporation, properly registered and approved by the government. Our national and international activities, tho small, are extremely useful in the artistic world: we supply cash and comfort to artists and poets harried by society, police, themselves and the universe; or ill; or too poor to do their proper work. Monies I receive from poetry readings are made over to Committee on Poetry (COP for short) Inc., and given to poets less fortunate than others.

I notice that the C.I.A. has been giving money to groups rather arbitrarily chosen in the past. I am therefore asking for a proper redress of that secret balance, by means of a large grant from the C.I.A. thru its fronts, or preferably, directly from CIA to COP. I don't see why, in the balance of things, C.O.P. — President Peter Orlovsky, Vice President Ed Sanders of *Fuck You / A Magazine of the Arts* and the Fugs — doesn't deserve equally to receive government stipend as did more conservative socially-minded organizations. In other words if social education is to be paid for, it should not be education so one-sided as to be communally square. Investment in some hip community is only fair. Otherwise one part of the citizenry has been unfairly defrauded of its prerequisites and dignities. And the government may be accused of brainwash. Certainly that is not the conscious intention of the CIA, and if it were it would have to be repudiated.

If your agency does not have information about my own educational activities and those of my fellow trustees, or of the activities of COP, I will be glad to supply more detail. Meanwhile I await your reply. The sum of $10,000,000.00 would be useful the next few years to begin to right the unbalance of cinema, poetry, publishing, legal protection for artists and persons of new consciousness — their poverty and second class alienated status where government

---

57 Richard Helms (1913–2002). Director of the CIA.

monies have been going in more aggressively angry and war making direction, specifically anti-communist in an ambivalently intemperate way.

While I am at it I would like to know if the CIA has a dossier on the undersigned? This may be a paranoid question, but in case of paranoia it is always comforting to check back to the reality, by open question.

Yours truly

Allen Ginsberg

[*In 1967 a controversy arose when a nude photograph of Ginsberg by Richard Avedon appeared in a college newspaper. The offending issue was suppressed and Allen came to the defense.*]

Allen Ginsberg [New York, NY] to Whom It May Concern [Portland, OR] May 29, 1967

Dear Sirs, Journals, Committees, Presidents and Other Poetry Lovers:

Such a great nonsensical flap has been made over the circumstances attending a poetry reading I gave at Portland State University on May 27, 1967, that I would like to add a few clear words and perhaps calm those curious who are calmable.

I arrived in Portland after a reading tour of various respectable universities throughout the nation—private and state supported colleges where I had been invited by student organizations often but mostly by English departments many of which include texts by me in their academic curricula—and had thus visited U of Texas, Iowa State, Kenyon, U of Southern California, Nashville's Vanderbilt, U of New Mexico, U of Colorado, etc., as well as U of Oregon and Oregon State and Reed, the later Portland State's near neighbors.

Monies gained from these poetry readings are all turned over to a pleasant tax exempt educational foundation and redistributed among poets and artists whose work has not been properly rewarded otherwise by larger institutions.

Portland State's student newspaper published a photo story prior to my reading. The text included an inaccurate report that the school had requested and I had complied with a request to behave at Portland State with some especial "propriety." Fortunately for everybody's sanity no such request had been made. It would have been a provincial and ill-educated request: it remains a provincial and ill-educated fantasy.

The fantasy was complicated by the student newspaper's printing a photograph of me by the celebrated photographer Richard Avedon, originally printed in his book on American persons, *Nothing Personal*. The book has been reprinted nationally in paperback, has sold calmly in Portland for a year. The photograph, a remarkable one, is of myself as a poet mostly naked, except that the controversial groin is modestly covered by the left hand with a Buddhist mudra (hand gesture) signifying contemplation. The right hand is raised palm out in Abhya Mudra, gesture of reassurance.

There is nothing in the picture to offend, unless one is offended by the sight of not quite naked person; in which case any slick magazine or local newspaper carrying bathing suit or shower soap advertisements might be found offensive, but they are not.

The fantasy was complicated further by an inaccurate rumor, that in college "performances" I remove my clothes. It is not generally known that I am initiated into a school of Hinduism some members of which do go abroad in the city ash-smeared and naked; this is Shivaite Hinduism but I am not a practicing Naga (naked) holyman. So I have not removed my clothes at a public reading for, alas, ten years. The one occasion in 1957 on which I did remove my clothes is, as an anecdote, too oft repeated (as in an issue of *Life* magazine a year ago) to be worthy of further repetition; but since such a small tale has never reached Portland in accurate form, apparently, I do bear witness that in a private house once upon a time a red haired lush from Hollywood interrupted fellow poet Gregory Corso in the midst of his long poem *Power* and shouted "Whatter you guys tryana prove?" and I spontaneously shouted back, "Nakedness!" and he shouted back "Whadya mean nakedness?" and so thinking over my own language I silently disrobed, and then clothed myself again, and then Corso continued the reading of *Power*.

All this has very little to do with Portland State, except that I do find it surprising that educated journalists would expect me to give the same answer twice.

The Portland State College fantasy over my body was further complicated by President Millar's late discomfiture over the Avedon photograph. I explained to President Millar that, as far as I was concerned, the photograph was representative of my own self, so to speak; I had stood still for it, and certainly had no objection to seeing it in the newspaper reproduced. It had been reproduced in various student papers before, for that matter. So there was nothing unusual there. Yet I found a Portland newspaper supposedly quoting President Millar days after my arrival and departure from Portland to the effect that the Avedon photograph was mis-representative of the invited poet and some sort of insult. I therefore hasten to reassure President Millar, and Portland media, and the

State Legislature itself if necessary, that I am not one to be insulted by my own physical image, especially photo'd in the act of making religious hand signs.

All gossip I have heard to date emphasizes the fact that all this great flapping and fantasy are traceable back to groups of ladies and gentlemen over college age who neither attended the poetry reading nor understood the significance of the photograph, and who assume that I am some sort of obscene quack ripping off my clothes in public, mouthing four letter words exclusively and mouthing them exclusively at Portland State, all this supposedly done for private financial gain or in an un-American attempt to subvert our tender youth who should be in training to die in Vietnam rather than listening to filthy poetry readings. This mentality has invaded the editorial columns of local and supposedly serious Portland newspapers; and in fact, one hears, it is a similar opinionation held by various State Legislators that has caused President Millar to take rash action, issue statement about my nudity to newspapers, suspend and burn the Portland State student newspaper, etc.

Reviewing the entire situation, I judge that there is a sickness of language and opinionation in Portland, a clear lack of basic information, a failed sense of humor, overwhelming anxiety for no real reason—almost all official persons concerned seem subject to nineteenth century fainting spells, the official kind that our Eastern grandmothers complained of.

Thank you for your attention,

Allen Ginsberg, poet

[An indication of just how busy Ginsberg was during the 1960s is given in this letter.]

Allen Ginsberg [London, England] to Gary Snyder [Kyoto, Japan]
July 26, 1967

Dear Gary:

Been in London—arrested for reading "Who Be Kind To" poem in Spoleto —opera Bouffe. Since here had great time at Poetry International for British Arts Council, reading as a team with 78 yr. old [Giuseppe] Ungaretti, Italian friend of Apollinaire—nicest old poet I met since W.C.W. Met Pound [at the Spoleto festival], silent just like Julius—looked in my eye tiny blue friendly pupils for 5 minutes, held my hand wordless.

Evening with Paul McCartney, and several evenings with Mick Jagger of the

Stones—we plan to make a side of Hari Krishna together for next Stones album—what beautiful Karma! Spent one nite watching Jagger, Lennon and McCartney composing "Dandelion Fly" hairy new record at studio. Looked like 3 graces w/ beads and Persian shirts. They're all turned on and dig the Diggers and new Fresh Planet. McCartney—"We're all one." They got out of their fame paranoia this year—treated me like familiar holy phantom and all turned on yaketing about high soul—chanted prajnaparamita to all, and all understood already—beautiful blue skies in London.

Now International Dialectics of Liberation—[Stokely] Carmichael angry and yelling, I stayed calm and kept chanting prajnaparamita. Gregory Bateson says auto CO_2 layer gives planet half-life: 10–30 years before 5 degree temp rise irreversible melt polar ice caps, 400 feet water inundate everything below Grass Valley[58]—to say nothing of young pines in Canada dying radiation—death of rivers—general lemming situation. P. [Paul] Goodman sez welfare should save money by paying folks to live in the country. He has great ideas on rural reconstruction. Enclosed note from Gershon Legman.

I'm making big TV British poetry conversation chanting scenes—wearing bright red satin shirt hand painted by McCartney—color TV—Hari Om Namo Shivai. Maretta [Greer] here. Peter may come, and my father in one month, I'll take him 3 weeks London Paris Rome. Love to Philip—love to you. Emmet [Grogan] here too, organizing vast circus Hells Angels, Dead, McClure travel Europe.

Allen

[*Ginsberg's relationship with Orlovsky was always rocky, but as drugs became more important to Peter in the 1960s, Allen began to write letters from afar to calm situations that had spun out of control back home.*]

Allen Ginsberg [London, England] to Peter Orlovsky [New York, NY]
August 10, 1967

Dear Peter:

Irving [Rosenthal] wrote and Barbara [Rubin] wrote, said you were on meth, thin, thinking house was afire, window moldings bugged or electrified,

---

58 Grass Valley. The location of Gary Snyder's house in the Sierra Mountains.

etc. and had begun taking them out. I don't know how far you are into that thought process, but I am worried about the house, my manuscript etc. I can't do much from here if things blow up. I wish you would quit playing with meth completely, you've seen in others it's always created sensory or idea quirks that you didn't like from the outside. There's now so much chaos and craziness on all sides that I wish we two could be calm and not swept up into violence. I say, fix up the house, fix windows fast, quit all needles and all meth, clean up, and come over here to England.

Apparently Julius is more talkative now. Let that responsibility slide off your shoulders, quit that as much as possible, let Barbara and others take care of him for the summer.

I'm just talking straight rather than avoiding facts to you. If you get in such state that you lose weight, are obsessed with spy-bugging, call fire dept. for imaginary fires, wind up with police in house and yourself temporarily in Bellevue—things is gone too far.

I'd rather be with you than without you. Stop meth, cool everything, come over here. Phone me collect at Panna's [Grady]. I'll send you ticket immediately. Panna has big house, plenty room for both of us. My father and mother [Edith] will be here August 15, I'll take them for 3 weeks on continent—you can stay here in England and groove with Miles and others in big backyard artist's studio that Panna has, she told me to tell you come here. I come back after I see my father off and we can all go to Russia.

Whatever you do please stay off meth. It's always created problems bigger than can be cleaned up. It's not a way of efficiency or accomplishment or getting things done, just the opposite.

That's what I think is facts. [...]

I give reading here tomorrow night. Went up to Wales and took lovely acid trip, nature, lambs, cows, fogs drifting over mountain, immense float of air thru valley fanning the foxgloves and ferns. No worries, I fell on moist grass, it smelled like sweet brown vagina, and sighed with pleasure.

Sigh with pleasure and relax honey. I'll write Barbara and Irving. Maretta was here with her Tony, needed money to leave and camped in my bed for weeks, they left an hour ago.

OK—Love

Allen

[Orlovsky didn't go to Europe and Ginsberg didn't return home, but he tried via correspondence to straighten things out between the two of them. It was really an impossible situation from that distance, but Allen tried to reassure Peter nonetheless.]

**Allen Ginsberg [Milan, Italy] to Peter Orlovsky [New York, NY]
October 7, 1967**

Dear Peter:

Sorry to be so slow writing. I received all the mail forwarded. I'm sorry also I've left you with all the ambiguity and anxiety of dealing with a lot of the financial problems which are strictly of my own making like the high phone bill and car insurance worries, etc. Now: enclosed find two checks signed to your name totaling $114.51. I also enclose the phone bill. Can you pay that bill (cashing checks at Ted or Grove) and that leave almost 30 dollars extra for your own use?

I have money coming to me here from Italian book (Nanda's *Hydrogen Juke-box*) so I have extra money now and no finance problems. I think I will come home soon—I really want to settle down quiet several months and do nothing social, just work on poetry books. I don't know when yet—want to see Pound in Venice again first. I'll send you another hundred in a few days, as soon as I get the Italian money (may be 600 or more so no worry). Have you got the tanpura yet or has money been too short? Please let me know. Your harmonium is in good health, and I use it daily and sing to everyone—practicing St. Francis Canticle to the Sun in Italian, and singing prajnaparamita in Italian too.

I hope you live years "594 yrs., now," but I never heard of anyone doing that except Methuselah in Bible. I don't want to be a wet blanket except sometimes making simple plans for our life time when we are together you and me, I would be happier to be able to feel some security and make practical plans for the next year to come or at most next decade. Beyond that I'm no prophet.

Well I'm happy making it with you alone as long as we make it. I just chase after boys as substitute when I get the idea that you don't want to be stuck with me and that I'm generally too old and repulsive to you now after so much familiarity. I mean I really got the idea the last year especially that you basically don't dig making it with me and so as not to lay my needs on you I diverted sex lovemaking to others and accepted the situation cheerfully rather than getting hung up on it and laying guilt on you or me. I don't in any case want to monopolize all your sex imagination and don't fantasize monogamy for you or me. If you've been at all avoiding lovemaking with me because you think I need or deserve younger various cats, well stop that thought and let's make it more again, I'd rather stick with you, if it were still pleasant to you. But basically—I think you've told me—that I'm getting physically too unappealing—which is no betrayal or fault of yours, that's nature—so I've not wanted to force myself on you lest I seem even more unappealing in the cold light of detached awareness. I have need for love touch and sex come but I'm not so nuts as to think that you or anyone has to find me sexy—so I've just been taking what comes to me without my having to force the situation by willpower. Anyway, all I meant was, don't get nervous about having to keep making it with me for 594 years or 45 if it ceases to be pleasing. The money situation and some inter-dependencies in household complicates our subjective schemes and fantasies.

The worst thing has been the meth—I never know who you are or where you are in the universe—and yet as long as there are practical attachments, as long as there are sex attachments of some kind also, there has to be some reliable meeting place. Otherwise I get scared my manuscript will disappear or you'll change your mind in the middle of a trip and denounce me for being an old singing fink.

Well well finish later. Spent 3 days with Inge Feltrinelli in castle in countryside of Lombardy, just got back. I'll send another hundred soon hopefully tomorrow. Working with Nanda. Inge asked after you and so does Nanda and Ettore say hello. Julius OK?

Love

Allen

[*Ginsberg stayed in Europe longer, in part, so he could visit Ezra Pound. That was a very important meeting for Allen, and he described it in detail.*]

Allen Ginsberg [New York, NY] to Robert Creeley [Buffalo, NY] November 28, 1967

Dear Bob:

Came back to Lower East Side 2 weeks ago, cleaned house up and foot thick pile of letters war resistance brochures books telegrams off desk answered finally, Peter back from driving Irving Rosenthal cross-country to settle near [Dave] Haselwood in S.F., Julius living with Barbara Rubin and girlfriends up on

3rd Ave and talking and socializing a little at last; so I finally started picking thru last 7 years poetry for City Lights book, house clean quiet and phone off.

The bulk of the scribblings difficult to range together because except for 'historic' paeans like *The Change* or *May King* or *Who Be Kind To*, the mass of other occasional journal-writing has "too many words" (said Bunting); what I got is a lot of spontaneous music and natural language gaiety but I can put my finger thru holes in every other line. So I'm revising a little mostly blue-pencil to condense words already there, put them closer together and cut syntactic fat. Only fear is the stiffness that comes from revision, unnatural compression. I'd like a surface you can read clearly like clear talk and not have to "study." So now about a third thru the poems, maybe done in couple weeks; then put together another book re U.S. Vietnam-States-Volkswagen tape machine *Wichita Vortex*, that's about 100 pages I hope.

I'm scheduled to read in Buffalo March 5, not seen correspondence (handled by agent)—is that a poetry festival? Will you be there then? I heard rumor you were going back to New Mexico, and then opposite gossip. John W. [Wieners] with long peroxide blond hair?

Got busted by local cops in Spoleto over *Who Be Kind To* text (came for me in coffeehouse half hour after reading, out of blue, unexpected, in fact surprising, I didn't do nothing, in fact I thought when they said 'come with us' it must have something to do with dope which fortunately I didn't have any on me). Menotti said he'd take care of legalities (according to Italian law anything formally "art" is exempt from obscenity bust so everything is ultimately safe.) Trouble is that Italian legal structure (prosecutors and upper courts) is still operating on fascist premises, i.e. laws and personnel the same, unchanged, as in Mussolini's day. Opposite U.S. where best chance is elders of Supreme Court, the last appeal Constitutional Court in Italy is all old men who were respectable judges during fascist days and so all Vatican and old order oriented; and the laws were patchwork thru 30s uncancelled by postwar constitution—requiring definite legislative revision or Constitutional Court decision to liberalize in line with theoretically liberal constitution. So to this day all public gatherings over 5 people require formal authorization by police as "manifestation"—except for political gatherings which don't require license. That's fine except it excludes anybody unorganized as a political party i.e. you can't have be-ins. So everything in Italy's ossified, as far as polis goes; so for years police vans have been swooping down on Duomo Sq. Milan or Spanish Steps Rome arresting "Capelloni"—longhairs—so naturally by good fortune when I went with family to Italy *en famille* staying at Hotel Engleterre 2 blocks from Keats' death room over Spanish Steps, and sat down on steps one dusk to converse furtively with local ragazzi I did by god get busted again for 3 hours. I tried to get out of it by sneaking across street when vans rumored arriving but got nabbed just after I thought I was safe.

Anyway that was later: went to England from Spoleto and stayed in style with Panna Grady and ran around a lot, finished proofs small book now published Cape-Goliard, yakked on TV and sang Hari Krishna in Hyde Park pot picnic, spent evening with Paul McCartney (He says "We are all one" i.e. all the same mystic-real being), spent a lot of evenings with Mick Jagger singing mantras and talking economics and law-politics during his court crisis—found him very delicate and friendly, reading Poe and Alistair Crowley—on thick carpets with incense and wearing ruffled lace at home—later spent nite in recording studio with Jagger, Lennon and McCartney composing and fixing voices on pretty song "Dandelion Fly Away" everybody exhilarated with hashish—all of them drest in paisley and velvet and earnestly absorbed in heightening the harmonic sounds inch by inch on tape, turning to piano to figure out sweeter variations and returning to microphone to try it out—lovely scene thru control booth window, I got so happy I began conducting like a madman thru the plate glass.

Waited in London for my father and stepmother, they stayed a week at Panna's in garden studio, we gave a reading together at Institute Contemporary Arts and he came on so vibrant (first time in Europe after 71 years) one of the smaller publishers offered him a book, which he needs and hasn't been able to get since his last, 30 years ago, so that was a capital event; then we went on to Paris and sat on Pont des Arts and looked at the summer trees along the Seine and sat in cafes and sightsaw, I got hotels and taxis and carried luggage and had the pleasure of him realizing how much I knew of the outer world, and him experiencing that dimension, outside of images of movies and newspaper books—his big dream always was to stroll by wooden bookstalls on Left Bank, and so we did just that and bought views of wooden bookstalls etchings. Then a week in Rome where my arrest livened things up (he came down to the *questura* to try and get me out and saw the scene and so in reality and person was on my side in what otherwise would've been for him a faraway dubious newspaper scandal hallucination) (Tho I was already out of jail, nonetheless he said he enjoyed striding into police station resolved to get an explanation from the culprit authority.) And saw Vatican and a lot of statues, family began getting tired, a couple days in Venice refreshing, then they left for U.S., he wept—old nostalgia—going thru ticket taker to plane ramp.

So I stayed in Milan with Nanda Pivano a month, worked on translations with her—rewrote poems into Italian word by word for next book—amphetamine babble syntax difficult but I think we did something novel in the tongue. FINALLY, got reply from Olga Rudge and went to Rapallo to spend afternoon with Pound, he wouldn't talk except "Would you like to wash your hands, she asks?" before lunch; and during lunch said *"Ouvert à la Nuit"* when Olga R and I asked him name of book by Paul Morand 30 years ago—drove to Portofino with him for hour's silent sit in cafe, he nodded negative when I asked if he's ever tried hashish. Sang Prajnaparamita and Hari Krishna. I babbled a bit, but basically he's stubborn as Julius was, I figured probably for similar reasons (Julius thought good was battling evil in universe and all the evil was coming from him so figured it was best to not do or say anything.)

Then went back to Milan and worked some more and wrote asked Rudge for date again in Venice, she wrote yes so I went alone to Venice and stayed in pension round corner from her tiny house. First day came to lunch as invited and brought gift *Sgt Pepper's Lonely Hearts Club Band* and *Blonde on Blonde* and more Beatles and Dylan and Donovan, drank some wine and smoked a stick of pot at table over coffee (without calling attention) looked Pound in eye and said, "Well old man, how old <u>are</u> you?" so he finally spoke "82 in several days." Then turned on Beatles and Dylan, recited lyrics so he could distinguish "Sad Eyed Lowland Lady" words, he wouldn't say nothing but sat thru ³/₄ hour of loud rock smiling, then I sang for an hour and went away and got drunk in Harry's Bar.

Then for the next 2 ¹/₂ weeks I hung around, saw him on street, we went to concert Vivaldi in church one night, ate occasionally together in pension on days when Rudge didn't cook, Italian TV was there making birthday documentary (he was 82 October 30). After a day or so I began asking specific questions textual. "Where are the soap-smooth stone posts at San Vio, I went and looked and there they're all rough" and he began answering. I kept record of everything he said, so, in sum stringing it all together exact words but sans context over 2 weeks: "No! No! (to Rudge's demand he have more Zucchini)...Yes, when the font was filled, now they've changed it, it used to be like that (to my question about "in the font to the right as you enter / are all the gold domes of San Marco" in *Pisan Cantos*)...Don Carlos the <u>pretender</u> (what's this "house that used to be of Don Carlos"?)...Yes but my own work does not make sense...Too late (when I asked if he'd like to read in Buffalo)...Bunting told me there was too little presentation and too much reference...A mess...my writing, stupidity and ignorance all the way through...the intention was bad, anything I've done has been an accident, in spite of my spoiled intentions, the preoccupation with stupid and irrelevant matters...I do (give me, Allen, his blessing, after I demanded it)...but my worst mistake was the stupid suburban anti-Semitic prejudice, all along that spoiled everything...I found after seventy years that I was not a lunatic but a moron...I should have been able to do better...No (smiling) he never said that to me (when I reported W. C. Williams told me Pound had a mystical ear)...(*Cantos*) it's all doubletalk...it's hard for me to write anything...I didn't read enough poetry...(*Cantos*) it's all tags and patches...a mess...my depression is mental not physical...it would be ingenious work to see any influence (his on younger poets as I described it including quoting from memory some of your poems, Robert)...Williams was in touch with human feelings...You know a great deal about the subject (replying after I'd explained LSD pot scene asking if I was making sense to him)...Worse, and alive..." That's weeks boiled down.

So, I hung around till I thought my presence was getting heavy and left for States—having delivered many concise accurate pep-talks—nicest evening was his birthday, Olga R. invited me in to sing for him by fireplace late in evening, alone, sang Prajnaparamita "No Nirvana no path no wisdom and no attainment because no attainment" he sat quietly, sad, ate some birthday cake, sipped some champagne, said no he hadn't read Crane's *Atlantis* (which I thereat recited 20 lines from memory), signed 110 Canto pamphlet for "Alan Guinzberg dall'autore." (Had said he hadn't read any of my poetry, knew yours or recognized your name quickly knew who you were—also responded very fast yes head nod he'd received *Briggflats* [by Basil Bunting]).

Olga Rudge says that oddly nobody has invited him to the U.S. lately, the last invitations situation wasn't sure and Laughlin I think'd interfered, or someone had. I asked if it would be alright to make discrete inquires at Buffalo or Berkeley. I think if it were handled gently, without too much fuss, he could be invited to Buffalo (Rudge knows about your and poesy activity there, as a center) especially for a festival. She said there is an invite for Opera Villon from Buffalo. But if situation is OK there, is it possible to invite him to appear like for a short poetry reading,—which he can and does still do—(as he still does write)? I think they would come. It would be glorious if it worked. They're worried about a fuss (political and otherwise) being made—need a smooth journey and comfort/privacy/attention for an old man—would presumably have quiet dinners with few people, maybe attend a concert or reading, and give a reading. He has spry physical strength. Don't know how much money they'd need. But we could all get together and contribute. Mainly I said I'd inquire (said to Rudge) if inquiries could be made without large gossip. Meant to write you earlier. I told Rudge the great scene also would be for him to visit SF read perhaps at Berkeley or SF State. If something can be done at Buffalo, and Rudge and Pound are willing, maybe contact Parkinson. I don't think they'd be able to do more in public than that, if that. Rudge sort of takes care of him, food, letters, visitors, travel arrangements, etc. Can write her, she said not to circulate address, otherwise.

OK—Bravo! Cheers! love to Bobbie, and where's Olson? Tell John Wieners *salve*. Peter says "Tell him a lotta good things."

As ever

Allen

Tone of this letter strange to me. I waited so long to write, the letter got to be long, and I couldn't figure out where to begin about Pound so kept describing other things. Also saw Pasolini, Antonioni, Quasimodo, Montale, Ungaretti and all the Feltrinellis, Mondadoris and Balistrinis and Nonos in sight.

[*At the urging of his close friend, Barbara Rubin, Ginsberg decided to buy a farm in upstate New York as an artists' retreat. He hoped friends like Kerouac, Orlovsky, Corso, and Huncke would use the farm as an escape from the city and a place to break their various addictions. He wrote a beautiful letter to the old woman who owned the land, coaxing her to sell it to him, which she eventually did.*]

Allen Ginsberg [New York, NY] to Mrs. LaSalle [Buffalo, NY]
May 9, 1968

Dear Mrs. LaSalle:

The farm land that you own on East Hill is to my heart quiet, green pines at the state-land edge where there's still a stream in May with trees I don't know names of except pussywillows which I remember from New Jersey where I grew up near woods—we had a house on what's now main street. I've lived in New York most of my adult life, but traveled a lot in Far East and done some wilderness-backpacking and mountain climbing so have developed more taste for mother nature that I had not known younger. I live now in Lower East Side New York in what would be called stone slum and am cheerful here and do my work but I become increasingly conscious that all the noise, metal motor, stone, gas smog, no green life is not healthy for me or others, and so want more and more to find a place where I can see sky, clear air, movement of wind on trees and trembling of branches and flowers and weeds. I know the city well, and have prospered, have some grey hairs in my beard as my great grandfather did (whom I remember alive) and while I have energy want to learn to live and learn more of Earth than I know.

I write poetry and live modestly in the city, but more money comes to me than I need, and so half year ago with friends began to look around for a place of retreat that I could buy for myself and a few other old or young sensible people that felt it was time to turn back and look at the land and cultivate it, or try to learn how to plant and grow some organic food for ourselves—we are mostly accustomed to vegetables and not much meat at all. The main idea was a quiet retreat in nature where we could learn something by working, where we could find some peace.

Your old farm is like a lonely Eden, the people we have met there like Ed Eurick [Urich] have been friendly and helpful and understood our lack of experience and we've followed Ed's advice how to cheer up the valley—begun by digging out the muck/dust from the well so it'll work (get rid of the foot of silt at the bottom)—planning to lay a plastic pipe to kitchen and install a pump thru Mr. Keller who came up and advised us—then later get a back-hoe dig a trench and lay the pipe under frost line—then later put in storm windows, get in gas for heat, fix up the house for winter use cozy, (they tell us it's snowbound as far as machines)—and begin now (as Ed was arranging) get an acre or two ploughed for planting some vegetables in the next weeks. Begin slow and do one thing at a time. There's a young couple there, who want to stay thru winter, (as I will be often away teaching or lecturing, and then back for weeks at a time). And one or two other friends who've worked on farms before and appreciate the beauty and isolation of East Hill, and like Ed Eurich [Urich]—so it all seems to be working out fine as we'd all hoped since we first saw the land and offered to buy it; Mr. Watrous and Mr. Kramer said $7500, and because I've just finished a poetry reading tour of about twenty colleges from Buffalo U. to Sacramento State U and Houston State, all over the country Salt Lake and all, I have the cash on hand to buy it without having to borrow from banks or complicate matters with delay in payment. So the day I saw it I put down $100 Mr. Watrous asked.

My brother who is a lawyer (with five children who would love to run around in the woods down by that stream) tells me that there is technical difficulty with the title, and that seems to be the only cloud in the sky, and says that should be cleared up or I shouldn't take a big step like this. I guess I should follow his advice, and tho the situation seems to be unclear, I am hoping that some way will be found that we can all go through with the purchase in a way which would be happy for everybody concerned.

I feel strongly enough about the purity and goodness of the land itself that I think that if we humans can solve our complications East Hill will show itself a good and healthy place to live—I talked to the Simmons' who had lived there after the turn of the century and they encouraged the project too. So I would like to make an effort as strong as possible to win the place by trying first to resolve the technical difficulties of the title, title insurance, etc.—so that everyone will feel secure and reassured. I would like to come up to see you in Buffalo with a friend who'll help on the farm, you can look us over and see if we look fit to care for your land with the right attention it deserves, and maybe sitting down together we can figure some way to straighten out all our problems and worries together—that's always the sensible-est thing to do when there's doubts. I wouldn't be happy to buy the land unless you also felt it a good thing in the end, I pray that you will.

Respectfully yours,

Allen Ginsberg

[*Once settled on the farm, Ginsberg wrote to Gary Snyder to tell him about it. He referred to building a cabin on land he had also purchased next to Gary's property in the Sierras. He also hinted at his involvement in the upcoming 1968 Chicago Democratic National Convention.*]

Allen Ginsberg [Cherry Valley, NY] to Gary Snyder [Kyoto, Japan]
July 8, 1968

Dear Gary:

Kept putting off writing because I had so much to say, so I'll be brief. I bought (or am buying) a farm upstate NY, isolated 2000 feet up near Cooperstown, surrounded by State Forest—70 acres and old 8 room house $9,000.00, spending a few thousand more to fix up for the winter. Peter and Julius been up there several months, Gregory Corso and his girl, Barbara Rubin pining for me (ugh!) (ouch I mean) and a young competent film-maker farm couple. We have 3 goats (I now milk goats) 1 cow 1 horse (chestnut mare for pleasure) 15 chickens 3 ducks 2 geese 2 fantail pigeons, small barn right size, nearby a friendly hermit been up there sans electric since 1939 teaching us how to manage and what to repair. More Kibbutz than commune, very loose, but the place is getting organized, Julius has work to do and speaks, Peter's mostly off meth and calm. No electric, now hand pump, we're digging well up in our woods so as to have gravity fed running water. 15 acres of woods one side, the other sides all state woods permanent— pine oak and maple etc. Got lotsa books on flowers. Table is meatless, we eat fish tho. So that's started. Will also build simpler place sooner or later in California land. Visited Tassajara finally one nite.

Local (U.S.A.) sociopolitics confusing. This yippie hippie be-in shot in Chicago has been a big drag since undercurrents of violence everywhere (state and street Black Mask etc.) make peaceful gestures seem silly. Yippie organiza- tion's in wrong hands sort of. Would like to get out or redirect it to some kind of prepositional new nation confabulation, but I don't have time.

Finished proofs of *Planet News Poems 61–67* for Ferlinghetti, and *Indian Jour- nals* for Auerhahn Haselwood. Next, collected poesy volume and collected interview/essay/manifesto volume to compile—all work's done except edit- ing that.

Skandas Snyder??? Sounds Norwegian (Poor l'il Skandas). Well let's see, a name—let's see the body of bliss first. Other gossip—I'd spent $^3/_4$ hour w/ Robert Kennedy discussing pot, ecology, acid, cities, etc. a month before he started running for Prexy and died. Peter/ meth big Karmaic problem. Gave up (drifted off) sex with him to take off pressure if that was it. Lightens our rela- tions a lot.

I'm driving to Mexico w/ brother and 5 nephews and sister in law, 2 weeks and thence to SF again meet my father and show him around 2 weeks—then likely back to the farm—maybe trip out to convention Chicago and back, hole in for several months.

Wrote one fantastical poem about being screwed in ass with repeated refrain "please master" which really got me a little embarrassed, but read it at last SF Poesy Renaissance big reading and it turned out to be, as usual, univer- sal, one hole or another, one sex or another. Really amazing year after year I stumble on to areas of shame or fear and their catharsis of community aware- ness takes off the red-cheeked bane.

How's fatherhood? Babyhood? I wrote Kapleau and he sent me his prajna- paramita translation—he chants it English monosyllables one of the Tassajara Senseis or Roshis is a Sanskrit expert, we can check out w/ him on your next trip here. Any plans? OK.

Love, as ever

Allen

I keep straying on mental anger warpaths, and then come back to milking the goats.

[*The farm never became the escape from addictions that Ginsberg had hoped. Everyone just smuggled drugs in under Allen's nose, but he eventually tried to be more strict. In the end he was unsuccessful.*]

Allen Ginsberg [Cherry Valley, NY] to Herbert Huncke [New York, NY] February 16, 1969

Dear Herbert:

Leaving for NY tonite to lecture at New School, arrived here last night. Maybe see you in NY. In case I miss you and you return here while I'm gone hello.

Louis [Cartwright] left this afternoon, to get job in NY; David went with him, unable to sleep most of last night, still sick, saying he was going into city to work music and stay clean. I tried persuading David to stay, but as I was leaving today myself it lacked force. I told him he was welcome to rest / cure /, but NOT welcome to wobble back and forth between here and NY scoring weekly which he, you and Louis have been doing.

As you remember this place was set up as refuge from chemical city conditions, and it worked with difficulty reasonably well for you the first months. Since Louis and then David been here and since you've been adamantly guarding yr spike [syringe] the last month, that original condition has degenerated more and more till the issue's muddy.

So I'm taking it on myself to clarify the original proposition to which you originally agreed, and repeat it clearly: you're welcome to home here, but no needle drugs and no needles on the premises. If there are no needle drugs here there's also no function for needles. Their presence is not sentimentality, it's practical. If this condition doesn't meet with your approval, then the whole house is not a viable situation for you and I suggest you make some other arrangement, and go back to the city.

This is nothing new, just repeat of the old conditions. If you don't think it's suitable that's up to you, and you're free to choose another household elsewhere.

I mean this seriously enough, once for all, to be understood. As you do have a tendency to deceive and burn yourself and others I will have to insist on your following the ground rules already agreed to. If I have any suspicion that you are creating illusions, speaking false words on the subject, I will not hesitate to search your room and your person.

As you may remember the last time round your words did not mean what they said and were meant to confuse me.

My own words above mean what they say: you're welcome here without needle, without needle drugs. You are not welcome here with needle and needle drugs. You're welcome here to kick and lay out. The house-social and town-social situation won't support the strain of needle drugs.

I'm leaving this explicit here, including the flat statement that I won't hesitate to search if I'm being double-crossed on the matter. It's not very pleasant but there seems to be no other way of definitively, actually, clearly and straightforwardly ending a problem which has been too long prolonged by my hesitancy and your insistency on having needle and drugs here. OKOKOK.

As ever,

Allen

I'm showing this note to all concerned and leaving it to be given to you on yr return if I'm not here, so there will be no ambiguity.

[During the late 1960s, Allen joined the War Tax Resisters and refused to pay income taxes that would go toward military spending. He clearly stated his position in this letter to the Secretary of the Treasury, David Kennedy.]

**Allen Ginsberg [New York, NY] to David Kennedy [Washington, DC]
July 16, 1969**

Dear Mr. Kennedy:

This is response to your Department's notice of 11 July, 1969 concerning tax assessment against me of $1488.68 plus interest asserted as $21.25 for the year 1968.

I am not able to pay this money into our Treasury to be expended in the present illegal and immoral effort to kill or subdue more Vietnamese people.

I have retained attorneys with regard to your claim against me and am instructing them to present the appropriate documents and authorities to your office as necessary to manifest my anxiety and inability to pay for this painful war.

I am obliged to inform you that I spent all of the modest amount of money I earned that last year in keeping alive and helping others maintain their lives. You should also know that I am physically, mentally and morally unable to earn moneys to pay for the Vietnam war. Basic, traditional ethics of my profession of poetry prohibit me from assigning money earned incidental to the publication of literary compositions pronouncing the inhumanity and ungodliness and un-American nature of this war toward funding the very same war. My religious feeling is of a divine nature in persons so I wish to waken the divine in yourself by clearly explaining that I conscientiously object to and am incapable of paying money into the Treasury for war use in Vietnam. Equally clear is an awareness that so much as I may finance violence to others, equal measure of such violence shall be returned inevitably to my own person. I am absolutely afraid of this retribution.

As my religious apprehensions and convictions and my psychological condition prevent me from paying taxes into the treasury of the Vietnam war, an equally commanding practical and personal awareness of socially and economically deprived millions of fellow persons in America prevents me from supporting an inequitable and unfair tax system which places the costs of an horrific war so heavily upon poor, ecologically disoriented and hungry people, and transfers so much money as profit to investors in questionable military-industrial enterprises encouraged by and consequent to this constitutionally inappropriate war.

I am willing to pay your tax assessment by donating what money I will have to any tax exempt program acceptable to your department which will benefit money-poor Americans or protect natural resources wasted as consequence of war-haste.

I humbly request an appointment to meet with you with my attorney to discuss the policy decision which you must soon make as to how the numbers of persons who feel as I do are going to be treated by your department. We plan to offer reasonable alternative to paying taxes supporting the Vietnam war. I can't live in peace with myself and pay taxes into a fund which goes directly into the Vietnam war. This prospect has made me physically ill. If our tax system is so inequitable it cannot find a reasonable alternative such as payment of these taxes into a fund which is not used in this war then I am willing to go to jail.

Sincerely yours,

Allen Ginsberg

[Ginsberg's greatest political debates continued to be with his father. This letter was in response to Allen's support of the militant Black Panthers. Louis disapproved of their tactics, in part due to Panther support of Arab interests in Israel.]

Allen Ginsberg [Cherry Valley, NY] to Louis Ginsberg [Paterson, NJ] February 15, 1970

Dear Lou:

Take it easy don't blow your top, I took it easy & didn't blow mine this last few weeks despite attacks of rage similar to yours in letter "My rage will know no bounds." I think probably the Panthers feel exactly the same emotions we do, and the Arabs feel that precise violent sense of outrage, and the Jews identifying with Israel feel that adrenaline brilliance pounding in the gorge & forehead.

I do imagine that it's as Burroughs suggests some sort of trust of giant insects from another galaxy operating thru manipulation of images to drive everybody out of their skulls in states of outrage so blind it will blow up the planet so the insects can take over. Or if the metaphor's too outlandish, it's a trust of secret military bureaucrats (Israeli military vs. Egyptian military, Russian military vs. Pentagon) who have an interest in each other's mounting opposition — symbiosis like Narcotics Police & Mafia who have a mutual interest in keeping the junkies (100,000 in NY) persecuted as badly as Jews or Arabs or Blacks anywhere.

My direct experience of the Panthers hasn't been the same as your newspaper clips. I spent time smoking pot with [Eldridge] Cleaver & [Stokely] Carmichael in Nashville while the *Nashville Banner* newspaper incited a riot to coincide with Carmichael's presence in Nashville & was with both of them the night of a violence which was blamed directly on them by U.P.I. and *NY Times.* Panther means fight back when attacked. As I don't believe in this strategy I part ways with them there; and I think they've stuck to fighting back when attacked, and they have been attacked illegally & grievously, despite accountings of Reisel & others, in accounting by *Life* and ACLU & enormous mass of weekly reports I've read from dozens of cities in underground press for 2 years now, material which you haven't seen. Which I can send as I keep it all here in boxes, tho it will only fatigue the reader with such a welter of "institutionalized" violence that you realize the Panther cries are just what we hear, of an unnumbered & unreported myriad illegalities, beatings, false arrests, insults, unconstitutional force & illegal court process so deep and vast from south where it's acknowledged to north where it's complained about, suffered thru, & bears scars from head from. Panthers in context are Irgun[59] in context. The amazing thing is that Black Violence and Zionist Violence come head on like immovable force & unpushablé object round the corner of the world, each with the same fear of extermination and violent sense of outrage. It is precisely the same anxiety that motivated Panthers-like military competence in Israel that motivates Dayan-like[60] language and behavior & propaganda among the Panthers.

As I would not see myself as Black if I were black, I don't see myself as a Jew as I am a Jew, & so don't identify with nation of Jews anymore than I would of nation of America or Russia. Down with all nations they are enemies of mankind! And nationalism is disease. If this be renegade treason etc. remember that's precisely the rhetoric the Panthers apply to blacks who cooperate with white culture police.

You can't have Jewish integrity at the expense of Panther sympathy or Arab reality any more than you can have Arab integrity at price of Jewish extermination. Napalm & violence & bombing from Jewish or Arab hands has already escalated the problem beyond reasonable solution. I don't have a solution except not to take sides that involve bloodying anyone's ass or any kind of political violence. If however everyone insists on being violently right, then we will all have to suffer it through & die violently at various idiots' hands, Jewish idiots, Arab idiots, American idiots, Maoist idiots, liberal idiots, reactionary idiots. All the same violence and it's always proved wrong. By hindsight I wonder if WW II actually solved anything? How many more would've been killed unnaturally if Hitler had his madness enacted, than have already been killed as we've had our madness enacted? I dunno. Obviously no reality to that thought except as it's a thought entertainable among many nowadays.

I didn't read Dave McReynolds' circular. Generally his judgment is good. He was among the first to protest A-bomb drills, and in the 1960's was early organizer with [David] Dellinger and others of anti-war movement. He then took a pacifist position on war buttressed with reasonable arguments against the Vietnam war which arguments are now considered universal—i.e. we have no right fighting their war, we shd hold elections as per Geneva Convention, it's wrong war wrong place etc. He also gave 10 years working against that war while others including myself had not yet had our consciences roused. He's not "communist." He may have different opinion re Panthers than you but his sincerity is

---

59 Irgun. Militant Zionist group operating in Palestine from 1931–1948, credited with bombing the King David Hotel in Jerusalem.

60 Moshe Dayan (1915–1981). Israeli military leader.

unquestionable and it doesn't help reconciliation to refuse his essay any dignity. It's reconciliation or death for everyone, that includes you as well as Arabs and Panthers. So don't blow your top.

I'm meanwhile worried about Dellinger going to jail, & the rest of the conspirators, because I suppose it's getting nearer. I'm next unless I begin to shut up & give in and participate (i.e. pay taxes) for the war. The thing that really amazes me is slow discovery of how much of my comfort & ability is the result of labor of others and suffering of other forms of life. I don't think that we in U.S. with all our ease are in a position to be very much outraged at disturbances being made by people living in subhuman or nonhuman circumstances. Be glad you're not black & living on River Street or behind the market by the docks in Port Au Prince & that I have a nice typewriter & comfy light to write you a letter with. Remember most people ain't got what to eat, and it's going to get worse.

Until we can recognize & solve Black problems we've created—like, in N.J. mafia dominated police and politics that we've refused to acknowledge for over a decade tho blacks were outspoken about it—& that includes Paterson especially you know—we're not in position to lecture Panthers. I once asked Carmichael what he'd do if he were me—he said sensibly, "Pacify the white violence, calm the whites." Obviously that's one thing we <u>can</u> do, it makes no sense to lecture Panthers on their violent rebellion against the police until you can, at very <u>least</u> say that the police and mafia are not working together in NJ as well as Chicago, Cleveland, Detroit, etc.

Well ok, don't blow yr top, realize the actual problems drive people mad because they are maybe insoluble with present population pressure anyway. I blew my top with Eugene like you blew your top with me, rather than lay it back on you, & that's the net result of violence—passing it on down the line till it returns to the self. Well this is all obvious.

Regarding Reisel, Evans & Novak articles: They have reduced the number of probably killed by police to a dozen or 10 depending on count; & blamed all violence on the Panthers. This is just doublethink. The number of publicized deaths may well be only a dozen. ACLU has more extensive analysis and details, even *Life* shows a different picture. I remember that the Panthers first began on West Coast after <u>years</u> of abuse of Blacks in Oakland, & I remember the context, Panther as "fight back when & only when attacked" from the beginning. You'd have to rewrite all the newspaper work SF 1960–65 to eliminate that context. Read Cleaver's book. OK

Allen

[*A short note from Ginsberg to Carolyn Cassady described Kerouac's funeral a few months earlier. It showed just how deeply Allen was moved by the loss of his friend.*]

Allen Ginsberg [Cherry Valley, NY] to Carolyn Cassady [Los Gatos, CA]
February 19, 1970

Dear Carolyn:

Jack's funeral very solemn, I went with Peter and Gregory and John Holmes in Holmes' car, saw Jack in coffin in Archambault funeral home on Pawtucketville Street Lowell, same name and funerary home from Jack's own memory—and pallbore thru high mass at St. Jean Baptiste. Jack in coffin looked large headed, grim-lipped, tiny bald spot top of skull begun but hair still black and soft, cold skin make up chill to finger touch on his brow, fingers wrinkled, hairy hands protruding from sports jacket holding rosary, flower masses around coffin and shaped wrinkle-furrow familiar at his brow, eyes closed, mid-aged heavy looked like his father had become from earlier dream decades. Shock first seeing him there in theatric-lit coffin room as if a Buddha in Parinirvana pose, come here left his message of illusion—wink and left the body behind.

Sad I didn't call you before, but too much woe, life and business on my desk till this dusk. Take care of yourself.

OK—as ever

Allen

[*Once again writing to Gary Snyder, Ginsberg touched on a wide range of topics from practical matters such as a wind charger to his continued interest in drug experimentation.*]

Allen Ginsberg [Cherry Valley, NY] to Gary Snyder [Nevada City, CA]
August 24, 1970

Dear Gary:

Home on farm since mid-May, I'm finally catching up with masses of unanswered letters a year old, and cleaning desk.

Have been continuing organ practice and can now notate and play and sing melodies and chords simultaneous; so been setting new songs more elaborately than before. If you didn't receive the Blake record (and also *Indian Journals*) send me a card.

Wind-charger's now set up here on platform next to the ram house, with batteries and a solid state inverter set down below frost line in ram house, and wires leading to remote switch in house by radiophonotape machine units. And it all doesn't work.

At least not in summer, we're told winter winds much more ample will provide plenty of electric. As it is the batteries just run down slower than before. We may have defective batteries. All these kinks to be ironed out in the next year, by then we'll have some workable system to produce 400 watt's worth—four hundred watt litebulbs. Using neon lights you get brighter illumination for 20-30 watts by the way, if electric's scarce. Meanwhile, if you're interested, you can run TV or minor electric equipment off car or golf cart batteries. I'll let you know what we work out.

I wake every morning totally depressed, 4 or 5 AM, Leary and [John] Sinclair in jail in my mind, the weight of sustaining the farm heavy in light of apparent continuing disintegration of social order. Vast garden crops coming in, and we'll have canned 100 cases of vegetables (corn peas stringbeans etc.) enough, really, for winter survival, I'm amazed to see—by the end of harvest. Great organic garden this year, 3'd year of Gordon Ball's experience and study —also planted orchard of fruit trees and permanent strawberry and asparagus beds on hill above house.

I got 12 dollar sleep bag and sleep out under stars in full moon now—stayed out for Perseid meteorite shower last week.

Not getting much literary writing done but now recently converting 4AM depression energy raw consciousness of disaster into articulate notes in notebook at bedside, so it lightens my mind load and in a few months I'll know or be able to read back and see what's bothering me.

Ferlinghetti got invite 13 readings Australia next May so I said I'd go along (as I was invited) if the money was all right, and spend a month down under. Thence see Bodrubadur or Polynesia or Philip Whalen, return via India Persia take time. I think I need to go around the world again (like pulling a chain—"I think I need to go to the bathroom again").

Don Allen phone today said you were starting your house walls, beams and rafters and roof must be in? What's happening? In brief, send me a postcard.

The cities—I went to Yale Panther Rally May Day and saw Genet, he gave a great "commencement" speech which I got a copy of and prefaced for City

Lights to publish—teargassed there chanting om a hum. Then to Washington May 9 and teargassed there singing plain Om. Have been immersed here ever since, walking in woods and sleeping recovering from city shock—catching up with paperwork.

O! I got one cylocybin Mexican authentic mushroom (silk-smooth purplish cap) and ate it—with Maretta and others—tastes fine unlike peyote or any other preparation—absolutely easy, natural, not a trip i.e. no departure from any normal custom, you just eat some food, some food, soma-esque food, but basically just regular body food that tastes like ordinary Jap dried mushroom if you soak it halfway and chew it—found myriad tiny fish making ripples in the green backwater behind the beaver dam, frog sitting haunch in mud, head stuck out looking around the woods where we passed—walked 6 hours all over neighbor's hills and found old woods familiar and neighbor lake set in valley below reminiscent of Tolkien landscape. First such experience since 67 and just about imperceptibly smooth transition from quotidian activity and perceptions. So all's well there. Collecting fly agaric here as per Wasson's *Soma* book but won't try till I find expert.

Saw Sakya Lama last spring in Seattle—he said "Marijuana? O that's fine" —but hadn't tried LSD. Saw Trungpa Tolku and had long happy high talk, sang and chanted. He demonstrated proper phat sound—a "hike!" in back of throatskull like a soprano baby shriek, very lovely.

Maretta Greer here, back from street sadhu begging sadhana year in Rawalpindi—she wants to go back and settle in Ladakh. Very good shape, meditates and does mantra quietly all day like the Sakyapa old man did, she also reads extensively now, got herself together quite neat, everyone remarks on her beauty and quiet demeanor, and she helps out here and there with gardening or canning or curry cooking—we take long silent walks in woods. Ray Bremser and wife and babe here almost half year. Peter strong and marvelously straight compared to last year—he don't drink smoke or speed—I don't smoke now also. Practically no sex also—all dem vegetables. OK luv, regards to Masa and kids. I hear you're overproducing your scheduled *Changes*? Well I guess we'll have to colonize the sun.

As ever

Allen

[Ginsberg often cited the British system in which they dealt with junkies as a medical issue and not a legal problem as a step in the right direction. He was never able to get much support from politicians in this country, however. In this letter he made his case to his congressman, Ed Koch.]

Allen Ginsberg [New York, NY] to Ed Koch [New York, NY]
September 22, 1970

Dear Representative Koch:

I've by now read and pondered March 30, 1970 *NY Times'* survey of British easy handling of junk problems, and a series of associated articles, by Richard Severo, which you cited to me as influencing you to impression that my proposition of total medicalization of U.S. addict problem is unsupportable by British experience. I've also been in brief correspondence with Severo, who has not been communicative. I have the impression he's a philosophical conservative who probably thinks I'm mad, or immature. In any case I can't get any dialogue going with him, to discuss his position. That's why it's taken so long for me to get back to you on this point we spoke of at Moratorium May 9, D.C.

OK—my conclusion is that, again, *NY Times* and Severo are continuing same vast misjudgment that's been going on for decades and has created the U.S. junk problem.

Put simply, the British practice has been effective in CONTAINING the number of addicts and avoiding all the hideous fallout characteristic of police and police-mentality dominated system in U.S.A.

It would take more time to document criticism of Severo's evaluation of British system than I have right now but briefly bear these obvious facts in mind:

NYC with population similar to London has 100 to 200 thousand addicts and they're multiplying while London has one hundredth the number—2000 presently "known."

Now that simple fact is the whole story. Present narco bureau line, and Severo's reasoning, is that there is a huge jump in addiction in Britain in last 10 years. Yes that's so, but for various reasons (see below) NOT mentioned by Severo. Causes of rise in number of British addicts include:

1. General historic escalation of drug culture adding a limited few hundred more junkies to rolls, not a mortal problem.
2. Confusion and spotty black market caused by shift over from individual doctor to clinic system and stricter "state" control. At beginning many

junkies were cut off from doctors and assigned to clinics which didn't
yet exist except on paper during transition year 1965 or 7 around then.
This caused slight black market, and junk-spread.

3. Invasion-influence of panicked neurotic U.S. addicts who sought refuge
   in London bringing their U.S. "criminal" paranoia with them—I know
   many personally, i.e. overflow of anxiety from U.S. and overflow of U.S.
   malpractice by addicts conditioned to police state black market
   conditions. Continuous pressure by high level U.S. drug-police
   bureaucracy and police-connected MD's on British to change their
   system and persecute junkies led also to some unsettlement of
   conditions there, i.e. premature and possibly unnecessary shift to clinic
   system and depersonalization of medical attention. What was needed
   was slightly more supervision of doctors as a few were overwriting.
   Transition to clinic system was influenced by U.S. pressure.

4. Increased efficiency in statistics gathering and registration due to
   transition from relatively unsupervised and basically workable private
   doctor system to strictly registered clinic system. This latter is probably
   one of the biggest factors in paper rise of addiction statistics in Britain.

If you examine Severo's articles closely you find they are based on a paper
statistical rise in number of registered or "known" addicts (Opiate addicts)
from 437 in 1960 to 2,782 in 1968. The greatest numerical rise came after stiffen-
ing of registration procedures. Severo and narco bureau reasoning does not
include any of the 4 key considerations above—and Severo and narco bureaus
in non sequitur extrapolate this paper-large but practically small rise in addic-
tion to the following scare argument which I propose is irrational:

"What would happen if the present (U.S.) addiction problem grew geomet-
rically, spawned by a free heroin program...?" (later *Times* article May 30, 1970.
Severo)

This is non sequitur because:

1. "Geometrical growth" of British addiction was mainly on paper and
   due to factors outlined above, and not "spawned" by medically
   supervised legal opiate supply, which is improperly termed "free
   heroin."

2. Best medical sociology in U.S. attributes giant growth of U.S. addiction
   quite specifically to the opposite: cash nexus of black market. This
   historic point completely ignored by Severo and U.S. drug bureaucracy,

is a major point made officially by historic and frequently ignored 1963 NY Academy of Medicine Bulletin Report on Drug Addiction: "It is reaffirmed that profit is a major force in the spread of addiction."

All these conditions and considerations are completely ignored by Severo who has presented a partial and prejudicial view of what is in fact the successful containment of the same problem which in the U.S. is the single largest cause of breakdown of urban morale law and order. The fact that in Britain the entire problem is contained mainly to small group in medical control, and does not overflow to be the cause of vast street and house crime, overload of courts, breakdown of legal procedure, alteration of constitutional propriety in stop and frisk laws, etc., has simply not been taken into consideration. Severo's analysis in the end relies on a slight rise in physical addiction and huge rise in paper addiction, all of which he attributes, in his own prejudicial and inflammatory phraseology to "free heroin." The rest of his article is sensationalist interviews with a few lost junkies in London. His articles do not take into account the comparative sociology of NY-London junk scene, crime fallout, breakdown in fabric of society. Nor are basic constitutional and humane considerations taken into account. In the long run common sense and humane treatment of sick addicts by medical service rather than police service is the only sane way, both practically and sociologically and also from human-relations emotional point of view. U.S. policy of police state control in this area has been deliberately brutal, and we are now paying for that breach of common civility. "Do unto others"—200,000 junkies in NY are doing unto middle class exactly as middle class has done to them—i.e. violence and corruption.

I enclose a little documentation of the present crisis escalation of the junk problem in NY. Please Xerox and return this to me rapidly.

1. Overwhelming mass of informed medical opinion thinks U.S. system is historically crazed.
2. Bulk of lobbying for police nonmedical system comes from police not from qualified medical experts. Report after official report says police system is wrong and criticizes police pushiness.
3. Bulk of narcotics police Federal State and local in U.S. themselves historically have been pushing, and thus have self interest in scarcity drug market. This third point is a key point, with all its implications, and it is entirely documentable from the *NY Times* over last few years, see enclosed clippings.

Present repressive drug bureaucracy inside U.S.A. is itself responsible for the entire junk plague. Until that point is understood in all its shocking grandeur, you will never understand the entire breakdown of law and order in U.S.

Please remember: There exists documentation of the assertion that the bulk of U.S. drug police themselves sell. As you may remember, Ramsey Clark indicted 32 out of 80 Federal Narcs in 1967. He recently remarked that 1) that was all he could get evidence against, 2) this condition had been going on for at least a quarter century. That's what he told me.

My documentation of drug peddling and extortionary activities of police comes mostly from the press, oddly. There is now sufficient data on this fact on public record. It is completely ignored as crucial to understanding of drug problem. On one page we read of universal corruption in drug police bureaus; on another, fascist demands for more police to solve the drug problem. No politician has ever put these idiot facts together in one analysis.

As ever

Allen Ginsberg
Scribe

[*Ginsberg's continued frustration with the articles he read in the* New York Times *is evidenced in this letter to columnist C. L. Sulzberger. Allen continued to correspond in this manner with Sulzberger and years later won an apology from him concerning some of his points about CIA involvement in drug smuggling.*]

Allen Ginsberg [Cherry Valley, NY] to C. L. Sulzberger [New York, NY]
November 26, 1970

Dear Mr. Sulzberger:

U.S. agents immediately became active with the "new authorities" in Cambodia according to Charles Meyer *New York Times* November 20, 1970; followed by vast U.S.-Saigon invasion, as well as enormous open military aid to strengthen pro U.S. Cambodian Government. Given the history of covert CIA and infra-CIA activity all thru the area it would seem likely that Prince Sihanouk was headed in "that direction," as you put it, mainly because of U.S. activity (including your own depressing verbal activity, cosmic military babble, etc.)

Despite fragmentary objections to covert invasions and destruction of democratic politics by CIA in SE Asia and elsewhere there still has been no comprehensive exact inventory of that activity in the *Times* over last 20 year period. This may not be news fit to print for you but it is news I am interested in.

I enclose the notes from Greek jail I mentioned. As you will see there is assertion that Greek secret police KIP and U.S. CIA share offices in Athens. Plus a good deal of other information that might be checked regarding shift in heroin manufacturing to Greece from fabled Marseilles. Given KIP CIA connection, and older history, I don't see how I can accept your "personal conviction" that CIA had nothing to do with prospectus, planning and consolidation of Colonel's Coup. And later growth of heroin traffic in Athens.

In column after column your consideration of cold war balance of forces depends entirely on limiting your arguments' range of thinking to interests of the secret police/army bureaucrats of both sides, rather than to larger interests of citizens not involved in jobs making money in cold war. Yet your rhetoric strays: "The argument is that democratic societies can no longer limit themselves to weapons known to be outmoded..." etc.

The sloppiness of your use of the word democratic here strikes me as same vagueness of language or pseudo-reference as old U.P.I. habit of referring to U.S. dominated military dictatorships in South America as "Free World Governments."

From your letter: "You know, Allen, we really went through those original 'tips' on 'the CIA and Dope' and the findings are very, very slim—often invisible. Everybody knows lots of opium is grown in Laos and everybody knows the CIA is active in Laos but it is hard to draw invidious conclusions from that—especially ones that are not libelous."

You know, Cy, my "tips" weren't original, where they linked CIA with Indochinese opium trafficking activity, they were drawn from Senatorial statement backed by learned Princeton area-specialists from WHO [World Health Organization] field researchers on the spot (Dr. [Joel] Fort); scholars, newsmen, Senatorial subcommittee conclusions, labor experts in area, etc.

If you have examined the Xerox material I left with you carefully you will see that a relationship is already so heavily established between CIA and opium traffic, that you already have the story. It would be advisable for the *Times* could do some real research into it but I don't feel there's the will there. Because the material I gave you completes one aspect of the story that "everyone" (yourself for instance) didn't know or believe, I suggest that you simply publish the material as it stands; i.e. that Sen. Gruening's Subcommittee report says Marshall Ky made money on dope in CIA operation Haylift; that Sen. Tunny asserts CIA had made deal with Meos (on basis of Princeton Prof. McAlister's research); that Nationalist Chinese armies in SE Asia have always been opium traffickers as Stanley Karnow reports at great length in September February 22, '64 which I've now read; that Madame Anna Chennault owns Air America, a CIA franchise outfit for covert military activities long hidden from U.S. public, which according to innumerable scholars reporters newspapers etc. transports opium, and that also Mme. Chennault's a close friend to [Melvin] Laird, [John] Mitchell and J. E. Hoover at Watergate parties; that the proprietress of "Air Opium" as it is called did heavy fundraising for Nixon '68; etc. etc. All this material's already on record. That you can say all the above is "invisible" or "thin," Cy, is about as astonishing as your use of the phrase "democratic societies." Are we talking the same language? A little professionalism, please!

As ever

Allen Ginsberg
Have you actually read all that Xerox material I gave you?

[*New York politico Donald Maness was quoted as calling Ginsberg a "Commie," which drew an immediate response from Allen. The letter also showed how Ginsberg had refined his explanation about what had happened in Cuba and Czechoslovakia in 1965.*]

**Allen Ginsberg [New York, NY] to Donald Maness [New York, NY]
December 22, 1970**

Dear Mr. Maness, and Others Concerned:

I am not, as a matter of fact, a member of the Communist Party, nor am I dedicated to the overthrow of this or any government by violence. I am in fact a pacifist and object to the actions of the United States in attempting to subvert and overthrow Indochinese and Latin American governments by violence, just as I object to Soviet Bloc use of internal and external police violence to overthrow popular governments. I must say that I see little difference between the armed and violent governments both Communist and Capitalist that I have observed; or more precisely that the problem on both sides is police bureaucracy armed and violent against respectable citizens both in U.S.A. and in Russia, with differences of degree and different forms of exploitation and oppression practiced by such governments not only against their own citizens but also against Mother Nature herself. I have experienced police state conditions in Cuba, which I count a police state much like Florida for some of her minority citizens; I was in fact expelled from Cuba in February 1965. This situation rosé because I had consistently criticized the police bureaucracy of Cuba for persecution of homosexuals, repressive laws against marijuana use, and harassment of bearded hiply dressed youths. Taken by uniformed guards from my hotel room and cut off from communication with other officials or friends, I was put on a plane for Czechoslovakia.

As I have spoken my mind freely against party hacks and repressive police in Chicago, and in favor of legalization of mind manifesting drugs and end of government war violence during 1968 Convention, so also I had spoken in favor of psychedelic drugs, sexual freedom, and liberty from oppressive police bureaucracy in Prague, Czechoslovakia in 1965. For that I was elected May King by 100,000 Prague citizens on May Day at a student's festival; and to spite that election the Prague police bureaucracy arrested, detained and expelled me from Czechoslovakia on May 7, 1965. The poem "Kral Majales" in my book *Planet News* records that incident and contains an attack on Marxist police bureaucracy. That same year I found myself arrested on the steps of the Whitehall New York draft board with Dr. [Benjamin] Spock for protesting the draft of young American fellows to fight in an unjust tyrannical war inspired by U.S. police bureaucracies including the CIA.

All the above information and political opinion is, however, irrelevant in a discussion of a literary text which cannot be judged, either here or in Russia, as to whether it toes the correct party line — just as in Russia, authors are stupidly attacked by party hacks and loud mouthed art-hating agitators, so here in America authors and their texts can be attacked by small organized groups representing special political interests, like Jacksonville's United White People group whose spokesman at Duval County's School Board special meeting claimed that "Allen Ginsberg, is an admitted communist, but actually has written some of the most filthiest, vulgar books that was ever written in America." Such claims, aside from their perverse grammar, inaccuracy of fact, and silly overstatement, are exactly like the claims of Communist party hacks attacking authors like Solzhenitsyn, Voznesensky, or Alexei Ginzberg in Russia. The whole school board meeting was parallel to a particularly confused meeting of Communist bureaucrats and outraged so-called workers chewing over the supposed "anti-patriotic" or "degenerate" tendencies of any number of communist poet free spirits who've been censored or jailed or suicided from Mayakovsky in the 30s to Moscow's rebel poet-editor Alexei Ginzberg (a friend of mine incidentally) in jail this year 1970 in Russia. The White Citizen's Council and friends' rhetoric sounds similar in tone and abusiveness and impoliteness and insensitivity and authoritarian insistency and imprecise accusation to the worst of Communist literary criticism. As a poet, I would say that they are, in lack of free human spirit, the same people in fact. And I believe that these enemies of humor and liberty on both sides of the cold war need each other, feed on each other, and often make their living from each other's mythical existence. And that, precisely, is the point and humor of the text "America," a take-off on U.S. police-military-industrial bureaucracy hysteria.

That poem and "Wichita Vortex Sutra" are widely known as examples of respectable legitimate poetry, are taught in hundreds of schools and colleges in the U.S.A. and outside of it, and are included in a number of standard anthologies, some, like Grove Press' *New American Poetry*, already a decade old, others among several dozen, published in the last year, like Wadsworth Publishing Company's custom anthology, *Readings for Composition* [*by Logic*, edited by Sidney P. Moss], for English 1-2-3 Freshman English. In my own travels for poetry readings in schools and colleges throughout the country over the last 15 years —hundreds of readings, and extensive teaching—I've been informed that "America" particularly, and later "Wichita Vortex Sutra" are commonly used as texts in high schools and colleges, and are particularly acceptable to a new generation of open and thoughtful minded students. The "America" text's been used for years in New York State, Pennsylvania, California, Kansas and Texas high schools among other places, according to letters I've received which are on file at Columbia University Library's special collections archive, where my literary papers are now housed.

For these and other poems I received a Guggenheim Foundation Fellow's grant in 1963 and a National Institute of Arts and Letters grant in 1968, was elected to PEN Club Executive Board and am now a member of that international literary organization's four-man Committee on Censorship. The poem "Kral Majales" above-mentioned received $500 award from the U.S. Government's National Council of Arts in 1968. If any abusive critic wishes to found the right of juniors in an American literature class in high school in Duval County, Florida, to read what I have written, they will have to measure their opinions against that of the above Establishments, as well as every anthology of XX Century American Poetry issued in the last decade, as well as the January 1970 opinion of a Federal Court in Miami which declared my poems to be protected by the U.S. Constitution.

The United States is going through many changes, as is the entire planet. This country with a small percentage of the world's population consumes half the world's raw material supply, and according to respectable essayists in the

New York Times each of us Americans pours more poison waste into fresh water and ocean than any thousand Asians. The world's oceans may be dead as Lake Erie by the time Duval's high school students are middle-aged, near 50 years old in the year 2000, if we have not stopped our war on Mother Nature and our wars on our own human kind. The study of natural wisdom has always been the subject of youths' education from classical time, and that natural wisdom always lies within human heart and mind if it is not drowned by violence or unnatural electronic fantasy: education means, historically, the lead out that wisdom from heart and mind: that is the root of the word education—from Latin *duc* (to lead) plus *e* (out). Poetry has always served that function of bringing out in public what is within heart and mind privately, and was among all races and climes the chief ritual of social communication, carrying prophecy, history and natural science in its rhythmic language in human memory preserved for the community whilst cities have burned and culture and pyramids risen and disintegrated. Poetry is the most sensitive speech we know, poetry is the tender heart of man uttered on the tongue. Attack and insult and ban poetry to our youths and you dumb their hearts, defend and praise and teach poetry to our youths and you lead their own natural hearts to utterance. The visionary poet William Blake, a revolutionary and friend of Tom Paine, prophesied for us singing two hundred years ago in "The Schoolboy":

> O! father & mother, if buds are nip'd
> And blossoms blown away,
> And if the tender plants are strip'd
> Of their joy in the springing day,
> By sorrow and cares dismay,
>
> . . .
>
> How shall the summer arise in joy
> Or the summer fruits appear.
> Or how shall we gather what griefs destroy
> Or bless the mellowing year,
> When the blasts of winter appear.

So till that summer when children live with poetry safe on American earth, I remain,
        Your faithful Bard,

    Allen Ginsberg

[*Ginsberg was asked to sit on the National Book Awards committee for poetry. He was happy to be recognized as an authority in the field, but when his fellow committee members chose to give the top prize to Mona Van Duyn, Ginsberg couldn't believe it and wrote a formal protest to the committee.*]

Allen Ginsberg [Cherry Valley, NY] to National Book Award Committee [New York, NY] January 20, 1971

Dear National Book Award Literary Fellow Lady Judges:

We are on odd modern committee, odious formalistic place to be, comparison bureaucracy of Muses, if we are poets our dramatic intuitions and sympathies for Poesy's history must be unerring, clear hearted and bold; to sign our names to laurel mediocrity or merely good verse, smart verse, useful verse, shapely verse, fine verse for this or that work horse or mare, excellent packaged verse for *New Yorker* magazine or even *Poetry*, charmingly printed slightly jagged original attempts at variations for literature, or occasional strands of haikuesque observation, would be to continue counterfeiting an official literary life in the same tradition of stultification and boredom and small time careerist politicking in arts and letters officialese as over half a century ago disheartened Pound, Williams and new creative Steiglitz friends attempting to waken native aesthetic consciousness in these States; and similarly two decades ago roughly all of us present witnessed or partook, in various radiant or dismaying roles, in similar crisis in public consciousness not only in Poesy—freeing it from mind-forged shackles of an archaic prosody—but also in American Person.

That change of Person has affected all of us as poets willingly or not, and has affected the manner of presentation of almost all poetry books 1970 we attempted to judge, loosening up the verse of poets whose forms had once been unnaturally rigid and unoriginal, imitative of a "tradition" which never actually existed outside of the minds of second-rate poets of earlier times, enemies of Pound's and Williams' aesthetic praxis—to say nothing of Whitman. Remember how hideous current taste for the "acceptable" has always been, from the Hall-Pack-Simpson[61] exclusion of all originally form'd verse in their last gasp of '50s decade menial survey of poetrics, a choice which given 20 years experience seems nonsensical enuf to scratch head puzzling on't, back to the Academy Classics Series *American Poetry Anthology*, Allyn and Bacon, Boston,

---

61 Reference is to several editors of academic anthologies that were published at the time.

1923 which traced the line of acceptable letters forward thru turn of century from Sidney Lanier thru Ina Coolbrith, John Boyle O'Reilly, John Bannister Tabb, Eugene Field, Edwin Markham, Henry Van Dyke, James Whitcomb Riley, Henry Culyer Bunner, Katherine Lee Bates, Danske Dandridge, Frank Dempster Sherman, Hamlin Garland, Clinton Scollard, Louise Imogen Guiney, Ernest McGaffrey, Benjamin Sledd, Henry Holcomb Bennett, Richard Hovey, Madison Cawein, Edwin Arlington Robinson, Robert Frost, Joyce Kilmer, Alan Seeger, Amy Lowell, Carl Sandburg, Witter Bynner, Vachel Lindsay, Charles Hansen Towne, Archibald Rutledge and Theodosia (Garrison) Faulks. That was only 1923, a glance at Oscar Williams' anthology later choices shows more professional involvement but similar irrelevant judgments; the history of prizes Pulitzer and NBA and otherwhere generally dreary even from '55 times on when there was definite Renaissance in U.S. poetic world both East coast and West more notoriously. None of that historic alteration, from what was called silent generation well groomed or combed poetry, basically academic in nature in a more open form (variously practiced in fact by 9 of 10 poets nominated by ourselves for prize considerations '70) has been acknowledged properly by the journalistic and academic prize giving system in which we are participating, particularly for specific poets who were heroes of the original effort of our own generation to transform that poetry, even against the wishes and practices of most of the judges on the present committee. Now it is true that we have all come to some friendly social terms, and that the first despairing arguments I myself had with fellow judges Kizer, Snodgrass and Howard appear'd to have been superseded by mutual affections, maturation of their taste to include poets as worthy whom they thought once formless or frivolous, or prosodic alteration of the judge's own poetic style following general cultural impulse initiated by earlier technicians of open breath poetries but when we come now down to case and person in present ruminations over comparative value of our fellow poets books for 1970, ancient history repeats: Snodgrass now, as then, is convinced that no "major" work has been done (I think 1960 NYC E 2 Street I threw a copy of Snyder's *Myths and Texts* out window at Snodgrass after long conversation in which he declared same boredom with his previous decade). Mike McClure's philosophically subtle *Star* perceptions unreadable to all judges except myself and Howard and Howard as ever myopically convinced of McClure's blob inadmissibility as proper culture and texts poetry. Philip Lamantia, old veteran of poetic wars and completely disinterested in the whole world of prize yatter and prosaic well made poetry that engages our attention, published again, rare event, with surrealist texts dis-

missed immediately by every judge tho Snodgrass rightly complained about
the deadness of language of most of the books considered considerable—at
any rate, here Lamantia pure poet, out of it altogether, in our attention, yet in
it for immortal attention, because his poems have more live mad free language-
highs than the reasonable poets preferred by majority of jury, this prophecy
Merlin shall make for I live before his time: and I've had to defend Lamantia
before from Howard's critical unhipness or more precisely language-stupidity,
i.e. insensitivity to the magic humors of this poe-esque genre of language and
which thus mis-takes Lamantia's proposal to "Be firm and take over the corpo-
rations with dog pudding" as inflated adolescent rhetoric rather than kindly
Pythagorean utterance; all judges preferring the high serious prosaic bombast
of, "I think of Jeffers' / obsessed will to arrive at the inhuman / view..." (MVD
[Mona Van Duyn]). And it's this sort of deficiency of poetic inspiration, settling
for a little wit, a little humane generalization, a little understandably flat moral,
even a little quatrain here and there, or a lot of comfy even blank verse lines
that look like solid "work"—that makes the present tendency of the judges
(toward Van Duyn, Swenson and Merwin) so dispiriting to me, historically and
poetically, and it will be dispiriting for the multitude of poets in America and
the revolutionarily sensitive-minded youthful readers of poetry if prizes con-
tinue to be awarded to poets whose work is not even exciting—who methodi-
cally denounce inspiration—in fact! Isn't this the same old argument for
proportion order and work we went thru a decade ago, that WCW [William
Carlos Williams] went thru all his life? Whalen's book last year mentioned at
Rexroth's insistence I presume, and this year's at my last minute intervention, it
seemed so little part of the mainstream of acceptable writing, tho obviously
likeable to judges other than myself—although I gather from Carolyn Kizer
'twas accepted probably more to placate my possible egotistic fury than for the
quality of the man or his work itself. Snyder having been miraculously ignored
in prize giving for the decade now maybe acknowledged as worthy of inclusion
on our list of runners up, though single-handedly he's introduced the entire
planetary ecological crisis into U.S. poetry, so to speak, and in this book altered
the whole revolutionary practice of the younger generation (probably as usual
unbeknownst to present judges as they were insensitive to his re-introduction
of Buddhism and political Bodhisattvic radicalism into poetry over a decade
ago) (into poetry and into national mind-consciousness) with his famous and
"immortal" (if there be any human memory after this century's left) redefini-
tion of the exploited masses, *Long Hair* section *Regarding Wave*, "the most /
Revolutionary consciousness is to be found / among the most ruthlessly

exploited classes / animals, trees, water, air, grasses" which statement with other phrasings in this book distributed widely amongst nonacademic youths thru underground newspapers has already broken thru Marxist revolutionary youth culture rhetoric and naturalized and humanized the revolutionary perceptions of thousands and thousands of active heads. Popularity or politics is not proposed as criteria here: the prophetic function of poetry is, the active tho unacknowledged legislative precision is, and notice must be taken—as it has not this year or any previous—that some poets like Corso or Snyder have actually defined large areas of our communal consciousness and that, particularly this year again, whether the judges are aware of it or not, some of the texts under consideration—Snyder's *Revolution within the Revolution within the Revolution* and Corso's Kerouac–death text *Elegiac Feelings American* (that text alone as published in *Ramparts* out of whole book of varying prophecies and inventions) already have, overtly, instructed and defined large numbers of people's imaginative action and sense of history on East and West coasts thru underground dissemination.

So what are you proposing: That Mona Van Duyn has a better EAR than Gregory Corso, a greater economy, a more fertile sense of invention, a greater grasp of history, a greater involvement of person with poetics, a superior shrewdness in phrasing, a loftier metaphysic, even a more practical band? Are you all mad? Have you no sense of modesty or proportion to your dreadful ambition to reduce all poetic judgment to domesticated mediocrity? There is nothing wrong with Van Duyn's book except that it is not the work of Genius, and there is nothing right about Corso's book except that it is the work of Genius, absolutely, irrevocably, line by line, invented phrase by invented phrase, death thrill by politic prophecy, scratched Egyptic reverie by learned Druid reverie, contemporary Elegy by Amerindian loaded requiem, an entire book of thought-language unrivaled by any book proposed for electric-crackle of weird classic poetics phrase by phrase, dense dense dense like Rimbaud or Crane or Corso is dense—so dense too hard to read overnight unless you're already a pure poet reading for poetry not second-rate humanistic ideas comfortable to read and propose as "magazine verse." Yes remember Spicer's category, "Magazine Verse." That's what you'd substitute for the inspired public prophetics of McClure, Corso or more rarified Lamantia, much less the practical sutra-text-like solid discourses of McClure's *Surge,* or *Poisoned Wheat* (*Star,* out of consideration); or Whalen's *Birthday Poem* summation of recent history; or Snyder's *Revolution,* etc.

Merwin is intelligent, and begins to experiment formally tho icily with warmer metrics out of Smart, already a genre extended by Corso a decade ago; Strand is bright-precise of idea at best, at mediocre also moving humanely experimenting with Smart's mystic line to good effect for himself, but magazine verse silly in *New Poetry Handbook*, "Darker." May Swenson certainly the most liberated formally, and precisely observant (except for Van Duyn in illness alone) like an intelligent lady in "Geometrid," "Iconographs," or other nature / insect / ocean touches, paper wings, "Everything Happens" waves, — and that is the limit: formal liberation a bit gaga tho charming and intelligence, "precisely observed" as they used to say re. Marianne Moore for a quality of attention rare enuf tis true ground to walk on eye to see with tis true but not yet Genius, not yet the Poet's poet or Teacher to Age and Youth, not prophetic, for all the rhetorical blurb from Stafford attenuated down page to Howard—I keep saying there is nothing wrong with many choices Harper Finkel Swenson Van Duyn except lack of historic overwhelming genius, and there is nothing right with the poets I've so insistently proposed to your attention this year as previous decades except the genius of their life—works inclusive of important texts named above in books present before us.

I had not seen myself as participant in bureaucracy of letters, working within system, as so oft proposed by nonpoets and nonrevolutionaries, but felt for peace's sake drawn to participate in this jury as invited, knowing the gulfs and pitfalls and previous disagreements on precisely similar issues over a decade ago between all of us (with exception of Thorpe Mann alas innocent bystander of this literary gangbopping)—but as I see the same inexorable closedown of safe bad taste, limited and unimaginative sophistication, and goopy personal alliances move to limit your perceptions—once again: to the poetic genius confronting you in the McClure Lamantia Whalen Snyder Corso line up—I am forced again to break the proprieties of the literary game played, not "be reasonable," not let you forget the past—(and I haven't till now even brought up here the genius of Kerouac as poet which none of you've ever caught on to, which wanting, all your perceptions of contemporary composition fall awry)—not, as I'm slightly tempted for peace and time saving's sake let it slide—or was tempted before I blew it on phone and essayed this epistle as of yore—but I cannot as Mona Van Duyn wittily advises in her charmingly literate quatrains mistake beaky nose for Divine Swan visage for I have constant warning even more wittily phrased from Corso: "What blessed knockout O Champ of Heaven / nears in thy fist of sky / my visionic eye / all its stars of kayo." So that rather than sit still with the committee to determine Genius and let it function dully and satisfactorily to the trade, my duty as poet judge here is to disrupt present consciousness and convenience including my own and resist what appears to me to be your tendency to make the same life-mistake again, wet-blanket Poesy, and present to outer world a prized poet/ess whose naming is repetitious Unenthusiasm, a poet whose victory no one with sense will thrill and sigh with happiness to know announced, — or more precisely to point. A prize to Snyder is just and announces a sacred political Bodhisattva presence officially; a prize to Whalen enriches a poor sage and publicizes an under- ground wiseman; a prize to Corso gives a prize to History, shocks mediocre academy habit, safeguards his sick person, flashbulbs intelligence among the young, and would probably engage the prize givers in all sorts of awkward con- frontations with the Poet at laurel—dinner. McClure Lamantia Duncan others as prizewinners would've ratified history also but like much of history these were early eliminated from our consideration, formally speaking.

I began to say I'd not earlier conceived myself in judge's role especially because comparisons are odious so I've attempted to avoid heavy negation in my critiques above: but one fantasy I hold to, in this situation, bureau system establishment committee power judge, not to·participate if it means, in the end affirming prizes to mediocre muse while genius is present alive in the country: this is a horror fantasy I'm sure we all share who remember our own youthful outsider's vision of poetic politics of yore. Disrupt the social situation as it may, I insist on my own responsibility to that politic-social-poetic vision and your own responsibility to historically articulated genius.

As ever,

Allen Ginsberg

[*Ginsberg was always generous with his time, but sometimes people expected more of him than he could deliver. This letter is a good example of what happened when Allen lost patience with a poet who wanted him to make them instantly successful.*]

Allen Ginsberg [New York, NY] to Norman Moser [Austin, TX]
January 2, 1972

Dear Norm:

I'm sorry I haven't been able to help you or more poets but I've been help- ing the poets I knew and whose work moved me spontaneously as much as I've been able. Most all of the bread I make from readings gets recycled via farm-retreat or direct bread to a lot of poets over last seven years—more than I make on my books, and I live on what I get from books, not readings. But it also comes to difficulty that too many people hit me up for bread, or help, or prefaces, or pull, etc. and get angry if I'm incompetent to do more than I physically can. I have been stuck literally all this last 2 weeks writing preface to Ed Marshall's poetry, which I've wept over, admired it for 17 years—but also working on Marshall's manuscript has prevented me from moving ahead typing up the last year's poems of my own. So my own work has been cut in half because of divided attention, like this, and because I still try to answer letters, like this. I'm now in debt, from spending and giving too freely. If you wonder why I never gave money in your direction, it's because there was a limited amount, going mostly to people in bad trouble that I knew well and people like Corso or Whalen or Huncke who I felt were my teachers. I'm not Ford Foundation.

I can't make Ferlinghetti publish against his will, we don't agree on all poetry text matters, so it isn't a "'united front,' as long as you, Gary, Ferlinghetti do not publish or acknowledge newer poets like myself, Joe, etc." Ferlinghetti won't publish Marshall, nor Charlie Plymell—both of whom I felt strongly enough about to write prefaces—and I don't know Joe's poetry, and I don't feel strongly enough moved to tears by yours as I have been by Marshall's or Plymell's—and so what should I do? I am not "chief honcho" tho I have influence and use it where I can, but it is much more haphazard and weak than you set it up to be—so that I get upset by your letter blaming me for your situation as if I or Snyder—or Ferl!—were the only way of moving the nation, poetically. Our loose liaison is one of myriad, and it's too loose to be a Pure Gate—as I said Ferl doesn't publish all poets I recommend so I only recommend poets rarely when I really know, want, and mean it. Your idea assumes that all I have to do is write a note, whether I feel it or not, and it's done! On top of that Ferl publishes less poetry now and wants prose—published Plymell's prose refused his poetry.

Snyder has a whole set of different poetic interests and younger poets of his own concern—doesn't coincide with mine.

I send out most of my work to mimeo mags run by small presses or nearly unknown—about $1/5$ of my poetry gets to large magazines—or less—it's a random matter as I don't have secretary so whenever I get a poem typed I send it to whatever letter asks nearest to reach—it's about that haphazard since I have no index file of requests, I get say 100 requests a year, only have 20 poems or less a year, and have no way to keeping it straight.

I am actually overloaded with mail from poets, I answer what I can most all of it and put my support there looking over a few pages at a time and writing marginal comments as W.C.W. did for me.

You have no idea how much mail I get and answer, and how much extra curricular literary activity I do—I once made vow not to do mechanical prefaces and letters of recommendation. I find now that the poets I do love and would labor for are too many as it is. I get overloaded, and do more, trying to answer honestly, than I can without cutting into my own muse time. So for that reason my own poetic life's been slightly crippled. It's my Karma—as it is my Karma to have to try explain this way in specific detail rather than sending you a cheery New Years postcard saying Sure Sure Happy Destiny Good Luck.

The national reading circuit ("How does one get on the national reading circuit?")—usually is managed professionally by high powered professor poets like Dickey or Ciardi and is a commercial prestige matter I don't know how they do it. Snyder or his wife answers mail and makes his own arrangements. Ferl does same. I have an agent do mine because, after reading 1956–1965 free, refusing money except expenses, I was already so well known that I needed agent to handle letters, phone calls, he has a secretary for that and she's paid $3.00 per hour. The agent I use, Charles Rothschild, approached me 6 years ago and is honest. However he did not work out for McClure, Corso or others I suggested to him, as they are less easy show-biz than I am, so this probably be no help in your situation. The situation I have is eccentric and jerry-built and not a prefabricated structure I can hand on to anyone else by push-button or even letter or even long conversation.

I remember *Desert Review* and have published there years ago but can't (now) remember editor, never heard of *Gar*. "If you and your friends ordered" —Oh No! Shit Norman, what am I going to do, write Ferl and Gary and insist that they get together and publish your friends, whether Ferl and Gary agree or not? As if Ferl and Gary didn't have their own poets they admire and gotta take on my business, and gotta throw my weight around like "chief honcho" and make them read poems I don't have time to read, write round robin letters on this occasion also as well as the dozens I already got waiting years behind—and also write *Gar* from Zeus' Heaven throwing Ginsbergian thunderbolt "publish Moser! and Joe! and Jim Cody! and everyone who deserves!" Help!

I mean, you're laying a life's trip on me, and I try to stagger along with as many life's trips as I can including my brother Eugene (just wrote a preface for his book, which he's mimeographing himself—couldn't get a publisher even with my preface). But what upsets me Norman is I keep thinking you're blaming me for what you interpret as your difficulties, as if I had a $ commercial monopoly on the national poetry scene. I keep saying, I have weight and influence spottily where my word is backed up by my feeling, but it's a random spontaneous matter and can't be turned on and off like Billie Holiday's love faucet—but I never finished a thought from several pages previous—which is that you're blaming me for not helping younger poets, but you have no clear idea of how many situations I do try—and now am overloaded, I keep saying it's my own Karma as I've left myself open to be bugged as I did cultivate a reputation for being helpful as I could, my own—ego, I suppose the reason for this is my wounded ego—but shit on my wounded ego, it's no more wounded than yours or anyone's... and you're laying your wounded poetic ego on me—and Joe and Jim's and "sundry supporters" as well!—Heaven help us all!

Ach, this is long enough—"Death is a letter that was never sent"—thanks for your letter anguishing though it was—send a xerox of this to *Gar* or *Desert Review*—I'm going back to my own poetry—no! Help—I still have to retype Marshall preface—tonite—I'm still not free. Hum Hum Hum—please don't make me write big letters! Ah ah ah—maybe I can do Marshall tomorrow!—when do I get to do my own typing? next week? No! Now! No! Marshall! No! Moser! No! Me! No! Buddha!

Love

Allen

[*Abbie Hoffman was arrested in a drug bust in 1973, and Ginsberg, a long-time friend, led the fight in his defense. In this letter he tried to show that Abbie had been a target of the government and was intentionally singled out for arrest.*]

Allen Ginsberg [New York, NY] to Gerald Lefcourt [New York, NY]
August 29, 1973

To Whom It May Concern:

On behalf of political poet Abbie Hoffman reported arrested with friends and a group of government men over three pounds of cocaine, I wish to share my thoughts:

First I bear witness to his special experience in the honorable cause of peace protest in the face of violent denial of human civil rights to citizens in America and out of it, especially during course of Indochinese War activity foisted on this nation by government. Abbie Hoffman has already been jailed many times for seeking, with peaceful fire and good humored street theatre and astonishing public drama, redress of grievances for the bad luck of the Vietnam War.

Reviled and insulted at first for articulating a now commonly held opinion of that war, he defended himself and others against defeated government accusations of conspiracy, illegal speech, gesture and public assembly in urging the war end. In this situation he became a hero in a nation engulfed with moral catastrophe, and no man of any generation in right mind can be but grateful for Abbie Hoffman's inventive national communication of the war's madness and folly. I remain grateful for his righteous indignation over the Vietnam War, the moral power of his deeply-felt resistance to the injustice of it, and his demonstration of free imagination against mass complacency at the mass murder in which we were all involved.

Abbie Hoffman was one of the first souls in the nation to make consciousness sensitive to the Eichmann-like nature of our public war-guilt. Thus any legal case in which he is involved is a matter of deep political consideration, requiring special attention, straight heart judgment and exquisite moral care— that public resentment against him as god-fool of conscience not crush him in present legal difficulty.

We are now in midst of national scandal of government misbehavior called Watergate. High politicians preaching law and order were themselves habitually breaking Bill-of-Rights laws in the interests of the creation of some sort of police state. Patriotism was as usual the refuge of these scoundrels, who wrapped themselves in the language of the flag, in order to trash the Constitution. This is an age-old pattern. Unauthorized wiretapping, spying, use of agents-provocateurs and double agents, spooks, burglaries, police set-ups, official perjury, in-government conspiracy to deprive citizens of protection against excess government snooping and illegal infra-war activity, domestic surveillance of political enemies. This pattern of Watergate crooked-heartedness was precisely the government pattern denounced prophetically by Abbie Hoffman. Some of these same Watergate actors defamed and prosecuted Abbie Hoffman precisely for his vocal and theatrical resistance to their war machine. He too wrapped himself in the flag, threw free money off the balconies of the stock market, wrote forbidden words on his brow, woke the young to national disaster, and practiced exorcism of a black magic operating in the highest reaches of respectable government—illusory statistics, lying, public deception, conspiracy mania even mass assassination in Vietnam, Operation Phoenix confessed in public before Congress. Constriction by government on his own liberty, such as wiretapping, has I believe been proven in court in the course of numerous trials by which the government tried to knock Abbie Hoffman and his peace friends out of action against war and growth of police state.

So I bear witness that Abbie Hoffman is not an ordinary citizen, member of a silent majority of citizens compliant with 1984-style bureaucracy and acquiescent to remote-control war. Hoffman is a patriot who has fought the Good Fight to waken his fellow Americans to the corruption of their own traditional ideals. Like Tom Paine, he is a classic example of philosophic and poetic dramatist of public ideals, a pamphleteer and book man, seeking liberty for his illegal war and police state, not touched deeply by the courts, till late—they were touched deeply by Abbie Hoffman.

Thus his social position as a leader or theorist of new survival society credits him with deliberation and reason. In recent conversation Abbie explains his arrest as the following circumstance: He was researching relationship between Mafia drug dealing and police for a new text he was preparing for publication. Thus he got trapped in the middle of a coke sale surrounded by police dealing with each other while posing as big time gangsters.

In time of communal apathy synchronous with Abbie Hoffman's recent disillusioned withdrawal to private life (after crises of his public efforts to confound government police bureaucracy and war led him to be attacked left and right), Mr. Hoffman is now to be congratulated on an arrest which by its very surprise, its simultaneous whimsicality and seriousness, re-unites many of his fellow workers once again to resist the steamroller of police state power crushing another live citizen's body.

Mr. Hoffman's arrest for cocaine dealing does not bear toward resolution of the real "hard drug" problem in America, in any way, shape or form. Government's visioned sentence of life for Abbie Hoffman resolves no whit the real tormenting drug problem in America, but only adds more pain and hysteria to the scene.

What is the actual "hard drug" mess in America? Politicians, police, drug bureaucrats, and criminal syndicates run wild over the public, and over sick junkies, against professional medical-scientific advisement—greed and money is their addiction, and violence and hypocrisy their works.

The real drug problem in America is that government narcotics bureaucracies and organized crime have had a status quo working relationship for decades. This arrangement denies legitimate opiate addicts reasonable access to their specific medicines. The black market for opiates consequently created serves to increase the number of addicts, not decrease it, serves only to increase the social disorientation of addiction, not cure it, serves to discredit helpless sick citizens, not minister to them. This arrangement increases the pain of addiction. This arrangement profits only Narcotics Control Agencies and Organized Crime Networks. Both depend on continued criminalization of addicts to maintain their complementary parasitic existences. Both groups have grown with the growth of the black market they have created. In this situation the medically sick junkie is a victim, treated like a Jew under Hitler, driven mad in the streets to seek relief from unendurable pain and social degradation imposed on him by police bureaucracy and organized crime.

This moral and political running sore, uncured by self-righteous anger at heroin addicts, further infected with hysteria by current draconian law, is opened afresh in an operation in which agents of the drug bureaucracy represent themselves over dramatically buying pounds of old Bohemian cocaine from Abbie Hoffman and friends. Cocaine in my experience is a drug neither hard nor soft, offering too short a flash of common use, too expensive for psychological habit generally, traditionally the sport of self indulgent millionaires more recently gaga rock stars.

The seriousness of punishment promised by vengeful prosecutors—one of whom characterized Abbie Hoffman's hapless alleged dabbling in cocaine as "insidious and treacherous as homicide"—opens up the great drug question—not so much of Hoffman's legal or moral guilt, which notion is considerable whimsical in fact. His arrest raises the publicly suppressed drug question: How can we endure longer the total insanity sadism incoherence and incomprehensibility of past and fresh present narcotics law politics? Mr. Hoffman's arrest, by its own built-in heaviness of consequence, raises challenge to the entire fabric of law that confuses foolish sensational cocaine or serious philosophic psychedelics as "hard drugs" with the strong-habit-forming opiates and overplentiful brain-cooking amphetamines. How dare government bureaucracy impose penalties on use and sale of hard drugs for the last half century without providing (as do other countries successfully) reasonably satisfactory easily accessible medical services for the majority of addicts who now outnumber and for 150,000 reasons don't fit into recent but limited scope of monolithic NY police-bureaucracy-supervised methadone maintenance services.

Beyond this colossal infliction of pain on heroin addicted citizens, present law perpetuates discomforting sanctions against marijuana use, contrary to the best counsel of reason and science codified into innumerable public reports, and contrary to vast community experience, by what unconstitutional proscription of liberty and pursuit of happiness must the drug bureaucracy maintain its heavy criminal penalties for securing gardening and distributing sociable noncommercial quantities of hemp weed. What state violence is used to suppress herbal cigarette smokes. The soft drug situation remains undefined, except by official presumption and violence, confused and complicated by law and crime where it might be simply free of law and crime but regulated as in other societies by common sense of situation.

News of Abbie Hoffman's arrest proposes shock dismay and mental rejection of the idea that life imprisonment for cocaine drug entrapment by police (with no eligibility for parole for 15 to 25 years, depending on pronouncement of the judge) is a sane response to the fact of cocaine and its elitist use in U.S.A. Mandatory life for cocaine is neurotic, irrational, a hysterical swipe at people's souls, a polyphemus body crusher punishment, a killer idea—it is not sober social response to cocaine usage and special problems, it is no help to old ladies in the street mugged by ignorant junkies conditioned to depravation violence and pain with police bureaucracy and mafia fattening on the illegality of addiction. Life in jail for anti-war hero Abbie Hoffman and friends is national folly. Threat of life behind bars for Hoffman over cocaine sale is not an image of Law and Order, it is an image of bureaucratic dictatorship and confusion, it is misrule and chaos, national folly.

I pray with body speech and mind OM AH HUM for courts and government and public to recognize the strange delicacy and historical charm of the situation in which they are placed together with peace poet Abbie Hoffman

And myself sincerely yours

Recommending Hare Krishna to one and all

Allen Ginsberg

[*Early in the 1970s, Ginsberg began to take formal Buddhist training from Tibetan lama Chögyam Trungpa. In this letter, he described some of his meditation practice to his French translator and friend, Jean Jacques Lebel.*]

Allen Ginsberg [Cherry Valley, NY] to Jean Jacques Lebel [Paris, France] January 6, 1974

Dear Jean Jacques Lebel:

Spent from September to December in Wyoming. Yes was Chögyam Trungpa who I've been seeing last few years, he's been teaching me meditation —just sitting at moment following breath out nostril dissolving into space thus mixing breath with space, mind with breath, thus mixing mind with space in front of face thus short-circuiting discursive thought daydream & sleepiness with each attentive breath thus opening up awakened space, more precisely, wakening awareness of space around the room, the planet, etc. Other tendency he's turned me on to much like Kerouac is improvisation. Now when I give poetry readings I try to do something usually blues form with harmonium, made up on stage on spot, from whatever theme politics Dharma-chakra or sex is hanging over the hall. Also been teaching Trungpa U.S. poetry—Kerouac, W. C. Williams and Whitman—& we gave some poetry readings together to raise money for his monasteries—so spent 3 months [at] his Buddhist seminary about 60 of his pupils together we sat 25 days for 10 hours a day, rest of time studied old texts on meditation and he expounded a large-scale map of Tibetan Buddhist exercises from Hinayana breath mindfulness exercises to ultimate tantric return to spontaneous passions & return to world mindful of suffering as essential condition. Also he'd suggested to me for Miami antiwar conventions last year to use AH as mantra rather than OM for mass protection against police. He reminds me of Kerouac, drinks & cries, full of sharp minded ancient prac- tices. Lovely guru. Gossip from friends traveling thru India is that he's famous among Tibetan community as good meditation teacher & trained in highest tra- ditional doctrines empowered to teach all the mysteries Artaud was curious about so to speak—tho all the Lamas are a little worried about his health— drinking & fucking. His basic attitude is that there's no nirvana wisdom etc., just disillusionment from fantasies & hopes & mind trips which cover up basic suffering & boredom—in that sense much like later Kerouac—but that realiza- tion of basic suffering & emptiness of personality & continuous chaos of world leads to compassionate action to relieve people of daydream they're going somewhere ideal, thus relieving the worst cause of suffering. Ignorance of the basic egoless situation we're all in. That's putting it all in nutshell. No vision just total boredom till examining the texture of the boredom the wall the skin etc. everything comes into compassionate focus. This is mostly his language.

Regarding politics, any action taken in hostile emotion or with aggression as motive leads to more hostility & aggression, & aggression in form of capital monopoly or psychic power monopoly is root of personal & social woe— aggression to maintain & reinforce illusion of separate egohood & its powers. This is classic Buddhist notion, terminology updated. [...]

As ever

Allen

[*Timothy Leary was also in trouble with the law during the 1970s and as an old friend, Gins-berg wanted to be of help. In Leary's case, however, he was being held in prison incommuni-cado and mixed signals were being sent about whether he wanted or needed help.*]

**Allen Ginsberg [Cherry Valley, NY] to Timothy Leary
[California prison system] January 28, 1974**

Dear Tim:

Spent 3 months Teton Village Wyo studying Buddhism with Chögyam Trungpa Lama and about 60 of his disciples/students. He lectured on Hinayana, Mahayana and Vajrayana giving rough technical map of the proce-dures and intentions of each style. I'd never had a comprehensive idea before —and did 10 hour a day sitting cross-legged watching or attending breath leave nostrils and dribble off into space (i.e. mix breath with space, mix mind with breath, mix mind with space) for 25 days of that time. The effect is dis-illusioning in the sense that many of my Blake vision trips and memories tended to fade or become transparent, as mere thought forms, as present space (the room, my body sitting there) became more clear. Finally awareness of each breath could be used as Manjushri sword to cut thru discursive thought, daydream, and sleepiness. What results is a profile of recurrent thought-forms and familiarity with mind-in-anger, mind-in-sleepiness, mind thinking about Leary, mind doing this and that. It doesn't end thought, merely outlines thought as thought so it doesn't displace present time for too many breaths in a row. That's it in a nutshell. Basic Hinayana mindfulness practice. Back in NY state in attic I've been sitting 6–8 hours a day the last few weeks, will travel a week, see Dylan concert, read in Maine, do nonviolence work-shop benefit in Atlanta and come back and sit another couple weeks.

The effect of long sitting (sesshins as Zen people call them) is similar to psy-chedelic trip in very slow slow motion thought by thought stretched out weeks immobile attention fixed on neutral reliable changing-but-ever-same breath as resting place. The attention and time given and patience cause subtle changes of fixed idea and personality, which are grounded in the sense of taking place in such slow motion you can examine every thought form as it rises passes and disappears. The moment of split second of shift from a thought (about money say) back to the breath space in front of your nose is the interesting gap—Cut! as they said in movie prose! Meditation also surprisingly similar, thus, to Bur-roughs' cut-ups.

Burroughs returning to U.S. next month—will teach at CCNY English

Dept. February-May, first such scene for him. He's interested in ESP Pyramids Gimmicks Orgone Boxes Yogas EEG's Sensory Deprivation etc. and has been practicing his own very definite home-made mindfulness sitting or lying for years. I spent time with him this summer London.

Long letter from Michael Horowitz gives me general idea of your literary plans, and the idea of writing your way-out is sound, it seems to me. I don't fully understand the script—it seems so abstract, dependent on undependable abstract symbols like Kohoutek [comet]—but almost any kind of respectable literary activity will do, despite confusions of content. Thought a precise clear outline of practical legal and social predicament, summary, outline of all previous trials and future hazards at Millbrook, parole boards, etc., and account of lawyers and fees needed, and logical motions, and of your present state of mind and situation, in one package suitable for *Liberation* magazine (or *Penthouse*) and for mailings by "movement" organizations to raise money—simply a realistic inventory of the political-legal fix you're in—would produce some practical results I guess, I hope. See there doesn't seem to be any center organized for people to rally to—Joanna was in N.Y. while I was in Wyoming. Tho her visit was in some ways helpful, I hear from gossip, and the film a real discovery (I read text in Philadelphia underground *Distant Drummer* paper), the general tone was so "far out" that any practical organization was bypassed in favor of confidence in Kohoutek answering everyone's hopes. "Don't worry Kohoutek will take care of the details" seemed to be the message several months ago in NY, as your basic word. I hesitate to criticize any more since I'm not at hand to execute my own suggestions, and Joanna has carried a heavy lonesome burden spiritedly. But some down to earth practical humanistic-liberal-civil liberties clarity home pad would be helpful as base from which to travel to other planets.

NY's Mayer Vishner is in touch with Michael H. in case some move in that direction is organized—collection of money for legal fees, civil liberties appeals etc. A basic essay by you or an inspired lawyer is necessary—something straight and simple.

I'll be out in California in May with my father to read with him, then stay on May 15 to September building a little cabin in the Sierras so I can do some more extensive sitting (doing nothing). I'll see Ram Das in August in Boulder for a week we'll both be teaching at Chögyam's Naropa Institute.

Peter is in great shape, he has big tractor. Maretta Greer just arrived after 3 years on streets of Rawalpindi and Islamabad with scabies and scurvy and months in jail but she's OK. Peter's girlfriend Denise [Feliu] has a rock and roll band. I've read "Starseed" in *Village Voice*—some of the rhetoric Part II was passionate and lovely. Michael or someone will send me other later Terras.

As ever

Allen

I can do benefits anytime anything's organized, etc. as before. I did have space-ship earth to Andromeda all mankind on trip fantasy Newton Mass I remember. Didn't develop it.

TV Baby Poem, *Planet News* "... calling all Beings! in dirt form the ant to the most frightened Prophet that ever clomb tower to vision planets.—crowded in one vast space ship to Andromeda..."

Doesn't mean much to me now except general prophecy for 1,000,000 A.D. or something.

[*On occasion Ginsberg would include poetry with letters, but this is one of the very few examples where his whole letter takes the form of a poem. He wrote to his father about the construction of his cabin in the Sierra mountains next to Gary Snyder.*]

Allen Ginsberg [Nevada City, CA] to Louis Ginsberg [Paterson, NJ]
July 10, 1974

Dear Louis:

> Hard work for me potbellied city-lax,
> pushing wheelbarrows empty up hill, shoveling red dirt
> into a sieve, shaking out fine Mexican-red dust,
> lifting iron spoons full w/ clay into flat-bed jeep,
> mixing gravel from old gold mines with measures of grey concrete
> with red clay dust, to color kitchen floor, then
> watering hardened concrete with hose so it won't crack
> And logs, draw knives strip bark, chisels smooth out branch holes,
> tumbling round posts over each other a bed of two pine laid parallel,
> helping dig foot deep holes for porch stone foundation
> all work done in a month—then unseasonable rain—
> days under apartment—high ponderosa's dripping water
> onto lean-to roofed with black and white plastic rolls,
> sleeping bags muddy wet at dawn, squirrels scampering away from our apples,
> deer at Gary Snyder's pond-edge in garden—

Unexpected rain ending sweaty labor, a few days
sheltered indoors, reading Zen koans or Lu Yu's
eleventh century laughter about his drunken white hair —
Now sun's out, Wednesday sky's blue,
Cool wind in pines dries housetops and grass fields —
Trail to re-stack wet lumber to dry in sunlight,
Load the truck with second hand windows to take to Marysville
to dip in vats of chemical paint remover, and on to Frisco
to poetry reading this Friday w/ McClure & Snyder,
Benefit small island attacked by Yamaha Industries tourism —
Small sample of great natural world eaten by human cancer —
I read your friend Bluefarb's letter but could not make head or tail of it —
Yes he reasons well, but poems my stepmother likes he thinks are off track,
He doesn't believe in Jahweh but he wants me to believe,
He doesn't practice religion but wants me to practice what he rejected —
He doesn't respect my learning but wants me to respect his bookishness —
He takes things personally and denounces my vanity —
It's too confusing to argue when neither of us know what we're discussing
and meanwhile pseudo-peace in mid-east makes all previous reasons vain —
assertions of sovereignty yesteryear today are bargained away today —
Meanwhile lumber must be piled properly or it'll warp
And what I'm learning is not history or Kabbalah
but bruises on my hands and knees, splinters from rough cut wood
and how difficult it is to master the "primitive"
the old story, how I lost track of shelter and food, given them in cities,
and how hard and beautiful both seem when worked for by hand.
I'll write in a few days when returned from the white-hilled city —
Meanwhile we have each other's love while still alive —
Son,

Allen

[*Chögyam Trungpa asked Ginsberg to found a poetry department at his new Buddhist college, Naropa Institute. During the next decades, the Jack Kerouac School of Disembodied Poetics at Naropa was to take up much of Allen's time. In this newsy letter he tried to coax Gary Snyder to visit the school, much as he did all his friends. In addition, now that his cabin next to Snyder's was finished, Ginsberg had numerous household matters to discuss.*]

Allen Ginsberg [Boulder, CO] to Gary Snyder [Nevada City, CA]
July 11, 1975

Dear Gary:

Forgive me for not writing, long slow lethargy after hospital[62] and lotsa work and people here. I just let mail pile up and sent messages with Phil [Whalen].

To the point: Enclosed your $50 check returned, I'll charge rent on the place normally but between us it's a family matter and there doesn't seem to be need for so formal a rent arrangement, especially for Masa's [Snyder's wife] parents. Besides which the amount of attention and work you've put into the house and general overseeing you do balances out any rent etc. if reasons are necessary. Gimme a kiss instead.

Anne Waldman and Michael Brownstein plan to spend part or all of September there—Michael has a poetry reading October 9 in Bay Area—so they'll be there till at latest October 5, probably leave a week earlier.

I haven't written to Jonathan or Bob Ericson about general state of construction, tho both've written me, inquiring a bit. Haven't been writing letters —but received note from Bill Crosby saying he needs shelter for next winter and offering work-exchange, which sounds fine, if he can accommodate to early October move-in. Says he can put in firewood during summer and build woodshed, which'll be great improvement. I'm going to take a month solitary retreat this fall maybe September but I think I'll do it on some Chögyam land to get experience how they organize it traditionally and then can use cabin later for any similar solitudes with some quasi-formal experience. I'll be in SF maybe in December—Anne mentioned that Michael McClure mused on setting up a 6 Gallery memorial reading then.

How does Bill Crosby sound as tenant? Had you any other idears? I'd write him directly but want to check with you first. If it's OK let him know if not write or phone me collect here.

Naropa Kerouac School of Poetics been lovelier and livelier even than imagined. Burroughs was here a month, he and Trungpa circling each other warily and finally meeting drunk last nite of his stay long talk, taped. "Well if Mr. Burroughs wants to take a typewriter with him into month retreat, maybe we make special dispensation." "Well if the Trungpa says no typewriter,

---

62 Ginsberg had suffered an attack of Bell's palsy.

maybe I won't take a typewriter." Gregory Corso here outrageous shithead borrowing money from students calling Trungpa a "dumb asshole" in midst of all sangha assembled speech, SHUT UP! vajra voice from Trungpa's chair— and then they had tea the next day, and we all taught a poetry class together— final exam all the students wrote poems about how they all loved Gregory and everyone taking Gregory as some kind of human koan. What to do with him. He's been in basically good shape for him—with French girlfriend no dope but darvon. Up in the mountain W. S. Merwin—sitting and coming to classes on Vajrayana and having intelligent suppers with Gregory and Anne and Joanne and Peter Warshall. My parents here for 2 weeks in my big apartment. Ed Sanders and wife and babe here now. Philip been here, and Ted Berrigan and New York poets Anne brought in Dick Gallup—local poets Jack Collum —extended meeting, and we're all housed in 8 apartment ghetto one big house with Lama Karma Tinley and Francesco Freemantle sanskritist just published new translation *Book of Dead*. Merwin and John Ashbery read next all-school reading—been having big readings every Wednesday. Bill and Gregory to start, then me and Phil, then Diane di Prima and Berrigan and Anne Waldman, then Sanders and Brownstein—Peter due out here to teach bucolic poesy in a month.

Will you be passing thru? Session runs July 21-August 23, then maybe I'll take off for retreat or a weeks sesshin to begin with—dunno. If you're still planning Utah trip let me know—plenty room here for stopover. Warshall taught all the poetry classes too with slides on animal aesthetics. Gregory taught my class the first week I was sick. Merwin, Anne, Gregory and me each read Shelley's *[Ode to the] West Wind* our own interpretations in one class—3 or 4 older poets listening in each class. I started with seafarer and read thru Shelley and Marvell and Smart when I discovered half my class never read nothing but Snyder and Kerouac and *Howl* in high school and college—half the class had never read *West Wind*, so I went back in time and taught weird selected survey course "Scepter and Crown must tumble down" etc. Winding up tonight with WCW and Kerouac and session—my father taught Keats my last class.

So—Ed Sanders may drop by before September he's in 4 wheel drive land rover headed west to Bolinas.

Joanne [Kyger] acts crazy when she's drunk—Chögyam told her sit more she seemed relieved.

I'm recovering tho still my stamina is low. Going to homeopathic doctor.

Finished book of songs and sent it to printer Full Court Press care of St. Marks Project—illustrated with lead sheets music for half the songs.

OK—love to Masa. I hear your little retreat cabin's great beauty and done already.

Love

Allen

[*In 1975 Bob Dylan asked Ginsberg to tour with his Rolling Thunder Revue and help him make a movie at the same time. The result was the film,* Renaldo and Clara. *While on tour near Lowell, Massachusetts, Ginsberg and Dylan took the opportunity to film in Kerouac's hometown.*]

Allen Ginsberg [Lowell, MA] to Louis Ginsberg [Paterson, NJ]
November 4, 1975

Dear Louis

Beautiful day with Dylan in Lowell Mass, beginning early afternoon visiting Kerouac's grave plot & reading the stone "He honored the world"[63]—We stood in the November sun brown leaves flying in wind & read poems from *Mexico City Blues,* then we sat down, Dylan played my harmonium, Peter beside him, & we traded lines improvising a song to Kerouac underground beneath grass & stone. Then Dylan played blues chords on his guitar, while I improvised a ten stanza song about Jack looking down with empty eyes from clouds. Dylan stopped guitar to stuff a brown leaf in his breast pocket while I continued solo voice, & he picked up his guitar to pluck it on the beat perfect to the end of my stanza—little celestial inspired ditty on Kerouac's grave—all recorded for movie then shot many other scenes in Catholic statue grotto Jack wrote about, near an orphanage—Dylan conversing w/ statue of Christ.

Staying here a few days, then to Stockbridge.

Dylan wants to do some scene related to Sacco & Vanzetti when we get to Boston. Thoreau near Walden. A Bicentennial picture. We shot some scenes on Mayflower replica, & at Pilgrim Plymouth Rock.

Stay well, hang on, more work to do to come.

Love

Allen

63 The actual epitaph reads, "He honored life."

[Barry Miles had been Allen's friend since the 1960s and was instrumental in helping Allen make and organize his recordings. It was through Miles, who wrote a good deal about rock music, that Ginsberg met many of the British rock stars of the era, including the Beatles.]

Allen Ginsberg [New York, NY] to Barry Miles [London, England]
ca. **May 10, 1976**

Miles:

I've been in the studio with John Hammond producing *First Blues* record. Columbia approved rough mixes for issue — dirty songs and all. Hard on Blues, Guru Blues, CIA Dope Calypso, etc. and new songs. Arthur Russell and Jon Sholle played, and a 19 year old genius musician David Mansfield from Dylan Rolling Thunder Band — he plays pedal steel, dobro, violin, rhythm guitar, bass, piano, mandolin, and drums. Sholle says it's the best 16 track work we've done so far. I'll make final mix with Hammond July in NY. We did it in three 3 hour sessions, need another 3 hours to mix, all mostly first or second takes. Russell and Sholle knew the music for years and Mansfield picked up overnight with celestial sympathy. I mean celestial bell-like sounds on mandolin and pedal steel, somehow intuitively accenting and punctuating my own native sense of time so that a lot of riffs came out of 3 dimensions like I hear music in my head. Happy chances!

I may go to Berlin briefly in September if Louis's health permits,[64] and if he's gone, go with Peter to Trungpa's 3 month tantra seminary as I did in 1973 — Peter wants to go sit now. Life is closing, death is nigh, in fact it already happened. I recorded all my songs solo with harmonium last year at Chelsea Hotel in Harry Smith's Wollensack room. No action from Fantasy. If I lay out money to pay you (I still have an account at Jonathan Cape) can you go to up to Cambridge and arrange Blake album to illustration-transparencies, when and if time comes I can get Fantasy (or maybe Columbia) to put them out? MGM has now discontinued Volume 1 after re-issuing it with horrible irrelevant gray mafiaesque photo cover in Archetype series. Rights to both albums probably have reverted to me: if I can get Rothschild to get masters back from MGM and Fantasy I can put them out double album at last. Rothschild is now inquiring. Do you remember if we have copies of both masters at Columbia library? My own head is so dispersed, fragmented I can't remember.

I was passing by Dakota Apartments last month, phoned upstairs and vis-

---

64 Allen's father was dying of cancer at this time.

ited John Lennon and Yoko Ono for an hour. Lennon said he was retired tem-
porarily from Los Angeles music scene, staying home with baby and extreme
clean diet. They went on 40 day fast after baby birth—he said he couldn't live
happily with all the cocaine, alcohol madness on the L.A. music scene. Said he
was lying sleepless one night listening to WBAI earphones and heard someone
reciting a long poem, he thought it was Dylan till he heard the announcer say it
was Ginsberg reading HOWL. He said he'd never read it or understood it
before, his eye'd seen the page but "I can't read anything, I can't get anything
from print" but once hearing it aloud he suddenly understood, he said, why
Dylan had often mentioned me to him and suddenly realized what I was doing
and dug it—said he himself at the moment was interested in spoken word and
did I have any more that I could send him on tape cassette. I explained to him
what you and I had been doing in 1971, assembled vocalized poems for Apple—
he said oh so that's what it was—said he didn't understand at the time. He'd
seen me as some kind of strange interesting American supposed to be a poet
hanging around but didn't understand exactly what my role was. Now he said
he understood how close my style was to Dylan's and how it influenced Dylan
and also dug my voice reciting, the energy. So I'm sending him a bunch of cas-
settes of HOWL, KADDISH and Blake. I wish I had cassettes of our 16 albums
which Fantasy/Bendich once promised. It sure was nice hearing Lennon close
that gap, complete that circle and treat me like a fellow artist as he walked me
to the door goodbye.

Love,

Allen

[*Ginsberg's father grew weaker and died on July 8, 1976. Just before the end, Allen wrote
this letter which showed elements of his poem, "Don't Grow Old," in prose form. It also
revealed Allen's growing interest in music as a pleasure of its own and a means to reach
larger audiences.*]

Allen Ginsberg [Boulder, CO] to Gregory Corso [Paris, France]
June 12, 1976

Dear Gregory,

[...] I'm in a light brown apartment on Broadway, Boulder, with a fire
siren wailing and whooping distant under slow white clouds, dandelion

seeds drifting past second floor balcony under streetlamp telephone wires. Naropa's broke. Only 500 students, budget cut but lots of poets. Duncan and Helen Adam just here, McClure next week couple weeks, June. John Ashbery and Dick Gallup same time next door. Who's Diane Wakoski? Ted Berrigan early July, Burroughs and Giorno arriving mid July, will stay til summer end, Phil Whalen, Diane di Prima and Creeley and wife named Bobbi Louise Hawkins also will be here August. Peter and Denise maybe come then too.

Aspen Institute Rockefeller Foundation offered to pay you roundtrip fare from New York after July if you ever got that close to Amorika's shores and house you week in Aspen for reading, free food and cigarette money. Maybe could arrange small fees, Denver improvised reading, $200 Naropa reading, and bedroom here. This is just in case you do get to America.

Have you had a chance to check your translations? Demand xeroxes instantly. Didja see Soupault Michaux again under old folks home cafe awnings? Is Orpheo[65] singing yet? I finished recording *First Blues* with young genius Botticelli faced violin, mandolin, pedals, street pianist, guitarist, borrowed from Rolling Thunder, exquisite Ginsy-Dylanesque 1920's razzmatazz, best I done sung the blues yet. It's gonna be pretty on 2010 AD, beauteous jukeboxes. Full band sound like Glenn Miller, Benny Goodman, Nigger Heaven-Hell Billie Holiday. In fact, some blues almost pretty as Holiday, as they are recorded by same man, John Hammond, recorded last Bessie Smith sessions, Billie fine and mellow. I got ten secretaries to dictate to and phone ringing.

Louis is dying in Paterson. Wasted thin arms and wrinkled breasts, big belly, skull nose, speckled feet, thin legs, can't stand up out of bathtub. I read him Wordsworth, he says, "It's correct, but not true." About "trailing clouds of glory, we come from God who is our Home." He says that when he was Newark child on Boyd Street, he mysteried about green bush sprout-leaved back tree back lot and wondered what was behind the yard. When he grew up, he walked around the block and finally discovered what it was there. It was a glue factory.

His cap covered with futuristic old Willkie buttons. I may have to leave Naropa to go help him out of bed to die. Waiting for a call. Whalen take over my job here. I spent half each week since Paris with Louis in Paterson. Write

---

65 Max Orfeo Corso. Gregory's son.

him cheery card, full of ghoulish glee, annuncio energy. I'm here in Boulder. Phone. [...]

Love,

Allen

Went with Dylan again on tour last month for week and a half. Wichita Colorado Salt Lake. He sent me out to read poem. I read one short at intermission in Fort Collins front of 27,000 people in the rain on Neal's ashes. In Salt Lake, Holy Ghost on the Nod, 22,000 ears 11,000 folk.

[*Ginsberg was so devoted to Naropa and Trungpa that when times got tough for the college financially, Allen did the one thing he was most reluctant to do. He asked some of his famous friends for money. He received no reply from Dylan, but Naropa survived the monetary crisis without his help.*]

Allen Ginsberg [Boulder, CO] to Bob Dylan [Los Angeles, CA]
June 29, 1976

Dear Bob,

And this letter composed also is for eye of Joni Mitchell, and extra eyes Yoko Ono and John Lennon, for consolidation of effort:

As you know Anne Waldman and I for several years have been establishing teaching works Jack Kerouac School of Disembodied Poetics in collaboration with Tibetan Lamas' ancient traditions of mindfulness of spontaneous consciousness (awareness of what you think). Now you know we're not perfect and we're fools, but we been around long enough to have some common sense and sense of direction for teaching younger generations what we've learned— and we've hooked in to the best poets we could, Corso, Burroughs, Robert Creeley, Diane di Prima, Philip Whalen from San Francisco renaissance now Zen Monk, even Ramblin' Jack Elliott teaching a class, Mike McClure just here 2 weeks, Robert Duncan, others all this summer, Ted Berrigan too, John Ashbery surrealist academic champ this year etc. setting up whole institute center for poets to meet cross-country, fuck students, open mind actual inside teaching—this coupled with authentic legal real real access to the oldest almost, most sophisticated and technical wisdom of the east heretofore secret, i.e. actual availability of Tantric Vajrayana (traditional Crazy Wisdom) "reincarnate" Lamas and official Zen masters, right here in one place—a necessary progression, historically logical, from older useful Americanist drug and poetry experiments—so we got a good thing going historically, and Whalen and Burroughs and Corso wise fools all agree worth our time—not obviously Big Time Market Commerce but something which can ultimately enter in to Big Time Commerce and Art Song by introducing tradition of Emptiness and Non-grasping Non-Addictive Consciousness into more chaotic pop improvisation lives. You know total hermit in his basement room by one bright thought can blast thru history, we've all done this one way or another before—and we're working small scale with just such relatively obscure poets' poets and lamas' lamas, not a big deal but culturally rock bottom reality—examination of first-thought sense perception, order of sequence of sensory flashes of mind, gaps between thoughts—home mind reality—with advantage of our poesy experience and Buddhist consciousness-experts all poets themselves. So we're all broke, most schools rely on government and foundations, we've relied on self support, working with tiny salaries or none, school administrative people secretaries all meditators working for $50 a week sustenance or free, students contributing much as they can. Got 500 students, about 100 poetry students most of them doing empty-mind open eye meditation or learning, the poets passing thru also learning, if they don't know already, basic classical Buddhist meditation-on-breath practices to use if they want or not, but at least to learn it and get it down for later reference or scholarly or practical insight.

Total summer debt for this whole enterprise is $90 thousand dollars—libraries, taping lectures and readings, building and housing rents, airfares for half hundred teachers including Zen masters poets theologians from Harvard biologists tai chi experts Peter Lieberson charge of classical music, Don Cherry due next month.

Present situation seems to be we'll have to close down the whole project in a month, abandon second five week session due to begin July 18 unless we can get $90,000 to pay off bank loans private loans housing rents some salaries, debts due.

As a business apparently Naropa is not unworkable in long run—just that we started abruptly 2 years ago without sufficient investment capital they call it. Need several years to start a school and get government and foundation support.

Can you supply any or all money in form of tax exempt contribution, or loan with ordinary interest, or fast solitary concert? I think latter could be handled by Lieberson (son of Goddard who's in charge of special events such-like) in Boulder-Denver area?

Enclosed is an abstract financial report and can supply you with voluminous exact accountings and presentations of certified whatevers, there's a staff to handle that, it's relatively well organized that way. Just this fast note with rudimentary facts all you or I can handle this instant. I know you're besieged with information messages and demands, special pleadings of the most distinguished and OK nature as well as crank and hype and ambiguous spiritual vegetarian futuristic projects and so as usual would not bother your brains more with guilt anxiety woe of another possible fantasy, or worthy prayer, but this situation is also real, already accomplished, workable and solidly already being done, and ancient and venerable as far as characters types personnel and intention, so I don't feel worried about your fragility in writing asking Help! I don't know your financial situation, I'm not presuming, No Blame, no wall to get up against except the solid wall of gold this letter is off of.

I'll be here till June 10, then home Paterson to stay by my dying father he's got maybe 2 months left—Whalen, Burroughs and Waldman be here all rest of summer, with other poets passing thru a week or 2 each.

Let me know if anything's possible, if you can help any way small or large, need large actually to sustain the situation, otherwise afraid we'll have to let it collapse next month. No ultimate disaster if that's the case, meditation practices and poetics go on all over anyway but here seems historical opportunity to center refine and speed up the process of benevolent mindfulness genius near Rockies' spine height.

As ever

Allen Ginsberg, Bard

[*Ginsberg always took interest in the work of younger poets. After reading Antler's poem, "Factory," Allen wrote this letter showing the same genuine enthusiasm and generosity of spirit as he had given to members of his own generation.*]

Allen Ginsberg [New York, NY] to Antler [Milwaukee, WI]
August 27, 1976

Dear Antler:

What's your name born? Yes, I remember last summer returning your book, I had your person mixed up with another ghost and completely forgot our City Lights correspondence and your Clapping and Laughing poems which

I liked then as you remind me, but when I opened the *Factory* book you sent and read it through from 3 AM to 5 AM Monday nite, returned from Boulder, memory came back and I regretted I didn't look at you more closely at Morton Grove, I have only faint recollection and you must've been disappointed at my blankness, so forgive me and send me a picture so I can see your face and eyes.

Factory inspired me to laughter near tears, it's the most enlightening and magnanimous American poem I've seen since *Howl* of my own generation, and I haven't been as thrilled by any single giant work like that by anyone of 60s and 70s decades as I was by your continuing inventions and visionary transparency—Muse-aic inspiration culminating in the solitary scene blazing erection end of section VII. Nakedness honesty beautified by your self confidence and self-regard and healthy exuberance that exuberance a sign of genius, Bodhisattva wit come from losing yourself in the reality of your own presence and pushing that realism to the limit, or following it to complete exhibition of your secret imagination of your best self—seems you have developed your sincerity and natural truth and come through to eternal poetic ground, unquestionable and clear. I mean there are questions of honesty they're questions of range or amplitude—I thought, well what kind of vision was Whitman's getting a heart kiss or blowjob from the comrade who lay across his breast? Your moment, like that, of bodily glory in the sunlight, turned me on poetically and sexually and mentally, it was the reality of your awareness of the scene which makes it immovable—everybody does it or would do it or did it—but you recognized that naked natural moment—near *Factory* no less—and made it home—grounded immortal—memoried.

So it seems from these manuscript you've hardened your poetic page line and ripened and solidified the promise we both noted 1971, thank god you have that solidity now. Yes and your letter was very gentle with me thank you. You certainly did find a place somewhere inevitable to stop and wait for me to catch up and recognize myself, or yourself.

All the poems were unique, your own energy and amazing intelligence in development of idea, and terrific technical vocabulary and strong factual-realistic-naturalistic descriptive grasp when necessary, and theatrical tact (Tired of reading this text) when necessary, all-humored inclusiveness aware of reader, that's heart generosity . . . also the *Metropolis*-like or *Howl*-esque spacious march-of-robot panoramas're well accomplished: your ear is humorous and elongated and balanced. More fineness than I thought probable to see again in my lifetime from younger solitary unknown self-inspirer U.S. poet. I guess it's so beautiful to see because it appears inevitable as death, that breakthrough of beauty you've allowed yourself and me.

One basic problem, basic but not disastrous depressing or heavily trouble-some, is the conflict between poetic condensation possible, and the natural-syntax easy manly-kidlike talk-syntax you're using. You have the advantage of absolutely natural real Milwaukee speech extended lines. That's a special charm. It carries disadvantage of being (in Basil Bunting's words, as he told me re *Howl* and *Kaddish*) *too many words,* apparently lax sentences. You gotta find some way of intensifying the sentences without becoming gnomic arty or stiff-spoken—so as to keep the authentic talking-to-yourself style and its inspira-tional cheerful ease—at the same time not waterdown the density of poetical mind-speed or page gleam possible. In other words how intensify the line to make it brilliant within itself, not depend on ambient idea-structure to give it its twist and sharpness (developing ideas preceding with weird twists and new renewed takes line after line)? There still is an element of prosaic flatness in tak-ing the lines isolated. There is in Whitman too, tho each line does have some cranny or whorl within it, in Whitman. I tried a surreal speedup in *Howl* to give lines individual poetry.

It may be possible thru simple condensation, elimination of unnecessary articles, possessive words, prepositions, etc.; that's an operation to experiment with further tho I see you have used my own and Corsoesque condensations often. The styles do seem to proceed from Whitman and my own energy yap-ping, and Corso's combination idea-phrasings, the best adaptations and devel-opments I've seen, I mean the most personally-genuine-appearing. Thanks for doing that because I was wanting to have created some method of poesy that was developable and practically usable by others, extendable thru other lives and generations and not just my own cranky phrase-way. Your own application takes its main power from your own experience and intelligence rather than be minor spin-off from my perception of line bounce and length and soul-bounce of acceptancy of self sex and person heroism. That was my first thought, with delight, that here was a poem I could recognize my own poetic nature in, but done independent of my own mythology and details and social place.

Speaking of which, it's the isolation (American isolato) you're writing in and the solitude that is part subject of the poem, your own heroic awareness all by yourself, and I'm afraid this book will break that isolated necessity-place from which you rhapsodize. As I am completely surrounded by public scene even in privacy, everything I say ready to be eyed by nation sometime— whereas poignancy of your present attack comes from having no direct recourse to public complaint. Well that's a bridge to cross.

If you're free and still poverty-surrounded next summer (or for 2 weeks next March 1977 for that matter) come to Naropa and be my teaching assistant, so you get free tuition and discount on rent and maybe $100 cash, we'll figure practical problems out. I need an intelligent poet who can type to help me teach and order class. Had good poet half last summer Michael Scholnick of NY but he couldn't type and relieve me of type burden. I'm in touch with half a dozen your contemporaries seem ripened poetry practitioners based on Williams-groundedness and Kerouac-Corso playfulness — David Cope, in Grand Rapids, Marc Olmsted in SF, Scholnick in NY, one miniature Williams-Buddhist in Boulder Walter Fordham (older, 30) and another precise eyeball husband in Boulder Tom Swartz. There's lots of poets.

I sent word to Ferlinghetti he should do your *Factory* book, or *Last Words*, I hope he does: and mentioned your name and address in last 2 days to various publishers [James] Laughlin at New Directions and cat whose name I can't remember phoned me yesterday. If you have choice you might consider smaller independent publisher, just to support general decentralization of powers in U.S.; tho New Directions is fine or Fred Jordan Grove Press, was interested in seeing your manuscript; when I spoke of it. I'll be glad to write small preface if needed.

Your work is firm enough to last so you should take your time independent of public and perfect your manuscript or book and publish it at leisure not be tempted by speedy acceptance to throw together whatcha got. Do you need your Xerox back or can I keep it?

I tried tinkering with "Trying Remember What I Learned," but it's incomprehensible, my cutting, but I'm enclosing that confusing page anyway, some half-baked suggestions.

Send me photo I said, and phone me some evening collect, I'd like to hear your voice, I didn't pay attention properly before.

I'll leave here for Berlin with Burroughs September 19–Oct 10 and then with Orlovsky (who's almost finished reading *Last Words*) go to Buddhist meditation seminary northern Wisconsin — Oct 10 or so to Dec 4, isolated w/100 Buddhists sitting and breathing and reading and teaching poetry to sitters. Wisconsin! so maybe I'll see you on the way in if the route's in your way. I go to King's Gateway Hotel, Land O'Lakes, Wisc. near Rhinelander airport I think. Wherezat? No visitors once I get there. I'll try stopover.

God is unworkable, there's no God to appeal to, that's my empty minded conclusion. Don't need god idea for death, or for what we're doing, I think — don't appeal to that dead end in your imagination, I wasted 25 years crying after that theory vision. Better off stay with the vast space we're in, work with what's awake in that, than divert energy to ideals conception that IS NOT. If 'twere be only vast projection of Self, which also has no permanent existence, tho it has persistence awhile in the measured breaths of poesy.

I haven't got into details, i.e. specific lines noticed in your rhapsodies, but save that for later, what I like precisely —

"Beyond Call of Duty" the only poem that seemed relatively flat. You sure are poet of sleek turds! There is some relation to the submission of being fucked anal erotic and the ecstasy of submission and prayer to immortality in poesy. Or there's that class of classic inspirationatory mood.

Also enclosed a page of "Tyranny Images," several lines I cut into to condense, please send it back or copy of it, as I'd like to keep complete text. Enclosed the whole poem. Pencil checked lines are those seemed WOW when I read them.

It'll be hard for me to correspond but I'll try to reply if you communicate. Forgive this delay. Thank god you grew up and ripened patient and expansive. I have my eyes so close to earth on purpose I'd forgotten self-independent rhapsody poetry. Maybe it's still possible for me. Since there doesn't seem to be a permanent Self (much less God self) I'd curbed my selfish rhapsody to train in detail'd ground thoughts—but some outburst of crazy wisdom as yours is not totally self-ish, there's independence from heaven and earth there. I was too long dependent on idea of Heaven so I had to come down and start all over, that's the purpose of my Buddhist trainings.

Love to you.

Allen

[Ginsberg never stopped his running argument with Diana Trilling over what he wrote on his Columbia dorm window thirty years earlier. He continued to be irritated every time she mentioned the incident, feeling that her inaccuracy muddled the mythology.]

Allen Ginsberg [Boulder, CO] to Diana Trilling [New York, NY]
January 15, 1979

Dear Diana:

Peter showed me your note to him of a month ago, I'd hoped to answer before I left NY but was due here to teach Blake (mostly Vala The Four Zoas) and am only now catching up on mail.

What I finger-traced in dust on Livingston Hall dorm window to attract attention and cause window-cleaning by Irish lady whom I sophomorically contemned as inattentive to her duty to a window thick enough with dust to write on was as follows:

BUTLER HAS NO BALLS

[2 drawings]

FUCK THE JEWS

The first slogan was paraphrased from a local "Barnard" song "No balls at all / No balls at all / She married a man who had no balls at all." The second slogan, jejune as it was, was also in the mode of college humor aimed at the cleaning lady who I thought was, being Irish, anti-Semitic, and therefore maybe not cleaning up my room. The drawing was a cock and balls and also (unless my memory's mistaken on this final detail only) a death's head.

I wouldn't have thought the matter of serious importance but the cleaning lady, who did apparently have some edge of querulousness, reported these dusty terrors to the authorities instead of cleaning the window and obliterating any evidence of my evident depravity.

As it happened that very weekend Jack Kerouac who'd been banned from setting foot on the campus as an "unwholesome influence" on his friends among students (Dean McKnight's phrase) came to see me after a long talk with Burroughs who'd warned him solemnly that if he continued to cling to his mother's apron strings he'd find his destiny to be closed in narrower and narrower circles around her figure—an uncannily factual prophecy that astounded Jack! So he appeared in my dorm room on Friday midnight, just as I was finishing my most immense piece of juvenilia, *The Last Voyage* a poem modeled on both *Bateau Ivre* of Rimbaud and *Le Voyage* of Baudelaire done in iambic quatrains imitative of my father's poetries, saying young farewell to "Society."

We talked of life and art long into the night, and as it was too late for him to return to Ozone Park he bedded down with me, chastely as it happens, since I was a complete virgin, much too shy to acknowledge loves that dare not speak names, as far as I understood, on that campus, in that time and of that place.

Morning came and with it a Dean of Student-Faculty Relations coach to athletic department and football team that Kerouac had quit to study poesy (thus losing his football scholarship)—was it Mr. Furman? [*sic*: Furey] who rapped loudly on the suite entrance, then burst in the unlocked door, we were still snoozing innocent in bed. Kerouac opened an eye, saw the enemy coach loose in the dorm-suite jumped out of bed in his skivvies, rushed into the entrance room and jumped into the bed there—(my roommate William Wort Lancaster Jr. son of Chairman of National City Bank, head of Amer-Soviet Friendship Society, whose mother as member of Karen Horney Society'd paid for years of adolescent analysis for him as he had an awful tic round eye and mouth, had risen early and gone to class)—as I writ, Kerouac jumped into bed and pulled the covers over his head and went to sleep leaving me alone trembling bare legged in my underwear to face the fury of the Assistant Dean who pointed angrily at the window and demanded: "Who is responsible, who did this?" "Me," I admitted my guilt and he insisted, "Wipe that off immediately." I grabbed a towel and dirtied it clearing the window of what charwoman and assistant dean considered speakably objectionable. "The Dean will want to see you later," and he departed. When I went downstairs an hour later, I found a $2.75 dorm bill for an overnight guest and a note informing me I was wanted at the Dean's Office in an hour. Entering Dean McKnight's office he greeted me, "Mr. Ginsberg, I hope you realize the enormity of what you've done."

Actually I hadn't done much of anything, and on Burroughs' advice I'd been reading C. F. Céline's *Journey to the End of the Night* wherein the second chapter the hero finds himself in the middle of a World War I battlefield and recognizing that everyone about him is completely mad, crazily shooting and being shot at near a ravaged woods, decides to flee the scene immediately.

"Oh yes I do, Sir, I do, whatever can I do to explain or make amends." This seemed to be the best tactic. "Mr. Ginsberg, I hope you realize the enormity of what you've done."

Diana, by the time the story got to you and Lionel I have no idea what it sounded like but I assume the only devil that remained imprinted in faculty memory was "Fuck the Jews" as if in some awful psychological self-mutilation this poor sensitive mad-mother'd student was internalizing the torments of rejection he might have supposed were being laid on him by an authoritative society or class beyond his innocent comprehension etc. I'm not sure what psychological system was devised to "understand" this case. However, no evidence of the situation remained after dust and whispered gossip (I hope) had vanish'd to oblivion, other than the single "shocking" or "old" slogan "Fuck the Jews" which seemed to be the only thing remembered of the entire comedy when, a decade and half later, you recollected "The Other Night at Columbia."

So, around that time, after your essay, I wrote you, or Lionel, or both, a long letter on mailgram stationary, from San Francisco I think, explaining in detail, as I have again just now, the entire contents of the vanished windowpane, and the context, pleading for some common sense and humor, as well as accuracy, also hoping to disburden you and he of whatever weight of anxiety you might have felt about my poor relation to my "Self" or heritage.

I was somewhat disappointed to get a 1959 reply from Lionel that you had both read my letter, and understood it, but that I was making a mountain out of a molehill, that it was not so serious a matter that it made any difference what I particularly wrote on the window. I was disappointed because I thought that much had been made by you of the phrase "Fuck the Jews" out of context of "Butler has no balls" etc.; yet it made me seem foolish to take it seriously enough to correct and write you about it. Did you feel it was important but he didn't feel so? Did I feel it was important but you didn't? I never could figure it out. But in any case I'd written the matter up in detail, sent you the account, and done my best to be reasonable. Still, decade after decade, Columbia wits who read your essay do ask me, is it true you wrote "Fuck the Jews" and did get kicked out of Columbia? "Oh yes" I reply, "but you see it was like this etc...." And as a matter of fact I've laid out in scholarly print one place and another public and private the Full Compleat and Unexpurgated Tale of the Rape of the Windowpane . . . but especially to you and Lionel back around 1959 as above described, and so if you have access to old letters from me you may locate it, and Lionel's reply is sitting available at 801 Butler in Special Collections, where he so kindly helped me place my papers for archive.

So it was a little jolting to see your note to Peter saying "because he had written in the dust on a window in one of the halls "Nicholas Murray Butler has no balls!" But this is not at all what Allen wrote. Surely he must remember that he wrote: "Fuck the Jews."

Now I have gone through all these three pages to give you precise detailed accounting, as I went through two pages same a decade or more ago, yea two decades, about an event 3 $^1/_2$ decades mellowed in the cask. I hope it relieves you of the fear that all these decades I have been nursing some terrible neurosis of Jewish Self, a shameful secret more awful to recollect than the openly joyful recollection of most "terrible" family tragedies in the poem *Kaddish*. See? Don't worry, I've been alright all along.

Meanwhile, as the precise Text on the Vanish'd Windowpane has been established for scholars (actually I was dismayed your scholarly husband didn't seem to recognize that I was doing that, formally, in 1959 letter, as this as well) I've taken the liberty recently, when the matter rose among scholars, to empha-size the phrase "Butler Has no Balls" as co-equal to and, in fact, on one rare occasion, pre-eminent above "Fuck the Jews."

I reasoned that since half of my impertinent remarks in the dust were so exclusively emphasized in the past, I might take at least one time, in graybeard maturity, the liberty of making emphatic notice of the other half of this entirely trivial text which has, much through your efforts, appear'd to've gained temporary immortality. Doubtless, patient scholars future will see thru this recent college humor.

It is not your information or opinions I am contesting, correcting or challenging here: what I'm aiming at is decades old, an attitudinal vanity masked as moral responsibility, and inability to get basic facts straight disguised as superior sinceritas.

"Don't strike at the heart" say Buddhist slogans. True. Goodnight. I've written you a long long letter, I don't believe in eternal damnation, you probably do, poor girl . . . it's not important to be right.

As ever

Allen Ginsberg

[*One of the more troubling events of Ginsberg's later years took place at Trungpa's 1975 Vajrayana retreat in Aspen. Ginsberg wasn't even on the retreat, but the poets W. S. Merwin and Dana Naone were. At one point Merwin was invited to a party hosted by Trungpa, but he did not want to attend. That angered Trungpa and he ordered his supporters to strip the couple and drag them to the party by force if necessary. That incident created a stir in the Buddhist community and people took sides over who was right and who was wrong. Publicity fueled the fire of controversy and Allen found himself caught in the middle after he spoke candidly to a reporter, Tom Clark.*]

Allen Ginsberg [New York, NY] to Bill (W. S.) Merwin and Dana Naone [Hawaii] *ca.* March 10, 1979

Dear Bill and Dana:

As you may know an article appeared in *Harpers* lately "Spiritual Obedience" discussing Trungpa Naropa Vajrayana and in disguised form using odd initials your disagreement with Trungpa at the '75 Seminary. It drew on the Sanders class report. Following that an article in *Boulder Camera* appeared, using your names, rebuking Trungpa for public drunkenness. Several weeks ago Tom Clark—who had made a kind of heroic interview with me in *Paris Review* thirteen years ago—asked me to sit with him for an interview on the subject—"the Merwin incident" and the *Harpers* piece. I was hesitant since I've tried to avoid talking publicly on the whole matter for many reasons including my own paranoia, the delicacy of the subject, divided loyalties, unwillingness to subject either Trungpa or yourself to the vulgarity of my own loudmouth on the situation whereat I wasn't present and was still uncertain as to the details and their significance. However Tom is an old friend and poet, he came with Ed Dorn whom I've know since 1955, and whatever might be done as an interview, I would have felt like a creep not talking to them as poet companions, since we never discussed the matter at intimate length and they were troubled by it and probably by my ambiguous attitude. I said I thought the matter was too delicate to deal with except very gently, should be done with long consideration, and in any case, since the *Harpers* article used off initials, we should follow the same format, and also not rush it into print, I was leaving for a week in NY and wanted a chance to read and correct transcription. Tom said his magazine was in a rush, I said this shouldn't be treated so hastily; if he found himself pressured, at least show the text to Anne Waldman. However I basically trusted his judgment and that of Ed Dorn, so we talked for several hours, recording probably ²/₃ the conversation.

I later became apprehensive and spooked when I returned from NY. Since I learned that the *Boulder Magazine* was going to print my conversation/ interview with Tom and Ed Dorn along with a chapter of the Sanders Report, and I couldn't reach Tom Clark to get a copy of the transcript, and it hadn't been shown to Anne. A copy was finally delivered to my door, I reedited it and corrected transcript, and brought it back in a day to the *Boulder Magazine* office with a note saying that I thought you should be consulted before your name was bandied about so in public, I wasn't sure the magazine, or Sanders, had checked with you as to your wishes before publishing their 'investigation'. Al Santoli had been canvassing the class in vote on publication and I'd asked him to contact you for your own permission or advice before proceeding.

When I finally met Tom at the *Boulder Magazine* office I found printed copies of the magazine with portions of Sanders report and my own text printed, already in distribution. I was freaked out and yelled at Tom, thinking he'd betrayed my trust and purposely got me in hot water. My main worry was that indiscreet put downs of your poetry, hyperbolic fantasies of Buddhist fascism, low grade gossipy opinions about scenes where I wasn't present, distorted paraphrases of conversations with Trungpa, inaccurate conversational references to Burroughs as murderer and Corso as total dope fiend, on top of mis-transcriptions of phrase would not only reveal my own basic hypocrisy but also confuse the public issue (if there was one) with my unedited private and hysteric or irritable conversation with friends; I'd thought I'd have a chance to correct the interview or Clark have the friendly commonsense to edit it and clean up my stoicisms.

Tom didn't edit it all himself nor transcribe everything I thought significant, so there may be some additional disproportion added to my original inanities and ill-willing frankness. Remarks comparing your poetry to Trungpa's were left in adding insult to injury to your person, and a paragraph of appreciation of your character and sensitive behavior was edited out.

I stopped yelling at Tom when I realized it was a *fait-accompli* irreversible, and that he thought he was doing it (aside from pressure from the magazine) as the rare bold action of an honest reporter, and that my yelling was only making the situation worse by solidifying my own and Tom's self-righteousness. I also breathed a sigh of relief, that I had hit bottom, and my own hypocrisies were unmasked to fellow poets and fellow Buddhists, and that was almost a service rather than a stumbling block.

Please accept my apologies for my objectionable remarks about your writing—ill considered even for private yatter among friends, some kind of vanity got into me there, which is not my whole mind, an irritable and nasty arrogance in me which I can't disown since I spoke it, except to acknowledge it as bad character on my part and ask for forgiveness.

I'll send under separate cover a copy of the *Boulder Magazine*, as well as a copy of the interview as I edited it and brought to Tom Clark at his office before I knew it had been published, i.e. as I would have had the text, had it been given to me to publish as an edited revised perfected statement of my opinions. I've marked the paragraphs edited out of the published version by Tom and his editor, including the one appreciative of your public relation to Trungpa (and my own school scene).

I also enclose a Xerox of the note I'd brought along with my edited copy to the magazine, suggesting they consult you before publishing all that gossip. I'm still not sure whether Sanders—who is privately publishing his book in about 1500 copies—ever did contact you for advice, i.e. whether or not to do it and in what form and with what discretion.

My main shame is in having discussed your situation in public (re the Seminary conflict) when you've had the delicacy to leave the situation ripen on its own without aggression on your part. Of all people, I certainly owed you equal courtesy, and am humiliated to find my own vanity and meanness in print, a situation somewhat of my own making since I did sit down to talk with Tom Clark and Ed Dorn, and knew that Tom wanted the interview for his magazine.

I simply didn't think to have them sign papers requiring my approval of final text, and was self deceived in thinking that Tom understood my feelings, or thought them worthy of respect for that matter. Perhaps he was right; "Drive all blames into One" is the Mahayana slogan.

Well, this letter has gone far enough. Through my own ineptness the disrelation between yourself and the local Trungpa Buddhist scene has been exacerbated. Be that as it may both Tom Clark and Ed Sanders are scheduled to visit here and teach in the Poetics school this summer. Rather than allow the emotional or literary situation to fester with gossip or misunderstanding or in communication or absolutist mutual rejection or unwholesome recrimination or snakes mistook for ropes in everybody's mind, I wish you and Dana would revisit Boulder and teach at the Kerouac School when it is possible for you, if you're willing. Not so much a matter of forgive and forget, or papering over some basic disagreement irreconcilable, as our making a mutual effort to accommodate to each other's understandings or mis-understandings, and be in a place together where we can talk in community—in this case Naropa Buddhist oriented but free school, not Trungpa Shrine Room or Vajrayana camp. The conflict has been a great difficulty to me—literally six months of headache illness trying to reconcile my mind—which oddly enough the Clark interview did, making me realize that despite my own paranoia I did trust in Trungpa's basic sanity—despite the fact that his Crazy Wisdom lineage is also Mistake or Mishap lineage (i.e. learn from mistakes, alchemize shit to roses)— and the unreconciled conflict or paranoia has I think slightly unbalanced Tom Clark and Ed Sanders as well as myself. So that it's occurred to me often (as well as other, Anne Waldman and Billy McKeever who's now executive officer i.e. manager of administration at Naropa) to ask you to visit here and help break through the fear, hesitation, ideologic gossip and anxiety that smogs the Poetics school. Basically the school is stable and brilliant and the summer coming probably be the ripest; I am here half year this year teaching Blake's prophetic books line by line (now finished with Lambeth books to 1795 and beginning on Urizen—a project that will take 2 years to complete with students here); and I'll be teaching 9 months next year,—since we're accredited, effort's necessary to build infant school bones. So I'm even more committed than before to trying to interrelate meditation and poetics for the long range health and glory and practical usefulness of both in America. I know you have deep grievance, and if my own anxiety is any measure of yours it must be an awful anchor drag. Or perhaps not, I remember you said you never wanted to see Trungpa again, though you'd learned something from him at first. Still the basic humane as well as traditional Bodhisattva attitude is never cut off completely from any sentient being asking help or teaching. So with great respect I'm asking you to help me, and the Kerouac School, and the U.S. Buddhist community of poets and gossips, by visiting here, teaching or reading, talking to poetry students and fellow Buddhists and help attempt to uncoil the snake and find the rope, if there is one, which I think we can do. I don't think it means anybody—yourself, Dana or Trungpa—need compromise any basic principle or betray any absolute regulation. It means, for myself, letting go of conceptions, and solidifications of thought (as I had to to stop yelling at Tom Clark and let the situation be as it is unjudged and unprejudiced by my own resentment at having been found out, so I thought)—letting go of painful interpretation and trying to approach our whole mutual relationship fresh and new. Otherwise I'm caught, and maybe you, maybe not, I only know my own experience, in past causes and effects as seen in the past unchanged still somewhat a bummer to outsiders and ourselves.

Please let me hear from you, I hope this letter reaches you soon, let me know your reaction to the *Boulder Magazine* and if you have words of rebuke to me for my own behavior or speech please frankly lay them on me, I am both bewildered and tranquil enough to listen.

As ever,

Allen Ginsberg

[*Ginsberg's habit of writing to his elected representatives continued with this note to President Carter asking that a writer be appointed to the National Council on the Arts.*]

Allen Ginsberg [New York, NY] to Jimmy Carter [Washington, DC]
October 26, 1979

Dear Mr. President:

It has recently been brought to my attention that no writer currently sits on the National Council on the Arts. Although the performing and visual arts have their own lobbying groups, there's not a commercial market for poetry large enough to support a heavy pressure group. Some assistance is open to writers within the National Endowment for the Arts, but Literature has the smallest budget in the N.E.A.!

Poetry practices control awareness and purification of language, it makes up penetratingly communicative word pictures. Because poetry is like the central nervous system of the body politic, poetic projection of image has a compelling role in the history of human actions. That's why Shelley said, "Poets are the unacknowledged legislators of the World." That's why someone representing poetry and prose word arts should sit on the National Council on the Arts and have some say in national arts monies. Maybe it would be better to give no money to arts at all, see what happens, if arts have been bought up by national patronage, and made lethargic to the pain of America's present history, politics, etc. Painters have an industry with vast slush funds flowing up and down Madison Avenue. Because poetry comes out in little magazines, non-commercial, it would be best to beef up the least fat-cat art. If we're going to have subsidization at all, put on a poet to buffer it from commerce, censorship, and government interference. You need somebody with brains on top to figure out how to do it right — namely some writers on the National Council on the Arts.

Sincerely,

Allen Ginsberg

[*With age came an increasing mention of Ginsberg's health in his correspondence. By the 1980s, Allen had a full-time secretary and teaching assistants at Naropa to help him, but it only gave him the opportunity to create more work. He decided after a decade of year-round teaching at Naropa to try to limit himself to the summer writers' program.*]

Allen Ginsberg [Boulder, CO] to Philip Whalen [Tassajara, CA] November 5, 1982

Dear Philip:

A letter you sent me a month ago arrived in N.Y., Peter packed it with a few other papers to bring to me in Boulder, and somehow that folder's disappeared. So I never got your letter, tho I know you wrote.

I've been in simultaneous sublime and awful health — superb activities in rocknroll, poesy, teaching, meeting Chinese writers with Gary, getting *L.A. Times* book prize in a week, (big secret don't tell the masses' networks) etc. etc. but I have hi blood pressure, a half-thumbnail-sized kidney stone hovering around the urethra corner waiting to drop into my bladder, a backache, and complete aversion to paperwork, letters, business, teaching schedules, in fact the whole prison of my life to date. So I am about to change my schemes in the next 2 years. Drift off from Naropa, more retreats, more privacy, more r⌄⌄ home alone and writing. Fat chance.

I visited Maezumi Roshi in LA and Eido Roshi in Livingston Manor N.Y. Eido said, "Sit more, and sing more." My singing is getting better satire, Maezumi said, "Go out and get angry about the Bomb, anything."

I heard your zendo rent got escalated and you gave up the house, and are in Tassajara. If you ever want a change of scene, you can always use my apartment in N.Y.—I have an extra private room—or the cabin at Kitkitdizze, or if you'd like to come out to Boulder to teach for an extended period we could definitely arrange a 2 $^1/_2$ or 5 month stay here with a couple hundred a week pay. If you would like that for a season I'd try to get it together. As is, Larry Fagin and I are main props of poetry school. The Buddhists (Billy McKeever and Reginald Ray) have often asked if you could come.

I've been teaching Beat Gen. Lit. History 1957–60 this year—going thru Gary's work on that time, a whole section chronologically arranged out of *Interglacial Age* and *Like I Say*, Lew Welch's 55–59 poems and correspondence with you and Gary. And McClure's *Torture/Dark Brown* to come this week.

Amazing thing, the students know so little of that period, and are so delighted by the texts read aloud, that it's pleasurable to teach. I spent last 2 hour class reading Kerouac's <u>Heaven</u> poem and all thru Lamantia's 58–59 expostulations (Put Down of Whore of Babylon) which none in the class (17 year olds very bright, to 35 year old Alaska workers on vacation) already knew —it lit their faces—Lamantia's energy, your humor and detachment, Welch's common sense sentences etc.

However I still couldn't explain your remark about my not appreciating your consonantal music as you never explained it to me, o teacher.

Mornings I dawdle and before the claustrophobic mass of cloudy Karmic thoughts closed down on my mind I have a cup of tea, take a walk, or do nothing—look out the window and write a haiku or just take in the sky. Ösel Tenzin (the regent) recommended that dawdle for my high blood pressure. Suggested checking out the space around as way of meditating rather than narrower attention to breath. A sort of Ati-related practice.

What's new? I was happy to hear you'd written and frustrated not to have received the epistle. I weigh 170 and am wearing a red shirt, I just bought a brown cashmere overcoat for $35.00 at Salvation Army. I have this immense Salvation wardrobe accumulated here in Boulder over 10 years—delightful Brooks Brothers indestructible suits, myriad regimental striped ties, ill fitting and also neat-hung blue and black blazers with silver buttons. Peter got Kesey's

Kerouac Day Prize for being both worst dressed and best dressed poet at conference: brown sandals, pink stockings, red or baby blue pants—bright green summer sports jacket, lavender shirt, green and red flowered tie, big stomach, and blue railroad cap.

Well, love you as ever. Write again, please!

Love

Allen

Gregory Corso has new poem "Day After Humankind" I think is his sublimest Shelleyan vision of after-bomb spirits in the swirling dust—that he's ever produced. His last 3 years poems (see *Autochthonic Spirit* book) and new poems are magical and simple. He's still tough to be with but mellowing. Ever see him in S.F.?

[*Ginsberg gave all of his money away to friends and poets in need, so he tried to win a MacArthur Foundation grant to subsidize himself for a while, but had no success. The letter he wrote as application was a tremendous summary of his career.*]

Allen Ginsberg [Boulder, CO] to Charles Rothschild [New York, NY]
November 13–14, 1982

Dear Charlie:

You asked me to state case for getting MacArthur Foundation award, and it's taken me weeks to answer, mainly distraction of other work, illness, and hesitancy to commit my fantasies to paper; in organized fashion. It sounds like work.

Peter's father died last night, he's been ill these last weeks, Peter flew back to New York and had been tending him in hospital (Cabrini). That's taken some of my attention. To the point:

I'm considered by some people in U.S. and Europe to be the greatest poet in the world; by others to be the most famous or celebrated, one model of what poet should be as aesthetic innovator and also public personage.

I think Corso is a more perfect poet, unique and independent of modes and manners. And Burroughs more voluminous genius as prose poet. Otherwise in U.S.A. I may be more poet than anyone else.

At a time of poetic and cultural inertia in official culture, my first book *Howl* spearheaded a world-wide artistic and cultural revelation or breakthrough: a new international-style poetic form, of radical spiritual content; also proposes a new post industrial political mind.

That book and works that followed (*Kaddish*, etc.) were picked up by avant-garde almost instantly in nearly every literary culture and affected the style and perception and spirit of both older and younger poets all over Europe and South America, and even had impact in India, Japan, even later China, as well as throughout Socialist countries.

This effect depended mostly on a literary style that consolidated many different XX Century movements and tendencies into one blockbuster poem followed by a series of other back-up experiments in forms and subjects. The innovation was as follows:

In taking the long democratic-minded inclusive verse-line of Whitman (and Bible and Blake)

joining that with the swift modern surrealist dada and futurist tone and mind-jump poetic intensification of unexpected syntax combinations

joining that with pragmatic American naturalism developed by Imagists Pound and Williams, with a touch of populist "ashcan school" pictorial realism

joining that with spiritual record, accounting of vivid states of consciousness actually experienced

joining that with revival of vocalized dimension of poetry practice (in the West, only in Russia that was preserved among whites)

joining that with modernization of diction to include popular idiomatic matter

joining that with concern for "measurement" of the line of verse in the new open freestyle spontaneous composition—concern with shapes and "forms," as W. C. Williams had been preoccupied with measuring his line of free verse

joining that with modern frankness in personal information and theme and language, breaking down the barrier between what was considered public knowledge and what was usually held private information.

The result was immense impact on all aspects of culture and art in myriad languages. My own breakthrough was visibly part of a legendary "movement" in community with fellow artists working in the same direction—Kerouac Burroughs Snyder and others among writers.

1. Poetry took on new popularity and public force in the West.

2. Popular singers such as Dylan spread that style all over U.S. and the world, acknowledging *Howl* and *Kaddish* as models.

3. Movement toward vernacular, vocalizable, open form, idiomatic and self-expressionistic style became active in France, Italy, was reinforced in Spanish, Hungarian and Yugoslav languages, Japanese, *etc.* and strengthened in Russia.

4. *Howl, Kaddish* and later poems were translated into most modern languages. In Italy and France the bulk of my poetry (and much prose) has been published bilingual, in many editions, with scholarly apparatus. *"Hydrogen Jukebox,"* translated brilliantly by Nanda Pivano with my collaboration was for a decade the single best selling book of poetry in Italian language. There are full books in Danish, Finnish, Hungarian, Yugoslavian, Spanish, Portuguese, Swedish, Dutch, Polish, German, Greek, Japanese among others; and large sections of my poetry, early and late, have been anthologized in Russia, mainland China, Arabic, Czech, Rumanian, Bengali, Hindi, etc.

Extensive travel and readings in many of these countries has aided understanding of the translations, generated local revivals of oral tradition of poetry readings, stimulated popular appreciation of poetry among last few youth generations, and entered and affected mass culture thru influence on popular song, and rock and roll—especially in Hungary, Czechoslovakia and England.

All the above indicates world wide 1) Aesthetic 2) Cultural effect of texts, above and beyond another dimension of myself as notorious poet "folk hero," which later aspect is also remarkable, better known or more obvious, to nonliterary observers.

The quality of my work has been acknowledged by Guggenheim Foundation Grant 1963; American Academy of Arts and Letters Grant and election to American Institute of Arts and Letters 1973; several Rockefeller Foundation grants in late 1970s; National Endowment for Arts and NY State CAPS grants 1978; National Arts Club Medal 1978 for Lifelong Distinction in Poetry; also National Book Award 1973 and *L.A. Times* Book Review poetry prize for *Plutonian Ode* 1982.

My texts have a major place with perhaps more space than any contemporary poet in standard prestigious university anthologies of poetry: the Norton Anthologies, Oxford Anthology, Trilling's Holt Rinehart *Experience of Literature,* revised Oscar Williams Anthology, etc.

For the last 22 years I've been consistently invited to an extended series of world-class international poets' gathering along with Günter Grass, H. M. Enzensberger, Voznesensky and Yevtushenko, Octavia Paz, Jorge L. Borges, Robert Graves, etc. in England, France, Italy, Mexico, Belgium, Holland, Cuba,

Chile and U.S.A. and have generally been among the most translated, most read, most visible, most respected and best attended of all international poets present, favored by both older and younger generations of critics and poets. In sum, it is probable that <u>I am</u> the best known and most widely read living American poet, in this country and abroad.

This fame is based on specific artistic forms I work with, adaptable to international use, and synthesized from international styles. It is also based on direct treatment of specific modern themes which have engaged international attention and respect or serious notice:

1) Gay Liberation and Sexual Liberation

2) Explicit citizenly assertion of individual civil and imaginative rights (arrested, jailed and censored often in U.S.A., 1965 Prague and Havana, and 1967 Italy).

3) Anti War Activism and Pacifist Pragmatics

4) Investigative scholarship into Secret Police activities

5) Initiative in psychedelic substance law reform and research

6) Revival of vocalization in poetry

7) Work with song: Blake, Dylan, New Wave and Clash band recently, recordings on Folkways, and with John Hammond, celebrated producer of U.S. song from Billie Holliday to Dylan.

8) Advancement of meditative tradition in Western Culture and literature (*How the Swans Came to the Lake,* by Rick Fields, Shambhala Press 1981, accounts myself, Snyder, Whalen and Kerouac as major secular introducers of Buddhism to America)

9) Innovative introduction of mantra chanting to U.S. culture (affecting jazz and popular music)

10) Pioneer exploration of Orient and Indian culture for my own generation and subsequent decades since 1961–3 trip with Snyder. (See *Indian Journals*, City Lights, 1970.)

11) Literary Editorship: collaboration with major seminal innovative poetry magazines, publishing houses and anthologies over last decades:

Yugen—ed. LeRoi Jones

Black Mountain Review—ed. Robert Creeley

Evergreen Review—ed. Barney Rosset and Don Allen

New American Poetry Anthology—ed. Don Allen

Chicago Review—Big Table

12) Innovative teaching: Lectures at every major American University as well as Oxford Cambridge Heidelberg Tubingen Warsaw Prague Benares;

founded School of Poetics Naropa Institute 1974; repeated residencies at Harvard, Yale, Berkeley.

13) Seminal participation in "Underground" cinema classics: Collaboration with Robert Frank, Larry Rivers, Nam June Paik, Ron Rice, Jonas Mekas, Bob Dylan, Harry Smith, Alan Kaprow, Andy Warhol and others in U.S., England, Prague, Budapest, in improvised film form, as actor and producer and writer.

14) Breakthrough of my texts against censorship: *Howl* Trial 1956–7 was first of series of mid-late 1950s legal contests involving D. H. Lawrence, Henry Miller, Jean Genet, Nabokov, Burroughs and others (including older classics Catullus, Petronius Arbiter, Lord Rochester, *Fanny Hill*).

15) Advancement of lineage and techniques of modern experimental verse forms in tradition and under direct guidance of W. C. Williams.

16) Encouraging, agenting, subsidizing, and editing works of my contemporaries, Burroughs, Kerouac and many others, in formative years.

17) Introduction of the word "Fuck" into college textbooks as integral literary word in poems.

18) Role model innovation in integrating persona of poet as spiritual meditative aesthetic private personage and public activist "generation leader" democratic citizen, thus expanding possibilities of "public figure" to be frank in public.

19) Innovative relationship to various marginal or unusual social groups—Hells Angels, Rock and Roll Punk and New Wave groups, Hare Krishna and Buddhist practitioners, Underground Press, etc.

20) Participation in anti-nuclear movement, Rocky Flats arrests, as well as production of prize literary texts on subject.

21) Unique openness as well to Establishment vehicles: American Institute of Arts and Letters, *Atlantic*, *Washington Post*, *Life*, National TV programs, etc. Collaboration with Les Whitten, in investigative research, collaboration with Al McCoy in S.E. Asia research for Harper and Row books, work with Institute of Policy Studies.

All this indicates a range of activity that very few artists could—or would even care to—encompass, but now it's my desire to lay off, complete a few long range projects of poetry and song and prose, and have money and leisure to conclude the following deeds:

First, my financial situation is as follows:

I am $8,000 in debt, (for the first time in my life in debt).

I make $8,000 a year more or less from City Lights my main publisher.

I can make another 10–20 thousand by poetry reading tours, but have not been able to catch up to my expenses—telephones, secretaries, typing, recording, archiving, traveling, and 7 months yearly teaching at Boulder Naropa with no salary, despite the expense of a second residence. I also contribute $4,000 a year to the poetics department for salaries of other poets in residence.

I want to diminish my public activities as I am now in strained physical health:

1) Active kidney stone problem

2) High blood pressure

3) Critical mass of paperwork driving me nuts

4) General mental fatigue, from overextended workaholic and sedentary labors.

SOME PROJECTS I WANT TO FINISH BEFORE I DIE:

1) Collected Poems, contracted this year by Alfred Knopf Co. a document of 1500 pages requiring a year or two of close attention without disturbance and distraction.

2) Collected Interviews—texts already assembled over 25 year period now require my attention, already edited by Don Allen.

3) Collected Literary Essays: Compiled complete 1957–1982 but requiring my direct attention and collaboration in editing, likely with Dr. Gordon Ball, Asst. Prof English Old Dominion U., Norfolk, who previously edited my *Journals Early 50s–60s* (Grove, NY, 1977) and *Allen Verbatim* (McGraw Hill, 1972)

4) Journals: The 1950s—Now being edited by myself and Dr. Ball, slowly, for Dial Press, Grove or Knopf. 400 + pages.

5) A mass of journals unedited but already typed, starting 1948 and continuing to present—about 5,000 pages, or more. They are typed, some already proofed, half not; not yet edited and cut to gist for publication. Would be about 2,500 pages of equal quality to the two vols. already published. (including *Indian Journals*). For late or posthumous publication.

6) Complete "Songs of Innocence and Experience by William Blake tuned by Allen Ginsberg." I've completed music and satisfactory recording of about 30 of the 45 poems in this series. I have about 5 more songs to score, and another ten to record and re-record satisfactorily: a project I began in 1968 with MGM release of 22 songs. Folkways will issue the complete set when I collect it together. I have to buy back the out-of-print recording from MGM, and spend another $5,000–6,000 recording the rest. I wish to complete this work. What is available has found favor with Blake scholars and high school and college teachers and has been used as teaching aid in introducing students to Blake. Dylan placed one "Nurses Song" in his film *Renaldo and Clara*.

7) I have a large archive of all my papers at Columbia U Special Collections, and a mass of material—letters, manuscripts, tapes, that needs to be catalogued, transcribed, filed etc. I need a full time secretary, and a typist-transcriber. The same amenities and help that a major university professor has for research and preparation of manuscript I am years behind in preparing my own writings for publication. I have had some help at Naropa thru an apprentice program, but this is too intermittent. And my main files are in NY.

8) Collected Poetry Vocalized. In 1970, B. Miles (Burroughs' bibliographer) edited several hundred hours of my taped poetry readings down to a 16 hour (16 album) set which was broadcast several times thru Pacifica Stations in SF and LA. I need equipment and secretary to update the collection which begins with records as early as 1948. I sold the set (up to 1970) to Fantasy Records in Berkeley for $7,000 and need to buy it back for Folkways to start a project of issuing them. Moses Asch of Folkways has offered to find funding for the pressing. Fantasy has no present plans to issue them, but wants remuneration to give them back to me.

Since my specialization has been the vocalization of poetry, reviving that traditional practice, and since the bulk of this project is already physically done (in a 3 year period 1967–70) I'd like to complete it.

9) I have no house of my own suitable for completing all the above projects. I live in Lower East Side NY in a $300 a month apartment with 5 small rooms, not enough room for library, tapes, archive work and privacy. I don't know how long my rent will be stabilized as is. I'd like to move to a larger permanent space, perhaps a single family house or a loft where papers, tapes and documents can be filed safely and worked on properly. I can't manage such a move with present income and debt. And the travel necessary to raise enough money for space, materials and assistance would preclude an extended period of residence quietly at home to finish work.

10) Finally, I would like enough money to put aside all these projects but the few that require my direct attention (like Collected Poems) and have the leisure to do nothing but muse, daydream, and write more extended works.

I am advised by my doctor, my family and friends that it's time for me to cut out present excessive public activity, readings and work travel, and to rest and write, perhaps teach. I am committed to travel and teach thru Fall 1983. IF I had a sizeable grant I would retire to live more closely with friends and family, cultivate reading and meditation practice, and spend more long mornings and afternoons at a desk. With a word processor. As you may have noticed I have not at present a really efficient typewriter. This is a second hand $75.00

Portable Royal. As indeed I am one of the best or most celebrated or most read of all poets alive in the world, I can make good use of leisure time and more handy equipment to work with. I'm not complaining, I chose the life I live, but the intervention of a massive amount of money for the next years would allow me to put my life and work in order. Body-strain overwork, travel, to earn money, poor housing and materials have led to backlog of paper and domestic disorder.

I think this covers my case. MacArthur Grants include stipend for nonprofit teaching institution—which Naropa is. As I am attached here it would make the burden of teaching much easier—It's total financial drain right now, and we can not even afford a teaching assistant. (Another project presently in progress is transcribing some of my 8 years' Naropa discourses on Blake, Williams, Pound, Beats, Intnl. Poetics, etc.) (WBAI NY edited one term's 1976 taped discourses on W. C. Williams, which series was broadcast twice, 10 one-hour lectures on W.C.W. in NY area, over radio).

I leave this Friday Nov 19 for LA where I'll get *LA Times Book Review* 1982 Poetry Prize for *Plutonian Ode (Poems 1977–1980)* City Lights 1982. (Paul Mariani's huge biography of W. C. Williams got the nonfiction award so it's harmonious environment.) December 10 I'll be in Paris for UNESCO War On War international poetry readings with the Russian Voznesensky. Ferlinghetti and I are the American poets, everything (all poems we read) translated into 26 languages. Big responsibility. Then Peter and I and musician will tour Scandinavia till February 15, maybe come home with enough dollars to pay debts.

I'm not sure I've completed all the details, nor summarized any Big Picture. Tho I am an awkward jerk or thru Joseph K's eyes I may seem charlatan, or merely notorious, I really am a National Treasure, probably more so than anyone recently given awards (unless I. B. Singer); and I'm treated that way in Europe, "cher maestro," and some times here too, depends which circles you trip. That's based on the odd good fortune that the humor of my fame is above and beyond the basic fact that my poetry has elements of genius in melody, rhythm and intellectual scope—considering the subtle adaptations I've made of esoteric Blakean visionary and specialized tantric study to intelligible American idiomatic "ordinary mind." I have traveled a range of intelligence from Williams to Martin Buber to Ezra Pound (who gifted me with his apologia regarding his "stupid suburban anti-Semitic prejudice" as he phrased it 1967 Venice) to Burroughs to Henri Michaux to most of the Zen Masters Yogis and Buddhist Lamas in U.S.A., and have been instrumental in bringing this esoteric infusion of classical spirituality to America, introducing that international element to our material scene, and that's no mean intellectual and historically practical feat — in addition to altering the entire course of Western Poetics in a single generation. I've done all this on modest income and means, hunt and peck on typewriter, thru poetic body rhythm, humane attentiveness, and a kind of spiritual self confidence or certainty based on my own inner experience and the willingness to serve and apprentice myself to spiritual teachers from Neal and Huncke and Kerouac and Burroughs to Swami Shivananda, Swami Muktananda, and various Tibetan Lamas and Zen Masters and W. C. Williams and Bob Dylan, and take teaching from all — and thus consciously re-create the role of poet as sacramental conscience of national sanity. To do that without going nuts, and retain vulnerability as an asshole or innocent jerk, and blunder into J. E. Hoover's Dangerous Security list as well as Prague and Havana police shitlists and then at age 55 get up and sing on Broadway with punk new wave big band Clash is some kind of Gnostic miracle I learned taking care of my mortal mother when she was mad and I was too young to resist the realization that the world was hopeless, and therefore wide open to poetic imagination.

Well that's enough. I hope you can get me that grant — I can use it for art creation as few of my contemporaries can — and it might add a few years to my life — which is a literal consideration. On the other hand I probably could retire without making so much of a fuss about it.

I have delayed this letter so long it's probably unusable — it's taken six hours and I don't often have that much straight free time to dwell at a typewriter. That's why I've been so slow answering, besides inhibition at revealing my real estimate of myself which may seem megalomaniac to others, yet I've committed myself to this declaration here and so I'll have to live with it.

Love, as ever

Allen

Yes thanks for galvanizing me to write all this down.

P.S. Recent work "Father Death Blues" and "Plutonian Ode" is as famous in Europe as my early work, as highly regarded. So there's been no diminution of energy or art over 30 year period. Voznesensky's translation of *Plutonian Ode* was printed in *Isvestia* several years ago.

P.P.S. I might also want to get married and have children, had I sufficient means.

[*Ginsberg did not receive a grant, but in 1983 he hired Andrew Wylie to act as his literary agent. Things improved financially for Allen when Wylie landed him a book contract with Harper & Row. In this letter he notified Lawrence Ferlinghetti and assured him that he would preserve City Lights' right to continue publishing his Pocket Poets Series books.*]

Allen Ginsberg [Boulder, CO] to Lawrence Ferlinghetti and Nancy Peters [San Francisco, CA] September 28, 1983

Dear Larry and Nancy:

Enclosed a clipping re Shepherd [Sam Shepard] City Lights book, I brought it from NY as I emplaned to Florida thence Boulder. Enclosed also a nice interview in St. Petersburg, Mrs. Stella Kerouac's had a stroke, and is living with a sister in Lowell. I have the phone if you need it. She's recovering somewhat.

I hired Andrew Wylie to reconstruct my publishing life and get a N.Y. publisher for *Collected Poems*, essays, interviews, mid-1950s journals that Gordon Ball is editing now in Japan etc.

I woke up a month ago $6,600 in debt for the first time in my life that big. After 27 years of publishing I'd like to make a living from writing, even if it is mostly poetry. I was spurred to action when Miles came to town and said he couldn't find a copy of *Kaddish* anywhere in Village or East Village or uptown. There must be some copies in NY but he had trouble finding them. Maybe N.Y. publishing house distribution would ease that situation for a collected poems and selected, etc. I'll leave it up to Andrew Wylie, who'll be in touch with you. I instructed him basically to make the best deal he could, at the same time preserving City Lights editions which are traditional and beautiful.

I'm back in Boulder, with Peter till December, then I'll be Co-Director Emeritus and move my goods here to NY—books and clothes—and come visit summers like I used to. Although August trip to NY's poisonous smog heat made me wonder why live there. In Maine I saw Berenice Abbott and she said that after lung operation 20 years ago or so, her doctor told her she'd die within a few years if she stayed in NY.

Larry how was Italia? Did Phil Whalen see the sights? Just got a letter from him, says he saw some but doesn't say what. Delightful to imagine him wandering round the Forum and huffing and puffing up Michelangelo's staircase onto Capitoline Hill. Was Nanda there?

Peter's girlfriend Juanita Lieberman has typed up his book-length collection of his letters to Kate his deaf mother—1956 thru Europe and India and 60s I think. Full of gossip and details, Juanita says. Would City Lights be interested in manuscript to look at?

I'll be here till December and then return next summer 1984. Probably Creeley Whalen di Prima and maybe Snyder again, with me and Peter and Waldman and [Larry] Fagin and a prose conference—for which [Norman] Mailer said likely OK (last nite on phone) and Burroughs be there. We also invited [Susan] Sontag. Summer 1985 we're planning music and poetry (Greece antique thru India thru Punk.)

Love

Allen

[Around the same time as his new book contract, Ginsberg's interest in photography was rekindled. Especially helpful to him was old friend, Robert Frank, who gave him pointers and encouragement. Also helpful was a visit to see photographer Berenice Abbott at her home in Maine. She also gave him a few professional tips from time to time.]

Allen Ginsberg [New York, NY] to Berenice Abbott [Monson, Maine]
ca. **January 18, 1984**

Dear Miss Abbott:

Our visit last August (with Hank O'Neal and Shelley Skier and young scholar Jonathan Robbins) catalyzed some memory of 1930s and my mother, and I had a dream, a sort of epilogue 25 years later to a long poem I once wrote, *Kaddish*. In dream I met my long-dead mother as an old shopping-bag lady in an alleyway in the Bronx, and your figure and your photographs were part of the background scene. There's a composite description (with many details clear but dream-wrong) of some of your photos which had stuck in my mind and which I return to look at often in book-edit of your pictures. Particularly the frontispiece, "hundred thousand windows shining electric-lit," the "Fifth Avenue Coach" (which in dream I confused with "Tramcar in September Sun"), the "General View from Manhattan Bridge," and "Herald Square" with straw hats I recomposed in the dream, described in the new poem White Shroud.

I tried to stick to the Breughel-like principle you stated—universal panorama and maximum fine detail (by means of large negative,) in the poem. I hope you have time to read it or find someone to read it to you.

I gave your respects to Robert Frank whom I see often and with whom I am working again. He's experimenting with video, and I read him this poem for the first time, and he video-filmed it, chair squeaking on soundtrack as he moved and Peter Orlovsky coming in and out of the little room on the Lower East Side E 12 Street and 1st Avenue where I live.

I would like to buy from you prints of several of the photographs I mentioned above. Do you have any for sale, or could they be printed, and what would it cost? Particularly the "thousands of windows electric lit at midnite midtown" and "Herald Square" because some versions of them entered my dream of my mother.

I talked with the Ezra Pound *Paedeuma Magazine* professors at Orono, U. of Maine, and think that they may re-publish Marsden Hartley's poems. Hank gave me Xerox of the pamphlets you had, and I already had Hartley's Viking Press 139 page hardcover *Selected Poems* of 1945. I've been reading his writing since 1950 when W. C. Williams suggested Hartley as model for open-form American vernacular verse.

I learned a lot from the brief visit and want to thank you for your hospitality then. What I learned? Mainly old art-life attitude, and that one specific notion of large negative for maximum detail in a panoramic perspective. Thank you. I hope your energy and health stay spry till we can meet again.

Respectfully yours,

Allen Ginsberg

[*In late 1984 Ginsberg took a tour of China as a guest of the Chinese Writer's Union with a group of American writers including Gary Snyder. After the official tour, Allen stayed in China to teach and tour more. Postcards were the main form of Allen's communiqués during this period. This one illustrated how he could typically cram more information on a post-card than most people do in entire letters.*]

Allen Ginsberg [Kunming, China] to Tom Pickard and Joanna Voit [London, England] December 20, 1984

Dear Tom and Joanna:

I've been in China traveling two months, down Yangtze River gorges in steamer, cement factories lining the wide banks before and after, mines and scum, and soft coal smog hovering over river town. Mao's 1954–76 career a series of disasters, Great Leap Forward wrecked industry, Hundred Flowers followed by "Anti Rightist Campaign" of 50's sent 1,000,000 into work camps—Cultural Revolution 1966–76 halted most industrial activity 80%, sent 20,000,000 (recent official figures) professors, cadres, old ladies, mothers and technicians to pig farms where many suicided or died, now all supposed to be rehabilitated. New economic "4 Modernizations" opens up a whole new world of activity, peasants now prosperous for first time in decades (maybe centuries?) Students eager to hear latest old and new waves, "Blowing in Wind" well known tho voice of America pipes them John Denver instead of the Clash or Dead Kennedys. Folks exquisitely polite, one to one they talk frankly—but three's a crowd!! Fun! Happy New Year

　　Allen Ginsberg

[*Ginsberg's oldest friend was Lucien Carr. Carr had introduced Allen to Jack Kerouac back in the early 1940s and in this letter, Allen comments again on Kerouac's mistreatment by literary critics.*]

Allen Ginsberg [Boulder, CO] to Lucien Carr [Washington, DC]
August 6, 1985

Dear Lucien:

　　Thanks for sending me *Hong Kong Sunday Post* review of Nicosia-Kerouac biography—a reprint certainly from *London Times Literary Supplement.* The reviewer Ian Hamilton did the same evil job on my *Collected Poems* that English Viking put out this last April—same tone, insult, i.e. Kerouac "not very gifted," thickheadedness and meanness—"Kerouac's dreadful life"...etc. It's not Nicosia's fault, nor Jack's (nor yours nor mine)—it's strictly an English problem of Xenophobic Provincialism. There's a whole strain of intelligent open-form poets somewhat influenced by W. C. Williams and American ideas of fresh idiomatic language and open experimental forms,—Tom Pickard, his mentor Basil Bunting who died this year—Gael Turnbull, Roy Fischer, etc.— and they are consistently ignored or put down by the English literary "establishment" as represented in *Times Lit Sup* by Ian Hamilton—who, as various friendly professors of London tell me, is a consistent limey snob, and doesn't perceive what he reads or hears. My own fat book got the same treatment from him and others, sort of excruciatingly more insensitive and neoconservative Thatcherite maliciousness than even Podhoretz who tho he had moral objections still had some distant respect for the effort of art.

What you read was the real "Establishment" tone, I've had lots of experience of it in my own trips there and heard lots of complaints from Pickard and Bunting over the years, tho I never saw it so nasty as this year. I've been tempted to go over (as invited) and read up and down the country and politic and fight back—as it does finally poison the well of poesy and art in Albion, and there are hearty poets suffering the same insult—and lack of cash respect—poverty—because of that establishment yak—but it's too much work. It seems also tied in with the conservative political dominance. This year funds for Greater London Council and other local arts councils, which are more left and experimental—have been cut by Thatcher in effort to consolidate conservative power into a central bureaucracy (controlled by folks like Ian Hamilton likely)—so as to push aside radical art tendencies public funding which'd been going on since Labor Government days, popular on local elected council level. This may be too detailed. Anyway I don't think it's Nicosia's fault—that reviewer also laid crap on Jack's prose—which he may never actually have read—I don't think he really read my book which he reviewed. It's an old story. I've been here 3 weeks. Burroughs come and gone, Gregory and Amiri Baraka here, Anne Waldman, Nanao Sakaki my Jap poet friend, Philip Whalen 2 weeks gone back to his Zendo in Santa Fe. I'll be done with school poetry summer next week, travel to west coast and come back for three weeks' retreat.

No word from Peter, he's still up in Karmê Chöling, Vermont meditation center. Mail piling up here, it's depressing, I can write and edit my poetry, and enjoy taking photos right now, but the weight of unedited prose, letters, journals, essays and interviews to plough thru depresses me totally—Karma trap.

Read biography of T. S. Eliot this week—he had same case, plus mad wife who rubbed both with ether, took morphine for nervous headaches and continually bled "purulent discharges" from her yoni—wound up in madhouse after 18 years of mutual torture—he himself wrote wild filthy epic of King Bolo (nobody's seen in public yet) full of assholes and Jewboys and cunts and pricks; and "was addicted to Nembutals" (goofballs) *aetat.* 60. Happy ending however the last 8 years of his life married his secretary who said the "little boy" finally came out in him, and he lived smiling ever after, said "Hurrah Hurrah!" carried back home thru his portal from the hospital the last time, and died calling his new wife's name. And he smoked Galouise almost to the end, with heavy emphysema!

Love as ever,

Allen

[*Norman Podhoretz was a classmate of Ginsberg's at Columbia and proved to be his lifelong nemesis. Still Allen kept in touch with him and tried to point out errors in Podhoretz' way of thinking.*]

Allen Ginsberg [Boulder, CO] to Norman Podhoretz [New York, NY]
ca. 1986

Dear Norman:

I've been in Latin America a bit, even Central America. They <u>don't</u> want to be tied up with red police state, you're right. <u>But</u> U.S. policy is <u>forcing</u> it on them—by having long ago eliminated most viable middle of road democratic and left non-violent alternatives. The boycott and blockade of reforms and revolution pursued by U.S. <u>over a longer period</u> than the existence of red police states in this century, is what has brought about the polarization.

Further push in the direction of right-wing terror tactics can only make matters worse, as it did in Vietnam. You should re-think your policy of ignoring the mass of Latin-and-Central American public opinion and forcing terrorist governments of the right on these nations. It's obviously unethical and immoral—unjust!—but also counter-productive, a loser policy. You/we lose because the tyrannic politicians you/we back are more intolerable than their middle of road or mildly left opponents who are more popular. By subverting middle road and mild left rebellious you/we polarize the situation and create conditions where you/we yourself/ourself would likely be forced to ally yourself/ourself with Cubans and Russians—it's that bad, don't you realize?

10% of Indian population in Guatemala has been genocided by government troops. The Mosquito Indians, pushed around as they were, had it comparatively easy with Sandinistas, in comparison. Think the problem thru before you help create more painful bad Karma for all of us.

As ever,

Allen Ginsberg

[*Ginsberg's relationship with Orlovsky was falling apart. Following one particularly bad incident with Peter, Ginsberg decided to write him a letter since Peter was beyond the point of rational discussion. Allen still believed that Peter could "snap out of it" if he wanted to, but Peter's problems would require serious professional help in the years to follow.*]

**Allen Ginsberg [Boulder, CO] to Peter Orlovsky [New York, NY]
June 29, 1987**

Dear Peter:

[. . .] Ronnie Laing[66] had a big blue swollen lip where you hit him I think when he was on his knees. I've had the walls washed to get rid of streaks of apple and grapefruit juice left over when you threw juice bottles at the wall. I had to clean up (with the Jap priest Soiku) all the books which got splashed and soiled by apple juice. Some of the books were rare, and some old Zukofksy essays on Apollinaire in antique "Westminster" review.

You poured milk and apple juice over the harmonium as well as R. D. Laing when he was playing it on the floor. I've cleaned it off as best I could, only one upper key no longer works. I may be able to clean it inside when there's time. The harmonium yellow-saffron Shiva cloth spread out on the rug, wet with juice and milk, left a big saffron stain on the rug. Jackie Gens[67] said she'd get someone in to clean it. A teapot lid was broken, tiny fragments, no vacuum cleaner yet and I was too injured to get thing straight till now. One cigarette burn on rug, one on hallway linoleum. My shin got kicked when you overturned the coffee table while I was sitting on the couch watching you and Laing go at it.

The violence had escalated so high after you bit Laing on the mouth that, after knocking you down in anger myself, and you throwing a chair at me (I ducked behind the entrance wall) I finally called the police. One cop pushed you back so violently hard you fell back naked on me on the lawn outside and I slammed back onto the pavement, fracturing a pinky as I hit the concrete, and bruising the bottom of my spine, my left knee and my hip.

I woke up at 3AM in state of shock, mouth dry, trembling. I'd tried to clean up the house, pick up all the overturned chairs and tables and the smashed avocado on the rug, clean the juice and harmonium in a state of shock, but the pain in spine, etc. hit me in middle of night. Fortunately I had some codeine. Next day Dr. Weber sent me for X-rays, no bones cracked except pinky, and I was on crutches till yesterday, tho I'm still limping and slightly crippled and have coccyx (bottom of spine) ache.

What Laing did was mirror your gestures and tone of voice, "entering your world of communication" and that escalated. Probably I shouldn't have invited

66 R. D. Laing (1927–1989). Author and psychologist who was teaching at Naropa at the time.
67 Jacqueline Gens. Ginsberg's housekeeper and assistant.

him over. He made a circle on the floor and planted himself there, and kept pointing out to you that you were invading his space, and he wasn't invading yours, while he mirrored your voice and gestures. But you seemed too intoxicated to get the point, and wound up socking him in the mouth, which brought him to his knees holding his face, groaning. I'm detailing all this because it is not certain you remember how irrational and violent, possibly dangerous, you get when on top of depression you drink, as I found several vodka bottles around in the kitchen.

Anne Waldman and others blame me for "enabling" you, and re-activating a double-bind psychological set up between us wherein you become dependent on me, and infantile with mockery and tantrums and imitation—parody—as in class where you yowled into microphone with harmonium instead of teaching haiku or Milarepa as scheduled; and then snapped pictures incessantly, a foot from me while I was trying to teach, in sum sabotaging the normal situation and sabotaging what I wanted to do, as has happened before on stages from here to Europe. One view is that the Vajrayana situation, intensive teaching, and economic dependency on me—or some element of our relation where I am the father or power figure and you think yourself dependent or subservient, and resent it, in combination, these elements set you off.

As it worked out I paid tuition and groceries and offered Halifax ticket (which escalated to $600) and camera ($300) without discussion of how you'd repay or work it off, one condition of my giving you money was that I get service in return, so that you wouldn't feel bad and I wouldn't have you in my debt and thus dominate you with guilt or money power. Trungpa had also said "Let him go, be there for emergencies, don't let him become dependent."

I never quite credited the "dependency" theory of our relationship since it seemed so easy and natural for us to be inter-dependent in various ways, but maybe I've had a blind spot. Certainly there seems when you're drunk or manic a tendency to revenge yourself on my role toward you by sabotaging my scene. This has gone on since 1967 or 1968 when you worked out in red tights on stage with barbells behind me while I was, unknowingly, trying to read Wichita Vortex in New Jersey. But at this point the aggression you get into has become too violent and dangerous to play with anymore. We will have to figure how to get out of this double bind.

I've written all this down to give you a clear picture of what actually happened. I haven't ever been able to find out from you whether you remember these episodes clearly or not. If you did remember all the steps of the way, I'd think you'd take steps to stop the process before it escalated, if it were in your power. At one point when I asked why you'd quit the antabuse you said, ruefully sweet, "I just wanted to drink a beer." So there seemed to be some element of will or choice. Marianne Faithfull[68] who came out of A.A. mother hospital in Minnesota, Hazelden, says you've got to continue to love the person but reject the behavior which is part of a sickness, like cancer or any physical illness, with no "moral" judgment involved. On the other hand your cycle also seems willful, and that's what's confusing. The appearance of a sort of malicious-humor in you, which gets into violent behavior.

R. D. Laing pointed out to you, while drunk, a strong element of "arrogance" in the way you were directly insulting everyone, threatening people and furniture with your enormous strength. That seemed to fit in with David Rome's insight into "pride"—all the reverse of your usual humility and self-doubt and shy lack of belief or awareness of your own true value which is enormous. Everyone basically respects and loves you as man and artist, and that respect never seems real to you, tho it is to others.

So what's to be done? I've tried to talk about these things but you rarely respond enough to go over and clarify the reality or mistake in our mutual projections, so I'm writing this all down. For you to read at leisure.

[*Later that year Ginsberg wrote a short newsy letter to Snyder touching on Orlovsky's problems among many other things. Ginsberg was now teaching at Brooklyn College and since he hadn't been able to get Snyder to visit Naropa, he tried to get him to come to Brooklyn for a reading and lecture. They had also planned a trip back to India and Tibet together, but that never worked out.*]

Allen Ginsberg [New York, NY] to Gary Snyder [Nevada City, CA]
December 21, 1987

Dear Gary:

Lhasa-Kashgar trip! I don't know if I've physical stamina! My left knee healing tho weak, lost some thigh muscle, taking physiotherapy.

Well, anytime you're in N.Y. area give me some notice and please spend a few hours reading at Brooklyn for students and small crowd, it would likely

---

68 Marianne Faithfull (b. 1946). Singer, songwriter.

also do me good toward fast tenure track I'm already on. Faculty and students all consensus ask for you. As is this spring Ashbery Koch Baraka Waldman Cope di Prima Wieners and locals Bob Rosenthal, Eileen Myles, New Jerseyian James Ruggia, and [Ed] Sanders, Tuli Kupferberg and Steven Taylor and Eliot Katz (N.J.)—have all OK'd series for "Living Poets." Course, undergrad excitement Mondays. Also Simon Pettit downstairs and Alice Notley a few blocks away will read—good full program one semester.

I finished mixing on 24 track computerized studio in Woodstock—a spoken poetry record with lively haunting jazz melodies, somewhat an innovation since the musicians chose the poems and extended their art with deliberate compositions allowing for improvised solos—which they don't often get with their pop songs—and they went all out [*The Lion For Real* (Island Records)]. My "producer" may next try Burroughs w/ symphony and old time Glenn Milleresque background.

Burroughs in town new *Western Lands* novel his late period best. "The old writer has run out of words..." + 300 pps. and then had gala art gallery vernissage 60 or more of his shotgun art painting collages. He'd been doing calligraphic mazes and collage books since 1958 but last 2 years in burst of energy employing shotguns chance and paint filled balloons he got activated. Tout N.Y. was there—the European star painters [Francesco] Clemente and Sandro Chia—and many younger artists who've been returning to narrative and dreams and chance after long minimalist arhat dryness, so it was a prize cultural party.

Peter's more or less stable these weeks, Julius stayed with me a month, talkative—we'll try to get him moved down to an Adult Home nearer the city so he can socialize again after years rusticating in distant halfway houses. I think I mentioned, I spent a week intensive in Minneapolis Hazelden Institute the mother hospital for A.A., Family Services Co-dependent program run by one Terence Williams ex-drunk former Special Collection librarian of U. of Kansas Lawrence at whose house I stayed February 1966 writing *Wichita Vortex* series. Old home week for us broken-down reprobates, Beverly Isis[69] came with me but Peter wouldn't. Interesting—most all of us suffering from low self esteem and worthlessness illusions—the crux of codependency w/ alcoholics and junkies and nuts. Love to Masa and kids if you see them.

As ever

Allen

69 Beverly Isis. Peter Orlovsky's girlfriend.

[*Orlovsky wasn't Ginsberg's only problem. Since he helped support so many people with problems of one sort or another, he frequently felt he was in over his head and sometimes wrote formal letters to try to correct problems. The following letters, one to old genius friend Harry Smith and one to Gregory Corso, are both good examples that show Allen's patience sometimes wore thin.*]

Allen Ginsberg [New York, NY] to Harry Smith [Boulder, CO]
September 8, 1988

Dear Harry:

Probably best to stop conversation on phone as I was overwhelmed by realization of how deep into a hole we had got. I sent you a summary of outlays yesterday, saw Rani[70] and spoke to Jacqueline Gens this morning. Enclosed find summary of Rani's bill to me itemized for your food, hours of work, and loans to you unpaid back, it comes to $388.25. Jacqueline put out $58.27 for medicines. And I had forgotten to include the $150 advance Bob [Rosenthal] had given you in June against Don Yannac fee-to-come from jury CU [Colorado University] showing. So altogether since late June, i.e. from June 23 to today September 8 my outlays for you have totaled:

Advance on C.U. Yannacito Showing	$ 150.00
Expenses previously itemized 6/23 – 9/7 88	3280.81
Payment to Rani Singh 9/7/88 itemized as enclosed	388.25
Repayment Jackie Gens medicine and food 9/8/88	68.27
Memorable Expenses for Harry Smith 6/23 – 9/8 1988	3887.23
Unpaid Medical Bill Dr Beasley	865.00
Total Commitment AG to Harry Smith 6/23 – 9/8, a 10 week period	$4752.23

This approximates $475 a week potentially if I'm stuck with Dr. Beasley's bill, if you don't get Medicaid or SSI, and if you do it comes to $388 a week, or approximately $20,000 a year. Well, Harry, I can't afford this subsidy of all your needs including your book buying habits. Jackie said this morning you had been out all night after pneumonia recurrence, you'd spent your daily stipend on other than food, and you were now both sick and down to your last can of soup.

This may seem religious or noble behavior to you, but the fact is that it is at

70 Rani Singh. Ginsberg hired Singh to act as Harry's "Gal Friday" while he was in Boulder.

my expense, and others, financially. Small amounts of money in the past have been ok, but such subsidy as $3887 for ten weeks is impossible for me to maintain, and even you must recognize this unless you are so imperceptive and habituated that I would be advised to kick our relationship cold turkey as far as money. If you force me to, I will do that.

You have other sources for money: Grants (Guggenheim, NEA or Smithsonian, whatever) or sale of your archives and collections or pictures, or getting SSI.

SSI will automatically take care of medical bills / which I can't ignore since they were incurred dependent on my credit and the bills were sent to me. Joe Gross said he was working on that several weeks ago but it will be easier and clearer to get it in Colorado. Bureaucracy less vicious there. Please work on this, I discussed it with Rani and Joe Gross. She would help, and I'd pay for time unless you become obstructive. Please help, and Dr. Weber will write the evaluation forms etc. Rani will have to do it with you. I'll send for Guggenheim application forms. Enclosed Xerox of NEA Arts Grant. Please consult Yannicito and Brakhage to get this done. I'll call Spitzer, in Washington to inquire further. Regional might be easier, please find out from Brakhage and Yannicito, I think his voice answers that phone number in Boulder, I already called and left him a message inquiring.

Henceforth I will send half of your $140.00 food money to Rani or whomever you designate to buy you food, shopping for 5 hours a week and send you 70 or whatever's left. The $10 a day was always intended for food maintenance. You simply have no right to take money from me for your book buying. If you designate someone else to handle your food money they will have to make phone arrangements with me first. This will begin September 23, the next check time.

By September 23 you might complete arrangements for SSI benefits and if Rani and Weber inform me that that process has begun, I'll send food check to Rani and your $70 to you. If you haven't moved by then to get SSI, I'll send only food check. Equally, if you haven't moved on regional NEA or other NEA grant, and I hear nothing on that from you or Rani, I won't send anything more than food check. I'll continue that through October 7, and pay October rent. After October's over if you've applied to both NEA and Guggenheim, I'll continue some minimal subsidy till SSI comes through. If SSI and Guggenheim and NEA grant are not applied for and paperwork completed, I'll stop paying any money at all even for rent, and you can take care of yourself after November 1.

I will not pay for a return ticket to New York, and you cannot stay in my house if you do come back here. It's too expensive for me now. If you say so I'll pay the Anthony house $44 rent from now to September 23 (September 9–23). After that I quit. Alan Steinfeld offered to help me pack and ship them [Smith's collection of books and records] to you or store them for you. I won't pay to have you come back and do it in style you're accustomed to, but we would do it neatly and safely.

Once you apply for SSI you get Medicaid faster than the SSI, says Joe Gross. He has not done anything at all here on SSI. He said you can't get Medicaid if not paid taxes, except thru SSI. Says not to worry about other income threatening your SSI that can be offset by the gigantic medical bill you owe him. I spoke to Weber Phil Dr. and he and Gross can write it up for you, the necessary letters saying you're unable to earn a living normally. If you don't apply for SSI and leave me stuck with this giant bill $865 Beasley $240 Brown plus Weber's, I'll come out there and cut your heart out . . . unless you pay it yourself.

The above restrictions and directions about your subsidies may be complicated but just read this letter over couple times and you'll figure it out.

Your similarity to Alan [Ginsberg's nephew] is that you both try to evade looking directly at your dependency, and indulge in magical thinking and evasive yak to keep the dependency going and a little muddled, in a state of continual crisis. When I asked you yesterday about SSI on the phone you said you were already having something done about it in Boulder when that was a fib. That's why I got so mad, you were obscuring the situation and delaying action making a muddle confusing the facts evading the issue thus continuing to drain me of money as long as I would put up with it.

Harry I've tried to be friendly and somewhat helpful, but can't do it, on your terms any more, and we will either work with your problems gracefully with your cooperation or I won't help at all.

If you have a more practical plan than immediate SSI application let me know. I haven't heard anything real from you for years on this subject, and fear my subsidies have enabled you to avoid simpler solutions like SSI. I don't feel your art work or sound taping is as valuable to me as having you put your energy to relieving me of the financial burden.

I am in touch with Debbie Freeman, and explained our mutual situation to her tonight. Perhaps you've compartmentalized our efforts too long. I hope you're well, watch out for Kefflex, if you're allergic to penicillin.

XX

OK as ever

Allen

**Allen Ginsberg [New York, NY] to Gregory Corso [New York, NY]
November 13, 1988**

Dear Gregory:

I'm sorry our meetings in NY have turned out badly. I respect you as old friend & poet & do love you; but as I've said for years I'm increasingly allergic to being bombarded psychically by alcoholic pressure.

I'd willingly have you stay with me, supply money, ask you to teach with me at Brooklyn, and be old friend.

When we meet, and you've been drinking as at my house with cola can of spirits the other night—your mind body & speech become very volatile, sometimes seeming overbearing. For instance, hard to conduct common 4 way conversation in a room as with Ewert's father, Nanda [Pivano] & Carl Weissner—you ask for complete separate attention, like unhappy tantrum child. And when that's refused or hesitant, you get angry i.e. "Do you love me?" and someone can say yes, but then it seems that you're testing, or mocking, or needy, or setting me up for a contest—a confusing situation—so that I withdraw, embarrassed in front of other. Then your face darkens, you glower and begin to turn dark and threatening—a moment after demanding a kiss—and I think you're trying to trouble me—No! You really need love! No! You want something else, maybe money a pillow! No, it's love! By that time you're threatening to "cash in your chips forever" and that I'm insulting you. By that time, I look at you, realize you've been drinking and get the idea, like in a Céline novel, that you're completely absent, just crazed, weeping and insulting in rapid succession, nothing really to do with me, whatever my reaction you'd be just the same. Finally I resolve not to take it, "Gregory I'll only see you when you're sober."

Last nite Peter spent the day bellowing up and down the street, drunk or on crack, threatening to kill me blocking the doors or break Steven's guitar as he was trying to get out to catch a train to Boston. Finally he ended dancing on the fire escape, yelling bellowing as he'd been doing for hours, neighbors leaning out the window, choruses of answering bellows from the gangs on the street, a *Daily News* truckdriver stopped to yell up, "Jump! Jump!"—and ambulances and 20 cops and emergency squads. I let them in, he was taken to Cabrini 9 PM and out at 7 AM—no place to put him there—God knows where this will end.

This is the context wherein you demand to be accepted and kissed in front of strangers no matter how demanding and difficult and insulting you are to me. I don't think you realize what it looks like, how it feels—what madness it seems—thru my own mind and eyes.

I'm trying to explain to you what's wrong between us. I'm <u>allergic</u> to being ordered or pushed around or yelled at by people who are drinking, or out of their skull. I can't stand it any more and see no reason to.

It's your choice: if you want my direct contact friendship or help it's here, but not when you're in that state of volatile drinking.

If the alcohol volatility is something you need on the street in present situation, but regret as permanent condition, you could go (as I have) (for co-dependency) out to Hazelden Hospital in Minneapolis or some other detox. I don't know how to set up safe haven for you but could try if you were interested.

Or be glad to see you in company on your own terms—but calmly—but apparently I can't tell you what's on my mind without your becoming so upset you run away and refuse to talk further.

I had brought down a check for more money the other day but you were so "volatile" you didn't want to deal with <u>me</u> at all, just wanted the $20 immediate.

And then accused me of rejecting you, as you went away cursing me. I had come down to talk.

OK. I hope you do OK. This seems the only way—in writing—that you'll accept words from me, if you even read this.

OK Love

Allen

[*Even when people wrote adulatory articles about Ginsberg, Allen was sometimes suspicious of underlying themes hidden in the praise. This was evident in this letter to a journalist he had known for thirty years, Al Aronowitz.*]

Allen Ginsberg [New York, NY] to Al Aronowitz [Elizabeth, NJ]
January 10, 1989

Dear Al:

I haven't changed my mind about the fathead awkward dishonesty of your prose where you center the attention on yourself—it's embarrassing, as embarrassing as the awful scene you describe hogging the stage praising me in terms I actually find insulting and stereotyped and really demeaning. Well, you're entitled to your opinions but I don't feel obliged to agree with the tone, attitude, phrasing, etc.—or even put up with it in silence. It's sort of ass-licking in an embarrassing and obnoxious way, and underneath it there's a subtle negative stereotype of me—making me a kind of conniving thing—that I actually find repulsive.

I've said this to you in various ways before so I'll repeat it tho you seem so thick skinned that you don't really care or react, tho you ask my approval or opinion.

You were more artistic as an objective and passionate reporter (as I remember it) and you either hid or disguised your "attitudes" or self-consciousness and focused on a world outside of yourself but still of yourself truly because the details and particulars were your direct observations.

But most of this writing is still about yourself and your neuroses, paranoias ego trips exaggerations and childish self-preoccupation—and when you describe others it's always with an in-joke know-it-all referential stereotype that scants details and particulars and slips into an obnoxious pseudo hip stereotyped (abstract) set of cultural generalizations which are your own not common to me or anybody literate, but sort of smarmy hippy style not only anachronistic but mishandled even if it were 1960s back again—Big Daddy type stereotypes awful then and worse now.

Why don't you just write common spoken English not exaggerated hip talk, and write as you can about others and leave yourself out except for objectively written record of context of personal facts (to explain context) but not this exaggerated self praise and masochistic breast-beating and obsessional references to your struggles and failures which by hindsight seem to have been self-inflicted? And don't blame me or Rimbaud for your idiotic bouts with coke or overuse of grass. Nobody told you to derange your senses, that's really crass laying that trip on me as if I ever was monomaniacal enuf to take Rimbaud without a big grain of salt—and explain his classic "derangement of the senses" without a big dose of humor and irony—unless I had to give a kindergarten lecture on what Rimbaud wrote, for beginners.

I find the whole tone of your essay objectionable and the worst kind of "New Journalistic" stylized over stylized second-rate slush.

I've said this politely to you numerous times and you always come back with the same egocentric crap, slightly disguised one way or another every few years! No more! Why subject me to this test every time?

I value your friendship and help for old times' sake but please don't depend on me for approval or empowerment or reference for prose which you already know I'm ashamed and embarrassed to see you, a friend, write.

Beside the sort of subliminal sabotage you work into your praise of my persona as you perceive it—reducing me to some kind of manipulative macher conniver as you portray yourself, perhaps equally unconscious of the impression you leave with this self-adulatory buffoonery—a trip you also project on me, which I shrink from.

Okay? This is what I really think, I've said so before to you over and over and you don't listen so why go thru it again and again? Write straight, or lay off sending me manuscript. Take care of yourself.

Allen Ginsberg

[By the late 1980s censorship in America had once again become a hot topic for Ginsberg. The Moral Majority had begun pressuring politicians to put new restrictions on the freedom of speech and Ginsberg's work was once again banned from the public airwaves, so he wrote to the New York Times.]

Allen Ginsberg [New York, NY] to Michael Oreskes [New York, NY] August 29, 1989

Dear Mr. Oreskes:

Your politically knowledgeable story on Jesse Helms' antics seemed to make sense if his NEA censorship bill were only a one-shot deal—Mapplethorpe, and that's the end of it.

But he's introduced a bill to impose his art views permanently. Furthermore, he got thru a bill a year ago to impose his literary views on the FCC and Pacifica, resulting in the chilling out of my poetry off Pacifica and other stations. So these are chronic attacks on the First Amendment.

The notion that the public is up in arms is nonsense. Helms, Heritage Foundation, the Moonies and Moral Minority are engaged in a PR campaign for political purposes to deconstruct not only the art "left" but also the middle road nonconservative Democrats. It's strictly a nasty political cutthroat deal reminiscent of Nazi-Stalinist racist homophobic chauvinism.

Note Helms' comment in the *NY Times*, "There's a difference between 'The Merchant of Venice' and a photograph of two males of different races"...

If Jackson's forced to repudiate Farrakhan, why aren't Bush and Atwood and Gingrich forced to repudiate Helms' overt racist comments, much less homophobia?

Since my own work's been kicked off the air, I don't think a "Don't make waves" stand is any more useful here than it was in Germany 1930s or under Stalin. Remember truck drivers in Georgia still have Stalin's picture on their windshields.

The media is cooperating with this con game as it did with ACLU attack during 1988 campaign.

What was Bush criticizing? The word "American?" The word "Civil?" The world "Liberties?" The word "Union?" The phrase "Civil Liberties?"

I heard no one question this outrageous hype. It was seen by cynical media as a charming P.R. ploy, distasteful—but allowed to pass unchallenged.

Perhaps you would dig into Helms' tobacco financing and racist statements, as well as homophobic pronouncements. Doesn't he want to reverse 1963 Civil Rights decisions? The other *Times* story headlined "No lose position." That's if you allow him to bamboozle you with his second rate language. You can do better than that.

Yours,

Allen Ginsberg, Poet

[*Ginsberg also praised people whose writing seemed intelligent and thoughtful, as in this letter to Thom Gunn. Gunn had just published a laudatory article about Allen in the* European Gay Review.]

Allen Ginsberg [New York, NY] to Thom Gunn [San Francisco, CA] September 21, 1989

Dear Thom Gunn:

Martin Duberman sent me Xerox of your essay "Allen Ginsberg—A Record" and reading it I was moved—almost to tears—by your sympathetic perceptions, poem by poem, and by a gentler attitude toward my poetics practice than I'm used to hear of.

I do know what I'm doing—it's all I can do, so to speak, "no choice" —and I resolved to stick with it long ago, but I'd got thick-skinned and after all do underneath recoil when I read criticism or critique—even or especially in Miles' biography—less sensitive than yours. I mean I read your essay with relief, at being understood on my own ideal terms rather than terms more vulgar—stereotype and buzzword is my critical portion usually—not that I don't have understanding friends among poets from Corso to Creeley—but to see such extensive thoughtful consideration in print is a heart-relieving novelty— like a fresh love, someone likes me or someone articulate as yourself under- stands the poetic persona as based on experience of real persona. A few notes —re "awkwardness"—yes Hardy! and also Herman Melville's *Collected Poetry* —the same ungainly genius of phrasing—as in *The Swamp Angel*, "There is a coal-black Angel / With a thick Afric lip"...(i.e. a cannon overlooking Vicks- burg.)

I'm glad you noticed the anecdote / Narratives—my model for that's been Marsden Hartley's poetry (recommended to me 1951 by W.C.W. [William Car- los Williams]) and Charles Reznikoff whom I dote on more and more for teach- ing epiphanous vignette.

The Chicago Bouffante girl I always liked (including the redoubled "whose" turn of phrase)—and the minor narratives "Uptown" "Imaginary Universes" "Dream Record" and "White Shroud" are all stories, naturalistic, W.C.W.-Zola naturalism [?] or charged with Apollinaire zone montage swiftness—my for- mula was Whitman and Apollinaire (or Lorca's *Ode to Walt Whitman*: "cor- duroy shoulders worn down by the moon" [*sic*: "corduroy shoulders frayed by the moon"]). Dream gives the surreal super reality, but the texture is naturalis- tic, social realist almost. I liked the fact that the "Satanic thistle" seems to have caught in your mind sufficiently that you (mis)quote it (by habit?) as raising its "horned geometry" rather than its "horned symmetry." I don't know which is better but the "symmetry" is close to Nijinsky's drawings and Blake's Tyger talk.

Re Bunting: I knew him relatively well, stayed over at his house in 1965, paid his Hotel Chelsea bill here years later and split my Albert Hall fee to give him the bulk of it 800 pounds for his last reading in London a few years ago. 1965 at Morden Tower I read thru *Howl*, *Kaddish* up to poems 1965 and asked him what he thought. "Too many words," he said and it clicked in my head. My effort was to condense syntax thereafter, not condense idea or catalogue —not much I could do about that discursiveness of mind but at least short- hand it syntactically.

I used "suggested" that poetry "be equated with condensation" because Pound quotes Bunting's formulation using an = mark: Dichter = condense. So I said "Equate." I didn't have the text at hand writing footnote so I settled on the moderate noun suggest. Certainly it was a more firmly nailed down thought, typical of Bunting's laconic definiteness and stubbornness. I just wanted a newsreel/time capsule 360 degree description of Piccadilly (midnite or so) after leaving the Albert Hall reading alone marooned haunting Piccadilly—trying to condense not the image or idea to an image but condense the syntax of the catalogue. Whitman and Bunting's "rut thuds the rim." Kerouac taught me accumulation—and is a much more seminal poet (to McClure, Snyder, Whalen, Creeley, myself and others) than is known—great poet. Alas Rexroth's 1960 wrong-headedness set the wrong course of mis-appreciation of *Mexico City Blues* for decades and poets have not yet generally understood Kerouac as magnificent poet—only Bob Dylan did (in 1959–60) and credits Kerouac for introducing him to his own style. "It blew my mind" Dylan said in Kerouac's Lowell graveyard when we once visited—14 years ago.

I don't think anyone else noticed *Manhattan May Day Midnite's* utterance "Ur."—and hardly anyone's looked at *Many Loves* directly tho I cherish it as narrative, and truthful ("awkward" "and mine stuck out of my underwear.") (awful!) (or so real it's a naked telepathic shock). (what oft was thought but ne'er...expressed.)

Mugging some people have noticed tho rarely part II, which I think is lesser than #1 but I'm glad you find something useful in it.

Nobody's ever commented on "ignorant girl of family silence" *Aunt Rose* line before, tho it's another raw line that's purest poetry for me—and that's Kerouac's "spontaneous mind" influence. That's the essence of it—that ignorant raw even embarrassing slip of mind that tells the truth.

Or (I don't know if you didn't notice) it's summed up in the dream I had of W.C.W. instructing me in China: "Take your / chances / on / your accuracy.") (*White Shroud* book)

Yes certainly "sacramental" reverence in *Many Loves*, for Cassady.

Well thank you for the effort it took to write a formal essay, and the empathy with which you read my scribblings.

As ever,

Allen Ginsberg

[*Ginsberg wrote a newsy letter to Japanese poet and friend, Nanao Sakaki. Allen's meditation teacher, Chögyam Trungpa, had died in 1987, and Allen was now under the direction of Gelek Rinpoche. Gelek is mentioned in relation to Allen's fascination with death. Health continued to be a recurrent theme in most of Allen's letters from this and later years.*]

Allen Ginsberg [New York, NY] to Nanao Sakaki [Japan]
February 11, 1992

Dear Nanao:

Enclosed find all sorts of souvenirs of New York. What's happened here in the last year?

1. Put on my tie in a taxi, short of breath, rushing to meditate.
2. I can still see Neal's 21 year old corpse when I come in my hand.
3. Two blocks from his hotel in a taxi, the fat lama punched out his mugger.

Last 2 years I visited Gelek Rinpoche (the "fat lama") in Ann Arbor—discussed the mind at moment of death. "Cultivate compassion for all sentient beings in the universe...go to whatever meditation you're most familiar with"...and some sense of emptiness or openness? Weeks later he said "Better not take a chance on emptiness, try to remember meditation...don't look back, it's too late anyway!" So I've been seeing him and doing a little more regular sitting daily...also in buses, dentists' chairs, in front of TV.

I took part in some outdoor protests over Iraq War in front of Rockefeller Center a year ago; kept going with a series of black poets reading at Brooklyn College, saw a lot of Chinese poets, collaborated on opera *Hydrogen Jukebox* with Philip Glass, musician.

Peter's in Bellevue Hospital again the last few months, getting out to live in supervised half-way house in Brooklyn ghetto—see how that works.

Forgot if I told you, I spent week teaching with Gordon Ball at Virginia Military Institute, a state college where he's a professor in uniform, during the Iraq War—advised the students to stay in the army to prevent a military putsch (take over, palace revolution) in U.S.A. 20 years from now. Did a lot of traveling, enjoying poetry reading more and more: Shreveport on Mexican Gulf, LA, SF, Wisconsin, Florida, all over U.S.A.—signing books since new big photograph book (91 11″ × 14″ photos) came out (printed in Japan—fine rotogravure process). Visits to Naropa with Philip Glass—working with artists—Karel Appel (Dutch "Cobra" movement), and Francesco Clemente, with him we've begun giant 2′ × 4′ page 5 verses a page 108 page illuminated hand-written *Howl*.

Saw Voznesensky often in NY and read his English a few times. Visited Bob Dylan in his house to take his photo with Rolliflex camera. We went to Tompkins

Square Park earlier and got chased out by homeless folk throwing bottles at us thinking we were taking their picture. At home, Dylan said, unshaven face, "Fame is a curse, without redeeming value." People have broken into his bedroom window at night, he has to have gates and guards and guard houses.

So, I made my will, itemized by Steven Taylor, everything in my house. Recorded Whitman's *Crossing Brooklyn Ferry* for a film last June, and also large portion of Kerouac's *Dharma Bums* for an educational cassette. July month long at Naropa, then a week's retreat with Gelek Rinpoche in park near Ann Arbor. Visited northwest and saw painter Robert LaVigne and read poetry with McClure, Seattle and Portland. A whole month retreat at Rocky Mountain Dharma Center with Peter living in a tent on the land and sitting every day, with month-long lectures on Mahamudra by a football-player looking Lama— taught "Literary History of Beat Generation" at City University Graduate School for doctoral students, Jack Shuai Shu[71] was in my class. He's still living in my apartment, cooking, cleaning, and making a lot of money teaching in colleges—American Literature to negroes at Medgar Evers College, Chinese conversation at New York University. Cheerful as ever, affectionate as a Chinese nephew taking care of an uncle. What a pleasure! Cooking brown rice (a huge evolution from Chinese white rice as you can guess.)

So I traveled and sang and performed in our opera in Los Angeles and stayed up late at night trying to answer mail, and was exhausted and short of breath in December, so called up my doctor and in a few days had an x-ray and blood tests and then before Christmas went into a hospital suffering heart failure. Water accumulated around the lungs put the heart to too much work: "put on my tie in a taxi, short of breath, rushing to meditate." Not enough sleep, too much "low-salt" salty Kikkoman or Eden Soy sauce in my morning savory oatmeal!

Recovered, slept and went to Holland with Anne [Waldman], Benn Posset arranged Paradiso Club reading, then spent two weeks with Gelek Rinpoche at his Jewel Heart center there—his students cooked leeks, potatoes, skinless chicken, salt free bread—a new diet no salt (no more than a gram a day—an English muffin has 250 mg.) no sugar no grease. Steamed or slow pan fried no grease vegetables taste great! Huge chicken vegetable soups! No salt all veggies! Then went to join Philip Glass, big reading with music filling the Opera House at Turin—then to Modena to the best country restaurant in Italy (in the

71 Jack Shuai Shu. A young man Ginsberg met on his trip to China, and Allen sponsored him to study in New York.

agricultural plain, always the richest area) at the "Clinica Gastronomica"—!—discovered how really good food is plain without salt—a little few drops of rich olive oil make spinach sublime!

OK so now I'm mostly home tho at this moment in my office which is now on 14th floor overlooking Union Square at 17th St.—11 PM. That's my account of the year. Harry Smith died at the Chelsea Hotel the day before Thanksgiving—exertion of that, safeguarding his archives—helped exhaust me before Christmas.

My gallery agent in Los Angeles is arranging a show in Japan at a gallery unconnected with big industry, so all's well there, I'll let you know. *White Shroud* was published in Japanese translation, I asked the publisher to send you a copy, did it arrive? How's the translation? My first big book of poems was published in mainland China—not so good Chinese versions of all *Howl* book, *Kaddish*, selections really generous all the way to *White Shroud* poem. I'm lucky to have a book there, but one thing I realized in Italy—"Immortality comes later."

Love to you and friends

Allen

[*As the years passed, Ginsberg tried to keep in touch with old friends and mentors. In December 1992 he wrote to Paul Bowles to fill him in on gossip about all the people they had known decades earlier. A year later, Allen visited Bowles in Morocco, one of the few times in Allen's busy life when he allowed himself to enjoy a few days of nostalgia for his past.*]

Allen Ginsberg [New York, NY] to Paul Bowles [Tangier, Morocco]
December 23, 1992

Dear Paul:

Happy Chanukah, Merry Xmas and Happy New Year—so have been longing to write you—constantly reminded of your ineffable charming presence by my own memories—and books that come in the mail—biographies, festschrifts (plural) and histories of Tangier.

Well you have fondest regards from us. Bill B's due in NY in a week for a vernissage of his recent paintings at Gagosian Gallery, very high class. James Grauerholz's[72] friend Michael Emerton suicided himself w/ pistol in mouth 3

---

72 James Grauerholz. Close friend and companion of William S. Burroughs.

months ago, Bill was sad. We'd spent time together (all of us) at a sweat-lodge ceremony in Lawrence KS last May.

Gregory's OK in N.Y. living with faithful friends; a Japanese admirer supplies rent, some food money and allowance weekly and methadone clinic weekly fee, so Gregory's relatively stable. In any case his poetry is always pure and wise and untouched by life-woes but reflecting them in enlightened style.

Peter Orlovsky's been in and out Bellevue with alcoholism and some coke problems adding to his melancholia—enthusiasms quasi manic depressive cycle. Young lads around, his admirers, have been typing up his 1955–65 letters from Europe Tangier India etc. a huge book and City Lights has asked for an "Orlovsky Reader." I'm in some time throes of tears and grief codependent on his suffering so spent a week at Hazelden Hospital (Minneapolis) for family therapy—Hazelden the mother hospital for Alcoholics Anonymous. Gregory spent January there detoxing and thought it was a sympathetic place. You've been thru similar grief with Jane so I guess you understand some of the sadness I feel about Peter. Nothing much I can do that doesn't enrage him more tho underneath who knows what grief he feels that drives his extreme inebriation and violence to himself—howling on street and captured by cops to hospitals now several times a year lately—once a year in the past 80s? Alan Ansen in Athens as ever, perhaps you hear from him, heavy arthritis keeps him housebound.

By hindsight it seems to me we were quite boorishly behaved with Montgomery Clift at Libby Holman's house decades ago (we, i.e. Peter, me and Gregory) (too fresh!) (and God knows what Clift was suffering).

Jane as I remember was finally quite gracious toward us once we met so I'm sorry that the impression her biographers have given on basis of chatty letters or casual remarks doesn't carry the relative amity she showed at her house offering couscous, and at other encounters.

Brion Gysin's reputation grows, various younger flash artists like the late Keith Haring now do venerate him—Philip Taafe you met—I see him now and then happily—your recent Mrabet translation wonderfully readable—at one sitting. I've been working with painter Francesco Clemente, a Blakean aristocrat well mannered family Italian gent who has big studio on Broadway and Great Jones Street. And I see Buddhist Dharma-brother Philip Glass often. We have a piano-vocal duet declamation number we developed for Dharma benefit performances, have put together an opera with fragments of my poetries 1960–80, which toured Spoleto and U.S.A., and are preparing more duets. I think when he works with my words he tends toward heart-felt melodrama and aria and romantic exuberance so I feel comfortable with him. I don't know if you know his early and later work, beginning with "minimal" cycles of tune or progression (inspired by Indian modes and Bach it sounds like, arithmetic variations)—but he's developed some full blown operatic choral and orchestral thunder and melody—and I like him. We study with same Buddhist Lama.

Oddly I've been working with musicians a lot since India and sing a lot, so now am preparing a 4 CD box set of oldie but goldie poetry and music works done from 1953 (earliest tape of *a capella* song) to 1990—including collaborations done in studio with Elvin Jones (Coltrane drummer), Don Cherry (jazz trumpeter), Bob Dylan singing backup on Blake and playing tunes to my vocal lyrics, a cellist Arthur Russell much liked by some avant-garde friends here in music circles, an old lover who recently died of AIDS, lived upstairs from me.

I guess you heard or received the CD's done 2 years ago by Bill [Burroughs] (*Dead City Radio*) and me (*Lion For Real*) on Island Record label. Produced by excellent simpatico younger professional Hal Willner. Did these discs ever reach you? Anyway when my CD set comes out June or later I'll ship it over. But I'm pleased that a lot of recordings I paid for 20 years ago and later are at last put together for public ear. I'd been storing "treasures in eternity" but despaired of having them issued while I was still around. Old Blake record, and Hammond *First Blues* albums will be selected from and re-issued as part of the 4 C.D.s.

Recovered from diabetes insulin needle crisis of last May, I'm now eating macrobiotic foods—mostly pleasant varied grains and vegetables and fish and no meat no dairy no salt no sugar no raw food lots of seaweed soy bean curds and "rice-milk" (liquefied rice powder sweet tastes like milk)—and no longer need pills or needles for late-onset diabetes; also took off weight and feel fit tho sad tho happy to be alive; at least "happy not yet to be a corpse." Hope you're well as can be and similarly not unhappy.

Best wishes as ever,

Allen Ginsberg

I hope you can read this scribbled hand—impulsively writ, now or never—it's been on my mind!

**Allen Ginsberg [Tangier, Morocco] to Peter Orlovsky [New York, NY?]
December 22, 1993**

Dear Peter:

Wherever you are, thought of you all day, arrived in Tangier from Athens, 4 nites to stay till return for Buddhist retreat till January 5 or so with Gelek. Got hotel this afternoon and walked up Blvd. Pasteur past Café de Paris, several blocks longer than I'd remembered down to the corner turn left down a block toward Villa Muniria[73]—went inside and on stairway up to our old 1957 verandah room (now $10.00 a nite) I cried to think how innocently happy we were together that trip to Europe, how much I loved you and miss your presence now, what happened to our lives together and can't we ever return to each other if we can't return to our light-hearted youthtime? The upstairs room seemed smaller, the verandah now cracked concrete but still can go out on it. I went downstairs into the garden all overcrowded with big leafy plants—where we took pictures against a big palm tree. The garden smaller and more cluttered than I'd remembered also. And Bill's French door! a housekeeper portly man and his family live in two rooms there now (Portman's and Bill's)—yes second time less happy for our harmony but we survived thru all India thru years with Trungpa and now? How do you choose? I'm still waiting, tears in my eyes, hoping you wind up safe, happy, calm genius as you are dear Peter. Well I'll go see Paul Bowles age 82 tomorrow. Went down to Soco Chico, longer walk than I'd remembered, at dusk, one Moroccan in cafe at end of square said, "You look like a Jewish peoples you going to get killed, someday make you dead." And an old Arab friend of Bill and Gysin has antique shop across from hotel.

Love as ever

xxx

Allen

Allen Ginsberg [Tangier, Morocco] to William S. Burroughs [Lawrence, KS] December 22, 1993

Dear Bill:

Spent 4 nights in Athens and visited Alan Ansen twice, he's housebound by arthritis, has 3 sizeable rooms crowded with books in steel shelves, on bed, and has his own chair and lamp—a worn out pair of silk pajamas and undershirt about a week old, says his illness fits him perfectly as he wants to stay home with books. A friend English School principal provides him with Polish boys to help him shop and launder—says he's content. [I] had come from Dublin Oslo Munich Paris Berlin Prague, then met Lucien in Barcelona, we spent 4 days sightseeing, I gave big reading (500 in theater) there and in Madrid. Lucien left

73 Villa Muniria. The hotel where Ginsberg, Orlovsky, Burroughs, Kerouac, and Ansen stayed on their 1957 visit.

for home, we both caught flu in same room. He's retired and in mild humor grizzled grey and limping from old drunk car wrecks. Then Cordoba and Malaga a nite each, Athens as above, today at last arrived in Tangier after 32 years' absence—just walked streets, found Villa Muniria, rented balcony room (seems smaller) (and less pristine) (but same verandah) and wept to see it and your garden again, some snapshots inside and by door with owner. Walked down to Soco Chico, accosted by 10 year old spoke English, and another older guy to show me around but I had no money changed left after buying an azure shirt, said "No," I heard muttering nearby from cafe at corner of Soco Chico. "You look like Jewish people, someday they're gonna kill you, you be dead..." as I passed. Wandered uphill back to Blvd. Pasteur. Soco and Grand Chico unchanged, smaller Soco than I remember. I'll see Paul B. tomorrow. Ah, the years past, poor Peter.

Love

Allen

Panama Café no longer serves food alas! I realized I was quite happy here 1957 and in Europe.

[As time passed Ginsberg's letters became shorter and more infrequent. Telephones, the deaths of close friends, and a busy schedule kept him from writing very much. From time to time he'd sit at his desk and catch up with people in a hurried manner, never enough time to do all he wanted.]

Allen Ginsberg [New York, NY] to Gary Snyder [Nevada City, CA]
January 12, 1995

Dear Gary:

[...] Dreamt I saw Jack K. last nite, told him he'd done enough work, he should take it easy and maybe write one book every ten years and live to be 80 or 90 years old. I guess that's advice to me.

Spent December in London and Paris, new books out bilingual from Bourgois ed. (*White Shroud*, 1 volume, *Mind Breaths* and *Plutonian Ode*, 2nd volume) and *Cosmopolitan Greetings* in Penguin edition—so I did a lot of interviews and went to museums. Assistant Peter Hale came along to carry bags and laptop with modem, so could fax from Ritz Hotel to office in N.Y. *Nouvelle Observateur* put us up in Ritz for 3 nites @ $690 per room per nite)—so saw Paris hi life a few days. I'll start teaching February 1. Enclosed last week's poem. Best to Carol and your family. Did anyone send you my 4 CD set *Holy Soul Jelly Roll?* Vol. 3 w/ Blake is easy listening. Living alone in my apartment. Peter Orlovsky now 6 months clean, at present at Spring Lake Ranch in Vermont, I'll visit him this weekend, after 3 months in rehab in New Jersey. So there's some hope after 10 years, maybe he hit bottom after all.

My heart's still pumping but especially in travel I get out of breath easily, feel older and less energetic—so I guess the Kerouac dream applies. Hope to finish *Collected Essays* and blurbs, *Selected Interviews* and *Selected Correspondence* in next year's and *Selected Poems*—different editors working on all books except myself last—all done in-house (i.e. people I assigned and pay to edit)—Bill Morgan bibliographer, Miles, etc.

I'll be at Stanford and in S.F. February 9–13. Stanford w/ [Carl] Rakosi, and to look over my archive site.

Love XX as ever

Allen

[*About the only time Ginsberg stopped to write longer letters was to address political issues. Even in these cases Ginsberg would often ask someone to compose the letter and then he would go back over it to "Ginsbergize" it with his own special words and phrases.*]

Allen Ginsberg [New York, NY] to Randy "Duke" Cunningham [Washington, DC] April 4, 1995

Dear Legislator:

I strongly oppose any diminishment of the National Endowment for the Arts. I find this proposition's motives ingenuous and a politicization of arts grants.

If you examine the testimony of legislators denouncing the NEA, all of their comments were political—it wasn't that they really objected to the art or government subsidy of art. They don't mind subsidizing military brass bands. They have a political agenda, and they were accusing the artists and broadcasters of having a political agenda. It's all part of Newt Gingrich's "declaration of war" against the so-called "counterculture."

The attack on the arts is an attack on counter-culture. In 1965 when the Beatles were around the Birch Society would hand out pamphlets saying that the

Beatles were trying to hypnotize kids and teach them degenerate behavior. Even the innocent pretty Beatles. But in those days they were attacked by the right wing, the John Birch Society. Those days the Birchites were the mirror image of Communists who were saying the same thing. I remember visiting Central Europe around that time, Czechoslovakia to Russia and found a big cultural battle 1965 between youths rock-n-roll and the totalitarian bureaucracy. Marxists felt that rock-n-roll gave the youth culture a voice of its own and they'd become too loose and independent for mind control by the Marxist governments and their secret police.

These aggressive neo-cons fund military brass bands but they won't fund the civilian arts. The artist is self-empowered and outside the control of government; the original NEA was designed to be independent of political whims, political pressures. Senator Helms and the theopolitical right wing politicized NEA, trying to reimpose censorship. The terminology they use parallels the old Stalinoid terminology. Their partisan argument against NEA is "Why should these individuals have the right to taxpayers' money to pay for their elitist art?" That was actually Stalin's complaint about writers who opposed him. They were unRussian cosmopolitans, "Why should the Soviet citizen have to pay for this elitist individualism?" Nazi terms were similar to the American demagogue's terms: "Degenerate Art." And the Maoist terms for censorship were the same as Rev. Donald Wildmon, Pat Robertson and Pat Buchanan's use now: "Spiritual corruption." It's the same authoritarian police state language, and the intention of Mao Tse-tung and Stalin was mind control, and that's exactly what these televangelists and corrupt politicians are after, monopoly thought control.

Religious fanatics and demagogic superpatriots are trying to take over U.S. culture, and they say so themselves. Pat Buchanan says it's a spiritual war for the soul of America. Theopolitical televangelist money changers have abandoned their spiritual prayers to take worldly power, and impose their religious self-righteousness on the majority of us Americans.

Although the party-line says, "Get government off our backs," Jessie Helms and the Republicans imposed their thought control on the radio-television in the form of a law passed in October 1988 by Senator Helms, signed by Pres. Reagan, directing the FCC to forbid all so-called and undefined "indecent" language off the air. This has eliminated my own poetry from broadcast on the listener supported stations like Pacifica that don't get funds from the government. A group of broadcasters and PEN Club writers took this law to the Supreme Court and won half the battle. Now the ban is only 6am to 8pm; so far 8pm to 6am is so called "Safe Harbor."

The excuse is to guard the ears of minors from "indecency," but these same *Howl* and *Kaddish* poems of mine under ban are read in high school and college anthologies during the very hours the poems are banned off the radio. When neo-conservative theopoliticians originally objected to NEA grants to Robert Mapplethorpe or Karen Finley, they said this wasn't censorship, just guarding taxpayers' money. However these same people have imposed censorship on non-taxpayer money on the listener supported radio networks that don't get money from the government. So their authoritarian party-line cover story is a fraud.

I repeat: the neo-cons say it's just "government money," not censorship, and then they turn around and censor non government supported venues. Back in 1957–1962, books were censored also, and new generations don't realize that. *Howl* survived a censorship trial. Henry Miller was protected by Constitution, said the courts. D. H. Lawrence's *Lady Chatterley's Lover,* Burroughs' *Naked Lunch,* and Catullus were liberated. Now censorship is re-imposed on what is at present the main marketplace of ideas: radio, TV, and even now the information highway.

The only useful alteration of the current system of arts funding is to make it more independent of political demagogues.

Sincerely,

Allen Ginsberg

[Ginsberg's health took over more and more time and this letter reflected his concern. Allen had a good attitude, but the doctors had trouble diagnosing his most serious ailment which turned out to be liver cancer.]

Allen Ginsberg [Amboise, France] to Gary and Carole Snyder [Nevada City, CA] June 22, 1995

Dear Gary and Carole:

[. . .] I'd a painful week in bed late May with a pulmonary embolism, knife-like hurt in right chest with blood clot detached from thickened and slightly corrugated right hand heart valve—fortunately not left side of heart which would've been dangerous. As it was, fatigue and lassitude and codeine and I recovered in time for two brief obligations at NYU Kerouac/Poetry (J.K. as *littérateur* and poet) Conference. Then June 7 flew to Venice for show of 108 photos during Bienniale week—great deal of interest since there's another crest of admiration in "Beat" literary character in Italy and Milan publishers are preparing a big "Collected Poems" translated by Fernanda Pivano—first book with new poems since 1974 when Maoist and multinational egotists took over Mondadori.[74] Mondadori's gay nephew now in charge.

There were a couple photos of you in the Venice show—but alas the bulk of my negatives from *Indian Journals* disappeared in early 70s when book was published. I'd asked David Haselwood, City Lites and Berkeley UC Special Collections—nobody knew where they vanished. Suddenly I got a call from Haselwood, he'd found them after 25 years at the bottom of his trunk when cleaning house. So the original negatives now are safe in my office in N.Y.—enough for a small show this fall. Photo activity more remunerative and expansive, I have secretary-curator lady who's efficient and big museum shows in Japan and Europe are in preparation.

So, after Venice I went down below Naples to Amalfi where Francesco Clemente's wife Alba was born, grew up, and had ten days of convalescence in Mediterranean sun on a veranda overlooking town and ocean and sky, eating fresh pasta and local veggies and fruit—hundreds of thousands of lemons in terraces up and down town hillsides. Then strength recovered have been traveling with Clementes and their four kids by overnite wagon-lit train to Loire Valley where he has opening in a few days of 108 pastels he did over last year in N.Y., India, Amalfi, New Mexico—huge display of poetic images, he's an excellent poet mind and Pound devotee—intelligent sensitive couple who honeymooned age 21 in India for 2 years. We've worked on projects together the last decade. He did collaborations with McClure, Creeley, Wieners and Gregory C. Grew up in 60s and treats Beat Culture with serious European insight and charm. So now vacationing with his family and 82 year old father in Loire Valley visiting chateau which'll get a million visitors this year, most during summer.

Before I left I talked with Rick Fields[75] whose voice was whispery, he's got cancer, lung or esophagus. And a call from Timothy Leary inquiring means to sell his archives to Stanford, which offered a deal. He said "I don't now if you've heard of my condition, I have terminal cancer." He seemed ready and cheerful or as J.K. said "coach-like," Irish football coach, said he had 75 years, was satisfied and ready. Prostate, with metastasis awhile back aggravated by fatigue

---

74 Mondadori. Ginsberg's Italian publisher.
75 Rick Fields (1942–1999). Fellow Buddhist and author of *How the Swans Came to the Lake*.

from foolish 15 city lecture tour to support his extended family. Gregory fine in NY financially secure with monthly stipend from Japanese painter Hiro Yamagata who sponsored my photo show in Venice and donated a quarter million $ to Naropa last year and sez he'll continue yearly — with extra stipend for Anne Waldman to ease her penury directing Poetics Department.

I keep writing — journals and poems, much about physical aging or obvious deterioration of body — w/ $^2/_3$ of my heart working I have less physical energy approaching age 70 — tho I feel like 16 emotionally — but sightseeing I've got energy for one castle a day and lots of naps. Peter Orlovsky now OK in Hazelden Fellowship Halfway House six blocks from our apartment, for a few months.

With $^1/_3$ left of my Stanford archive sale million, after Fed. State Local Taxes, $^1/_{10}$ to Bibliographer/Archivist Bill Morgan for 14 years work, every item retrievable catalogued, and 5% to agent [Wylie] — I purchased a nice big loft around the corner from my apartment from painter Larry Rivers. So I'll move in the fall and Peter gets our old apartment.

PPS: New loft 2100 sq. feet, lots of open space, windows on 3 sides 5 flights up with new stainless steel elevator with keys.

[Ginsberg didn't have much energy during his final months and didn't write many letters. This letter was written in answer to a question from Bob Wilson, the retired owner of the Phoenix Book Shop, about Ginsberg's very first publications, the mimeos of Howl and "Siesta in Xbalba."]

Allen Ginsberg [New York, NY] to Bob Wilson [St. Michael's, MD]
February 18, 1997

Dear Robert:

Howl mimeo wasn't handed out at Six Gallery or Berkeley reading a few months later — wasn't even finished except for Part 1 at Six Gallery, that's all I read then — by Berkeley March 56 I'd inaugurated the rest — see original Berkeley tapes (or hear) 4 CD box set Holy Soul Jelly Roll Poems 1949–1996, Rhino records — first reading of entire 3 (or 4, I forget part Howl, and first public reading of "America" and "Sunflower Sutra." This mimeo you mentioned was typed by Creeley, run off on a ditto machine at S.F. State, later, before City Lights pamphlet arrived, by Martha Rexroth.

I was employed as yeoman storekeeper on a military sea transport ship

(M.S.T.S.)—then living with Peter when ship was in dock in S.F.—our ship re-supplied the D.E.W. line at Icy Cape, Alaska. I had no liaison with Coast Guardsman, nor was smuggled on ship, I was allowed like other sailors off ship in port (see *Journals Mid-50s*, Harper 1996)—had mimeo machine as ship store-keeper—no Coast Guardsman alas, (that a brave story). Never heard of that Guardsman before—where'd you get that screwy gossip? Pay from that ship trip carried us to Mexico City [to] see Jack [Kerouac], thence to N.Y. and Europe. The poem—a single poem was "Siesta in Xbalba."

I thought you'd be amused to hear the actual tale—I had a year's sea time including that 2 or 3 month's work on ships by then, with Union trip card, hav-ing gone thru MSTS training at Sheepshead Bay NY 1945 and got my Coast Guard certification then.

As ever,

Allen Ginsberg

[*Ginsberg planned a trip to Italy in the spring of 1997, still unaware that he was terminally ill. This letter to an Italian publisher, Il Saggiatore, touches on that visit and his health as well. He addressed the new translations of his poetry and compared it to Nanda Pivano's earlier translations. Since Allen didn't want to offend his old friend Pivano, he suggested that Il Saggiatore publish both the new and old translations in the same volume.*]

Allen Ginsberg [New York, NY] to Luca Formenton [Milan, Italy]
March 17, 1997

Dear Luca:

I consulted a few intelligent literary Italians here in New York about the *Howl* translations and the consensus was: Nanda's is grounding language, rig-orous, classic. Luca's is more inventive, flies higher, why not—? It's heartfelt, but "inventive," i.e. flamboyant, yet widens the scope of the poem. Sandro Chia thought Luca's was superior, more true to the language. Since the poem takes only 10 or 12 pages of Italian is it possible to include both? That would give both aspects, retain Nanda's classic language and please her, and give place for Luca. The English need not be repeated twice. How does this sound?

I'm still in bed, miserable with hepatitis. Maybe another month bed rest as ordered by the doctor. I still hope to get to Italy. I'll spend a few days in Milan for poetry convocations and then try to find a little one room studio—where

Peter Orlovsky and I can cook—located somewhere like Florence, Venice, Bologna, Sienna, or Rappalo, or anywhere in driving distance or fast train from Milan. Do you know of any inexpensive accommodation I can make for convalescence for a week or so? I can pay moderate rent. Ideally I would like to leave Milan for convalescence on the 24th, but if necessary I will stay for the Burroughs' vernissage that day. Staying any longer in the limelight will be a strain. I need to return to the U.S. by May 5th. Are any other American poets coming?

   As ever,

   Allen

[*The last letter that Allen wrote was also the only letter he drafted after he learned he had terminal liver cancer. He died at home on April 5, 1997, a few days later.*]

Allen Ginsberg [New York, NY] to Bill Clinton [Washington, DC]
ca. April 1, 1997

Dear President Clinton:

   Enclosed some recent political poems.
   I have untreatable liver cancer and have 2–5 months to live.
   If you have some sort of award or medal for service in art or poetry, please send one along unless it's politically inadvisable or inexpedient. I don't want to bait the right wing for you. Maybe [Newt] Gingrich[76] might or might not mind. But don't take chances please, you've enough on hand.
   Best wishes and good luck to you and Ms. Hillary and daughter (name).
   Home office #: lunchtime noon and 6–7 pm supper.

   Allen Ginsberg

---

76 Newt Gingrich (b. 1943). Conservative Republican, Speaker of the House.

INDEX

Treasury Department (U.S.), narcotics, legal battles and, 238
Tremblay, Paul, 110
Trial, The (Kafka), 304
Trilling, Diana, 36, 216, 224, 225, 299, 325
    letter to, 393–397
Trilling, Lionel, 35, 36, 68, 205, 216, 298, 395, 396
    letters to, 10–15, 22–24
Trocchi, Alex, 270
Troilus and Cressida (Shakespeare), 100
Tropic of Cancer (Miller), 130
Trungpa Tolku, 353
Turnbull, Gael, 416

Ubo, George, 93
Underground cinema, Ginsberg's seminal participation in, 408
Ungaretti, Giuseppe, 332, 341
University of Chicago, 221
Urich, Ed, 342

Van Doren, Mark, 35, 36, 37, 43, 55, 68, 116
    letters to, 10, 28–30
Van Duyn, Mona, 363, 365, 366, 367
Van Dyke, Henry, 364
Van Gogh, Vincent, 54, 153, 181
Van Meter, Peter, 107
Vancouver, poetry reading in, 288
Velasquez, Diego Rodriguez, 164
Verlaine, Paul, 323
Viereck, Peter, 298
Vietnam, Ginsberg's visit to, 286–287
Vietnam War, 321, 349
    Ginsberg's role in anti-war movement during, 296, 301, 309, 310–313, 316, 346–347, 360, 371–372
Viking Press, 89, 183, 124, 136, 148
Villa Muniria (Tangier, Morocco), 438n73, 439
Village Voice, 150, 379
Villiers Printers, 130, 257
Vishner, Mayer, 378

Visions of Cody (Kerouac), Ginsberg's references to, 76, 78–80, 81–82
Visions of Neal (Kerouac), 115, 116, 189, 210
Voit, Joanna, letter to, 415–416
Voltaire, François Marie Arouet de, 3–4, 193
Voznesensky, Andrei, 281, 282, 302, 308, 325, 360, 406, 411, 412, 433

Wadsworth Publishing Company, 361
Wain, John, 196
Wakoski, Diane, 386
Waldman, Anne, 381, 382, 387, 398, 400, 417, 420, 422, 434, 444
Wallace, Henry A., 3n2
Wang (meditation initiation mantra), 261n47, 262
War and Peace (Tolstoy), 11
War Tax Resisters, 346
Warhol, Andy, 408
Warshall, Peter, 382
Washington Post, 408
"Wasted Illness, A" (Harding), 35
Watergate scandal, 372
Wattress, Jane, 61
Watts, Alan, 241
Weaver, Raymond, 204
Weissner, Carl, 426
Weitzner, Richard, 29, 50, 55
Welch, Lew, 318, 403
Wernham, Guy, 119
West, Nathaniel, 88
"Western Ballad, A" (Ginsberg), 28
Western Lands (Burroughs), 422
Weyden, Roger Vander, 164
Whalen, Philip, 148, 173, 174, 180, 257, 290, 323, 327, 352, 365, 367, 381, 388, 413, 432
    Ginsberg helps to finance publishing costs for, 219, 369
    letters to, 402–404
    at Naropa Institute, 386, 387, 414, 417
    San Francisco Poetry Renaissance and, 142, 144, 145, 200, 211, 213, 225, 322, 368
White, Ed, 55
White Pony, The (Payne, ed.), 108